Contents

Section A *Forces and movement*
Section B *Energy*
Section C *Waves*
Section D *Electricity and magnetism*
Section E *Atomic physics*
Section F *The Earth and space*

Section A

Chapter 1	**Describing motion**	**1**
1.1	Measuring speed	2
1.2	Distance–time graphs	8
1.3	Changing speed	12
1.4	Velocity–time graphs	16
1.5	The equations of motion	20
Chapter 2	**Forces and motion**	**26**
2.1	Forces produce acceleration	27
2.2	Balanced and unbalanced forces	31
2.3	Friction and drag	36
2.4	The force of gravity	39
Chapter 3	**Forces and momentum**	**49**
3.1	Collisions and explosions	50
3.2	Momentum and force	56
Chapter 4	**Turning effects of forces**	**63**
4.1	The moment of a force	64
4.2	Stability and centre of mass	68
Chapter 5	**Forces and matter**	**71**
5.1	Density	72
5.2	Forces acting on solids	74

Further questions Section A   **79**

Section B

Chapter 6	**Energy resources**	**84**
6.1	The energy we use	86
6.2	Storing energy	90
6.3	Renewable energy technologies	93
Chapter 7	**Energy transformations, energy transfers**	**98**
7.1	Forms of energy	98
7.2	Conservation of energy	104
7.3	Energy efficiency	108
Chapter 8	**Work and power**	**112**
8.1	Gravitational potential energy	113
8.2	Kinetic energy	115
8.3	KE–GPE transformations	117
8.4	Doing work	120
8.5	Power	124
Chapter 9	**The kinetic model of matter**	**127**
9.1	Changes of state	128
9.2	Particles, forces and the kinetic model	131
9.3	Thinking about the kinetic model	136
9.4	Internal energy	138
9.5	Temperature and temperature scales	140
Chapter 10	**Thermal energy transfers**	**147**
10.1	Conduction	148
10.2	Convection	152
10.3	Radiation	154
10.4	Effective insulation	158
10.5	Specific heat capacity	160

Section B

Chapter 11 The gas laws — 164
11.1 Properties of a gas — 164
11.2 Boyle's law — 167
11.3 Charles' law — 170
11.4 The pressure law — 173
11.5 Combining the three gas laws — 175

Further questions Section B — 178

Section C

Chapter 12 Sound — 183
12.1 Making sounds — 184
12.2 At the speed of sound — 185
12.3 Seeing sounds — 189
12.4 How sounds travel — 194
12.5 Using ultrasound and infrasound — 197

Chapter 13 How light travels — 200
13.1 Travelling in straight lines — 201
13.2 The speed of light — 202
13.3 Reflecting light — 205

Chapter 14 Refraction of light — 210
14.1 Refraction effects — 211
14.2 Total internal reflection — 215
14.3 Lenses — 218
14.4 Light and colour — 224

Chapter 15 The electromagnetic spectrum — 227
15.1 Extending the visible spectrum — 228
15.2 Infrared and ultraviolet radiation — 232
15.3 Radio waves and microwaves — 235
15.4 X-rays and gamma rays — 238

Chapter 16 Waves — 241
16.1 Describing waves — 242
16.2 Speed, frequency and wavelength — 247
16.3 Reflection and refraction of waves — 249
16.4 Diffraction — 253

Further questions Section C — 259

Section D

Chapter 17 Static electricity — 263
17.1 Charging and discharging — 265
17.2 What is electric charge? — 270
17.3 The hazards and uses of static electricity — 274

Chapter 18 Electric circuits — 278
18.1 Current in electric circuits — 280
18.2 Electrical resistance — 285
18.3 Resistive components — 291
18.4 Combinations of resistors — 295

Chapter 19 Electricity and energy — 300
19.1 Using electrical appliances — 301
19.2 Voltage and energy — 304
19.3 Domestic electricity supply — 308

Chapter 20 Electromagnetic forces and electric motors — 315
20.1 Electromagnets — 316
20.2 Uses of electromagnets — 319
20.3 How electric motors are constructed — 323
20.4 The motor effect — 326
20.5 Electric motors revisited — 331

Chapter 21 Electromagnetic induction — 333
21.1 Generating electricity — 334
21.2 The principles of electromagnetic induction — 336
21.3 Power lines and transformers — 339

Chapter 22 Electronic control circuits — 347
22.1 Electronic processors — 348
22.2 Input devices — 353
22.3 Output devices — 356

Further questions Section D — 360

Section E

Chapter 23 Atoms, nuclei and electrons   366
23.1 The size of atoms   367
23.2 Electrons   368
23.3 Inside atoms   372
23.4 Protons, neutrons and electrons   375

Chapter 24 Radioactivity   380
24.1 Radioactivity all round   381
24.2 The microscopic picture   384
24.3 Using radioactive substances   388
24.4 Radioactive decay   391

Chapter 25 Nuclear fission   399
25.1 Nuclear fission   401

Further questions Section E   408

Section F

Chapter 26 The active Earth   411
26.1 Inside the Earth   412
26.2 Plate tectonics   415

Chapter 27 Around the Earth   420
27.1 Gravity   421
27.2 Into orbit   424
27.3 Spacecraft at work   427

Chapter 28 The Solar System   430
28.1 The moving Earth   431
28.2 Moon and Sun   433
28.3 The nine planets   434

Chapter 29 The Universe   443
29.1 Stars and galaxies   444
29.2 The life of a star   447
29.3 The life of the Universe   449

Further questions Section F

A glossary of terms and answers to questions can be found on the Cambridge University Press website. Go to http://uk.cambridge.org/education/secondary/SANG

Acknowledgements

1.1, ©Penny Tweedie/Panos Pictures; 1.2, Collections/John Callan; 1.3, 7.5, 11.11, 14.17, 14.19, 15.15, Nigel Luckhurst; 1.6, 3.14, 12.21, Stephen Dalton/NHPA; 1.7, Instruments Direct; 1.11a, Milepost 92½; 1.11b, courtesy of Northern Spirit; 1.16, 8.5, 10.14, 15.11, 22.12, Roger G Howard Photography; 1.18, 3.1, 15.9, 15.16, 19.2, Images Colour Library; 1.26, 2.12, 10.12, 19.1, Shout! Picture Library; 1.27, ©Crown copyright. Reproduced with the permission of the Controller of HMSO; 1.29, Department of Transport; 2.1, 2.14, 6.2b, 8,2, 15.4, 27.1, 27.8, 27.11t, 28.13r, NASA/Science Photo Library; 2.4, Trinity College, Cambridge, UK/Bridgeman Art Library; 2.10, ©Sez. di Zoologia 'La Specola' del Museo di Storia Nat. dell'Universita di Firenze/INDEX, Florence, Italy; 2.15, Tom Mackie Images; 2.21, ©MSI Sutton, USA; 2.27, 9.2a, Mehau Kulyk/Science Photo Library; 2.30, Didier Kline/Allsport; 3.2, Neil Tingle/Action Plus; 3.5, Kieran Doherty/Reuters/Popperfoto; 3.7, I Virga Regt; 3.8, Courtesy of CERN; 3.9, TRH Pictures/QAPI; 3.17, 22.1, courtesy of Ford Motor Company Ltd; 4.1, Neale Haynes/Action Plus; 4.4, ©Clint Clemens/Int'l Stock/Robert Harding Picture Library; 4.10, NCNA/Camera Press; 5.1, Popperfoto; 5.4, Professor Harold Edgerton/Science Photo Library; 5.5, Arnaud Fevrier/Camera Press; 5.9,Courtesy of Volkswagen-presse; 6.1, B. Murton/Southampton Oceanography Centre/Science Photo Library; 6.2a, David Ducros/Science Photo Library; 6.4, Sally Morgan/Ecoscene; 6.5, Martin Land/Science Photo Library; 6.6, 25.2, 25.10, 25.11, BNFL; 6.7, Gerard & Margi Moss/Still Pictures; 6.8, 7.12a, 9.12, 9.15, 10.9, 10.15, 11.1, 11.2a, b, 11.4a, b, 11.12, 12.4, 12.10, 13.2a, b, 13.9a, 14.2, 14.3, 14.6, 14.12, 14.14, 14.20, 15.8, 15.10, 15.14, 16.4a, b, 16.10b, 16.11b, 16.15a, b, 16.17, 17.10, 18.2, 18.3a, 18.6, 18.14, 18.15a, 18.16a, 18.17a, 19.3, 19.4, 19.5, 19.9, 19.10, 19.11, 20.15, 20.20, 22.9a, 23.6, 24.10, 24.11, Andrew Lambert; 6.10a, b, courtesy of BP Solar; 6.11, Tony Craddock/Science Photo Library; 7.1, ANT/NHPA; 7.3, Mick Hutson/Redferns; 7.4a, European Space Agency/Science Photo Library; 7.10, Martin Bond/Science Photo Library; 7.11, Mark Baker/Reuters/Popperfoto; 8.1, Brian Shuel/Collections; 8.4, 8.7, Glyn Kirk/Action Plus; 8.9, Angelo Hornak Library, 8.10, ©National Maritime Museum Picture Library, London; 8.16, Lesley Howling/Collections; 9.1, Eichhorn/Zingel/FLPA–Images of Nature; 9.2b, c, Claude Nuridsany & Marie Perennou/Science Photo Library; 9.17, 21.2, 29.8b, Science Photo Library; 10.1, Andy Rouse/NHPA; 10.2, Daryl Balfour/NHPA; 10.8, Simon Hazelgrove/Collections; 10.11, Alfred Pasieka/Science Photo Library; 11.7, 20.1, Mary Evans Picture Library; 12.1, Jill Douglas/Redferns; 12.2, ©J.G. Fuller/Hutchison Photo Library; 12.3, courtesy of Dr Bernard Richardson, Department of Physics and Astronomy, Cardiff University; 12.5, David Redfern/Redferns; 12.6, 15.7a, NASA; 12.17, Jonathan Evans/Reuters/Popperfoto; 12.22, Saturn Stills/Science Photo Library; 13.1, Corbis Stock Market; 13.4, QA Photos Ltd; 13.6, Joe Pasieka/Science Photo Library; 13.7, Mark Bowler/Tom Bowler Pictures; 14.1, Royal Observatory, Edinburgh/Science Photo Library; 14.9, 24.14, TEK Image/Science Photo Library; 14.10, Deep Light Productions/Science Photo Library; 14.11, Eye of Science/Science Photo Library; 14.21, 16.1, ©David Hosking/FLPA – Images of Nature; 15.2a, b, Leonard Lessin/Science Photo Library; 15.7a, b, 29.1, ©Anglo-Australian Observatory/photo by David Malin; 15.12b, NRAO/AUI/Science Photo Library; 15.17, Addenbrooke's Hospital Photographic Department; 16.2, Steve Bardens/Action Plus; 16.12, ©SilvestrisFotoservice/FLPA – Images of Nature; 17.1 The Granger Collection, New York; 17.2, The Library Company of Philadelphia; 17.12, Høyanger Aluminium Production Plant, Norway/photo courtesy of Norsk Hydro; 18.1, Maximilian Stock Ltd/Science Photo Library; 18.19, ©Guzelian/Professor C J Humphreys, Cambridge University; 20.2, G. Brad Lewis/Science Photo Library; 20.4, Alex Bartel/Science Photo Library; 20.5, courtesy of Moorfield Eye Hospital, London; 20.7, 26.1, Ann Ronan Picture Library; 15.12a, 20.22a, b, courtesy of CERN, Geneva; 21.4, Bill Longchore/Science Photo Library; 21.6, 21.13, The Royal Institution, London, UK/Bridgeman Art Library; 21.9, supplied courtesy of The National Grid Company plc; 21.10, Popperfoto/Reuters/photo by Michael McCaugherty; 21.14, Innogy plc/courtesy of Photobition Jupiter; 22.2, Hank Morgan/Science Photo Library; 23.1, ©David Simson; 23.2, Philippe Plailly/Science Photo Library; 23.3, Cavendish Laboratory, University of Cambridge, England; 17.6, 23.4, Science Museum/Science & Society Picture Library; 24.1, 24.12, ©National Radiological Protection Board; 24.2, US Air Force/Science Photo Library; 24.3, courtesy of Addenbrooke's Hospital, Cambridge; 24.5, Bibliothèque Centrale de l'Ecole Polytechnique, Paris, France; 24.6, Pascal Goetgheluck/Science Photo Library; 24.9a, Klaus Guldbrandsen/Science Photo Library; 24.9b, Martyn F. Chillmaid/Science Photo Library; 24.19, Popperfoto/Reuters/photo by Claudio Papi; 25.1, Martin Bond/Science Photo Library; 25.3, Popperfoto/Reuters/photo by Volodymr Repik; 25.7, Michael Marten/Science Photo Library; 26.2, The Natural History Museum, London; 26.4, Carlos Munoz-Yague/Eurelios/Science Photo Library; 26.9b, Popperfoto/Reuters/photo by Fred Prouser; 27.2, CNES, 1990 Distribution SPOT Image/Science Photo Library; 27.11b, NASA; 28.2, 29.3, Space Telescope Science Institute/NASA/Science Photo Library; 28.3, Dr Jeremy Burgess/Science Photo Library; 28.10, John Thomas/Science Photo Library; 28.12, courtesy of Institute of Physics; 28.13l, Popperfoto/Reuters; 29.2, Lund Observatory, Sweden; 29.6, John Sanford/Science Photo Library; 29.8a, Harvard College Observatory/Science Photo Library

Every effort has been made to contact copyright holders; Cambridge University Press would be happy to hear from anyone whose rights have been unwittingly infringed.

Describing motion

Topics in this chapter

◆ distance, speed and time

◆ displacement, velocity and acceleration

◆ scalar and vector quantities

◆ graphical representations of motion

◆ measuring and recording motion

◆ equations of motion

Today, people are on the move (Figure 1.1). You may have to travel several kilometres to get to school each day. Members of your family may live in a different part of the country, so that you have to travel hundreds of kilometres to visit them. Holidays may involve flying to another country, or even to another continent. You might choose to become a student at a university a long way from home.

For some people, movement is a more desperate business. They may be refugees, fleeing from a war zone. They may be economic migrants, travelling great distances to find work and a decent standard of living.

Life in today's industrialised countries is very different from how it was two centuries ago. If you had lived then, your life would probably

Figure 1.1 We live in a world of contrasts. For some people, daily movement is limited to a few kilometres, on foot. For many people from the industrialised world, travelling hundreds of kilometres in a day is commonplace, thanks to cars, trains and planes.

Figure 1.2 This image from a traffic camera shows a speeding car, together with its speed as determined by an electronic measuring device. The driver will be contacted and may be fined, or have to appear in court. A driver who speeds past the same camera every day may soon have committed enough offences to lose his or her licence.

have been tied to farming and the land. You would have lived in a village, and married someone from the next village. A journey to the nearest town would have been a rare event. News travelled no faster than a galloping horse. Then came the Industrial Revolution, with work concentrated in the new cities. The railways made it easier to travel longer distances; then came cars and aeroplanes; motorways and fast and reliable air transport followed.

In this chapter, we will look at ideas of motion, speed and acceleration. In later chapters, we will look at how physicists came to understand the forces involved in motion, and how we control these forces to make everyday travel possible.

1.1 Measuring speed

If you drive along a major highway or through a large city, the chances are that someone is watching you. Cameras on the verge and on overhead gantries keep an eye on traffic as it moves along. Some cameras are there to monitor the flow, so that traffic managers can take action when blockages develop or when accidents occur. Others are equipped with sensors to spot speeding motorists, or those who break the law at traffic lights. In the busiest places, traffic police may observe the roads from helicopters circling above – see Figure 1.2.

Drivers should know how fast they are moving – they have a speedometer to tell them their speed at any instant in time. Traffic police can use a radar speed 'gun' to give them an instant read-out of another vehicle's speed (such 'guns' use the Doppler effect to measure a car's speed). Alternatively, they may time a car between two fixed points on the road. Knowing the distance between the two points, they can calculate the car's speed.

Distance, time, speed

As we have seen, there is more than one way to determine the speed of a moving car or aircraft. Several methods rely on making two measurements:

● the **distance travelled** (or moved) between two points;
● the **time taken** to travel between these two points.

Then we can work out the **average speed** between the two points:

$$\text{average speed} = \frac{\text{distance travelled}}{\text{time taken}}$$

$$v = \frac{s}{t}$$

Figure 1.3 Timing a cyclist over a fixed distance. Using a stopwatch involves making judgements as to when they pass the starting and finishing lines, and this can introduce an error into the measurements. An automatic timing system may be better.

Notice that this equation tells us the vehicle's average speed. We cannot say whether it was travelling at a steady speed or whether its speed was changing. For example, you could use a stopwatch to time a friend cycling over a fixed distance – say, 100 m (see Figure 1.3). Dividing distance by time would tell you their average speed, but they might have been speeding up or slowing down along the way.

Table 1.1 shows the different units that may be used in calculations of speed. SI units are the 'standard' units used in physics; SI stands for *Système Internationale*, or International System. In practice, many other units are used. In US space programmes, heights above the Earth are often given in feet, while the spacecraft's speed is given in knots (nautical miles per hour). These awkward units didn't prevent US astronauts from reaching the Moon, but confusion over units contributed to the crash-landing of a probe on Mars in 1999.

Quantity	Symbol	SI unit	Other units	
distance	s	metre, m	kilometre, km	miles
time	t	second, s	hour, h	
speed	v	metres per second, m/s, m s^{-1}	km/h	miles per hour, mph

Table 1.1 Quantities, symbols and units used in measurements of speed. Take care not to confuse s (italic) for distance with s (not italic) for seconds (or even with speed, for which we use v, for magnitude of velocity).

Rearranging the equation

The equation $v = s/t$ allows us to calculate speed from measurements of distance and time. We can rearrange the equation to allow us to calculate distance or time. For example, a railway signalman might know how fast a train is moving and need to be able to predict where it will have reached after a certain length of time:

distance travelled = average speed × time taken

$$s = vt$$

Similarly, the crew of an aircraft might want to know how long it will take for their aircraft to travel between two points on its flight path:

$$\text{time taken} = \frac{\text{distance travelled}}{\text{average speed}}$$

$$t = \frac{s}{v}$$

Later in this chapter we will see some more equations which apply to an object that is speeding up or slowing down at a steady rate.

A note on learning equations

What is the best way to learn the relationship between speed, distance and time? The most important thing is to understand what the equation is telling you. In the form $v = s/t$, it says that speed is a distance divided by a time. You may find it easier to think in terms of units: speed is measured in metres per second, so we need to divide a distance by a time. Remembering a relationship like this will remind you of the underlying physics.

We have seen that there are three forms of the equation; it is probably best to learn one form, and be able to rearrange it.

Finally, you may find it helpful to learn the 'formula triangle' that represents this equation – see Figure 1.4. The problem with this is that, in learning the triangle, you are ignoring the important physical relationship between speed, distance and time, so only resort to the formula triangle if you have serious difficulties in rearranging equations.

Figure 1.4 The 'formula triangle' method for rearranging a simple equation. To find the formula for one of the quantities, cover it up; then you can see whether to multiply or divide the other two quantities.

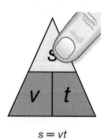
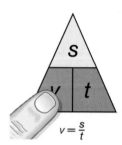

$s = vt$

$v = \dfrac{s}{t}$

Worked example 1

Figure 1.5 A spacecraft orbiting Earth.

[This example illustrates the importance of keeping an eye on units. Because speed is in km/s and distance is in km, we do not need to convert to m/s and m. We would get the same answer if we did the conversion:
$t = (40\,000\,000\,\text{m})/(8000\,\text{m/s})$
$= 5000\,\text{s}.$]

A spacecraft is orbiting the Earth at a steady speed of 8 km/s – see Figure 1.5. How long will it take to complete a single orbit, a distance of 40 000 km?

Start by writing down what you know, and what you want to know:

average speed $v = 8\,\text{km/s}$

distance travelled $s = 40\,000\,\text{km}$

time taken $t = ?$

Now choose the appropriate equation, with the unknown quantity t as the subject:

$$t = \frac{s}{v}$$

Substitute numerical values, and remember to include units:

$$t = \frac{40\,000\,\text{km}}{8\,\text{km/s}}$$

Perform the calculation:

$t = 5000\,\text{s}$

This is about 83 minutes. So the spacecraft takes 83 minutes to orbit the Earth once.

Measuring speed in the laboratory

The multi-flash photograph in Figure 1.6 is a record of an insect taking off. You can see that the images start off close together, indicating slow speed. As the insect speeds up, the images become further apart.

A video camera linked to a computer can provide a similar sequence of images. The camera makes a succession of images at equal intervals of time – see Figure 1.7. Then the image distance can be measured to find the speed of the object as it moves.

Figure 1.6 To make a multi-flash photograph like this, the camera's flash gun is programmed to flash at regular intervals of time, perhaps every tenth of a second. From the spacing of the images, you can tell where the insect is moving slowly, and where it is moving quickly.

In a similar way, the **ticker-timer** records the motion of a moving trolley in the laboratory (Figure 1.8). Dots are marked on the ticker-tape at a regular rate, and these provide a record of the trolley's movement. From the pattern of dots, you can tell whether the trolley was moving at a steady speed, speeding up or slowing down.

From the ticker-tape you can also calculate the average speed of the trolley over an interval of time. Dots are usually marked on the tape at intervals of 1/50th of a second (0.02 s). So each *gap* between adjacent dots shows how far the trolley travelled in 0.02 s. If we take, say, five gaps and measure their total length, this tells us the distance the trolley travelled in 0.1 s. We can then calculate its average speed over that distance.

Figure 1.7 In the laboratory, a video camera can record a series of images of a moving object. The images are made at regular intervals of time, and you can vary the time interval to suit the speed of the object. It helps if the object is moving past a scale, so that its position can be read directly from the images.

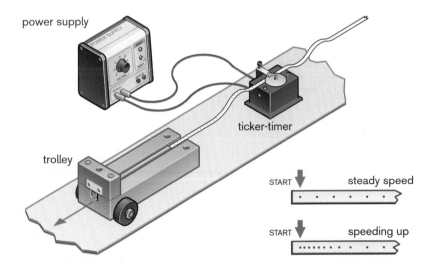

Figure 1.8 The trolley pulls the tape through the ticker-timer. Dots are made at equal intervals of time, to provide a record of the trolley's motion. It's important to know which end of the tape represents the start of the trolley's motion!

One problem with a ticker-timer is that the trolley must drag the tape through the timer. This tends to slow down the trolley, so that it moves more slowly than if the tape was free.

A second method uses two **light gates** – see Figure 1.9a. In light gates a beam of (invisible) infrared radiation is received by a detector. When the moving trolley breaks the beam of the first gate, the electronic timer is started. When the second beam is broken, the timer stops. This tells you the time the trolley has taken to travel between the two gates; if you measure the distance between the two, you can then calculate the trolley's average speed between them.

An alternative method uses a single light gate and an **interrupt card**, fixed to the trolley – see Figure 1.9b. The front edge of the card breaks the beam and starts the timer. When the trailing edge passes the gate, the beam is unbroken and the timer stops. Given the length of the interrupt card, you can calculate the trolley's average speed. (If the timer is connected to a computer, it may do the calculation for you.)

Infrared gates like this are used to check the positions and speeds of cars on roller-coaster rides at fairgrounds. It is important that the ride's computer system knows where each car is, so that it can take action to avoid a collision if a fault occurs. You may also have noticed

Figure 1.9 **a** The peg on top of the trolley breaks the infrared beam of the first light gate as it passes through. This provides an electronic signal to start the timer. The timer stops when the peg breaks the second beam. Given the distance travelled by the trolley between the two gates, the trolley's average speed can be calculated.
b An alternative method uses a single gate. The timer starts when the leading edge of the card passes through the gate, and stops when the trailing edge passes through. The trolley's average speed is then the length of the card divided by the recorded time interval.

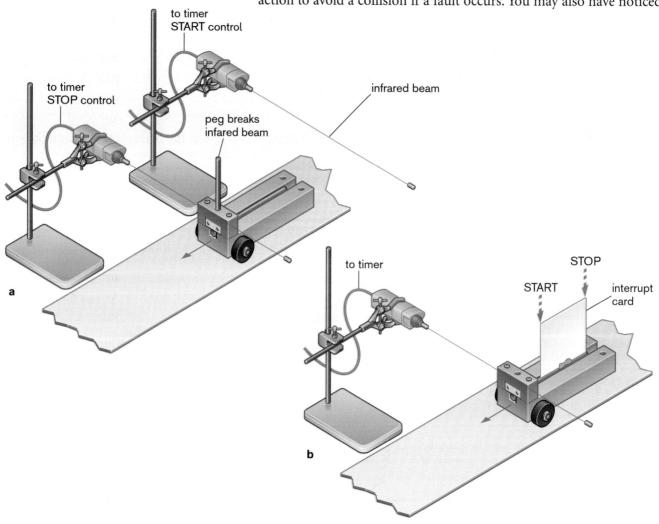

the infrared gate that controls the conveyor belt on a supermarket checkout. When an item reaches the end of the belt, the beam is broken and the belt stops automatically.

Instantaneous speed

The two methods for measuring speed described above both tell us about the *average speed* of the moving object, that is, the object's average speed over an interval of time. In the case of the ticker-timer, we might use a five-gap segment of the tape, representing 0.1 s, so we calculate the trolley's average speed during this time interval. In the case of two light gates, we find the trolley's average speed while it is travelling between the two light gates.

A car's speedometer tells us its **instantaneous speed**. The driver can glance down at the dial and see that the car is moving at 70 mph. This is the car's speed at that instant. The speedometer does not time the car over a certain distance; it works in an entirely different way, to give an instant read-out of the speed. (It works using a magnetic device attached by a cable to the gear-box. The faster the drive-shaft is turning, the more the magnet is dragged round and the higher the needle rises up the scale.)

If you are using a distance-and-time method to measure speed, you can only find an average speed. To get a closer approximation to the instantaneous speed, you must make the time interval as short as possible. With light gates, for example, it is best to keep them close together so that the trolley does not take long to pass between them. Alternatively, using a single light gate, the interrupt card should be short – perhaps 5 cm in length. Then the trolley's speed is unlikely to change significantly whilst the timer is operating.

Speed and velocity

Although the words *speed* and *velocity* have the same meaning in everyday speech, there is an important distinction between them in physics: **speed** tells us about how fast something is moving; **velocity** tells us how fast it is moving *in a particular direction*. So, if you are cycling east along a road at 10 m/s, your speed would be 10 m/s, but your velocity would be 10 m/s *towards the east*. To state your velocity completely, it is essential to include the direction in which you are moving.

Velocity is an example of a **vector quantity**. Vector quantities have both magnitude (size) and direction. Another example of a vector quantity is force (see Chapter 2). If you are lifting 20 kg, you would say that the force with which you are lifting it is 200 newtons *vertically upwards*. You need to state the direction of the force if someone else is to know the full details of your lifting force.

You may also come across another vector quantity, **displacement**. This specifies the position of an object after a particular time, in relation to its starting point.

A simpler type of quantity is a **scalar quantity**. This is a quantity that has magnitude but no direction. Speed is a scalar quantity, because we do not need to give a direction when we state an object's speed. Another scalar quantity that we have already discussed is total distance travelled.

? Questions

1.1 Which of the following could not be a unit of speed?

km/h, s/m, mph, m/s, m s

1.2 Mental arithmetic: A runner travels 400 m in 50 s. What is her average speed?

1.3 Mental arithmetic: How far will a bus travel in 30 s at a speed of 15 m/s?

1.4 In a multi-flash photograph (such as Figure 1.6), how can you tell whether the object is moving quickly or slowly?

1.5 Sketch a length of ticker-tape that represents the following motion: a trolley moves at a steady speed for a short time; then it moves an equal distance, slowing down.

1.6 Which of the following are vector quantities, and which are scalars?

speed, displacement, velocity, distance, time

1.2 Distance–time graphs

You can describe how something moves in words:

> 'The coach pulled away from the bus stop. It travelled at a steady speed along the main road, heading out of town. After five minutes, it reached the motorway, where it was able to speed up. After ten minutes, it was forced to stop because of congestion.'

We can show the same information in the form of a distance–time graph – see Figure 1.10. The graph is in three sections, corresponding to the three sections of the coach's journey:

● *Section A* The graph slopes up gently, showing that the coach is travelling at a slow speed.

Figure 1.10 A graph to represent the motion of a coach, as described in the text. The slope of the graph tells us about the coach's speed. The steepest section (B) corresponds to the greatest speed. The horizontal section (C) shows that the coach is stationary.

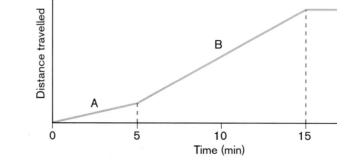

- *Section B* The graph becomes steeper. The distance of the coach from its starting point is increasing more rapidly; it is moving faster.
- *Section C* The graph is flat (horizontal). The distance of the coach from its starting point is not changing; it is stationary.

The slope of the distance–time graph tells us how fast the coach is moving. The steeper the graph, the faster it is moving (the greater its speed). When the graph becomes horizontal, its slope is zero. This tells us that the coach's speed is now zero. Notice that the total distance travelled can never decrease.

Distance–time data

The Settle to Carlisle railway follows a very picturesque route across the hills of northern England. Figure 1.11 shows a train crossing a viaduct on the line, together with part of the timetable. This suggests another way to represent the motion of a moving object: in the form of a table.

Figure 1.11 **a** A train crossing the Ribblehead Viaduct in the north of England. **b** Part of the timetable for this line. Information from the timetable allows us to draw a distance–time graph like the one shown in Figure 1.12.

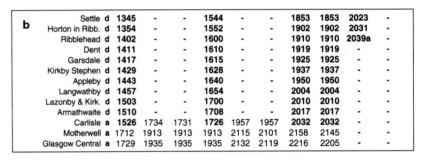

b											
Settle	d	1345	-	-	1544	-	-	1853	1853	2023	-
Horton in Ribb.	d	1354	-	-	1552	-	-	1902	1902	2031	-
Ribblehead	d	1402	-	-	1600	-	-	1910	1910	2039a	-
Dent	d	1411	-	-	1610	-	-	1919	1919	-	-
Garsdale	d	1417	-	-	1615	-	-	1925	1925	-	-
Kirkby Stephen	d	1429	-	-	1628	-	-	1937	1937	-	-
Appleby	d	1443	-	-	1640	-	-	1950	1950	-	-
Langwathby	d	1457	-	-	1654	-	-	2004	2004	-	-
Lazonby & Kirk.	d	1503	-	-	1700	-	-	2010	2010	-	-
Armathwaite	d	1510	-	-	1708	-	-	2017	2017	-	-
Carlisle	a	1526	1734	1731	1726	1957	1957	2032	2032	-	-
Motherwell	a	1712	1913	1913	1913	2115	2101	2158	2145	-	-
Glasgow Central	a	1729	1935	1935	1935	2132	2119	2216	2205	-	-

Table 1.2 shows how far the train has travelled at different points along its journey, together with the time taken. The same information is plotted as a graph in Figure 1.12. The graph does not always have the same slope; this shows that the train's speed was changing as it went along. It was moving fastest where the graph is steepest.

Calculating speed

Figure 1.13 represents the motion of a runner in a 400 m race. You can see that, for most of the race, the graph is a straight line. This shows that the runner was moving at a steady speed. The graph also shows

Table 1.2 This table represents the motion of a train; the data were used to plot the graph shown in Figure 1.12.

Station	Distance travelled (km)	Time taken (minutes)
Settle	0	0
Horton	10	8
Ribblehead	18	16
Dent	28.5	26
Garsdale	34	31
Kirkby Stephen	47	43
Appleby	60	56

Figure 1.12 A distance–time graph for a train, based on the data shown in Table 1.2 (see page 9). From the slope of the graph, we can deduce the train's speed.

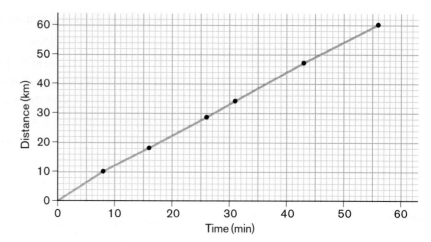

how to calculate the runner's speed. Here, we are looking at the straight section of the graph, where the runner's speed was constant. We need to find the value of the slope of the graph, which will tell us the speed:

speed = slope of distance–time graph

- *Step 1* Identify a straight section of the graph.
- *Step 2* Draw horizontal and vertical lines to complete a right-angled triangle – for accuracy, as large as possible.
- *Step 3* Calculate the lengths of the sides of the triangle.
- *Step 4* Divide the vertical height by the horizontal width of the triangle ('up divided by along').

Here is the calculation for the triangle shown in Figure 1.13:

vertical height = 200 m
horizontal width = 25 s

so

$$\text{slope} = \frac{200\,\text{m}}{25\,\text{s}} = 8\,\text{m/s}$$

The runner's speed was 8 m/s for most of the race. It is important to include units in this calculation. Then the answer will automatically have the correct units – in this case, m/s. If we used the data for the train (Figure 1.12), where distances are in km and times in minutes, the speed would have been in km/minute.

Figure 1.13 This graph represents the motion of a runner in a race. The short curved section at the beginning represents the runner setting off; for most of the time, the graph is a straight line, indicating steady speed. At the end, the graph becomes a little steeper, indicating that the runner put on a final spurt in a dash for the tape.

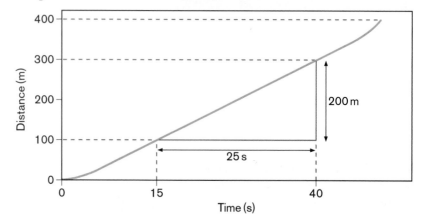

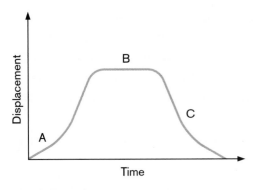

Figure 1.14 Displacement–time graphs are not always straight lines. This graph is for a car moving along a road. The curved section **A** shows it speeding up; section **B** shows where it has stopped; section **C** has a negative slope, showing that the car is returning towards its starting position.

Graphs of different shapes

We have seen the following points about distance–time graphs:
- the slope of the graph gives the object's speed;
- the steeper the slope, the greater the speed;
- a horizontal graph (slope = 0) indicates that the object is not moving.

We can also draw displacement–time graphs to represent the motion of an object along a straight line. Recall that displacement is a vector quantity. An object's displacement may increase or decrease, according to the direction in which it is moving. The displacement–time graph in Figure 1.14 shows the following points:
- where the graph is curved, the object's speed is changing;
- where the graph slopes downwards (negative slope), the object is moving in the opposite direction.

For a negative slope, we can still work out the speed from the slope, but we have to remember to include a minus sign.

Graphs in the laboratory

A **motion sensor** connected to a computer can be used to follow the motion of a moving object in the laboratory, and to produce a distance–time graph on the computer screen. As shown in Figure 1.15, the sensor is directed at a moving trolley. As the trolley moves back and forth in line with the sensor, the graph on the screen slopes up and down.

The sensor works by sending out pulses of ultrasound (high-pitched sound, too high to be heard). The pulses reflect off the trolley and are detected by the sensor. The computer determines the time between the transmission of the outgoing pulse and the reception of the reflected pulse. Knowing the speed of the ultrasound, it can calculate the distance of the trolley.

This is rather like the way in which a bat senses its surroundings, by listening to reflected bursts of ultrasound. An estate agent who is surveying

Figure 1.15 Using a motion sensor to detect the motion of a moving trolley. Ultrasound waves from the sensor are reflected back by the trolley. The closer the trolley is to the sensor, the shorter the time interval between transmission and reception. From these data, the computer can draw a displacement–time graph.

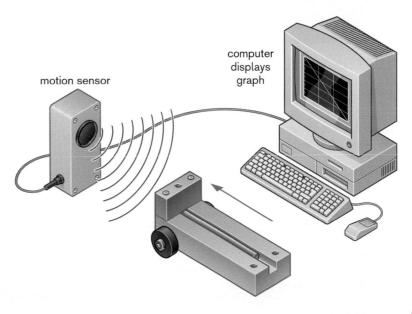

computer displays graph

motion sensor

a house for sale may use a device similar to the motion sensor to measure the dimensions of rooms without the need for a long tape measure.

You can investigate your own motion using a motion sensor. Walk towards it holding a small board to reflect the ultrasound waves. Try to walk steadily; it is surprisingly difficult to generate a smooth, straight-line graph on the screen.

?

Questions

1.7 Sketch a distance–time graph that represents the following motion: a trolley moves at a steady speed for a short time; then it moves an equal distance, speeding up.

1.8 A car is moving along a road. Its distance–time graph gradually becomes steeper. Is the car speeding up, slowing down, or travelling at a steady speed?

1.9 Scientists have calculated the distance between the Earth and the Moon by reflecting a beam of laser light off the Moon. They measured the time taken for the laser light to travel to the Moon and back. What other piece of information is needed to calculate the Earth–Moon distance? How would the distance be calculated?

1.3 Changing speed

An express train is capable of reaching high speeds – perhaps in excess of 300 km/h. However, when it sets off on its journey, it may take several minutes to reach this top speed. Then it takes a long time to slow down when it approaches its destination. The famous French TGV trains (Figure 1.16) run on lines that are reserved solely for their operation, so that their high-speed journeys are not disrupted by slower, local trains. It takes time to accelerate (speed up) and decelerate (slow down).

A bus journey is full of accelerations and decelerations. The bus accelerates away from the bus-stop; ideally, the driver hopes to travel at a steady speed until the next stop. A steady speed means that you can sit comfortably in your seat. Then there is a rapid deceleration as the bus slows to a halt. A lot of accelerating and decelerating means that you are likely to be thrown about as the bus changes speed. The gentle acceleration of an express train will barely disturb the drink in your cup; the bus's rapid accelerations and decelerations would make it impossible to avoid spilling the drink.

Calculating acceleration

Some cars, particularly high-performance ones, are advertised according to how rapidly they can accelerate. An advert may claim that a car goes 'from 0 to 60 miles per hour (mph) in 6 s'. This means that, if the

Figure 1.16 France's high-speed trains, the TGVs (trains à grande vitesse), run on dedicated tracks. Their speed has made it possible to travel 600 km from Marseille in the south to Paris in the north, attend a meeting, and return home again within a single day.

car accelerates at a steady rate, it reaches 10 mph after 1 s, 20 mph after 2 s, and so on. We could say that it speeds up by 10 mph every second; in other words, its **acceleration** is 10 mph per second.

The express train may take 300 s to reach a speed of 300 km/h. Its acceleration is 1 km/h per second.

These are not very convenient units, although they may help to make it clear what is happening when we talk about acceleration. To calculate an object's acceleration, we need to know two things:

- its change in velocity;
- the time taken for the change.

Then its acceleration is given by:

$$\text{acceleration} = \frac{\text{change in velocity}}{\text{time taken}}$$

In the case of the car above, its velocity increased by 60 mph in 6 s, so its acceleration was (60 mph)/(6 s) = 10 mph/s.

We can write the equation for acceleration in symbols. We use the symbol a for acceleration. We need two symbols in order to show the change in velocity: we use u and v to represent the velocities at the start and finish of the time interval t (remember that u comes before v in the alphabet):

u = initial velocity

v = final velocity

a = acceleration

Our equation is

$$a = \frac{(v - u)}{t} \quad \text{or} \quad a = (v - u)/t$$

Worked example 2

An aircraft accelerates from 100 m/s to 300 m/s in 100 s. What is its acceleration?

Start by writing down what you know, and what you want to know:

$u = 100$ m/s

$v = 300$ m/s

$t = 100$ s

$a = ?$

Now substitute into the equation for acceleration:

$$a = \frac{(v - u)}{t} = \frac{(300 \text{ m/s} - 100 \text{ m/s})}{100 \text{ s}}$$

The brackets will help to remind you to calculate the change in velocity before you divide by the time taken:

$$a = \frac{200 \text{ m/s}}{100 \text{ s}} = 2 \text{ m/s}^2$$

Units of acceleration

In worked example 2, the units of acceleration are given as m/s^2 ('metres per second squared'). These are the standard units of acceleration. The calculation shows that the aircraft's speed increased by

2 m/s every second, or 2 metres per second per second. It is simplest to write this as 2 m/s^2, but you may prefer to think of it as 2 m/s per second, as this emphasises the meaning of acceleration.

Other units for acceleration are possible – earlier we saw examples of acceleration in mph per second and km/h per second, but these are unconventional. It is usually best to work in m/s^2.

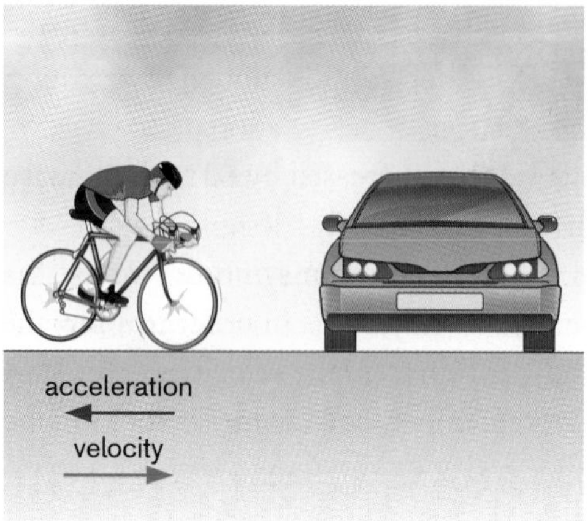

Worked example 3

A car driver suddenly pulls out from a side road in the path of a fast-moving cyclist (see figure 1.17). The cyclist brakes hard to avoid riding into the car. His speed decreases from 15 m/s to 3 m/s in 3 s. What is his acceleration?

This example illustrates the calculation of acceleration when an object is slowing down (decelerating).

From the question, we have:

$u = 15 \text{ m/s}$

$v = 3 \text{ m/s}$

$t = 3 \text{ s}$

Substituting into the equation for acceleration gives

$$a = \frac{(3 \text{ m/s} - 15 \text{ m/s})}{3 \text{ s}} = \frac{-12 \text{ m/s}}{3 \text{ s}} = -4 \text{ m/s}^2$$

So the cyclist's acceleration is -4 m/s^2 (*minus* 4 metres per second squared). The value is negative since this is a deceleration.

Figure 1.17 This cyclist (worked example 3) is slowing down to avoid hitting the car. The cyclist's velocity is to the right (positive) but his acceleration is to the left (negative).

Velocity and acceleration

In worked example 3, the cyclist's *change* in velocity is negative (he is slowing down), and so his acceleration is also negative. This is illustrated in Figure 1.17. The cyclist is always moving forwards (in a positive direction), but his acceleration is in the opposite direction (backwards). This shows that acceleration has a direction; it is a vector quantity, like velocity. So, we should always talk about 'change in velocity' when we are considering acceleration, rather than 'change in speed'.

Some people get a lot of pleasure out of sudden accelerations and decelerations. Many fairground rides involve sudden changes in velocity. On a roller-coaster (Figure 1.18), you may speed up as the car runs down-hill. Then, suddenly, you veer off to the left – you are accelerated sideways. A sudden braking gives you a large, negative acceleration (a deceleration). You will probably have to be fastened in to your seat to avoid being thrown out of the car by these sudden changes in velocity.

Figure 1.18 A roller-coaster ride involves many rapid changes in velocity. These accelerations and decelerations help to give the ride its thrill. The ride's designers have calculated the accelerations carefully to ensure that the car will not come off its track and the riders will stay in the car.

Measuring acceleration in the laboratory

If you place a trolley at the top of a sloping ramp, it will run downhill, picking up speed as it travels down the ramp. It is accelerating. To

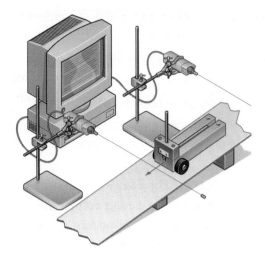

Figure 1.19 To measure the acceleration of a trolley on a sloping ramp, you need two measurements of its velocity. One method uses two light gates. The computer calculates the trolley's velocity as it passes through each gate, and then calculates its acceleration.

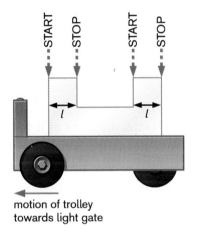

motion of trolley
towards light gate

Figure 1.20 With a single light gate, the trolley must be fitted with an interrupt card that breaks the infrared beam twice. The computer then records four measurements of time; it is also programmed with the length of the sections of the interrupt card. From these data, it can calculate two velocities and the time interval between them, and hence the trolley's acceleration.

measure its acceleration, you need to make two measurements of its velocity (initial and final), and you also need to know the time interval between the two measurements. Here are two ways of doing this, using light gates connected to a timer or computer:

1 With two light gates (Figure 1.19), the trolley has a rectangular interrupt card attached. The card breaks the infrared beam of the first light gate; then it breaks the beam of the second light gate, but for a shorter time, because it is moving more quickly. Knowing the length of the interrupt card, the computer connected to the light gates can then calculate the trolley's average velocity as it passes the first gate, and then its average velocity as it passes the second gate. (These are the initial and final velocities.) It can also calculate the time taken by the trolley to travel from one gate to the next. This is enough information for the computer to work out the trolley's acceleration.

2 With a single light gate (Figure 1.20), the trolley must be fitted with a different interrupt card. This is cleverly designed, with two sections of equal lengths sticking up to break the infrared beam. The first section breaks the beam for a short time; the second section breaks the beam for a shorter time, because the trolley is speeding up. The computer is programmed with the length of each of the sections; it then calculates the trolley's average velocity as each section passes the gate. Using the timer interval between these two measurements, it calculates the acceleration.

Accelerating downwards

The trolley on the sloping ramp accelerates down the slope. The steeper the ramp, the greater its acceleration. A falling object also accelerates. If you hold a ball at arm's length and let it go, the force of gravity pulls it downwards, causing it to speed up as it falls. You can see the pattern of its acceleration using a ticker-timer. A heavy weight has a ticker-tape attached, and is then allowed to fall. The tape records its fall; the spacing of the dots on the tape increases steadily, showing that the weight is accelerating. (The pattern is like that shown in Figure 1.8 for an object speeding up.)

It is possible to analyse such a ticker-tape to determine the weight's acceleration. However, as mentioned earlier, the tape is slowed down by friction as it passes through the timer, and this means that the answer is less than if the weight was falling freely.

You can find out more about the motion of falling objects in Chapter 2.

> **? Questions**
>
> **1.10** Which of the following could not be a unit of acceleration?
> km/s^2,   mph/s,   km/s, m/s^2

Questions continued

1.11 Give one word that means the same as 'moving with a negative acceleration'.

1.12 Sketch three lengths of ticker-tape to show the following: **a** an object moving with steady speed; **b** the same object accelerating; **c** the same object moving with a greater acceleration.

1.13 Draw an 'interrupt card' that could be used with a single light gate to find the acceleration of a moving trolley. Indicate the direction in which the trolley is moving; indicate also the edges of the card which start the electronic timer, and those which stop it.

1.14 Mental arithmetic: A runner accelerates from rest to 8 m/s in 2 s. What is her acceleration?

1.4 Velocity–time graphs

Just as we can represent the motion of a moving object by a distance–time graph, we can also represent it by a velocity–time graph. (It is easy to get these two types of graph mixed up. Always check out any graph by looking at the axes to see what their labels say.) A velocity–time graph shows how the object's speed changes as it moves.

Figure 1.21 shows a velocity–time graph for a bus as it follows its route through a busy town. (To keep things simple, we assume that the velocity is always in the same direction, so that the bus moves in a straight line.) The graph often drops to zero because the bus must keep stopping to let people on and off. Then the line slopes up, as the bus accelerates away from the bus-stop. Towards the end of its journey, it manages to move at a constant velocity (horizontal graph), as it does not have to stop. Finally, the graph slopes downwards to zero again as the bus pulls in to the terminus and stops.

The slope of the velocity–time graph tells us about the bus's acceleration:

● the steeper the slope, the greater the acceleration;

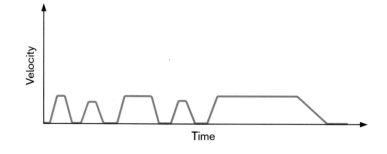

Figure 1.21 A velocity–time graph for a bus on a busy route. At first, it has to halt often at bus-stops. Towards the end of its journey, it keeps to a steady velocity.

- a negative slope means a deceleration (slowing down);
- a horizontal graph (slope = 0) means a constant velocity.

By calculating the slope of the graph, we can find the acceleration:

acceleration = slope of velocity–time graph

Worked example 4

Velocity (m/s)	Time (s)
6.0	0
6.0	10
6.0	20
8.0	30
10.0	40
12.0	50
14.0	60

Table 1.3 Velocity–time data for a train.

A train travels slowly as it climbs up a long hill; then it speeds up as it travels down the other side. Table 1.3 shows how its velocity changes. Draw a velocity–time graph to show these data, and use the graph to calculate the train's acceleration during the second half of its journey.

Before starting to draw a graph, it is worth looking at the data in the table. The values of velocity are given at equal intervals of time (every 10 s). The velocity is constant at first (6.0 m/s); then it increases in equal steps (8.0, 10.0, etc.). In fact, we can see that the velocity increases by 2.0 m/s every 10 s, and this is enough to tell us that the train's acceleration is 0.2 m/s². However, we will follow through the detailed calculation to show how to work out acceleration from a graph.

Figure 1.22 shows the velocity–time graph drawn using the data in the table. You can see that it falls into two parts:

- the initial horizontal section shows that the train's velocity was constant (zero acceleration);
- the sloping section shows that the train was then accelerating.

The triangle shows how to calculate the slope of the graph. This gives us the acceleration:

$$\text{acceleration} = \frac{(14.0\,\text{m/s} - 6.0\,\text{m/s})}{(60\,\text{s} - 20\,\text{s})} = \frac{8.0\,\text{m/s}}{40\,\text{s}} = 0.2\,\text{m/s}^2$$

So, as we expected, the train's acceleration down the hill is 0.2 m/s².

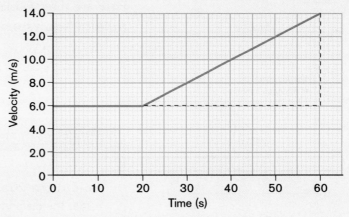

Figure 1.22 Velocity–time graph for a train, based on the data in Table 1.3. The triangle is used to calculate the slope of the second section of the graph; this tells us the train's acceleration.

Graphs of different shapes

Velocity–time graphs can show a lot about an object's movement. Was it moving at a steady velocity, or speeding up, or slowing down? Was it moving at all? The graph shown in Figure 1.22 is a bit unrealistic; it is

Figure 1.23 An example of a velocity–time graph (for a train during part of its journey). This illustrates how such a graph can show acceleration, constant velocity, deceleration and zero velocity.

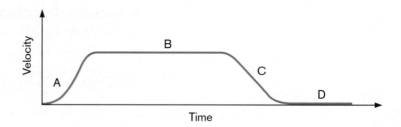

made up simply of two straight-line sections. Figure 1.23 shows a more realistic graph for a train journey. If you study the graph, you will see that it is in four sections, each of which illustrates a different point:

- *Section A* Sloping upwards – velocity increasing – the train was accelerating.
- *Section B* Horizontal – velocity constant – the train was travelling at a steady velocity.
- *Section C* Sloping downwards – velocity decreasing – the train was decelerating.
- *Section D* Horizontal – velocity has decreased to zero – the train was stationary.

The fact that the graph lines are curved in sections A and C tells us that the train's acceleration was changing. If its velocity had changed at a steady rate, these lines would have been straight.

Finding distance travelled

If we want to find the total distance travelled by a moving object, we can use a speed–time graph. To do this, we have to make use of the equation

distance travelled = average speed × time taken

Here are three worked examples to illustrate how to find distance travelled from a speed–time graph.

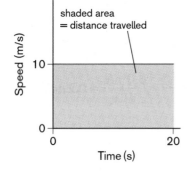

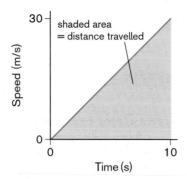

Figure 1.24 Speed–time graphs for
a constant speed and
b constant acceleration from rest (see worked examples 5 and 6). In each case, the distance travelled is represented by the shaded area under the graph.

Worked example 5

You cycle for 20 s at a constant speed of 10 m/s – see Figure 1.24a. The distance you travel is:

distance travelled = 10 m/s × 20 s
= 200 m

This is represented by the shaded area under the graph. This rectangle is 20 s long and 10 m/s high, so its area is 10 m/s × 20 s = 200 m.

Worked example 6

(This is a little more complicated.) You set off down a steep ski slope. Your initial speed is 0 m/s; after 10 s you are travelling at 30 m/s – see Figure 1.24b. Your average speed is 15 m/s. The distance you travel is:

$$\text{distance travelled} = 15\,\text{m/s} \times 10\,\text{s}$$
$$= 150\,\text{m}$$

Again, this is represented by the shaded area under the graph. In this case, the shape is a triangle whose height is 30 m/s and whose base is 10 s. Since area of a triangle $= \frac{1}{2} \times$ base $\times$ height, we have area $= \frac{1}{2} \times 10\,\text{s} \times 30\,\text{m/s} = 150\,\text{m}$.

Worked example 7

Calculate the distance travelled in 60 s by the train whose motion was described in worked example 4 (Figure 1.22 and Table 1.3).

The graph in Figure 1.25 is the same as that in Figure 1.22, but it has been shaded to show the area that gives the distance travelled by the train (this is why we use speed rather than velocity). This area is in two parts:

● a rectangle of height 6 m/s and width 60 s, with

$$\text{area} = 6\,\text{m/s} \times 60\,\text{s} = 360\,\text{m}$$

which tells us how far the train would have travelled if it had maintained a constant speed of 6 m/s;

● a triangle of base 40 s, and height $(14\,\text{m/s} - 6\,\text{m/s}) = 8\,\text{m/s}$, with

$$\text{area} = \frac{1}{2} \times \text{base} \times \text{height}$$
$$= \frac{1}{2} \times 40\,\text{s} \times 8\,\text{m/s} = 160\,\text{m}$$

which tells us the *extra* distance travelled by the train because it was accelerating.

The total area then gives

$$\text{total distance travelled} = 360\,\text{m} + 160\,\text{m} = 520\,\text{m}$$

So, in 60 s, the train travelled 520 m. We can check this result using an alternative approach. The train travelled for 20 s at a steady speed of 6 m/s, and then for 40 s at an average speed of 10 m/s. We get

$$\text{total distance travelled} = (6\,\text{m/s} \times 20\,\text{s}) + (10\,\text{m/s} \times 40\,\text{s})$$
$$= 120\,\text{m} + 400\,\text{m} = 520\,\text{m}$$

(The brackets are included as a reminder to perform the multiplications before the addition.)

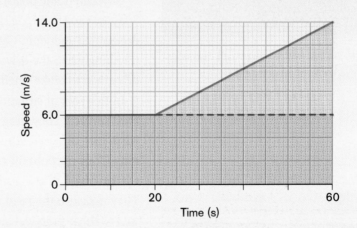

Figure 1.25 Calculating the distance travelled by a train. Distance travelled is represented by the area under the graph. To make the calculation easier, this area is divided up into a rectangle and a triangle, as shown.

In fact, the total distance travelled by a moving object can always be found from the area under the speed–time graph:

distance travelled = area under speed–time graph

In more complicated situations, you may have to divide the area under the graph into rectangles and triangles, and add up their separate areas – worked example 7 illustrates this. Alternatively, you can use the technique of counting the squares on the graph paper.

? Questions

1.15 Sketch a velocity–time graph to show the following motion: a car accelerates uniformly from rest for 5 s; then it travels at a steady velocity for 5 s.

1.16 On your sketch graph from question 1.13, shade the area that represents the distance travelled by the car in 10 s.

1.17 The velocity–time graph for part of a train journey is a horizontal straight line. What does this tell you about the train's velocity, and about its acceleration?

Figure 1.26 Traffic police carry out investigations at the scene of an accident.

Quantity	Symbol	Unit
displacement	s	m
time taken	t	s
initial velocity	u	m/s
final velocity	v	m/s
acceleration	a	m/s^2

Table 1.4 The important quantities that we have met so far. Speed is not included because it is velocity (speed in a particular direction) that is important in calculations.

1.5 The equations of motion

After a road accident, traffic police (Figure 1.26) may be sent to examine the scene. They are looking for evidence that may show whether any of the drivers involved were breaking the law. They may look for skid marks on the road, or anything that may have obstructed the view. They will have taken statements from those involved, and they will want to check whether what witnesses say matches up with the situation on the ground.

How can traffic police reconstruct the events leading up to an accident? Suppose they find long skid marks, left on the road when one of the cars decelerated suddenly. Can they deduce how fast the car must have been travelling when the driver braked? Can they work out how much time a driver had to brake when a problem arose ahead?

In this sort of situation, the police carry out experiments to test the road surface. They drag a device called a sledge along the road, to see what sort of acceleration they can achieve without slipping or skidding. They may obtain a car of the same make and model as that which was involved in the accident and test it on the same stretch of road. They measure the road and make a map of the accident situation. As well as these practical approaches, they make use of a set of equations which relate the important quantities that we have looked at already in this chapter. These quantities are shown as a reminder in Table 1.4.

There are four equations that link these quantities, known as **the equations of motion**. Note that they only apply in situations where an object is moving with constant acceleration. In other words, its velocity is changing at a steady rate. The four equations are as follows.

1 We have already seen one equation linking these quantities:

$$a = \frac{(v - u)}{t} \qquad \text{or} \qquad a = (v - u)/t$$

This equation defines what we mean by acceleration. It is often more useful in the form

$$v = u + at$$

This tells us that the final velocity v of an object is equal to its initial velocity u plus the amount by which it increases when it moves with acceleration a for time t:

final velocity = initial velocity + change in velocity

2 The next equation comes from the definition of average velocity:

$$s = \frac{(v + u)}{2} t \qquad \text{or} \qquad s = \frac{1}{2}(v + u) t$$

This tells us that the displacement s is the average velocity $\frac{1}{2}(v + u)$ multiplied by the time taken t.

3 If we do not know the object's final velocity v, we can use an alternative equation to work out how far the object has travelled:

$$s = ut + \frac{1}{2}at^2$$

Note that, if the object was not accelerating ($a = 0$), this would simply be $s = ut$, or displacement = velocity × time.

4 Finally, if we know the displacement of an accelerating object, rather than the *time* during which it is accelerating, we can find its final velocity using the equation

$$v^2 = u^2 + 2as$$

Again, for zero acceleration ($a = 0$), this would simply give us $v^2 = u^2$, so that the final velocity would equal the initial velocity.

The four equations of motion are collected together in Table 1.5. Worked examples 8 and 9 show how they can be used.

$$v = u + at$$
$$s = \frac{1}{2}(v + u)t$$
$$s = ut + \frac{1}{2}at^2$$
$$v^2 = u^2 + 2as$$

Table 1.5 The four equations of motion, for an object moving with constant acceleration.

Worked example 8

A car is travelling at 20 m/s along a road. A child runs out into the road, 50 m ahead, and the car driver steps on the brake pedal. What must the car's acceleration be if the car is to stop before it reaches the child? The police have estimated that no vehicle can achieve a greater deceleration than −5 m/s². Will the driver be able to stop in time?

● *Step 1* Write down what you know, and what you want to know:

$u = 20$ m/s
$v = 0$ m/s
$s = 50$ m
$a = ?$

(This first step is crucial in helping you to decide which equation to use.)

continued on next page

Note that the answer is negative because the car is slowing down (decelerating). This is less than the maximum estimated by the police, so the driver should be able to stop the car in time provided its brakes and tyres are in good condition.

- *Step 2* Choose the equation of motion that links these quantities, and rearrange it to make the unknown quantity a the subject:

$$v^2 = u^2 + 2as$$
$$a = \frac{(v^2 - u^2)}{2s}$$

- *Step 3* Substitute in values and solve:

$$a = \frac{-(20\,\text{m/s})^2}{2 \times 50\,\text{m}} = \frac{-400\,\text{m}^2/\text{s}^2}{100\,\text{m}} = -4\,\text{m/s}^2$$

Worked example 9

A car joins a motorway travelling at 15 m/s. It accelerates at 2 m/s² for 8 s. How far will it travel in this time?

- *Step 1* As before, write down what you know, and what you want to know:

$$u = 15\,\text{m/s} \qquad t = 8\,\text{s}$$
$$a = 2\,\text{m/s}^2 \qquad s = ?$$

- *Step 2* Choose the equation of motion that links these quantities. In this case, there is no need to rearrange it, because the unknown quantity, s, is already the subject:

$$s = ut + \tfrac{1}{2}at^2$$

- *Step 3* Substitute in values and solve:

$$s = 15\,\text{m/s} \times 8\,\text{s} + \tfrac{1}{2} \times 2\,\text{m/s}^2 \times (8\,\text{s})^2$$
$$s = 120\,\text{m} + 64\,\text{m} = 184\,\text{m}$$

Thinking and braking

The Highway Code is a booklet that tells drivers and others how to use Britain's roads safely. On its back cover it carries a diagram (Figure 1.27) showing the shortest distances in which a car can come to a halt if the driver has to stop in a hurry. A car travelling at 20 mph, for instance, requires at least 12 m in which to stop. From the diagram, you can see that the **stopping distance** is made up of two parts:

- **Thinking distance** is the distance that the car travels in the time between the instant when the driver realises he or she must stop, and the instant when the brakes are applied. It takes a fraction of a second for the driver to react and for their brain to send a message to their foot. The car travels at a steady speed in this time.
- **Braking distance** is the distance travelled by the car as it slows down to a halt. Its speed decreases steadily (constant deceleration) during this time.

So we have

stopping distance = thinking distance + braking distance

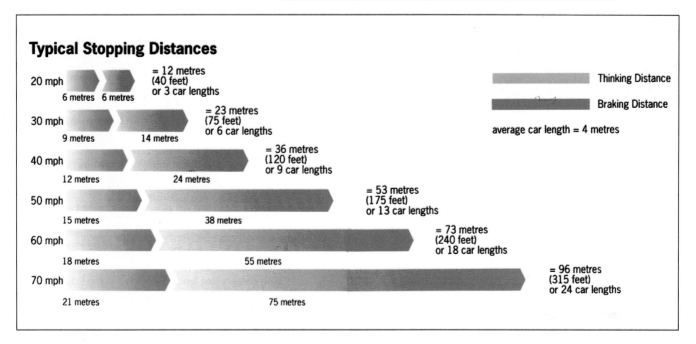

Figure 1.27 A chart of stopping distances, from *The Highway Code*. These distances assume an alert driver in good road conditions with a well-maintained car.

The distances in the chart assume that the conditions of both the road and the car are good, and that the driver's reactions are quick. The braking distance, in particular, may be greater if the road surface is slippery, or if the car's brakes or tyres are faulty. The thinking distance may be greater if the driver has been drinking alcohol, for example, or if they are sleepy.

Table 1.6 shows the same information, with speeds converted to m/s. The data in the table, and the graphs shown in Figure 1.28, show the following points.

- *Thinking distance* increases in proportion to speed. If the car is travelling twice as fast, it will travel twice as far during the **thinking time**. From the graph (Figure 1.28a), we can see that, by dividing any speed (in metres per second) by the thinking distance at that speed, the thinking time is about two-thirds of a second ($\frac{2}{3}$ s).
- *Braking distance* increases more and more rapidly as the car's speed increases – see Figure 1.28b. Look at the values for 20 mph and

Table 1.6 Data on stopping distances, taken from *The Highway Code*. Stopping distance increases more and more rapidly at high speeds.

Speed (mph)	Speed (m/s)	Thinking distance (m)	Braking distance (m)	Stopping distance (m)
20	9.0	6	6	12
30	13.4	9	14	23
40	17.9	12	24	36
50	22.4	15	38	53
60	26.9	18	55	73
70	31.4	21	75	96

a

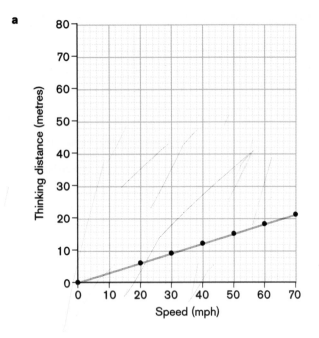

b

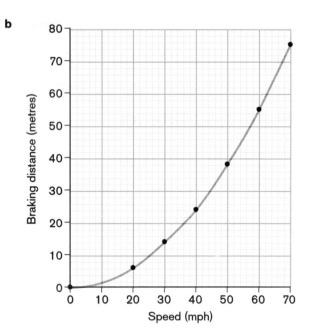

Figure 1.28 Graphs representing data on stopping distances, taken from *The Highway Code*. They show how
a thinking distance and
b braking distance depend on a car's speed.

Figure 1.29 Safety markings on a motorway. Drivers can keep a safe distance by keeping two sets of chevrons between their vehicle and the vehicle in front – this is easier than trying to judge the distance.

40 mph. Braking distances are 6 m and 24 m. Doubling the speed gives four times the braking distance. Similarly, trebling the speed from 20 mph to 60 mph gives nine times the braking distance. This gives the curved graph shown in Figure 1.28b. The braking distance is proportional to the *square* of the car's speed. This is what we might expect from one of the equations of motion: $v^2 = u^2 + 2as$. The final speed $v = 0$. Rearranging gives us $s = -u^2/2a$, which shows that the distance s is proportional to the square of the initial speed, u^2.

The Highway Code also advises drivers to maintain a good distance from the car ahead. Some drivers habitually 'tailgate' the car in front; that is, they drive very close to its back bumper. The advice suggests that drivers should maintain a gap of at least 2 s, considerably more than the minimum thinking time of $\frac{2}{3}$ s; at a speed of 70 mph (31 m/s) on a motorway, this means a gap of 62 m. In the UK, distance markers are positioned every 100 m on the motorway verge, and these can help drivers to keep to a safe separation. Some European motorways have double chevrons (V-shapes) marked at intervals along their length to help drivers maintain a safe distance behind the vehicle in front – see Figure 1.29. Drivers are also encouraged to use the 'two second rule' to keep a safe distance behind the car in front. Watch for the car in front to pass a prominent marker; if you pass the marker less than 2 s later, you are too close.

Questions

1.18 If you are going to use any of the four equations of motion to calculate some aspect of the motion of an object, what must be true about the object's acceleration?

1.19 Which of the equations of motion is the same as the definition of acceleration, i.e. acceleration = (change in velocity)/(time taken)?

1.20 When a car stops suddenly, the stopping distance is the sum of the thinking distance and the braking distance. Which of these two factors might be affected by a slippery road surface? Explain why both factors might be affected if the driver had consumed alcohol or drugs.

Summary

◆ Average speed is calculated as follows:

$$\text{average speed} = \frac{\text{distance travelled}}{\text{time taken}}$$

$$v = \frac{s}{t}$$

◆ Speed is the slope of a distance–time graph.

◆ Acceleration is calculated as follows:

$$\text{acceleration} = \frac{\text{change in velocity}}{\text{time taken}}$$

$$a = \frac{(v - u)}{t}$$

◆ Acceleration is the slope of a velocity–time graph.

◆ Distance travelled is the area under a speed–time graph.

◆ A scalar quantity (e.g. speed, distance travelled) has only magnitude. A vector quantity (e.g. velocity, acceleration) has both magnitude and direction.

◆ *The resultant of two or more vectors is found by drawing a vector diagram.*

◆ The equations of motion are used in calculations where an object moves with a uniform (constant) acceleration.

◆ Stopping distance is the sum of the thinking distance and the braking distance.

◆ Thinking distance is affected by tiredness or consumption of alcohol. Also, it increases in proportion to speed.

◆ Braking distance is determined by speed, road surface, mass of the vehicle and condition of the brakes.

Forces and motion

Topics in this chapter

◆ force, mass and acceleration

◆ the newton as the unit of force

◆ balanced and unbalanced forces

◆ Newton's first and second laws of motion

◆ friction and drag

◆ gravity and weight

◆ motion under gravity

ℯ circular motion

Figure 2.1 The Space Shuttle accelerating away from its launch pad. The force needed is provided by five rocket engines; two of these are booster rockets which are jettisoned once they have used all their fuel, to reduce the mass that is being carried up into space.

It takes an enormous force to lift the giant Space Shuttle off its launch-pad, and to propel it into space (Figure 2.1). The rocket engines that supply the initial thrust provide a force of several million newtons. As the spacecraft accelerates upwards, the crew experience the sensation of being pressed firmly back into their seats. That is how they know that their craft is accelerating.

Forces change motion: one moment, the Shuttle is sitting on the ground, stationary; the next moment, it is accelerating upwards, pushed by the force provided by the rockets.

In this chapter, we will look at how forces – pushes and pulls – affect objects as they move. You will be familiar with the idea that forces are measured in newtons (N). To give an idea of the sizes of various forces, here are some examples.

● You lift an apple. The force needed to lift an apple is roughly 1 newton (1 N).

● You jump up in the air. Your leg muscles provide the force needed to do this – about 1000 N.

● You reach the motorway in your high-performance car, and put your foot down. The car accelerates forwards; the engine provides a force of about 5000 N.

● You are crossing the Atlantic in a Boeing 747 jumbo jet. The four engines together provide a thrust of about 1 000 000 N – that's about the same as the thrust provided by each of the Space Shuttle's rocket engines.

2.1 Forces produce acceleration

The car driver in Figure 2.2a is waiting for the traffic lights to change. When they go green, she moves forwards. The force provided by the engine causes the car to accelerate. In a few seconds, the car is moving quickly along the road. The arrow in the diagram shows the force pushing the car forwards. If the driver wants to get away from the lights more quickly, she can press harder on the accelerator. The forward force is then bigger, and the car's acceleration will be greater.

The driver reaches another junction, where she must stop. She applies the brakes. This provides another force to slow down the car – see Figure 2.2b. The car is moving forwards, but the force needed to make it decelerate is directed backwards. If the driver wants to stop in a hurry, a bigger force is needed. She must press hard on the brake pedal, and the car's deceleration will be greater.

We have seen several things about forces:

- They can be represented by arrows. A force has a direction, shown by the direction of the arrow.
- A force can make an object accelerate. The object accelerates in the direction of the force.
- The bigger the force acting on an object, the bigger the acceleration it gives to the object.

This last idea (the greater the force, the greater the acceleration) can be represented mathematically. We say that the acceleration a produced by a force F is *proportional to* the force. In symbols:

$$a \propto F$$

'Proportional' means that doubling the force produces twice the acceleration, three times the force produces three times the acceleration, and so on.

The car driver uses the accelerator pedal to control the car's acceleration; this alters the force provided by the engine. There is another factor that affects the car's acceleration. Suppose the driver picks up some friends from the airport and they have lots of heavy luggage. She will notice the difference when she moves away from the traffic lights; the car will not accelerate so readily, because its mass has been increased. Similarly, when she applies the brakes, it will not decelerate as readily as before. The mass of the car affects how easily it can be accelerated or decelerated. Drivers learn to take account of this. To summarise:

- The bigger the mass of an object, the smaller the acceleration it is given by a particular force.

Again, we can represent this idea mathematically. The greater the mass, the *smaller* the acceleration, so we say that the acceleration a produced

a

b

Figure 2.2 A force can be represented by an arrow.

a A forward arrow represents a forward force; the forward force provided by the engine causes the car to accelerate forwards.

b A backward arrow represents a backward force; the backward force provided by the brakes causes the car to decelerate.

by a given force is *inversely proportional* to the mass m of the object acted on by the force. In symbols:

$$a \propto \frac{1}{m}$$

'Inversely proportional' means that if we double the mass of the object its acceleration for a given force will be halved.

Force, mass, acceleration

These relationships between force F, mass m and acceleration a can be combined in a single, very useful, equation:

> force = mass $\times$ acceleration
> $F = ma$

Using this equation, we can say that it takes a 2000 N force to give a car of mass 1000 kg an acceleration of 2 m/s² (2000 N = 1000 kg $\times$ 2 m/s²). If we want to find the acceleration produced by a particular force, we can rearrange the equation as follows:

> $$\text{acceleration} = \frac{\text{force}}{\text{mass}}$$
> $$a = \frac{F}{m}$$

The quantities involved in these relationships, and their units, are summarised in Table 2.1. The worked examples that follow illustrate how the relationships can be used in some very simple situations. Later, we will see how to make use of the same ideas in more complex situations.

Table 2.1 The three quantities related by the equation $F = ma$.

Quantity	Symbol	SI unit
force	F	newton, N
mass	m	kilogram, kg
acceleration	a	metres per second squared, m/s²

Worked example 1

When you strike a tennis ball that another player has hit towards you, you provide a large force to reverse its velocity and send it back towards your opponent. You give the ball a large acceleration. What force is needed to give a ball of mass 0.1 kg an acceleration of 500 m/s²?

We have

$m = 0.1$ kg

$a = 500$ m/s²

$F = ?$

Substituting in the equation to find the force gives

$F = ma = 0.1 \text{ kg} \times 500 \text{ m/s}^2 = 50 \text{ N}$

Worked example 2

Figure 2.3 A jumbo jet has four engines, each capable of providing a quarter of a million newtons of thrust. When the aircraft lands, the engines are put into 'reverse thrust' mode, so that they provide a decelerating force to bring it to a halt.

A Boeing 747 jumbo jet (Figure 2.3) has four engines, each capable of providing 250 000 N of thrust. The mass of the aircraft is 400 000 kg. What is the greatest acceleration that the aircraft can achieve?

The greatest force provided by all four engines working together is $F = 4 \times 250\,000\,N = 1\,000\,000\,N$. Now we have

$F = 1\,000\,000\,N$

$m = 400\,000\,kg$

$a = ?$

The greatest acceleration the engines can produce is then given by:

$$a = \frac{F}{m} = \frac{1\,000\,000\,N}{400\,000\,kg} = 2.5\,m/s^2$$

[We could now go on to calculate the length of runway needed for this aircraft. Suppose it must reach a speed of 85 m/s to achieve take-off; using $v^2 = u^2 + 2as$ with $u = 0$ gives $s = 1445\,m$. In practice the runway must be even longer than this, because air resistance means that the aircraft cannot maintain an acceleration of $2.5\,m/s^2$. Runways capable of taking jumbo jets are usually about 3 km long.]

What is a newton?

We can learn more by looking at the equation $F = ma$. What force is needed to give a mass of 1 kg an acceleration of 1 m/s²? The answer is $F = 1\,kg \times 1\,m/s^2 = 1\,N$. The equation tells us what we mean by a newton:

One newton (1 N) is the force that will give a mass of 1 kg an acceleration of 1 m/s².

This is the **definition of the newton**, the SI unit of force. It is named after Isaac Newton, the English scientist who made great strides in developing a scientific picture of forces and how they affect motion (Figure 2.4).

What is mass?

The equation $F = ma$ also tells us something about mass. Imagine being stopped in the street by a motorist. He has broken down; will you help by giving him a push? When you get round the corner, you find that he is the driver of a large delivery van! It is much easier to push a small car such as a Mini (mass about 500 kg) than a large van (mass 2000 kg).

You may feel that the problem is friction. There is more friction with a large van, so it is harder to get it moving. Now think about a similar problem, this time on the surface of a frozen lake. The ice is perfectly

Figure 2.4 Isaac Newton (1642–1727), after whom the newton is named. He investigated how forces affect moving objects; one of his greatest achievements was to show that the movements of the Moon and planets were governed by the same physical laws as the motion of objects here on Earth.

smooth, so that there is no friction to worry about. (You will need to wear shoes with spikes, so that you can grip the ice.) Which is easier to push, a small rock or a large one? You may be able to give the small rock a push so that it goes skidding off over the ice. The same force will give the more massive rock a much smaller acceleration, so that it will slide much more slowly over the ice.

In the same way, the mass of an object affects how easy it is to slow down the object. Picture a fly (mass 0.1 g) and a cricket ball (mass 0.15 kg) coming towards you at the same speed. It takes a much bigger force to catch the ball than the fly; that is, to decelerate the ball or fly so that its speed becomes zero.

So the mass of an object tells us how easy it is to accelerate or decelerate the object; the smaller the mass, the easier it is to change an object's speed.

Investigating $F = ma$

In the laboratory, you can investigate the equation $F = ma$ using a linear air track – see Figure 2.5. (Alternatively, you could use a trolley.) The track has a row of tiny holes along either side. Air is blown out through these holes, and this provides a cushion of air on which a glider can float smoothly from one end of the track to the other. The feet of the track can be adjusted so that the track is horizontal; then, when the glider is given a gentle push to start it moving, it moves at a steady speed from one end of the track to the other.

To provide a force to accelerate the glider, a thin string is attached to one end and passed over a pulley. Masses are hung on the end of the string. Each 100 g mass provides a pulling force of (approximately) 1 N. When the masses are released, they pull the glider along the track, causing it to accelerate. The acceleration can be measured as described in Chapter 1, using an interrupt card and a single light gate.

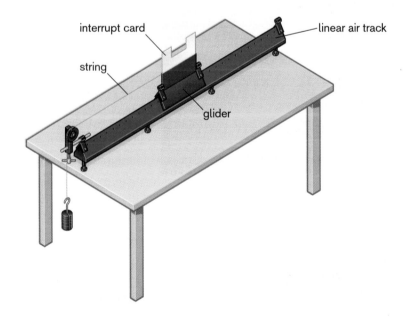

Figure 2.5 Using an air track and glider to investigate how acceleration depends on force and mass. There is no friction to slow the glider because it is supported on a cushion of air. Acceleration is measured using an interrupt card and light gate. It is a good idea to make several measurements of each value of acceleration, to see how closely the results can be repeated. Take an average of the values found.

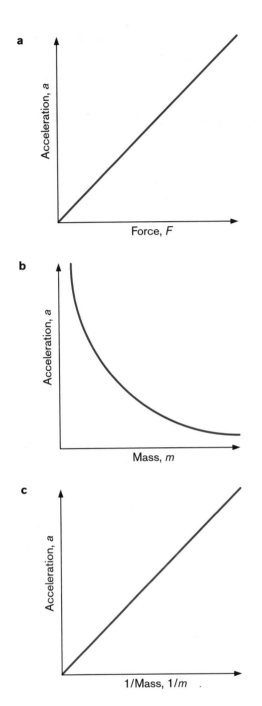

The force pulling the glider can be varied by adding more masses to the hanger on the end of the string. In practice, this is done using ten 100 g masses as follows. Initially, one mass is hung on the end of the string. The other nine are attached to the glider, and its acceleration measured. Then one mass is transferred to the end of the string, leaving eight on the glider. The acceleration is measured again, another mass transferred to the end of the string, and so on. To understand the reason for doing this, it is important to realise that it is not *just* the glider that is being accelerated; the masses are also accelerating. By transferring masses from the glider to the hanger, the total mass accelerated remains constant. Only the force increases; the greater the force, the greater the glider's acceleration.

To investigate how acceleration depends on mass, the accelerating force must be kept constant. A fixed number of masses (say, four) is hung on the end of the string. Gradually, masses are added to the glider and its acceleration measured for each value of mass. Again, it is important to include the mass of the masses hanging on the end of the string, since they are also being accelerated by the force.

Figure 2.6 shows the shapes of the graphs that can be drawn to represent the results of these experiments.

? Questions

2.1 What are the units of mass, force and acceleration? How are these units related to one another?

2.2 Why is it sensible on diagrams to represent a force by an arrow? Why should mass not be represented by an arrow?

2.3 Which will produce a bigger acceleration: a force of 10 N acting on a mass of 9 kg, or a force of 9 N acting on a mass of 10 kg?

2.4 What force is needed to give a mass of 20 kg an acceleration of 5 m/s²?

Figure 2.6 Graphs to represent the results that can be found from the experiment shown in Figure 2.5. Graph **a** is a straight line passing through the origin. This shows that acceleration is proportional to force. Graph **b** shows that, as the mass of the glider increases, its acceleration decreases (for a given force). To show that acceleration is inversely proportional to mass, it is necessary to draw graph **c**. This is another straight line through the origin, showing that acceleration is proportional to 1/mass. (These are idealised graphs; the results of an experiment may not show these patterns quite so clearly.)

2.2 Balanced and unbalanced forces

Imagine that you are travelling on a bus, and it breaks down. The driver asks the passengers to get off and push. You all push your hardest, but the bus will not move. You are applying a force, but it is producing no acceleration. Why not? Of course, your force is not big enough. But why does it need to be bigger? The answer is that there is another force, opposing your pushing. This force is friction, and if you can provide a big enough push, you can overcome friction and the bus will start to move.

Figure 2.7 shows the situation. At first, a small push is balanced by a small frictional force, pushing in the opposite direction. The forces are **balanced**, and nothing happens. Push harder, and the frictional force gets bigger. Push very hard, and your push is greater than the force of friction. Now the forces are unbalanced, and the bus moves.

We say that the bus accelerates because there is a **resultant** or **unbalanced force** acting on it.

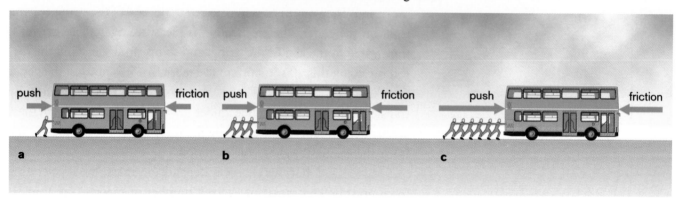

Figure 2.7 Pushing a bus. In **a** and **b**, the pushing force is cancelled out by the opposing frictional force. In **c**, the pushing force is greater than the frictional force, and the bus will start to move.

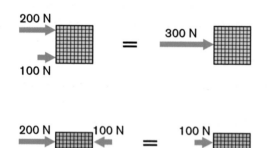

Figure 2.8 Adding forces. To take account of the directions of the forces, here it is convenient to say that forces to the right are positive, forces to the left are negative.

Adding forces

It is not difficult to work out the **resultant** of two or more forces if they are acting in a straight line, as shown in the examples in Figure 2.8. (These diagrams should remind you that force is a vector quantity; to describe a force fully, it is necessary to state its size in newtons *and* the direction in which it is acting.)

● If the forces are pointing in the same direction, they add up.
● If the forces are acting in opposite directions, they subtract.

Worked example 3 illustrates this, and shows how to find the direction of the resultant force.

If there are several forces acting on an object, we can still find its acceleration. First, we find the resultant force acting on it; then we calculate its acceleration (this is also illustrated in worked example 3):

$$\text{acceleration} = \frac{\text{resultant force}}{\text{mass}}$$

$$a = \frac{F}{m}$$

Worked example 3

A car has a mass of 800 kg. Its engine provides a forward force of 400 N. There is a frictional force of 160 N, acting to oppose the car's motion. What is the resultant force acting on the car? What is its acceleration?

The first step in a problem like this is to draw a diagram, to represent all of the information we have – see Figure 2.9 on page 33. The two forces are represented by arrows. The car's mass is given below the car, but it has no arrow, since mass has no direction.

We have two forces, 400 N to the right (+400 N), and 160 N to the left (−160 N). We can thus find the resultant force:

$$\text{resultant force} = (+400\,\text{N}) + (-160\,\text{N}) = +400\,\text{N} - 160\,\text{N}$$
$$= +240\,\text{N}$$

continued on next page

Worked example 3 continued

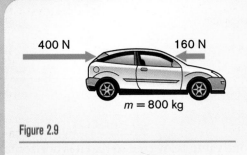

400 N   160 N

$m = 800$ kg

Figure 2.9

The resultant force is positive, meaning that it acts to the right. (You would have expected this, because the forward force is greater than the frictional force.)

Now we can calculate the car's acceleration:

$$\text{acceleration } a = \frac{\text{resultant force}}{\text{mass}} = \frac{+240\,\text{N}}{800\,\text{kg}} = +0.3\,\text{m/s}^2$$

We have kept the positive sign for the resultant force. The acceleration is also positive, and this tells us that the car's acceleration is towards the right, as you would have expected.

Galileo – and Newton's first law

Galileo Galilei (usually known more simply as Galileo) was born at Pisa in Italy in 1564. He spent his lifetime carrying out experiments on motion and astronomy. His great strength was his ability to design experiments that showed the truth of the theories he developed. Previously, it had been commonplace for scientists to dream up theories that they believed must be true, without carrying out experiments to test them. Galileo lived at a time when scientific discussion was very fashionable, and his work was supported by some of the noble families of the day. He built equipment to demonstrate his ideas. Figure 2.10 shows one of his demonstrations.

Figure 2.10 A nineteenth-century painting showing Galileo demonstrating one of his experiments at Court. Scientific discussion had become very fashionable, and scientists were sponsored by dukes and counts. That is how Galileo could afford to live and work as a scientist. Today, you can see many of his original pieces of equipment in the Science Museum in Florence. In this experiment, the ball rolls down the slope; Galileo showed that, in 2 seconds, it rolled four times as far as in 1 second. This is what we would expect from the equation $s = ut + \frac{1}{2}at^2$.

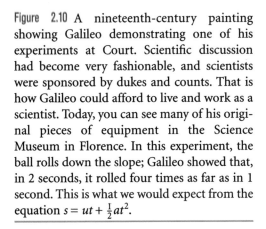

In the illustration, Galileo is rolling a ball down a ramp. He showed that the ball accelerated as it ran down-hill, and deduced a relationship between the distance rolled and the time taken. In an extension of this experiment, he attached a second ramp at the end of the first one. The ball rolled down one ramp and up the other. It reached a height equal to the original height from which it was launched – see Figure 2.11. Then he lowered the second ramp. This time the ball rolled further, again stopping when it reached its original height. Now, asked Galileo,

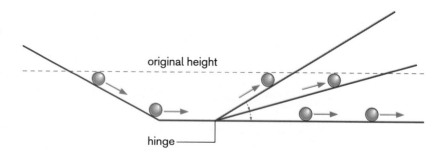

Figure 2.11 Galileo's demonstration that a moving object will keep on moving, unless an unbalanced force stops it. The ball keeps rolling, until it returns to its original height. With the second ramp horizontal, it can never get back to that height, so it must roll for ever. Of course, Galileo could not prove that it would roll for ever. His demonstration is interesting because it requires us to imagine what would happen in an impossible world where friction did not slow the ball.

what will happen if the second ramp is lowered so that it is horizontal? His answer was that the ball would never be able to reach its original height – it would roll on for ever.

Of course, we know that the ball would eventually come to a halt – friction would see to that. But Galileo was imagining a world without friction, in which case the ball would roll for ever. This was a surprising idea at the end of the sixteenth century. Everyday experience suggested the opposite – nothing would keep moving for ever. If the ox stopped pulling the wagon, the wagon ground to a halt. If you stopped rowing the boat, you would get nowhere.

Galileo's idea was that a moving object keeps moving, unless an unbalanced force stops it. In the cases of the wagon and the boat, it is the force of friction that stops them.

We need to be clear what we mean when we say that 'a moving object keeps moving'. We are talking about an object moving at a steady speed in a straight line; in other words, with constant velocity. This is referred to as **uniform motion**. Galileo's idea was that such an object will continue to move at the same speed and in the same direction, i.e. with the same velocity, unless an unbalanced force acts on it. His idea also applies to a stationary object; it will remain stationary unless an unbalanced force starts it moving.

Isaac Newton (born just a few months after Galileo's death in 1642) took up Galileo's ideas on motion, and extended them. Galileo's ideas about uniform motion became **Newton's first law of motion**:

> A body will stay at rest or in a state of uniform velocity unless acted on by an unbalanced force.

If you have pushed a heavily loaded trolley around a supermarket, you have probably experienced Newton's first law. The trolley tends to keep moving forwards in a straight line, provided its wheels are turning freely. If you want to turn a corner, you have to struggle to apply an unbalanced force that will slow it down and change its direction. Figure 2.12 illustrates another example of this. An articulated lorry has jack-knifed. The driver applied the brakes, and this provided the force needed to stop the front section of the lorry. However, there was insufficient force to stop the rear half, which continued forwards, pushing the front section to the side.

Figure 2.12 A jack-knifed lorry. Drivers of articulated lorries have to brake with caution. The brakes stop the cab section of the lorry. The back section may carry on regardless, particularly on an icy road.

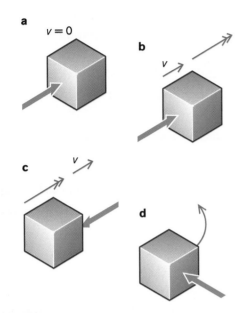

Figure 2.13 Four objects, each acted on by an unbalanced force.
a A stationary object starts to move.
b A moving object speeds up when the force is in the same direction as its velocity.
c A moving object slows down when the force is in the opposite direction to its velocity.
d A moving object changes direction when the force pushes it sideways. In each case, the object's velocity changes – it accelerates.

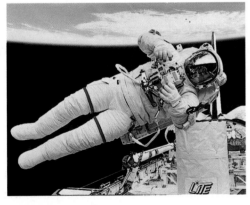

Figure 2.14 An astronaut on a space walk. His back-pack has jets that are used for manoeuvring when free from the spacecraft. These work in the same way that you can make a balloon fly around the room, by inflating it and then letting it go. Pressurised nitrogen gas blows backwards out of the jets to start the astronaut moving forwards. To stop, he must fire the jets in the opposite direction.

Newton's second law

Newton's first law tells us what happens if no unbalanced force acts on an object: it remains stationary, or it continues to move at a steady speed in a straight line. His second law tells us what happens if there is an unbalanced force acting on an object: it makes the object accelerate or decelerate.

Figure 2.13 shows four different situations where an unbalanced force acts on an object.

a The object is stationary. The force makes it accelerate. It starts to move in the direction of the force.
Example: A car setting off; the force is provided by the engine.

b The object is already moving to the right. The unbalanced force acts to the right. This makes the body accelerate to the right.
Example: A car speeding up; the force is provided by the engine.

c The object is again moving to the right. Now the unbalanced force acts to the left. This makes the object slow down.
Example: A car slowing down. The force is provided by its brakes.

d The object is again moving to the right. This time, the unbalanced force pushes it sideways. This makes the object gradually change direction.
Example: Someone is rowing a boat straight across a river. The current of the river pushes the boat sideways, so that it ends up further downstream.

In each of these situations, the velocity of the object is changed by the unbalanced force. The object speeds up, slows down, or changes direction. The object is accelerating; its acceleration is caused by the unbalanced force, and is in the same direction as the unbalanced force. This is **Newton's second law of motion**:

An unbalanced force causes an object to accelerate; the acceleration is proportional to, and in the same direction as, the unbalanced force.

We have already met Newton's second law in the equation $F = ma$. This equation tells us how to calculate the acceleration a of an object of mass m when it is acted on by an unbalanced force F.

Astronauts have to understand Newton's laws. When in weightless conditions, objects may float freely around inside the spacecraft. A tool that is accidentally moved will continue to move, according to Newton's first law until it collides with the opposite side of the cabin, so most objects are held down by clips or straps.

Figure 2.14 shows an astronaut floating freely in space. In the early days of space travel, astronauts on a space walk had to remain tethered to their craft, or they were in danger of drifting gradually away with no way of getting back to safety. The astronaut in the photograph is wearing a manned manoeuvring unit (MMU), which allows him to move about in a controlled way. The MMU uses jets of nitrogen gas to push the astronaut around. The first firing of the jet starts him moving; he

Figure 2.15 Inside an old water-mill. Grain is ground between two stones to make flour. The machinery turns one stone on top of the other, and the force of friction grinds the grain. Eventually the stones become worn away, and the grooves on their surfaces have to be re-cut. There is friction between the large cog-wheels too. There is some ingenious design here. One cog has wooden teeth. These get worn away but are easily replaced. This helps to preserve the metal cog-wheel, which would be expensive to replace.

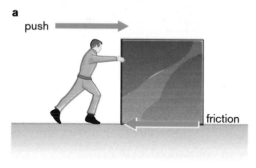

Figure 2.16 **a** If you try to push a box along rough ground, friction will oppose your push. **b** Friction opposes the motion of a skater on an icy surface.

will then move at a steady speed in a straight line. To stop, the jet must be fired again, pointing in the opposite direction. In cartoon films, this is often shown incorrectly. Spacemen are shown with their jets firing continuously as they move at a steady speed; when they switch off their jets, they stop. The cartoonist is imagining a universe where Newton's second law does not apply!

? Questions

2.5 In which of the following situations are unbalanced forces acting?
a box sits on a table;
a stone rolls down a hill at a steady speed;
a car travels along a straight road at 20 m/s.

2.6 Mental arithmetic: A car's engine provides a forward force on it of 850 N. Friction causes a backward force of 300 N. What is the resultant force acting on the car?

2.7 What is meant by 'uniform motion'?

2.3 Friction and drag

If you slide down the banisters, you will experience the force of friction – the experience can be quite painful! One surface, your skin, is trying to slide over another, the banisters. As the surfaces rub together, they produce the force of friction. (You can feel the same force in a less painful way by rubbing your hand on a desk.) You will observe two things about the force:

- The two surfaces get hot as they rub together.
- The two surfaces can become damaged – they may wear away.

Friction is often a problem, but it can also be useful – see Figure 2.15. You make use of friction every time you use an eraser to rub out pencil marks on paper. The frictional force wears away the surface of the paper. You will have noticed that the eraser also gets worn away.

Friction and motion

If you try to push an object along the ground, the force of friction is directed against your push – see Figure 2.16a. If you push gently, the friction is a small force exactly equal to your push, and pushing back against you. The forces on the object are balanced; we can tell this from Newton's laws – if the object doesn't accelerate, the forces on it *must* be balanced. Push a bit harder, and friction increases to balance your push. Eventually, friction cannot increase further, and your push is enough to overcome it. The forces are unbalanced and the object moves.

If you slide along a smooth surface, such as an ice-rink, friction acts to slow you down – see Figure 2.16b. Ice-skaters can glide a long way without pushing themselves forwards, but eventually they will come to a halt.

We can summarise these ideas by saying that 'friction is a force that tends to oppose motion'. If something is stationary, friction will tend to stop it from moving. If something is moving, friction will tend to act to slow it down.

In fact, you would find it very difficult to move without friction. We all rely on friction in order to walk about – think about the difficulty of walking on an icy surface. In the same way, it is difficult for a car to start moving on an icy or oily surface. Figure 2.17 shows the part played by friction when we walk, or when a car moves along the road.

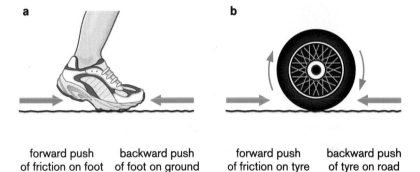

Figure 2.17 We need friction to get us moving.
a The force that moves a walker forwards is the frictional push of the road on their foot, *not* their push on the road.
b The backward push of the car tyre on the road produces frictional force. This allows the wheel to grip rather than slip, so that the car can start moving forwards.

forward push of friction on foot   backward push of foot on ground

forward push of friction on tyre   backward push of tyre on road

To start walking, you use your feet to push *backwards* on the ground. This may seem surprising; what you are doing is making use of friction to push you forwards. Your backward push is opposed by the forward push of friction, and it is this force that makes you move. Think about the starting-blocks used by sprinters. The athlete 'kicks back' against the blocks in order to be pushed forwards at the start of the race.

Similarly, the bottom of the car's wheel, where it touches the road surface, is pushing backwards. Friction pushes in the opposite direction and allows the car to start moving. The force of the car tyre on the road is pushing backwards, to produce the friction.

Measuring friction

Friction is a force, and can be measured in the laboratory using a **forcemeter** (also known as a **newtonmeter**). Figure 2.18 shows one method.

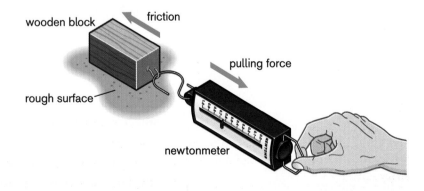

wooden block   friction

pulling force

rough surface

newtonmeter

Figure 2.18 An experimental arrangement to measure the force of friction. The forcemeter shows the pulling force, not the amount of friction. However, when the book moves at a steady speed, the pulling force is equal to the force of friction.

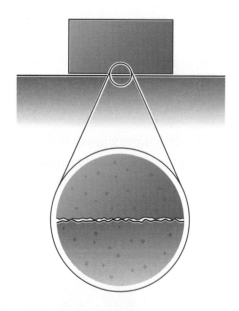

Figure 2.19 Friction comes about because of the roughness of surfaces, often on a microscopic scale. Pushing one surface over the other causes the surfaces to lock together. A force is needed to push one surface past the other.

The forcemeter is attached to a large object; the object is pulled using the forcemeter, and we can read the pulling force from the scale on the meter. A gentle pull may not be enough to pull the object; gradually increasing the force will eventually start it moving. The aim is to pull the object at a steady speed. Newton's first law then tells us that the forces on it are balanced. At this point, the pulling force must equal the frictional force, and so the reading on the meter tells us the size of the frictional force.

Friction, drag and air resistance

Friction comes about because surfaces cannot be perfectly smooth. On a microscopic scale, all surfaces are rough. This means that they tend to interlock with one another, as shown in Figure 2.19. A force is needed to push the irregularities on one surface past the irregularities on the other. As they are pushed past one another, the surfaces may be damaged – this is why surfaces tend to wear away as they slide over one another.

Drag is a similar force to friction, and occurs when an object is moving through a fluid (a liquid or a gas). If a whale or a boat, for example, is moving through water, it has to push the water aside. At the same time, the water rubs against its sides. You will have experienced the same thing if you have ever run into the sea; the deeper the water, the greater its resistance to your motion. In deeper water, it is easier to swim forwards than to walk.

Air resistance is the same as drag, and occurs when an object is moving through air. An aircraft, for example, moves rapidly through the air, and the air resistance tends to slow it down. Air resistance has much less effect than the drag of water because air is much less dense than water, so air is more easily pushed aside. However, for a supersonic aircraft like *Concorde*, air resistance is very important. Flying at 600 m/s, friction with the air causes its surface to become very hot. This makes it expand by several centimetres, and this has been taken into account in its design. For example, wiring that stretches from one end of the aircraft to the other must be fixed slackly, so that, when the aircraft expands, the wires do not get stretched. The US Space Shuttle is covered with heat-resistant tiles to protect it from the high temperatures generated as it enters and travels through the Earth's atmosphere at high speed when it comes in to land.

Top speed

Every car has a top speed – the fastest it can go. The speedometer may go up to 150 mph, but the top speed of a typical family car is usually much less than this, perhaps 100 mph. What stops the car from going any faster? The answer, of course, is air resistance. The driver can press on the accelerator to make the car go faster. However, the faster the car moves, the greater the air resistance becomes. Eventually, the car

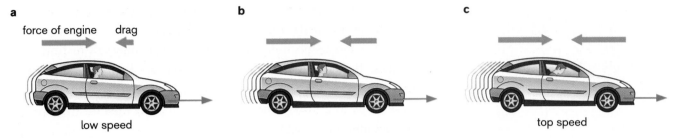

a

force of engine   drag

low speed

b

c

top speed

Figure 2.20 **a** At low speeds, a car can accelerate because the force of its engine is greater than the drag opposing its motion.
b As the car's speed increases, the drag on it also increases.
c At top speed, the drag has increased further until it equals the engine force.

reaches a speed at which the backward force of air resistance equals the forward force provided by the engine – see Figure 2.20. At this speed, the forces on the car are balanced, and it can go no faster. Figure 2.21 shows a racing car, designed to have a much higher top speed than a family car. The same is true for trains and planes. They can usually go faster than a car, but their top speed is limited by air resistance.

Figure 2.21 A racing car has a streamlined shape (to reduce drag) and a powerful engine. This means that it has a high top speed. However, it is in danger of taking off, so it is fitted with 'ailerons' as part of the rear-wing assembly. These have the same cross-sectional shape as an aircraft wing, but upside down. This means that there is an extra force pushing downwards on the car, keeping it in contact with the road. This gives good 'grip' between the tyres and the road surface, so that there is plenty of friction to help the car go round corners.

? Questions

2.8 What *two* effects occur when friction acts on a surface?

2.9 How can changing the *shape* of an object alter friction? How can changing the *surface* of an object alter friction?

2.10 What is a fluid? Give two names for the force of friction when an object moves through a fluid.

2.4 The force of gravity

The Earth's gravity is a familiar force that we experience every day. Jump up in the air and you fall back down. Let go of a book and it falls to the floor. When we are standing up, our muscles keep working to ensure that our bodies remain upright; if our muscles stopped working, we would collapse in a heap on the ground.

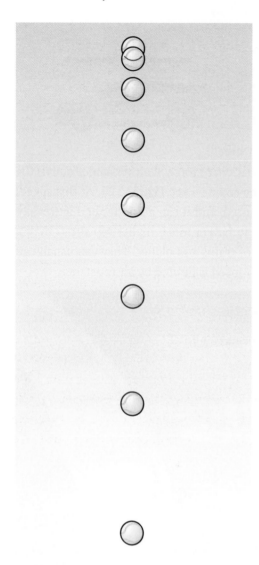

Like any other force, gravity can make things accelerate. You can see this in the multi-flash photograph of Figure 2.22. A ball has been dropped, and its position is shown at regular intervals of time. The images become increasingly far apart as the ball accelerates downwards. You can see the same effect using a ticker-timer. Attach a ticker-tape to a heavy object and let it fall. The dots on the tape get further and further apart.

Measuring the acceleration

You could make measurements on the artwork in Figure 2.22 to find the ball's acceleration. You would need to know the time interval between each image, and the distance of each image below the ball's starting point. An alternative method is shown in Figure 2.23.

A steel ball is held by a spring-loaded clamp. When the ball is released, the electronic timer automatically starts. The ball lands on a receptor pad and switches off the timer. The timer then indicates the time taken for the ball to fall from the clamp to the receptor pad.

Here is one way to calculate the ball's acceleration: Suppose the ball falls 0.8 m in 0.4 s. Then

$$\text{average speed} = \frac{0.8\,\text{m}}{0.4\,\text{s}} = 2\,\text{m/s}$$

Since the ball's initial speed was zero, its final speed must be twice its average speed:

$$\text{final speed} = 4\,\text{m/s}$$

Its speed has changed from 0 to 4 m/s in 0.4 s, so its acceleration is

$$\text{acceleration} = \frac{\text{change in speed}}{\text{time taken}} = \frac{4\,\text{m/s}}{0.4\,\text{s}} = 10\,\text{m/s}^2$$

Figure 2.22 An artwork based on a multi-flash photograph of a ball falling. The images of the ball are made at equal intervals of time. Gravity makes the ball accelerate, so the images become further apart. An image like this can be analysed to work out the ball's acceleration.

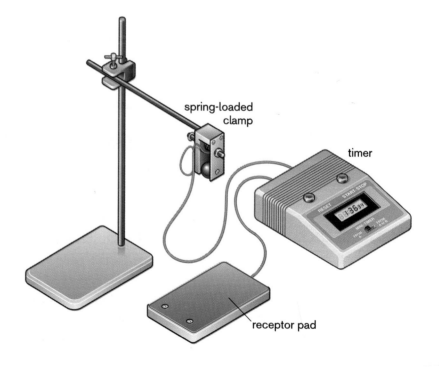

Figure 2.23 An experiment to measure the acceleration of a falling ball. The timer starts when the ball is released from the spring-loaded clamp. It stops when the ball lands on the receptor pad. The height through which the ball falls must be measured. This is the distance between the bottom of the ball before release and the top of the receptor pad.

The measurements must be repeated several times, and for several different heights, to increase the accuracy of the final result.

A motion sensor can also be used to measure the acceleration of a falling object. The sensor is fixed above the ground, facing downwards. A ball is held below the sensor and released. The sensor produces a graph to show how the ball's speed increases as it falls. (This is a better method than letting the ball fall down onto the sensor, which is easily broken.)

Measurements show that the acceleration of a falling object is about 10 m/s^2. (A more accurate value is 9.8 m/s^2. The precise value of the acceleration caused by gravity depends on just where you are on the Earth's surface.) For your work (unless you are told otherwise) you can assume that, at the Earth's surface

acceleration g due to gravity = 10 m/s^2

Weight

Gravity is one of the fundamental forces of Nature. The Earth's gravity pulls on everything on it or near it. If we look around us, everything we see is being pulled downwards by the force of gravity – see Figure 2.24. If an object of mass m is dropped, then it will fall with an acceleration g. By Newton's second law (force = mass × acceleration) the force on the object must be mg. But this force is the force of gravity, its **weight** W. So

$$W = mg$$

or

weight = mass × acceleration due to gravity

Because weight is a force, it is measured in newtons.

The acceleration due to gravity, g, is also referred to as the **gravitational field strength** (gravitational force on each unit mass) and can be given as 10 m/s^2 or 10 N/kg. A car of mass 500 kg has a weight of 5000 N. An apple of mass 100g (0.1kg) weighs 1N.

The origin of gravity

If we could step back and see the Earth as a whole (Figure 2.25), we would see that the weight of every object is directed towards the centre of the Earth. In a similar way, if you went to the Moon, you would find that you were pulled on by a force directed towards the centre of the Moon. However, the force would be considerably less than on the Earth – about one-sixth as strong; the acceleration of falling objects is only one-sixth of its value on Earth. Astronauts who have visited the Moon have been able to demonstrate this.

The Moon is much smaller than the Earth, and its mass is much less. Gravity is caused by the pull of one mass on another; because the Moon's mass is smaller than the Earth's, its pull is weaker.

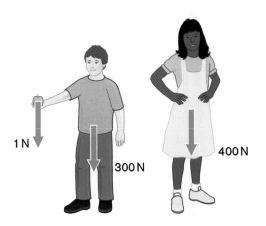

Figure 2.24 Everything on or near the Earth is pulled downwards by the Earth's gravity. The weight of an object depends on its mass. The greater its mass, the greater its weight.

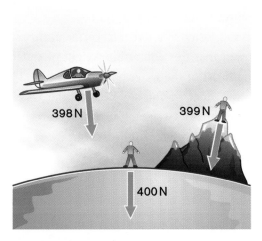

Figure 2.25 The force of gravity acts towards the centre of the Earth. If you move further away from the Earth's centre, for example by climbing a mountain or travelling in an aircraft, your weight gets less. Strangely, at the centre of the Earth, you would have no weight. This is because you would be pulled equally in all directions by the mass of the Earth, and the forces would all cancel out.

The pull of the Earth's gravity also depends on the mass of the object being pulled. If your mass is greater than your friend's mass, the Earth's gravitational pull on you will be greater than its pull on your friend – your weight will be greater than theirs.

This connection between mass and gravity means that it is easy to confuse the ideas of mass and weight:

- Your **mass** is measured in kilograms (kg); it remains the same wherever you are. It determines how readily you can be accelerated (see page 29).
- Your **weight** is a force, measured in newtons (N); it varies from place to place. It is the force caused by gravity pulling on you.

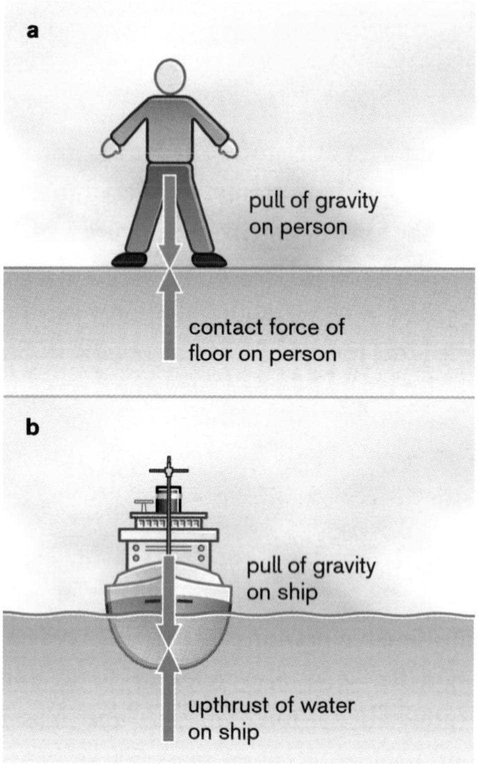

Staying still

Gravity is pulling on you all the time, but you don't accelerate downwards through the floor. There is another force acting to stop you. The floor pushes back up on you with a force called the **contact force** – see Figure 2.26. Usually, these forces are balanced. If you step on thin ice – beware! The ice may not be able to push back up with a sufficiently large contact force, and you will fall through.

Contact forces are important, because they help objects to remain stationary. However, we do not usually think about their existence. The contact force of the floor comes about because the floor has a slight springiness. When you stand on the floor, your feet push downwards on it. The floor is compressed very slightly, so that it pushes back against you. You would notice this effect if you stood on a springy mattress, or on a trampoline. Your feet would push down, compressing the mattress until its upward force matched your weight.

An object floating in water is supported by another force, the **upthrust** of the water; Archimedes showed that this equals the weight of water displaced by the object. The upthrust of the water balances the object's weight. A ship, for example, can float in the sea because the water provides the upthrust needed to balance its weight. If the ship is carrying a heavy load, it sinks down in the water until the upthrust is great enough to balance its weight again.

Old ideas

Earlier in this chapter, we saw how Galileo and Newton helped to develop our modern ideas of forces and motion. Previously, people followed the ideas of ancient Greek thinkers, who thought that horizontal motion was different from vertical motion.

They thought that anything moving *horizontally* would naturally come to a halt. Today, we explain this by saying that friction makes things slow down. Without friction, things can move for ever.

They thought that *vertical* motion was different. Things naturally fell downwards, to their natural level. Apples drop from trees, water runs

Figure 2.26 For an object to remain stationary, a force is needed to balance its weight. **a** The contact force of the floor supports you when you are standing. **b** The upthrust of the sea supports a ship. Air can provide upthrust too, for example to support a hot-air balloon.

Figure 2.27 Recreating the guinea-and-feather experiment using a hammer and a feather. The air was pumped from a glass tube. A hammer and a feather were then released. In the absence of air resistance, both fell at the same rate.

down-hill. They called this property 'gravity', meaning heaviness. Some things naturally moved upwards – smoke and gases, for example. These things possessed a property called 'levity', the opposite of gravity. Now we know that even light substances, such as air, are pulled downwards by gravity. That is what keeps the Earth's atmosphere in place.

If you drop a stone, it is hard to see that it is accelerating. People imagined that things fell with a steady speed; as soon as the stone left your hand, it was moving quickly. Photographs like Figure 2.22 show that this is not the case. When Galileo rolled a ball down a slope (Figure 2.10 on page 33), he was trying to show that gravity made things accelerate. The slope meant that the ball accelerated more gradually, so that the effect was easier to see. If the ramp was steeper, the acceleration was greater, and if it was vertical, the ball would accelerate freely downwards.

One reason why people did not have a good understanding of gravity was that they were used to seeing things fall at different rates. A stone falls more quickly than a feather. Today, our explanation is that the feather is affected more by air resistance. If the stone and the feather are released in a vacuum (where there is no air), the feather will fall at the same rate as the stone. This is an experiment that could not be done in ancient times; but the invention of gas pumps that could evacuate a glass tube made the experiment possible in the eighteenth century. Famously, the two objects used were a golden guinea and a feather – see Figure 2.27. Today the experiment has been repeated by astronauts on the Moon, where there is no atmosphere to cause air resistance.

In the absence of air resistance, all objects on the Earth's surface fall with equal acceleration, approximately $10\,\text{m/s}^2$.

Moving with gravity

How do things move when the force of gravity is pulling on them? Figure 2.28 shows the path of a ball thrown upwards and forwards. You can see that the images get closer together as the ball moves upwards, and then further apart as it falls back downwards. We can think of these two parts of its motion separately:

● The ball starts off with an upward velocity. Its velocity steadily decreases. This means that it is decelerating upwards, or accelerating downwards.

● As the ball falls, its velocity increases. It is accelerating downwards.

So in both halves of its motion, the ball has a downward acceleration. This is, of course, caused by the downward pull of gravity. In practice, we do not need to consider the ball's upward motion separately from its downward motion.

Figure 2.28 also shows the force acting on the ball as it moves. The force is constant; the ball's weight does not change. In the past, before the work of Galileo and Newton, people had a different way of explaining the ball's motion. They said that the ball was given a 'force' by the hand

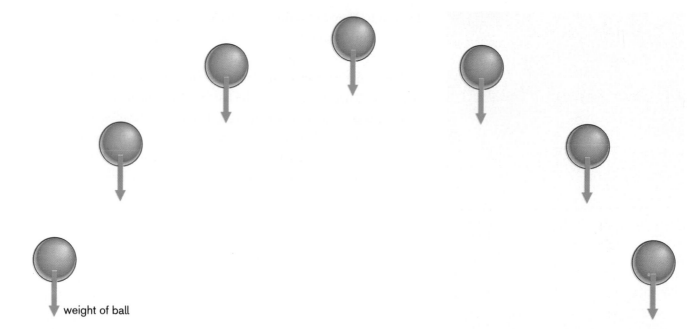

weight of ball

Figure 2.28 As a ball moves through the air, it is acted on by the force of gravity. This force, its weight, is always directed vertically downwards. Its size does not change as the ball moves, so that the ball has a constant acceleration downwards.

that threw it; this force got weaker as the ball went upwards; eventually, the ball ran out of force, and fell back down to the ground. Today, we do not imagine that the force of our hand continues to have an effect once the ball has left it. Once the ball is free, gravity is the only force on it (apart from air resistance). Worked example 4 shows how we can use this idea to calculate how high a ball will rise.

Worked example 4

A ball is thrown vertically upwards with an initial velocity of 20 m/s. How high will it rise in the air?

The trick here is to realise that, at its highest point, the ball's velocity has reduced to zero; it is stationary for an instant.

Step 1 Write down what we know, and what we want to know (see Figure 2.29):

initial velocity $u = 20$ m/s

final velocity $v = 0$ m/s

acceleration $a = g = -10$ m/s^2

height reached $s = ?$

(Note that the acceleration is negative; upwards is positive, and the ball is accelerating downwards.)

continued on next page

Worked example 4 continued

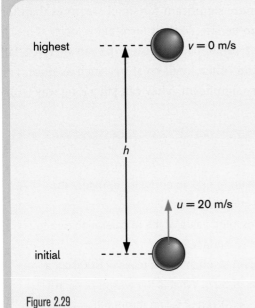

highest — — — $v = 0$ m/s

h

$u = 20$ m/s

initial — — —

Figure 2.29

- *Step 2* Choose the appropriate equation of motion:

  $v^2 = u^2 + 2as$

- *Step 3* Rearrange to make *s* the subject:

  $v^2 - u^2 = 2as$

  $$s = \frac{v^2 - u^2}{2a}$$

Now substitute in values:

$$s = \frac{0 - (20\,\text{m/s})^2}{2 \times (-10\,\text{m/s}^2)}$$

$$s = \frac{-400\,\text{m}^2/\text{s}^2}{-20\,\text{m/s}^2} = 20\,\text{m}$$

So the ball will rise 20 m in the air before it falls back to earth.

Here is another way to think about this problem: The ball's acceleration is 10 m/s², so it slows down by 10 m/s every second. Since the ball started moving at 20 m/s, it will take 2 s to come to a halt. Its average speed in this time is 10 m/s (half of its maximum speed). At 10 m/s, in 2 s it will travel 20 m.

Figure 2.30 A free-fall parachutist, before she opens her parachute. She can reach a terminal velocity in excess of 100 mph (45 m/s).

Falling through the air

Gravity makes you fall, but air resistance can save you. That is the idea used by parachutists (Figure 2.30). A free-fall parachutist jumps from an aircraft. At first, she accelerates downwards with an acceleration of 10 m/s², just like any other falling object. However, air resistance gradually comes in to play. There is friction between her body and the air, and this creates an upward force that reduces downward acceleration. The faster she goes, the greater the force of air resistance; eventually, air resistance equals weight, and the forces are balanced – see the second 'snapshot' in Figure 2.31. The parachutist has reached her top speed, known as her **terminal velocity**. (This is just like the top speed of a car, discussed earlier, on page 38, where the forward force of the car's engine is balanced by air resistance.) Terminal velocity for a person in free fall is over 50 m/s, considerably faster than the speed limit for traffic on a motorway.

A free-fall parachutist can adjust his speed by changing the position of his body. Head-first is a streamlined shape, reducing air resistance and giving a greater terminal velocity. Spread-eagled, with legs and arms spread out horizontally, is a slower way to travel.

Opening the parachute (see the third 'snapshot' in Figure 2.31) greatly increases air resistance. Now there is a much bigger force upwards; the forces on the parachutist are unbalanced, and he slows

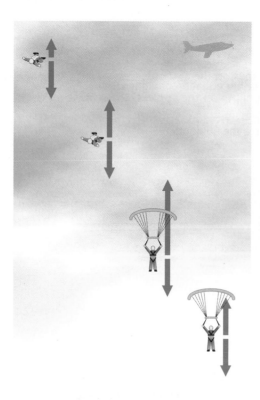

Figure 2.31 The forces on a falling parachutist. Notice that his weight is constant. When air resistance equals weight, the forces are balanced and the parachutist reaches a steady speed. The parachutist is always falling (velocity downwards), although his acceleration is upwards when he opens his parachute.

down. The idea is to reach a new, slower, terminal velocity of about 10 m/s (fourth 'snapshot') before reaching the ground.

Air resistance is much more significant for small creatures than for people. Cats are lighter than people, so their terminal velocity is much less than that reached by a free-fall parachutist. A cat can survive a fall from a high building, as can other small creatures such as mice. For insects, air resistance is very significant. They can fall a long way without being damaged.

Questions

2.11 Why is it appropriate to use an arrow to represent the weight of an object in diagrams?

2.12 What is the approximate value of the acceleration due to gravity at the Earth's surface?

2.13 Mental arithmetic: An elephant has a mass of 5000 kg; a mouse has a mass of 50 g. What is the weight of each?

2.14 A sky-diver of mass 100 kg is falling through the air. Sketch a diagram to show the forces acting on her when she reaches terminal velocity. What is the force of air resistance acting on her? What resultant force acts on her?

Extension material

Motion in a circle

The Earth moves around the Sun in an orbit that is roughly circular. The Moon also follows a roughly circular orbit, around the Earth. Many other objects follow curved paths – a train on a curved section of track, an aircraft changing direction, the hands of a clock as they move around the clock face, and so on. These objects may move at a steady *speed*, but their *velocity* is not constant, because its direction is always changing.

You can see this from Figure 2.32. The toy train is travelling around a circular track at a steady speed; at the far side, its

velocity is to the left; when it comes round to the near side, its velocity is to the right.

If an object's velocity changes, there must be an unbalanced force causing the change. Think about the toy train: as it goes around the track, it is constantly turning to the left. There must be a force pushing it sideways. This force is provided by the track, pushing on the wheels. If the track wasn't curved, there would be no sideways force on the train and it would go straight ahead.

Any object moving in a circle has a force acting on it; this force is always at right-angles to the object's velocity, directed towards the centre of the circle. A force that points towards the centre of a circle is called a **centripetal force**. Here are some examples.

● The Moon orbits the Earth; it is pulled on by the Earth's gravity – see Figure 2.33a. Similarly, the Sun's gravity keeps the Earth in its orbit.

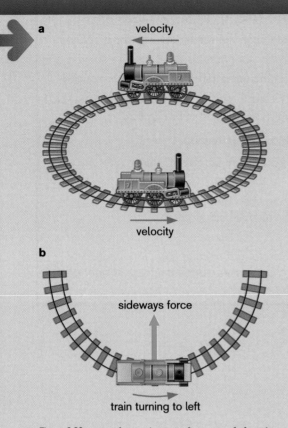

a velocity

b

sideways force

train turning to left

Figure 2.32 a As the train travels around the circular track, its velocity changes direction. For this to happen, a force must be acting that causes the direction of its motion to change.
b Seen from above, the train is always turning to the left. A sideways force acts to push it round the circle.

- If you whirl an apple around on the end of a piece of string, the tension in the string keeps pulling on the apple. If the string breaks, the apple flies off at a tangent – see Figure 2.33b.
- When an aircraft banks to turn a corner, it tilts its wings. The lift force on the wings then acts partly sideways – see Figure 2.33c.

The size of the centripetal force must be just right, or the object will not move along the desired circular path. The factors that determine the size of the force are:

- the mass of the object – the bigger the mass, the bigger the force needed to push on it so that it stays on the circular path;
- the velocity of the object – the faster it is moving, the bigger the force needed;
- the radius of the circle – the smaller the radius, the bigger the force needed.

You may be able to understand this by thinking about what it is like to try to change direction when cycling. If you carry a heavy load on your bike, it is harder to turn a sharp corner. Your bike wants to carry on in a straight line. Again, if you travel fast, it is harder to turn a sharp corner. And finally, the sharper the corner, the harder it is to turn, particularly at speed.

There is more about circular motion in Chapter 27.

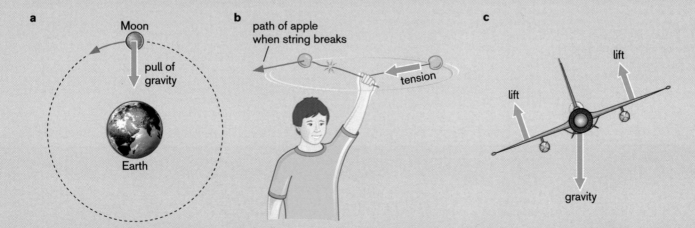

Figure 2.33 Examples of circular motion. In each case, there is a sideways force pushing the object around in a circle; these forces are called centripetal forces.
a Gravity is the centripetal force that keeps the Moon orbiting the Earth.
b Tension in the string keeps the apple whirling round – until the string breaks.
c As it banks, the lift on the wings of an aircraft provides the centripetal force needed to make it change direction.

Summary

◆ Newton's first law of motion: A body will stay at rest or in a state of uniform velocity unless acted on by an unbalanced force.

◆ Force, mass and acceleration are related by Newton's second law: $F = ma$.

The acceleration a is in the same direction as the unbalanced force F.

◆ The unit of force is the newton (N). $1\,N = 1\,kg\ m/s^2$.

◆ Frictional forces tend to oppose motion.

◆ Weight is the force of gravity on an object's mass. We can write it in three ways

Weight = mass × acceleration due to gravity
Weight = mass × gravitational field strength
$W = mg$

◆ When an object travels along a circular path, its direction of motion is constantly changing. A centripetal force is needed to keep it moving in a circle.

Forces and momentum

Topics in this chapter

◆ momentum

◆ conservation of momentum

◆ momentum in collisions and explosions

◆ force and momentum

◆ Newton's third law of motion

◉ *impulse of a force*

Cycling in town can be dangerous, with cars passing at speed and pedestrians to be avoided (Figure 3.1). Being followed by a large truck can be even more nerve-racking. What happens if you have to stop suddenly? It is not so easy for a truck to stop. It has a lot of mass and may be travelling quite fast, so, even if the driver applies the brakes promptly, it may not stop in time to avoid an accident.

Mass and velocity are important in many sports, too. Here are some examples.

● In tennis, your opponent may hit the ball towards you so that it is travelling very quickly. If your return stroke is weak, you may not give the ball enough velocity for it to get over the net.

Figure 3.1 Cycling in fast-moving traffic is hazardous. Large, fast-moving vehicles cannot stop quickly. Cyclists may feel that they are safe, because they are agile and can move quickly. However, in case of accidents, it is advisable to wear a safety helmet.

Figure 3.2 Jonah Lomu, the New Zealand rugby player, has a large mass and can run fast. This makes it very difficult for his opponents to stop him as he runs for the line. It is much easier to tackle a lightweight opponent who is running slowly.

- If you play tennis in wet weather, the ball may absorb water and become waterlogged. Then it is more difficult to strike it so that it travels a long way. Its mass has increased, so the effect of your hit is less.
- In rugby, it is difficult to stop an opposing player who is large and moving fast (Figure 3.2). It is much easier to tackle a small, slow-moving player.
- In hockey or cricket, if you strike the ball very hard with your stick or bat, you can make it move very fast. The force of the stick hitting the ball is transmitted to your hand – it can give you quite a jerk. It is easier to make the ball move fast if you strike it as it goes past, so that you increase its velocity. It is much harder to hit it head-on, so that it stops and flies off in the opposite direction.

If you play a sport, you develop an intuitive grasp of these ideas. Your experience allows you to predict where a ball will go, or where a player's movement will take them. Physics can help us to explain these and other observations of how things move.

3.1 Collisions and explosions

Here are two situations that show how, in physics, we can think about what happens when two objects collide:

- In a game of snooker, the white ball rolls across the table and strikes a red ball. The collision is head on, rather than a glancing blow. What happens? The white ball stops dead, while the red ball moves off. It moves in the same direction in which the white ball was originally moving, and with the same speed. The 'movement' of the white ball has been transferred to the red ball.
- Indentical twin brothers are skating on an ice-rink. One is stationary in the middle of the rink. The other skates towards him, and they collide. They move off together, but at a slower speed than that of the brother who was originally moving. His 'movement' has been shared with his brother.

Collisions can be much more complicated than this, with objects bouncing off one another, striking each other at glancing angles, and so on. To understand how to give a scientific description of what is going on, and to be able to predict what will happen, we can start with two simple experiments. (These correspond to the two collisions described above.)

In the first experiment (Figure 3.3a), a trolley moving with velocity v collides with an identical stationary trolley. To make the collision springy, the spring-load of the moving trolley has been released. When it hits the stationary trolley, it stops moving, and the second trolley moves off with a velocity v equal to that of the first trolley. This is just how the snooker balls behaved. Before the collision, we have a single trolley of mass m moving with velocity v; after the collision, we again have a trolley of mass m moving with velocity v.

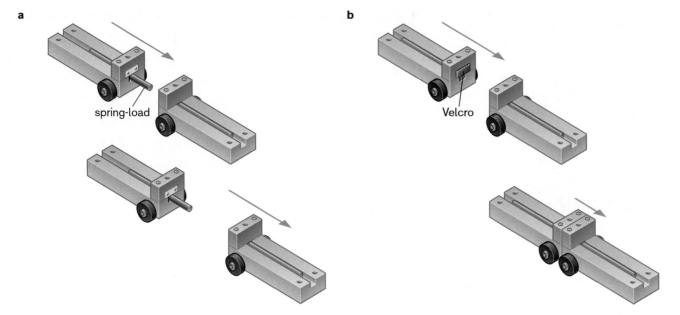

a

b

spring-load

Velcro

Figure 3.3 In both of these collisions, a moving trolley runs into a stationary one. In both **a** and **b**, the trolleys are shown before collision (above) and after collision (below).
a The collision is springy; the second trolley moves off, leaving the first one stationary.
b The collision is sticky; the trolleys stick together and move off together after the collision.

In the second experiment (Figure 3.3b), the collision is sticky, rather than springy. The first trolley collides with the second, they stick together and move off, just like the ice-skating twins. Measurements of the velocities of the trolleys show something that you might have guessed: if the first trolley's velocity is v, then the velocity of the two trolleys together is $v/2$. After the collision, the mass that is moving has doubled, but its velocity has halved.

Predictability

These experiments suggest that, in order to understand collisions, we need to think about both mass m and velocity v. They hint at a very important quantity that combines both of these; this quantity is **momentum**. To calculate the momentum of a moving body, we simply multiply together its mass and velocity:

$$\text{momentum} = \text{mass} \times \text{velocity}$$
$$= mv$$

In the springy collision, the first trolley starts off with momentum mv; in the collision, it transfers all of its momentum to the second trolley. In the sticky collision, the first trolley again has momentum mv; this time, after the collision, we have a double trolley (mass $= 2m$) moving more slowly (velocity $= v/2$). The momentum of the double trolley is $2m \times v/2 = mv$. So the first trolley has shared its momentum with the second.

In the discussion of the snooker and ice-skating collisions above, we said that 'movement' was being transferred or shared. Now we can see that the correct quantity to describe this is 'momentum'. This is a very important understanding, because it helps us to predict what will happen in the event of a collision, and predicting the outcome of events is one of the main aims of science.

Calculating momentum

When thinking about the difficulty of tackling a rugby player (Figure 3.2), it seemed obvious that both the mass and the velocity of the player were important. The greater the player's mass and the faster he is moving, the more difficult (and painful) it would be to stop him. In other words, the more momentum a player has, the harder it is to stop him.

Units: momentum is calculated as mass (in kg) × velocity (in m/s), so its units are kg m/s. (There is no special name for this unit in the SI system.) An alternative unit is newton seconds (N s). This is the same as kg m/s, because (as we saw in Chapter 2), $1\,N = 1\,kg\,m/s^2$.

Worked example 1

Who has more momentum, a rugby forward of mass 125 kg running at 8 m/s, or a fly-half of mass 80 kg running at 10 m/s?

In each case, we can calculate the momentum using the equation:

momentum = mass × velocity

We get

momentum of forward = 125 kg × 8 m/s = 1000 kg m/s
momentum of fly-half = 80 kg × 10 m/s = 800 kg m/s

So the forward has more momentum. He is moving a little more slowly than the fly-half, but his mass is much greater.

Momentum is conserved

The trolley experiments above suggest something very important about momentum: there is as much momentum after a collision as there is before. This is true in any situation, not just in collisions. The total amount of momentum is always the same before and after a collision, an explosion or any other event. We say that 'momentum is conserved'. This is the **principle of conservation of momentum**:

> In a closed system, the total amount of momentum remains constant.

(A 'closed system' means that the object or objects we are considering interact with each other but they are not acted on by any external forces.) The principle of conservation of momentum can allow us to calculate the outcome of events, as is shown in the next worked example.

Worked example 2

A trolley of mass 2 kg is moving at 5 m/s. It collides with a second, stationary, trolley of mass 8 kg; it bounces back with a velocity of 3 m/s. With what velocity does the second trolley move off?

In problems like this, it is best to draw a 'before and after' diagram to show the information provided in the question – see Figure 3.4. One half of the diagram shows the situation *before* the collision; the other half shows the situation *after* the collision. The trolleys are marked with their masses and velocities. The only unknown quantity is *v*, the velocity of the second trolley after the collision.

continued on next page

Worked example 2 continued

before collision

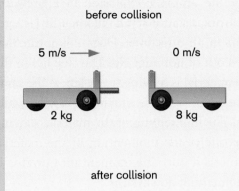

5 m/s →   0 m/s

2 kg   8 kg

after collision

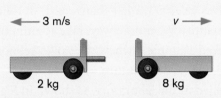

← 3 m/s   v →

2 kg   8 kg

Figure 3.4 Diagram for worked example 2. This shows the situations before and after the collision of the two trolleys. Velocities are shown with arrows, because their directions are important.

Step 1 We calculate the total momentum of the two trolleys before the collision. (Note that the velocity of the second trolley is zero.) We get

$$\text{momentum} = [2\,\text{kg} \times 5\,\text{m/s}] + [8\,\text{kg} \times 0\,\text{m/s}] = 10\,\text{kg}\,\text{m/s}$$

Step 2 We write down the momentum of the trolleys after the collision. In this case, the first trolley is now moving backwards, so its velocity is negative. We obtain

$$\text{momentum} = [2\,\text{kg} \times (-3\,\text{m/s})] + [8\,\text{kg} \times v] = (8\,\text{kg} \times v) - 6\,\text{kg}\,\text{m/s}$$

Step 3 Because momentum is conserved, the momentum after the collision equals the momentum before the collision.

$$(8\,\text{kg} \times v) - 6\,\text{kg}\,\text{m/s} = 10\,\text{kg}\,\text{m/s}$$

Rearranging gives

$$8\,\text{kg} \times v = 10\,\text{kg}\,\text{m/s} + 6\,\text{kg}\,\text{m/s}$$
$$8\,\text{kg} \times v = 16\,\text{kg}\,\text{m/s}$$
$$v = \frac{16\,\text{kg}\,\text{m/s}}{8\,\text{kg}} = 2\,\text{m/s}$$

So the second trolley moves off to the right at a speed of 2 m/s.

Checking: In calculations like this, it is a good idea to check the final answer by calculating the total momentum before and after the collision. We need to be sure that no momentum has appeared or disappeared. As we calculated above:

momentum before collision = 10 kg m/s

$$\begin{aligned}\text{momentum after collision} &= [2\,\text{kg} \times (-3\,\text{m/s})] + [8\,\text{kg} \times v]\\ &= [2\,\text{kg} \times (-3\,\text{m/s})] + [8\,\text{kg} \times 2\,\text{m/s}]\\ &= -6\,\text{kg}\,\text{m/s} + 16\,\text{kg}\,\text{m/s}\\ &= 10\,\text{kg}\,\text{m/s}\end{aligned}$$

A useful formula

From worked example 2, we can see that another way to write down what is meant by the principle of conservation of momentum is to say that:

| total momentum before collision | = | total momentum after collision |

You may prefer to remember how to do the type of calculation in worked example 2 using a formula. We imagine object 1 colliding with object 2. Then we have:

$$m_1 u_1 + m_2 u_2 = m_1 v_1 + m_2 v_2$$

Here, m_1 is the mass of object 1, u_1 is its initial velocity and v_1 is its final velocity. The subscript 2 shows the same quantities for object 2.

Figure 3.5 Fireworks exploding. The sparks have momentum; the momentum of particles moving to the left is balanced by the momentum of particles moving to the right. We would be very surprised if all the sparks flew off to the left, with nothing moving to the right.

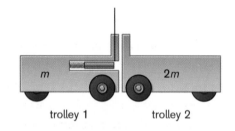

trolley 1   trolley 2

Figure 3.6 A model explosion. When the peg in trolley 1 is tapped, its spring-load is released and the trolleys fly apart. Trolley 2 has twice the mass of trolley 1 and moves at half the speed.

Momentum is a vector quantity

The idea of momentum can also help us to predict what happens in an explosion. Figure 3.5 shows the dramatic explosion of a firework. Before the explosion, the firework is stationary; its momentum is zero. Afterwards, material flies off in all directions. Does this mean that momentum has been created out of nothing? No. The clue lies in the words *in all directions*. Some material is moving to the left; at the same time some is moving to the right. Some is moving upwards, while some is moving downwards. The momentum of the material moving to the left is equal and opposite to the momentum of the material moving to the right, and cancels it out. The momentum upwards is equal and opposite to the momentum downwards.

Because momentum involves *velocity* (rather than speed), it follows that momentum is a vector quantity. We must always take account of its direction. (We did this in worked example 2, where the trolley rebounded with a negative velocity, so that its momentum was –6 kg m/s.)

An explosion can be modelled in the laboratory, as shown in Figure 3.6. Two trolleys, one having twice the mass of the other, are placed in contact. The spring-load of one is released and they fly apart. The trolley with the smaller mass moves more quickly – twice as fast as the other. Trolley 1 has negative momentum, as it is moving to the left. The momenta of the two trolleys are

momentum of trolley 1 $= -mv$

momentum of trolley 2 $= 2m \times v/2 = mv$

Adding these gives:

total momentum $= mv + (-mv) = 0$

Although each trolley has momentum, their combined momentum is zero. This is the same as their momentum before the explosion, when both were stationary. So momentum has been conserved.

More explosions

When a bullet is fired from a gun, it flies off at high speed. The person firing the gun must be prepared for its recoil. The bullet is an object of small mass moving at high speed; the gun has a much greater mass, so it moves backwards at a much smaller speed. You may have seen the same effect in a historical drama where soldiers are firing a cannon (Figure 3.7). They ignite the fuse and jump aside; the cannon-ball flies off, and the cannon jerks backwards. Similarly, cannon-fire from early naval ships had to be carefully controlled. As the cannon recoiled, it transferred its momentum to the ship, which moved back slightly. If all the cannons on one side of the ship were fired at the same time, it was in danger of capsizing.

Rockets and jet engines also rely on recoil for their motion. A rocket is a controlled explosion. As its fuel burns, hot gases rush out of the back end. They gain momentum backwards; the rocket itself is given

Figure 3.7 Recoil can be dangerous. When the cannon is fired, it leaps backwards. In the process of giving momentum to the cannon-ball, the cannon is given an equal amount of momentum in the opposite direction. Because the mass of the cannon is much greater than that of the ball, its velocity is much smaller.

momentum in the opposite direction. Similarly, jet engines blast hot gases backwards to give an aircraft momentum forwards.

Here is an example that may not seem like an explosion. An astronaut is repairing the outside of a spacecraft. Her tether breaks free, and she finds herself drifting away from the craft. How can she get back? Newton's first law of motion says that she will drift further and further away. She needs to give herself some momentum towards the spacecraft. She can do this by throwing something – a spanner, for example – in the opposite direction, away from the spacecraft. If she gives the spanner enough momentum, she will start moving back towards safety. She may have to throw the spanner quite hard to overcome her momentum as she drifts away.

More collisions

A tennis racket strikes a ball; the ball slows down, stops for an instant, and then flies back in the opposite direction. This is an example of a collision. How is momentum conserved here? The ball is given momentum to reverse its velocity. At the same time, the racket slows down as it strikes the ball. Because the player is holding the racket and is also in contact with the Earth, the racket *and* the player *and* the Earth are all affected. Their momentum is reduced by an amount equal to the ball's change in momentum.

What happens if you are running along and collide with a wall? You come to a sudden halt. Where has your momentum gone? You transfer it to the wall. Since the wall is attached to the ground, your momentum is transferred to the whole of the Earth. You make the Earth accelerate. However, the Earth has an enormous mass, so you won't notice its velocity change.

Figure 3.8 shows a collision involving sub-atomic particles. The yellow track shows a particle entering from the bottom of the picture. It collides with another particle in the middle of the picture. The particles that fly off (purple and orange tracks) share the momentum of the original particle. Physicists can analyse these tracks to deduce the masses and velocities of the particles. In the picture, one particle leaves no visible track, but its properties can be deduced using the principle of the conservation of momentum.

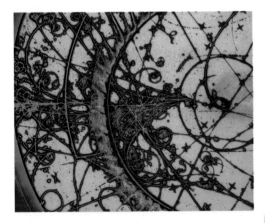

Figure 3.8 This image is from a bubble chamber, a machine for detecting sub-atomic particles. The particles' tracks have been coloured to make them clearer.

? Questions

3.1 Which has more momentum, spacecraft A (mass 500 kg, velocity 1000 m/s) or spacecraft B (mass 1000 kg, velocity 500 m/s)?

3.2 Mental arithmetic: What is the momentum of a child of mass 40 kg running at 4 m/s?

Figure 3.9 *Concorde* has been the only commercially operated supersonic passenger aircraft. It uses turbo-jet engines to push it to twice the speed of sound. These engines use a great deal of fuel, so a flight on *Concorde* is very expensive. A jumbo jet can carry five times the load for the same amount of fuel.

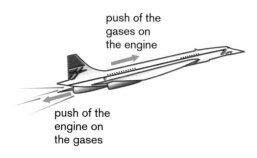

Figure 3.10 *Concorde's* engines provide the thrust force needed to move it through the air. The engines exert a backward force on the exhaust gases; the gases exert a forward force on the engines. It is this forward force that accelerates the aircraft.

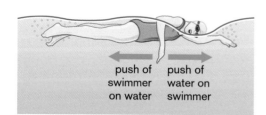

Figure 3.11 Forces are created in pairs. The swimmer pushes backwards on the water, and the water pushes forwards on the swimmer. These forces are equal and opposite. Compare this with the pair of forces in the diagram of *Concorde*, Figure 3.10.

> **Questions continued**
>
> **3.3** Momentum is measured in kg m/s. What is an alternative SI unit for momentum?
>
> **3.4** Is momentum a vector or a scalar quantity?
>
> **3.5** Mental arithmetic: An astronaut of mass 100 kg is floating in space. He throws a hammer of mass 2 kg with a velocity of 10 m/s to the right. What will be the astronaut's velocity after the throw?

3.2 Momentum and force

If you have ever heard *Concorde* fly over, you will know that its engines are exceedingly noisy (Figure 3.9). They burn 20 tonnes of fuel every hour, as they blast hot exhaust gases backwards to propel the aircraft forwards. They enable *Concorde* to travel at 600 m/s, almost twice the speed of sound in air.

Inside a jet engine, there is a controlled explosion going on. Fuel and air are mixed and burned at a steady rate, and the exhaust gases push their way out of the back of the engine. We can describe what *Concorde's* jet engines do in two different ways – in terms of momentum, and in terms of forces.

In the *momentum* picture, the exhaust gases gain momentum backwards. Since we know that momentum is conserved, we know that the aircraft gains an equal amount of momentum forwards (ignoring drag). So the aircraft moves off in the opposite direction to the exhaust gases. (This is like inflating a balloon and then releasing it. As the air rushes out in one direction, the balloon rushes off in the other.)

In the *forces* picture, we say that a force pushes the exhaust gases out of the back of the engine. An equal force pushes the aircraft forwards. These forces are shown in Figure 3.10. The forces are represented by arrows, to show their directions. Notice how the arrows are labelled:

- on the left, the push of the engine on the gases,
- on the right, the push of the gases on the engine.

It is important to say what is providing the force, and what the force is pushing on.

Pairs of forces

Figure 3.11 shows another situation involving movement. Imagine being stationary in a swimming pool. If you can swim, imagine how you can get moving. You use your hands to push the water backwards. This provides the force to move you forwards. In momentum terms, you give the water some momentum backwards; it gives you an equal amount of momentum forwards.

Here we have two forces: your push on the water, and the water's push on you. These forces are equal in size, and opposite in direction.

Figure 3.12 Magnets attract and repel one another with equal and opposite forces. Even if one magnet was replaced by a piece of unmagnetised iron, the forces of attraction would be equal and opposite.

One is exerted by you, and acts on the water. The other is exerted by the water, and acts on you. Without the force of the water on you, you would not start moving forwards.

Isaac Newton realised that forces are always created in pairs. Just as momentum cannot be created out of nothing (momentum is conserved), nor can a single force be created out of nothing. Here are two more examples of these equal-and-opposite pairs of forces.

- If you hold two bar magnets so that the north pole of one faces the south pole of the other, they will attract one another (Figure 3.12). You will feel that they attract each other equally strongly. Even if one magnet is more strongly magnetised than the other, you will feel that they are pulled equally. Reverse one of the magnets, and you will feel that they now repel each other with equal forces.

  Suppose the forces were *not* equal. Then, if the two magnets in the diagram were held apart on a frictionless surface, and then released, one magnet would gain a greater speed as they flew together. They would end up together moving in the faster magnet's original direction – which would violate the principle of conservation of momentum (see page 52).

- On page 37, we saw how friction is necessary for walking. To walk, you push backwards on the ground. Your foot is tending to slide backwards on the ground, so a frictional force pushes forwards to oppose you. There are thus two frictional forces acting: one which acts backwards on the ground, and the other which acts forwards on your foot.

We are used to the idea that the Earth's gravity pulls on us. If we fall down, it is because of gravity. The force of gravity on us is our weight – say, 500 N. But at the same time, we pull on the Earth. We pull upwards on the Earth with a gravitational force of about 500 N. However, because the Earth's mass is so great, this force has very little effect on it.

An important example of a pair of equal-and-opposite forces is shown in Figure 3.13a. Contact forces act when two objects are touching one another. It is important to realise that contact forces, too, come in pairs. If you stand on the ground, you push down on the ground and the ground pushes up on you. If we concentrate on the point where your feet touch the ground (Figure 3.13a), we can see this pair of

Figure 3.13 **a** When any two objects touch, each exerts a contact force on the other. These forces are an equal-and-opposite pair.
b Now we can think about the forces acting on the person. On this diagram, we only show the forces acting on the person; we do not show the forces exerted by the person on anything else.

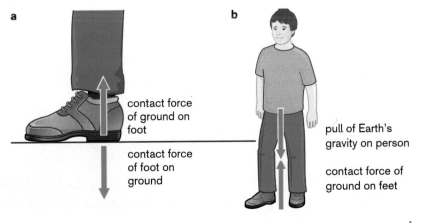

forces. (If you don't believe that they exist, imagine putting your hand between the foot and the ground. It would be squashed between the upward and downward forces.) Now if we look at the person as a whole (Figure 3.13b), we must consider only the forces acting on him. These are his weight downwards and the contact force upwards. If these forces are equal the person is in equilibrium. If the contact force is smaller than his weight, the person will accelerate downwards through the floor.

Newton's third law

The idea that forces are always created in pairs is known as **Newton's third law of motion**:

> When bodies interact, they exert equal and opposite forces on each other.

The forces in such a pair must be:

- equal in size;
- opposite in direction;
- of the same type.

'Of the same type' means that both forces are either gravitational, or contact, or frictional, or magnetic, etc. In addition, one force acts on one of the bodies; the other acts on the other body. *They don't act on the same body.*

Why is this a law of motion? Newton realised that forces make things speed up or slow down – they cause acceleration. Thus forces change momentum. Suppose two objects – say a foot and a ball – collide. Then by Newton's third law, the force of the foot on the ball and the force of the ball on the foot are equal and opposite, and the total momentum is *unchanged*. In this way, we can begin to see that Newton's second and third laws together lead to the principle of conservation of momentum.

You may sometimes hear a pair of forces like this referred to as *action* and *reaction*. So the third law is sometimes stated as:

> For every action, there is an equal and opposite reaction.

However, you need to be careful that you understand what the terms 'action' and 'reaction' mean.

Figure 3.14 To stay in flight, this owl pushes downwards on the air with its outstretched wings. If it kept its wings in the same position on the upward stroke, it would push itself back downwards. Instead, it tips its wings so that they can slice cleanly through the air, rather than pushing on it. Swimmers do the same thing. They push backwards in the water with their hands and arms to move forwards; then they lift their arms out of the water as they bring them forwards (air is much easier to push through than water), ready for the next backward stroke.

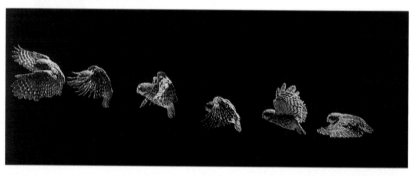

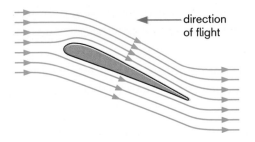

Figure 3.15 The cross-sections of the wings of birds and aircraft allow air to flow smoothly over them. Their shape and the angle at which they are tilted causes the airflow to be directed downwards and an upward force on the wing. If the aircraft stopped moving forwards, there would be no lift.

Fear of flying

We can use these ideas to think more about how birds and aircraft fly. Birds have more than one way of flying; flapping flight is one. Figure 3.14 shows an owl in flapping flight. As its wings beat downwards, they push air downwards. The downward force on the air results in an upward force on the bird. In terms of momentum, the bird gives the air some downward momentum. The bird gains an equal and opposite upward momentum.

As the bird raises its wings, it must avoid pushing air upwards. To do this, it tips its wings sideways so that they slice through the air. There is a small force on the air, so that the bird drops slightly, but then it is ready to push downwards again. You can see why a child cannot fly by flapping its arms. Arms are not designed for pushing air downwards, or for slipping through the air on the upward stroke.

Birds have another method for remaining airborne. In gliding flight, they make use of the shape of their wings – see Figure 3.15. The diagram shows how air flows past the wing. The shape of the wing and the slight tilt give an upward push on the wing, known as **lift**, enough to keep the bird in the air. Some species of bird, such as the albatross, can glide for days like this without having to use flapping flight.

An aircraft uses this same method. Its engines provide the thrust to push it forwards through the air. Its wings are shaped and tilted and give a lift force which counteracts the force of gravity. The forces acting on an aircraft in level flight at steady speed are shown in Figure 3.16.

Figure 3.16 In flight, an aircraft (or a bird) is acted on by four forces. The lift on the wings is created by pushing air downwards. If the air-craft is travelling horizontally at a constant velocity, the forces on it are balanced. The lift force balances its weight and the thrust of its engines balances the drag of the air.

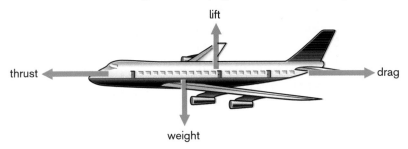

Extension material

Impulse of a force

Cats in New York live a dangerous life – falling from a skyscraper is no fun! When some New York vets investigated their records, they were surprised to find that cats which fell from higher than the third floor were more likely to survive than those which fell from lower down. How could this be? When a cat lands on the ground, it uses its legs to break its fall. (It is advisable for people to do the same thing – allowing your legs to bend as you land results in a smaller force for a longer time and a smaller chance of a bro-ken limb.) The vets found that, if a cat fell from high up, it had enough time to twist its body round and have its legs ready to break its fall.

When an object falls to the ground, it has momentum. It shares its momentum with the Earth; if it can spread this sharing over a longer period of time, the force will be smaller. Many modern cars have crum-ple zones (Figure 3.15) to reduce the force of impact during a collision. A cat's crumple zone is its legs, which it bends as it lands on the ground. A dog cannot do this.

Figure 3.17 The front section of this car's body is the crumple zone. On impact, it collapses during a fraction of a second. This is enough to reduce the force of impact. A rigid body results in a sudden impact with a much larger force. (In the same way, a jumper can reduce the force of impact on landing by bending her legs.) Some cars have 'bull-bars' attached at the front. These can have fashion appeal, but they transfer the impact force directly to the car's chassis, by-passing the crumple zone and increasing the danger to the driver.

Newton's second law, $F = ma$, can be written as

$$F = m(v - u)/t = (mv - mu)/t$$

You can see that $mv - mu$ is the change in momentum of the body. So we have

$$\text{force} = \frac{\text{change in momentum}}{\text{time}}$$

which can be rewritten as

$$\text{force} \times \text{time} = \text{change in momentum}$$

The quantity 'force × time' is known as the **impulse** of the force. Worked examples 3 and 4 show how we can use these ideas to calculate a force.

Worked example 3

Rockets

The Ariane rocket travels into space carrying liquid oxygen and hydrogen as its fuel supply (Figure 3.18). Its third stage burns fuel at the rate of 14.2 kg/s, and the exhaust gases leave the rocket at a speed of 4440 m/s. What thrust does the rocket provide?

We have:

$$\text{thrust force} = \frac{\text{change in momentum}}{\text{time}}$$

In 1 s, 14.2 kg of fuel is given a speed of 4440 m/s. So the momentum gained by the fuel in 1 s is: 14.2 kg × 4440 m/s = 63 048 kg m/s and this is the change in momentum.

Thus:

$$\text{thrust force} = \frac{63\,048\,\text{kg m/s}}{1\,\text{s}}$$

$$= 63\,048\,\text{N}$$

This is about 63 kN (kilonewtons).

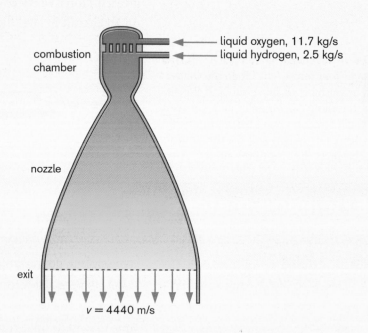

liquid oxygen, 11.7 kg/s
liquid hydrogen, 2.5 kg/s
combustion chamber
nozzle
exit
$v = 4440$ m/s

Figure 3.18 The third stage of an Ariane rocket. Because this rocket travels well above the Earth's atmosphere, it has to carry its own oxygen supply. The calculation shows that it provides a thrust of 63 kN.

Worked example 4

Helicopters

Like aeroplanes and birds, helicopters fly by pushing air downwards. They do this using their rotor blades. Each blade is slightly tilted, and is shaped rather like an aircraft wing – see Figure 3.19a. As the blades rotate, they push down a cylinder of air – see Figure 3.19b. We can explain how the helicopter stays up in two ways.

- In terms of momentum, the blades are giving downward momentum to the air, and so the air gives upward momentum to the blades.
- In terms of forces, the blades exert a downward force on the air, so the air exerts an upward force on the blades.

The blades of a large helicopter push air downwards with a velocity of 200 m/s. How much air must be pushed down each second to provide the upward force of 50 kN needed to support the helicopter?

- *Step 1* Write down what we know, and what we want to know:

  velocity of air = 200 m/s
  force = 50 kN
  time = 1 s   (because we want to know how much air
                        must be pushed down *each second*)
  mass in one second = ?

- *Step 2* Write down the impulse equation:

  force × time = change in momentum

- *Step 3* Write the change in momentum in one second as mass × velocity, and rearrange the equation to make mass its subject:

$$\text{mass} = \text{force} \times \frac{\text{time}}{\text{velocity}}$$

- *Step 4* Substitute values and solve:

$$\text{mass} = 50 \times 10^3 \, \text{N} \times \frac{1}{200 \, \text{m/s}} = 250 \, \text{kg}$$

So the blades must push 250 kg of air downwards each second at 200 m/s for the helicopter to stay in the air. From this sort of calculation, helicopter designers can work out how long the blades must be and how fast they must rotate. Figure 3.19c shows how the helicopter moves forwards.

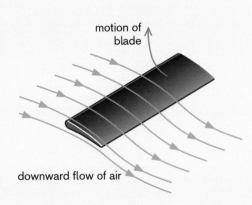

motion of blade

downward flow of air

a

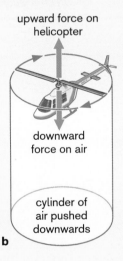

upward force on helicopter

downward force on air

cylinder of air pushed downwards

b

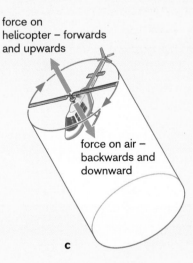

force on helicopter – forwards and upwards

force on air – backwards and downward

c

Figure 3.19 This is how a helicopter manages to fly.
a The blades are shaped and tilted so that, as they rotate, they push air downwards.
b The blades push a cylinder of air downwards. The reaction to this push is an upward force on the blades, which keeps the helicopter up. **c** To fly forwards, the pilot tips the helicopter so that the cylinder of air is pushed slightly backwards. Now there is a forwards force on the blades and, in turn, the helicopter accelerates forwards.

Questions

3.6 Sketch a diagram to show how a jet engine provides a force to move an aircraft forwards.

3.7 A girl stands on the floor. She exerts a downward force of 500 N on the floor. What force does the floor exert on her?

3.8 Sketch a diagram to show the forces two objects exert on each other when they are touching.

3.9 State Newton's third law of motion.

3.10 Your weight is the force of the Earth's gravity on you. What is the equal and opposite reaction to this force?

3.11 Why would an aircraft be unable to fly on the Moon?

Summary

◆ The momentum of an object is the product of its mass and velocity:

momentum = mass × velocity = mv

◆ The SI unit of momentum is kg m/s, or N s.

◆ The principle of conservation of momentum states that in a closed system, the total amount of momentum remains constant.

◆ Newton's third law of motion states that when bodies interact, they exert equal and opposite forces on each other.

⊖ *The impulse of a force is the product of the force and the time for which it acts.*

Turning effects of forces

Topics in this chapter

- moment of a force
- balancing moments
- equilibrium
- levers
- stability
- centre of mass

Human beings are inherently unstable. We are tall and thin, and walk upright. Our feet are not rooted into the ground, so you might expect us to keep toppling over. Babies learn to stand and walk at the age of about 12 months. It takes a lot of practice to get it right. We have to learn to coordinate our muscles so that our legs, body and arms move correctly. There is a special organ in each of our ears (the semicircular canal) that keeps us aware of whether we are vertical or tilting. Months of practice and many falls are needed to develop the skill of walking.

We have the same experience later in life if we learn to ride a bicycle. A bike is even more unstable than a person, and it can take years to master the stunt skills that some teenagers can demonstrate (Figure 4.1).

Figure 4.1 Stunt bikers are constantly trying to remain upright while gravity and momentum try to topple them over. Riders make continuous adjustments to the position of their bodies in order to remain vertical.

a

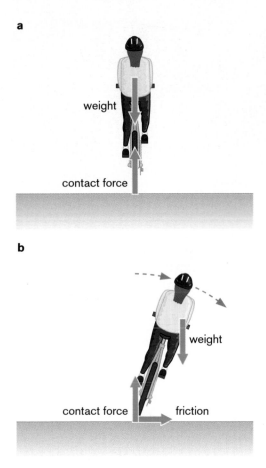

b

Figure 4.2 **a** When the cyclist is vertical, the two forces acting on her are balanced and she is in equilibrium.
b As she tilts, she is no longer in equilibrium. While the bottom of her wheel is in contact with the ground, this point acts as a pivot, and her weight causes her to tip around the pivot.

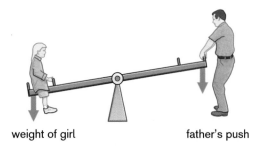

Figure 4.3 Two forces are causing this see-saw to tip: the girl's weight causes it to tip to the left, while her father provides a force to tip it to the right. He can increase the turning effect of his force, either by increasing the force, or by pushing down at a greater distance from the pivot.

If you ride a bike, you are constantly adjusting your position to maintain your stability and to remain upright. If the bike tilts slightly to the left, you automatically lean slightly to the right to provide a force that tips it back again. You make these adjustments unconsciously; you know intuitively that if you let the bike tilt too far, you will not be able to recover the situation, and you will end up sprawling on the ground.

4.1 The moment of a force

Figure 4.2 shows the forces that act on a cyclist as she tries to remain upright. If she is vertical, only two forces act (Figure 4.2a). The force of gravity (the weight of the rider and bicycle) acts vertically downwards, and the contact force of the road pushes back upwards. These forces are equal to one another, and they point in opposite directions. In these circumstances, the forces on the cyclist are balanced and we say that she is **in equilibrium**.

If the cyclist tilts to the right, the forces are as shown in Figure 4.2b. Her weight still acts downwards, and the contact force of the road acts upwards, but these forces are no longer in line with one another. There is also an additional force: friction. The wheel is tending to slip to the left, and this is opposed by the force of friction pushing to the right. (You can imagine that, on a very slippery road, the bottom of the wheel would slip off to the left and the cyclist would fall straight down.) You can see from the diagram that the forces on the cyclist are not balanced, so she is not in equilibrium. She will topple over to the right, following a curved path as shown on the diagram. If she wanted to avoid this, she would have to move some of her weight back to the left, but it is too late!

In this situation, it is the cyclist's weight that pulls her over. This force does not make her accelerate straight downwards — the sort of situation considered in Chapter 2. Instead, it causes her to tip. The point where the wheel touches the ground acts like a hinge or **pivot**, and the cyclist's weight has a **turning effect** about this pivot. The further she tips, the greater is the turning effect of her weight.

Moment of a force

The situation of the toppling cyclist is a difficult place to start analysing the turning effects of forces. An easier situation is shown in Figure 4.3. A small child is sitting on the left-hand end of a see-saw. Her weight causes the see-saw to tip down on the left. Her father presses down on the other end; if he can press with a force that more than balances her weight, the see-saw will tip to the right and she will come up in the air.

Now, suppose the father presses down closer to the pivot. He will have to press with a greater force if the turning effect of his force is to overcome the turning effect of his daughter's weight. If he presses at half the distance from the pivot, he will need to press with twice the force to balance her weight.

Figure 4.4 The wind blowing on the sail of this yacht is causing it to topple over. To prevent this from happening, the yachtsmen lean out as far as they can in the opposite direction, so that their weight provides a moment that will balance the moment of the wind's force. The further they lean out and the greater their weight, the greater their effect.

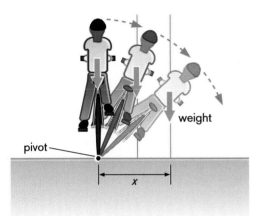

Figure 4.5 The cyclist's weight acts vertically downwards. As she topples over, its line of action moves further to the right. The perpendicular distance x from the pivot to the line of action increases.

The quantity that tells us the turning effect of a force about a pivot is its **moment**. There are two ways to increase the moment of a force (see Figure 4.4):

● increase the size of the force;
● increase the perpendicular distance from the pivot at which the force acts.

This last point needs some detailed consideration. Figure 4.5 shows the cyclist of Figure 4.2b as she topples over. As she topples, the turning effect of her weight increases, although her weight does not increase. You can see why this is from the diagram. The pivot is the point where the wheel touches the ground. The distance that matters is the perpendicular distance x between the pivot and the line of action of the force. As she topples over, x increases, and so the moment of her weight increases.

The other two forces (friction and contact force) in Figure 4.2b both pass through the pivot. Their perpendicular distance from the pivot is therefore zero, and they have no moment about the pivot.

Now we can write an equation for calculating the **moment of a force**:

moment = force × perpendicular distance from pivot to force

Units: since moment is a force (N) multiplied by a distance (m), its unit is simply the newton metre (N m). As we shall see later, newton metres are the same as joules: 1 Nm = 1 J.

Worked example 1

A trapdoor, hinged at one end, is supported by a cable as shown in Figure 4.6a. The tension (force) in the cable is 200 N. What is the moment of this force about the hinge?

Figure 4.6b shows the force and its distance from the hinge.

● *Step 1* Identify the pivot. The hinge is the pivot.
● *Step 2* Identify the line of action of the force. The force acts along the cable, as shown.
● *Step 3* Starting from the pivot, draw a line perpendicular to the line of action of the force.

continued on next page

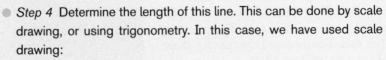

Worked example 1 continued

Figure 4.6 The cable is attached to the end of the trapdoor, but to find the moment of the tension in the cable, it is necessary to draw a perpendicular line from the hinge to the cable (from the pivot to the line of action of the force).

● *Step 4* Determine the length of this line. This can be done by scale drawing, or using trigonometry. In this case, we have used scale drawing:

perpendicular distance from pivot to line of action of force = 1.2 m

● *Step 5* Calculate the moment of the force:

moment = 200 N × 1.2 m = 240 N m

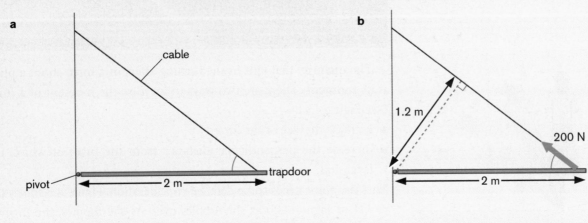

Balancing moments

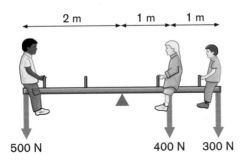

Figure 4.7 A balanced see-saw. On his own, the child on the left would make the see-saw turn anticlockwise; his weight has an anticlockwise moment. The weight of each child on the right has a clockwise moment. Since the see-saw is balanced, the clockwise moments must equal the anticlockwise moment.

Young children enjoy playing on a see-saw. They can learn to balance it; two small children can balance the weight of a larger one – see Figure 4.7. The weight of the child on the left is tending to turn the see-saw anticlockwise; it has an anticlockwise moment. The weights of the two children on the right have clockwise moments. From the data in the diagram, we can calculate these moments:

anticlockwise moment = 500 N × 2.0 m = 1000 N m

clockwise moment = (300 N × 2.0 m) + (400 N × 1.0 m)
= 600 N m + 400 N m = 1000 N m

(The brackets are included as a reminder to perform the multiplications before the addition.) We can see that in this situation:

total clockwise moment = total anticlockwise moment

and the see-saw is balanced.

We can use this idea to find the value of an unknown force or distance, as shown in worked example 2.

Worked example 2

The beam shown in Figure 4.8 is 2.0 m long and has a weight of 20 N. It is pivoted as shown (at the point indicated by the small triangle); a force of 10 N acts downwards at one end. What force *F* must be applied downwards at the other end to balance the beam?

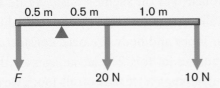

Figure 4.8 Note that the weight of the beam (20 N) is represented by a downward arrow at its midpoint.

● *Step 1* Identify the clockwise and anticlockwise forces. Two forces act clockwise:

20 N at a distance of 0.5 m and 10 N at 1.5 m

One force acts anticlockwise:

F at 0.5 m

● *Step 2* Since the beam balances, we can write:

total clockwise moment = total anticlockwise moment

● *Step 3* Substitute in the values from step 1, and solve:

$$(20\,N \times 0.5\,m) + (10\,N \times 1.5\,m) = F \times 0.5\,m$$
$$10\,Nm + 15\,Nm = F \times 0.5\,m$$
$$25\,Nm = F \times 0.5\,m$$
$$F = \frac{25\,Nm}{0.5\,m} = 50\,N$$

So a force of 50 N is needed.

[You might have been able to work this out in your head, by looking at the diagram. The 20 N weight requires 20 N to balance it, and the 10 N at 1.5 m needs 30 N to balance it. So the total force needed is 50 N.]

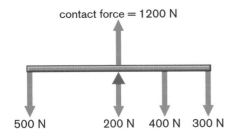

Figure 4.9 A force diagram for the see-saw shown in Figure 4.7. The contact force of the pivot on the see-saw balances the downward forces of the children's weights. Because it acts through the pivot, the contact force has no moment about the pivot. We are ignoring the weight of the see-saw itself; this is another force that acts through the pivot, so it also has no moment.

In equilibrium

In the drawing of the three children on the see-saw (Figure 4.7), three forces are shown acting downwards; there is also the weight of the see-saw – 200 N. If these were the *only* forces acting, they would make the see-saw accelerate downwards. Another force acts to prevent this from happening: a **contact force** where the see-saw sits on the pivot. Figure 4.9 shows all five forces.

Because the see-saw is in **equilibrium**, we can calculate this contact force. It must balance the four downwards forces, so its value is (500 + 200 + 400 + 300) N = 1400 N, upwards. The contact force and the weight have no turning effect because they act through the pivot.

Now we have two conditions that must be met if an object is to be in equilibrium:

● there must be no resultant or unbalanced force acting on it;
● total clockwise moment = total anticlockwise moment.

?

Questions

4.1 Write down a word equation for the moment of a force about a point.

4.2 What are the units of the moment of a force?

Figure 4.10 This high-wire artiste is using a long pole to maintain her stability on the wire. If she senses that her weight is slightly too far to the left, she can regain her balance by moving the pole to the right. Frequent, small adjustments allow her to walk smoothly along the wire.

Questions continued

4.3 What is the value of the moment of a force about a point if the force passes through that point?

4.4 Mental arithmetic: Which has the greater moment, a force of 10 N acting at 4 m from a point, or a force of 6 N acting at 7 m from the point?

4.2 Stability and centre of mass

People are tall and thin, like a pencil standing on end. Unlike a pencil, we do not topple over when touched by the slightest push. We are able to remain upright, and to walk, because we make continual adjustments to the positions of our limbs and body. We need considerable brain power to control our muscles for this. The advantages are that, with our eyes about a metre higher than if we were on all-fours, we can see much more of the world and our hands are free to do other things.

Circus artistes such as tightrope walkers (Figure 4.10) have developed the skill of remaining upright to a high degree. They use items such as poles or parasols to help them maintain their balance. The idea of moments can help us to understand why some objects are stable while others are more likely to topple over.

A champagne glass (which is tall and thin, with a long stem) is easily knocked over – it is unstable. It could be described as top-heavy, because most of its mass is concentrated high up, above its stem. Figure 4.11 shows what happens if the glass is tilted.

a When the glass is upright, its weight acts downwards and the contact force of the table acts upwards. The two forces are in line, and the glass is in equilibrium.

b If the glass is tilted slightly to the right, the forces are no longer in line. There is a pivot at the point where the base of the glass is in contact with the table. The line of the glass's weight is to the left of this pivot, so it has an anticlockwise moment, which tends to tip the glass back to its upright position.

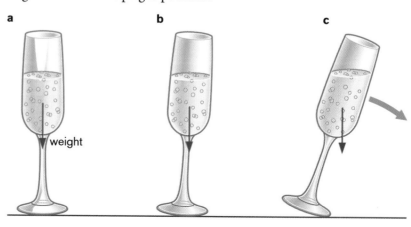

Figure 4.11 A tall glass is easily toppled. Once the line of action of its weight is beyond the edge of the base, as in **c**, the glass tips right over.

c Now the glass is tipped further. Its weight acts to the right of the pivot, and has a clockwise moment, which makes the glass tip right over.

We say that an object is **stable** if, when displaced from equilibrium, it returns to its original position.

Centre of mass

In Figure 4.11, the weight of the glass is represented by an arrow starting at a point inside the liquid in the bowl of the glass. Why is this? The reason is that the glass behaves as if all of its mass were concentrated at this point, known as the **centre of mass**. The glass is top-heavy because its centre of mass is high up. The force of gravity acts on the mass of the glass; each bit of the glass is pulled by the Earth's gravity. However, rather than drawing lots of weight arrows, one for each bit of the glass, it is simpler to draw a single arrow acting through the centre of mass. (Because we can think of the glass's weight acting at this point, it is sometimes known as the centre of gravity.)

Figure 4.12 shows the position of the centre of mass for several objects. A person is fairly symmetrical, so their centre of mass must lie somewhere on the axis of symmetry. (This is because half of their mass is on one side of the axis, and half on the other.) The centre of mass is in the middle of the body, roughly level with the navel. A ball is much more symmetrical; its centre of mass is at its centre.

For an object to be stable, it should have a low centre of mass and a wide base; the pyramid in Figure 4.12 is an example of this. (The Egyptian pyramids are among the wonders of the world. It has been suggested that, if they had been built the other way up, they would have been even greater wonders!) The tightrope walker shown in Figure 4.10 has to adjust the pole so that her centre of mass remains above her 'base' – the point where her feet make contact with the rope.

Figure 4.12 The weight of an object acts through its centre of mass. Symmetry can help us to judge where the centre of mass lies. An object's weight can be considered as acting through this point. Note that, for the table, its centre of mass is in the air below the tabletop.

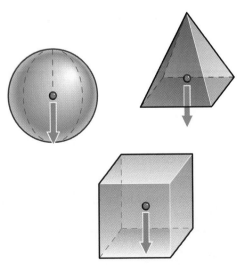

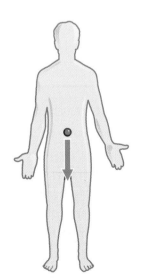

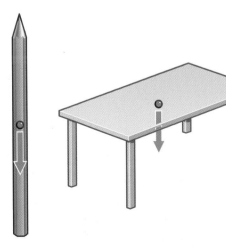

Figure 4.13 Finding the centre of mass of an irregularly shaped piece of card. The card hangs freely from the pin. The centre of mass must lie on the line indicated by the plumb-line hanging from the pin. Three lines are enough to find the centre of mass.

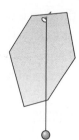 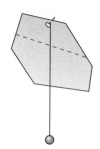 

Finding the centre of mass

Balancing is the clue to finding an object's centre of mass. A metre rule balances at its midpoint, so that is where its centre of mass must lie.

The procedure for finding the centre of mass of a more irregularly shaped object is shown in Figure 4.13. In this case, the object is a piece of card. The card is suspended from a pin; if it is free to move, it hangs with its centre of mass below the point of suspension. (This is because its weight pulls it round until the weight and the contact force at the pin are lined up. Then there is no moment about the pin.) A plumb-line is used to mark a vertical line below the pin; the centre of mass must lie on this line.

The process is repeated for two more pinholes. Now there are three lines on the card, and the centre of mass must lie on all of them, that is, at the point where they intersect. (Two lines might have been enough, but it is advisable to use at least three points to show up any inaccuracies.)

 Questions

4.5 What is meant by the centre of mass of an object?

4.6 Where is the centre of mass of the Earth? And of a book?

4.7 Give an example of an object whose centre of mass is outside the object. Sketch the object and mark its centre of mass.

4.8 Use the idea of centre of mass to explain why a tall thin object is less stable than a short wide one. Use diagrams in your answer.

 Summary

◆ The moment of a force about a pivot is given by:

moment = force × perpendicular distance from pivot to force

◆ For an object to be in equilibrium:
  • there must be no resultant or unbalanced force acting on it;
  • total clockwise moment = total anticlockwise moment.

◆ The mass of an object can be considered to be concentrated at a single point, its centre of mass.

Forces and matter

Topics in this chapter

◆ density

◆ elastic and plastic deformation

◆ Hooke's law

The air around us feels very thin. We have no trouble walking through it; at times, it is hard to believe there is anything there. However, when the air starts to move, it can wreak terrible damage. Figure 5.1 shows the effects of moving air. A tornado struck these houses. Roofs have been destroyed and scattered around as though a giant demolition crane had been at work. Trees have been snapped like matches and lie scattered on the ground.

Air seems thin because its density is very low. Water is almost 800 times denser, so we notice its effects more readily. However, air does have mass; when it moves it has momentum. From the photograph, you can see that it packs quite a punch when it moves at high speed.

This chapter looks at the effects of forces on matter: in particular, how they can deform and break solid objects.

Figure 5.1 A tornado is just moving air, but it can cause terrible damage. This one hit Atlanta in the USA. Many people were killed or injured.

5.1 Density

Air has a low density – approximately $1.29 \, kg/m^3$; that is to say, a cubic metre ($1 \, m^3$) of air has a mass of $1.29 \, kg$. This may seem like very little. However, the mass of all the air in a typical school classroom is likely to be about $100 \, kg$ – more than the mass of a typical pupil.

The density of air is low because its molecules are widely separated – see Figure 5.2. Most of the volume of air is made up of empty space. This makes it easy to change the density of air, by compressing it. You do this when you blow up a balloon, or inflate a bicycle tyre. The density of air inside a car tyre is three times the density of the air outside it. Cooling air also increases its density. At very low temperatures (about $-200\,°C$) it condenses into a liquid with a density similar to that of water. If all the air in the room you are in now were suddenly to condense, it would form a layer two or three millimetres deep on the floor.

Figure 5.2 **a** Under everyday conditions, the molecules in air are widely separated; more than 99.8% of the volume of air is empty space. **b** Compressing the air increases its density. The molecules are pushed closer together; the volume of the molecules themselves does not change, but there is less empty space between them.

a 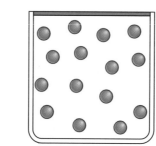 b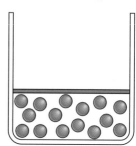

Defining density

These thoughts about the density of air remind us of the meaning of density. Density is a property of a material; it tells us how concentrated its mass is. In everyday speech, we might say that lead is heavier than wood; we mean that, given equal volumes of lead and wood, the lead is heavier. In scientific terms, the density of lead is greater than the density of wood. So we define **density** as follows:

$$\text{density} = \frac{\text{mass}}{\text{volume}}$$

$$\rho = \frac{M}{V}$$

The symbol ρ (rho, Greek letter r) is used to represent density; D is sometimes used as an alternative.

Units: The SI unit of density is kg/m^3 (kilograms per cubic metre). You may come across others, as shown in Table 5.1.

Table 5.1 Units of density. These depend on the units chosen for measuring mass and volume.

Unit of mass	Unit of volume	Unit of density
kilogram, kg	cubic metre, m^3	kilograms per cubic metre, kg/m^3
kilogram, kg	litre, l	kilograms per litre, kg/l
gram, g	millilitre, ml	grams per millilitre, g/ml
	(or cubic centimetre, cm^3)	(or grams per cubic centimetre, g/cm^3)

Material	Density (kg/m^3)
Gases	
air	1.29
hydrogen	0.09
helium	0.18
carbon dioxide	1.98
Liquids	
water	1000
alcohol (ethanol)	790
mercury	13 600
Solids	
ice	920
wood	400–1200
polythene	910–970
glass	2500–4200
steel	7500–8100
lead	11 340
silver	10 500
gold	19 300

Table 5.2 Densities of some substances. For gases, these are given at a temperature of 0 °C and a pressure of 1×10^5 Pa.

Our eyes can deceive us. When we look at an object, we can judge its volume. However, we can only guess its mass, and we may guess incorrectly because we misjudge the density. You may offer to carry someone's bag, only to discover that it contains heavy books. A large box of chocolates may have a mass of only 200 g, a great disappointment!

Values of density

Some values of density are shown in Table 5.2. Here are some points to note.

● Gases have much lower densities than solids or liquids.
● Hydrogen and helium are much less dense than air. This means that they can be used for filling balloons, which will then float upwards. It also helps to explain why there is very little of either of these gases in the Earth's atmosphere. They are so light that they float up towards the top of the atmosphere, and can then escape into space. Jupiter's atmosphere consists mostly of hydrogen and helium. It is a much more massive planet than the Earth, so its gravitational pull is stronger. It is also much colder, so some gases condense to form solids.
● Density is the key to floating. Ice is less dense than water. This explains why icebergs float in the sea, rather than sinking to the bottom.
● Many materials have a range of densities. Some types of wood, for example, are less dense than water and will float. Others (such as mahogany) are more dense and sink. The density depends on the composition.
● Gold is denser than silver. Pure gold is a soft metal, so jewellers add silver to make it harder. The amount of silver added can be judged by measuring the density.

Worked example 1

A balloon is filled with 2000 m^3 of hydrogen of density 0.09 kg/m^3. The mass of the (unfilled) balloon is 2000 kg. Will the balloon float in air of density 1.29 kg/m^3?

When the balloon is filled, its total mass is the mass of the balloon plus the mass of the hydrogen it contains, so we first have to calculate the mass of the hydrogen:

mass of hydrogen = density × volume
= 0.09 kg/m^3 × 2000 m^3 = 180 kg

So we get the mass of the filled balloon as:

mass of filled balloon = 180 kg + 2000 kg = 2180 kg

To find whether the balloon will float, we need to find its average density and compare this with the density of air:

$$\text{density of balloon} = \frac{\text{mass}}{\text{volume}} = \frac{2180\,\text{kg}}{2000\,\text{m}^3} = 1.09\,\text{kg/m}^3$$

The balloon will float in air. However, its average density is not much less than that of air, so it will not be able to carry a heavy load.

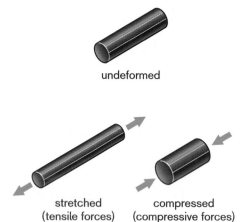

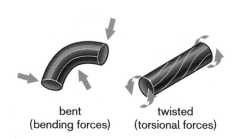

stretched
(tensile forces)

compressed
(compressive forces)

bent
(bending forces)

twisted
(torsional forces)

Figure 5.3 Forces can change the size and shape of a solid object. These diagrams show four different ways of deforming a solid object.

Questions

5.1 Write down an equation that defines density.

5.2 Material A: 5 kg occupies 20 cm³. Material B: 20 kg occupies 90 cm³. Which has the greater density?

5.3 Will silver (density 10 500 kg/m³) float in mercury (density 13 600 kg/m³)?

5.4 Mental arithmetic: The density of water is 1000 kg/m³. What is the mass of 3 m³ of water?

5.5 A block of steel is placed in a measuring cylinder that contains water. The water level rises from 100 cm³ to 300 cm³. If the mass of the steel is 1500 g, what is its density in g/cm³?

5.2 Forces acting on solids

Forces can change the shape of an object. They can stretch, squash, bend or twist it. Figure 5.3 shows the forces needed for these different ways of deforming an object. You could imagine holding a cylinder of foam rubber, which is easy to deform, and changing its shape in each of these ways.

Foam rubber is good for investigating deformation because, when the forces are removed, it springs back to its original shape. We say that it deforms in an *elastic* way; this is known as **elastic deformation**. Some materials do not return to their original shape. They deform in an *inelastic* way; this is known as **plastic deformation**.

Examples of elastic and plastic deformation

Here are some examples of materials deforming in an elastic way.

● When a rugby ball is kicked, it is compressed for a short while – see Figure 5.4. Then it springs back to its original shape as it leaves the foot of the player who has kicked it. The same is true for a tennis ball when struck by a racket. It is hard to believe it, but it is also true for a snooker ball when hit by the cue. The ball is very hard, so it does not compress very much. It returns to its original shape when it leaves the end of the cue.

● A floor bends very slightly when you walk on it. It has to do this to provide the contact force that pushes up on you, to prevent you falling through the floor – see page 58. Wood is a good material for this because it is slightly springy. This makes it more comfortable to walk on than a rigid concrete floor.

● Bungee jumpers rely on the elastic deformation of the elastic rope that breaks their fall when they jump from a height. If the rope became permanently deformed, they would stop suddenly, at the bottom of their fall, rather than bouncing up and down and gradually coming to a halt.

Figure 5.4 A rugby ball is compressed when it is kicked. It returns to its original shape as it leaves the player's boot. (This is an example of an elastic deformation.) The boot is also compressed slightly but, because it is stiffer than the ball, the effect is less noticeable.

Figure 5.5 A goldsmith at work. Gold is a relatively soft metal at room temperature, so it can be hammered into shape without the need for heating. In contrast, blacksmiths have to get iron red-hot before they can hammer it into a desired shape.

Here are some examples of materials deforming in a plastic way.

- Gold is a metal that can be deformed inelastically – see Figure 5.5. People have known for thousands of years how to shape rings and other ornaments from gold.
- Steel pylons carry electricity cables over large distances. They can stand up to most weather conditions, but occasionally hurricane-force winds prove too strong. The steel buckles and the lines come crashing to the ground.
- Aluminium drinks cans are made from an alloy of aluminium that is readily deformed. A can starts off as a flat disc of metal. A piston then stamps out the shape of the can. The metal forming the walls of the can is stretched so much that its thickness is only about one-tenth of the thickness of the original disc.

Stretching springs

To investigate how objects deform elastically, it is simplest to start with a spring. Springs are designed to stretch a long way when a small force is applied, so it is easy to measure how their length changes.

Figure 5.6 shows how to carry out this investigation. A spring is hung from a rigid clamp, so that its top end is fixed. Weights are hung on the end of the spring; these are referred to as the **load**. As the load is increased, the spring stretches and its length increases.

The red broken line in Figure 5.6 also shows the pattern observed as the load is increased in regular steps. The length of the spring increases (also in regular steps). At this stage the spring will return to its original length if the load is removed. However, if the load is increased too far, the spring becomes permanently stretched and will not return to its original length. It has been inelastically deformed.

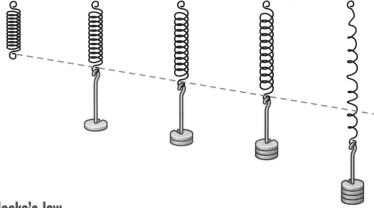

Figure 5.6 Stretching a spring. At first the spring deforms elastically: it will return to its original length when the load is removed. Eventually, however, the load is so great that the spring is damaged. It has been inelastically deformed.

Hooke's law

The mathematical pattern of the stretching spring was first described by the English scientist Robert Hooke. He realised that it was important to consider the *increase in length* of the spring. This quantity is known as the **extension**. So

length of stretched spring = original length + extension

Hooke realised that, when the load on the spring was doubled, the extension also doubled. Three times the load gave three times the extension, and so on. This shows up in the graph (Figure 5.7a). The graph shows how the extension depends on the load. At first the graph is a straight line, leading up from the origin. This shows that the extension is proportional to the load.

At a certain point, there is a kink in the graph, and the line slopes up more steeply. At this point, the spring has been permanently damaged. If the load is removed, the spring will not return all the way to its original, undeformed length (Figure 5.7b). The point beyond which this happens is known as the **elastic limit**. The spring deforms elastically before the elastic limit, but inelastically after it.

Figure 5.7 **a** A load–extension graph for a spring. The extension is the amount by which the spring's length increases for a given load. Beyond the elastic limit, the spring is permanently deformed. **b** The small graph shows what happens when the load is removed: the extension does not return to zero, showing that the spring is now longer than at the start of the experiment.

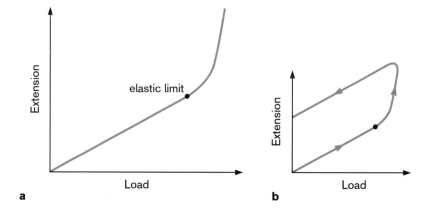

The behaviour of the spring is summed up by **Hooke's law**:

The extension of a spring is proportional to the load applied to it, provided the elastic limit is not exceeded.

Stretching other materials

A rubber band can be stretched in a similar way to a spring. As with a spring, the bigger the load, the bigger the extension. However, if the weights are added with great care, and then removed one by one without releasing the tension in the rubber, the following can be observed.

- The graph obtained is not a straight line. Rather, it has a slightly S-shaped curve. This shows that the extension is not exactly proportional to the load; rubber does not obey Hooke's law.
- Eventually, increasing the load no longer produces any extension. The rubber feels very stiff. When the load is removed, the graph does not come back exactly to zero.

Copper wire can also be stretched, as shown in Figure 5.8. It will only extend a short distance elastically. With a greater load, the elastic limit is exceeded, and the copper starts to deform inelastically. The copper becomes longer and longer, and will not return to its original length.

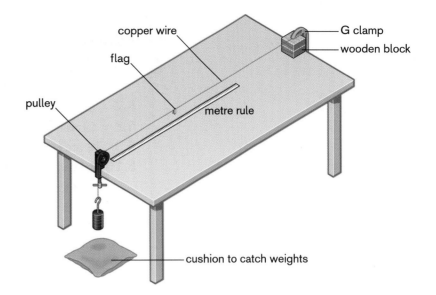

Figure 5.8 Stretching a copper wire. The wire is rigidly clamped at one end. It is stretched along the bench and over a pulley. Weights are hung on the end. To see the effect of increasing the load, a 'flag' made from Sellotape is attached about 50 cm from the pulley. Careful observation shows that, beyond the elastic limit, the copper gradually stretches even without increasing the load. The flag moves along the bench for several seconds. This behaviour is known as 'creep'.

Beyond the elastic limit

Copper is an interesting material because it shows both elastic and plastic (inelastic) behaviour. Many coins are made of copper (with other metals added to make it a bit stiffer). If you drop a coin, it bounces. In bouncing, it deforms slightly, then springs back to its original shape. However, a greater force can deform it permanently – for example, if the coin is hit with a hammer. This property of copper is used in making copper wires. The manufacturer starts with a thick rod of copper. This is stretched in stages to make it thinner and thinner, until it is a long, thin wire. The force stretching the wire must be great enough so that the elastic limit is exceeded.

Glass shows slightly elastic behaviour. If you press gently on the centre of a window-pane, the glass bends a little. This is elastic deformation. If you press too hard, the glass breaks. The elastic limit has been exceeded, but the glass does not deform – it shatters. Because it breaks in a brittle way, glass is referred to as a brittle material.

The bodywork of a car is usually made from steel. The particular type of steel chosen must be reasonably easy to deform, so that the different panels can be readily pressed into shape – see Figure 5.9. (Pressing the panels into shape actually makes the metal harder.) In normal circumstances, the bodywork retains its shape, even if someone leans on the bonnet or slams the door. However, in a collision, the elastic limit is exceeded and the bodywork gets dented – it is inelastically deformed. Use is made of this property in the crumple zone of a car, which is made of material that will deform in a collision. It is better for the crumple zone to be crushed, rather than the bodywork of the people inside the car!

Figure 5.9 The bodywork panels of a car are made from flat sheets of steel. They are pressed into shape by a giant press, which provides a force that allows the elastic limit of the steel to be exceeded. Unfortunately, this means that the panels are vulnerable in a collision and are easily dented.

Questions

5.6 What is the difference between *elastic deformation* and *plastic deformation*?

5.7 Explain what is meant by the term *extension*.

5.8 Explain what is meant by the term *elastic limit*.

5.9 State Hooke's law.

5.10 An unstretched spring is 12 cm long. A load of 5 N stretches it to 15 cm. Assuming that it obeys Hooke's law, to what length will it stretch under a load of 15 N?

5.11 Sketch a load–extension graph for glass, which deforms according to Hooke's law, and then breaks.

◆ Density is the mass per unit volume of a material:

$$\text{density} = \frac{\text{mass}}{\text{volume}}$$

$$\rho = \frac{M}{V}$$

◆ Density is measured in kg/m^3.

◆ Hooke's law: The extension of a spring is proportional to the load applied to it, provided the elastic limit is not exceeded.

◆ Beyond the elastic limit, a material deforms plastically and will not return to its original dimensions when the load is removed.

Further questions

The numbering is continued from the in-chapter questions.

Chapter 1

1.21

An ice-skating race consists of three sections with a total length of 5000 m. One skater completes the first section, of length 1200 m, in 100 s. She completes the next section, of length 2400 m, in 240 s.

a Calculate the skater's average speed over the first section, over the second section, and over the two sections together.

b If the skater maintains an average speed of 10 m/s over the third section of the race, what is the time she takes to cover the whole track?

1.22

The table shows the distance travelled by a car as it sets off from traffic lights, at intervals of 1 second.

a Use the data to plot a distance–time graph for the car.

b What can you say about the speed of the car during the first 4 s?

c From the graph, deduce the car's speed after 6 s.

Distance (m)	Time (s)
0	0
1	1
4	2
9	3
16	4
24	5
32	6
40	7

1.23

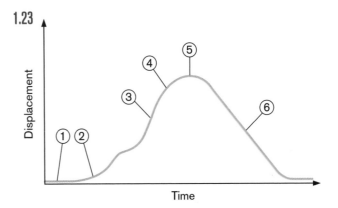

Figure Q1.23 Displacement–time graph for a roller-coaster car.

The graph shows the displacement of a car on a roller-coaster ride, at different times along its trip. It travels along the track, and then returns to its starting position. Study the graph and decide which point best fits each of the following descriptions. In each case, give a reason to explain why you have chosen that point.

a The car is stationary.

b The car is travelling its fastest.

c The car is speeding up.

d The car is slowing down.

e The car is on its return journey.

1.24

A car travels for 10 s at a steady velocity of 20 m/s along a straight road. The traffic lights ahead change to red, and the car slows down with a constant deceleration so that it halts after a further 8 s.

a Draw a velocity–time graph to represent the car's motion during the 18 s described.

b Use the graph to deduce the car's deceleration.

c Use the graph to deduce how far the car travels during the 18 s described.

d Use the equations of motion to check your answers to parts **b** and **c**.

1.25

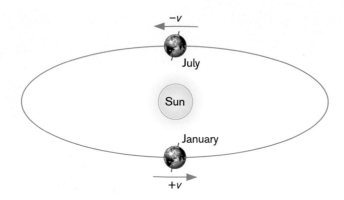

Figure Q1.25 The Earth in its orbit around the Sun.

The Earth orbits the Sun once every year (approximately 3.15×10^7 s). It travels at a steady speed along a roughly circular path of radius 150 million kilometres. As shown in the figure, in January, the Earth is travelling to the right. Six months later, in July, it is travelling to the left.

a Calculate the Earth's average speed v around its orbit. (Circumference of a circle $= 2\pi \times$ radius.)

b The Earth's *speed* is more or less constant, but its *velocity* changes as it orbits the Sun. Explain how this can be.

c Between January and July, the Earth's velocity changes from $+v$ to $-v$. Calculate its change in velocity in this time.

1.26

At an amusement park, a small child slides down a water flume with a constant acceleration of 1.5 m/s^2. The child starts from rest (zero velocity), and the flume is 12 m long.

a How long will it take the child to reach the foot of the flume?

b How fast will the child be travelling at the foot of the flume?

c An older child pushes herself off at the top of the slide, so that her initial velocity is 4 m/s. How fast will she be travelling at the foot of the flume? (Her acceleration is the same as that of the small child.)

1.27

A truck pulled out from a side road. The driver had not noticed an approaching car, and they collided at a distance of 8.5 m from the junction. The police asked the truck driver to accelerate the truck from rest, for a distance of 8.5 m. They found that the average time for this was 2.9 s.

a Estimate the truck's acceleration.

b Estimate the speed with which it struck the car.

c Explain why your answers are only estimates.

Chapter 2

2.15

A car of mass 1200 kg is moving along a level road at a speed of 10 m/s. Its engine provides a forward force of 400 N. The car's motion is opposed by a frictional force of 100 N, caused by air resistance. (Gravitational field strength at Earth's surface = 10 N/kg.)

a Draw a diagram to show the horizontal and vertical forces acting on the car. Indicate the size and direction of each force.

b Calculate the resultant (unbalanced) force acting on the car.

c Calculate the car's acceleration.

d If the car's acceleration remains constant, how long will it take to reach a speed of 15 m/s?

e Explain why the car's acceleration is unlikely to remain constant as it speeds up.

2.16

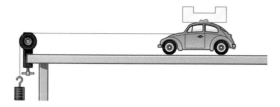

Figure Q2.16

The diagram shows the way in which a group of students set about investigating how the acceleration of a small toy car depended on the force causing it to accelerate. They attached a string to the car and passed it over a pulley. The weights on the end of the string pulled the car and made it accelerate. They measured the acceleration using an interrupt card and a single light gate.

The table shows the students' results, which were not what they expected.

Mass on end of string, m (kg)	Weight pulling car, F (N)	Acceleration, a (m/s^2)
0.1	1.0	3.5
0.2	2.0	5.0
0.3	3.0	6.2
0.4	4.0	6.8
0.5	5.0	7.1

a The students expected to find that doubling the force F would produce double the acceleration a. Draw a graph to test whether this is true, for the data in the table. Comment on the shape of your graph.

b The problem was that the car had a very small mass, only 0.2 kg. When a mass of 0.1 kg was hung from the string, the total mass being accelerated was therefore 0.2 kg + 0.1 kg = 0.3 kg. Calculate the acceleration you would expect this mass to be given by a force of 1 N. Compare your answer with the first row in the table, and comment on your answer.

c Suggest how the experiment could be re-designed to give a good test of the relationship between force and acceleration.

2.17

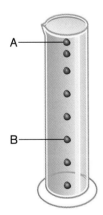

Figure Q2.17

A spherical pebble was dropped into a tall glass container filled with water. The diagram shows the position of the pebble at equal intervals of time.

a Describe how the pebble's velocity changed as it fell through the water.

b For positions A and B, draw diagrams to show the forces acting on the pebble. Explain whether the forces are balanced or unbalanced at each position.

c Where was the pebble's acceleration greatest?

2.18

A spacecraft is carried up into space by a rocket that provides a constant force, vertically upwards. As the rocket moves upwards, its store of fuel is gradually used up. Explain what will happen to the rocket's acceleration as it rises upwards.

2.19

a The unit of force is the newton. Define the newton.

b It is useful to remember that 'the weight of a typical apple is roughly 1 newton'. What does this suggest is the mass of a typical apple?

c Under what circumstances might the weight of an apple be very different from 1 newton?

2.20

Galileo is said to have carried out an experiment in which he dropped two heavy objects, cannon-balls of different sizes, from the top of the Leaning Tower of Pisa. (Unfortunately, there is no historical evidence to prove that he ever did this.) He is supposed to have shown that, when released simultaneously, they reached the ground at the same instant.

a Explain why this is what you would expect to observe if you could repeat the experiment today.

b If Galileo had thrown one ball horizontally at the same time as releasing the other, what would you predict that he would have observed?

c It has been suggested that, if Galileo had truly carried out these experiments, his results would have been affected by air resistance. What difference would this make to your answers to parts **a** and **b**?

Chapter 3

3.12

Two trolleys are moving directly towards one another. Trolley A has a mass of 2 kg and is moving at 4 m/s; trolley B has a mass of 3 kg and is moving at 3 m/s. When they collide, they stick together.

a Calculate the momentum of each trolley before the collision.

b In which direction will they move after the collision? Explain how the principle of conservation of momentum helps you to answer this.

c How fast will they move after the collision?

3.13

A toy cannon of mass 100 g fires a ball of mass 20 g horizontally. The ball leaves the gun with a speed of 10 m/s. The cannon recoils. What is its speed of recoil?

3.14

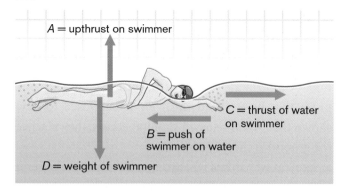

Figure Q3.14

The diagram shows a swimmer who is just setting off to swim a length of a pool.

a Of the four forces shown on the diagram, which two form a balanced pair of forces, both acting on the swimmer?

b Which of these pairs of forces is an action and reaction pair, as described by Newton's third law of motion?

c Is the swimmer in equilibrium? Explain your answer.

Chapter 4

4.9

Two children sit on a 6 m long see-saw that is pivoted at its midpoint. One child, who weighs 400 N, sits at one end of the see-saw. The other, who weighs 600 N, sits 1 m from the other end. Is the see-saw balanced?

4.10

Figure Q4.10

The diagram shows a 3 m uniform wooden beam, pivoted 1 m from one end. The weight of the beam is 200 N.

a Copy the diagram, and mark the beam's centre of mass.

b Add arrows to show the following two forces: the contact force on the beam at the pivot; the beam's weight.

c A third force F presses down at the end of the beam (point A). What value of F is needed to balance the beam?

d When this force is applied, what is the value of the (upwards) contact force that the pivot exerts on the beam?

4.11

Use the ideas of *stability* and *centre of mass* to explain the following:

a Double-decker buses have heavy weights attached to their undersides.

b The crane shown in the diagram has a heavy concrete block attached to one end of its arm, and others placed around its base.

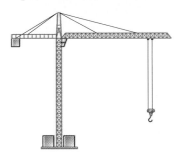

Figure Q4.11

Chapter 5

5.12

A group of students carried out an experiment in which they stretched a length of wire by hanging weights on the end. For each value of the load, they measured the length of the wire. The table shows the results.

Load (N)	Length (m)	Extension
0	3.200	
10	3.207	
20	3.215	
30	3.222	
40	3.230	
50	3.242	
60	3.255	
70	3.270	

a Fill in the column showing the extension for each load.

b Draw a graph of extension against load for the wire.

c From your graph, determine the extension produced by a load of 25 N.

d Estimate the value of the load at the elastic limit?

Energy resources

Topics in this **chapter**

◆ fossil, nuclear and biomass fuels

◆ stored energy

◆ energy units

◆ renewable and non-renewable energy resources

◆ the meaning of 'energy'

Here on Earth, we rely on the Sun for most of the energy we use. The Sun is a fairly average star, 150 million kilometres away. The heat and light we receive from it have taken about eight minutes to travel through empty space to get here. Plants absorb this energy in the process of photosynthesis; animals are kept warm by it.

There are some forms of life that do not depend on the Sun's rays. Deep in the oceans, where continents are pulling apart from one another, scientists have discovered places where scalding hot water is bubbling up from deep inside the Earth. These vents are known as 'smokers' – see Figure 6.1. Conditions around these 'smokers' seem very hazardous to life – high temperatures, high pressures, high

Figure 6.1 A 'smoker' deep in the mid Atlantic Ocean. The bacteria and worms that live here rely on energy supplied by the hot water and the nutrient chemicals it contains. The temperature of the water coming up from under the sea-bed may be as high as 400 °C; the worms live around the cooler edges of the smoker.

concentrations of noxious chemicals such as sulphides (which would be harmful to us) – and, yet, specialised forms of life including species of worms and shrimps have evolved to live there.

These creatures obtain their energy supply from the hot water and from the chemicals that it contains. They are not dependent on energy from the Sun. The water brings heat from inside the Earth, heat produced by radioactive materials decaying slowly away. These materials have been inside the Earth since it first formed, 4500 million years ago. We can imagine that, even if the Sun ceased to shine, these strange animals would continue to live on a darkened Earth.

The Earth is at a convenient distance from the Sun for living organisms. The Sun's rays are strong enough, but not too strong. The Earth's average temperature is about 15 °C, which is suitable for life. If Earth were closer to the Sun, it might be intolerably hot, like Venus, where the average surface temperature is over 400 °C. Farther out, things are colder. Saturn is roughly ten times as far from the Sun, so the Sun in the sky looks one-tenth of the diameter that we see it, and its radiation has only one-hundredth of the intensity. Saturn's surface temperature is about –180 °C.

This poses a problem for space exploration. Most spacecraft rely on solar panels to power them. Energy from the Sun is converted directly into the electricity that is needed to operate the on-board instruments. An alternative energy supply is required for spacecraft travelling out into the depths of the Solar System.

One solution is to use a radioactive material – plutonium. This is a waste product of some nuclear power stations. Because plutonium decays fairly rapidly, it is warm. This energy is used to generate electricity for spacecraft – see Figure 6.2.

Figure 6.2 **a** The Cassini–Huygens spacecraft was launched towards Saturn in October 1997. **b** The instruments on board the spacecraft are powered by plutonium batteries, which rely on heat produced by radioactive decay to generate electricity. Saturn is so far from the Sun that the Sun's radiation is too weak to provide the necessary power.

Here, we have looked at two unusual energy resources – 'smokers' and plutonium batteries – and the importance of the Sun as an energy source. In the rest of this chapter, we will look further at energy resources and begin to get an idea of just what we mean by the term 'energy'.

6.1 The energy we use

Most of the energy we use comes from the Sun, but only a very little is used *directly*. On a cold but sunny morning, you might sit in the sunshine to warm your body. Your house might be designed to collect warmth from the Sun's rays, perhaps by having larger windows on the sunny side. However, most of the energy we use comes only *indirectly* from the Sun.

Figure 6.3 is a chart which shows the different fuels that contribute to the world's energy supplies. This chart shows patterns of energy consumption (use) at the start of the twenty-first century. Many people today live in industrialised countries and use large amounts of energy, particularly from fossil fuels (coal, oil and gas). People living in less developed countries use far less energy; mostly they use biomass fuels, particularly wood. A thousand years ago, the chart would have looked very different. Fossil fuel consumption was much less important; most people relied on burning wood to supply their energy requirements. We will now look at these groups of fuels in turn.

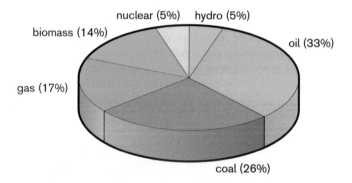

Figure 6.3 World energy use, by fuel type. This chart shows the contributions made by different fuels to energy consumption by people today, across the world. Three-quarters of all energy is from fossil fuels.

Biomass fuels

For many people in the world, wood is the most important fuel. It warms their homes and provides the heat necessary for cooking their food. Wood is made by trees and shrubs. It stores energy that the plant has captured from sunlight in the process of **photosynthesis**. Most plants contain the green pigment chlorophyll, which is the substance that traps energy from the Sun, enabling photosynthesis to take place. The energy is used to make carbohydrates from water and carbon dioxide:

water + carbon dioxide + energy $\rightarrow$ carbohydrates + oxygen

Carbohydrates are then stored in the plant, and act as its food. When the plant needs energy, it breaks down the carbohydrate to release the

Figure 6.4 Coppicing is a way of growing wood rapidly. A tree is cut down, and new stems grow from the base. After a few years, these are cut and used as fuel. New stems grow, and so on. By managing an area of woodland in a cycle, wood can be available at all times. Today, farmers in industrialised countries are being encouraged to grow coppiced wood for burning in power stations to generate electricity.

stored energy. In the same way, by burning wood we release the energy it stores. This energy came from the Sun in the recent past, perhaps ten or a hundred years ago.

Sometimes, people simply collect wood from their surroundings. This can be satisfactory if the population density (number of people per square kilometre) is low. However, as populations grow it becomes necessary to manage reserves of trees – see Figure 6.4. In the past, whole civilisations have disappeared when they have cut down all available forests and laid waste the land. (This seems to be the most probable explanation for the downfall of the human population of Easter Island in the Pacific Ocean, famous for the giant stone head sculptures that they created.)

Wood is just one example of a biomass fuel, or **biofuel**. Others include animal dung and biogas generated by rotting vegetable matter. These can be very important fuels in societies where most people live by farming. As you can see from Figure 6.3, biofuels account for about one-seventh of the world's energy consumption. This figure can only be a rough estimate, because no-one keeps track of all the wood consumed as fuel. However, we can say that this segment of the chart represents the energy consumption of about three-quarters of the world's population. The remaining one-quarter (who live in developed, industrial nations) consume roughly six times as much.

Fossil fuels

Oil, coal and gas are all examples of **fossil fuels**. These are usually **hydrocarbons** (compounds of hydrogen and carbon only). When they are burned, they combine with oxygen from the air. The carbon becomes carbon dioxide; the hydrogen becomes 'hydrogen oxide', which we usually call water; and energy is released:

hydrocarbon + oxygen $\rightarrow$ carbon dioxide + water + energy

You can see that this reaction is essentially the reverse of the reaction taking place in photosynthesis: burning – or **combustion** – reverses the process of photosynthesis.

Hence, we can think of a fossil fuel as a store of energy. More correctly, the energy is stored in the fuel and the oxygen together. Where has this energy come from?

Fossil fuels are the remains of organisms – plants and animals – that lived in the past. Many of the Earth's coal reserves, for example, formed from trees that lived in the Carboniferous era, between 286 and 360 million years ago ('Carboniferous' means 'coal-producing'). These trees captured sunlight by photosynthesis; they grew and died. Their trunks fell into swamps, but they did not rot completely, because there was insufficient oxygen. As material built up on top of these ancient trees, the pressure on them increased. Eventually, millions of years of compression turned them into underground reserves of coal – see

Figure 6.5 Coal is a fossil fuel. A fossil is any living material that has been preserved for a long time; usually, its chemical composition changes during the process. Coal sometimes shows evidence of the plant material from which it formed. Sometimes, as here, you can see fossilised ferns or creatures that lived in the swamps of the Carboniferous era. They died along with the trees that eventually became coal.

Figure 6.6 A nuclear power station generates electricity; its fuel is uranium. As the fuel is used up, highly radioactive waste products are produced, and these have to be dealt with very carefully to avoid harm to the surroundings. Here, checks are being carried out to ensure that the level of radioactivity near the power station is safe.

Figure 6.5. Today, when we burn coal the light and warmth have their origins in the sunlight trapped by trees hundreds of millions of years ago.

Oil and gas are usually found together. They are formed in a similar way to coal, but from the remains of tiny shrimp-like creatures called microplankton, which lived in the oceans. The oilfields of the Persian Gulf, North Africa and the Gulf of Mexico, which contain half of the world's known oil reserves, all formed in the Cretaceous era, 75 to 120 million years ago.

(Oil is found underground. Some scientists have suggested that oil might have formed from the remains of bacteria rather than microplankton. Their idea is that bacteria live deep underground, in tiny cracks in the rocks of the Earth's crust, and the remains of these bacteria may be the origin of today's oil reserves.)

Nuclear fuels

Nuclear power was developed in the second half of the twentieth century. It is a very demanding technology, which requires strict controls because of the serious damage that can be caused by an accident.

The fuel for a nuclear power station (Figure 6.6) is usually uranium, sometimes plutonium. These are **radioactive** materials. Inside a nuclear reactor, the release of nuclear energy is speeded up so that the energy they store is released much more quickly. (There is more about this in Chapter 25.)

Uranium is a very concentrated store of energy. A typical nuclear power station will receive about one truck-load of new fuel each week. Coal is less concentrated; a similar coal-fired power station is likely to need a whole train-load of coal every hour. A wind farm capable of generating electricity at the same rate would cover a large area of ground – perhaps 20 square kilometres.

In some countries that have few other resources for generating electricity, nuclear power provides a lot of energy. In France, for example, nuclear power stations generate three-quarters of the country's electricity, and excess production is exported to neighbouring countries, including Spain, Switzerland and the United Kingdom.

Nuclear fuel is a relatively cheap, concentrated energy resource. However, nuclear power has proved expensive because of the initial cost of building the power stations, the cost of disposing of the radioactive spent fuel, and the costs of making such power stations safe (called decommissioning) at the end of their working lives.

Water power

The final contribution to the chart in Figure 6.3 is water or hydro-power. For centuries, people have used the energy of moving water to turn water-wheels, which then drive machinery of all sorts – for grinding corn and other crops, for pumping water, for weaving textiles. Today, water power's biggest contribution is in the form of **hydro-electricity** –

Figure 6.7 This giant dam is on the Panama River on the border of Brazil and Paraguay.

see Figure 6.7. Water stored behind a dam is released to turn turbines, which make generators spin. This is a very safe, clean and reliable way of producing electricity, but it is not without its problems. A new reservoir floods land that might otherwise have been used for hunting or farming. People may be made homeless, and wildlife destroyed.

Most hydro-power comes ultimately from the Sun. The Sun's rays cause water to evaporate from the oceans and land surface; this water vapour in the atmosphere eventually forms clouds at high altitudes; rain falls on high ground and can then be trapped behind a dam. This is the familiar water cycle. Without energy from the Sun, there would be no water cycle and much less hydro-power.

A small amount of hydro-power does not depend on the Sun's radiation energy. Instead, it is generated from the tides. The Moon and the Sun both contribute to the ocean's tides; their gravitational pull causes the level of the ocean's surface to rise and fall every twelve-and-a-quarter hours. At high tide, water can be trapped behind a dam; later, it can be released to drive turbines and generators. Because this depends on gravity, and not on the Sun's heat and light, we could rely on tidal power even if the Sun ceased to shine.

> **Questions**
>
> **6.1** Name three fossil fuels, and three non-fossil fuels.
>
> **6.2** Name two energy resources for which the original energy source is not radiation from the Sun.
>
> **6.3** **a** What name is given to the process whereby plants store energy from sunlight?
>
> **b** What name is given to the process whereby energy stored in plant material is released by burning it?
>
> **6.4** **a** What other substance is needed to obtain the energy stored in a fuel?
>
> **b** What substances are produced when a hydrocarbon is burned?

6.2 Storing energy

We have now considered each segment of the diagram showing the world's energy sources (Figure 6.3). There are other energy sources that contribute in small ways: solar panels and cells, wind and wave power, batteries and so on. We will consider these later in this chapter and in Chapter 7. However, their contribution is not great enough for them to appear on the chart.

What is a fuel?

The term 'fuel' is difficult to define. We have looked at fossil fuels and biofuels. What these have in common is that they must be burned (with oxygen) to release the energy that they store. So a very strict definition of a fuel might be:

A fuel is a substance that is burned with oxygen to release the energy it stores.

However, we talk about uranium and plutonium as 'nuclear fuels'. They are stores of energy, but they are not burned with oxygen to release their stored energy, so they do not fit the strict definition above. Sometimes electricity is referred to as a fuel. If you are asked, 'What fuel do you use for cooking at home?', your reply might be 'electricity'. Electricity is even less like a fuel that you burn, but we may sometimes think of it as a fuel.

We might try an even more general definition of a fuel. Perhaps a fuel is anything that stores energy. This would include water behind a dam – this is a store of energy. A battery stores energy in the chemicals it contains – are the chemicals inside a battery a fuel?

From this, we can see that the term 'fuel' is used rather loosely, both in science and in everyday language. However, this discussion should show some important features of the energy resources that we use. A little of the energy we use comes to us directly from the Sun; most of it comes indirectly from the Sun. What we find most useful are *stores* of energy. We want to be able to release stored energy at a time and place convenient to us. We might release the energy by burning a fuel or by some other process; it might be released as heat or electricity, or in some other way.

So a better way to think of fuels, stored water, sunlight and so on, is as **energy resources**:

An energy resource is anything available to us from which we can obtain a useful supply of energy.

The word 'energy' itself is another term that needs defining carefully. In science it has a strict meaning, stricter than the meaning of 'fuel'. In the rest of this chapter, and in the other chapters of Section B, we will gradually build up a scientific definition of energy.

How much energy?

We need food as the energy supply of our bodies. Food comes from plants, which have captured and stored energy from the Sun. Their energy stores are sugar and starch. We may also eat meat from animals, which have, themselves, eaten plants. Food is our fuel – we 'burn' it in the process of **respiration** to release the energy we need for our daily activities, and simply for maintaining the activity of the cells of our bodies.

Most packaged foods have a label that indicates the composition of the food and the energy it can supply. Some examples are shown in Figure 6.8. The energy content per 100 g or per serving may be quoted in two units: calories (kcal – no longer a scientific unit) and kilojoules (kJ). Food scientists determine the energy value of a food by burning it and measuring the energy released. Because combustion and respiration are simply different methods of releasing the stored energy, the energy released by burning a food is the same as the energy value it has for the person who eats it.

A typical breakfast cereal such as cornflakes with milk provides about 1000 kJ (or 1 MJ, one megajoule) of energy. A healthy lifestyle requires about 10 MJ a day, so the cornflakes and milk together supply about one-tenth of a day's energy needs.

Fuels also have an energy value. Table 6.1 shows the energy values of some fossil fuels and biofuels. These values are slightly variable, depending on the precise composition of the fuel. If you look at a gas bill, you may see on it the energy value of the gas supplied; this is given so that consumers can compare the cost of using gas with that of using electricity.

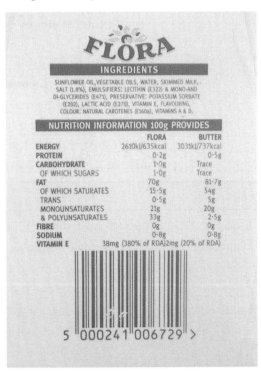

Figure 6.8 Packaged foods are labelled to indicate their nutritional value. One important piece of information is their energy content. Fats have the highest energy content per gram; carbohydrates such as sugar, starch and alcohol also contain a lot of energy.

Fuel	Energy value (MJ/kg)
wood	20
peat	21
coal	22–32
carbon/charcoal	34
petrol (gasoline)	35
oil	42
natural gas	55
hydrogen	142

Table 6.1 Energy values of some fuels. Values are given in megajoules per kilogram, that is, the energy in MJ released when 1 kg of the fuel is burned with oxygen.

From Table 6.1, you can see that wood and peat are relatively poor stores of energy. So is coal, which we can think of as compressed wood. The best coal is almost pure carbon, and this is reflected in its higher energy value.

When choosing a fuel, a high energy value is obviously desirable. Then you can carry around a relatively small amount of fuel to supply your energy needs. Why do we not make more use of hydrogen, the 'best' fuel in Table 6.1? The answer is that hydrogen is not available as a natural fuel. Any hydrogen that existed in the Earth's atmosphere has either escaped from the Earth or has long since combined with oxygen to form water. In order to produce hydrogen gas from water, we need to use an electric current to split up the water. (This is the process of electrolysis.) That takes energy – exactly the same amount of energy as we would get back by burning the hydrogen – so we have gained nothing.

However, hydrogen is likely to become a useful fuel in the future. In sunny countries, solar cells may be used to produce electricity from sunlight, and this can then be used to electrolyse water to produce hydrogen. This will be worthwhile because the energy of sunlight is effectively free. Several car manufacturers have developed prototype hydrogen-fuelled cars, and a network of hydrogen 'gas' stations is planned in California.

How do foods compare with fuels? Cornflakes (without milk) have an energy value of about 15 MJ/kg, rather less than that of wood. A day's energy requirements for an active adolescent would be supplied by eating about two-thirds of a kilogram of cornflakes (or half a kilogram of wood! Don't try this though; humans can't digest wood).

Energy units

The SI unit of energy is the joule (J). The way in which the joule is defined and how it is related to other SI units will be explained in Chapter 8 (see page 122). Table 6.2 shows how larger quantities of energy may be expressed in kilojoules, megajoules and so on.

You will come across other units of energy. Calories (kcal) were mentioned above. Kilowatt hours (kWh) are a unit used to measure energy that is supplied electrically – see Chapter 19. Traditionally, oil was measured in barrels; one barrel was equivalent to 5600 MJ of energy.

Table 6.2 Energy measurements in joules and multiples of joules.

Abbreviation	Unit	Example
1 J	1 joule	It takes about 1 J to lift an apple 1 m above the floor
$1\,kJ = 10^3\,J$	1 kilojoule	A single cornflake provides about 2 kJ of energy
$1\,MJ = 10^6\,J$	1 megajoule	One litre of petrol supplies about 35 MJ of energy
$1\,GJ = 10^9\,J$	1 gigajoule	A large power station might produce 1 GJ per second
$1\,TJ = 10^{12}\,J$	1 terajoule	The average American consumes about 0.5 TJ every year
$1\,PJ = 10^{15}\,J$	1 petajoule	The UK's annual energy consumption is about 10 000 PJ
$1\,YJ = 10^{24}\,J$	1 yottajoule	The Earth's fuel reserves are estimated at 0.1 YJ

?

Questions

6.5 Look at Table 6.1.

    a Which of the fossil fuels listed has the lowest energy value?

    b Which fossil fuel has the highest energy value?

6.6 Carbohydrates are foods that supply energy. Name three types of carbohydrate.

6.7 **a** What is the SI unit of energy?

    b What do kJ and MJ stand for?

6.8 Name two other units of energy not mentioned in Question 6.7.

6.3 Renewable energy technologies

Renewable or non-renewable?

Fossil fuel reserves are mined or extracted from under the ground. As we have seen, they were mostly formed tens or hundreds of millions of years ago. This means that when we burn coal, oil or natural gas, we are making use of energy that came from the Sun all that time ago. Once these fuels are used, they cannot be used again. They are known as **non-renewable energy resources**. In the same way, the uranium that fuels nuclear power stations has to be mined. Once it has been used, it can never be used again. (With fossil fuels, we could wait around for 50 million years or so for new supplies to be formed. The uranium we use, on the other hand, dates from the formation of the Earth, 4500 million years ago. No new reserves are being formed.)

It is difficult to be sure how long our reserves of fossil fuels can be expected to last. At present, oil and gas stocks may last 50 years. Coal should last longer. It all depends on the amounts of new fossil fuel reserves that are discovered, and how fast we use them. However, we can be sure that prices will go up as the reserves gradually decrease. If more people are to benefit from energy-rich lifestyles then alternative, **renewable energy resources** must be exploited.

Another reason for trying to make better use of renewable energy resources is that the burning of fossil fuels increases the amount of carbon dioxide in the atmosphere – see Figure 6.9. This increases the greenhouse effect, causing global warming. The first effects of global warming are now being seen, with changes to the normal weather patterns causing serious problems for people in many parts of the world.

You might think that burning biofuels such as wood would also put more carbon dioxide into the atmosphere and further increase global warming. While it is true that burning wood produces carbon dioxide, this is absorbed by new trees growing in place of the ones cut down. Thus, provided new trees are planted to replace those cut for fuel, there will be no net increase in the carbon dioxide level in the atmosphere.

Figure 6.9 The level of carbon dioxide (CO_2) in the atmosphere has been monitored over a long period of time. This graph shows that the level has gradually increased; you can also see that the level goes up and down during the year. This is because trees and other plants absorb a lot of CO_2 in the summer while they are growing rapidly; in the winter, they grow much more slowly. At the same time, power stations are busier in the winter, so they produce more CO_2 then as well. Data courtesy of the National Oceanic and Atmospheric Administrationm (NOAA).

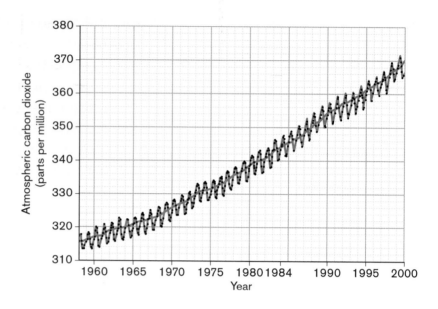

Renewable energy resources

For most renewable energy resources, we can trace their source back to the Sun. We expect the Sun to keep shining (well, at least, for the next five billion years!) and so these resources are constantly being made available. We have already looked briefly at two examples, biofuels and hydro-power. Here are some further examples.

- The Sun's rays fall on a **solar panel** on the roof of a house. This absorbs the energy of the rays, and water inside the panel heats up. This hot water can then be stored in a tank for washing and bathing purposes.
- We can also make electricity directly from sunlight (Figure 6.10). The Sun's rays shine on a **solar cell** (also known as a **photovoltaic cell**). The energy of the rays is absorbed, and electricity is produced. As this technology becomes cheaper, it is finding more and more uses,

Figure 6.10 Two applications of solar cells. **a** These houses in Amsterdam have solar panels built into their roofs to provide electrical power for the occupants. **b** In Zambia, many people in remote areas rely on local health centres. Solar cells can provide the electricity needed to power the refrigerator that stores vaccines. These cells also power the lights, so that medical staff can continue to work after sunset.

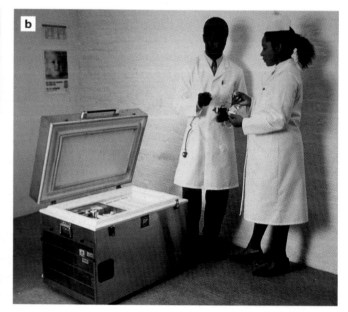

Figure 6.11 Denmark has put a lot of effort into developing wind power. These giant turbines are part of a wind farm on the Jutland Coast, Denmark. They produce as much electricity as a medium-sized coal-fired power station.

particularly in remote places. Solar cells, for example, may run a refrigerator that stores medicines in central Africa, or power roadside emergency phones in the Australian outback. In isolated parts of Scotland, telephone boxes are powered by solar cells. Solar cells have also been used a great deal for powering spacecraft. Ideally, a solar cell is connected to a rechargeable battery, which stores the energy collected, so that it can be available during the hours of darkness.

- Wind and waves are also caused by the effects of the Sun. The Sun heats some parts of the atmosphere more than others. Heated air expands and starts to move around – it forms a convection current (see Chapter 10). This is the origin of winds. Most wind energy is given up to the sea as waves are formed by friction between wind and water. There are many technologies for extracting energy from the wind. Windmills for grinding and pumping are traditional, and modern wind turbines can generate electricity – see Figure 6.11. Wave technology is more complicated; the up-and-down motion of waves must be used to spin a turbine, which then turns a generator. This is tricky to achieve, and rough seas are a hazardous place to work. On calm days, the system produces no power.

All of these energy resources are renewable, because they are constantly replenished as the Sun keeps shining. Small amounts of energy are also extracted from other renewable resources that are not dependent on radiation from the Sun. We have already mentioned tidal power, which gets its energy from the gravitational pulls of the Moon and the Sun. Another example is geothermal energy, where heat is extracted from rocks deep underground. These get their energy from radioactive substances decaying inside the Earth, (as do the deep-sea 'smokers' mentioned at the beginning of this chapter.)

Keep it clean

Burning fossil fuels releases carbon dioxide into the atmosphere. We have already seen that this is a cause of global warming. Carbon, trapped safely underground for millions of years, has become a major concern of the twenty-first century. Fossil fuels also release other substances when they are burned, most notably sulphur dioxide. This is produced because fossil fuels are not pure carbon; they contain other elements from the living materials from which they formed. Oxides of nitrogen (which we can write in shorthand as NO_x) are produced in hot engines, where the gases of the air react with each other at high temperature.

These oxides are acidic compounds; they dissolve in rain-water and produce **acid rain**. Acid rain causes damage to trees and other plants, and to fish and invertebrates (creatures without a backbone, such as worms, shrimps, snails, etc.) living in lakes and rivers.

So, could we switch entirely to renewable energy resources? The problem is that each has its drawbacks as well as its advantages. Here are some typical drawbacks that may arise when we start to think about using renewable energy resources.

- *Cost* Although there is no fuel cost, renewable energy technologies can be expensive. Solar cells are costly, so that the electricity they produce is currently two or three times the cost of electricity from a fossil-fuel power station. Wave power has had little money spent on its technical development, so little use is made of it at present.

- *Environmental damage* The energy in many renewable resources is **dilute**, that is, not very concentrated. This means that a wind farm that can supply as much electricity as a large gas-fired power station is likely to cover several square kilometres. This can be an eyesore, and it can also be noisy for local residents.

- *Supply and demand* We expect to be able to use electricity at the flick of a switch. We use more at night (when people are at home), and in cold weather. So demand varies, but at the same time, supply can vary, particularly from renewable energy resources. Sunlight is only available for half the day; the wind cannot be relied on to blow constantly; the tides occur at different times from one day to the next. The answer may be to use a range of resources. Then the Sun may be shining when the wind isn't blowing, and so on. With some way of storing energy, a practical system might be developed that could match supply to demand.

A word about 'energy'

In everyday life, we use the word 'energy' in a lot of different ways. Sometimes these even seem contradictory, although we know what the speaker means:

> 'If you exercise regularly, you will have more energy.'
>
> 'I did so much exercise, I ran out of energy and felt exhausted.'

In this chapter, we have looked at some aspects of what we mean by energy in science. We have looked at energy resources that stem from the Sun; we have briefly mentioned some of the things we can do when we make use of these resources – generating electricity, grinding and pumping, keeping warm and so on.

Here, in Section B of this book, we will gradually build up a picture of what we mean by energy. We are working towards a more formal definition of the word. We are also building up a mental picture of energy. It is not the easiest scientific concept to grasp. In fact, Isaac Newton had never heard of it. He died in 1727, and the concept wasn't developed until almost a century later. Yet he still managed many great achievements in physics, despite this 'ignorance'.

Questions

6.9 Which one of the following is a non-renewable energy technology?

photovoltaic cells, windmills, nuclear power, tidal power

6.10 In many applications, photovoltaic cells are connected to rechargeable batteries. Why is this?

6.11 Why would photovoltaic cells be a good way of powering a telecommunications link between remote islands in the Pacific Ocean?

6.12 Explain how the Sun's radiation gives rise to wind energy.

6.13 Explain what is meant by 'geothermal energy'.

6.14 Why would it be unsatisfactory to rely on a single renewable source of energy for all our energy requirements?

Summary

◆ Most of the energy resources that we use are non-renewable – particularly fossil fuels. Reserves are dwindling, and burning fuels damages the environment.

◆ Fossil and nuclear fuels are concentrated stores of energy. Renewable energy resources tend to be more dilute, and this adds to the difficulty and expense of exploiting them.

◆ Energy is measured in joules (J).

◆ Most renewable energy resources can be traced back to radiation from the Sun. These include solar heating and electricity, biofuels, water, wind and wave power.

◆ Tidal energy comes from the gravitational pull of the Moon and Sun; geothermal energy comes from radioactive substances decaying underground. Both of these count as renewable resources.

Energy transformations, energy transfers

Topics in this **chapter**

◆ forms of energy

◆ energy transformations

◆ conservation of energy

◆ transferring energy

◆ energy efficiency

Figure 7.1 Crocodiles are cold-blooded creatures, so it is relatively safe to approach them on a cold day. On a hot day, they are much more active. Crocodiles are not big eaters, but they make efficient use of the energy supplied by their food.

Crocodiles are efficient creatures. Their jaws snap down on their prey, and there is no escape. You might imagine that a crocodile has a big appetite (Figure 7.1), but that is not so. A crocodile needs very little food – it can exist on just one-quarter of its own body weight each year. This is the equivalent, for a human being, of surviving on fish and chips once a week!

There are several reasons for this. It doesn't take much energy to lie in wait in a water-hole. The water supports your weight, and you don't have to move around a lot. Also, crocodiles (like all reptiles) are cold-blooded, so that their body temperature is close to that of their surroundings. On a cold day, they are sluggish and much more approachable. On hot days, their system is more active, and they are much more agile and dangerous. Their bodies make good use of the food they consume. Finally, unlike you, whose brain uses up a lot of your energy supply, a crocodile doesn't have a very large brain. So, a crocodile's energy is stored and only released when it's time to grab a snack.

In this chapter, we will look at how energy is wasted, and how it can be used efficiently.

7.1 Forms of energy

Scientists don't all agree about forms of energy. Some suggest that we should simply talk about 'energy' and how it is transferred from place to place. Others think that it is useful to be able to describe events in terms of changes from one form of energy to another. Here, we will look at how we can describe events in terms of such energy transformations.

In later chapters (Chapters 8, 10 and 19), we will see how such descriptions can help us to do useful calculations involving energy changes. Now we will list some different forms of energy. Here again, scientists do not agree on what makes a complete list, or on what name should be given to each form. However, provided you have an understanding of what each term means, you should be able to understand any alternative names you may come across.

- *Kinetic energy* A moving object has kinetic energy (KE). We know this because we need to transfer energy to an object to get it moving. Also, if you stand in the path of a moving object so that it runs into you, it will move more slowly. It has transferred some of its energy to you. In Chapter 8, we will see how to calculate kinetic energy.

- *Gravitational potential energy* If you lift an object upwards, you give it gravitational potential energy (GPE). If you let the object fall, you can get the energy back again. This is made use of in many situations. The water stored behind a hydro-electric dam has GPE. A grandfather clock has weights that must be pulled upwards once a week; then, as they gradually fall, they drive the pendulum to operate the clock's mechanism.

- *Chemical energy* Fuels such as coal or petrol are stores of chemical energy. As we saw in Chapter 6, it is more correct to say that the energy is stored in the fuel-plus-oxygen mixture. We know that there is a store of energy because, when the fuel burns, the stored energy is released, usually as heat and light. There are many other stores of chemical energy – see Figure 7.2. As we saw above, energy is stored by chemicals in our bodies. Batteries are also stores of energy; when the battery is part of a complete circuit, the chemicals start to react with one another and an electric current flows, carrying energy to the other components in the circuit.

- *Nuclear energy* A close relation of chemical energy is nuclear energy. Uranium is an example of a nuclear fuel, which is a store of nuclear energy. All radioactive materials are stores of nuclear energy. In these substances, the energy is stored in the nucleus of the atoms – the tiny positively charged core of the atom. To release the energy, a nuclear reaction must occur. The nucleus either splits, or emits some radiation, or two light nuclei may join together, thereby releasing its stored energy. (This is different from chemical energy. To release a store of chemical energy, a chemical reaction must take place. This changes the arrangement of bonds between the atoms; the nuclei of the atoms are not affected.)

- *Elastic energy* If you stretch a rubber band, it becomes a store of elastic energy. The band can give its energy to a paper pellet and send it flying across the room. Elastic energy (also known as *strain energy*) is the energy stored by an object that has been stretched or squashed in an elastic way (so that it will spring back to its original

Figure 7.2 Some stores of chemical energy – petrol, bread and batteries. Our bodies have long-term stores of energy in the form of fatty tissues.

dimensions when the stretching or squashing forces are removed). The metal springs of a car are constantly storing and releasing elastic energy as the car travels along, so that the occupants have a smooth ride. Wind-up clocks store energy in a spring, which is the energy source needed to keep the clock mechanism operating.

- *Electrical energy* An electric current is a good way of transferring energy from one place to another. It carries electrical energy. When the current flows through a component such as a heater, it gives up some of its energy.

- *Heat energy* If you heat an object so that it gets hotter, you might say that it has heat energy. A better term for this is *internal energy* (or *random thermal energy*). We can picture the atoms of a hot object jiggling rapidly about – they have a lot of energy. This picture is developed further in Chapter 9. It is better to reserve the term 'heat energy' to mean energy moving from a hotter place to a colder place.

- *Light energy* Very hot objects glow brightly. They are giving out light energy. Light radiates outwards all around a very hot object.

- *Infrared energy* A hot object loses energy to its surroundings. This is often referred to as heat energy. If the energy is radiated outwards, a better term is infrared energy. This is similar to light energy. A cool or warm object gives out *only* infrared energy; as it gets hotter, it starts to glow; now it is emitting light energy. Both infrared and light, along with γ-rays, ultraviolet rays, microwaves and radio waves are electromagnetic radiation – see Chapter 15.

- *Sound energy* Another way in which energy can be transferred to an object's surroundings is as sound energy. An electric current brings electrical energy to a loudspeaker; sound energy (and heat energy) are produced – see Figure 7.3.

Figure 7.3 At a major rock concert, giant loud-speakers pour out sound energy to the audience. Extra generators may have to be brought onto the site to act as a source of electrical energy to power the speaker systems. Much of the energy supplied is wasted as heat energy, because only a fraction of the electrical energy is transformed into sound energy.

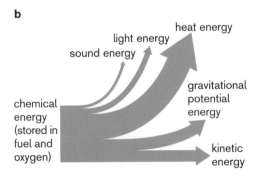

Figure 7.4 **a** This giant rocket uses rocket motors to lift it up into space. Each rocket motor burns about 1 tonne of fuel and oxygen every minute to provide the energy needed to move the rocket upwards. **b** This diagram represents the energy transformations going on as the rocket accelerates upwards. Chemical energy in the fuel and oxygen is transformed into five other forms of energy.

Transforming energy

When energy changes from one form to another, we say that it has been *transformed*. We have already mentioned several examples of energy transformations. Now we will look at a few more, and think a little about the forms of energy that are involved.

The rocket in Figure 7.4a is lifting off from the ground as it carries a new craft up into space. Its energy comes from its store of fuel and liquid oxygen. The fuel is liquid hydrogen. The liquid oxygen is required to burn the fuel because the space craft will rise above the atmosphere. The hydrogen fuel and oxygen are its store of chemical energy. When they burn together, energy is released.

The rocket is accelerating, so we can say that its kinetic energy is increasing. It is also rising upwards, so its gravitational potential energy is increasing. In the photograph, you can see light coming from the burning fuel. You can also imagine that large amounts of heat energy and sound energy are produced. This energy transformation is shown in Figure 7.4b. We can also represent the transformation as an equation:

$$\text{chemical energy} \rightarrow \text{KE} + \text{GPE} + \text{heat energy} + \text{light energy} + \text{sound energy}$$

The clockwork radio (Figure 7.5) is a famous invention. Where batteries or mains electricity are not available, or are too expensive, it allows people to listen to radio broadcasts with low running costs. The model shown in the photograph has an additional feature: a solar cell acts as an alternative energy source.

The wound-up spring of the clockwork mechanism is a store of elastic (strain) energy. But the radio requires electrical energy to function; so, as the spring unwinds, it turns a generator. The elastic energy of the unwinding spring first becomes kinetic energy of the turning mechanism, and then electrical energy carried by the current to the radio. Finally, the energy is transformed to sound energy. Along the

Figure 7.5 This clockwork radio is designed for use by people who do not have a ready supply of batteries or mains electricity. It operates from two alternative energy sources: a wound-up clockwork spring, and a solar cell. Since many users live in sunny parts of the world, the solar cell is a useful feature.

way, energy is wasted as heat energy. This is because no generator can transform all of the kinetic energy that it is supplied with into electrical energy; some becomes heat energy. Similarly, heat is produced by the electronic circuits of the radio, and by its loudspeaker. We can represent these transformations by an equation with several steps:

$$\text{elastic energy} \rightarrow \text{KE} \rightarrow \text{electrical energy} + \text{heat energy}$$
$$\rightarrow \text{sound energy} + \text{heat energy}$$

The solar cell transforms light energy directly into electrical energy. Again, some energy is wasted as heat. The whole transformation for the solar cell then becomes:

$$\text{light energy} \rightarrow \text{electrical energy} + \text{heat energy}$$
$$\rightarrow \text{sound energy} + \text{heat energy}$$

Extension material

Potential energy – energy of position or configuration

We have seen that lifting an object increases its gravitational potential energy (GPE). We can understand this term as follows: This energy is *gravitational* because, in lifting an object, we are pushing it upwards against the force of gravity. The word *potential* means that the object has the potential or the capacity to do something – for example, water with GPE has the potential to turn a turbine, and a raised hammer has the potential to fall and push a nail into wood.

Sometimes, GPE is referred to as 'energy of position'. An object has GPE because of its position relative to the Earth's surface. The higher it is, the greater its GPE. We will see how to calculate GPE in Chapter 8.

Other forms of energy are sometimes referred to as potential energy. One example is elastic (or strain) energy. If an object is attached to a spring and pulled to one side (see Figure 7.6a), then energy is stored in the stretched spring. Because the stretching is elastic, the energy can be recovered by releasing the object. The force of the spring pulling on it, will make it accelerate and gain KE. We can think of this as an example of potential energy gained by a change in configuration. The more the spring is stretched, the greater the potential energy it stores.

Figure 7.6b illustrates a further form of potential energy. Two magnets are placed so that they have opposite poles attracting one another. If the magnets are pulled apart, they gain magnetic potential energy. Let them go and they move back together. Their energy depends on their position.

Figure 7.6 Two examples of potential energy, illustrating how potential energy depends on an object's position or configuration. **a** The energy of a spring changes if its configuration changes – let the object go and the stored energy becomes kinetic energy. **b** You can give the magnets potential energy by pulling them apart – let them go and they snap back together again.

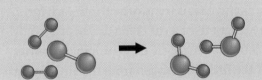

Figure 7.7 The atoms in molecules of hydrogen and oxygen have potential energy – together they have the potential to cause an explosion and release their store of chemical energy. In the process, water molecules are formed. Overall, the atoms of a water molecule are more tightly bound together than they were in the original hydrogen and oxygen molecules.

Now we can think a little more about chemical energy. This is another form of potential energy. Consider some hydrogen and oxygen atoms (red and green respectively, see Figure 7.7). They attract each other – they want to join together to form water, H_2O. Let them do this, and bang! – energy is released. Overall, the atoms in the water molecules are more closely bonded together than the gas molecules from which the water is formed, so they now have less potential energy.

Water molecules can be split up to form hydrogen and oxygen, but energy must be put in to do this. That is what happens when water is electrolysed. An electric current brings electrical energy, and this splits the hydrogen and oxygen atoms apart. This is the reverse of the process by which a mixture of hydrogen and oxygen explodes.

Electrolysing water is like pulling the magnets apart; they gain potential energy. Burning hydrogen and oxygen together to form water is like releasing the magnets so that they come back together again.

? Questions

Questions

7.1 What form of energy is possessed by a moving object?

7.2 What form of energy is stored by a stretched spring?

7.3 What form of energy is radiated even by a cool object?

7.4 **a** What do the letters GPE stand for?

  b How can an object be given GPE?

7.5 Our bodies have long-term stores of chemical energy. What form do they take?

7.6 Name a device that transforms electrical energy to sound energy. (It may also produce heat energy.)

7.7 Write an equation to represent the transformation of chemical energy stored in petrol (gasoline) when a car is speeding up. How would your equation be different if the car was travelling at a steady speed?

7.2 Conservation of energy

When energy is transformed from one form to another, it is often the case that some of the energy ends up in a form that we don't want. A light bulb produces light energy that we do want, but also heat energy that we don't want. The rocket motor (Figure 7.4b) transforms chemical energy into two forms that we do want (KE and GPE) and three that we may not (heat, light and sound).

These arrow diagrams that represent energy transformations are known as **Sankey diagrams**. The width of each segment of the arrow shows the proportion of the energy that is transformed into each form.

Figure 7.8 shows a Sankey diagram for a car being driven at a steady speed along a flat road. Its source of energy is the petrol that it burns, and the numbers show that the fuel plus oxygen from the air supplies 80 kJ (kilojoules) every second. Some heat energy escapes from the hot engine and in the exhaust gases; some is wasted as heat produced by friction within the workings of the car. The rest is used in overcoming

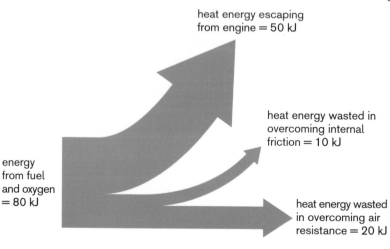

heat energy escaping from engine = 50 kJ

heat energy wasted in overcoming internal friction = 10 kJ

energy from fuel and oxygen = 80 kJ

heat energy wasted in overcoming air resistance = 20 kJ

Figure 7.8 A Sankey diagram for a car, showing the energy transformed by the car each second.

air resistance, another form of friction, so that the air is warmer after the car has passed through it.

All of the energy supplied by the car's fuel ends up as heat energy. If you add up the different amounts of heat energy, you will see that they come to 80 kJ. This is an example of a very important idea, known as the **principle of conservation of energy**:

> In any energy transformation, the total amount of energy before and after the transformation is constant.

This tells us something very important about energy: it cannot be created or destroyed. The total amount of energy is constant. If we measure or calculate the total energy of a system before a transformation, and again afterwards, we will always get the same result. If we find any difference, we must look for places where energy may be entering the system or escaping unnoticed.

There are two ways in which a Sankey diagram shows that energy is conserved: the total width of the arrows remains constant, and the figures also add up. It's rather like a form of book-keeping or accounting. Energy is like money: the amounts entering a system must equal the amount leaving it plus the amount stored within it.

Energy going to waste

Energy is expensive, and we don't want to waste it. Using more energy than necessary increases the damage we do to the environment, so it is important to avoid waste. Figure 7.9 shows a Sankey diagram that represents energy flows in the whole of the United Kingdom in one year. Most of the energy flowing into the UK comes from fuels, particularly coal, oil and gas. Energy is wasted in two general ways: when it is converted (transformed) into electricity, and when it is used (for example, in light bulbs).

Most wasted energy ends up as *heat* energy. There are two main reasons for this.

Figure 7.9 A Sankey diagram showing energy flows in the United Kingdom in 2000. A large proportion of the energy supplied by fuels is wasted in conversion processes and in final use. Some waste is inevitable, but better insulation and more efficient machines could reduce the waste and environmental damage, and save money. (All numbers are $\times 10^{18}$ J.)

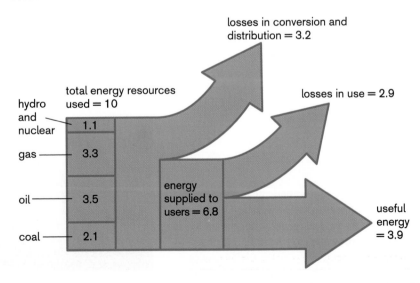

1 When fuels are burned (perhaps to generate electricity, or to drive a car), heat is produced as an intermediate step. Hot things readily lose energy to their surroundings, even if they are well insulated. Also, engines and boilers have to lose heat as part of the way they operate. For example, power stations produce warm water from the cooling process, cars produce hot exhaust gases.

2 When things are moving, friction is very often a problem. Lubrication can help to reduce friction, and a streamlined design can reduce air resistance. But it is impossible to eliminate friction entirely from machines with moving parts. Friction generates heat.

Another common form of wasted energy is *sound*. Noisy machinery, loud car engines and so on are all wasting energy. However, loud noises do not contain very much energy, so there is little to be gained (in terms of energy) by reducing noise.

Waste energy in the form of heat and sound is sometimes referred to as low-grade energy.

Reducing energy waste

Efforts are made to use waste heat energy. Power stations produce a lot of waste heat, so they are an obvious target for attention. Figure 7.10 shows a modern power station at Newcastle-upon-Tyne in the UK. This has two features designed to make it less damaging to the environment:

- it burns a lot of rubbish, collected by the local council;
- as well as generating electricity, it uses most of its waste heat to provide hot water to local homes and offices.

Other modern technologies can help to reduce energy wastage. Since cars are a major source of polluting chemicals and waste heat, cleaner cars are most desirable. The car shown in Figure 7.11 runs using solar cells. Its bodywork is covered in arrays of photovoltaic cells, which generate electricity from sunlight. This is supplied directly to electric motors that turn the wheels. Some electrical energy is passed to a battery, which can take over when the Sun is covered by cloud.

Figure 7.10 The combined heat and power (CHP) station at Byker, Newcastle-upon-Tyne, England. As well as generating electricity, it supplies hot water for heating purposes to local consumers.

Figure 7.11 This car runs on photovoltaic (PV) cells. It has been designed to take part in a race across 3000 km of the Australian desert, from Adelaide to Darwin. The best PV cells convert about 15% of the sunlight that falls on them into electrical energy, and so the car must be almost completely covered in cells to provide enough energy to keep it going. It must also be very lightweight. You can judge for yourself whether this would be an appropriate design to replace petrol-fuelled cars in your own country.

Another important technology that will help to clean up cars in the future is provided by fuel cells. These are a form of battery. Fuel such as petrol or hydrogen is put into one compartment, and oxygen into another. The two react and produce electricity. The fuel is oxidised, just as if it had been burned, but without producing the intermediate heat.

Conserving energy

The word 'conservation' has two slightly different meanings in connection with energy:

- Sometimes, consumers are urged to 'conserve energy'. This means that we are being encouraged to avoid waste, perhaps by insulating our homes or by using a more fuel-efficient car. As we have seen, there are good environmental reasons for this.
- However, when we say that 'energy is conserved', this has the rather different meaning that the total amount of energy is always constant; energy cannot disappear, or appear from nowhere.

So, in physics, energy conserves itself; in everyday life, we have to try to conserve it by stopping it from turning into forms that we don't want.

Transferring and transforming energy

We have discussed in detail how energy may be transformed from one form to another. Sometimes, we have mentioned energy being 'transferred'. It is easy to get these two terms confused.

> Energy is **transformed** when it is converted from one form to another.

You can see the word 'form' inside 'transformed'.

> Energy can be **transferred** from one object to another, or from place to place.

(Remember that a 'ferry' transfers people from place to place.) Here are four different ways in which energy can be transferred.

- *By a force* If you lift something, you give it gravitational potential energy. You provide the force that lifts it. Alternatively, you can provide the force needed to start something moving – you give it kinetic energy. When energy is transferred from one object to another by means of a force, we say that the force is **doing work**. This is discussed in detail in Chapter 8.
- *By heat* We have already seen how heat energy spreads out from hot objects. No matter how good the insulation, energy is transferred from a hot object to its cooler surroundings. This is discussed in detail in Chapter 10.
- *By electricity* An electric current is a convenient way of transferring energy from place to place. The electricity may be generated in a power station many kilometres away from where the energy is

required. Alternatively, a torch battery provides the energy needed to light a bulb. Electricity transfers the energy from the battery to the bulb. This is covered in Chapter 18.

● *By radiation* Light reaches us from the Sun. That is how energy is transferred from the Sun to the Earth. Some energy is also transferred as infrared and ultraviolet radiation. These are all forms of electromagnetic radiation – see Chapter 15.

? Questions

7.8 **a** What is the most common form of waste energy?
  b Name another form in which energy is often wasted.

7.9 How is a combined heat and power (CHP) station designed to waste less energy than a conventional power station?

7.10 What force makes it impossible to make a perpetual motion machine?

7.11 Energy may be transferred by a force. What name is given to this process?

7.12 Energy may be transferred by a force or by heat. Name two other ways in which energy may be transferred.

7.3 Energy efficiency

We have seen the importance of making good use of the energy resources available to us. Energy tends to get wasted, as heat energy, in almost everything we do. We must use resources efficiently. But how can we say just how efficient we are being? Sankey diagrams can give us a clue.

Figure 7.12 shows two types of light bulb and their Sankey diagrams. One is a filament lamp; the other is an energy-efficient lamp. We use light bulbs to provide us with light, and the Sankey diagrams show that the two bulbs produce the same amount of light energy. However, the energy-efficient lamp requires a much smaller input of electrical energy because it wastes much less energy as heat.

The filament lamp uses 100 J of energy every second; it provides 15 J of light energy. We say that its efficiency is 15%.

The other lamp provides 15 J of light from just 25 J of electrical energy. So $\frac{15}{25}$ of the energy supplied is converted to the form that we want (light); its efficiency is 60%.

Calculating efficiency

To calculate the efficiency of an energy transformation, we need to know two quantities:

● the energy input (the amount of energy supplied);

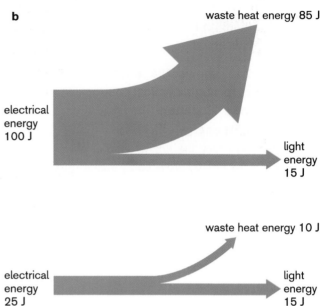

Figure 7.12 Each of these two light bulbs provides the same amount of light, but the energy-efficient lamp on the right wastes much less energy as heat.

Device	Typical efficiency (%)
electric heater	100
large electric motor	90
washing machine motor	70
gas-fired power station	50
diesel engine	40
car petrol engine	30
steam locomotive	10

Table 7.1 Energy efficiencies. Most devices are less than 100% efficient because they produce waste heat. An electric heater is 100% efficient because all the electrical energy supplied is transformed to heat – no problem about waste here!

● the useful energy output (the amount of energy that ends up in the form that we want).

The energy **efficiency** (which is usually given as a percentage) is then given by:

$$\text{energy efficiency} = \frac{\text{useful energy output}}{\text{energy input}} \times 100\%$$

Table 7.1 shows typical efficiencies for some important devices. You can see that even the most modern gas-fired power station is only 50% efficient; half of the energy it is supplied with is wasted.

Opting for efficiency

Energy-efficient (or low-energy) light bulbs sound like a good thing, so why don't more people use them? It is true that these bulbs use less electrical energy than a conventional filament lamp, and so their running costs are less. They also last a lot longer – perhaps ten times as long. However, they have the disadvantage that they cost a lot more to buy. Overall, the cost of an energy-efficient bulb and the electricity it consumes is less than that of the filament lamps that must be bought instead, but this is not how people see it. They see the initial price tag and think twice before buying. They may also feel that the energy-efficient bulb is larger and uglier than the other bulb.

We have also seen that many older power stations tend to be inefficient. Should the power companies shut them down and build new ones? Often the answer is no. It is cheaper, at least in the short term, to run an existing inefficient power station than to build and run a new, more efficient one.

Worked example 3

Figure 7.13 shows the energy that flows through a typical coal-fired power station in 1 s. Calculate its energy efficiency.

- *Step 1* Identify the energy input. This is the energy provided by the coal, so

  energy input $= 1200$ MJ

- *Step 2* Identify the useful energy output. This is the energy carried away by the electric current in the wires, so

  useful energy output $= 420$ MJ

Figure 7.13 Energy flow per second through a large coal-fired power station.

- *Step 3* Calculate the energy efficiency:

$$\text{energy efficiency} = \frac{\text{useful energy output}}{\text{energy input}} \times 100\%$$

$$= \frac{420\,\text{MJ}}{1200\,\text{MJ}} \times 100\% = 35\%$$

From this, you can see that the power station wastes almost two-thirds of the energy supplied to it. (Note that the energy units, MJ, cancel out and we are left with a number without units.)

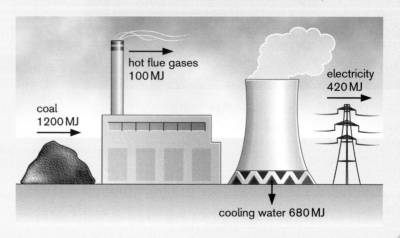

hot flue gases
100 MJ

electricity
420 MJ

coal
1200 MJ

cooling water 680 MJ

Questions

7.13 An electric heater transforms electrical energy to heat energy with 100% efficiency. Draw a Sankey diagram to represent this.

7.14 A hairdryer is connected to the mains electricity supply. It blows hot air at the user's wet hair. It whirrs as it does so.
  a What two desired forms of energy is it producing?
  b What form of waste energy is produced?

7.15 A particular electric light bulb is found to have an efficiency of 20%. Draw a Sankey diagram to represent the outcome of transferring 100 J of electrical energy to the bulb.

7.16 Mental arithmetic: A crane lifts a load of bricks to the top of a building. Every second, 20 kJ of electrical energy is supplied to the motor of the crane, and the bricks are given 8 kJ of GPE. What is the crane's efficiency?

Summary

◆ Energy can be transformed from one form to another.

◆ In any energy transformation, the total amount of energy before the transformation is equal to the total amount after the transformation. This is the principle of conservation of energy.

◆ In energy transformations, some energy often appears in forms that are not wanted, particularly as waste heat.

◆ Energy can be transferred from place to place, or from one object to another, by a variety of means.

◆ Energy efficiency indicates the fraction of the input energy that ends up in a useful form:

$$\text{energy efficiency} = \frac{\text{useful energy output}}{\text{energy input}} \times 100\%$$

Work and power

Topics in this chapter

◆ gravitational potential energy

◆ kinetic energy

◆ doing work

◉ *machines*

◆ power

Running up a mountain is hard work, although some people (Figure 8.1) do it for pleasure! As you move upwards, gravity is trying to pull you back down. Your legs have to push hard on the ground if you are to move quickly upwards. This takes energy and so you have to draw on the energy reserves stored in your body. Your blood supply brings the necessary oxygen to your muscles.

Figure 8.1 Racing uphill is very demanding on your legs. They have to push your body upwards, against the downward pull of the Earth's gravity. The higher you go, the thinner the atmosphere and the harder it will be for you to run.

If you are running at high altitudes, you may get short of oxygen. The air gets thinner the higher up you are, and you may suffer from altitude sickness. People who live at high altitudes have more haemoglobin in their blood, so that the blood has a greater oxygen-carrying capacity. When, in 1968, the Olympic Games were held in Mexico City, at a height of 2200 m above sea-level, athletes had to spend several weeks acclimatising themselves to the conditions before they could compete.

It is much easier coming down-hill. Now gravity is on your side. If you let yourself go, you could simply roll down to the bottom. Gravity will make you go faster and faster; friction will tend to slow you down. In practice, your legs will be working hard again, pushing down on the ground to stop you from going out of control.

In this chapter, we will look at the energy transformations involved when things move up and down, and when they speed up and slow down. These energy changes involve forces. (In the running example above, the forces are gravity, friction and the push of the runner's legs.)

8.1 Gravitational potential energy

Mountaineering on the Moon should be easy – see Figure 8.2. The Moon's gravity is much weaker than the Earth's, because the Moon's mass is one-eightieth of the Earth's even though at the Moon's surface you are nearer to its centre of gravity. The weight of an astronaut on the Moon is about one-sixth of his or her weight on the Earth: in principle, it is possible to jump six times as high on the Moon. Unfortunately, because an astronaut has to carry an oxygen supply and wear a cumbersome suit, this height cannot be reached in practice.

In Chapter 7 we saw that an object's gravitational potential energy (GPE) depends on its height above the ground. The higher it is, the greater its GPE. If you lift an object upwards, you increase its GPE. The heavier the object, the greater the energy transferred in lifting it, and hence the greater its gain in GPE. This suggests that an object's gravitational potential energy depends on two factors:

- the object's weight mg;
- the height h of the object above ground level.

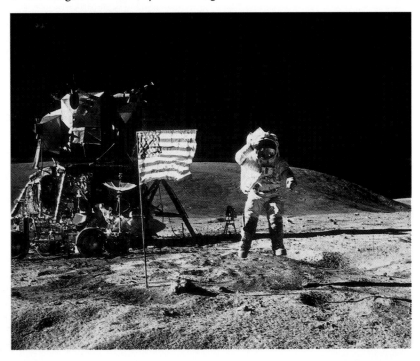

Figure 8.2 An astronaut on the Moon. Because the Moon's gravity is one-sixth of the Earth's, it should be possible to jump six times as high. The astronaut's bulky spacesuit and equipment make this feat impossible to achieve in practice. Experiments on the Moon have shown that a golf ball can be hit much farther than on Earth, because it will travel a much greater distance horizontally before gravity has pulled it back to the ground.

This is illustrated in Figure 8.3. From the values given in the diagram, you can see that the gain in GPE is simply calculated by multiplying weight and height:

> gain in gravitational potential energy = weight × height

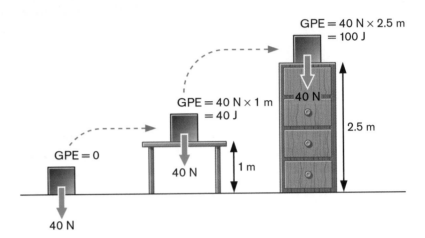

Figure 8.3 The gravitational potential energy of an object increases as it is lifted higher. The greater its weight, the greater its GPE. In being lifted from ground to table the gain in GPE is 40 J; in being lifted from table to chest of drawers there is a further gain of 60 J.

Here, for convenience we have taken the object's GPE to be zero when it is at ground level. If a stone is on the ground at the edge of a deep hole, we may say that its GPE is zero relative to the ground, but it is a lot more than zero relative to the bottom of the hole. It all depends on where we choose the zero of GPE to be. So we always consider *changes in GPE*:

> change in GPE = weight × change in height = *mgh*

When an object is lifted upwards, its GPE increases; when it falls, its GPE decreases.

Worked example 1

An athlete of mass 50 kg runs up a hill. The foot of the hill is 400 m above sea-level; the summit is 1200 m above sea-level. By how much does the athlete's GPE increase? [Acceleration due to gravity $g = 10\,\text{m/s}^2$]

- *Step 1* Calculate the increase in height:

  $h = 1200\,\text{m} - 400\,\text{m} = 800\,\text{m}$

- *Step 2* Write down the equation for GPE, substitute values and solve:

  change in GPE = weight × change in height

  $= mgh$

  $= 50\,\text{kg} \times 10\,\text{m/s}^2 \times 800\,\text{m}$

  $= 400\,000\,\text{J} = 400\,\text{kJ}$

So the athlete's GPE increases by 400 kJ.

Figure 8.4 This high-jumper curves her body in order to get over the bar. She cannot increase her GPE enough to get her whole body above the level of the bar. Her centre of gravity passes under the bar, so that at no time is her body entirely above the bar.

Figure 8.5 The word 'kinetic' means 'related to movement'. Many sculptors have had fun making kinetic sculptures, such as mobiles. These kinetic sculptures are at the Centre Georges Pompidou, an arts centre in Paris. Water squirts out of jets on the sculptures, pushing them around, so that the water makes great sprays in the air.

A note on height

We have to be careful when measuring or calculating the change in an object's height.

Firstly, we have to consider the *vertical* height through which it moves. A train may travel 1 km up a long and gentle slope, but its vertical height may increase by only 10 m. A satellite may travel around the Earth in a circular orbit. It stays at a constant distance from the centre of the Earth, and so its height doesn't change. Its GPE is constant.

Secondly, it is the change in height of the object's centre of gravity that we must consider. This is illustrated by the high-jumper shown in Figure 8.4. As she jumps, she must try to increase her GPE enough to get over the bar. In fact, by curving her body, she passes over the bar, but her centre of gravity passes under it.

Questions

8.1 In the following examples, is the object's GPE increasing, decreasing or remaining constant?

 a an apple falls from a tree

 b an aircraft flies horizontally at a height of 9000 m

 c a rocket is fired into the sky

8.2 Mental arithmetic: A girl of weight 500 N climbs on top of a 2 m high wall. By how much does her GPE increase?

8.3 Mental arithmetic: A stone of weight 1 N falls downwards. Its GPE decreases by 100 J. How far has it fallen?

8.2 Kinetic energy

It takes energy to make things move. You transfer energy to a ball when you throw it or hit it. A car uses energy from its fuel to start moving. Elastic energy stored in a stretched piece of rubber is needed to fire a pellet from a catapult. So a moving object has energy; this energy is known as its **kinetic energy** (KE) – see Figure 8.5.

We often make use of an object's kinetic energy; to do this, we must slow it down. For example, moving air turns a wind turbine. This slows down the air, reducing its KE. The energy extracted from the air can be used to turn a generator to produce electricity.

The KE of an object depends on two factors:

● the object's mass m;

● the object's speed v.

These are combined in a formula for KE:

$$\text{kinetic energy} = \tfrac{1}{2} \times \text{mass} \times \text{speed}^2$$
$$\text{KE} = \tfrac{1}{2}mv^2$$

Note that the formula is not simply mass × velocity – that is the object's *momentum* (see Chapter 3). Worked example 2 shows how to use the formula to calculate the KE of a moving object.

Note also that kinetic energy, like all forms of energy, is a scalar quantity, despite the fact that it involves *v*. It is best to think of *v* here as speed rather than velocity.

Worked example 2

A van of mass 2000 kg is travelling at 10 m/s. Calculate its kinetic energy. If its speed increases to 20 m/s, by how much does its kinetic energy increase?

- *Step 1* Calculate the van's KE at 10 m/s:

$$KE = \tfrac{1}{2}mv^2$$
$$= \tfrac{1}{2} \times 2000\,kg \times (10\,m/s)^2$$
$$= 100\,000\,J = 100\,kJ$$

- *Step 2* Calculate the van's KE at 20 m/s:

$$KE = \tfrac{1}{2}mv^2$$
$$= \tfrac{1}{2} \times 2000\,kg \times (20\,m/s)^2$$
$$= 400\,000\,J = 400\,kJ$$

- *Step 3* Calculate the change in the van's KE:

$$\text{change in KE} = 400\,kJ - 100\,kJ = 300\,kJ$$

So the van's KE increases by 300 kJ when it speeds up from 10 m/s to 20 m/s.

Comments on worked example 2

It is worth looking at worked example 2 in detail, since it illustrates several important points.

When calculating KE using $\tfrac{1}{2}mv^2$, take care! Only the speed is squared. Using a calculator, start by squaring the speed; then multiply by the mass, and finally divide by 2.

When the van's speed doubles from 10 m/s to 20 m/s, its KE increases from 100 kJ to 400 kJ. In other words, its speed increases by a factor of 2 but its KE increases by a factor of 2^2, which is 4. KE depends on speed squared. If the speed trebled, the KE would increase by a factor of 3^2, which is 9 – see Figure 8.6.

When the van starts moving from rest and speeds up to 10 m/s, its KE increases from 0 to 100 kJ; when its speed increases by the same amount again, from 10 m/s to 20 m/s, its KE increases by 300 kJ, three times as much. It takes a lot more energy to increase your speed when you are already moving quickly. That is why a car's fuel consumption

Figure 8.6 The faster the van travels, the greater its kinetic energy – see worked example 2. Double the speed means four times the kinetic energy, because KE depends on speed squared. The graph shows that KE increases more and more rapidly as the van's speed increases.

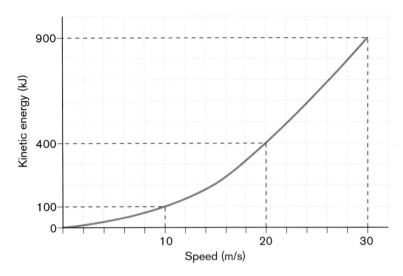

starts to increase rapidly when the driver tries to accelerate in the fast lane of a motorway.

Questions

8.4 Is kinetic energy a scalar or a vector quantity?

8.5 What does *v* represent in the formula $KE = \frac{1}{2}mv^2$?

8.6 Mental arithmetic: How much KE is stored by a 1 kg ball moving at 1 m/s?

8.7 Mental arithmetic: Which has more KE, a 2 g bee flying at 1 m/s, or a 1 g wasp flying at 2 m/s?

Figure 8.7 Energy transformations are going on as a ski-jumper performs in the air. Accelerating downhill, GPE is transformed into KE. As he rises from the end of the take-off ramp, KE is being transformed back into GPE.

8.3 KE–GPE transformations

The ski-jumper shown in Figure 8.7 has travelled uphill on a chair-lift. This increases his gravitational potential energy. Now he can ski downhill. His kinetic energy increases as his GPE decreases. GPE is being transformed into KE. As he jumps from the ramp, he starts to rise in the air. Now KE is being transformed into GPE.

There are many other situations where such transformations are going on. The following are some examples.

● An apple falls from a tree. It accelerates downwards. GPE is being transformed into KE.

● On a roller-coaster ride, a car runs downhill, then back up the next slope. GPE is being transformed into KE, and then back into GPE. Because of friction, some of the energy is wasted as heat, so the car cannot reach its original height.

● A pendulum is swinging from side to side – see Figure 8.8. At its highest point, it is momentarily stationary. Now its GPE is a maximum but it has no KE. As it swings downwards, it speeds up. GPE is being transformed into KE. At the lowest point of its swing, it is

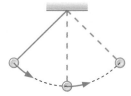

Figure 8.8 As a pendulum swings back and forth, there is a constant interchange of energy between GPE and KE. The mass on the end of the pendulum has maximum KE at the lowest point of its swing, where it is moving fastest. Its GPE increases as it rises upwards towards the ends of its swing.

moving at its fastest. It slows down again as it swings back up. KE is being transformed back into GPE.

We can use these ideas to perform some useful calculations – see worked example 3. We will state the principle of conservation of energy for a falling object in the following useful form:

decrease in GPE = increase in KE

We can write this as an equation assuming that speed v is gained as the object falls from rest through a height h:

$$mgh = \tfrac{1}{2}mv^2$$

This equation can be solved to give v when we know h, or to give h when we know v.

Worked example 3

Figure 8.9 The Leaning Tower of Pisa.

Galileo is said to have carried out experiments on the effect of gravity on objects, by dropping them from the top of the Leaning Tower of Pisa. Suppose that he drops a cannon-ball of mass 2 kg from the top of the tower, 55 m above the ground below. How fast is it moving when it reaches the ground?

● *Step 1* Write down the equation that represents the transformation of GPE to KE:

$$mgh = \tfrac{1}{2}mv^2$$

The mass m cancels, so we get

$$gh = \tfrac{1}{2}v^2$$

● *Step 2* Rearrange to make v^2 the subject:

$$v^2 = 2gh$$

● *Step 3* Solve for v:

$$v = \sqrt{2gh}$$
$$= \sqrt{2 \times 10\,\text{m/s}^2 \times 55\,\text{m}}$$
$$= \sqrt{1100}\,\text{m/s} = 33\,\text{m/s}$$

So the ball will be moving at 33 m/s when it reaches the ground. Note that, to get this answer, we have assumed that all of the ball's GPE will be transformed to KE; none is lost as heat due to friction with the air.

Galileo and gravity

No-one knows for sure whether Galileo (Figure 8.10) performed the experiment described in worked example 3. In his old age, he mentioned it to a young student when discussing his work in Pisa; and he

Figure 8.10 Galileo Galilei (known as Galileo) at the age of 42 in 1606.

certainly had a heated debate with other scholars at the time. The question was this: which falls faster, a heavy object or a light one? Galileo claimed that they would fall at the same rate, provided there was no friction to slow them down. The opposing view was that heavy objects fell faster. In particular, if one object weighed ten times as much as another, it would fall ten times as fast.

Today, we agree with Galileo. However, when he was working (in the early 1600s), scientists did not look for the answers to questions in experiments. Rather, they studied the writings of revered Greek and Arabic philosophers. So, because Aristotle had said that heavy objects fall faster, they stuck to that view.

It is said that Galileo tried to convince them that they were wrong by dropping large and small cannon-balls from the top of the Leaning Tower of Pisa. The larger one touched the ground *just* before the smaller one – it was less affected by air resistance. 'Just as we predicted', said his opponents. Of course, their prediction would have been that the heavier one would reach the ground *much* sooner than the lighter one. Galileo grumbled that they were splitting hairs, and that the experiment justified his view. This is what he wrote:

'Aristotle says that a hundred-pound ball falling from a height of a hundred arm-lengths hits the ground before a one-pound ball has fallen one arm-length. I say they arrive at the same time. You find, on making the test, that the larger ball beats the smaller one by two finger-widths. Now, behind those two finger-widths you want to hide Aristotle's ninety-nine arm-lengths and, speaking only of my tiny error, remain silent about his enormous mistake.'

We can understand why Galileo was correct by looking at the equation that is based on the principle of conservation of energy:

$$mgh = \tfrac{1}{2}mv^2$$

As we saw in worked example 3, both sides of this equation include *m*, so we can cancel it out:

$$gh = \tfrac{1}{2}mv^2$$

Rearranging gives an equation for v^2:

$$v^2 = 2gh$$

This shows that the speed *v* with which a falling ball reaches the ground does *not* depend on its mass but only on the height *h* from which it falls and the acceleration due to gravity *g*.

Of course, Galileo did not have the idea of energy to help him to prove that his idea was correct. He used another way of thinking about the same problem. He argued like this:

Suppose it were true that a small mass falls slowly and a large one falls more quickly. Imagine tying a small mass to a larger one. Now we have an even larger mass, which should fall even faster. However, we can imagine the small mass trying to fall more slowly, because it is pulled more weakly by gravity. It will slow down the larger one. Similarly, we would expect the larger one to speed up the smaller one. Their speed, when joined, should be in between their separate speeds, not greater than either.

The solution to this disagreement is to suppose that they fall at the same rate. Then it makes no difference whether they are tied together or not. The large and small masses will fall at the same rate.

Today we would explain this as follows: A larger mass needs a bigger force to make it accelerate, but gravity provides this bigger force because it pulls more strongly on a larger mass. Hence, objects fall with the same acceleration, regardless of their different masses.

Questions

8.8 A ball rolls down a smooth slope. What energy transformation is taking place here?

8.9 A skier comes down a hill. We could calculate his speed using $mgh = \frac{1}{2}mv^2$. What assumption are we making if we use this equation?

8.10 Use the equation $mgh = \frac{1}{2}mv^2$ to explain why an object dropped on the Moon is moving more slowly when it hits the ground than if it had been dropped from the same height on the Earth.

8.11 A pendulum is a mass hanging on the end of a string. Pull it to one side and it swings back and forth. Which would you expect to swing faster, one with a large mass or one with a small mass?

8.4 Doing work

Figure 8.11 shows one way of lifting a heavy object. Pulling on the rope raises the heavy box. As you pull, the force on the box moves upwards.

To lift an object, you need a store of energy (as chemical energy, in your muscles). You give the object more gravitational potential energy.

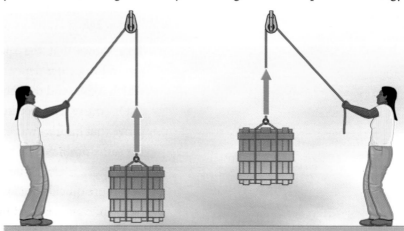

Figure 8.11 Lifting an object requires an upward force, pulling against gravity. As the box rises upwards, the force also moves upwards. Energy is being transferred by the force to the box.

The force is your means of transferring energy from you to the object. The name that we give to this type of energy transfer by a force is **doing work**.

The more work that a force does, the more energy it transfers. The amount of work done is simply the amount of energy transferred:

work done = energy transferred

We use the symbol W to represent the amount of work done. Since this is the same as the amount of energy transferred, it is measured in joules (J), the unit of energy.

Figure 8.12 Three examples of forces doing work. In each case, the force moves as energy is transferred.

Some further examples of forces doing work are shown in Figure 8.12:

a Pushing a shopping trolley to start it moving. The pushing force does work; it transfers energy to the trolley; and the trolley's kinetic energy increases.

b An apple falling from a tree. Gravity pulls the apple downwards. Gravity does work; and the apple's kinetic energy increases.

c Braking to stop a bicycle. The brakes produce a backward force of friction, which slows the bicycle. The friction does work; and the bicycle's kinetic energy is reduced. Energy is transferred to the brakes, which get hot.

Calculating work done

Think about lifting a heavy object, as shown in Figure 8.11. A heavy object needs a big force to lift it. The heavier it is, and the higher it is lifted, the more its GPE increases. This suggests that the amount of energy transferred by a force depends on two things:

● the size of the force – the greater the force, F, the more work it does;

● the distance moved by the object in the direction of the force – the further the distance moved, d, the more work it does.

We can write

> work done = force × distance moved in the direction of the force
> $$W = Fd$$

Joules and newtons

The equation for work done by a force ($W = Fd$) shows us the relationship between joules and newtons. If we replace each quantity in the equation by its SI unit, we get

$$1\,J = 1\,N \times 1\,m \qquad \text{or} \qquad 1\,J = 1\,N\,m$$

So a joule is a newton metre. More formally:

> A joule (1 J) is the energy transferred (or the work done) by a force of one newton (1 N) when it moves through a distance of one metre (1 m) in the direction of the force.

Worked example 4

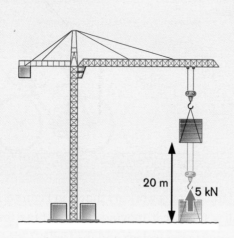

A crane lifts a crate upwards through a height of 20 m. The lifting force provided by the crane is 5 kN (see Figure 8.13). How much work is done by the force? How much energy is transferred to the crate?

- *Step 1* Write down what you know, and what you want to know:

  $F = 5\,kN = 5000\,N$
  $d = 20\,m$
  $W = ?$

- *Step 2* Write down the equation for work done, substitute values, and solve:

  $W = F \times d$
  $\quad = 5000\,N \times 20\,m$
  $\quad = 100\,000\,J$

So the force does 100 000 J, or 100 kJ, of work. Since work done = energy transferred, this is also the answer to the second part of the question: 100 kJ of energy is transferred to the crate.

20 m
5 kN

Figure 8.13 A crane provides the upward force needed to lift a crate. The force transfers energy from the crane to the crate; the crate's GPE increases.

Work done and *mgh*

Worked example 4 (the crane lifting the crate) illustrates an important idea. The force provided by the crane to lift the crate must equal the crate's weight mg. It lifts the crate through a height h. Then the work it does is force × distance, or $mg \times h$. Hence the gain in GPE of the crate is mgh. This explains where the equation for GPE comes from.

In figure 8.14 the child slides down the slope. Gravity pulls her downwards, and makes her speed up. To calculate the work done by gravity, we need to know the vertical distance h, because this is the

Figure 8.14 It is important to use the correct distance when calculating work done by a force. Gravity makes the child slide down the slope. However, to calculate the energy transferred by gravity, we must use the vertical height moved.

Figure 8.15 Three examples of forces which are *not* doing work. **a** When you sit still on a chair, there are two forces acting on you. Neither transfers energy to you. **b** The spacecraft stays at a constant distance from the Earth. Gravity keeps it in its orbit without transferring any energy to it.

distance moved in the direction of the force. If we calculated the work done as weight multiplied by distance moved down the slope, we would get an answer that was too large.

Forces doing no work

If you sit still on a chair (Figure 8.15a), there are two forces acting on you. These are your weight *mg*, acting downwards, and the upward contact force *C* of the chair, which stops you from falling through the bottom of the chair.

Neither of these forces is doing any work on you. The reason is that neither of the forces is moving, so that they do not move through any distance *d*. Hence, from $W = Fd$, the amount of work done by each force is zero. When you sit still on a chair, your energy doesn't increase or decrease as a result of the forces acting on you.

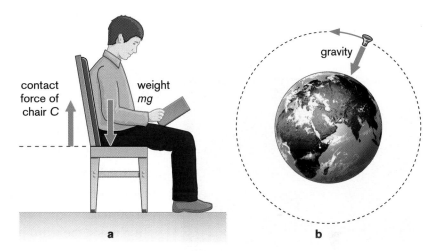

Figure 8.14b shows another example of a force that is doing no work. A spacecraft is travelling around the Earth in a circular orbit. The Earth's gravity pulls on the spacecraft to keep it in its orbit. The force is directed towards the centre of the Earth. However, since the spacecraft's orbit is circular, it does not get any closer to the centre of the Earth. There is no movement *in the direction of the force*, and so gravity does no work. The spacecraft continues at a steady speed (its KE is constant) and at a constant height above the Earth's surface (its GPE is constant). Of course, although the force is doing no work, this does not mean that it isn't having an effect. Without the force, the spacecraft would escape from the Earth and disappear into the depths of space.

You will by now understand that 'work' is a word that has a specialised meaning in physics, different from its meaning in everyday life. If you are sitting thinking about your homework, no forces are moving and you are doing no work. It is only when you start to write that you are doing work. To make the ink flow from your pen, you must push against the force of friction, and then you really are working.

Work and power | 123

Questions

8.12 What units are used in measuring the work done by a force?

8.13 A fast-moving car has 0.5 MJ of kinetic energy. The driver brakes and the car comes to a halt. How much work is done by the force provided by the brakes?

8.14 How much work is done: **a** by a force of 1 N moving through 1 m, and **b** by a force of 5 N moving through 2 m?

8.15 Mental arithmetic: Which does more work, a force of 500 N moving through 10 m or a force of 100 N moving through 40 m?

8.16 A steel ball of weight 50 N hangs at a height of 5 m above the ground, on the end of a chain 2 m in length. How much work is done on the ball: **a** by gravity, and **b** by the tension in the chain?

Figure 8.16 It's hard work down at the gym. It's easier to lift small loads, and to lift them slowly. The greater the load you lift and the faster you lift it, the greater the power required. It's the same with running on a treadmill; the faster you have to run, the greater the rate at which you do work.

8.5 Power

Exercising in the gym (Figure 8.16) can put great demands on your muscles. Speeding up the treadmill means that you have to work harder to keep up. Equally, your trainer might ask you to find out how many times you can lift a set of weights in one minute. These exercises are a test of how powerful you are. The faster you work, the greater your power.

In physics, the word **power** is often used with a special meaning. It means the rate at which you do work (that is, how fast you work). The more work you do, and the shorter the time in which you do it, the greater your power P. We can write this as an equation:

$$\text{power} = \frac{\text{work done}}{\text{time taken}}$$

$$P = \frac{W}{t}$$

Since work done = energy transferred, we can also write:

$$\text{power} = \frac{\text{energy transferred}}{\text{time taken}}$$

Units of power

Power is measured in watts (W). One watt (1 W) is the power when one joule (1 J) of work is done in one second (1 s). So

1 watt = 1 joule per second

1 W = 1 J/s

We also have

$$1000\,\text{W} = 1\,\text{kilowatt (kW)}$$
$$1000\,000\,\text{W} = 1\,\text{megawatt (MW)}$$

Take care not to confuse *W* for work done (or energy transferred) with W for watts. In books, the first of these is shown in *italic* type, but you cannot tell the difference when they are written by hand.

Worked example 6

A car (mass 800 kg) accelerates from rest to a speed of 25 m/s in 10 s. What is its power?

- *Step 1* Calculate the work done. This is the increase in the car's kinetic energy:

$$\text{KE} = \tfrac{1}{2}\,mv^2$$
$$= \tfrac{1}{2} \times 800\,\text{kg} \times (25\,\text{m/s})^2$$
$$= 250\,000\,\text{J}$$

- *Step 2* Calculate the power:

$$\text{power} = \frac{\text{work done}}{\text{time taken}}$$
$$= \frac{W}{t}$$
$$= \frac{250\,000\,\text{J}}{10\,\text{s}}$$
$$= 25\,000\,\text{W} = 25\,\text{kW}$$

So the energy is being transferred to the car (from its engine) at a rate of 25 kW, or 25 kJ per second. As we discussed earlier (Chapter 7), car engines are not very efficient. In this example, the car's engine may transfer energy at the rate of 100 kW or so, although most of this is wasted as heat energy.

We can apply the idea of power to any transfer of energy. For example, electric light bulbs transfer energy supplied to them by electricity. They produce light and heat. Most light bulbs are labelled with their power rating – e.g. 40 W, 60 W, 100 W and so on – to tell the user about the rate at which it transfers energy. We will find out more about electrical power in Chapter 19.

Questions

8.17 How many watts are there **a** in a kilowatt, and **b** in a megawatt?

8.18 It is estimated that the human brain has a power requirement of 40 W. How many joules is that per second?

8.19 Mental arithmetic: A light bulb transfers 1000 J of energy in 10 s. What is its power?

8.20 An electric motor transfers 100 J in 8 s. If it then transfers the same amount of energy in 6 s, has its power increased or decreased?

Summary

◆ Gravitational potential energy = weight × height
$$GPE = mgh$$

◆ Kinetic energy = $\frac{1}{2}$ × mass × speed^2
$$KE = \frac{1}{2}mv^2$$

◆ When a force moves, it transfers energy. We say that it does work. (The distance moved is measured in the direction of the force.)

◆ Work done = energy transferred

◆ Work done = force × distance moved by the force
$$W = Fd$$

◆ Power is the rate at which energy is transferred, or the rate at which work is done.

◆ Power = $\dfrac{\text{work done}}{\text{time taken}}$

$$P = \frac{W}{t}$$

◆ Power = $\dfrac{\text{energy transferred}}{\text{time taken}}$

The kinetic model of matter

Topics in this chapter

◆ changes of state

◆ kinetic theory

◆ models in physics

◆ diffusion and osmosis

◆ internal energy

◆ temperature and temperature scales

Young people usually enjoy snow. You may live in a country where snow is rarely seen (Figure 9.1); alternatively, you may be snow-bound for several months of the year. If you do experience snow, you will know the excitement of the first fall of the winter. Everyone rushes out to have snowball fights, or to go tobogganing or skiing.

Living with a lot of snow can be very daunting. Houses must be specially insulated. Cars may need electric heaters to keep their engines warm when they are not running. Roads must be cleared or salted regularly. You may have to go shopping in a covered mall heated to perhaps 40 degrees above the sub-zero temperatures outside.

Figure 9.1 Most parts of the world experience snow at some time, even tropical areas. High in the atmosphere, temperatures are much lower than at ground level. Water vapour in the air condenses to form snow, and the flakes may survive their fall through warmer air. Mount Kilimanjaro, on the border between Tanzania and Kenya, stands just south of the equator. Because it is almost 6000 m high, its peak is permanently glaciated and snowstorms are frequent.

Figure 9.2 Snowflakes all have six-fold symmetry. They grow fairly slowly in the atmosphere. This tells us that the conditions in which they form must be very uniform, otherwise one arm of the flake might grow faster than the others and the flake would be lopsided.

Snow is remarkable stuff. It is simply frozen water – and yet, people such as the Inuit, who live among it, have many different words for snow, depending on how it is packed down, for instance. If you are interested in winter sports, such information about snow can be vital, since it determines the avalanche risk. Each snowflake is different from every other one, yet they all share the same six-fold symmetry (Figure 9.2). Snow is similar to ice, but it forms high in the atmosphere where low temperatures cause water vapour in the air to condense. Because of their spiky shapes, snowflakes do not pack closely together, so snow has a low density. When a 10 cm depth of snow melts, it leaves about 1 cm of water.

We are familiar with the changes that happen when snow or ice melts. A white or glassy solid changes into a transparent, colourless, runny liquid. Heat the liquid and it vanishes into thin air. Although this sounds like a magic trick, it is so familiar that it doesn't strike us as surprising. The Earth is distinctive among the planets of the Solar System in being the only planet on which water is found to exist naturally in all three of its physical states. In this chapter, we will look at what happens when materials **change their state** – from solid to liquid to gas, and back again. By thinking about the particles – the atoms and molecules – of which the material is made, we can build up a picture or model that describes changes of state and explains some of the things we observe when materials change from one state to another.

9.1 Changes of state

Figure 9.3a shows one way to investigate a liquid material as it solidifies. The test-tube contains a waxy substance, octadecanoic acid. It is warmed and becomes a clear, colourless liquid. Then it is left to cool down, and its temperature is monitored using an electronic thermometer probe and data-logger. The graph of Figure 9.3b shows temperature against time and is known as a **cooling curve**. From the graph, you can see that there are three stages in the cooling of the material.

1 The liquid wax cools down. Its temperature drops gradually. The wax is hotter than its surroundings, so it loses heat. Notice that the graph is slightly curved; this is because, as the temperature drops, there is less difference between the temperature of the wax and its surroundings, so it loses heat more slowly.

2 Now the wax's temperature remains constant for a few minutes. The tube can be seen to contain a mixture of clear liquid and white solid – the wax is solidifying. During this time, the wax is still losing heat, because it is still warmer than its surroundings, but its temperature does *not* decrease. This is an important observation that needs explaining.

3 The wax's temperature starts to drop again. It is now entirely solid, and it continues cooling until it reaches the temperature of its surroundings.

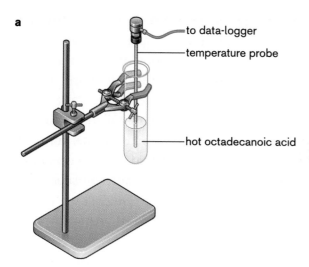

Figure 9.3 **a** As the warm liquid (octadecanoic acid) cools, its temperature is monitored by the electronic probe. **b** The graph shows how the temperature of the octadecanoic acid drops as it loses heat. The temperature remains constant as the liquid solidifies. (Octadecanoic acid is also known as stearic acid.)

Figure 9.4 Naming changes of state. Sublimation is the direct change from solid to gas; there is no special name for the reverse process.

Table 9.1 Melting and boiling points of some pure substances. Mercury is interesting because it is the only metal that is not solid at room temperature. Tungsten is a metal; it has the highest boiling point of any substance. Helium has the lowest melting and boiling points of any element; in fact, it will only solidify if it is compressed as well as cooled.

From the horizontal section of the graph (stage 2), we can draw a horizontal line across to the temperature axis and find the substance's melting point.

Naming the changes

We think of matter as existing in three states: solid, liquid and gas. Heat a solid and it melts to become a liquid. Heat the liquid; some **evaporates** and the rest finally boils to become a gas. Cool the gas and it becomes first a liquid and then a solid. The names for these changes are shown in Figure 9.4.

At atmospheric pressure, some solids change directly into a gas. An example is solid carbon dioxide, known as 'dry ice'. This is the material often used to create 'smoke' effects in concerts and stage shows. It starts as a hard white solid and turns into a cold gas. The gas makes water vapour in the air condense, so that it looks like clouds of white smoke. A direct change from solid to gas is known as **sublimation**.

From the experiment shown in Figure 9.3, you can see that a pure substance changes from solid to liquid at a particular temperature, known as the **melting point**. (If we think of the process in reverse, we might call this temperature the **freezing point**.) At its **boiling point** a liquid changes into a gas. Table 9.1 shows the melting and boiling points of some pure substances.

Substance	Melting point (°C)	Boiling point (°C)
helium	−272	−269
oxygen	−218	−183
nitrogen	−191	−177
water	0	100
mercury	−39	257
iron	2080	3570
diamond (carbon)	4100	5400
tungsten	3920	6500

Notice that we have to be careful here to talk about *pure* substances. Salty water boils at a higher temperature than pure water, and freezes at a lower temperature. Salty water is a **solution** of salt in water. Any dissolved substance changes the temperature at which a pure substance melts or boils.

However, a **mixture** of substances may melt or boil over a range of temperatures. Candle wax is an example: it is not a single, pure substance, and some of the substances in it melt at lower temperatures than others. Similarly, crude oil is a mixture of different substances, each with its own boiling point. You may have studied the process of fractional distillation, which is used to separate these substances at an oil refinery.

There are other ways in which materials can behave when they are heated: some burn; others decompose (break down) into simpler substances before they have a chance to change state.

Figure 9.5 shows what happens if you take some ice from the deep freeze and heat it at a steady rate. In a deep freeze, ice is at a temperature well below its freezing point (0°C). From the graph, you can see that the ice warms up to 0°C, then remains at this temperature while it melts. Lumps of ice float in water; both are at 0°C. When all of the ice is melted, the water's temperature starts to rise again. At 100°C, the boiling point of water, the temperature again remains steady. The water is boiling to form steam. This takes longer than melting, which tells us that it takes more energy to boil the water than to melt the ice. Eventually, all of the water has turned to steam; if we continue to heat it in a rigid container, the temperature of the steam will rise again.

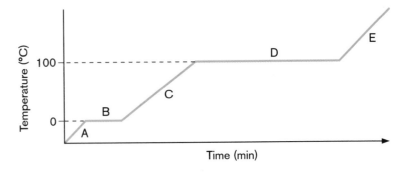

Figure 9.5 A temperature–time graph to show the changes that occur when ice is heated at a steady rate until it eventually becomes steam.

As mentioned above, water doesn't have to be heated to 100°C before it will turn into a gas. After a downpour of rain, the puddles eventually dry up even though the temperature is much lower than 100°C. We say that the water has become water vapour in the air by **evaporation**. If you smell the linseed oil that is the solvent in an artist's oil paints, you are detecting another sort of vapour.

In fact, even ice can evaporate. Sometimes snow turns directly to water vapour, particularly if its temperature is close to 0°C and there is a wind blowing to carry away the water vapour. Water can also evaporate from food in a deep freeze. If you look at food that has been stored for several months, you may find that it is covered with white crystals of 'snow'. These have formed from water vapour that has evaporated from the food, and then refrozen. It is a cause of deterioration of frozen food, and explains why frozen food can only be stored for a limited time in a domestic freezer. Large commercial cold-stores are kept at temperatures as low as $-40\,°C$ to reduce the problem.

> **? Questions**
>
> **9.1** What name is given to the temperature at which a gas condenses to form a liquid?
>
> **9.2** What name is given to the process in which a solid changes directly into a gas?
>
> **9.3** What name is given to the process in which a liquid changes into a gas at a temperature below its boiling point?
>
> **9.4** Look at Figure 9.5. **a** What is happening in the section marked C? **b** Name the state or states of the substance present in the section marked D.
>
> **9.5** Look at Figure 9.3. From the graph, deduce the melting point of octadecanoic acid.
>
> **9.6** Table 9.1 shows the melting and boiling points of nitrogen and oxygen, the main constituents of air. Why can we not talk about the melting point and boiling point of air?

9.2 Particles, forces and the kinetic model

Several questions arise from our discussion of changes of state.

- Why do different substances melt at different temperatures? Why do they have different boiling points?
- Why does it take time for a solid to melt? Why doesn't it change instantly into a liquid?
- Why does it take longer to boil away a liquid than to melt a solid?
- How can a solid evaporate? Why do liquids cool when they evaporate?

Here is an even more fundamental question:

- Why are there three states of matter?

In this part of the chapter, we will look at a model for matter that provides the way in which we can answer these questions.

The model we are going to consider is called the **kinetic model** of matter. As we saw in Chapter 8, the word 'kinetic' means 'related to movement'. In this model, the things that are moving are the particles of which matter is made. The model thus has an alternative name: the **particle model** of matter.

The particles of which matter is made are very tiny. They may be atoms, molecules or ions, but we will simplify things by disregarding these differences and referring only to particles. We will also picture a material as consisting of large numbers of identical particles. Thus we are considering a pure substance whose particles are all the same, rather than a mixture containing two or more types of particle. We will also think of the particles as simple spheres, although in reality they might have more complicated shapes. The molecules of a polymer, for example, may be like long thin strings of spaghetti, rather than like small, round peas.

The idea that matter is made up of identical spherical particles is a great simplification, but we can still use it to find answers to the questions that we have listed. Later, we will think about whether we are justified in using such a simplified model.

Arrangements of particles

Figure 9.6 shows how we picture the particles in a solid, a liquid and a gas. For each case, we will think about two aspects: how the particles are arranged, and how they are moving – see Table 9.2.

Figure 9.6 A simple model of a solid, a liquid and a gas. The arrangement and motion of the particles change as the solid is heated to become first a liquid and then a gas.

Table 9.2 The arrangement and movement of particles in the three different states of matter. Compare these statements with the pictures shown in Figure 9.6.

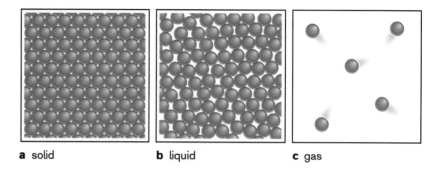

a solid   **b** liquid   **c** gas

Arrangement of particles	Movement of particles
Solid The particles are packed closely together. Notice that each particle is in close contact with its neighbours. In a solid such as a metal, each atom may be in contact with 12 neighbouring atoms	Because the particles are tightly packed, they cannot change places. However, they do vibrate about a fixed position. The hotter the solid, the more they vibrate
Liquid The particles are packed slightly less closely together (compared with a solid). Each particle is still in close contact with most of its neighbours, but fewer than for a solid. The general arrangement is more jumbled and disorderly	Because the particles are slightly less tightly packed than in a solid, they have the opportunity to move around within the bulk of the liquid. Hence the particles are both vibrating and moving from place to place
Gas Now the particles are widely separated from one another. They are no longer in contact, unless they collide with each other. In air, the average separation between the particles is about ten times their diameter	The particles are now moving freely about, bouncing off one another and the walls of their container. In air at room temperature, their average speed is about 400 m/s

These ideas can explain many observations. Here are some.

- Liquids take up the shape of their container, because their particles are free to move about within the bulk of the liquid.
- Gases fill their container, because their particles can move freely about.
- Solids retain their shape because the particles are packed tightly together.
- Gases **diffuse** from place to place so that, for example, we can smell perfume across the room. The perfume particles spread about because they are freely mobile.
- Similarly, a dissolved substance diffuses throughout a liquid. Sugar crystals in a drink dissolve, and sugar molecules spread throughout the liquid. In a hotter drink, the particles are moving faster and the sugar diffuses more quickly.
- Most solids expand when they melt. The particles are slightly further apart in a liquid than in a solid.
- Liquids expand a lot when they boil. The particles of a gas are much farther apart than in a liquid. We can think about this the other way round. Gases contract a lot when they condense. If you cooled all of the air in the room you are in now, it would condense to form a thin layer of liquid, two or three millimetres deep, on the floor.

Forces, energy and the kinetic theory

So far, we have seen how the kinetic theory of matter can successfully explain some observations of the ways in which solids, liquids and gases differ. However, we have not answered all of the questions we raised at the start of this part of the chapter. To deal with these questions, we need to build two more scientific ideas into the kinetic theory: we need to consider the forces between the particles, and their energies.

Why do the particles that make up a solid or a liquid stick together? There must be **attractive forces** between them. Without attractive forces to hold together the particles that make up matter, we would live in a very dull world. There would be no solids or liquids, only gases. No matter how much we cooled matter down, it would remain as a gas.

Another way to refer to these forces is to say that there are **bonds** between the particles. Each particle of a solid is strongly bonded to its neighbours. In a liquid, the bonds between neighbours are only temporary and each particle has one or two fewer than in the solid.

What happens to the attractive forces in a solid as it is heated? The particles start to vibrate more and more strongly. Eventually, they vibrate sufficiently for some of the bonds to be broken, and the solid becomes a liquid. Heat the material more and eventually the particles have sufficient energy for all of the attractive forces between particles to be overcome. The material becomes a gas.

The attractive forces between particles in a gas haven't disappeared; however, the particles are so far apart and moving so fast that they do

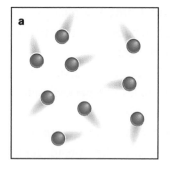 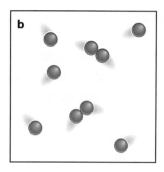 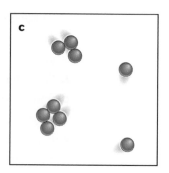 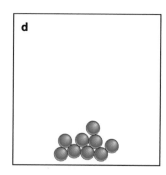

Figure 9.7 **a** As a gas is cooled to below its boiling point, it starts to condense. **b** The particles move more slowly and they start to stick together, because of the attractive forces between them. **c** As their energy gets less, they clump together in bigger and bigger groups until **d** they form a liquid.

not stick together. If you cool down a gas (Figure 9.7), the particles move more slowly. As they collide with one another, there is more chance that they will stick together. Keep cooling the gas and eventually, at one particular temperature, all of the particles stick together to form a liquid.

We can also describe changes of state in terms of energy. In a solid, the particles vibrate. They have kinetic energy. As they start to break apart to form a liquid, they are gaining potential energy. (Recall from Chapter 7 that potential energy is energy associated with position or configuration; in a liquid, the particles are further apart than in a solid, and so they have more potential energy.)

Heating a liquid makes its particles move faster, so their kinetic energy must be increasing. Finally, as they separate completely to form a gas, their potential energy increases dramatically. To summarise:

- When we heat a substance, the particles gain energy.
- If the temperature rises, the particles' kinetic energy is increasing.
- If the substance changes state, bonds are broken and the potential energy of the particles increases.

Using the kinetic model

Now we will return to the questions we posed earlier and see how the kinetic model can provide some answers.

- Why do different substances melt at different temperatures? Why do they have different boiling points?

This can be answered in terms of the forces between particles. A material with strong forces between its particles has a high melting point and a high boiling point. The atoms of helium attract each other only very weakly, and so it has to be cooled to an extremely low temperature before it will liquefy.

- Why does it take time for a solid to melt? Why doesn't it change instantly into a liquid?

If you put a lump of ice into a drink, the ice melts gradually. Heat is entering the ice and breaking some of the bonds between the particles. Enough energy must be supplied to break these bonds, and that takes time. Similarly, energy must be supplied to boil water. If you put a pan of water on the stove, it will come to the boil. Then it will take quite some time before it boils completely dry. You need to supply enough energy to break all of the bonds between the particles.

● Why does it take longer to boil a liquid than to melt a solid?

This is related to the previous question. When a solid melts, only a few bonds are broken between each particle and its neighbours (perhaps one or two bonds). When a liquid boils, all of the remaining bonds must be broken, and this may be as many as eight or ten. Hence more energy must be supplied for boiling than for melting.

● How can a solid evaporate? Why do liquids cool when they evaporate?

In a solid, some of the particles will have more energy than others. There is constant vibration. Particles jostle their neighbours, sharing their energy with them. A particle on the surface of the solid may gain a little extra energy and break free. (It only has relatively few bonds to break, because it is not surrounded on all sides.) Once it is free, it will be moving only slowly, and it may re-condense back on the surface of the solid.

A liquid evaporates in the same way, but more readily because its particles are relatively free already. The particles that escape are those with most energy. Hence the particles that remain have less than average energy, and so the liquid becomes cooler. Evaporation is something that happens only at the surface of a liquid, whereas boiling takes place throughout a liquid.

● Why are there three states of matter?

We can see that the kinetic model provides an explanation for the three states of matter. In a solid, the particles are tightly bonded to all their neighbours; in a liquid, a fraction of the bonds are broken; and in a gas, all of the bonds are broken.

Sometimes we talk about a fourth state of matter, known as **plasma**. If you heat a gas to a sufficiently high temperature, its atoms start to fall apart. Electrons break free, leaving positively charged ions. The gas has become a mixture of charged particles. Plasmas have been detected in some of the hotter regions of space. A type of plasma also exists inside a fluorescent light tube, created when an electric current passes through mercury vapour. The current strips electrons from the mercury atoms to create the plasma, which glows to give the light we need.

Questions

9.7 Why is the kinetic model of matter called *kinetic*?

9.8 What can you say about the forces between the particles that make up matter?

9.9 **a** In which state of matter are the particles most closely packed? **b** In which state are they most widely separated?

?

Questions continued

9.10 When a gas is heated, how does the motion of its particles change?

9.11 Tungsten melts at a much higher temperature than iron. What can you say about the forces between the tungsten atoms, compared to the forces between the iron atoms?

9.12 A particular solid material is heated but its temperature does not rise.

    a What is happening to the solid?

    b Where does the energy go that is being supplied to it?

9.13 Why do most substances expand when they melt?

a

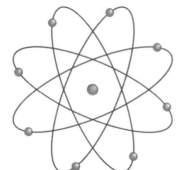

b

Figure 9.8 Two different models of the atom. **a** Particles (electrons) orbiting the nucleus, like a miniature Solar System. This picture of an atom is often used simply to mean that something is scientific, for example in advertisements, or as an icon in computer programs. **b** In this model, an electron is no longer imagined as a particle on an orbit but as a particle moving somewhere within a fuzzy region sometimes called an **orbital**. Three such orbitals are shown here; each has two lobes.

9.3 Thinking about the kinetic model

In physics (and in many other areas of study), we use **models** to help us to understand the world. Models take many different forms, but they all attempt to present a simplified version of the complex world we see around us. Because they are relatively simple, we can use them to explain things and to predict new things.

One model with which you may be familiar is that of the atom – see Figure 9.8a. We imagine that every atom has a tiny nucleus, with electrons whizzing around it. Your teacher might say that an atom is like a miniature Solar System. This makes it easier for us to have a mental image of an atom, because we already have an image of the Solar System, with the planets orbiting the Sun. With this model of the atom, we can go on to think about how atoms join (or bond) together, to form molecules. So this is a useful model. However, like all models, it has its limitations. Atoms are not really like miniature Solar Systems. Sometimes it is better to imagine the electrons as smeared out clouds, rather than as tiny particles (Figure 9.8b). To solve many problems, it is necessary to avoid models of the atom that are based on pictures and instead to use models based on equations.

The kinetic model of matter, which we have been studying in this chapter, shows some important features of models. Like all models, it starts from some basic ideas or assumptions. These are:

1 Matter is made of particles.
2 There are attractive forces between the particles.
3 The particles move about.

Now that you have studied the model, these ideas may seem obvious. However, if you look around you, you will realise that they are not. You cannot see that matter is made of particles. You can't experience the force that one particle exerts on another, and you can't see that they are

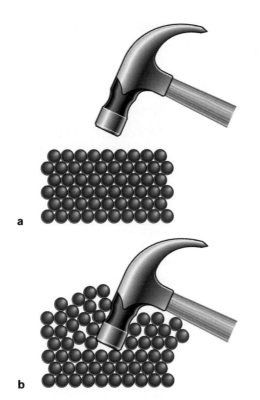

Figure 9.9 We can use the kinetic model to explain what happens when a hammer strikes a lump of lead and makes a dent in it. The atoms of the lead are only weakly bound together, so that the hammer can push them apart. To be more correct, we should picture the hammer head as being made of iron atoms. They are more strongly bound together than the lead atoms, so the hammer does not get dented.

Figure 9.10 One way of improving the kinetic model of matter is to take account of the fact that different molecules have different shapes. Iron atoms are more or less spherical, so they can pack together neatly. Water molecules are less spherical, so they pack less neatly. Polythene molecules are long and thin, like strands of cooked spaghetti; they may lie neatly side-by-side, or they may be more jumbled.

moving about. Today, we have some experimental techniques that allow us to see individual atoms and molecules, but these were developed only recently. Scientists developed the kinetic model long before there was such concrete proof of the existence of atoms. It was so successful in explaining many different phenomena that they felt sure that it was basically correct.

The ancient Greeks had an entirely different model for matter. They thought that there were four different 'elements' (we use the word with a very different meaning today). These were 'earth', 'water', 'air' and 'fire'. Anything solid was largely composed of 'earth', liquids were basically 'water', and so on. This early Greek model saw 'elements' as being *continuous*, without separate particles. Today we can understand where they might have got their idea from, but it was long ago replaced by the kinetic model.

Another thing that models must do is to explain new observations. Here is a challenge for the kinetic model. If you hit a lump of lead with a hammer, you will make a dent in it. If you warm the lead and hit it, it is easier to dent it. Why is this?

Figure 9.9 shows an explanation. The atoms of lead are packed closely together. It is a fairly soft metal, so the attractive forces between the atoms are fairly weak. When the hammer hits the metal, it pushes the atoms aside. When the lead is warmed, the atoms are vibrating more and bonds are weaker, so it takes less energy to push them aside.

Improving the model

Our version of the kinetic model is very simple. We can make a less basic model by changing some of its features. For example:

- We could change the shape of the particles – see Figure 9.10. Water molecules are not little spheres and some polymer molecules are very long and thin. Then we could use the model to explain why different materials behave in different ways.
- We could measure the forces between the particles, and the distances between them. Then we could do some useful calculations. We could explain, for example, why different substances have different melting points, and why some materials are stiffer than others.
- We could measure the speeds and masses of the particles in a gas. Then we could predict how hard they would strike the walls of the gas's container, and hence work out its pressure.

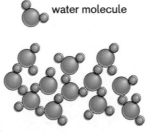

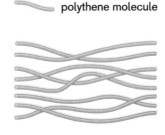

All these developments of the model have been carried out. You will learn about them if you continue with your studies of physics and chemistry.

In Chapters 10 and 11, we will see how the kinetic model can help to explain how heat energy moves around and how gases behave. Later, in Chapters 17 and 18, we will see how the model can be adapted to explain many of the ideas of electricity.

Questions

9.14 What are the three basic assumptions of the kinetic model of matter?

9.15 In the Solar System model of the atom: **a** what particles are the 'planets' and **b** what is the 'Sun'?

9.16 If a gas is heated, its molecules move faster. Use the kinetic model to predict what will happen to the pressure of the gas.

9.4 Internal energy

Imagine boiling some water to make a hot drink. You put the water in a container (a pan or a kettle), and heat it. Energy is supplied by burning a fuel such as natural gas, or by electricity. The energy goes into the water to make it hotter. How can we picture this energy?

The kinetic model gives us an answer to this. As the water gets hotter, its molecules move faster. They have more kinetic energy. You may not be able to see any difference in the water. It doesn't change colour, or glow. However, its energy has been increased. Rather than saying that the water contains more heat energy when it has been heated, we say that it stores more internal energy (or random thermal energy). Shortly we will see why this is a better term than 'heat energy'.

Earlier, we thought about the process of heating a block of ice so that it turned first into water and then into steam (Figure 9.5). Energy is supplied at a steady rate to the ice. After a while it reaches its melting point. Later, it is entirely water, and its temperature starts to rise again. It reaches 100 °C and starts to boil. In the end, all of the water becomes steam. The energy we have put into the ice does two things.

● It increases the kinetic energy of the particles – they move faster; the temperature rises.

● It increases the potential energy of the particles – bonds are broken; the substance changes state.

So now we can see what we mean by the **internal energy** of an object:

The internal energy of an object is the sum of the kinetic energy and potential energy of the random motion of all the particles that make up the object.

We should also expect that a large object would have more internal energy than a smaller one. Two litres of water at 100 °C contain twice as much internal energy as one litre at 100 °C. That's why it takes twice as long to boil two litres of water as one litre. A swimming pool full of water at 30 °C stores more internal energy than a cupful of water at 100 °C.

More ways than one

There are several ways of making something hotter. Here are four:

● You can place it next to a hotter object. The molecules of this object have, on average, higher kinetic energy and this will be gradually shared across the boundary.

● You can rub an object to make it hotter. The force of friction produces heat, and the two surfaces in contact warm up. The energy transferred to the object increases its internal energy. You can even melt ice in this way. Rub two pieces of ice together and they will start to melt.

● You can compress an object to make it hotter. This works best with a gas, because a gas is easily compressed. Put your finger over the end of a bicycle pump to stop the air inside escaping (Figure 9.11a). Compress the pump. The air gets hot; heat spreads out to the case of the pump. Release the gas, and repeat several times. You will find that the pump gets noticeably warm. Again, you are using a force to do work on the gas, and hence to transfer energy to it. Figure 9.11b shows how the pump increases the kinetic energy of the air molecules.

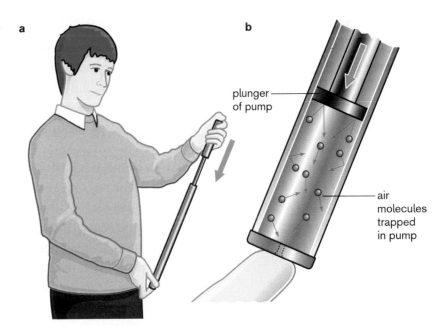

Figure 9.11 **a** Compressing air in a bicycle pump. **b** As the plunger of the pump moves downwards, it pushes the molecules of the air so that they move faster – their KE increases and the internal energy of the gas increases. It becomes hotter.

● You can make an object hotter using electricity. That's how an electric heater works. The current brings energy and transfers it to the heater. The heater transfers energy to the air in the room. The internal energy of the air increases.

So, we can see that there are several ways in which an object can be made hotter, and heating is only one of them.

There are also several ways of transferring energy to an object *without* increasing its internal energy. If you lift an object, you increase its gravitational potential energy, but you don't increase its internal energy. Similarly, you can use a force to accelerate an object; this increases its overall kinetic energy but not its kinetic energy of random motion. The speed at which a boat moves through the water does not affect the kinetic energy of random motion of the rats that live on the boat.

? Questions

9.17 Which of the following make up the internal energy of an object?

its overall kinetic energy	its gravitational potential energy
the kinetic energy of its particles	the potential energy of its particles

9.18 Which has more internal energy, 1 kg of water at 0°C or 1 kg of water at 100°C?

9.19 Which has more internal energy, 1 kg of ice at 0°C or 1 kg of water at 0°C?

9.20 Two ways of increasing the internal energy of an object are by *heating* it and by *doing work* on it. Name another way.

9.5 Temperature and temperature scales

We use thermometers for measuring temperature. Figure 9.12 shows two thermometers being used to measure human body temperature. One is a liquid-in-glass thermometer; in this type, a thin column of mercury expands inside an evacuated glass tube as it gets hotter. ('Evacuated' means that all the air has been pumped out of the tube.) The other is a liquid crystal thermometer; in this type, each segment shows up at a particular temperature. This type is much safer, particularly for use with children, who might bite a glass thermometer.

With each of these thermometers, it is important to wait for a minute or two if you want to see the correct reading. This is because the thermometer has probably been stored somewhere relatively cool, perhaps in a drawer at 20°C. The patient's temperature will be approximately 37°C, and it takes a short while for the thermometer to reach this temperature.

This gives us an idea of what we mean by **temperature**. The thermometer is placed in contact with the patient's body; it has to warm up until it reaches the same temperature as the patient. Energy from the patient is shared with the thermometer until they are at the same temperature. Then you will get the correct reading. (So the

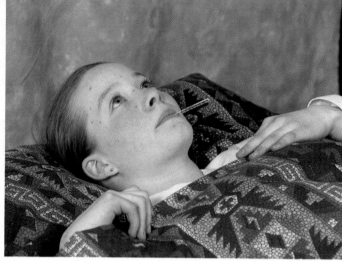

Figure 9.12 Measuring human body temperature using liquid crystal and liquid-in-glass thermometers.

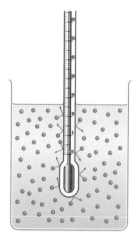

Figure 9.13 A cold thermometer placed in hot water is bombarded by the fast-moving water molecules. It absorbs some of their kinetic energy. Eventually it reaches the same temperature as the water and gives the correct reading.

thermometer doesn't tell you the patient's temperature; it tells its own temperature! But we know that the patient's temperature is now the same as the thermometer's.)

Figure 9.13 shows a thermometer measuring the temperature of some hot water. The molecules of the water are rushing about very rapidly, because the water is hot. They collide with the thermometer and share their kinetic energy with it. The bulb of the thermometer gets hotter; eventually it is at the same temperature as the water. (We say that the water and the thermometer bulb are in **thermal equilibrium** with one another. There is then no net transfer of energy from one to the other.)

You can see from this that it can be important to make a careful choice of thermometer. How could you measure the temperature of a small container containing hot water? If you chose a large, cold thermometer and poked it into the water, it might absorb a lot of energy from the water and thus make it much cooler. You would get the wrong answer for the temperature. A better solution might be to use an electronic thermometer with a very small probe; this would absorb less energy from the water.

A thermometer is thus telling us about the average kinetic energy of the particles in the object whose temperature we are measuring. It does this by sharing the kinetic energy of the particles; if they are moving rapidly, the thermometer will indicate a higher temperature. Placing a thermometer into an object to measure its temperature is rather like putting your finger into some bath-water to detect how hot it is. Your finger does not have a scale from 0 to 100 but it can still tell you how hot or cold the water is, from uncomfortably cold, to comfortably warm, to painfully hot.

Thus the temperature of an object is a measure of the average kinetic energy of its particles. We can compare internal energy and temperature:

● Internal energy is the *total* energy of *all* of the particles.

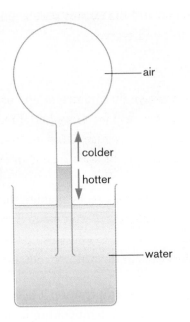

Figure 9.14 The principle of Galileo's thermometer, the first of all thermometers. It had only a narrow operating range and no scale. Since the water evaporated and air dissolved in the water, the reading became unreliable.

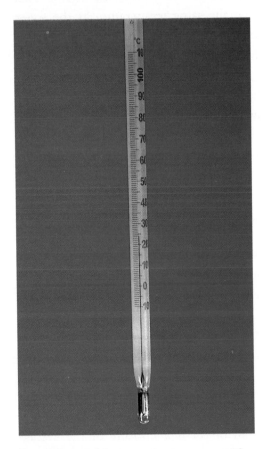

Figure 9.15 A Celsius-type thermometer, with a fixed quantity of mercury sealed in a glass tube.

● Temperature is a measure of the *average* kinetic energy of the *individual* particles.

So a bath of water at 50°C has more internal energy than a cup of water at the same temperature, but its individual molecules have the same average kinetic energy as the molecules of the water in the cup.

The Celsius scale

Galileo is credited with devising the first thermometer in 1593 (Figure 9.14). The air inside the flask expanded and contracted as the temperature rose and fell; this made the level of the water in the tube change. This could only indicate changes in temperature over a narrow range, and proved unsatisfactory because water evaporated from the reservoir.

A more successful thermometer was devised by Anders Celsius, working in Sweden in 1742. This had a volume of mercury in an enclosed and evacuated tube, with no chance of liquid loss by evaporation (Figure 9.15). Celsius also devised a scale of temperature which has two **fixed points**:

0°C – the freezing point of pure water at atmospheric pressure;
100°C – the boiling point of pure water at atmospheric pressure.

Each time he made a new thermometer, Celsius could calibrate it (give it a numbered scale) quite simply by putting it first in melting ice and then in boiling water, marking the scale each time. Then he could divide the scale into 100 equal divisions. (It is interesting to note that, with his first thermometers, Celsius marked the boiling point of water as 0 degrees and the freezing point as 100 degrees. It was a few years later that one of his colleagues decided that it was better to have the scale the other way up.)

There have been many different temperature scales down the years. The Fahrenheit scale is still used in weather-recording in many countries, including the USA. It was devised by Daniel Fahrenheit, working about 30 years before Celsius. He had two fixed points:

● 0°F – the freezing point of a mixture of ice, salt and ammonium chloride;
● 12°F – human body temperature.

He chose his zero as the lowest temperature he could achieve in the laboratory, imagining that no lower temperature was possible.

There were several things wrong with this scale. The two 'fixed' points were rather variable, depending on the composition of the freezing mixture and the health of the human body he chose to calibrate his thermometer. The scale divisions (degrees) were rather large, so he later sub-divided them into eight, so that human body temperature became 96°F. Nowadays, the scale has been re-defined, and average body temperature is taken to be 98.4°F or 98.6°F, depending on where you live. Water freezes at 32°F and boils at 212°F. These numbers are all rather inconvenient, and the Celsius scale is used for many measurements, both scientific and everyday.

Designing a thermometer

Mercury-in-glass (and alcohol-in-glass) thermometers are used in many different situations. They are attractive for a number of reasons.

- Mercury expands at a steady rate as the average KE of its molecules increases. This means that the marks on the scale are evenly spaced – we say that the scale is **linear**.
- The thermometer can be made very **sensitive**, by making the tube up which the mercury expands very narrow. Then a small change in temperature will cause the mercury to move a long way up the tube. In a typical clinical thermometer, used by doctors, the mercury rises several millimetres for a one degree rise in temperature.
- A mercury thermometer can have a wide **range**, because mercury is liquid between −39°C and +350°C. Some domestic ovens have mercury thermometers that read up to 250°C.

The problem with mercury thermometers is that they have to be read by eye. An alternative is to use an electronic thermometer. Some of these are based on **thermistors**, which are resistors whose resistance changes by a large amount over a narrow temperature range – see Figure 9.16. These can be very useful, especially as they are robust and can be built into electronic circuits. However, from the graph, you can see the following.

- The resistance of a thermistor changes in a **non-linear** way, so the intervals on a scale will not all be equal in size.
- The range of such a thermometer will be narrow, because the resistance only changes significantly over a narrow range of temperatures. You would need to choose a thermistor whose resistance changes most near the temperature you were trying to measure, if you want the thermometer to be sensitive.

A second alternative is to use a **thermocouple**, a device that gives an output voltage which depends on the temperature. Thermocouples are

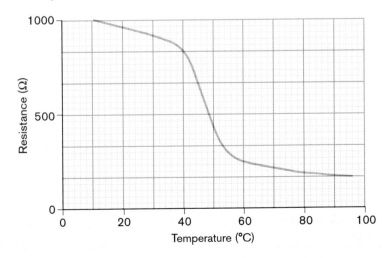

Figure 9.16 The electrical resistance of a thermistor changes over a narrow range of temperatures. This means that it can be used as a temperature probe for an electronic thermometer. However, it will only be sensitive over a narrow range, and its behaviour is non-linear.

Figure 9.17 William Thomson, who later became Lord Kelvin. Thomson was the first to propose an absolute temperature scale, now known as the Kelvin scale.

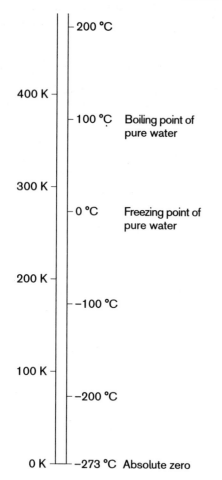

Figure 9.18 The Kelvin and Celsius scales of temperature. The divisions on the two scales are the same size, but their zeros are separated by 273 degrees.

made from two pieces of wire of different materials joined at a point; they can be made very small, they are robust, and they do not absorb much energy from the material whose temperature they are measuring. Thermocouples can be used to measure high temperatures (up to the melting point of the metals used). Because they are small, they heat up and cool down quickly, so they are useful for measuring rapidly varying temperatures.

The Kelvin scale

There is one other scale of temperature that is commonly used in physics, and that is the Kelvin scale, named after the Scottish physicist William Thomson, who later became Lord Kelvin (Figure 9.17).

Kelvin realised that there is a temperature below which it is impossible to go. Temperature is a measure of the kinetic energy of atoms. If all of the atoms in an object are slowed down so that they stop moving completely, they will have reached the absolute zero of temperature. (There is no absolute maximum of temperature, because you can always give atoms more energy.)

From experiments in which gases were cooled (see Chapter 11), it was possible to estimate a value for **absolute zero**, the lowest possible temperature. This was found to be −273 °C, or zero on the Kelvin scale, written as 0 K (zero kelvins).

The divisions on the Kelvin scale are the same size as on the Celsius scale, so the freezing point of water has the value 273.15 K. Usually we round this off to 273 K. Figure 9.18 shows how the two scales are related. To distinguish between temperatures on the two scales, we use different letters, T and θ (theta):

- T is a temperature on the Kelvin scale;
- θ is a temperature on the Celsius scale.

We can convert between the two scales simply by adding or subtracting 273:

- To convert from °C to K, add 273:
$$T = \theta + 273$$

- To convert from K to °C, subtract 273:
$$\theta = T - 273$$

Worked example 1

The boiling point of water is 100 °C. On the Kelvin scale, this is

(100 + 273) K = 373 K.

Worked example 2

Nitrogen gas condenses at 77 K. On the Celsius scale, this is $(77 - 273)°C = -196°C$.

Absolute zero (0 K) is a strange temperature. It is impossible to achieve a temperature of 0 K, for the following reason. When an object is cooled, it is only possible to extract *some* of its internal energy. Suppose that, each time you try to remove some of its internal energy, you can only extract half. The first time you remove some, half will remain. Try again, and one-quarter will remain. Try again, and one-eighth will be left. Keep going, and there will always be some (very small fraction) left.

Another oddity is that, even if you could get to absolute zero, some energy would remain in the atoms. They would continue to vibrate a small amount, according to quantum theory. At this extreme we have to take account of the wave nature of matter, and a wave cannot have zero energy – if it did it would cease to exist!

Absolute zero may be unattainable, but physicists are getting closer and closer. Techniques using lasers to extract the energy from small numbers of atoms have reached within one-billionth of a degree of absolute zero (0.000 000 001 K).

? Questions

9.21 Two buckets contain water at 30 °C. What three quantities are the same for the water molecules in the two buckets?

9.22 What are the two fixed points on the temperature scale devised by Celsius?

9.23 How is absolute zero written on the Kelvin scale?

9.24 Which is bigger, a degree on the Celsius scale or a degree on the Kelvin scale?

9.25 What symbol is used to represent a temperature on:
a the Celsius scale, and **b** the Kelvin scale?

9.26 Convert the following to the Kelvin scale: **a** 0 °C, **b** 27 °C, **c** −27 °C.

9.27 Convert the following to the Celsius scale: **a** 400 K, **b** 373 K, **c** 200 K.

Summary

◆ The kinetic model of matter assumes that matter is made of moving particles with attractive forces between them.

◆ The kinetic model explains why there are three states of matter, solid, liquid and gas.

◆ The internal energy of an object is the sum of the random kinetic energy and potential energy of all the particles that make up the object.

◆ The temperature of an object is a measure of the average random kinetic energy of its particles.

◆ During a change of state, the average kinetic energy and so the temperature of a pure substance remains constant. The external energy transferred to it increases the potential energy of its particles.

◆ To convert from °C to K, add 273:

$$T = \theta + 273$$

◆ To convert from K to °C, subtract 273:

$$\theta = T - 273$$

Thermal energy transfers

Topics in this chapter

◆ conduction

◆ convection

◆ radiation

◆ specific heat capacity

Mammals are warm-blooded creatures. They keep their body temperature at about 35–40 °C. The reason for this is that mammals are active creatures. If they are carnivores, they may have to sprint suddenly to catch their prey. Herbivores may have to graze for most of the day, occasionally running to avoid the carnivores. Muscles work much better at higher temperatures because the reactions that release energy go faster. People are mammals. If you have camped out overnight, you may have experienced the difficulty of getting your muscles to start working when you wake up on a cold morning.

There are problems with being warm-blooded. The polar bear (Figure 10.1) lives in a very cold climate. It is in constant danger of freezing to death. To avoid this danger, polar bears have thick coats of waterproof fur and layers of fat, so that heat cannot easily escape. They

Figure 10.1 The polar bear has thick fur to help it retain heat. It is a very bulky animal, so that its surface area is small compared to its volume. This is another way of retaining heat. Animals that live near the poles tend to be much larger than their relatives living near the equator. Deer provide another example: large elk and reindeer live in cold climates, but smaller roe deer and muntjac deer live further south.

Figure 10.2 An African elephant has large ear flaps, but these are not to improve its hearing. They help it to get rid of excess heat on a hot day, or when they have been very active. Blood flow to the veins in the ears is increased; this warms the nearby air, and the heat is carried away by convection. Wallowing in mud can also be cooling. As water evaporates from the elephant's skin, it carries heat energy away.

are also very bulky; this means that they have a relatively small surface area, compared to their volume. They have a lot more 'inside' than 'outside', and so they find it easier to retain their body heat. Grizzly bears also live in cold areas, and they too are bulky. Bears that live closer to the equator, such as the European brown bear, tend to be much smaller. They do not have such problems with retaining heat.

African elephants (Figure 10.2) have the opposite problem. They are large animals living in a hot climate, and they are in danger of overheating if they are too active. To cool off, they use their ears. On a hot day, more blood flows through the veins in their ear flaps; this warms the air nearby, so that heat escapes by convection. Flapping the ears increases the rate of heat loss. An elephant's ear flaps are thus the equivalent of a car's radiator – a way of getting rid of excess heat.

We often describe other creatures such as reptiles and insects as cold-blooded, but they still need to have warm muscles if they are going to be active. Butterflies generally do not start flying until their temperature reaches about 15 °C. They bask in the sun to capture heat with their wings, and this allows them to warm their muscles to a temperature where they can begin to work efficiently.

All creatures have ways of regulating (controlling) their body temperatures. They make use of all the different ways in which heat moves around – conduction, convection and radiation.

10.1 Conduction

Lying on the table are two spoons: one is metal, and the other is plastic. You pick up the metal spoon – it feels cold. But if you pick up the plastic spoon, it feels warm. In fact, both are at the same temperature, room temperature, as a thermometer would prove to you. How can this be?

What you are detecting is the fact that a metal is a good conductor of heat. Plastics are poor conductors of heat. Figure 10.3 shows what is going on.

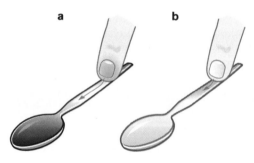

Figure 10.3 Metals feel cold; plastics feel warm. **a** Touching a piece of metal: Heat flows from your finger into the metal. Metals are good conductors of heat, so heat continues to escape from your finger – your finger gets colder. **b** Touching a piece of plastic: A small amount of heat conducts from your finger into the plastic, but it can go no further because plastics are good insulators – your finger stays warm.

- *The metal spoon* When your finger touches a metal object, heat is conducted out of your finger and into the metal. Because metal is a **good conductor**, heat spreads rapidly through the metal, leaving your finger colder than before. The temperature-sensitive nerves in your finger tell your brain that your finger is cold.

- *The plastic spoon* When you touch a plastic object, heat conducts into the area that your finger is in direct contact with. However, because plastic is a **good insulator**, the heat travels no farther. Your finger loses no more heat and remains warm. The message from your nerves is that you are touching something warm.

Note that the nerves in your finger tell you how hot your finger is, not how hot the object is that you are touching. This is similar to our discussion of thermometers in Chapter 9: a thermometer in water indicates its own temperature, and we have to assume that the temperature of the water is the same as this.

Your lips are very temperature sensitive. Try touching a metal object such as a paper-clip onto your top lip. Then try a plastic object such as a pen. Metals and some other substances feel much colder than plastic. This is used by jewellers to test diamonds. Real diamonds ('ice') are very good conductors of heat, so they feel cold on the lip. Fake diamonds ('paste') are poor conductors and feel warm.

Table 10.1 compares conductors and insulators.

Table 10.1 Comparing conductors of heat, from the best conductors to the worst. A bad conductor is a good insulator. Almost all good conductors are metals; polymers (plastics) are at the bottom of the list. Glass wool is an excellent insulator because it is mostly air.

best conductor	diamond	worst insulator
	silver, copper	
	aluminium, steel	
	lead	
	ice, marble, glass	
	polythene, nylon	
	rubber, wood	
	polystyrene	
worst conductor	glass wool	best insulator

Describing conduction

If you put a pan of water on the stove to heat, energy from the flame or hot-plate must travel through the metal of the pan to get to the water – see Figure 10.4. The metal is a conductor, so the heat travels through easily.

The temperature on one side of the metal is high – perhaps 500 °C. On the other side, the cold water is at a much lower temperature – perhaps 30 °C. This **temperature difference** makes the heat flow through the metal. If we could measure the temperature halfway through the metal, we would find that it was halfway between the two temperatures.

The rate at which heat flows depends on several factors.

- The bigger the temperature difference, the greater the rate of heat flow.
- The thicker the conductor, the slower the rate of heat flow.
- The bigger the area through which it can flow, the greater the rate of heat flow.
- The better the conductor, the greater the rate of heat flow.

Notice that, although energy is passing through the metal, the metal itself is not moving.

Table 10.1 shows that ice is a relatively poor conductor. However, this does not mean that ice does not conduct any heat; Figure 10.5 shows that heat conduction through ice is important, and explains how ponds and lakes can freeze over in cold weather.

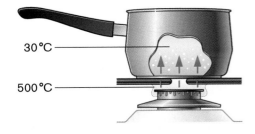

Figure 10.4 When heating water on a stove, heat must travel from the flame or hot-plate to the water. It travels through the metal base of the pan, because the metal is a good conductor. There is a temperature difference between the two sides of the metal, and this is what causes the heat to flow.

30 °C

500 °C

Thermal energy transfers | 149

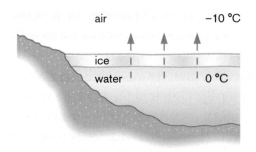

Figure 10.5 Although ice is a good insulator, it does conduct *some* heat. In cold weather, the surface of a lake freezes over. Now there is a temperature difference between the water below the ice and the air above it. Heat gradually conducts upwards from the water, so that it cools and freezes. The layer of ice becomes thicker, and this makes the rate of heat loss decrease. Deep ponds are not likely to freeze solid even in the depths of winter, so animals and plants survive until spring.

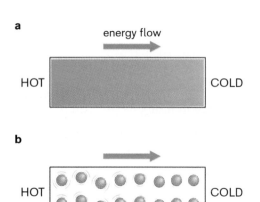

Figure 10.6 Conduction of heat in non-metals. **a** A glass rod, heated at one end and cooled at the other. Heat travels from the hot end to the cold end. **b** Energy is transferred because the vibrating atoms jostle one another. This shares energy between neighbouring atoms. The result is a flow of energy from the hot end to the cold end.

Explaining conduction in non-metals

Both metals and non-metals conduct heat. Metals are generally much better conductors than non-metals, and we need different explanations of conduction for these two types of material. We will start with non-metals.

Picture a long glass rod (Figure 10.6a). One end is being heated, and the other end is cold. So there is a temperature difference between the two ends, and heat flows down the rod. What is going on inside the rod?

We will picture the atoms that make up the glass as shown in Figure 10.6b. (They are shown as being identical, and fairly regularly arranged, but they are not really like this.) At the hot end of the rod, the atoms are vibrating a lot; at the cold end, they are vibrating much less. As they vibrate, the atoms jostle their neighbours. This process results in each atom sharing its energy with its neighbouring atoms. Atoms with a lot of energy end up with less; those with a little energy end up with more. The jostling gradually transfers energy from the atoms at the hot end to those at the cold end. Energy is steadily transferred down the rod, from hot to cold.

This is the mechanism by which poor conductors (such as glass, ice and plastic) conduct heat. It is also the mechanism in diamond, where the carbon atoms are tightly bonded to their neighbours. Any slight extra vibration of one atom is rapidly shared with its neighbours, and soon spreads through the whole piece of material.

Liquids can also conduct heat in this way, because the particles of which they are made are in close contact with one another. However, convection (see the next section of this chapter) is often more important than conduction in the transfer of heat through a liquid.

Explaining conduction in metals

Metals are good conductors of heat. They are also good conductors of electricity, and this gives us a clue to how they conduct heat.

If we look at the arrangement of atoms in a metal, we see the important difference between metals and non-metals (Figure 10.7a). In a metal, there are many tiny particles called **electrons** between the atoms; each atom has lost one (or more) electron. Electrons have a negative electric charge; an atom that has lost an electron is a positive **ion** (with a positive electric charge). The electrons in a metal are sometimes known as **free electrons**, because they have escaped from the atoms of the metal and are free to move about inside the metal. (They are also sometimes known as **conduction electrons**, because they are responsible for the conduction of heat and electricity.)

An electric current is a flow of these free electrons through a metal; there is more about this in Chapters 17 and 18. Because free electrons can carry energy, they can also transfer heat through a piece of metal. Here is how this happens.

a

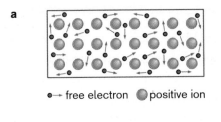

●→ free electron ● positive ion

b

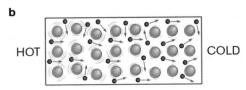

HOT   COLD

Figure 10.7 Conduction of heat in metals.
a Inside a metal, there are positively charged
ions and free electrons. In a typical metal,
there is one free electron for each ion. The free
electrons move randomly through the metal.
b Heat is transferred through the metal by the
free electrons. They collide with vibrating ions
at the hot end, gaining energy. They lose
energy when they collide with the ions at the
cold end.

Free electrons are constantly moving about inside a metal. As they
do so, they collide with one another, and with the vibrating ions of the
metal. Each collision results in a sharing of energy. Now picture a metal
rod that is hot at one end and cold at the other (Figure 10.7b). The ions
at the hot end are vibrating more than those at the cold end, because
they have more energy. The free electrons collide with these ions and
gain energy – they move slightly faster. As they move randomly
through the metal, they share their extra energy with any other electrons or ions with which they collide. When they collide with ions at
the cold end, they give energy to the ions, which start to vibrate more.
The overall result is that energy is transferred by the electrons from the
hot end of the metal to the cold end.

In a metal, energy is transferred partly by the free electrons, and
partly by the vibrating ions as they jostle their neighbours. In pure
metals, most of the energy is conducted by the electrons.

About heat flow

We have talked about 'heat' travelling through a conductor. (We could
have used the terms 'heat flow' or 'thermal energy flow' instead.) It is
important to think what we mean by this.

If we picture energy being conducted through a material, from a hot
part to a colder part, we might say that 100 J of heat passes through
each second. Here, we are not thinking about what is going on at the
level of the atoms, ions and electrons. The kinetic model gives us a
microscopic picture of the same energy transfer. The atoms (or ions
and electrons) at the hot end of a piece of material have more energy.
This energy is shared throughout the material, because the particles
interact with one another through collisions.

This spreading of energy through a material happens in a random
way. Atoms jostle one another randomly; free electrons move randomly through a metal. The outcome of this randomness is a non-random
sharing out of energy, so that energy moves from hotter places to
colder ones. If you heat one end of a metal bar and then wrap it in
insulating material, the energy will soon share itself within the bar so
that the whole bar reaches the same, uniform temperature.

? **Questions**

10.1 **a** Name a good conductor of heat (a thermal conductor).
  b Name a good thermal insulator.

10.2 What is needed for heat to flow through a conductor?

10.3 Which will conduct heat better, a long thin copper rod or a
  short fat one?

10.4 Look at Table 10.1. Which will feel colder to the touch,
  marble or polystyrene?

? Questions continued

10.5 Metals are good conductors of heat. What else can they conduct well?

10.6 a What particles in a metal make it a good conductor of heat?

 b What other particles are there in a metal?

 c What charge does each type of particle have?

10.2 Convection

'Hot air rises.' This is a popular saying, one of the few ideas from physics that almost everyone who has studied a little science can remember. Hot air balloons (Figure 10.8) make use of this idea.

When air is heated, its density decreases (it expands). Since it is less dense than its surroundings, it then floats upwards, just as a cork floats upwards if you hold it under water and then release it. In the case of a hot air balloon, the air in the balloon, plus the balloon fabric itself, plus the basket that hangs below, complete with occupants, must altogether have an average density less than that of the surrounding colder air.

The rising of hot air is just one example of **convection**. Hot air can rise because air is a fluid, and convection is a process that can happen in any fluid (liquid or gas). Figure 10.9 shows how a **convection current** can be observed in water. Above the flame, water is heated and

Figure 10.8 This mass launch of hot air balloons took place in Bristol, England. The uninflated balloons lie on the ground (bottom right). As hot air is blown into them, they start to inflate. Eventually, they are sufficiently light that they rise up into the air. The burners have to be switched on periodically to ensure that they stay fully inflated.

Figure 10.9 Because water is clear and colourless, it can be difficult to see how the water moves to form a convection current. Crystals of potassium manganate act as a purple dye to show up the movement of the water.

expands. Now its density is less than that of the surrounding water, and it floats upwards; the purple dye shows how it moves. Colder water, which is more dense, flows in to replace it.

A convection current is a movement of a fluid, which carries energy from a warmer place to a cooler one. This highlights an important difference between convection and conduction.

- In *convection*, energy is transferred through a material from a warmer place to a cooler place *by the movement of the material itself.*
- In *conduction*, energy is transferred through a material from a warmer place to a cooler place *without the material itself moving.*

Convection currents help to share energy between warm and cold places. If you are sitting in a room with an electric heater, energy will be moving around the room from the heater as a result of convection currents, rising from the heater. You are likely to be the source of convection currents yourself, since your body is usually warmer than your surroundings – see Figure 10.10a. This is made use of by many biting insects, for example bed bugs. They crawl across the bedroom ceiling, and can detect a sleeping person below by finding the warmest spot on the ceiling. Then they drop straight down on the sleeper. This is a lot easier than crawling about on top of the bedding.

Cold objects also produce convection currents. You may have noticed cold water sinking below an ice cube in a drink. The freezing compartment is positioned at the top of the refrigerator, so that cold air will sink to the bottom (Figure 10.10b). Warm air rises to be re-chilled.

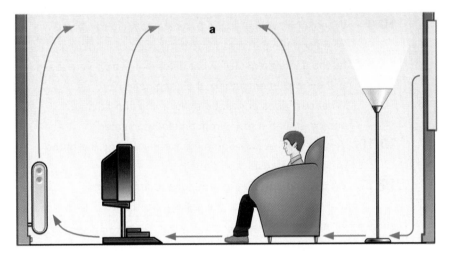
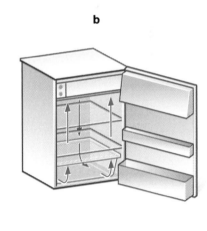

Figure 10.10 **a** Convection currents rise above the warm objects in a room. **b** In a fridge, cold air sinks from the freezing compartment. If the freezer was at the bottom, cold air would remain there and the items at the top would not be cooled.

At the start of this chapter, we discussed the ears of elephants (Figure 10.2). These are large, to provide a big surface area for heat to escape. The hot ear flaps warm the nearby air, which then carries the heat away as a convection current. By flapping its ears, the elephant can rid itself more quickly of the hot air. This is **forced convection**. You may come across another example when you use a computer. The components in the computer's electronic circuits produce unwanted heat, which must be helped to escape if the computer is not to overheat. A small fan starts to turn as soon as the computer is switched on.

This blows away the warm air around the components, helping to keep them cool. If you block up the ventilation slots on the sides (or front and back) of the computer, it will overheat. Computer monitors also have ventilation slots, but these rely on natural convection to allow heat to escape.

Explaining convection

We have already seen that convection results from the expansion of a fluid when it is heated. Expansion means an increase in volume whilst mass stays constant; hence, density decreases. A less dense material is lighter, and is pushed upwards by the surrounding denser material.

The particles in the hotter fluid have more kinetic energy – they move around faster. As they flow from place to place, they take this energy with them.

Convection depends on gravity. Without gravity, the denser fluid would not sink to replace the rising hotter fluid. (Without gravity, there *is* no 'upwards' or 'downwards'.) In a spacecraft in Earth orbit, everything is weightless. As a consequence, a candle flame does not have its normal pointed shape, caused by hot gases rising from it. Instead, the flame is spherical.

? Questions

10.7 'A thermal energy transfer by means of the motion of a fluid.' Is this a description of conduction or convection?

10.8 When a gas is heated, its particles gain energy. If you could see the particles of a hot gas and of a cold gas (at the same pressure), what difference would you see in:
a their movement and **b** their separation?

10.9 What part does convection play in the spreading of energy around a room from an electric heater?

10.10 Write a brief explanation of convection, using the terms *expansion*, *density* and *gravity*.

10.11 Why would it not be a good idea to fit an electric convector heater near the ceiling in a room?

10.3 Radiation

At night, when it is dark, you can see much farther than during the day. In the daytime, the most distant object you are likely to be able to see is the Sun, about 150 million kilometres away. At night, you can see much farther, to the distant stars. The most distant object visible to the naked eye is the Andromeda galaxy, about 20 000 million million million million kilometres away.

The light that reaches us from the Sun and other stars travels to us through space in the form of **electromagnetic radiation**. This radiation travels as electromagnetic waves. It travels over vast distances, following a straight line through empty space. As well as light, the Earth is bathed in other forms of electromagnetic radiation from the Sun, including infrared and ultraviolet. If we only received visible light from the Sun, the Earth would be a lot colder. On a sunny day, with the Sun directly overhead, we receive about 1 kW of power from the Sun on each square metre of the Earth's surface – that's 1000 joules each second.

The hotter an object, the more infrared radiation it gives out. You can use this idea to help you in doing a bit of detective work. Outside the house, a car is parked. How long has it been there? Hold your hands close to the engine compartment to see if you can detect heat radiating from it. Inside the house, the lights are out. Hold your hand close to the light bulb. Can you detect radiation? This would tell you that it was recently lit up.

Our skin detects the infrared radiation produced by a hot object. Nerve cells buried just below the surface respond to heat. You notice this if you are out of doors on a sunny day.

Here are the characteristics of infrared radiation that we have touched on so far.

- It is noticeably produced by warm or hot objects.
- It is a form of electromagnetic radiation.
- It travels through empty space (and through air) in the form of waves.
- It travels in straight lines.
- It warms an object that absorbs it.
- It is invisible to the naked eye.
- It can be detected by nerve cells in the skin.

Figure 10.11 shows another way of detecting infrared radiation, using a heat-sensitive camera. This image of a person shows that the camera is very sensitive to slight differences in temperature between different parts of the body. Figure 10.12 shows how the police may use such a camera, to detect people and cars at night. They are warmer than their surroundings, and so they show up well against the background.

Picturing infrared radiation

If you hold an object such as an iron nail in a Bunsen flame, and heat it, its appearance will gradually change. It will start to glow, first dull red, then bright orange, and perhaps eventually bright yellow. Its colour is an indication of its temperature. If you could heat it further, it would eventually glow white hot.

Take it out of the flame and it will cool down again. Its colour will change back through orange to red, and then it will no longer emit light. However, it will still be emitting invisible infrared radiation. The

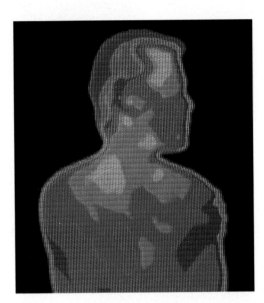

Figure 10.11 An infrared-sensitive camera was used to make this photograph of a person. Slight variations in body temperature show up as different colours. The brain is a great consumer of energy, and the head can be seen to be hotter than the rest of the body.

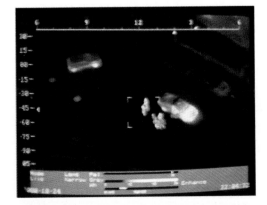

Figure 10.12 This photo was made at night from a police helicopter, using an infrared camera. It shows a group of people standing next to a car. Notice how warm the car is compared with the parked cars in the top right of the picture.

hotter the object, the more infrared radiation it emits. We picture its atoms vibrating and, as they do so, giving out infrared radiation (Figure 10.13a). A hot object loses energy to its surroundings by radiation, and so it cools.

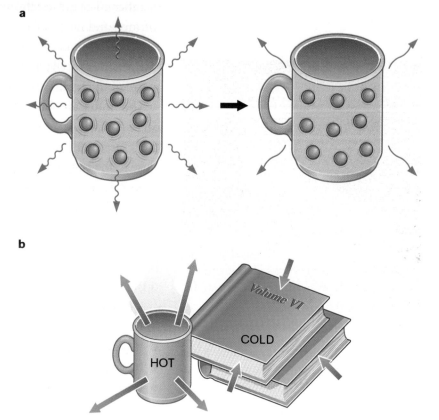

Figure 10.13 **a** As a hot object cools, its atoms vibrate less. They are losing energy to their surroundings as infrared radiation. **b** The surroundings of an object also give out infrared radiation. If the surroundings are cooler than the object, there is a net flow of energy from the object to the surroundings.

It is important here to think about the atoms that make up the surrounding objects. They, too, are vibrating and giving out radiation. However, if the surroundings are cooler than the object, they will be giving out less energy than they receive. The result is that the object gives out more energy than it receives; and the surroundings receive more energy than they give out. Hence there is an overall transfer of energy from the hot object to the colder one (Figure 10.13b), and the hot object cools down whilst the surroundings become warmer.

This is a rather strange idea to appreciate. Look around the room you are in now. Everything is emitting infrared radiation. You are probably warmer than the furniture, so there is a flow of energy from you to the furniture. If you have a hot drink nearby, some infrared radiation is spreading from you to the drink, but more is spreading from the drink to you.

All of the objects around us are constantly emitting infrared radiation. They don't get colder and colder, because they are also absorbing radiation from each other. Human beings don't cool down (whilst they are alive) because chemical reactions inside our bodies are steadily releasing energy to keep us warm and because we insulate our bodies against too much heat loss.

We can relate these ideas back to the idea of the absolute zero of temperature (Chapter 9). At absolute zero (0 K), the particles of a material have virtually zero energy. They emit no infrared radiation. As the material is heated, its particles emit increasing amounts of infrared radiation. The greater the temperature (measured on the Kelvin scale), the more infrared radiation is emitted.

Good absorbers, good emitters

On a hot, sunny day, car drivers may park their cars with a sunshield behind the windscreen (Figure 10.14). Such a sunscreen is usually white (or another light colour) because this reflects away light and infrared radiation, which would make the car get uncomfortably hot. The black plastic parts of the car (such as the dashboard) are very good absorbers of infrared, and they can become too hot to touch. On a hot day, you may also have noticed how the black surface of a tarred (metalled) road emits heat. Black surfaces readily absorb infrared radiation; they are also good emitters.

It is the surface that determines whether an object absorbs or reflects infrared radiation.

- A surface that is a good reflector is a poor absorber.
- A good absorber is also a good emitter.
- Shiny or white surfaces are the best reflectors (the worst absorbers).
- Matt black surfaces are the best absorbers (the worst reflectors).

The radiators that are part of a central heating system are often painted white. This might seem to be a bad idea, because white surfaces are poor emitters of heat. However, the paint or enamel that is used on such radiators is special. It is a good emitter of infrared radiation, and, if viewed with an infrared camera, it looks black. Furthermore, the energy from 'radiators' is transferred mainly by convection rather than by radiation.

Radiation and 'heat'

Now that we have discussed infrared radiation, we can see another reason why we have to be careful about our use of the word *heat*. We have seen three different ways of talking about heat energy moving around:

Conduction – in which energy is passed along by particles jostling their neighbours, or by free electrons moving through a metal.
Convection – in which the particles of a fluid themselves move around, carrying their energy with them.
Radiation – in which energy is transferred in the form of electromagnetic waves.

In all three cases, energy is transferred from a hotter place to a cooler one, but how we picture the energy flow is very different, particularly in the case of radiation. There is more about infrared and the other forms of electromagnetic radiation in Chapter 15.

Figure 10.14 A sunscreen reflects away unwanted radiation, which would otherwise make the car unbearably hot.

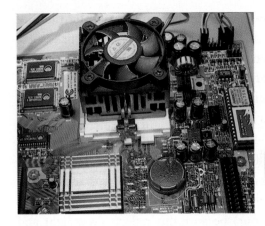

Figure 10.15 A heat sink is attached to the central processing unit of this computer. The CPU must not overheat or it will fail. The heat sink is made of metal, to conduct heat away readily. Its fins give it a large surface, to maximise contact with the air and so to increase convection. A fan is often included for forced convection. The surface of the sink is matt black, so that heat is radiated efficiently away.

Figure 10.15 shows a 'heat sink' attached to an electronic component (the central processing unit, or CPU) in a computer. This is designed to make good use of what we know about conduction, convection and radiation to remove as much heat as possible from the CPU, to avoid any problem of overheating.

Questions

10.12 By which of the following means can energy be transferred through the vacuum of space?
conduction, convection, radiation

10.13 On Earth, we receive visible light from the Sun. Name two other forms of electromagnetic radiation that we receive from the Sun.

10.14 If an object's temperature is increased, what happens to the rate at which it emits infrared radiation?

10.15 At what temperature does an object stop emitting infrared radiation?

10.16 What happens to the temperature of an object when it absorbs infrared radiation?

10.17 This book is constantly emitting infrared radiation. Why does it not get colder and colder?

10.18 Your body is constantly emitting infrared radiation. Why does it not get colder and colder?

10.19 **a** Which is a better absorber of infrared radiation, a matt black surface or a shiny black surface?
b Which is a better emitter of infrared?
c Which is a better reflector?

10.4 Effective insulation

Hot objects have a lot of internal energy. As we have seen above, energy tends to escape from a hot object, spreading to its cooler surroundings by conduction, convection and radiation. This can be a great problem. We may use a lot of energy (and money) to heat our homes during cold weather, and the energy simply escapes. We eat food to supply the energy we need to keep our bodies warm, but energy escapes from us at a rate of roughly 100 watts (100 J/s).

Because of this tendency to escape, internal energy is not a good way to store energy. A lump of coal stores chemical energy for millions of years. Uranium stores nuclear energy for billions of years. Water can be retained behind a dam and released when we want it. But a hot object (such as water in a tank) loses energy automatically.

To retain the internal energy in something that is hotter than its surroundings, we need to insulate it. Knowing about conduction, convection and radiation can help us to design effective insulation.

Home insulation

A well-insulated house can avoid a lot of energy wastage during cold weather. Insulation can also help to prevent the house from becoming uncomfortably hot during warm weather. Figure 10.16 shows some ways in which a building can be insulated, and more details of these are listed in Table 10.2.

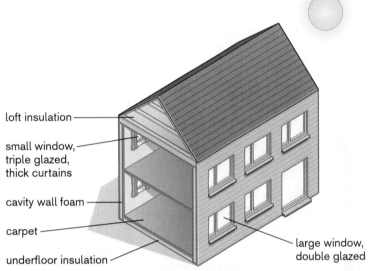

loft insulation

small window, triple glazed, thick curtains

cavity wall foam

carpet

underfloor insulation

large window, double glazed

Figure 10.16 This house has been well designed to reduce the amount of fuel needed to keep it warm. The windows on the sunny side are large, so that the rooms benefit from direct radiation from the Sun. The windows on the other side are small, so that little energy escapes through them.

Method	Why it works
Thick curtains, draught excluders	Cold air is prevented from entering and warm air from leaving
Loft and underfloor insulating materials	Conduction of heat through floors and ceilings is prevented
Double and triple glazing of windows	Vacuum between glass panes cuts out losses by conduction and convection
Cavity walls	Heat losses by conduction through the walls are prevented
Foam or rockwool in wall cavity	Heat losses by convection in the cavity are reduced

Table 10.2 Ways of retaining energy in a house.

Double-glazed windows usually have a vacuum between the two panes of glass. This means that energy can only escape by radiation, since conduction and convection both require a material. Modern houses are built with cavity walls, with an air gap between the two layers of bricks. It is impossible to have a vacuum in the cavity, and convection currents can transfer energy across the gap – see Figure 10.17a. Filling the cavity with foam means that a small amount of energy is lost by conduction, although the foam material is a very poor

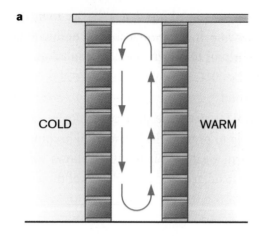

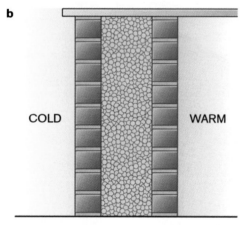

Figure 10.17 **a** A cavity wall reduces heat loss by conduction, because air is a good insulator. However, a convection current can transfer energy from the inner wall to the outer. **b** Filling the cavity with foam or mineral (glass or rock) wool prevents convection currents from forming.

conductor. However, this does stop convection currents from flowing (Figure 10.17b), so there is an overall benefit.

Hot water tanks should be well insulated. It is common to heat the water in the morning and the evening, when most hot water is likely to be needed. Some people argue that it is best to keep the water hot throughout the day, because allowing the water to cool is a waste of energy, and more energy will be needed to warm it up again in the evening. Does this make sense?

The hotter the water, the greater the rate at which energy escapes from it. Even the best-insulated tank loses some energy by conduction. By keeping the water hot all day, heat will escape more rapidly, and the total amount of energy that is lost will be greater. So it is more wasteful to keep the water hot throughout the day. [In fact, the most energy-efficient practice is to heat the water when you need it, and only to heat the amount you are going to need. Then there is no hot water being stored, and losing energy, all the time.]

Questions

10.20 List as many features as you can which can contribute to the insulation of a house in a cold climate. For each, state whether it reduces heat loss by conduction, convection or radiation.

10.21 Why do cold-blooded animals eat less food than warm-blooded ones?

10.22 Why is it important to wear a hat on a very cold day?

10.23 Why is the Moon colder than the Earth?

10.5 Specific heat capacity

To make a hot drink, you need to bring some water to the boil, i.e. increase its temperature. It is sensible to heat just the right amount of water. If you put too much in the kettle or pan, you will be wasting energy. The amount of energy you need to supply to boil the water depends on:

● the mass of the water;
● the desired increase in temperature.

In order to calculate how much energy must be supplied to boil a certain mass of water, we need to know one other fact:

● it takes 4200 J to raise the temperature of 1 kg of water by 1 °C.

Another way to express this is to say:

The **specific heat capacity** of water is 4200 J per kg °C (4200 J/kg°C).

> The specific heat capacity of a substance is the energy required to raise the temperature of 1 kg of the substance by 1 °C.

The cold water from the tap may be at a temperature of 20°C. To make your hot drink, you have to provide enough energy to heat it to 100°C. Its temperature must increase by 80°C. The amount of energy required to heat 2 kg of water by 80°C is $2 \times 4200 \times 80\,J = 672\,000\,J$.

We can write this as a formula. The energy required to raise the temperature of a certain mass of substance is given by:

> energy required = mass of substance × specific heat capacity
> × increase in temperature

Worked example 1 shows how to use this formula in more detail.

Worked example 1

A domestic hot water tank contains 200 kg of water at 20°C. How much energy must be supplied to heat this water to 70°C? [Specific heat capacity of water = 4200 J/kg °C]

- *Step 1* Calculate the required increase in temperature:

  increase in temperature = 70°C − 20°C = 50°C

- *Step 2* Write down the other quantities needed to calculate the energy:

  mass of water = 200 kg
  specific heat capacity of water = 4200 J/kg °C

- *Step 3* Write down the formula for energy required, substitute values, and calculate the result:

  energy required = mass × specific heat capacity
  × increase in temperature
  = 200 kg × 4200 J/kg °C × 50°C
  = 42 000 000 J = 42 MJ

So 42 MJ are required to heat the water to 70°C.

The meaning of specific heat capacity

Energy is needed to raise the temperature of any material. The energy is needed to increase the internal energy of the particles of the material. In solids, the particles vibrate more; in gases, the particles move about faster; in liquids, it is a bit of both.

We can compare different materials by considering standard amounts (1 kg), and a standard increase in temperature (1°C). Different materials require different amounts of energy to raise the temperature of 1 kg by 1°C. In other words, they have different specific heat capacities (s.h.c.). Table 10.3 shows the values of s.h.c. for a variety of materials.

From Table 10.3, you can see that there is quite a wide range of values. The s.h.c. of steel, for example, is one-tenth that of water. This means that, if you supplied equal amounts of energy to 1 kg of steel and 1 kg of water, the steel's temperature would rise ten times as much.

Type of material	Material	Specific heat capacity (J/kg °C)	Type of material	Material	Specific heat capacity (J/kg °C)
metals	aluminium	910	*non-metals*	polythene	2300
	steel	420		ice	2100
	copper	385		nylon	1700
	gold	300		glass	670
	lead	130			
liquids	water	4200	*gases*	methane	2200
	sea-water	3900		water	2020
	ethanol	2500		vapour	(at 100 °C)
	olive oil	1970		air	1000

Table 10.3 Specific heat capacities of a variety of materials.

The specific heat capacity of water

Water is an unusual substance. As you can see from Table 10.3, it has a high value of s.h.c. compared to other materials. This has important consequences.

● It takes a lot of energy to heat up water.
● Hot water takes a long time to cool down.

The consequences of this can be seen in our climate. In the hot months of summer, the land warms up quickly (low s.h.c.) whilst the sea warms up only slowly. In the winter, the sea cools gradually whilst the land cools rapidly. People who live a long way from the sea (in the continental interior of North America or Eurasia, for example) experience freezing winters and roasting summers. People who live in coastal areas (such as western Europe) are protected from climatic extremes because the sea acts as a reservoir of heat in the winter, and stays relatively cool in the summer.

? Questions

10.24 Look at Table 10.3.

    a Which of the materials listed has the greatest specific heat capacity?

    b In general, do metals or non-metals have greater values of s.h.c.?

10.25 In an experiment, 5 kg blocks of two different metals, A and B, are heated at the same rate. The temperature of metal A rises at twice the rate of that of metal B. Which metal has the greater specific heat capacity?

10.26 Mental arithmetic: The specific heat capacity of gold is 300 J/kg °C. How much energy is needed to raise the temperature of 2 kg of gold by 10°C?

Questions continued

10.27 When a dishwasher has finished washing, its contents are very hot. The china plates cool down very slowly, the metal cutlery more quickly.

  a Use the idea of specific heat capacity to explain this.

  b What other factors might affect the rate at which the different items cool down?

Summary

◆ Metals are good conductors of heat. Non-metals are poor thermal conductors (good insulators).

◆ In metals, free electrons carry energy throughout the material. In both metals and non-metals, energy is transferred between neighbouring ions or atoms.

◆ Convection currents form in fluids when the fluid is heated. The fluid expands, becomes less dense, and floats upwards. Colder, denser fluid flows in to replace it.

◆ Radiation is the transfer of energy by infrared waves, a form of electromagnetic radiation.

◆ All bodies radiate infrared radiation. The hotter they are, the greater the rate at which they radiate.

◆ Matt black surfaces are good absorbers and emitters of infrared radiation. Shiny or white surfaces are poor absorbers and emitters. A good absorber is a poor reflector.

◆ Energy must be supplied to raise the temperature of a material. The amount of energy required to raise the temperature of 1 kg of a material by 1°C is its specific heat capacity.

◆ The energy required to raise the temperature of a certain mass of a substance is given by

energy required = mass × specific heat capacity
× increase in temperature

The gas laws

Topics in this chapter

◆ pressure, volume and temperature of a gas

◆ Boyle's law

◆ Charles' law

◆ the pressure law

Figure 11.1 Your lungs provide the pressure needed to blow up a balloon. If the rubber was thicker, it would be too stiff for your lungs to blow up; if it was thinner, the air would escape too quickly through microscopic holes in the material.

When you blow up a balloon (Figure 11.1), your lungs provide the pressure to push air into the balloon. Tying the neck of the balloon traps the air. The pressure inside the balloon is greater than the pressure of the atmosphere outside. This pressure has to do two things: it has to push back atmospheric pressure and it has to stretch the rubber of the balloon.

If you blow up a balloon with a gas cylinder that has a pressure gauge fitted, you will see that the pressure needed is about 10% greater than atmospheric pressure. Car and cycle tyres are also inflated, but the pressure in these is usually much greater. The pressure inside car tyres is usually about three times atmospheric pressure. The pressure in the tyres on a large truck may be six times atmospheric; the same is true for the tyres of mountain bikes (all-terrain bikes). They make a terrific bang when they burst.

11.1 Properties of a gas

It is relatively easy to think about how to make measurements of a solid object such as a book or a stone. We could easily measure its mass, volume, temperature and so on. It is harder to picture a gas, because gases do not have a fixed volume – they fill up the container they are put in. If they are not in a container, they may spread out in all directions. It is easier if we think about a fixed amount of gas, and picture it in a container – that is why we started this chapter by thinking about the air trapped inside balloons and tyres.

What properties could we measure for a fixed mass of gas, such as the air trapped inside the flask shown in Figure 11.2? We will consider five.

Figure 11.2 **a** This glass flask contains 1 litre of air at atmospheric pressure. **b** When the air is pumped out, the mass of the flask is less, showing that air has mass.

1 The air in the flask has **mass**. The flask is sealed and weighed; then the air is pumped out and the flask re-weighed. The mass of the flask is found to be less. For a flask with a volume of 1 litre, its mass will decrease by about 1.3 g.

2 The air in the flask has **volume**. The air takes up the volume of the inside of the flask.

3 The air has **density**. As with any material, we can calculate its density from

$$\text{density} = \frac{\text{mass}}{\text{volume}}$$

4 The air exerts **pressure** on the walls of its container. If the air was compressed into the flask, it would exert a pressure greater than atmospheric pressure, and might blow the stopper out of the top of the flask.

5 The air has **temperature**. Heating the flask would transfer energy to the trapped air and it would get hotter. Putting it in the refrigerator would remove energy from the air, and its temperature would decrease.

Explaining the properties

In this chapter, we will look at experiments that show how these properties of a gas are related to each other. First, however, we will think about how we can relate these properties to the kinetic model of matter. This will make it easier to understand the laws that relate one property of a gas to another.

Figure 11.3a shows the particles that make up a gas. The gas is contained in a cubical box; the volume of the box is the volume of the gas. The gas has mass because each of its particles has mass. If we weighed all the particles individually and added up their masses, we would find the mass of the gas.

Figure 11.3 **a** The particles of a gas move around inside its container, bumping into the sides. **b** Doubling the number of particles means twice the mass, twice the density and twice the pressure. **c** At a higher temperature, the particles move faster. They have more kinetic energy, and this is what the thermometer records as a higher temperature.

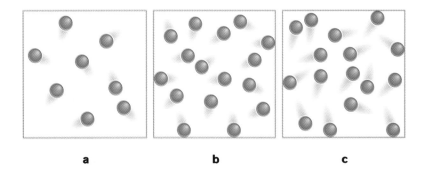

a　　　　　　　b　　　　　　　c

Figure 11.3b shows the same box with twice as many gas particles in it. The mass of the gas is doubled, and so is its density. A gas exerts pressure on the walls of its container because its particles are constantly colliding with the walls. As each particle bounces off the wall, its momentum changes because its velocity changes direction. Hence the particles exert a force on the walls. Compare Figures 11.3a and b: with twice as many particles, there are twice as many collisions, so the pressure is doubled.

Figure 11.3c shows the same amount of gas as in Figure 11.3b but at a higher temperature. The particles are moving faster; when they collide with the thermometer, they transfer more energy to it, and the level of the mercury rises.

The thermometer reading tells us about the average kinetic energy of the particles. (Remember that they don't all move at the same speed.) The more kinetic energy the particles have, the higher the temperature of the gas. You may recall from Chapter 9 that absolute zero is the lowest possible temperature, the zero of the Kelvin scale. At absolute zero, the particles of a gas have almost zero kinetic energy. As a gas is heated up from absolute zero, and the average kinetic energy of its particles increases, the absolute temperature rises. More exactly

> The average kinetic energy of the particles of a gas is proportional to its absolute temperature.

In other words, if one gas is at twice the absolute temperature of another gas, its particles are twice as energetic.

Note that the particles that make up the walls of the container are also vibrating. As the gas particles collide with the walls, they share their kinetic energy. If a cold gas is put in a hot container, the particles of the walls will have more energy than the gas particles. As they collide, energy will be transferred to the gas particles. The gas gets hotter and the container gets colder.

? Questions

11.1 A small sample of helium gas contains 5×10^{12} atoms. Each atom has a mass of 6.7×10^{-27} kg. What is the mass of the gas?

11.2 Look at Figure 11.3a. If half of the particles of the gas were removed from the container (and nothing else was changed), how would the following properties of the gas change?
   a mass,   **b** volume,   **c** density,   **d** pressure,
   e temperature

11.3 Gas A is at a temperature of 200 K; gas B is at 400 K. What can you say about the kinetic energies of their particles?

11.4 Use the kinetic model of a gas to predict what will happen to the pressure on the walls of the container shown in Figure 11.3a if the gas is heated. Explain your answer.

11.2 Boyle's law

Figure 11.4 shows two methods for investigating what happens when the pressure on a fixed mass of gas is increased.

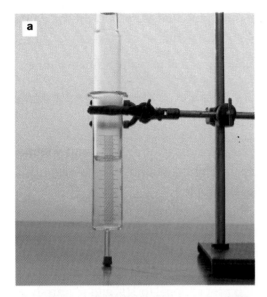

The gas syringe (Figure 11.4a) is similar to the syringes used for giving injections, only larger. The lower end is sealed to trap a fixed mass of gas inside the syringe. The plunger slides smoothly up and down, without allowing any air to escape. The volume of the gas can be read from the scale on the barrel. When weights are placed on top of the plunger, they increase the pressure on the gas and squash it so that it occupies a smaller volume. The force pressing down on the gas is provided by the weight of the plunger and the weights, and by the pressure of the atmosphere pushing down on the plunger. The pressure can be calculated as follows:

$$\text{pressure on gas} = \frac{\text{weight of (plunger + weights)}}{\text{cross-section area of barrel}} + \frac{\text{atmospheric}}{\text{pressure}}$$

In the hydraulic equipment (Figure 11.4b), some air is trapped inside the vertical glass tube. The oil in the bottom of the apparatus can be compressed with a pump, so that it pushes up inside the tube, compressing the air. The volume of the air can be read from the scale. The pressure exerted on the air by the oil can be read from the dial gauge.

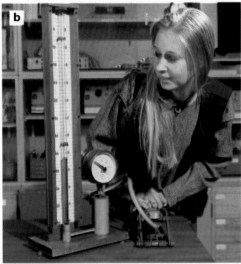

From both of these sets of apparatus, it is obvious that increasing the pressure on a gas decreases its volume. Table 11.1 shows some typical results. Can we find a mathematical relationship between the pressure p and the volume V of the gas? The relationship between p and V was investigated by Robert Boyle, an English physicist and chemist. He published his results in 1662. We can state the relationship in at least seven different ways:

1 If the pressure is doubled, the volume is halved. Three times the pressure gives one-third of the volume, and so on.

2 The graph of Figure 11.5a shows that increasing pressure leads to decreasing volume.

3 The figures in Table 11.1 also show this relationship. From the last column in the table, we can see that the quantity 'pressure × volume' is constant, so we can write

$pV =$ constant

Figure 11.4 Two methods for increasing the pressure on a gas. In each, a fixed mass of air is trapped inside the apparatus, and the pressure on it is increased. The volume of the gas can be read from the scale. **a** A gas syringe. **b** A hydraulic apparatus.

Table 11.1 Representative results for a Boyle's law experiment, to show their pattern. The temperature of the gas remains constant throughout.

Pressure, p (Pa)	Volume, V (cm³)	Pressure × volume, pV (Pa × cm³)
100	60	6000
125	48	6000
150	40	6000
200	30	6000
250	24	6000
300	20	6000

4 We can write the same idea in a way that is convenient for doing calculations:

initial pressure × initial volume = final pressure × final volume

or

$$p_1 V_1 = p_2 V_2$$

where p_1 and V_1 are one pair of readings of pressure and volume, and p_2 and V_2 are another pair. This equation is easy to memorise, and is made use of in worked example 1.

5 The graph of Figure 11.5b shows that plotting p against $1/V$ gives a straight-line graph, passing through the origin.

6 Because V decreases as p increases, we say that the two quantities are inversely proportional to one another. We say that 'V is inversely proportional to p' or that 'V is proportional to $1/p$', and we can show this as:

$$V \propto \frac{1}{p}$$

where the symbol $\propto$ means 'is proportional to'. Similarly, p is inversely proportional to V:

$$p \propto \frac{1}{V}$$

7 Finally, we can write the relationship in words:

> The volume of a fixed mass of gas is inversely proportional to its pressure, provided the temperature of the gas remains constant.

This statement is known as **Boyle's law**. It is important to understand why it includes the phrase 'provided the temperature of the gas remains constant'. When a gas is compressed, its temperature rises. We saw why this is in Chapter 9, page 139: the force compressing it does work, and so it transfers energy to the gas. However, in the Boyle's law experiment, the trapped air soon loses energy to its surroundings and cools back down to room temperature. While it is hot, its new pressure is above that predicted by Boyle's law. Only when it cools down will we find that it obeys the relationship pV = constant.

Figure 11.5 Two graphs to represent the results of a Boyle's law experiment. **a** A graph of pressure p against volume V shows that increasing the pressure causes a decrease in the volume. **b** The mathematical relationship between p and $1/V$ can be seen from this graph; since it is a straight line through the origin, we can say that pressure is inversely proportional to volume (and vice versa).

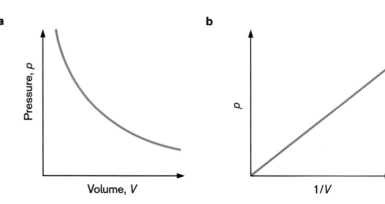

Worked example 1

[This example shows how the equation $p_1 V_1 = p_2 V_2$ can be used to find how the volume of a gas changes when the pressure on it is changed. You can use the same equation to work out how the pressure changes when the volume is changed.]

A piston contains 50 litre of air at a pressure of 120 kPa. What will its volume be if the pressure on it is increased to 400 kPa?

- *Step 1* Write down the initial and final values of the quantities that we know:

  $P_1 = 120\,\text{kPa}$
  $V_1 = 50\,\text{litre}$
  $p_2 = 400\,\text{kPa}$

- *Step 2* Write down the Boyle's law equation and rearrange to make V_2 the subject:

  $$p_1 V_1 = p_2 V_2$$
  $$V_2 = \frac{p_1 V_1}{p_2}$$

- *Step 3* Now substitute values:

  $$V_2 = \frac{120\,\text{kPa} \times 50\,\text{litre}}{400\,\text{kPa}} = 15\,\text{litre}$$

  So the volume of the air is reduced to 15 litre when it is compressed.

Notice an important feature of the equation $p_1 V_1 = p_2 V_2$. It does not matter what units we use for p and V, as long as we use the same units for both values of p (e.g. Pa or kPa), and the same units for both values of V (e.g. m³ or ml or litre).

Units of pressure

The SI unit of pressure is the pascal (Pa). You should recall that 1 Pa = 1 N/m². You may come across another unit for the pressure of a gas, the atmosphere (atm):

one atmosphere (1 atm) ~ 100 000 Pa (100 kPa)

Explaining Boyle's law

The kinetic theory of matter provides a simple explanation of Boyle's law – see Figure 11.6. When the volume of the gas is halved, the same number of particles occupy half the space. If the temperature remains constant then so does their average kinetic energy and therefore their average speed. However, they collide with the walls of the container twice as often. Hence the pressure is doubled.

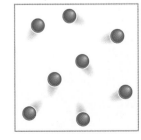

Figure 11.6 With the same number of particles in half the volume, there are twice as many collisions per second with the walls of the container. The result is twice the pressure.

?

Questions

11.5 The pressure on 6 litres of nitrogen gas is doubled at a fixed temperature. What will its volume become?

11.6 What is the meaning of the subscripts 1 and 2 in the equation $p_1 V_1 = p_2 V_2$?

11.7 Mental arithmetic: A container holds 600 litre of air at a pressure of 2 atm. If the pressure on the gas is increased to 5 atm at constant temperature, what will its volume become?

11.8 Draw diagrams of the particles in a gas to explain why, if the volume of the gas is doubled at constant temperature, its pressure is halved.

11.3 Charles' law

Jacques Charles was a French physicist who became interested in ballooning (Figure 11.7). He constructed a balloon of varnished silk and filled it with hydrogen gas. More than 400 000 Parisians came out to watch the balloon on its first (unmanned) flight in 1783. Unfortunately, after it had drifted for 25 km, it landed in a field where it was attacked by labourers with pitchforks and scythes.

Charles' pioneering ballooning exploits were related to his studies in physics. He wanted to know how the volume of a balloon would change if its temperature changed. This was important – it gets colder as you ascend through the atmosphere.

Figure 11.7 Many of the early attempts at balloon flight were carried out in France. This picture shows the first manned balloon flight in November 1783. The fire that provided the hot air was left on the ground as the balloon ascended.

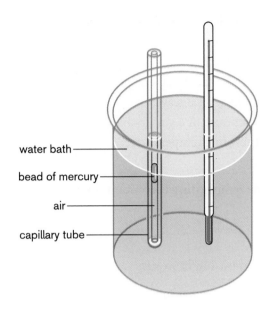

water bath
bead of mercury
air
capillary tube

Figure 11.8 A simple apparatus for investigating how the volume of a gas depends on its temperature. The capillary tube has a very fine, uniform bore. The air under investigation is trapped in the tube by the bead of mercury. As it is heated, the air expands and pushes the mercury further up the tube.

Figure 11.9 Graphs to represent the results of a Charles' law experiment. **a** With temperature varying between 0°C and 100°C, the volume of the gas changes only a little. We can extrapolate (extend) the graph backwards, to lower temperatures. This shows that the gas might be expected to have zero volume at a low temperature. **b** Re-plotting with temperature in kelvins (K) shows that the gas appears to expand from absolute zero. Its volume is proportional to its absolute temperature.

Varying the temperature of a gas

As with the pressure–volume experiment that led to Boyle's law, we have to consider a fixed mass of gas. Figure 11.8 shows a glass capillary tube that has been sealed at one end. A bead of mercury traps a length of air in the tube. The tube can be immersed in water; when the water is heated, the air expands and pushes the mercury up the tube. The length of the air in the tube indicates its volume. The pressure on the air is a combination of two things: atmospheric pressure pressing down on top of the mercury, and the effect of the mercury's own weight. The pressure stays constant throughout the experiment.

This apparatus is only really suitable for making measurements between 0°C and 100°C (using melting ice and boiling water). The volume of the air increases by about one-third as it is warmed over this range. How can we understand what is going on?

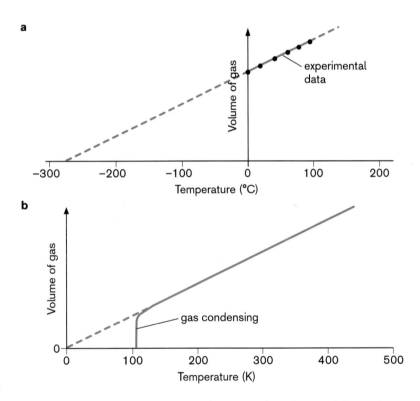

Figure 11.9a shows some typical results. The volume of the gas increases at a slow but steady rate as it is heated. Now, picture what happens if the gas is cooled from 100°C. Its volume decreases; if we could cool it below 0°C, we can imagine that the air would carry on contracting. This is represented by the lower broken line on the graph.

In drawing the broken lines, we say that we are **extrapolating** the graph. This means that we are taking it beyond the range of the available experimental evidence. Extrapolation suggests that eventually the volume of the air will reach zero, at a temperature close to −270°C. This should ring a bell – it is absolute zero, the lowest possible temperature.

By re-drawing the graph, with the temperature scale starting at 0 K (as shown in Figure 11.9b), we get a straight-line graph passing through the origin. As with Boyle's law, we can summarise the relationship between the volume V of a fixed mass of gas at fixed pressure and its absolute temperature T in several ways:

1 Doubling the absolute temperature of a gas doubles its volume.
2 Volume is proportional to absolute temperature:

$$V \propto T$$

3 Volume divided by absolute temperature is constant, so that:

$$\frac{V_1}{T_1} = \frac{V_2}{T_2}$$

4 Finally, we can write the relationship in words:

> The volume of a fixed mass of gas is proportional to its absolute (Kelvin) temperature, provided the pressure of the gas remains constant.

This statement is known as **Charles' law**. Note that in this experiment the pressure of the gas remains constant. We are dealing with three variables, p, V and T, so, in order to find the relationship between two of them (here V and T), we need to keep the third fixed. Changing the pressure of the gas during the experiment would give results that we could not readily interpret.

Of course, we cannot say that if we cool a gas down, it will carry on shrinking until the temperature reaches absolute zero. Something else will happen before this – as shown in Figure 11.9b. The particles of the gas move more and more slowly; the attractive forces between them take over and the particles stick together. The gas turns into a liquid.

Explaining Charles' law

We have found that the volume of a gas increases when it is heated at constant pressure. To use the kinetic theory to explain this, we have to picture the particles of the gas in a container that can expand (Figure 11.10). As the gas is heated, the particles move faster. They push harder on the walls of the container, and push the moveable side upwards. The pressure has remained constant (because there is still the same weight of atmosphere plus the weight of the piston on the moveable wall), so the volume of the gas must increase.

a

b

Figure 11.10 The gas is held in a container, one side of which can move. When the gas is heated, the particles push harder on the walls of the container and gradually the volume increases.

Questions

11.9 What two variable quantities are linked by Charles' law?

11.10 If the temperature of a fixed mass of gas increases from 300 K to 600 K, what will happen to its volume? (The pressure remains constant.)

? Questions continued

11.11 What word is used to mean 'extending a graph beyond the range of the available data'?

11.12 Draw diagrams of the particles in a gas to explain why, if the absolute temperature of the gas is halved at constant pressure, its volume is halved.

11.4 The pressure law

When fire-fighters are on their way to tackle a big blaze, two of the questions they have to consider are: Might there be gas cylinders in the burning building? Is there a danger of an explosion?

Many people use gas stored in cylinders, for a variety of purposes – propane gas for cooking, oxygen in hospitals, acetylene for welding, and so on (Figure 11.11). The gas is stored at high pressure in thick-walled metal cylinders. In the event of a fire, the cylinders may get very hot and explode. Suppose the cylinders are filled and stored at room temperature – that is roughly 20 °C, or about 300 K. In a fire, their temperature may reach 1500 K, five times room temperature. Charles' law tells us that the gas wants to expand to five times its original volume, but it can't. It is trapped inside the cylinders. We can picture the molecules rushing around inside, desperate to get out. They collide more and more violently with the walls of the cylinder, increasing the pressure as they do so. If the cylinder is not strong enough, the gas may burst out. The cylinder has exploded. (For fuel gases like propane and acetylene, there is then the additional danger of a *chemical* explosion, as the hot fuel meets the oxygen in the air and starts to burn.)

In this chapter, we have been thinking about three variable properties of a fixed mass of gas:

- its pressure, p;
- its volume, V;
- its absolute temperature, T.

Boyle's law tells us how p and V are linked (provided T is constant). Charles' law tells us how V and T are linked (provided p is constant). Now we come to a third law, the pressure law, which links the remaining pair of variables, p and T. The relationship between these two can be investigated using the apparatus shown in Figure 11.12.

The flask contains a fixed volume of air. As the water in the bath is heated, the temperature of the air rises; this causes its pressure to rise, as indicated on the pressure gauge. Because the gauge is not submerged in the hot water, we cannot be sure that all of the air reaches the temperature indicated by the thermometer. We hope that the volume of the air remains constant; this should be the case provided that the flask does not expand significantly.

Figure 11.11 These cylinders contain oxygen, used in a hospital for treating patients with breathing problems. They are stored outside the building where they are likely to do less damage in the unlikely event that one explodes.

Figure 11.12 Apparatus for investigating the pressure law. The air in the flask is heated by the water bath. Its pressure is indicated by the dial gauge.

The results of this experiment are represented by the graph shown in Figure 11.13. As with Charles' law, we find that the graph is a straight line, which can be extrapolated back to absolute zero. (You might have guessed this from our discussion of the problems of gas cylinders being heated in a fire.) We can state the relationship between the pressure and absolute temperature of a fixed mass of a gas in the following ways.

1 If the absolute temperature of a gas is doubled, its pressure doubles.
2 The pressure of a gas is proportional to its absolute temperature:

$$p \propto T$$

3 Pressure divided by absolute temperature is constant:

$$\frac{p_1}{T_1} = \frac{p_2}{T_2}$$

4 Finally, we can write the relationship in words:

> The pressure of a fixed mass of gas is proportional to its absolute temperature, providing the volume of the gas remains constant.

This statement is known as **the pressure law**. As with Boyle's law and Charles' law, we have to be careful about when this law applies. If the gas is at a low temperature where it is on the point of condensing, the law will no longer apply.

Figure 11.13

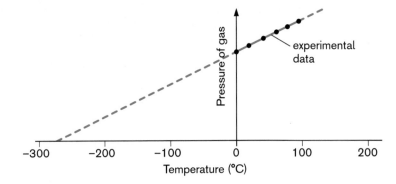

Explaining the pressure law

Raising the temperature of a gas gives energy to its particles. They move around more rapidly, so that they strike the walls of their container with greater force and more often. This increases the average pressure.

Questions

11.13 What two variable quantities are linked by the pressure law?

11.14 Write an equation to represent the pressure law.

11.15 Sketch a graph to represent the pressure law.

11.16 A fixed mass of gas in a rigid container is cooled so that its absolute temperature decreases from 600 K to 300 K. How will its pressure change?

11.17 Draw diagrams to explain why the pressure of a fixed volume of gas increases when its temperature is increased.

11.5 Combining the three gas laws

If a gas obeys all three gas laws, we say that it is an **ideal gas**. We have already seen that real gases can deviate from the gas laws, particularly when they are close to condensing. However, at higher temperatures the behaviour of real gases is predicted with good accuracy by the gas laws. We say that they behave like an ideal gas.

It is often the case that the pressure, temperature and volume of a gas are all changing at the same time. For example, you may have noticed an effect when using a camping gas stove. As the gas comes out of the cylinder, the cylinder gets cold. Condensation forms on the cold cylinder. Any gas is likely to cool as it expands into the air because it has to push the air aside. It does work, and this reduces its energy. So, as the gas comes out of the cylinder, its volume increases but both its pressure and temperature decrease. We can solve problems like this by combining the three equations linking p, V and T into a single equation, the **ideal gas law** (see below),

$$\frac{p_1 V_1}{T_1} = \frac{p_2 V_2}{T_2}$$

Worked example 2 shows how to use this.

Worked example 2

An oxygen cylinder of volume 40 litre is being filled. 2000 litre of oxygen at atmospheric pressure (1 atm) and 20°C are compressed into the cylinder. The cylinder is stored in a cold store at –20°C.
What will be the pressure of the gas in the cylinder?

Look at the figures in the question. The gas is being compressed to 1/50th of its original volume, so according to Boyle's law we might expect its pressure to be 50 atm. However, it is also getting colder, so its pressure will be less than this.

● *Step 1* Write down all the quantities we know; convert temperatures to the Kelvin scale:

$p_1 = 1$ atm
$V_1 = 2000$ litre
$T_1 = 20°C = (20 + 273)\,K = 293\,K$
$p_2 = ?$
$V_2 = 40$ litre
$T_2 = -20°C = (-20 + 273)\,K$
$\quad = 253\,K$

● *Step 2* Rearrange the ideal gas law to make p_2 the subject, substitute and solve:

$$\frac{p_1 V_1}{T_1} = \frac{p_2 V_2}{T_2}$$

$$p_2 = \frac{p_1 V_1 T_2}{T_1 V_2}$$

$$= \frac{1\,\text{atm} \times 2000\,\text{litre} \times 253\,K}{293\,K \times 40\,\text{litre}} = 43.2\,\text{atm}$$

So the pressure of the gas is 43.2 atm. This is somewhat less than 50 atm, as we guessed above.

? **Questions**

11.18 If the pressure and volume of a fixed mass of gas are both increased, will its temperature increase, decrease or stay the same?

11.19 If the pressure of a fixed mass of gas is doubled and its volume is found to have halved, has its temperature increased, decreased or stayed the same?

Summary

◆ Boyle's law states that the volume of a fixed mass of gas is inversely proportional to its pressure, provided the temperature of the gas remains constant:

$$V \propto \frac{1}{p} \quad \text{or} \quad p_1 V_1 = p_2 V_2$$

◆ Charles' law states that the volume of a fixed mass of gas is proportional to its absolute (Kelvin) temperature, provided the pressure of the gas remains constant:

$$V \propto T \quad \text{or} \quad \frac{V_1}{T_1} = \frac{V_2}{T_2}$$

◆ The pressure law states that the pressure of a fixed mass of gas is directly proportional to its absolute temperature, providing the volume of the gas remains constant:

$$p \propto T \quad \text{or} \quad \frac{p_1}{T_1} = \frac{p_2}{T_2}$$

◆ Combining all three gas laws, we have the ideal gas law:

$$\frac{p_1 V_1}{T_1} = \frac{p_2 V_2}{T_2}$$

Further questions

The numbering is continued from the in-chapter questions.

Chapter 6

6.15

Here are some examples of energy resources:

coal   wind   wood   water behind a dam
uranium   tidal energy   sugar

a Explain what is meant by a non-renewable energy resource.

b Classify each resource in the list as 'renewable' or 'non-renewable'.

c Choose one of the renewable energy resources and explain how its energy can be traced back to the Sun.

d Which renewable source cannot be traced back to the Sun's radiation?

6.16

Electricity supplied by solar cells is expensive. This is because, although sunlight is free, the cells themselves are made from sophisticated modern materials that are expensive to produce.

a Explain why solar cells are a suitable choice for powering a spacecraft, but are less likely to be used for providing domestic electricity to consumers in a city such as London or Hong Kong.

b Suggest some other situations in which solar cells would be a good choice, and justify each of your suggestions.

c Why are solar cells often used in conjunction with a battery?

6.17

Wind farms make use of a renewable energy resource and are often suggested as an environmentally friendly way of generating electricity. However, wind energy is described as a dilute resource when compared to coal or uranium.

a Explain what it means to say that wind energy is a *dilute resource.*

b What implications does this have for the design of a wind farm capable of producing large amounts of electricity? What impact can this have on the environment?

c Apart from its environmental impact, what other factors should be considered when deciding where to construct a wind farm?

d Why is it unlikely that a wind farm alone would be chosen to supply all of the electricity needs of a community?

Chapter 7

7.17

What are the energy transformations involved in each of the processes described below?

a Chemicals in the body of a glow worm react together to produce light and heat.

b An electric motor is used to start a computer's disk drive spinning round.

c A wind turbine spins and generates electricity.

d Friction in a car's brakes slows it down.

7.18

Low-energy light bulbs are designed to save energy, but do they also save money? An individual low-energy bulb is more expensive than the filament bulb it replaces; however, it lasts for much longer, typically 10 000 hours. The table shows typical costs, in pence (p).

a Copy the table and complete the first row to calculate

Type of bulb	Cost of one bulb	Number of bulbs needed for 10 000 h	Cost of electricity for 1 h	Total cost of electricity for 10 000 h	Total cost of bulbs plus electricity
low-energy	400 p	1	0.2 p		
filament	50 p	10	1.0 p		

the total cost of using a low-energy bulb for 10 000 hours.

b Complete the second row to calculate the cost of using ten filament bulbs instead of a single low-energy bulb.

c How much money is saved by using a low-energy bulb?

d Suggest reasons people might have for not using low-energy bulbs.

7.19

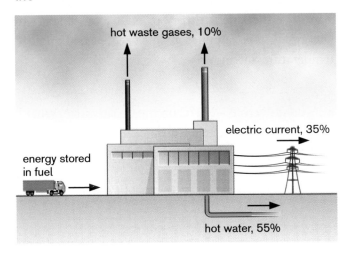

Figure Q7.19

The combined heat and power (CHP) station at Byker in Newcastle-upon-Tyne (see Figure 7.10 on page 106) burns rubbish in order to generate electricity. The diagram above shows the station's energy inputs and outputs.

a What useful energy forms are produced?

b What waste energy is produced?

c What is the station's efficiency?

7.20

Sketch a Sankey diagram to represent energy transformations when a petrol-fuelled car is moving uphill, accelerating as it goes.

7.21

Figure Q7.21

The figure shows an idea for a perpetual motion machine. The car runs on electricity. As it moves along, the air moving past the car turns the generator on the roof. This generates the electricity needed to power the car.

a Explain the energy transformations that are going on here.

b Explain why this idea will not work in practice.

Chapter 8

8.21

An astronaut on the Moon has a mass (including his spacesuit and equipment) of 180 kg. The acceleration due to gravity on the Moon's surface is 1.6 N/kg.

a What is the astronaut's weight on the Moon?

b The astronaut climbs 100 m to the top of a crater. By how much does his gravitational potential energy change?

c Does his GPE increase or decrease?

8.22

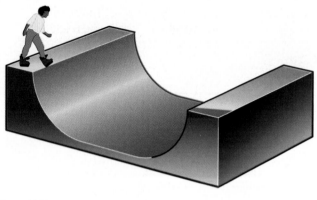

Figure Q8.22

The girl on the skate ramp in the diagram runs down one side of the slope and up the opposite side. She finds that she cannot quite reach the top of the slope, which is level with her starting position.

a What energy transformations are taking place as the girl moves downwards and then upwards?

b Use ideas about energy to suggest how the girl could reach the top of the slope.

8.23

A car of mass 750 kg accelerates away from traffic lights. At the end of the first 100 m, it has reached a speed of 12 m/s. During this time, its engine provides an average forward force of 780 N, and the average force of friction on the car is 240 N.

a Calculate the work done on the car by the force of its engine.

b Calculate the work done by the car against the force of friction.

c Calculate the increase in the car's kinetic energy as it accelerates.

d Explain whether your answers are consistent with the principle of conservation of energy.

8.24

Two boys are estimating each other's power. One runs up some steps; the other times him. Here are their results:

height of one step = 20 cm	number of steps = 36
mass of runner = 45 kg	time taken = 4.2 s

a Calculate the boy's weight. [Earth's gravitational field strength g = 10 N/kg.]

b Calculate the increase in the boy's gravitational potential energy as he climbs the steps.

c Calculate his power. Give your answer in kilowatts (kW).

Chapter 9

9.28

a According to the kinetic theory, matter is made of particles. What are the other fundamental assumptions of the theory?

b According to the kinetic theory of matter, how does the motion of the particles change as a material is heated from a solid to a liquid, and then to a gas?

9.29

As a block of ice melts, its temperature remains constant. Use the kinetic theory of matter to explain why energy must be supplied to melt ice even though its temperature does not rise.

9.30

a Absolute zero is –273 °C on the Celsius scale. What is its value on the Kelvin scale?

b What are the two fixed points on the Celsius scale of temperature?

c What are their values on the Kelvin scale?

Chapter 10

10.28

In cold climates, it is important to keep a house well insulated. Listed below are three ways of insulating a house. For each, explain how it reduces heat loss. In your answers, refer to *conduction, convection* or *radiation*, as appropriate.

a Heavy curtains, when closed, trap air next to a window.

b Shiny metal foil is fitted in the loft, covering the inside of the roof.

c Glass wool is used to fill the gap in the cavity walls.

10.29

Figure Q10.29

The hot water for a house's heating system is piped around the house through copper piping. The figure shows pipes of two different diameters. For the pipes shown, the thickness of the copper is the same.
Heat escapes from the pipes. Explain how you would expect each of the following changes to affect the rate of heat loss from the pipes.

a The temperature of the water is increased.

b The thickness of the copper is decreased.

c Plastic piping is used instead of copper.

d The radius of the pipe is doubled (compare the new and old volumes and surface areas).

10.30

a One end of a plastic rod is immersed in boiling water. The temperature of the other end gradually increases. Use ideas from the kinetic model of matter to explain how energy travels from one end of the rod to the other.

b If the experiment was repeated using a metal rod of the same dimensions as the plastic rod, what difference would you expect to notice in the outcome of the experiment?

c How are the particles in a metal involved in transfer-

ring energy from hotter regions to colder ones?

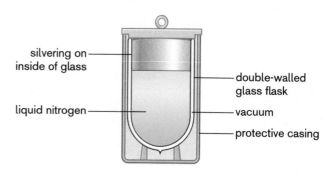

Figure Q10.31

10.31

Liquid nitrogen, at a temperature of −196 °C, is stored in a wide-necked thermos flask, as shown in the diagram.

a Explain the features of the design of this flask that help to keep the liquid nitrogen cold.

b When hot drinks are stored in a thermos flask, it is important to keep it stoppered. Why is it less important to have a stopper in a flask that is being used to keep things cold?

Chapter 11

11.20

a Here is an incomplete statement of Boyle's law:
   'The volume of a gas is inversely proportional to its pressure.'
   What two things must be added to this statement to make it complete?

b Sketch a graph to show how the volume of a gas (y-axis) depends on its pressure (x-axis).

c In an experiment, a sample of air at room temperature was enclosed in a cylinder of volume 0.6 m³; its pressure was 100 kPa. It was then compressed until its volume was reduced to 0.15 m³. What pressure was required to do this?

11.21

In an experiment to investigate how the volume of a fixed mass of gas changes with temperature, the results obtained in the table were obtained.

Temperature (°C)	Volume (cm³)
0	90
18	95
32	101
50	104
68	113
80	118
100	120

a With axes like those shown in the figure, draw a graph to show these data.

b Use your graph to estimate a value for absolute zero.

c How accurate do you consider this value to be?

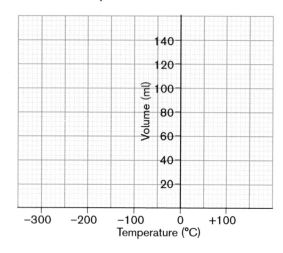

Figure Q11.21

11.22

a The kinetic model of matter suggests that a gas consists of particles moving rapidly about. How does this model explain the pressure exerted by a gas on the walls of its container?

b Use the kinetic model to explain why the pressure of a fixed mass of a gas increases when it is compressed to a smaller volume at constant temperature. Illustrate your answer with appropriate diagrams.

Sound

Topics in this chapter

◆ production of sound

◆ noise

◆ speed of sound

◆ reflection of sound (echoes)

◆ frequency and amplitude of sounds

◆ range of hearing, ultrasound and infrasound

◆ sound as a wave

◎ *resonance*

Most musicians have to tune their instruments before they start to play. Guitarists in a band adjust the tension of their strings so that they play the correct notes. If you have heard a symphony orchestra play, you may have noticed that the oboist usually plays a single clear note, and the other instrumentalists tune to this note. If they all played slightly different notes, the effect would be very uncomfortable on our ears.

Most music that we hear is played by instruments tuned to a standard scale, like the notes of a piano keyboard. However, not all instruments are tuned in the same way. The Scottish bagpipes, for example, play notes on a slightly different scale. A pipe band playing together can sound very exciting (Figure 12.1); but when mixed with

Figure 12.1 These pipers play instruments that produce notes on an unusual scale, different from the conventional scale of a piano. Because the scale is different from what we are used to, the music can at first seem off-key. Traditionally, bagpipes were often played before battles, to give the Scottish troops courage and to alarm the enemy.

Figure 12.2 Gamelan bands can be heard in Indonesia and other countries of the Pacific rim. They include string and woodwind instruments, and are specially noted for their range of percussion instruments – gongs, drums, chimes, marimbas, etc. For people who are used to listening to conventional western music (popular or classical), it can take some time to tune in to the complex rhythms and harmonies produced by a gamelan orchestra.

other instruments, the notes can clash to produce a very unpleasant effect. In a similar way, the instruments of an Indonesian gamelan band (Figure 12.2) play notes on a different scale.

In this chapter, we will look at musical sounds (and other sounds, too), how they are produced and how they travel. We will also look at why different instruments sound different to our ears.

12.1 Making sounds

Different musical instruments produce sounds in different ways.

- *Stringed instruments* The strings are plucked or bowed to make them vibrate. In most stringed instruments, the vibrations are transmitted to the body of the instrument, which also vibrates, along with the air inside it. This makes the sound much louder than if the strings alone were vibrating. The vibrations may be too small or too fast to see, but they can be shown up using laser techniques – see Figure 12.3.
- *Wind instruments* The 'air column' inside a wind instrument is made to vibrate, by blowing across or into the tube (Figure 12.4). The smallest instruments have a straight air column; bigger instruments capable of playing deeper notes (such as a horn or tuba) have an air

Figure 12.3 Although the player only plucks the *strings* of a guitar, the instrument's whole *body* vibrates to produce the notes we hear. This is shown up in this image, produced by shining laser light onto the guitar. Different notes produce different patterns of vibration, and this helps to give each note its particular quality.

Figure 12.4 Two recorders can sound very similar, but one is made of wood and the other of plastic. A flute may be of wood or metal. This tells us that it is not the *material* the instrument is made of that is important – what matters is the *air* inside, which vibrates to produce the desired note. Blowing into the instrument causes the air column inside it to vibrate, and the vibrations are transferred to the air outside.

Figure 12.5 Evelyn Glennie is one of the world's top solo percussionists, despite the fact that she is deaf. She has trained herself to be sensitive to vibrations that reach her body through the ground. This allows her to follow the rhythm of a piece of music, as well as to detect the subtle differences in tone between different percussion instruments.

column that is bent around so that the instrument is not inconveniently long. Some instruments have a reed in the mouthpiece; this vibrates as the player blows across it, causing the air to vibrate.

- *Percussion instruments* These instruments are played by striking them (Figure 12.5). This produces vibrations – of the skin of a drum, the keys of a xylophone, or the metal body of a gong.

In each case, part (or all) of the instrument is made to vibrate. This causes the air near the instrument to vibrate, and the **vibrations** travel through the air to the audience's ears. Some vibrations also reach us through the ground, so that they make our whole body vibrate (see Figure 12.5). If you sit close to a loud band or orchestra, you may feel your whole body vibrating in response to the music.

Sounds travel through the air as vibrations. These vibrations can travel through any material – through the solid ground, through the glass panes of a window, through water. If you put a battery-powered radio on the side of the bath and submerge your ears, you will hear the sounds from the radio travelling through the solid bath and the liquid water to your ears.

> **Questions**
>
> **12.1** Through which of the following materials can sound travel?
> wood, air, water
>
> **12.2** When a woodwind instrument such as a flute produces a note, what part of it vibrates?

12.2 At the speed of sound

Many military jet aircraft (Figure 12.6) are supersonic. This means that they can travel faster than the speed of sound in air.

The **speed of sound** in air is about 330 m/s, or 1200 km/h.

Such aircraft are able to reach speeds as high as perhaps 3000 km/h. They can cross the North Atlantic in under two hours. Computer control can help the pilot to make the split-second decisions needed when travelling so quickly. Most of us are unlikely to experience such travel, but you may hear the bang as a supersonic aircraft passes overhead.

When a supersonic aircraft 'breaks the sound barrier' (travels faster than the speed of sound), it creates shock waves in the air, rather like the bow waves of a speedboat racing across the sea. When these shock waves reach our ears, their vibrations cause us to hear a loud bang, a 'sonic boom'. The people inside the aircraft do not hear this boom – indeed, they notice no effect at all – because the waves do not pass their ears. The air inside the aircraft is being carried ahead of the boom.

Figure 12.6 This F-15 jet aircraft flies at more than twice the speed of sound (2650 km/h, Mach 2.2). The problem with designing a supersonic aircraft is that it needs relatively large wings for take-off and landing. At high speeds, much smaller wings are better because they cause less drag (see Chapter 2).

Travel time

The speed of sound in air (1200 km/s) is about 10 times the speed of cars on a major highway. When someone speaks, it seems to us that we hear the sound they make as soon as they make it. However, it takes a small amount of time to reach our ears. For example, if we are speaking to someone who is just 1 m away, the time for sounds to travel between us is about

$$\frac{1\,\text{m}}{330\,\text{m/s}} = 0.003\,\text{s} = 3\,\text{ms} \quad (3 \text{ milliseconds})$$

This is far too short a time for us to notice. However, there are occasions when we may notice the time it takes for sounds to travel. For example, imagine that you shout at a distance from a cliff or a high wall. After you shout, you may hear an **echo**. The sound has reflected from the hard surface and back to your ears – see Figure 12.7. Worked example 1 shows how to calculate the time it takes for the sound to travel to the cliff and back again.

Figure 12.7 An echo is heard when a sound reflects off a hard surface such as a cliff or a tall brick wall. Sound travels outward from the source, and bounces off the cliff. Some of it will return to the source. If there are several reflecting surfaces, several echoes may be heard.

If you watch people playing a game such as cricket or rounders, you may notice a related effect. You see someone hitting a ball; a split second later you hear the sound of the ball being struck. The time interval between seeing the hit and hearing it occurs because the sound travels relatively slowly to your ears, while the light travels quickly to your eyes. So the light reaches you first, and you see before you hear. When cricket matches are televised, the broadcaster may use a microphone buried in the pitch to pick up the sounds of the game so that there is no noticeable gap between what you see and what you hear.

For the same reason, we usually see a flash of lightning before we hear the accompanying roll of thunder. Count the seconds between the flash and the bang; then divide by 3 to find how far away the lightning is, in kilometres. This works because the sound takes roughly 3 s to travel 1 km, and the light travels the same distance in a few microseconds.

Worked example 1

A young child shouts loudly close to a high brick wall. If the child is 40 m from the wall, how long after the shout will the echo be heard? [Speed of sound in air = 330 m/s.]

- *Step 1* Calculate the distance travelled by the sound. This is *twice* the distance from the child to the wall (since the sound travels there *and back*). So

    distance travelled by sound = 2 × 40 m = 80 m

- *Step 2* Calculate the time taken for the sound to travel this distance:

$$\text{time taken} = \frac{\text{distance}}{\text{speed}} = \frac{80\,\text{m}}{330\,\text{m/s}} = 0.24\,\text{s}$$

So the child hears the echo 0.24 s (about a quarter of a second) after the shout.

Reflecting and absorbing sound

Sounds may be reflected or absorbed when they strike a surface, depending on the nature of the surface – see Figure 12.8.

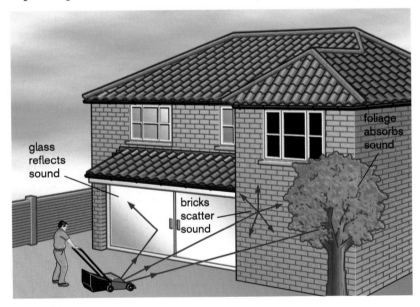

Figure 12.8 Sounds are reflected or absorbed differently by different surfaces.

- A hard, smooth surface gives clear echoes, because sounds are reflected directly.
- A hard, rough surface scatters sounds, so there is no clear echo.
- A soft surface tends to absorb sounds, so there is no echo.

Different materials, different speeds

We talk about 'the speed of sound' as 330 m/s. In fact, it is more correct to say that this is the speed of sound in dry air at 0 °C. The speed of sound changes if the temperature of the air changes, if it is more humid, and so on. (Note also that some people talk about 'the velocity

Material	Speed of sound (m/s)
Gases	
hydrogen	1280
air	330
oxygen	316
carbon dioxide	268
Liquids	
sea-water	1530
water	1500
mercury	1450
Solids	
iron, steel	5100
glass	5000
copper	3800
wood (oak)	3800
lead	1200

Table 12.1 The speed of sound in different materials (measured at standard temperature and pressure).

of sound' but there is no need to use the word 'velocity' here, since we are not talking about the direction in which the sound is travelling. In fact sound travels in all directions – see Chapter 1.)

Table 12.1 shows the speed of sound in some different materials. You can see that sound travels faster through solids than gases. Its speed in water (a liquid) is in between its speeds in solids and in gases.

Measuring the speed of sound

One way to measure the speed of sound in the laboratory is to find out how long a sound takes to travel a measured distance, just as you might measure the speed of a moving car or cyclist. Since sound travels at a high speed, you need to be able to measure short time intervals. Figure 12.9 shows one method.

When the student bangs the two blocks of wood together, it creates a sudden, loud sound. The sound reaches one microphone, and a pulse of electric current travels to the timer. The timer starts running. A fraction of a second later, the sound reaches the second microphone. A second pulse of current stops the timer. Now the timer indicates the time t taken for the sound to travel from one microphone to the next. The distance d between the microphones is measured; the speed of sound v can then be calculated using $v = \dfrac{d}{t}$.

It is important that the two microphones should be a reasonable distance apart – say, three or four metres. The farther apart the better, since this will give a longer 'time of flight' for the sound from one microphone to the other.

Figure 12.9 A 'time-of-flight' method for measuring the speed of sound. The wooden blocks and the two microphones are arranged in a straight line. The bang from the blocks is picked up by one microphone and then the other. The first activates the timer, the second stops it. The speed of sound is calculated from the distance between the two microphones and the time taken by the sound to travel between them.

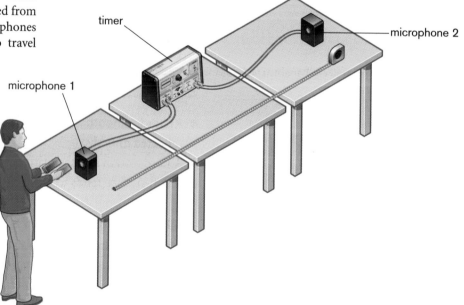

? **Questions**

12.3 Sound takes about 3 ms (milliseconds) to travel 1 m.

   a How long will it take sound to travel from the centre of a cricket pitch to some spectators, 100 m away?

   b What fraction of a second is this?

12.4 Some school rooms are fitted with carpets and curtains. Explain how this helps to reduce the noise made by a class.

12.5 Look at the experiment to measure the speed of sound shown in Figure 12.9. Explain why the wooden blocks and the two microphones must be in a straight line.

12.6 **a** Which travels faster, light or sound?

   b Describe one observation that supports your answer.

12.3 Seeing sounds

When a flautist plays her flute, she sets the air inside it vibrating. A trumpeter does the same thing. Why do the two instruments sound so different? The flute and the trumpet each contain an 'air column', which vibrates to produce a musical note. Because the instruments are shaped differently, the notes produced sound different to our ears.

An image of the notes can be produced by playing the instrument next to a microphone connected to an oscilloscope (Figure 12.10). The microphone receives the vibrations from the instrument and converts them to an electrical signal, which is displayed on the oscilloscope screen. The trace on the screen shows the regular up-and-down pattern of the vibrations that make up the sound. Figure 12.10 shows

flute

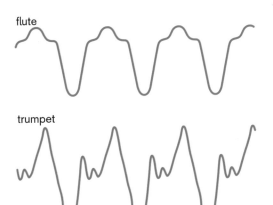

trumpet

violin

Figure 12.10 To display the vibrations of a musical note, it is converted to an electrical signal by a microphone and displayed on the screen of an oscilloscope. The trace on the screen shows the regular pattern of vibration of the sounds. Different instruments produce traces with different shapes, even though they are playing the same note. The bright, rounded tone of the flute and the less smooth, more abrasive sound of the violin are reflected in the shapes of their traces.

traces for three different instruments, each playing the same note. You can see that the three traces repeat themselves at the same rate across the screen, but the shape is different for each instrument.

Pure notes

A signal generator can produce pure notes, which have a very simple shape when displayed on an oscilloscope screen, as shown in Figure 12.11. This wavy shape is called a **sine curve** or **sine wave**. As shown in the diagram, we can make an important measurement from this graph – this is the time for one complete vibration, known as the **period** T of the vibration. This is related to the sound's **frequency** f:

> period T = number of seconds for one vibration
> frequency f = number of vibrations per second

Hence

$$f = \frac{1}{T}$$

Frequency is measured in hertz (Hz); a frequency of 1 Hz is one vibration per second. Worked example 2 shows how to find the frequency of a sound from an oscilloscope trace.

Figure 12.11 A pure note has the shape shown in this oscilloscope trace. The setting of the oscilloscope timebase is indicated on the right. It is important that the variable timebase control is set in the 'calibrated' position if you are to deduce values for the period and frequency of the note.

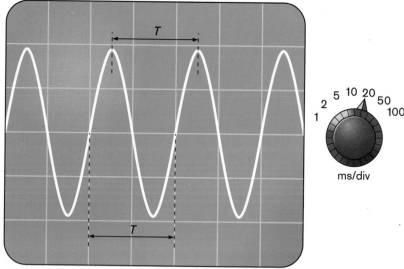

Worked example 2

What is the frequency of the sound represented by the oscilloscope trace shown in Figure 12.11?

- *Step 1* Measure the time for one vibration (marked T on the diagram) in divisions across the oscilloscope screen:

  one vibration occupies two divisions

- *Step 2* Note down the timebase setting, which tells you the time represented by each division across the screen:

  timebase setting = 20 ms/div

  (This means 20 milliseconds per division.)

continued on next page

Worked example 2 continued

● *Step 3* Use these two numbers to calculate the period of the vibration:

period $T = 2 \text{ div} \times 20 \text{ ms/div} = 40 \text{ ms}$

(Each division represents 20 ms, and one vibration occupies two divisions or 40 ms.)

● *Step 4* Calculate the frequency of the sound (it is easier to write 40 ms as 40×10^{-3} s):

$$\text{frequency } f = \frac{1}{T} = \frac{1}{40 \times 10^{-3} \text{ s}} = 25 \text{ Hz}$$

So the sound's frequency is 25 Hz (25 vibrations per second).

High and low, loud and soft

You can understand how an oscilloscope works by connecting it up to a signal generator. With a low-frequency note (say, 0.1 Hz), you will see that there is a single dot, which moves steadily across the oscilloscope screen. The electrical signal from the signal generator makes it move up and down in a regular way. Increasing the frequency makes the dot go up and down faster, until it blurs into a continuous line.

Changing the settings on the signal generator allows you to see the traces for notes of different frequencies and loudnesses. A loudspeaker will let you hear them as well. As shown in Figure 12.12, increasing the frequency of the note squashes the vibrations together on the screen. The note that you hear has a higher **pitch**. Increasing the **loudness** produces traces that go up and down further; we say that their **amplitude** increases. Take care: the amplitude is measured from the centre line to the peak, *not* from trough to peak. To summarise:

● higher pitch, higher frequency;
● louder note, greater amplitude.

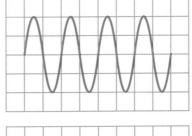 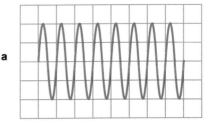

a

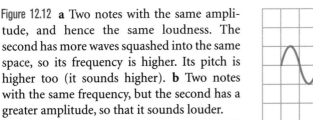 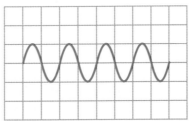 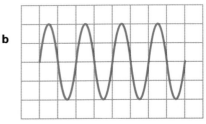

b

Figure 12.12 **a** Two notes with the same amplitude, and hence the same loudness. The second has more waves squashed into the same space, so its frequency is higher. Its pitch is higher too (it sounds higher). **b** Two notes with the same frequency, but the second has a greater amplitude, so that it sounds louder.

A piano keyboard covers a wide range of notes, with frequencies ranging from about 30 Hz at the bottom end to about 3500 Hz at the top end. Most other instruments cover a narrower range than this – for example, a violin ranges from about 200 Hz to 2500 Hz. The range of human hearing is greater than this. Typically, we can hear notes ranging from about 20 Hz up to about 20 000 Hz (20 kHz, or kilohertz). Sounds that are more high-pitched than this (above about 20 kHz) are too high to hear, and are known as **ultrasound**. Sounds below 20 Hz are too low to hear, and are known as **infrasound**. There is more about the uses of ultrasound and infrasound in section 12.5.

To determine whether someone's hearing has been damaged, perhaps because of working in a noisy environment or through listening to excessively loud music, doctors test hearing by playing notes of different frequencies to their patients through headphones. The doctor changes the frequency and amplitude of the notes, and the patient indicates when the note is too faint to hear. Then the doctor can plot audiograms such as those shown in Figure 12.13. This chart indicates whether the patient can hear clearly across all frequencies, or if their hearing has deteriorated.

Electronic sounds

A signal generator produces electrical signals which, when played through a loudspeaker, give pure notes. A synthesiser can do much more than this; it can produce notes that sound like many different musical instruments. Its electronic circuits produce waves having the appropriate shapes for the desired instruments, like those shown in

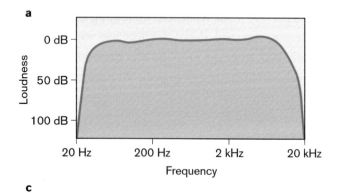

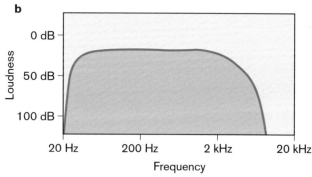

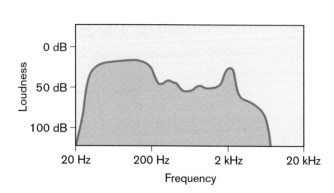

Figure 12.13 An audiogram shows the frequencies of sound that a person can hear, and how loud they must be to be heard. **a** For a young person with good hearing, this chart shows that they can hear well across the range from 20 Hz to 20 kHz. **b** This audiogram is for a middle-aged person. As we age, it becomes increasingly difficult to hear at higher frequencies. **c** This audiogram is for someone who has worked in industry. Exposure to noise has made their ears less sensitive to sounds across a wide range of frequencies. (Note the unusual scale on the horizontal axes: from one division to the next, the frequency increases by a factor of 10. On the vertical axes, the loudest sounds are at the bottom.)

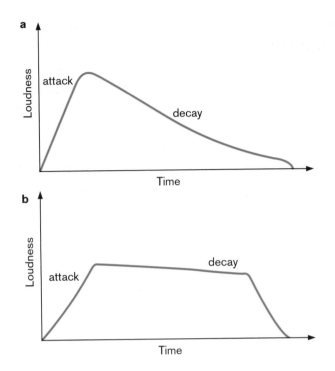

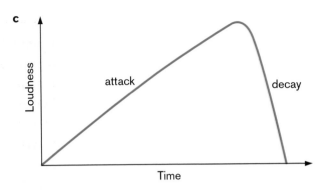

Figure 12.14 Some attack and decay envelopes. The loudness of a single note varies in a characteristic way for each musical instrument. An electronic synthesiser produces notes with the correct shape of vibration and the correct envelope to imitate almost any instrument the user might wish for.

Figure 12.10. However, there is more to it than this. Each note must also have the correct amplitude 'envelope' if it is to reproduce an instrument convincingly. Some envelopes are shown in Figure 12.14. Each consists of an initial attack phase, followed by a decay phase.

Think about how a piano produces a note. A hammer strikes a string; the string vibrates suddenly, with a large amplitude at first, and then fades away. The attack phase is rapid, the decay phase is slow and gradual. For another instrument, these might be the other way around. Some synthesisers allow the user to design their own attack and decay envelopes to create any sound they wish.

 Questions

12.7 What happens to the pitch of a sound if its frequency increases?

12.8 What happens to the loudness of a sound if its amplitude decreases?

12.9 a What is the approximate frequency range of human hearing?

b How does this change with age?

12.10 What is meant by *ultrasound*?

12.11 Think about how a cow says 'moo'. Now look at the attack and decay envelopes shown in Figure 12.14. Which corresponds to the way the loudness of a cow's 'moo' changes?

? **Questions continued**

12.12 Sketch the trace you would expect to see on an oscilloscope screen, produced by a pure note. On your diagram, indicate the distance that corresponds to the period *T* of the vibration.

12.13 An oscilloscope is set with its timebase at 1 ms/div. A complete vibration on the screen occupies two divisions. What is the frequency of the vibration?

12.4 How sounds travel

We can sum up some of our work so far in this chapter as follows:

● Sounds are produced by vibrating objects.

● Sounds are vibrations that travel through the air (or another material). How can we picture the movement of the molecules of the air as a sound travels through?

Figure 12.15 shows how the vibrations of a tuning fork are transmitted through the air. As the prong of the fork moves to the right, it pushes on the air molecules on that side, squashing them together. These molecules push on their neighbours, which become *compressed*, and which in turn compress their neighbours. In the meantime, the prong has moved back to the left, compressing the air molecules on the other side. As the prong vibrates back and forth, **compressions** are sent out into the air all around it. In between the compressions are **rarefactions**, areas in which the air molecules are less closely packed together, or *rarefied*.

Notice that the individual air molecules do not travel outwards from the vibrating fork. They are merely pushed back and forth; it is the compressions and rarefactions that travel through the air to our ears.

This picture of how a sound travels also explains why sound cannot travel through a vacuum: there are no molecules or other particles in a vacuum to vibrate back and forth.

Figure 12.15 also shows another way of representing a sound, as a wavy line rather like the trace on an oscilloscope screen. The crests on the wave match the compressions; the troughs match the rarefactions. Thus the wave represents the changes in air pressure as the sound travels from its source. It is much easier to represent a sound as an

Figure 12.15 A vibrating tuning fork produces a series of compressions and rarefactions as it pushes the air molecules back and forth. This is how a sound travels through the air (or any other material). We can relate this to the wavy trace on an oscilloscope screen.

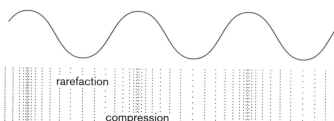

rarefaction

compression

up-and-down wave like this, rather than drawing lots of air molecules pushing each other back and forth.

Here we have used two different ways to represent sound:

- Vibrations travelling through a material – the particles of the material are alternately compressed together and then rarefied as the sound passes through.
- Sound as a wave – a smoothly varying up-and-down line, like the trace on an oscilloscope screen.

The first of these representations gives a better picture of what we would see if we could observe the particles of the material through which the sound is passing; the second is easier to draw. It also explains why we talk about **sound waves**. The wavy line is rather like the shape of waves on the sea. There is much more about sound waves (and other waves) in Chapter 16.

Extension material

Resonance

You can make a nice twanging sound by pressing one end of a ruler down on the edge of a table. Flick the free end and it vibrates up and down; with more of the ruler free to vibrate, the sound has a lower pitch – its frequency is less. The ruler has a **natural frequency** of vibration, its frequency when it vibrates freely. Any vibrating object has a natural frequency (see Figure 12.16), and use is made of this in musical instruments.

In stringed instruments, such as violins or guitars, the player can change the note by pressing down, along the neck, at different points on the string. A shorter string produces a higher note. Strings of different thicknesses have different masses. A thicker string gives a lower note. The tension of the string also alters its natural frequency, and this is how musicians can tune their instruments. A greater tension increases the frequency and so raises the pitch.

Figure 12.16 This springy toy is designed to be used by small children. They can rock rapidly back and forth, because the natural frequency is high. However, if a larger child (such as a teenager) tries to do the same, their mass is much greater, and this reduces the natural frequency. They cannot rock back and forth as quickly as the small child.

In wind instruments, the note produced depends on the length of the air column. A trombone is a good example. To play a low note, a trombone player pushes the slider away to lengthen the air column. Twice the length gives half the frequency.

To summarise, the natural frequency of vibration of an object depends on several factors, including:

- its size – bigger/longer objects vibrate at lower frequencies;
- its mass – objects with more mass vibrate at lower frequencies.

Bigger vibrations

You can use the idea of natural frequency to produce large vibrations. Picture how you can push a child on a swing. If you push once each time the child is moving forwards, the child swings higher and higher. You are giving energy to the swing, and the amplitude increases. Now picture what happens if you push at a different rate. Sometimes you push when the swing is coming towards you, and the swing slows down. You may even get knocked over! To produce large swings, you need to match the natural frequency of the swing.

Pushing with the natural frequency of vibration to produce bigger vibrations is known as **resonance**. It can have good effects and bad. In 1850, disaster struck a column of soldiers as they marched across a bridge at Angers in France. The regular movement of their marching feet resonated with the bridge. This caused it to swing more and more violently until it broke, and 226 men plunged to their deaths in the ravine below. Modern bridges can suffer from similar problems (Figure 12.17).

If washing is unevenly loaded in a washing machine, it may cause the machine to vibrate violently when it starts to spin. At a particular speed of rotation, the vibrations match the natural frequency of the whole machine, which

Figure 12.17 The Millennium Footbridge across the River Thames in London has an unusual design for a suspension bridge. When it was first opened in 2000, hundreds of people flocked to use it. As they walked across the narrow structure, it started to sway slightly. The pedestrians tried to regain their balance. Because they were all moving together against the sway of the bridge, their almost synchronised efforts pushed the bridge so that it swung more and more dangerously – an example of resonance. Engineers had to find ways of reducing the effect by absorbing the energy of the swaying bridge.

starts to vibrate wildly – it resonates. An automatic switch is usually fitted to stop the machine when this happens.

An entertaining example of resonance is shown in Figure 12.18. Start one weight swinging; its vibrations are transmitted by the string to the second weight, which starts to swing because it has the same natural frequency. The first weight slows down until it stops; then the second one slows down and the first one starts to swing again, and so on.

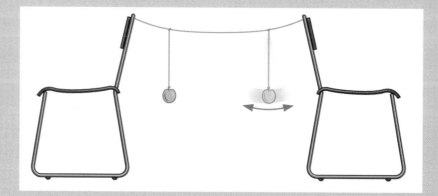

Figure 12.18 The two weights hang on equal lengths of string. Their natural frequencies of vibration are thus equal. Make one swing back and forth; it starts the second one swinging. This is an example of resonance.

? **Questions**

12.14 Why is it impossible for sounds to travel through a vacuum?

12.15 What is the difference between a compression and a rarefaction in a sound wave? Illustrate your answer with a sketch.

12.16 How could you convince a small child that, when you speak, it isn't necessary for air to travel from your mouth to the ear of a listener?

12.5 Using ultrasound and infrasound

Ultrasound is sound that is too high-pitched to hear – its frequency is above 20 kHz, which is beyond the audible range. Ultrasound can be used in a variety of ways:

- *Echo-sounding* Fishing boats may carry echo-sounding equipment that allows them to determine the depth of the water they are in, and to detect shoals of fish (Figure 12.19). Pulses of ultrasound are sent down into the water beneath the ship, and a detector picks up the reflected waves, which may come from the sea-bed or from fish. Electronic circuitry converts the detected signal into a display showing the depth. It can do this because it can measure the time taken for the pulse of ultrasound to travel down to the sea-bed and return to the boat. Knowing the time and the speed of the ultrasound waves in water, the distance can be calculated (just as in worked example 1 on page 187).
- *Quality control* In a similar way, ultrasound can be used to check for defects in solid objects such as metal castings. Ultrasound is directed into the object under investigation; some will be reflected by any flaws in its internal structure, and these flaws can be detected – see Figure 12.20.

Figure 12.19 Using ultrasound to detect features in the water below a ship. Some of the ultrasound is reflected by the shoal of fish; the rest is reflected by the sea-bed. The pulse reflected by the shoal takes less time to return to the ship because it has less distance to travel.

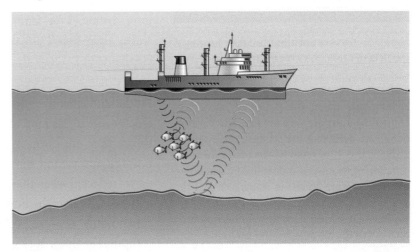

Figure 12.20 Quality control using ultrasound. Here, ultrasound is being used to check for cracks in a metal rail. The ultrasound is reflected by the flaw in the metal, and can be detected. In this way, solid objects can be checked without having to break or cut them open.

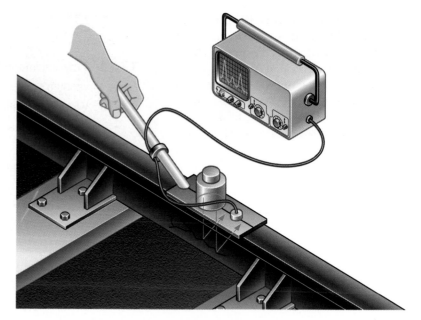

- *Cleaning* A rather different application of ultrasound is in cleaning small objects, such as items of jewellery. A dirty brooch, for example, is immersed in a bath of cleaning fluid and then ultrasound is directed at it. The brooch shakes at ultrasound frequencies, and the dirt is shaken off. This technique is also used for removing grease from tiny mechanical components and from electronic devices.

Animals, ultrasound and infrasound

Just because humans cannot hear ultrasound does not mean that other creatures cannot. Bats (Figure 12.21) are well known for using ultrasound to find their way around in the dark. The bat emits a sharp burst of ultrasound; then its ears pick up the reflections from all the surfaces around it. It can deduce two sorts of information about its surroundings:
- how close objects are – from the time taken for the echo to return to it;
- the nature of the surface, hard or soft, smooth or rough – from whether the echo is clear or more diffuse.

Elephants are thought to be able to hear at **infrasound** frequencies, below 20 Hz. They may be able to communicate with one another over long distances by stamping on the ground. Low-frequency sound waves then travel through the ground, to be picked up by other elephants that detect the waves through their legs.

Pre-natal scanning

Doctors use ultrasound to check on the health, position and sex of babies before they are born. A probe is moved over the mother's stomach, beaming ultrasound waves into her body (Figure 12.22). The waves are partly reflected when they strike the boundary between any two different materials, such as the boundary between the baby's body and the fluid surrounding it. The probe detects the reflected ultrasound, and a computer analyses the signal to produce an image on the screen.

Figure 12.21 Bats are not blind, but their hearing is much better than their eyesight. They have large ears to pick up ultrasound, reflected from the surfaces of objects, such as a moth. Although we cannot hear them, the pulses of ultrasound emitted by a bat are very intense. The bat is in danger of deafening itself, but it has a way of avoiding this. It switches its ears off for the short duration of its squeak. It does this by separating the ossicles (tiny bones) in its ears, so that the sound does not reach its cochlea. In a tiny fraction of a second, it switches its hearing back on to listen for the reflected ultrasound.

Figure 12.22 In many countries, pre-natal scanning using ultrasound is now routine. The probe that is moved across the mother's body both emits the ultrasound and detects the reflected waves. A high-power computer then produces an image of the baby on the screen. For many young people, such an image is now to be found in the family photograph album.

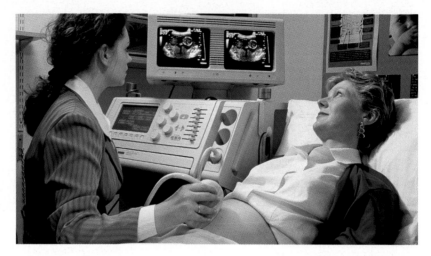

It isn't just expectant mothers who are scanned using ultrasound. Anyone can be scanned if there are suspected problems with their internal organs – perhaps a twisted or blocked digestive tract, or a damaged kidney. The risk posed by ultrasound to internal organs, or to a growing baby, is very much less than the risk from X-rays. This is a great advantage of ultrasound over X-rays. With even a small exposure to X-rays, there is a (very small) danger of cancer, so ultrasound scanning is greatly to be preferred.

? Questions

12.17 **a** Above what frequency is ultrasound?

   b Below what frequency is infrasound?

12.18 How can ultrasound be used in cleaning small objects?

12.19 Mental arithmetic: The speed of sound in sea-water is 1500 m/s. A pulse of ultrasound travels from a ship, to the sea-bed, and back again in 0.1 s. How deep is the sea?

12.20 What advantage does ultrasound scanning have over X-rays for looking at an unborn child?

Summary

- Sounds are vibrations, produced by a vibrating source. The vibrations travel through a material in the form of compressions and rarefactions of the particles that make up the material. Sounds cannot travel through a vacuum.

- Sound travels fastest through solids, and most slowly through gases.

- An echo is produced when a sound is reflected off a hard surface. Soft surfaces tend to absorb sounds.

- The frequency of a sound is the number of vibrations per second, measured in hertz (Hz). The greater the frequency, the higher the pitch.

- The greater the amplitude of a sound, the louder it is.

- The audible range of sounds is from about 20 Hz to about 20 kHz. Frequencies above this range are known as ultrasound; below this, infrasound.

- Ultrasound has a number of uses: for example, in echo-sounding, pre-natal scanning, and the cleaning of delicate items.

- *A vibrating object has a natural frequency of vibration. If stimulated at this frequency, it will vibrate more and more. This is resonance.*

How light travels

Topics in this **chapter**

◆ straight-line travelling

◆ speed of light

◆ law of reflection of light

ℯ *image in a plane mirror*

When *Apollo* astronauts visited the Moon, they left behind reflectors on its surface. These are used to measure the distance from the Earth to the Moon. A laser beam is directed from an observatory on Earth (Figure 13.1) so that it reflects back from the lunar surface. The time taken by the light to travel there and back is measured and, knowing the speed of light, the distance can be calculated. This is the same idea as echo-sounding, discussed in Chapter 12, page 197 but using light rather than ultrasound.

Figure 13.1 A laser beam travels in a straight line to the Moon. It is reflected by mirrors on the Moon's surface, so that it returns to Earth, where it can be detected. From the time taken for the round trip, together with the speed of light, the Earth–Moon distance can be found with great accuracy.

The Moon travels along a slightly elliptical orbit around the Earth, so that its distance varies between 356 500 km and 406 800 km. The laser measurements of its distance are phenomenally accurate – to within 30 cm. This means that they are accurate to within one part in a billion. The Moon is gradually slowing down and drifting away from the Earth, and it is possible with the help of such precise measurements to work out just how quickly it is drifting.

These measurements make use of three ideas that we will look at in this chapter: the way that light travels in straight lines, how fast it travels, and how it is reflected by mirrors.

13.1 Travelling in straight lines

Light usually travels in straight lines. It only changes direction if it is reflected, or if it travels from one material into another. You can see that light travels in a straight line using a **ray box**, as shown in Figure 13.2. A light bulb produces light, which spreads out in all directions. By placing a narrow slit in the path of the light, you can see a single narrow beam or ray of light. If the ray shines across a piece of paper, you can record its position by making dots along its length. Laying a ruler along the dots shows that they lie in a straight line.

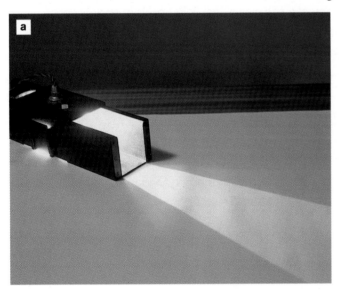
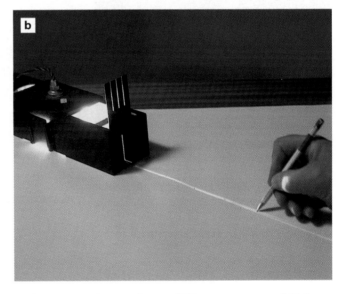

Figure 13.2 **a** A ray box produces a broad beam of light. **b** This can be narrowed down using a metal plate with a slit in it. Marking the line of the ray with dots allows you to record its position.

You may see demonstrations using a different source of light, a **laser**. A laser (Figure 13.3) has the great advantage that all of the light it produces comes out in a narrow beam. This is because the light bounces back and forth inside the laser, reflected by a mirror at either end. It gathers energy as it passes back and forth, and emerges as a single beam. All of the energy is concentrated in this beam, rather than spreading out in all directions (as with a light bulb). The total amount of energy coming from the laser is probably much less than the total amount from the bulb, but it is much more concentrated. That is why it is dangerous if a laser beam gets into your eye.

Figure 13.3 A laser gives a narrow, concentrated beam of light, which is more intense than the ray from a ray box. The light reflects back and forth between the two mirrors, and picks up energy as it passes through the gas mixture. One mirror lets through a small amount of light to form the beam, which emerges from the end.

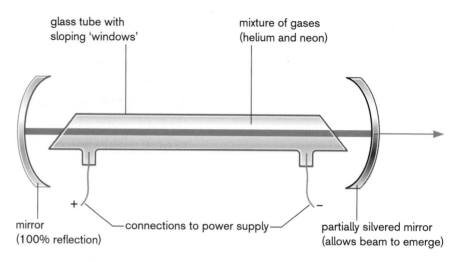

glass tube with sloping 'windows'

mixture of gases (helium and neon)

mirror (100% reflection)

connections to power supply

partially silvered mirror (allows beam to emerge)

When the Channel Tunnel was built, it was vital that the engineers tunnelling from the English end should arrive at exactly the same point as those working from the French end. This was achieved using laser beams (Figure 13.4) to guide the tunnelling equipment.

Figure 13.4 The red laser beam on the right was used to guide tunnelling equipment during the construction of the Channel Tunnel. This ensured that the two teams working from opposite ends met in the middle with pinpoint accuracy.

? Question

13.1 The beam of a cinema projector is often shown up as it reflects off particles of dust (and sometimes smoke!) in the air. You can see clearly that light travels in straight lines. Give two more examples of everyday phenomena that you have seen that show this.

13.2 The speed of light

Light travels very fast – as far as we know, nothing can travel any faster than light. Its speed as it travels though empty space is a fundamental quantity, which is given its own symbol, c, the same symbol as appears in Einstein's famous equation $E = mc^2$.

The **speed of light** c is exactly 299 792 458 m/s.

For most purposes we can round off the value to

300 000 000 m/s or 3×10^8 m/s

It is not obvious to our eyes that light takes any time to travel. When we see something happen nearby, perhaps in the same room as us, we assume that it happens at the instant that we see it. This is a safe assumption because the light takes only a tiny fraction of a microsecond to reach us, far too short a time interval for us to notice. Astronomers do have to worry more about the speed of light, because the distances to stars and galaxies are much greater than we are used to on Earth, and the time for light to travel such huge distances is much more significant. (There is more about this in Section F.)

When we discussed the gap between seeing lightning and hearing thunder (page 186), we explained that it came about because sound travels much more slowly than light – at about one-millionth of the speed of light. We see the lightning only an instant after it is produced, but the sound takes longer to reach us.

The first reasonably accurate measurement of the speed of light was made by Ole Romer, a Danish astronomer working in Paris in the 1670s. He made accurate records of the movement of Jupiter's moons; he wanted to be able to predict when they would be eclipsed as they passed behind the planet. He found that his records showed a strange variation. Sometimes, a moon was eclipsed a few minutes later than expected. He realised that this happened when the Earth was on the opposite side of the Sun from Jupiter, (Figure 13.5). Light from Jupiter had further to travel to reach the Earth than when the two planets were on the same side, so events appeared to happen later than he predicted.

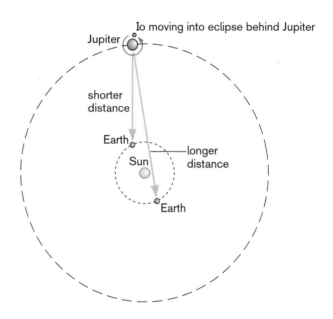

Figure 13.5 The Danish astronomer Ole Romer realised that, when Jupiter and the Earth were on opposite sides of the Sun, light had further to travel from Jupiter to reach Earth. Thus events such as the eclipsing of Jupiter's moon Io was seen later than expected, by up to 10 minutes. From this and the distances of the planets, he could deduce a value for the speed of light, about 225 000 km/s. This is reasonably close to today's agreed value.

The surveyor shown in Figure 13.6 is measuring a distance by timing a beam of light (or, more usually, a beam of infrared radiation – see Chapters 10 and 15). The beam is sent out by one instrument, placed on top of a tripod. It is reflected back by a prism on the second instrument. Knowing the speed of light, the distance between the two instruments can be found. These instruments can be used to track moving objects, so they have to calculate quickly using a built-in microprocessor (a computer microchip). Data from the survey can later be transferred to a larger computer, which generates a chart of the area surveyed.

Different materials, different speeds

Although we refer to c as 'the speed of light', we should remember that this is its speed in empty space (a vacuum). In any material, it travels more slowly, because the material slows it down. Table 13.1 shows the speed of light in some different materials.

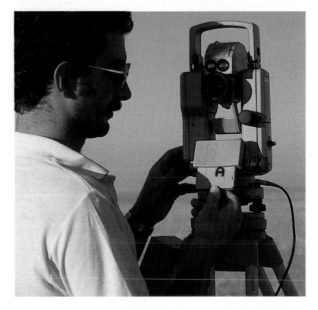

Figure 13.6 This surveyor is using an instrument that measure distances by timing a beam of light or infrared radiation. The beam is timed as it travels from one instrument to the other and back again. An on-board computer calculates the distance and stores the answer for downloading later into a more powerful computer, which draws an accurate plan of the area.

Table 13.1 The speed of light in some transparent materials. (The value for a vacuum is shown, for comparison.) Note that the values are only approximate. The third column shows the factor by which the light is slowed down. (This is the material's refractive index – see Chapter 14.)

Material	Speed of light (m/s)	$\dfrac{\text{Speed in vacuum}}{\text{Speed in material}}$
vacuum	2.998×10^8	1 exactly
air	2.997×10^8	1.0003
water	2.3×10^8	1.33
Perspex	2.0×10^8	1.5
glass	$(1.8\text{–}2.0) \times 10^8$	1.5–1.7
diamond	1.25×10^8	2.4

? Questions

13.2 Someone tells you that 'the speed of light is 3×10^8 m/s'. How could you make this statement more accurate?

13.3 Look at the values for the speed of light shown in Table 13.1.
  a In which of the materials shown does light travel most slowly?
  b Why do you think that a range of values is shown for glass?

13.4 The speed of light in empty space, c, is exactly 299 792 458 m/s. In calculations, we often use an approximate value for c. Which of the following are good approximations?
  300 000 000 m/s, 30 000 km/s, 300 000 km/s, 3×10^8 m/s, 3×10^9 m/s

13.5 Explain why the surveyor shown in Figure 13.6 would have problems if light did *not* travel in straight lines.

13.3 Reflecting light

Most of us look in a mirror at least once a day, to check on our appearance (Figure 13.7). It is important to us to know that we are presenting ourselves to the rest of the world in the way we want. Archaeologists have found bronze mirrors over 2000 years old, so the desire to see ourselves clearly has been around for a long time.

Modern mirrors give a very clear image. They are made by coating the back of a flat sheet of glass with mercury. When you look in a mirror, rays of light from your face reflect off the shiny surface and back to your eyes. You seem to see a clear image of yourself behind the mirror. (The 'extension material' on the next page will help you to understand why this is.)

For now, we will consider just a single ray of light, and see what we can learn about reflection. When a ray of light reflects off a mirror or other reflecting surface, it follows a path as shown in Figure 13.8. The ray bounces off, rather like a ball bouncing off a wall. The two rays are known as the **incident ray** and the **reflected ray**. By doing many experiments, the **angle of incidence** i and the **angle of reflection** r are found to be equal to each other. This is the **first law of reflection** of light:

> When a ray of light is reflected by a surface, the angle of incidence is equal to the angle of reflection.

In symbols:

$i = r$

Figure 13.7 Psychologists use mirrors to test the intelligence of animals. Does an animal recognise that it is looking at itself? Apes clearly understand that the image in the mirror is an image of themselves – they make silly faces at themselves. Other animals, such as cats and dogs, do not – they may even try to attack their own reflection.

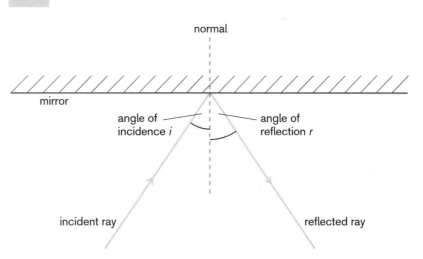

Figure 13.8 The first law of reflection of light. The normal is drawn perpendicular to the surface of the mirror. Then the angles are measured relative to the normal. The angle of incidence and the angle of reflection are then equal: $i = r$.

Note that, to find the angles i and r, we have to draw the **normal** to the reflecting surface. This is a line drawn perpendicular (at 90°) to the surface, at the point where the ray strikes it. Of course, the other two angles (between the rays and the flat surface) are also equal. However, we would have trouble measuring these angles if the surface was curved, so we measure the angles relative to the normal. The first law of reflection thus also works for curved surfaces, such as concave and convex mirrors.

The **second law of reflection** states that:
when a ray of light is reflected by a surface, the incident ray, the reflected ray and the normal all lie in the same plane.

If this were not the case, we would not be able to draw this diagram on a flat sheet of paper. The reflected ray would come out of the paper, or go back into the paper.

Extension material

The image in a plane mirror

Why do we see such a clear image when we look in a plane (flat) mirror? And why does it appear to be behind the mirror?

Figure 13.9a shows how an observer can see an image of a candle in a plane mirror. Light rays from the flame are reflected by the mirror; some of them enter the observer's eye. In the diagram, the observer has to look forward and slightly to the left to see the image of the candle. The brain assumes that the image of the candle is in that direction, as shown by the dashed lines behind the mirror in Figure 13.9b. (Our brains assume that light travels in straight lines, even though we know that light is reflected by mirrors.) The dashed lines appear to be coming from a point behind the mirror, at the same distance behind the mirror as the candle is in front of it. You can see this from the symmetry of the diagram.

The image looks as though it is the same size as the candle. Also, it is (of course) a mirror image; that is, it appears left–right reversed. You will know this from seeing writing reflected in a mirror.

The image of the candle is not a real image. A **real image** is an image that can be projected onto a screen. If you place a piece of paper at the position of the image in a mirror, you will not see a picture of the candle on it, because no rays of light from the candle reach that spot. That is why we drew dashed lines, to show where the rays *appear* to be coming from. We say that it the image in a mirror is a **virtual image**.

To summarise, when an object is reflected in a plane mirror:

- The image is the same size as the object.
- The image is the same distance behind the mirror as the object is in front of it.
- The image appears left – right reversed.
- The image is virtual.

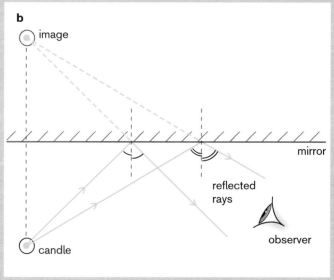

Figure 13.9 **a** Looking in the mirror, the observer sees an image of the candle. The image appears to be behind the mirror.
b The ray diagram shows how the image is formed. Rays from the candle flame are reflected according to the law of reflection. The dashed lines show that, to the observer, the rays appear to be coming from a point behind the mirror.

Ray diagrams

Figure 13.9b is an example of a **ray diagram**. Such diagrams are used to predict the positions of images in mirrors (or when lenses or other optical devices are being used – see Chapter 14) from the positions of the object and the mirror (or lens). The idea is as follows. First we draw in the positions of the things that are known (e.g. the candle and the mirror). Then we need to draw in some rays of light. But not just any rays! They must be carefully chosen if they are to show up what we want to see. The rough position of the observer (usually depicted by an eye) is marked. Two rays are drawn from the object to the mirror and then the reflected rays are drawn to the observer. Then these two reflected rays are **extrapolated** back, to show where they appear to be coming from. These are the dashed lines shown in Figure 13.9b. This is known as a **construction**, and it allows us to mark the position

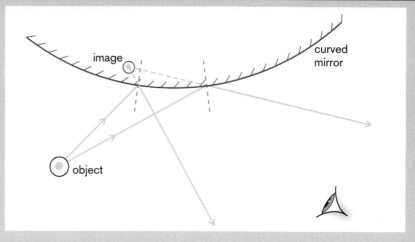

Figure 13.10 This ray diagram is drawn to scale. The curved mirror produces an image that is virtual and smaller than the object.

of the image. Worked example 1 shows the steps in constructing such a ray diagram.

Ray diagrams are often drawn to scale. An example, for a curved mirror, is shown in Figure 13.10. This shows that the image formed is behind the mirror, but closer to it, so that the image looks smaller. Such a mirror is often used as the rear-view mirror or wing mirror of a car, to give the driver a view over a wide area behind the car.

Today, designers of optical equipment such as cameras or microscopes use sophisticated computer software to draw ray diagrams so that they can be sure that their complicated systems of mirrors and lenses will give as clear an image as possible.

Worked example 1

A small lamp is placed 5 cm from a plane mirror. Draw an accurate scale diagram and use it to show that the image of the lamp is 5 cm behind the mirror.

The ray diagram is shown in Figure 13.11.

- *Step 1* Draw a line to represent the mirror, and indicate its reflecting surface. Mark the position of the object O. (It helps to work on squared paper.)

- *Step 2* Mark the rough position of the observer. From O to the mirror, draw two rays that will be reflected towards the observer. Where the rays strike the mirror, draw in the normal lines.
- *Step 3* Using a protractor, measure the angle of incidence for each ray; mark the equal angle of reflection.
- *Step 4* Draw in the reflected rays, and extend them back behind the mirror. The point where they cross is where the image is formed; label it I.

From the diagram, it is clear that the image is 5 cm from the mirror, directly opposite the object. The line joining O to I is perpendicular to the mirror.

continued on next page

Worked example 1 continued

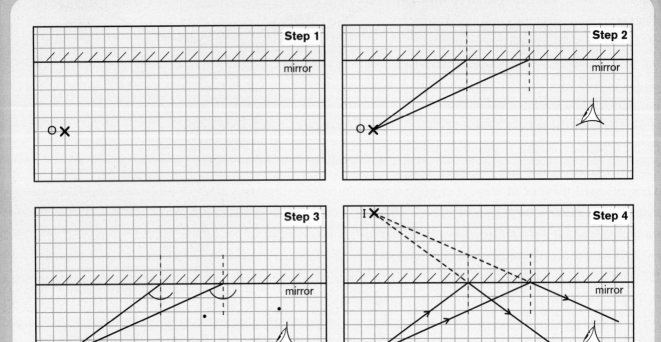

Figure 13.11 The steps in drawing a ray diagram for a plane mirror.

? Questions

13.6 Write the word AMBULANCE as it would appear when reflected in a plane mirror. Why is it sometimes written in this way on the front of an ambulance?

13.7 Draw a diagram to illustrate the law of reflection. Which two angles are equal, according to the law?

13.8 A ray of light strikes a flat, reflective surface such that its angle of incidence is 30°. What angle does the reflected ray make with the surface?

13.9 Some children think that we see an object because light from our eyes is reflected back by the object. Draw a diagram to represent this incorrect idea. Draw another diagram to show how diffuse reflection (scattering) explains correctly how we see things.

13.10 What does it mean to say that a plane mirror produces a *virtual* image?

Summary

◆ Light travels in straight lines.

◆ Light travels at a speed of almost 300 000 000 m/s in a vacuum. It travels more slowly in transparent materials.

◆ The first law of reflection states that, when a ray of light is reflected by a surface, the angle of incidence is equal to the angle of reflection ($i = r$). Angles are measured relative to the normal to the surface.

◆ The second law of reflection states that, when a ray of light is reflected by a surface, the incident ray, the reflected ray and the normal all lie in the same plane.

◆ *The image formed by a plane mirror is the same size as the object, is as far behind the mirror as the object is in front of it, appears left–right reversed, and is virtual.*

Refraction of light

Topics in this chapter

◆ describing refraction

◆ refractive index

◆ total internal reflection

◆ lenses

◆ dispersion and the spectrum

If you should ever become a professional astronomer, you might have the pleasure of working at a telescope set high on an exotic island – in the Canaries or Hawaii, perhaps (Figure 14.1). Your nights would be spent working at an advanced telescope. Being a physicist, you might wonder: Why is our telescope placed in such an unusual location? During the day (when you were not sleeping!), you could drive down the mountainside and enjoy a swim in a sunlit pool, surrounded by tropical plants. Idly floating in the pool, you notice the ripple pattern that the Sun's rays cast on the bottom of the pool, and again, being a physicist, you wonder: How is this pattern formed? These two questions have a shared answer.

Figure 14.1 This astronomical observatory is at La Palma in the Canary Islands, off the west coast of Africa. It is at a height of about 2400 m above sea-level, so that the telescopes are sited above most of the Earth's atmosphere. This gives them a much clearer view of the stars, without the twinkling effects produced by irregularities in the atmosphere.

Astronomers use telescopes to gather light. The lens of the telescope is much bigger than the lens of your eye, so it can gather more light and allow you to see fainter objects in the night sky. Light from distant stars travels for millions of years across empty space, carrying with it a record of the star's existence. In empty space there is nothing to interfere with the light, so it travels on and on, unimpeded. Then, just a few kilometres – and only a few microseconds – before it gets to your telescope, it reaches the Earth's atmosphere, and that's where the trouble starts.

The atmosphere is rather irregular. There are small patches that are denser, others that are less dense. As the starlight passes through these patches, it changes direction slightly. It moves from side to side, and that is why stars appear to twinkle in the night sky. Using a telescope positioned at sea-level, astronomers get a very poor view of the faintest stars. Looking at stars from sea-level is rather like trying to recognise a visitor when you see their face through a frosted glass panel in your front door.

The obvious answer is to get above the atmosphere. There are two ways to do this: put your telescope in space (like the Hubble Space Telescope) – but this is very expensive; or build your telescope on a high mountain. If the mountain is, say, 6 km high, you will be above most of the Earth's atmosphere, and you will get a much clearer view. Also, you will not need to worry about cloud and rain, because you will usually be above cloud level. Finally, choose a tropical location, where you won't have to worry about snow in the winter, and you have the ideal site for an observatory.

Why do we see patterns of shadowy ripples on the bottom of a pool? The surface of the water is irregular; there are always small disturbances on the water, and these cause the rays of sunlight to change direction, just like the irregularities in the atmosphere. Where the pattern is darker, rays of light have been deflected away, producing a sort of shadow. This bending of rays of light when the material they are moving through changes is called refraction, and it is the subject of this chapter.

As you drive back up the mountain to start your next night's work, you notice that the scenery around you looks blurred, rather like a mirage seen in the desert. There is a heat haze as warm air rises from the ground after a day in the baking sunshine. The warm air is less dense than the colder air it is moving through. It isn't difficult to explain why things look blurred through this irregular air.

14.1 Refraction effects

There are many effects caused by the refraction of light – the sparkling of diamonds, the way the lens in your eye produces an image of the world around you, the distorted image you see when looking through a bulls-eye window in an old house. The 'broken stick' effect (Figure 14.2)

Figure 14.2 The pencil is partly immersed in water. Because of refraction of the light coming from the part of the pencil that is underwater, the pencil appears broken.

is another consequence of refraction. The word 'refraction' is related to the word 'fractured', meaning broken. Picture a bent and fractured bone and you will remember the meaning of refraction.

Refraction occurs when a ray of light travels from one material into another. The ray of light may change direction. You can investigate this using a ray box and a block of glass or Perspex, as shown in Figure 14.3. Note that the ray travels in a straight line when it is in the air outside the block, and in a straight line when it is inside the block. It only bends at the point where it enters or leaves the block, so it is the *change* of material that causes the bending.

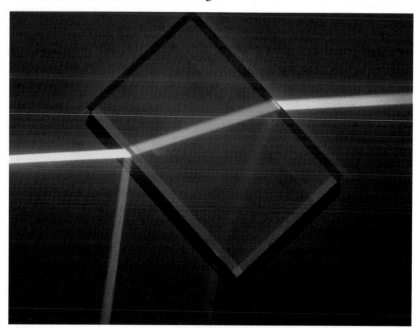

Figure 14.3 Demonstrating the refraction of a ray of light when it passes through a rectangular glass block. The ray enters from the left; it bends as it enters the glass; as it leaves, it bends back to its original direction. (Note that a fraction of the light is reflected as the ray enters and leaves the block.)

From Figure 14.3, you will notice that the direction in which the ray bends depends on whether it is entering or leaving the glass:

● The ray bends towards the normal when entering the glass.
● The ray bends away from the normal when leaving the glass.

One consequence of this is that, when a ray passes through a parallel-sided glass block, it returns to its original direction of travel, although it is shifted to one side. When we look at the world through a window, we are looking through a parallel-sided sheet of glass. We do not see a distorted image because, although the rays of light are shifted slightly as they pass through the glass, they reach us travelling in their original directions.

Changing direction

As with reflection, we define angles relative to the normal. Figure 14.4a shows the terms used. The **incident ray** strikes the block; the **angle of incidence** i is measured from the ray to the normal. The **refracted ray** travels on at the **angle of refraction** r, measured relative to the normal. (Note that, in Chapter 13, we used r for the angle of reflection; here it stands for the angle of refraction.)

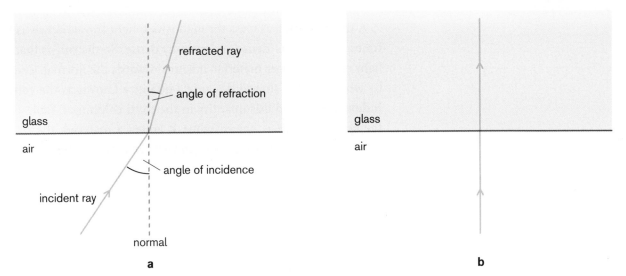

a

b

Figure 14.4 **a** Refraction: defining terms. The normal is drawn perpendicular to the surface at the point where the ray passes from one material to another. The angles of incidence and refraction are measured relative to the normal. **b** When a ray strikes the glass at 90°, it carries straight on without being deflected.

A ray of light may strike a surface head-on, so that its angle of incidence is 0°, as shown in Figure 14.4b. In this case, it does not bend; it simply passes straight through and carries on in the same direction.

Usually we say that:

Refraction is the bending of light when it passes from one material to another.

But we should bear in mind that, when the light is perpendicular to the boundary between the two materials, there is no bending.

Explaining refraction

Why does light change direction when it passes from one material to another? The answer lies in the way its speed changes. In Chapter 13, we saw that light travels fastest in a vacuum (empty space). Table 13.1 on page 204 shows that light travels very slightly slower in air, but much more slowly in transparent solid materials. Of all the materials shown in the table, light travels most slowly in diamond, where its speed is less than half that in a vacuum.

One way to explain why a change in speed leads to a change in direction is shown in Figure 14.5. A truck is driving along a road across the desert. The driver is careless, and allows the wheels on the left to drift off the road onto the sand. Here, they sink into the sand, so that the left-hand side of the truck moves more slowly. The right-hand side is still in contact with the road and keeps moving quickly, so that the truck starts to turn to the left.

The boundary between the two materials is the edge of the road; the normal is at right-angles to the road. The truck has veered to the left, so its direction has moved towards the normal. Thus we would expect a ray of light to move towards the normal when it enters a material where it moves more slowly, and this is indeed what we saw with glass (Figure 14.3). Light travels more slowly in glass than in air, so it bends towards the normal as it enters glass.

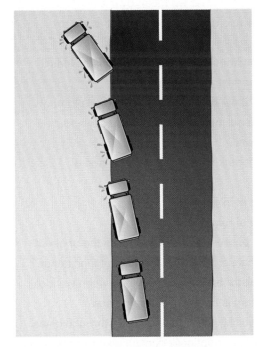

Figure 14.5 To explain why a change in speed explains the bending caused by refraction, we picture a truck whose wheels slip off the road into the sand. The truck veers to the side because it cannot move so quickly through sand.

A material such as glass through which light travels slowly is sometimes described as 'dense' or 'optically dense'. So the rule is that, when light enters a denser material, it bends towards the normal. The factor by which light is slowed down is a quantity known as the **refractive index** (we showed this quantity in the third column of Table 13.1). If the speed of light is halved when it enters a material, the refractive index is 2, and so on. Hence we can write an equation for the refractive index *n* of a material:

$$\text{refractive index } n = \frac{\text{speed of light in a vacuum}}{\text{speed of light in the material}}$$

Water has a refractive index $n = 1.33$. This means that light travels 1.33 times as fast in a vacuum, compared to its speed in water.

It is a *change* in refractive index that causes rays of light to bend; the bigger the change, the greater the effect. So, if one part of the atmosphere is warmer than another, it will be less dense and its refractive index will be less. This is what causes problems for astronomers as they try to look out through the atmosphere towards the distant stars.

? Questions

14.1 Draw a diagram to show what we mean by the *angle of incidence* and the *angle of refraction* for a refracted ray of light.

14.2 A ray of light passes from air into a block of glass. Does it bend *towards* the normal, or *away* from it?

14.3 Draw a diagram to show how a ray of light passes through a parallel-sided Perspex block. What can you say about its final direction of travel?

14.4 A vertical ray of light strikes the horizontal surface of some water.
  a What is its angle of incidence?
  b What is its angle of refraction?

14.5 When a ray of light passes from air to glass, is the angle of refraction greater than, or less than, the angle of incidence?

14.6 Why do we see a distorted view of the world when we look through a window that is covered with raindrops?

14.7 Light travels more quickly through water than through glass.
  a Which is denser (more optically dense), water or glass?
  b If a ray passes from glass into water, which way will it bend: towards or away from the normal?

14.8 Look back at Table 13.1 on page 204. What is the value of the refractive index of diamond?

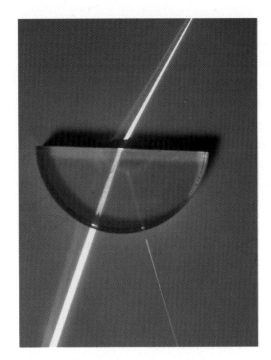

Figure 14.6 Using a ray box to investigate reflection when a ray of light strikes a glass or Perspex block. The ray is travelling upwards from bottom left. It enters the block without bending, because it is directed along the radius of the block.

Figure 14.7 How a ray of light is reflected or refracted inside a glass block depends on the angle of incidence. **a,b** For angles less than the critical angle, some of the light is reflected and some is refracted. **c** At the critical angle, the angle of refraction is 90°. **d** At angles of incidence greater than the critical angle, the light is totally internally reflected; there is no refracted ray.

14.2 Total internal reflection

If you have carried out a careful investigation of refraction using a ray box and a transparent block, you may have noticed something extra that happens when a ray strikes a block. Not only is the ray refracted; in addition, a reflected ray also appears. You can see this in Figure 14.3, but it has been ignored in Figures 14.4. When the ray strikes the block, some of the light passes into the block and is refracted; some is reflected. When it leaves the block, some is again reflected. These reflected rays obey the laws of reflection: the angle of incidence is equal to the angle of reflection.

These reflected rays can be a nuisance. If you try to look downwards into a pond or river to see if there are any fish there, your view may be spoilt by light reflected from the surface of the water. You see a reflected image of the sky, or of yourself, rather than what is in the water. On a sunny day, reflected light from windows or water can be a hazard to drivers.

To see how we can make use of reflected rays, you can use the apparatus shown in Figure 14.6. A ray box shines a ray of light at a semicircular glass or Perspex block. The ray is always directed at the curved edge of the block, along the radius. This means that it enters the block along the normal, so that it is not bent by refraction. Inside the block, the ray strikes the midpoint of the flat side, point X.

What happens next? This depends on the angle of incidence of the ray at point X. The various possibilities are shown in Figures 14.7a–d.

a If the angle of incidence is small, most of the light emerges from the block. There is a faint reflected ray inside the glass block. The refracted ray bends away from the normal, because the air is less dense than the glass.

b If the angle of incidence is increased, more light is reflected inside the block. The refracted ray bends even further away from the normal.

c Eventually, the refracted ray emerges parallel to the surface of the block. Most of the light is reflected inside the block.

d Now, at an even greater angle of incidence, all of the light is reflected inside the block. No refracted ray emerges from point X.

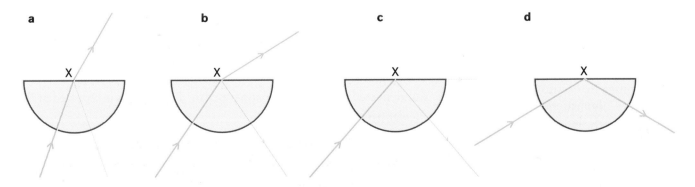

a   b   c   d

We have been looking at how light is reflected *inside* a glass block. We have seen that, if the angle of incidence is greater than a particular value, the light is entirely reflected inside the glass. This phenomenon is known as **total internal reflection** (or TIR):

- total – because 100% of the light is reflected;
- internal – because it happens inside the glass;
- reflection – because the ray is entirely reflected.

For total internal reflection to happen, the angle of incidence of the ray must be greater than a particular value, known as the **critical angle**. The critical angle depends on the material being used. For glass, it is about 42° (though this depends on the composition of the glass). For water, which has a lower refractive index, the critical angle is greater, about 49°. For diamond, with a very high refractive index, the critical angle is small, about 25°. Hence rays of light that enter a diamond are very likely to be totally internally reflected, so they bounce around inside, eventually emerging from one of the diamond's cut faces. That explains why diamonds are such sparkly jewels.

Using total internal reflection

It is the fact that TIR is 'total' that makes it so useful. A typical mirror reflects perhaps 90% of the light that falls on it; the rest of the light is absorbed. So the image in a mirror is dimmed slightly. However, with TIR inside a prism, 100% of the light is reflected, no light is lost, and the image is not dimmed. This means that suitably arranged prisms can be more effective than mirrors for some uses. Here are some important applications of TIR.

Periscopes

A basic, traditional periscope uses two mirrors to allow the user to see over a wall or over a crowd. You may have seen such periscopes in use at golf tournaments. For more technical applications, where it is important to get as clear a view as possible, a periscope fitted with two glass prisms is used. Periscopes like this are used in submarines. Figure 14.8a shows how this works.

A ray of light enters the upper prism. It is undeflected as it enters because it is travelling at 90° to the surface (that is, along the normal). When it reaches the sloping surface of the prism, its angle of incidence is 45°. This is greater than the critical angle (42°), and so TIR occurs. Its angle of reflection is 45°, and so it is reflected through 90°. It is undeflected as it leaves the upper prism. The process is repeated at the lower prism.

Binoculars

These often use pairs of prisms to reflect the light back and forth (Figure 14.8b). Without the prisms, the binoculars would have to be as long as a traditional telescope, perhaps 60 cm in length, which would

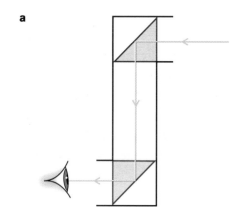

a

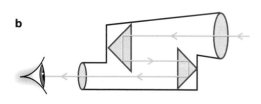

b

Figure 14.8 Two uses of prisms in optical instruments. **a** In a periscope, the ray of light is reflected through 90° by each prism. **b** In binoculars, the prisms are arranged so that each one reflects the light twice through 90°. In each case, the light is totally internally reflected so that no light is lost (as it would be with a mirror). This helps to ensure a bright image.

make them very unwieldy. In the case of binoculars, each prism reflects a ray of light twice through 90°, so that it ends up travelling in the reverse direction.

Optical fibres

A revolution in telecommunications has been made possible by the development of fibre optics. Telephone messages and other electronic signals such as internet computer messages or cable TV signals are passed along fine glass fibres in the form of flashing laser light – a digital signal. Figure 14.9a shows just how fine these fibres can be. Each of these fibres is capable of carrying thousands of telephone calls simultaneously.

Inside a fibre, light travels along by TIR – see Figure 14.9b. It bounces along inside the fibre because, each time it strikes the inside of the fibre, its angle of incidence is greater than the critical angle. Thus no light is lost as it is reflected. The fibre can follow a curved path and the light bounces along inside it, following the curve. For signals to travel over long distances, the glass used must be of a very high purity, so that it does not absorb the light.

Endoscopes

These are instruments with which doctors can examine their patients' insides. For example, they can view a patient's stomach by passing the flexible end of the endoscope down the throat. The endoscope contains a bundle of many parallel glass fibres, which bring an image back up to the doctor. Usually this is displayed on a video screen so that a whole team of assistants can observe as well (Figure 14.10).

Light travels up the glass fibres by total internal reflection, just as in an optical fibre for telecommunications. Usually some of the outer fibres are used to transmit light down into the patient, to illuminate the areas that the doctor wants to look at.

Figure 14.9 The use of fibre optics has greatly increased the capacity and speed of the world's telecommunications networks. Without this technology, cable television and the internet would not be feasible. **a** Each of these very fine fibres of high-purity glass can carry many telephone messages simultaneously. **b** Light travels along a fibre by total internal reflection. Because the reflection is total, and the glass is so pure, the light can travel many kilometres along a single fibre.

Figure 14.10 This medical team is looking at the patient's stomach using an endoscope. You can see where the long, flexible end of the endoscope enters the patient's body. Images of the patient's insides are then shown on a monitor for all to see. The endoscope may also include small tools that the surgeon can manipulate, for example to cut out any undesirable tissue.

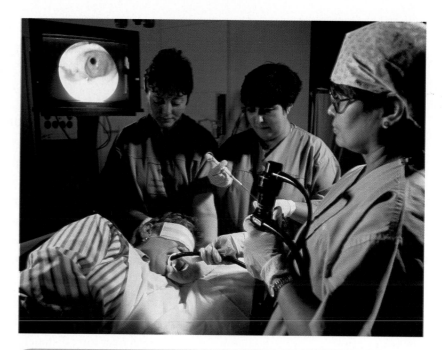

? Questions

14.9 Explain the meaning of the words *total* and *internal* in the expression 'total internal reflection'.

14.10 The critical angle for water is 49°. If a ray of light strikes the upper surface of a pond at an angle of incidence of 45°, will it be totally internally reflected?

14.11 Study Figure 14.8. Draw diagrams to show how a prism can be used to reflect a ray of light: **a** through 90° and **b** through 180°. Indicate the points where TIR occurs.

14.12 Sketch a diagram to show how a ray of light can travel along a curved glass fibre. Indicate the points where TIR occurs.

14.13 Most of the glass fibres in an endoscope carry light *out of* the patient. Explain why some are needed to carry light *into* the patient.

14.14 Why must high-purity glass be used for optical fibres used in telecommunications?

14.3 Lenses

We are all familiar with lenses in everyday life – in spectacles and cameras, for example. The development of high-quality lenses has had a profound effect on science. In 1609, using the newly invented telescope, Galileo discovered the moons of Jupiter and triggered a revolution in astronomy. In those days, scientists had to grind their own lenses starting from blocks of glass, and Galileo's skill at this was a major factor in his discovery.

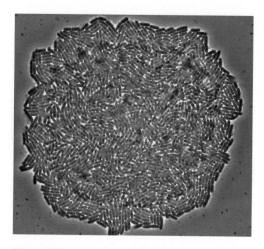

Figure 14.11 Bacteria that cause infections cannot be seen with the naked eye. This photograph, taken using a modern microscope, shows *E.coli* bacteria. Certain types of *E.coli* are known to cause food poisoning. The microscope uses two lenses to give an image that is 2000 times the size of the object being viewed.

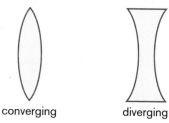

converging   diverging

Figure 14.12 The lenses on the left are converging lenses, which are fattest at the middle. On the right are diverging lenses, which are thinnest at the middle. Lenses are given these names because of their effect on parallel rays of light. Usually we simply draw the cross-section of the lens, as shown below the photograph, to indicate which type we are considering.

Later in the seventeenth century, a Dutch merchant called Anton van Leeuwenhoek managed to make microscope lenses that gave a magnification of 200 times. He used these to look at the natural world around him, and was amazed to find a wealth of tiny micro-organisms, including bacteria, that were invisible to the naked eye (Figure 14.11). This provided the clue to how infectious diseases might be spread. Previously people thought infections were carried by smells or by mysterious vapours. A revolution in medicine had begun.

Converging and diverging lenses

Lenses can be divided into two types, according to their shape (Figure 14.12):
- **Converging lenses** are fatter in the middle than at the edges.
- **Diverging lenses** are thinner in the middle than at the edges.

You have probably used a magnifying glass to look at small objects. This is a converging lens. You may even have used a magnifying glass to focus the rays of the Sun onto a piece of paper, to set fire to it. (Over a thousand years ago, an Arab scientist described how people used lenses for starting fires.) This gives a clue to the name 'converging'.

Figure 14.13a shows how a converging lens focuses the parallel rays of the Sun. On one side of the lens, the rays are parallel. After they pass through the lens, they converge on a single point, the **focus** or **focal point**. After they have passed through the focus, they spread out again. So a converging lens is so-called because it makes parallel rays of light converge. The focus is the point where the rays are concentrated together, and where a piece of paper needs to be placed if it is to be burned. The distance from the centre of the lens to the focus is the **focal length** of the lens. The fatter the lens, the shorter its focal length.

A diverging lens has the opposite effect on parallel rays: it makes them diverge, as shown in Figure 14.13b. They *appear* to spread out from a point behind the lens.

A converging lens can be used in reverse to produce a beam of parallel rays. If a source of light such as a small light bulb is placed at the focus, the rays that reach the lens are bent so that they become a parallel beam (Figure 14.13c). This diagram is the same as Figure 14.13a, but in reverse.

Lenses work by refracting light. When a ray strikes the surface of the lens, it is refracted towards the normal because it is entering a denser material. When it leaves the glass of the lens, it bends away from the normal. The clever thing about the shape of a converging lens is that it bends each ray just enough for them all to meet at the focus.

Forming a real image

When the Sun's rays are focused onto a piece of paper, a tiny image of the Sun is created. It is easier to see how a converging lens makes an

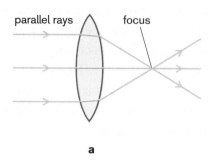
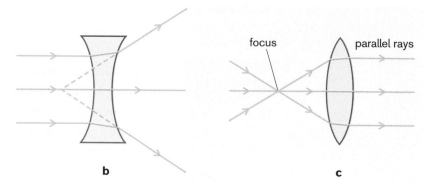

a   b   c

Figure 14.13 The effect of lenses on rays of light. **a** A converging lens makes parallel rays converge at the focus. **b** A diverging lens makes them diverge. **c** Rays from the focus of a converging lens are turned into a parallel beam of light.

image by focusing an image of a light bulb or a distant window onto a piece of white paper. The paper acts as a screen to catch the image. Figure 14.14 shows an experiment in which an image of a light bulb (the object) is formed by a converging lens.

We say that the image is **real**, because light really does fall on the screen to make the image. If light only *appeared* to be coming from the image, we would say that the image was **virtual**.

Figure 14.14 Forming a real image of a light bulb using a converging lens.

Provided the object is at least as far as two focal lengths from the lens:
- the image is inverted (upside down);
- the image is reduced (smaller than the object);
- the image is nearer to the lens than the object;
- the image is real.

We can explain the formation of this real image using a **ray diagram**, as shown in Figure 14.15. Here are the steps in drawing this diagram:
- *Step 1* Draw the lens – a simple outline shape will do – with a horizontal axis through the middle of it.
- *Step 2* Mark the positions of the focal points F on either side, at equal distances from the lens. Mark the position of the object O, an arrow standing on the axis.
- *Step 3* Draw ray 1, a straight line from the top of the arrow (the object) and passing undeflected through the middle of the lens.

Figure 14.15 A ray diagram can be used to show how an image is formed by a converging lens. The steps in drawing this diagram are given in the text.

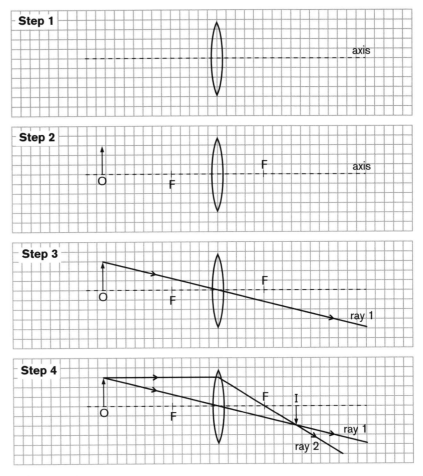

- *Step 4* Draw ray 2, from the top of the arrow (the object) parallel to the axis. As it passes through the lens, it is deflected down through the focal point (or focus). Look for the point where the two rays cross. This is the position of the top of the image I.

With an accurately drawn ray diagram, you can see that the image is inverted, reduced and real.

It is helpful to understand why we draw rays 1 and 2 as shown in Figure 14.15. Ray 1 passes through the middle of the lens. Here, the lens is thin and its sides are parallel, so the ray emerges undeflected. Ray 2 bends twice, at the two surfaces of the lens. It is easier to show it bending once in the middle of the lens, though this is not a correct representation of what really happens. Sometimes lenses are shown merely as a vertical line, with a small drawing above it to show the shape of the lens.

Cameras, eyes and projectors

A camera uses a single lens to capture an image of a scene on film. As you can see from the ray diagram in Figure 14.16, the image on the film is upside down. Some cameras can be focused, so that the picture will be clear if the object is close to the camera. To focus the image, the lens must be moved back and forth in front of the film. The closer the object, the further the lens must be from the film. (Many simple cameras cannot be focused. They assume that the scene being

Figure 14.16 How an image is formed on the film in a camera. **a** For a distant object, the single lens focuses rays onto the film. **b** If the object is close up, the image will form further from the lens, so the lens must be moved away from the film. This is what we do when we 'focus' a camera before taking a picture.

a distant object

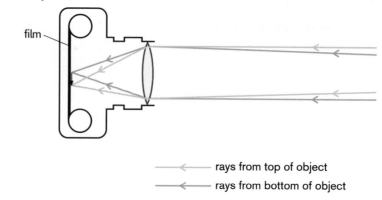

——◄—— rays from top of object

——◄—— rays from bottom of object

b close object

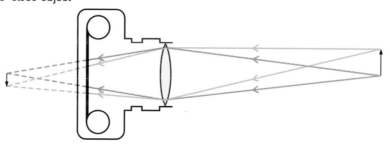

photographed is a reasonable distance from the camera – say, at least 2 m. Then the lens is fixed so that the film is at its focus. Anything too close to the lens will appear blurred.)

The human eye works in a slightly different way to a camera. The lens helps to focus rays of light onto the retina. The lens changes shape from thin to fat to focus objects that are close up. The image on the retina is upside down, but this is not a problem. Your brain is perfectly used to interpreting images like this – it knows which way up the world is. Psychologists have carried out experiments in which people wear spectacles that turn the image the other way up. At first, the world appears upside down, but soon the brain flips the wearer's mental image the right way up again. When they take the spectacles off, the world looks upside down again for a few hours.

A slide projector is like a camera working in reverse. A camera produces a small image of a large object. A projector produces a large image on the screen of a small object, the slide. To do this, the slide is placed close to the focus of the projector lens. Its position must be adjusted carefully to produce a focused image on the screen. If you have ever used a projector, you will know that the slides must be put in upside down so that the image on the screen is the right way up.

Extension material

Magnifying glasses

A magnifying glass is a converging lens. You hold it close to a small object and peer through it to see a magnified image. Figure 14.17 shows how a magnifying glass can help to magnify print for someone with poor eyesight.

The object viewed by a magnifying glass is closer to the lens than the focal point. This allows us to draw a ray diagram, as shown in Figure 14.18. We draw two rays from the top of the object O, the same two rays as in Figure 14.15:

- Ray 1 is undeflected as it passes through the centre of the lens.
- Ray 2 starts off parallel to the axis; it is deflected by the lens so that it passes through the focus.

Rays 1 and 2 do not cross over each other; they are diverging (spreading apart) after they have passed through the lens. However, by extending the rays backwards, as shown by the dashed lines, we can see that they appear to be coming from a point behind the object. This is the position of the image I. We draw dashed lines because light does not actually travel along these parts of the rays. This tells us that the image formed is virtual; we cannot catch the image on a screen, because there is no light there.

From the ray diagram, we can see the following features of the image produced by a magnifying glass:

- The image is upright (the right way up, not inverted).
- The image is magnified (bigger than the object).

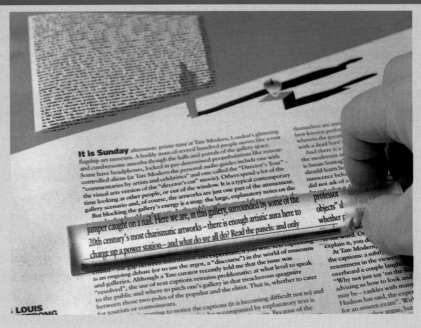

Figure 14.17   This large converging lens is designed to help people to read. It produces a magnified image of a line of print. The user simply slides it down the page.

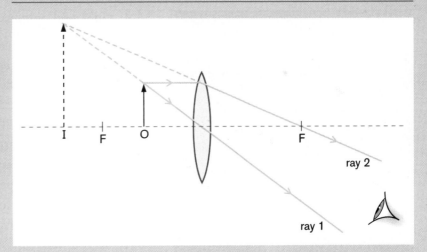

Figure 14.18   A ray diagram to show how a magnifying glass works. The object is between the lens and the focus. The image produced is virtual; to find its position, the rays have to be extended back (dashed lines) to the point where they cross.

- The image is farther from the lens than the object.
- The image is virtual (not real).

    So, if you read a page of a book using a magnifying glass, the image you are looking at is behind the page that you are reading.

? **Questions**

14.15 Draw and label a diagram to show the difference in shape between a converging lens and a diverging lens.

14.16 Draw a ray diagram to show how a converging lens focuses parallel rays of light.

14.17 How would you alter your diagram in the previous question to show how a converging lens can produce a beam of parallel rays of light?

14.18 What is meant by the focus (or focal point) of a converging lens?

14.19 What is the difference between a real image and a virtual image?

14.20 Look at the last ray diagram shown in Figure 14.15 on page 221. How does it show that the image formed by a converging lens is inverted?

14.21 A camera is focused on a distant scene. How must its lens be adjusted to focus on a nearby object?

Figure 14.19 Cut glass is used for ornaments and chandeliers, because it shows all the colours of the rainbow as it moves in the light.

14.4 Light and colour

Diamonds are attractive because they sparkle. As you turn a cut diamond, light flashes from its different surfaces. As we have seen, this is a result of total internal reflection of light within the diamond. You may also notice that you can see all sorts of colours in the diamond, even though the diamond itself is likely to be colourless. (Some diamonds are slightly yellow, because they contain impurities.) Where do these varying colours come from?

Cut glass is a lot cheaper than diamonds, and has many more uses (Figure 14.19). It is used for chandeliers, which move gently in the air. It is also used for glass ornaments; your eye is caught by the changing colours as you walk past. Again, the glass itself is colourless, so where do these colours come from?

The underlying principle is shown in Figure 14.20. A ray of white light is shone at a prism; it refracts as it enters and leaves the glass. At the same time, it is split into a **spectrum** of colours. You should notice that the colours merge into one another, and they are not all of equal widths in the spectrum.

Traditionally, we say that there are seven colours in the spectrum. The number seven was chosen because it had a mystical significance in the seventeenth century. It is very hard to distinguish between indigo and violet at the end of the spectrum, so you might say that there are really only six colours. Alternatively, you might suggest that there are many shades of red present, and of each of the other colours, so the

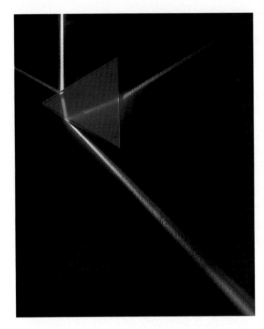

Figure 14.20 A spectrum can be produced by shining a ray of white light through a glass prism. The light is split up into a spectrum.

spectrum shows many more than seven colours. The standard list is as follows:

red orange yellow green blue indigo violet

There are different ways of remembering this list. One simple way is to remember the sequence of initial letters in the form of someone's name: Roy G Biv.

Explaining the spectrum

This splitting up of white light into a spectrum is known as **dispersion** (which means 'spreading out'). Isaac Newton set out to explain how it happens. It had been suggested that light is coloured by passing it through a prism. Newton showed that this was the wrong idea by arranging for the spectrum to be passed back through another prism. The colours recombined to form white light again. He concluded that white light is a mixture of all the different colours of the spectrum.

So what happens in a prism to produce a spectrum? As the white light enters the prism, it slows down. We say that it is refracted and, as we have seen, its direction changes. **Dispersion** occurs because each colour is refracted by a different amount. Violet light slows down the most, and so it is refracted the most. Red light is least affected.

A rainbow (Figure 14.21) is a naturally occurring spectrum. White light from the Sun is dispersed as it enters and leaves droplets of water in the air. It is also reflected back to the viewer by total internal reflection, which is why you must have the Sun behind you to be able to observe a rainbow.

Laser light is not dispersed by a prism. It is refracted so that it changes direction, but it is not split up into a spectrum. This is because it is light of a single colour, and is described as **monochromatic** (*mono* = one, *chromatic* = coloured).

Figure 14.21 A rainbow shows all the colours of the spectrum. White light from the Sun is split up into its constituent colours as it is refracted by water droplets in the air.

> **? Questions**
>
> **14.22** What colours are next to green in the spectrum?
>
> **14.23** Draw a diagram to show how white light can be dispersed into a spectrum using a glass prism.
>
> **14.24** Why are some colours of light more strongly refracted than others when they enter glass?

Summary

◆ A light ray changes direction when it meets the boundary between two different materials (unless it meets the boundary at right-angles). This bending is known as refraction.

◆ Refraction occurs because the speed of light changes as it travels from one material into another.

◆ A ray bends towards the normal as it enters a material where it travels more slowly (e.g. from air into glass), and away from the normal on entering a material where it travels more quickly.

◆ The higher the refractive index of a material, the slower light travels in that material.

◆ A ray is totally internally reflected when it strikes a boundary at an angle greater than the critical angle.

◆ Total internal reflection has many uses: in optical instruments, endoscopes, optical fibres for telecommunications, etc.

◆ Lenses make use of refraction. A converging lens makes parallel rays of light converge. A diverging lens makes parallel rays of light diverge.

◈ *A magnifying glass is a converging lens, used with the object closer than the focal point. It produces a magnified, virtual image.*

◆ White light may be split up into the colours of the spectrum by passing it through a glass prism. This is dispersion.

◆ Dispersion occurs because different colours of light travel at different speeds through glass, so some colours are refracted more than others.

The electromagnetic spectrum

Topics in this **chapter**

◆ electromagnetic radiation

◆ wavelengths and frequencies

◆ production and detection

◆ uses

◆ hazards

The rainbow is the most familiar example of the spectrum of visible light (Figure 15.1). Our eyes have evolved to allow us to see all the colours of the spectrum, from red to violet. The retina of the human eye contains rod cells, which allow us to see in low light levels, and three types of cone cell, which detect different regions of the spectrum – red, green and blue. When we see yellow light, it is because the red and green cells are stimulated most and our brain says – both red and green stimulated, must be in between, that's yellow. Scientists still argue as to whether other animals such as cats and dogs can see in colour, or merely in black and white. These animals are rather dull colours themselves, so it is possible that they cannot see the same range of colours that we can. Colourful parrots, however, use their colours to attract a mate, so they must have good colour vision.

Figure 15.1 Isaac Newton studied light, and wrote about the origin of rainbows: 'This Bow never appears but where it rains in the Sunshine.'

Figure 15.2 The top photograph shows a flower as seen by the human eye, which can only see the colours of the visible spectrum. Below, it is shown as seen by an insect that can see ultraviolet light, invisible to us. The photographic film used to make this photograph is sensitive to ultraviolet light. The insect can see a pattern of 'honey-guides' on the petals of the flower, and it follows these down to the store of nectar. As it does so, pollen is rubbed onto its body. Pollen from another flower may also be rubbed from the insect's body onto the stigma of the flower.

Insects and flowers have evolved together. They need each other: the insects need nectar from the flowers, and the flowers need the insects to pollinate them. Insects are attracted by the colours of flowers, and many flowers are specially patterned to guide insects to the source of nectar. Often, we cannot see these patterns. This is because they only show up in ultraviolet light, which is invisible to us, but visible to insects. Figure 15.2 shows how the appearance of a flower changes when it is viewed in ultraviolet light.

This chapter looks at ultraviolet radiation and the other types of invisible radiation that are around us but invisible to us. These different types of radiation make up the **electromagnetic spectrum**.

15.1 Extending the visible spectrum

Below the red

In 1799, William Herschel was examining the spectrum of light from the Sun. He was an astronomer, German by birth but working at Slough, near London. He knew that the Sun is a star and wondered what he might find out about the Sun by looking at its spectrum. He shone the Sun's light through a prism to produce a spectrum, then placed a thermometer at different points in the spectrum. The reading on the thermometer rose, because objects get warm when they absorb light. Herschel noticed an interesting effect – the thermometer reading grew higher as he moved towards the red end of the spectrum. What would happen if he moved just beyond the end? To his surprise, he found that the reading was higher still. There was nothing to be seen beyond the red, but there was definitely something there. A little further, and the mercury in the thermometer rose higher still. Further still, and it started to fall.

Herschel had discovered an invisible form of radiation, which he called **infrared radiation**. (The word *infra* means 'below', 'lower down' or 'further on'.) You can experience infrared radiation for yourself, using a kettle that has recently boiled. With great care, hold the back of your hand near to the kettle. You feel the warmth of the kettle as it is absorbed by your skin. The kettle is emitting infrared radiation. (We sometimes call this 'heat' – see Chapter 10 – but 'infrared radiation' is a better term.)

It isn't surprising to learn that we receive heat from the Sun. However, what is surprising is that this radiation behaves in such a similar way to light – it is as if it is just an extension of the spectrum of visible light.

Beyond the violet

In 1839, a French physicist called Edmond Becquerel was experimenting with photography, which had recently been invented. He made a photograph of the Sun's spectrum and, when he looked at his negative,

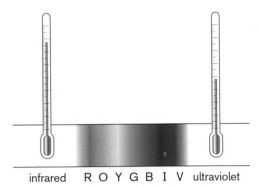

infrared R O Y G B I V **ultraviolet**

Figure 15.3 The spectrum of light from the Sun extends beyond the visible region, from infrared to ultraviolet. Thermometers placed outside the visible region will still be warmed by the Sun.

he discovered that the spectrum extended far beyond the violet region. He had discovered another extension of the spectrum, which he called **ultraviolet radiation**. (The word *ultra* means 'beyond', 'above' or 'extremely'.) Although our eyes cannot detect ultraviolet radiation, sensitive photographic film can – see Figure 15.3.

Both infrared and ultraviolet radiation were discovered by looking at the spectrum of light from the Sun. However, they don't have to be produced by an object like the Sun. Picture a lump of iron that you heat in a Bunsen flame. At first, it looks dull and black. Take it from the flame and you will find that it is emitting infrared radiation. Put it back in the flame and heat it more. It begins to glow, first a dull red colour, then more yellow. In a furnace it would eventually become white hot. It is emitting visible light. When its temperature reaches about 1000 °C, it will also be emitting appreciable amounts of ultraviolet radiation.

This experiment should suggest to you that there is a connection between infrared, visible and ultraviolet radiations. A cool object emits only radiation at the cool end of the spectrum; the hotter the object, the more radiation it emits in the visible and ultraviolet regions of the spectrum.

The Sun is a very hot object (Figure 15.4). Its surface temperature is about 7000 °C, so it emits a lot of ultraviolet radiation. Most of this is absorbed in the Earth's atmosphere, particularly by the ozone layer. A small amount does get through to us. The thinning of the ozone layer by chemicals released by human activity means that this amount is increasing. This increased exposure is disturbing because it increases the risk of skin cancer.

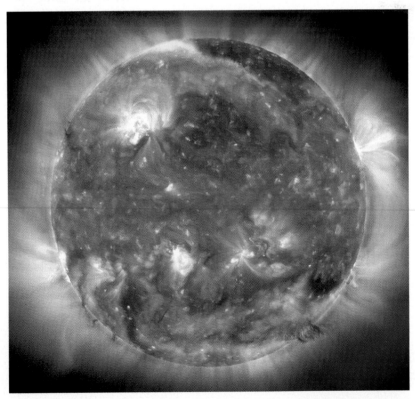

Figure 15.4 The Sun is examined by several satellite observatories. This image was produced by the SOHO satellite using a camera that detects the ultraviolet radiation given off by the Sun. You can see some detail of the Sun's surface, including giant prominences looping out into space. The different colours indicate variations in the temperature across the Sun's surface.

Electromagnetic waves

In Chapter 12, we saw that sound can be thought of as vibrations or waves travelling through the air (or any other material). Sounds can have different pitches: the higher the frequency, the higher the pitch. We could think of a piano keyboard as being a 'spectrum' of sounds of different frequencies.

In Chapter 14, we saw that a spectrum is formed when light passes through a prism because some colours are refracted more than others. The violet end of the spectrum is refracted most. Now we can deduce that ultraviolet radiation is refracted even more. On the other hand, infrared radiation is refracted less than red light. To explain the spectrum, and other features of light, we can think of light as being another form of wave. Physicists have developed the **wave model** of light:

- Visible light occurs as a spectrum of colours, depending on its frequency.
- Red light has a lower frequency than violet light.

A Scottish physicist, James Clerk Maxwell, eventually showed in 1860 that light was in fact small oscillations in electric and magnetic fields, or **electromagnetic waves**. His theory allowed him to predict that they could have *any* value of frequency. In other words, beyond the infrared and ultraviolet regions of the spectrum, there must be even more types of electromagnetic wave. By the early years of the twentieth century, physicists had discovered or artificially produced several other types of electromagnetic wave (see Table 15.1), to complete the electromagnetic spectrum. Maxwell also predicted that all electromagnetic waves travel at the same speed through empty space, the speed of light (almost 300 000 000 m/s). We now know the following about electromagnetic waves:

All electromagnetic waves travel in straight lines through empty space, at the speed of light.
All electromagnetic waves carry energy.

Wavelength and frequency

We can represent light as a wave, just as we represented the small changes in air pressure as a sound wave (page 194). Figure 15.5 compares red light with violet light. Red light has a greater wavelength

Type of electromagnetic wave	Discoverer	Date
infrared	William Herschel	1799
ultraviolet	Edmond Becquerel	1839
radio waves	Heinrich Hertz	1887
X-rays	Wilhelm Röntgen	1895
gamma rays	Henri Becquerel	1896

Table 15.1 Discoverers of electromagnetic waves. Henri Becquerel was the son of Edmond.

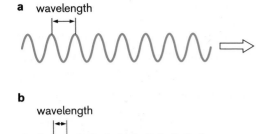

a wavelength

b wavelength

Figure 15.5 Comparing **a** red and **b** violet light waves. Both travel at the same speed, but red light has a longer wavelength because its frequency is less. The wavelength is the distance from one crest to the next (or from one trough to the next). Think of red light waves as long, lazy waves; violet light is made up of shorter, more rapidly vibrating waves.

than violet light – that is, there is a greater distance from one wave crest to the next. This is because both red and violet light travel at the same speed (as predicted by Maxwell), but violet light has a greater frequency, so more oscillations fit into the same length.

The waves that make up visible light have very high frequencies: over 100 million million hertz, or 10^{14} Hz. Their wavelengths are very small, from 400 nm for violet light to 700 nm for red light (1 nm is one billionth of a metre, so 400 nm = 400×10^{-9} m), so more than one million waves of visible light fit into a metre.

Figure 15.6 shows the complete electromagnetic spectrum, with the wavelengths and frequencies of each region. In fact, we cannot be very precise about where each region starts and stops. Even the ends of the visible light section are uncertain, because different people can see slightly different ranges of wavelengths, just as they can hear different ranges of sound frequencies.

In the rest of this chapter, we will look at each region of the spectrum, how the waves are produced and detected, how they are used, and their effects on living creatures such as ourselves.

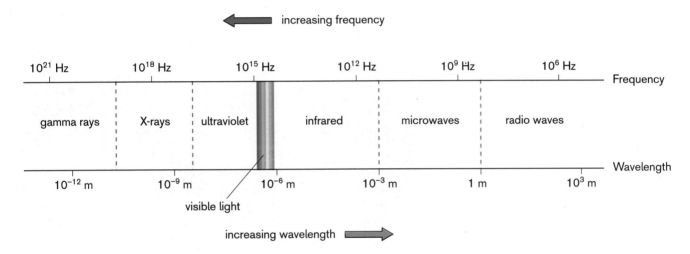

Figure 15.6 The electromagnetic spectrum. The scale of frequencies increases along one side; the scale of wavelengths increases in the opposite direction.

Questions

15.1 **a** Which has a longer wavelength, red light or violet light?

   b Which has a greater frequency?

15.2 **a** Which has a longer wavelength, red light or infrared radiation?

   b Which has a greater frequency?

15.3 Look at the spectrum shown in Figure 15.6.

   a Which waves have the shortest wavelength?

   b Which waves have the lowest frequency?

15.4 At what speed do electromagnetic waves travel through empty space?

? **Questions continued**

15.5 **a** Which travels faster in empty space, violet light or red light?

b Which travels faster in glass?

15.2 Infrared and ultraviolet radiation

Producing infrared radiation

Everything produces infrared radiation. We are used to the idea that warm objects are sources of infrared radiation. If an object is warmer than its surroundings, it cools down by emitting infrared radiation. In fact, even cold objects produce infrared radiation. As we saw in Chapter 10, an object that is colder than its surroundings absorbs infrared radiation more quickly than it emits it, so it warms up.

Infrared cameras can detect the radiation coming from an object. This is used by the police for detecting stolen cars or lost people at night; their warmth can be spotted by the camera (Figure 15.7).

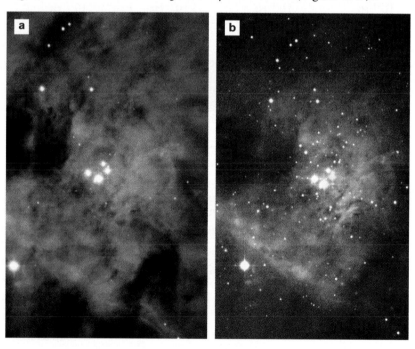

Figure 15.7 Astronomers often find that images of stars are clearer when they look at infrared wavelengths. These two images show the Orion Nebula **a** seen in visible light and **b** seen in infrared.

Just as some insects can see ultraviolet radiation, so some creatures can see infrared. Rattlesnakes and similar vipers can detect their warm-blooded prey in the dark, using special organs called pits, located near their eyes. This makes it difficult to get away from an attacking snake at night. (Insects that can see ultraviolet radiation are usually blind to red and orange light. Perhaps they would refer to these as 'infra-yellow radiation'.)

Uses of infrared radiation

- *Cooking* A conventional oven cooks by infrared radiation. The inside of the oven gets hot – say, 200 °C – and infrared waves radiate around inside it. Some are absorbed by the food, and this gets hot, so that the chemical reactions of cooking take place. An electric toaster is even hotter; the elements glow as the temperature rises above 500 °C. The infrared radiation is then intense enough to produce rapid browning of the bread.

- *Optical fibres* Most optical fibres found in telecommunications use infrared radiation. A tiny laser sends a beam of infrared radiation down the glass fibre. Total internal reflection (see page 215) ensures that the beam stays inside the fibre. In order for the fibre to be able to carry many signals (telephone or television messages), the beam is **modulated**. This means that the beam is switched on and off many millions of times a second so that the signal is carried in digital form, rather like Morse code. Infrared is used because it is less readily absorbed by the glass of the fibre, so the signal can travel further before it needs to be amplified.

- *Remote control* A television remote control (Figure 15.8) uses infrared radiation to change channels at a distance. The control emits a burst of infrared when a button is pressed. As with optical fibres, the infrared is modulated in an on–off pattern, a different pattern for each button. The television set detects the pattern and switches to the appropriate channel. Some cars have infrared 'keys' that lock and unlock the doors when the driver operates the button.

Figure 15.8 Many remote controls and car remote locks use infrared radiation. You cannot see the beam, but you can experiment by bouncing it off walls and windows to see its path to the detector on the television set or car dashboard.

Hazards of infrared radiation

We have nerve endings in our skin that allow us to detect infrared radiation. This is useful, because intense infrared can cause burns to skin and flesh.

Producing ultraviolet radiation

Very hot objects, glowing white hot, produce ultraviolet radiation. The hotter the object, the more intense is the radiation it produces, and the more penetrating it is. The Sun is the most intense source of ultraviolet radiation that we are likely to come across. However, some people have to work with ultraviolet radiation. For example, welders work with white hot material when they are joining two pieces of metal together, and they must wear protective clothing and eye-shields to avoid damaging themselves. Similarly, newly made steel as it is released from a blast furnace is white hot and emits large amounts of ultraviolet radiation; workers in the area wear protective clothing (Figure 15.9).

Uses of ultraviolet radiation

- *Fluorescent lights* Fluorescent lights, tubes and low-energy lamps produce ultraviolet radiation. They consist of a tube containing

mercury vapour. When switched on, an electric current flows through the vapour, causing it to glow faintly. Most of the radiation produced is ultraviolet. To convert this to light we can see, the inside of the tube is coated with a substance that absorbs the ultraviolet radiation and re-emits its energy as visible light.

- *Detergent additives* The process of absorbing ultraviolet light and re-emitting it as visible light is known as **fluorescence**. Many detergents for washing clothes contain chemicals called optical brighteners, which help to make the clothes look 'whiter than white'. Traces of these fluorescent substances are left on the clothes after washing, and they absorb ultraviolet radiation from sunlight and re-emit it as visible light. Hence the clothes look brighter and whiter than if they were simply pure white. Clothes that have been washed in this way show up as purple under ultraviolet lights. You sometimes see this effect at discos, and it is used for some stage effects in the theatre.

- *Security marking* Fluorescent markers are used in security coding (Figure 15.10). Valuable objects are marked using a pen that contains fluorescent ink. The markings cannot be seen under ordinary light, but they show up when ultraviolet light is shone on them.

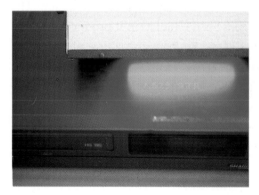

Figure 15.10 Security marking of valuables is often done using a fluorescent marker pen. The markings become visible when ultraviolet light is shone on them.

Hazards of ultraviolet radiation

Ultraviolet radiation can cause tanning of the skin. It is a penetrating form of radiation, and it stimulates the skin to produce a pigment called melanin. People from hot countries where the Sun's rays are more intense tend to have darker skin. The presence of melanin helps to protect them from the damage that ultraviolet radiation can do.

People with fair skin are particularly advised to avoid exposing themselves to too much strong sunlight (Figure 15.11), so beach holidays can be risky. The ultraviolet radiation can produce damage in the cells. The result can be reddening and burning of the skin, and skin cancer. Sun-tan lotion contains chemicals that absorb the ultraviolet radiation, but it is important to ensure that the skin is well-covered in the lotion to avoid any possible harm.

Figure 15.11 People with fair skin, in particular, should avoid excessive exposure to ultraviolet radiation. Today, many people from temperate climates have the opportunity to visit hot countries for holidays. At the same time, the damage to the ozone layer means that we are exposed to more intense ultraviolet radiation. As a consequence, the incidence of skin cancer is increasing rapidly.

Ultraviolet radiation can also damage the eyes, increasing the possibility of cataracts in the lens. This leaves the lens opaque, so that an artificial one may have to be fitted. That is why welders wear masks when they are working. The mask has a glass panel to see through. Glass is a good absorber of ultraviolet radiation, which is why people don't get tanned by sunlight coming through windows.

As well as beach holidays, winter sports holidays can also be risky. On snowy mountains, you are high up and there is less atmosphere above you to absorb dangerous ultraviolet radiation. Sunburn can happen quickly, so sun-tan lotion and protective clothing are advisable. Goggles protect eyes against the harmful rays.

Questions

15.6 Why is infrared radiation used in optical fibre communication systems, in preference to visible light or ultraviolet radiation?

15.7 **a** What two forms of damage to the skin can be caused by over-exposure to ultraviolet radiation?

b How can the eyes be harmed?

15.8 Which type of radiation is emitted by all objects?

15.9 Explain how security markings made with a fluorescent marker pen can be seen under ultraviolet light.

15.10 Which type of radiation is emitted by a television remote control?

15.3 Radio waves and microwaves

Radio waves are another form of electromagnetic radiation that we cannot see. However, they are around us all the time. Microwaves are similar to radio waves. There is no clear division between these two regions of the electromagnetic spectrum; in general, radio waves have longer wavelengths than microwaves. Like all forms of electromagnetic radiation, radio waves and microwaves travel in straight lines.

Figure 15.12 **a** This radio telescope is a giant dish, which acts like a mirror, focusing radio waves from distant objects in space. **b** An image obtained using a radio telescope. There is a massive galaxy at the centre of the picture. It is blasting material out into space, and this material is the source of strong radio waves, which are detected to make the picture. The giant bubbles of gas on the left are bigger than our own galaxy.

Producing radio waves and microwaves

A radio transmitter consists of an aerial, which may simply be a metal rod, with an electric current flowing up and down inside it. As the current changes, waves of electric and magnetic fields are radiated by the aerial, and these are detected by anyone with a suitable radio or television set. The waves make a current flow in the aerial attached to the radio or TV.

In addition to the waves used for broadcasting, radio waves come to us from space. Giant radio telescopes like the one shown in Figure 15.12a pick up the waves and convert them into images of objects in distant space (Figure 15.12b). Radio astronomers can detect dark objects in space which cannot be seen using ordinary telescopes. These objects may be too cool to produce visible light.

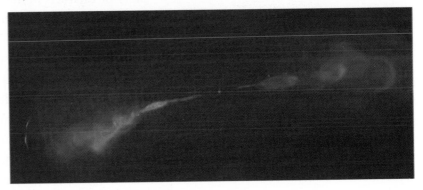

Using radio waves and microwaves

- *Radio and television* The discovery of radio waves, late in the nineteenth century, made broadcasting possible, both radio and television. Although radio waves and microwaves travel in straight lines, radio waves are reflected by layers of charged particles high up in the atmosphere. This means that radio signals follow the curve of the Earth, so that the signals do not disappear off into space (Figure 15.13). In the summer, the atmosphere becomes more highly charged and so radio signals are more strongly reflected. This means that it can be possible to pick up radio stations that are a long way off. It may be interesting to listen to broadcasts from thousands of miles away, or it may be a nuisance if these signals are using the same frequency as a local station to which you are trying to listen.

- *Satellite communication and tracking* Microwaves are not affected by the atmosphere (Figure 15.13). This means that they can be beamed directly out into space, so they can be used for communicating with satellites in Earth orbit, or elsewhere in the Solar System. Telephone messages are transmitted by microwave links around the Earth, passed from the ground up to communications satellites. The programmes beamed down to Earth from television satellites are sent up using microwaves. Microwaves are also used for the radar

Figure 15.13 Radio waves are bent when they reflect off the ionosphere, a charged layer in the atmosphere. This means that they travel around the Earth, following its curved surface. Microwaves are unaffected by the atmosphere, and so can be beamed directly into space. They are used for carrying messages up to communications satellites, for transmitting telephone calls or for broadcasting satellite TV programmes.

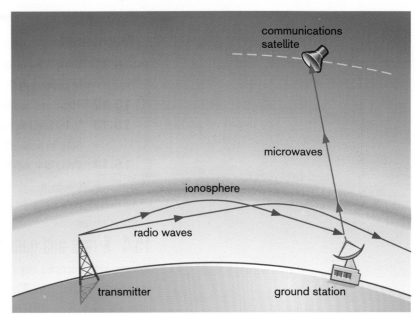

Figure 15.14 Looking inside a microwave oven, you may be able to see the rectangular hole through which the microwaves enter the oven. It is a few centimetres across, which gives you an idea of their wavelength. The microwave oven was invented by accident, by an American called Percy Spencer. He was working with microwaves when he noticed that some confectionery in his pocket had melted.

systems used by air traffic controllers to track aircraft, and on ships to check the positions of other ships nearby.

- *Microwave heating* Like all electromagnetic waves, microwaves cause heating when they are absorbed. Water is a good absorber of microwaves, and this is made use of in microwave cookers (Figure 15.14). Microwaves enter the cooker and bounce around inside, reflected by the metal walls. Any food that contains water absorbs the microwaves inside the cooker, gets hot and cooks. It is not strictly true to say that a microwave oven 'cooks food from the inside out'. Microwaves are gradually absorbed as they travel into the food. If the food is very thick, the middle may not be properly cooked when the outside is ready to eat.

Hazards of radio waves and microwaves

The microwave oven points to a hazard of microwaves and radio waves. The door of a microwave oven is fitted with a safety lock so that the source of microwaves is switched off as the door opens. Otherwise the user might be exposed to microwaves, which could be absorbed by the body.

Mobile phones transmit radio waves to carry their messages to a nearby receiving aerial. The aerial on the phone is very close to the user's ear, and this means that the head is exposed to radio waves. The brain contains water, which absorbs radio waves, and this can cause heating of the brain by around 0.1 °C. Young people, in particular, are advised to limit their use of such phones.

? **Questions**

15.11 Which have higher frequencies, radio waves or microwaves?

15.12 How are radio waves affected by the Earth's atmosphere?

15.13 Why are microwaves used for sending messages to satellites in space?

15.14 Why is it advisable to limit the use of mobile phones?

15.4 X-rays and gamma rays

X-rays and gamma rays are the shortest-wavelength forms of electromagnetic radiation. There is no strict division between X-rays and gamma rays. The difference is in the way in which they are produced. In general, gamma rays have shorter wavelengths and higher frequencies than X-rays.

Producing X-rays and gamma rays

In the X-ray machines used by doctors and dentists, a beam of fast-moving electrons collides with a metal target. The energy of the electrons is converted into X-rays, which are given off by the metal.

Gamma rays are produced by radioactive substances. They come from the nucleus of an atom when it decays. There is more about gamma radiation in Chapter 25.

Using X-rays and gamma rays

- *Medical imaging* The most familiar use of X-rays is in providing medical images of the insides of people or animals (Figure 15.15). A broad beam of X-rays is passed through the patient's body and detected using either a photographic film or an electronic detector, which can provide an image on a monitor screen. Bones absorb X-rays more readily than muscle or skin, so the patient's bones appear as a shadow on the image. To see soft tissues such as the gut, the patient may have to swallow a substance that absorbs X-rays. With exposure to the right dose of X-rays and a sensitive detector, a very clear image of bones and internal organs can be achieved.
- *CT scanning* In CT (computed tomography) scanning, the patient is subjected to much higher doses of X-rays. These are directed into the body at different points along it, and a computer then builds up a three-dimensional image of the patient's insides. Although this involves a much higher dose of harmful X-rays, in certain medical cases it provides the best diagnosis.
- *Security checks* X-rays are used to scan passengers' luggage in security checks at airports. A detailed picture appears on a screen

Figure 15.15 Vets use X-rays to examine the animals that are their patients. The animal's bones, which absorb X-rays more readily than soft tissue, show up as white shadows on the screen.

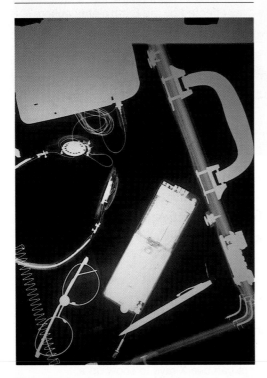

Figure 15.16 This image from an airport security X-ray machine gives a detailed view of objects in a briefcase. Guns and explosive materials may also be detected in this way.

(Figure 15.16), and the operator can identify suspect objects. Giant X-ray machines are also used at ports or other checkpoints to examine the contents of lorries without the need to open them up. Customs officers look at the images to see if they can detect illegal drugs, arms or stowaways.

- *Structural engineering* Gamma rays are used to examine large structures such as bridges. A beam of gamma radiation from a radioactive source is directed through the structure, and detected using photographic film or an electronic detector on the other side. This can show up any problems with the steel rods inside pre-stressed concrete without the need to break open the concrete.

Hazards of X-rays and gamma rays

Because these types of electromagnetic radiation are very energetic and penetrating, they have to be used with care. Large doses can damage cells, causing radiation burns. Even small doses can damage the genetic material in cells, and this can trigger cancer. When X-rays are used for medical imaging, the doctor must always balance up the possibility of starting a cancer against the benefit of having an image that will help with diagnosis.

Gamma rays are sometimes used to help destroy cancer cells (Figure 15.17). The patient is X-rayed to establish the exact position of their tumour, and then gamma rays are directed at the precise spot. The energy released kills the cancer cells.

Because gamma rays are so effective at killing cells, they are used for sterilising medical equipment. Items such as syringes and scalpels are first packed in cellophane wrappers. Then they are exposed to high-intensity gamma rays, which penetrate the packaging and destroy any bacteria or other living cells. When the doctor or nurse opens the package, they can be sure that the item is entirely sterile.

Some foodstuffs are also sterilised in this way. This is useful for hospital patients who are vulnerable to infections; it has also been used

Figure 15.17 This patient is suffering from cancer. The technician ensures that the gamma rays used to destroy the cancerous tissue are directed only at the tumour. The beam is sent in from different directions, so that the surrounding tissues receive a much weaker dose than the tumour.

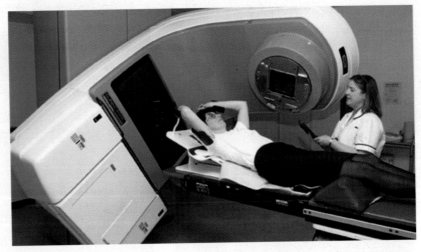

for in-flight catering for astronauts. Sterilised foods have a longer shelf-life because any micro-organisms that can make them go off have been killed. Different countries permit different foods to be sterilised using gamma rays, because there are still concerns that it may be hazardous to health.

Questions

15.15 Which have shorter wavelengths, X-rays or gamma radiation?

15.16 Explain how doctors can use X-rays to show up a patient's broken bone.

15.17 Give a non-medical use for X-rays.

15.18 How can gamma rays be used to treat cancer?

15.19 Give a non-medical use for gamma radiation.

15.20 Why should a patient's exposure to X-rays be kept to a minimum?

Summary

◆ The spectrum of visible light is only part of a much wider spectrum, known as the electromagnetic spectrum.

◆ All electromagnetic waves travel in straight lines through empty space, at the speed of light.

◆ The regions of the electromagnetic spectrum are:

longest wavelength		lowest frequency
↑	radio waves	↓
	microwaves	
	infrared	
	visible light	
	ultraviolet	
	X-rays	
shortest wavelength	gamma radiation	highest frequency

◆ Electromagnetic waves carry energy. When they are absorbed, the absorbing material gets hotter. Ultraviolet, X-rays and gamma rays can cause damage to cells, which may lead to cancer.

◆ We use electromagnetic radiation in many different ways. It is important to be aware of the hazards associated with them, to avoid dangerous levels of exposure.

Waves

Topics in this chapter

◆ describing waves

◆ transverse and longitudinal waves

◆ speed, frequency and wavelength

◆ explaining reflection and refraction

◆ diffraction

◉ *interference*

It can't be much fun to be adrift in a small boat on a rough sea. The waves toss you up and down, threatening to overturn your boat. You wonder if the next big wave will be your last.

For some birds, this is a regular experience. Many seabirds spend the whole winter on the open sea, at a time when the sea is at its roughest (Figure 16.1). The waves may be twenty metres high, enough to dwarf a two-storey house, but the birds feel safer here than they would on the cliffs where they nest in the spring. Guillemots, for example, cluster together in 'rafts', carried up and down by the waves. It is this up-and-down motion that is liable to make you feel sea-sick if you are on-board a ship in stormy weather.

Figure 16.1 Many seabirds such as guillemots spend the whole of the winter on the open ocean. They gather together in 'rafts', and spend their days and nights riding up and down on the waves.

Figure 16.2 Surfers look out for waves that are beginning to break. The top of the wave is tipping over, and this provides the push they need to start them moving along with the crest of the wave.

When waves reach the beach, they start to break. The bottom of the wave drags on the sea-bed and slows down. The top of the wave carries on and gradually tips over to form a breaker. Breaking waves like this are the natural home of the surfer (Figure 16.2).

Physicists talk about light waves, sound waves and electromagnetic waves. The idea of a wave is a very useful model in physics. It isn't obvious that light and sound are similar to waves on the sea. However, in this chapter we will see how water waves can act as a good model for both light and sound. When you think of waves, you may picture breakers on a beach. However, the water waves that we will be thinking about are more like those on the open sea.

16.1 Describing waves

Physicists use waves as a **model** to explain the behaviour of light, sound and other phenomena. Waves are what we see on the sea or a lake, but physicists have a more specialised idea of waves. We can begin to understand this model in the laboratory using a **ripple tank** (Figure 16.3). A ripple tank is a shallow glass-bottomed tank containing a small amount of water. A light shining downwards through the water casts a shadow of any ripples onto the floor below, showing up the pattern that they make.

Figure 16.4 shows two patterns of ripples.

a One way of making ripples on its surface is to have a straight wooden bar that touches the surface of the water. This bar vibrates up and down at a steady rate, and this sends equally spaced straight ripples across the surface of the water.

b A spherical dipper can produce a different pattern of ripples. Like the bar, the dipper touches the surface of the water. As the dipper vibrates up and down, equally spaced circular ripples spread out across the surface of the water.

In each case, the ripples are produced by something vibrating *up and down*, but the ripples move out *horizontally*. The vibrating bar or

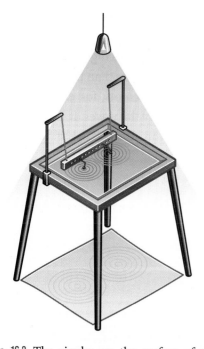

Figure 16.3 The ripples on the surface of the water in this ripple tank are produced by the bar, which vibrates up and down. The pattern of the ripples is seen easily by shining a light downwards through the water. This casts a shadow of the ripples on the floor beneath the tank.

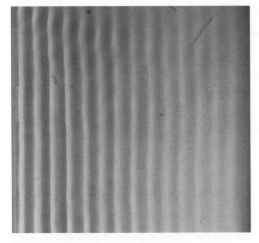

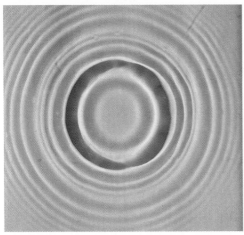

Figure 16.4 Two patterns of ripples on water. **a** Straight ripples are a model for a broad beam of light. **b** Circular ripples are a model for light spreading out from a lamp.

dipper pushes water molecules up and down. Each molecule drags its neighbours up and down; these then start their neighbours moving, and so on. This may make you think of the seabirds we discussed, floating on the rough sea. The waves go past the birds; the birds simply float up and down on the surface of the water.

How can these patterns of ripples be a model for the behaviour of light? The circular ripples spreading out from a vibrating dipper are like light spreading out from a lamp. (The dipper is the lamp.) The straight ripples are like a beam of light, perhaps coming from the Sun. The ripples move straight across the surface of the water, just as light from the Sun travels in straight lines. Throughout this chapter, we will gradually build up the idea of how ripples on the surface of water can be a model for the behaviour of light, other electromagnetic waves and sound.

Wavelength and amplitude

A more familiar way of representing a wave is as a wavy line, as shown in Figure 16.5. We have already used this idea for sound waves (in Chapter 12) and for electromagnetic waves (in Chapter 15). This wavy line is like a downward slice though the ripples in the ripple tank. It shows up the succession of crests and troughs of which the ripples are made.

The graph in Figure 16.5 shows a wave travelling from left to right. The horizontal (x) axis shows the distance travelled horizontally by the wave. The vertical (y) axis shows how far the surface of the water has been displaced from its normal level. Hence we can think of the x-axis as the level of the surface of the water when it is undisturbed. The line of the graph shows how far the surface of the water has been displaced from its undisturbed level.

From the representation of the wave in Figure 16.5, we can define two quantities for waves in general:

The **wavelength** λ of a wave is the distance from one crest of the wave to the next (or from one trough to the next).

Since the wavelength is a distance, it is measured in metres, m. The symbol λ is lambda, the Greek letter 'ell'.

The **amplitude** A of a wave is the maximum distance that the surface of the water is displaced from its undisturbed level; in other words, the height of a crest.

Figure 16.5 Representing a wave as a smoothly varying wavy line. This shape is known as a sine wave. If you have a graphics calculator, you can use it to display a graph of $y = \sin x$, which will look like this graph.

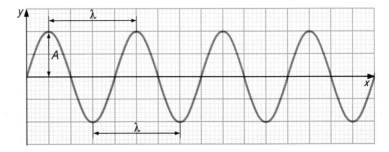

Notice that amplitude is measured from the undisturbed level up to the crest. It is not measured from trough to crest. For ripples on the surface of water, the amplitude is a distance, measured in metres, m.

For ripples in a ripple tank, the wavelength might be a few millimetres and the amplitude a millimetre or two. Waves on the open sea are much bigger, with wavelengths of tens of metres and amplitudes varying from a few centimetres up to several metres.

Frequency and period

As the bar in the ripple tank vibrates, it sends out ripples or waves. Each up-and-down movement sends out a single ripple. The more times the bar vibrates each second, the more ripples it sends out. This is shown in the graph of Figure 16.6. Take care! This looks very similar to the previous wave graph (Figure 16.5), but here the *x*-axis shows time, not distance. This graph shows how the surface of the water at a particular point moves up and down as time passes.

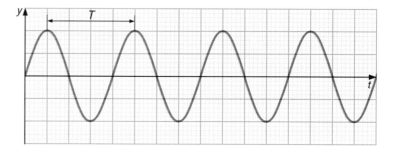

Figure 16.6 A graph to show the period of a wave. Notice that this graph has time *t* on its horizontal axis. Compare this with the displacement–distance graph shown in Figure 16.5

From the representation of the wave in Figure 16.6, we can define two more quantities for waves in general:

> The **frequency** *f* of a wave is the number of complete waves sent out each second.

Frequency is measured in hertz, Hz. One hertz (1 Hz) is one complete wave per second.

> The **period** *T* of a wave is the time taken for one complete wave to pass a point, measured in seconds, s.

It is important always to check whether a wave graph has time or distance on its *x*-axis.

The frequency of a wave is the number of waves passing a point per second; its period is the number of seconds for each wave. Hence *f* and *T* are obviously related to each other. Waves with a short period have a high frequency. We have

$$\text{frequency (Hz)} = \frac{1}{\text{period (s)}}$$

$$f = \frac{1}{T}$$

and

$$period\ (s) = \frac{1}{frequency\ (Hz)}$$

$$T = \frac{1}{f}$$

Waves on the sea might have a period of 10 s; their frequency is therefore about 0.1 Hz. A sound wave might have a frequency of 1000 Hz; its period is therefore 1/1000 s = 1 ms; a wave arrives every one millisecond. (Worked example 1 in section 16.2 uses this relationship.)

Transverse and longitudinal waves

Ripples in a ripple tank are one way of looking at the behaviour of waves. You can demonstrate waves in other ways. As shown in Figure 16.7a, a stretched 'slinky' spring can show waves. Fix one end of the spring (perhaps to a heavy wooden block) and move the other end from side to side and a wave travels along the spring. (You may notice it reflecting from the fixed end of the spring.) You can demonstrate the same sort of wave using a stretched rope or piece of elastic.

A second type of wave can also be demonstrated with a stretched slinky spring. Instead of moving the free end from side to side, move it back and forth (Figure 16.7b). A series of *compressions* travels along the spring, regions in which the segments of the spring are compressed together. In between are *rarefactions*, regions where the segments of the spring are farther apart. This type of wave cannot be demonstrated on a stretched rope.

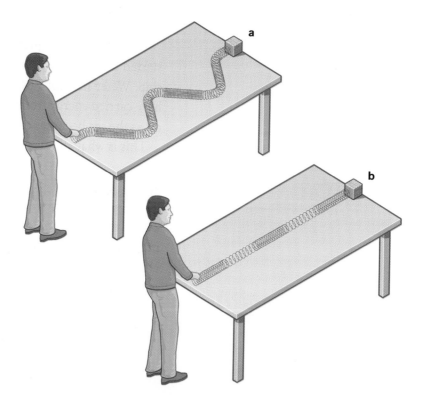

Figure 16.7 Waves along a stretched spring. **a** A transverse wave, made by moving the free end from side to side. **b** A longitudinal wave, made by pushing the free end back and forth, along the length of the spring.

These demonstrations show two different types of wave:

● *transverse waves* – in which the particles carrying the wave move from side to side, at right-angles to the direction in which the wave energy is moving;

● *longitudinal waves* – in which the particles carrying the wave move back and forth, along the direction in which the wave energy is moving.

A ripple on the surface of water is an example of a transverse wave. The particles of the water move up and down as the wave travels horizontally.

Table 16.1 Transverse and longitudinal waves.

Transverse waves	Longitudinal waves
ripples on water	sound
light and all other electromagnetic waves	

A sound wave is an example of a longitudinal wave. As a sound travels through air, the air molecules move back and forth as the wave travels through the air. Compare Figure 16.7b with Figure 12.15 on page 194 to see the similarity. Table 16.1 lists examples of transverse and longitudinal waves.

Waves and energy

What do all waves have in common? Imagine that it is a sunny day and you are floating in the calm sea. A large ship passes in the distance. It is sending out waves as its bow cuts through the water. Suddenly, the waves reach you. You start to move up and down. Then the waves pass by and your part of the sea becomes calm again.

Energy has been spreading out from the ship. You could not have started moving up and down if you had not received energy from the ship. Water has not flowed from the ship to you. Instead, the waves have carried energy from the ship to you. Eventually, the energy moves on as the sea becomes calm again.

This is what all waves have in common:

Waves transfer energy from place to place, without any material being required to carry the energy.

There may be a material through which the wave moves, but the material itself does not move from place to place. In the case of electromagnetic waves such as light, the waves can travel through empty space.

16.1 Describe the motion of molecules of water as a ripple moves across the surface of water in a ripple tank.

16.2 The two graphs shown in Figures 16.5 and 16.6 are very similar to each other. What is the important difference between them?

16.3 Draw a diagram to show what is meant by the amplitude of a wave.

16.4 How could you find the wavelength of the ripples shown in both Figures 16.4a and 16.4b?

16.5 If 10 waves occupy 15 cm, what is their wavelength?

16.6 Suppose that 100 sound waves reach your ear each second.
   a What is their frequency?
   b What is their period?

16.7 Are sound waves transverse or longitudinal?

16.8 Are radio waves transverse or longitudinal?

16.2 Speed, frequency and wavelength

How fast do waves travel across the surface of the sea? If you stand on the end of a pier, you may be able to answer this question. Suppose the pier is 60 m long, and that you notice that exactly five waves fit into this length (Figure 16.8). From this information, you can deduce that their wavelength is 12 m.

Now you time the waves arriving. The interval between crests as they pass the end of the pier is 4 s. How fast are the waves moving? One wavelength (12 m) passes in 4 s. So the speed of the waves is

$$\frac{12\,\text{m}}{4\,\text{s}} = 3\,\text{m/s}$$

Hence speed v, frequency f and wavelength λ are connected. We can write the connection in the form of an equation:

speed (m/s) = frequency (Hz) × wavelength (m)

$$v = f\lambda$$

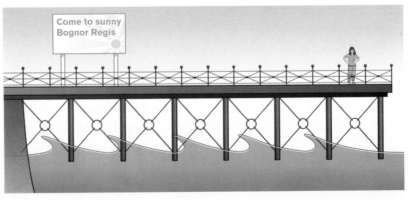

Figure 16.8 By timing waves and measuring their wavelength, you can find the speed of waves.

Another way to think of this is to say that the speed is the number of waves passing per second times the length of each wave. If 100 waves pass each second ($f = 100$ Hz), and each is 4 m long ($\lambda = 4$ m), then 400 m of waves pass each second; the speed of the waves is 400 m/s.

Worked example 1

An FM radio station broadcasts signals of wavelength 3.0 m and frequency 100 MHz. What is their speed?

- Step 1 Write down what you know, and what you want to know:

$f = 100\,\text{MHz} = 100\,000\,000\,\text{Hz} = 10^8\,\text{Hz}$

$\lambda = 3.0\,\text{m}$

$v = ?$

- Step 2 Write down the equation for wave speed, substitute values and calculate the answer:

$v = f\lambda$

$v = 10^8\,\text{Hz} \times 3.0\,\text{m} = 3 \times 10^8\,\text{m/s}$

So the radio waves travel through the air at 3.0×10^8 m/s. You should recognise that this is the speed of light, the speed at which all electromagnetic waves travel through empty space.

Worked example 2

A pianist plays the note middle C, whose frequency is 264 Hz. What is the wavelength of the sound waves produced? [Speed of sound in air = 330 m/s]

- Step 1 Write down what you know, and what you want to know:

$f = 264\,\text{Hz}$

$v = 300\,\text{m/s}$

$\lambda = ?$

- Step 2 Write down the equation for wave speed:

$v = f\lambda$

Rearrange it to make wavelength λ the subject:

$\lambda = \dfrac{v}{f}$

- Step 3 Substitute values and calculate the answer:

$\lambda = \dfrac{330\,\text{m/s}}{264\,\text{Hz}} = 1.25\,\text{m}$

So the wavelength of the note middle C in air is 1.25 m.

Changing material, changing speed

When waves travel from one material into another, they usually change speed. Light travels more slowly in glass than in air; sound travels faster in steel than in air. When this happens, the frequency of the waves remains unchanged. As a consequence, their wavelength must change. This is illustrated in Figure 16.9.

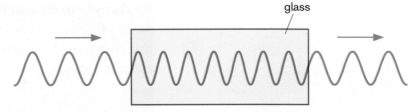

Figure 16.9 Waves change their wavelength when their speed changes. Their frequency remains constant. Here, light waves slow down when they enter glass and speed up when they return to the air.

The diagram shows light waves travelling quickly through air. They reach some glass and slow down; their wavelength decreases. When they leave the glass again, they speed up, and their wavelength increases again.

> ## ? Questions
>
> **16.9**   **a** Write down an equation relating speed, frequency and wavelength of a wave.
>
>   **b** Indicate the SI units of each quantity.
>
> **16.10** Mental arithmetic: If 10 waves pass a point each second and their wavelength is 30 m, what is their speed?
>
> **16.11** All sound waves travel with the same speed in air. Which has the higher frequency, a sound wave of wavelength 2 m or one with wavelength 1 m?
>
> **16.12** Which have the longer wavelength, radio waves of frequency 90 MHz or 100 MHz?
>
> **16.13** Light slows down when it enters water from air.
>
>   **a** What happens to its wavelength?
>
>   **b** What happens to its frequency?

16.3 Reflection and refraction of waves

If we look at ripples on the surface of water in a ripple tank, we can begin to see why physicists say that light behaves as if it were a form of wave. The ripples are much more regular and uniform than waves on the sea, so they are a good **model system** to look at.

Figure 16.10a shows what happens when a flat metal plate is placed in the ripple tank. Straight ripples ('plane waves') are reflected when they strike the flat surface. The metal plate acts like a mirror, and the ripples bounce off it. Figure 16.10b shows the pattern of the ripples. This shows an important thing about how waves behave; they pass through each other when they overlap.

In Figure 16.10c, you can see the same pattern, this time as a drawing. This is an 'aerial view' of the ripples; the blue lines represent the tops of the ripples. These lines are known as **wavefronts**. Also shown are lines to indicate how the direction of travel of the ripples changes. This diagram should remind you of the ray diagram for the law of reflection of light (Figure 13.8 on page 205). The ripples are reflected

a

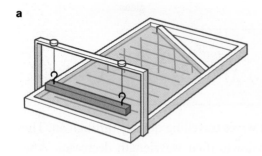

c

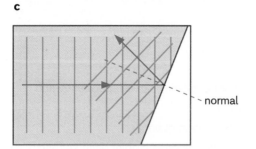

normal

b

Figure 16.10 a Plane waves travel down the ripple tank and are reflected by the flat metal plate. **b** The reflected ripples make a criss-cross pattern as they pass through the incoming ripples. **c** The arrows show how the direction of the ripples changes when they are reflected. The angle of incidence is equal to the angle of reflection, just as in the law of reflection of light.

by the metal plate so that the angle of incidence equals the angle of reflection.

The nature of light – waves or particles?

For two centuries, physicists argued about the nature of light. Does light travel in the form of waves, or as a stream of particles? The idea of sound travelling as a wave was well established. You could see or feel the vibrations of a drum or a guitar string, and imagine the particles of air being pushed back and forth as the sound travelled towards your ears. But what about light?

Experiments with ripple tanks show that waves are reflected in a similar way to light. However, this does not prove that light is a wave. Particles also reflect off hard surfaces in the same way – think about how a tennis ball bounces off the ground, so that its angle of incidence equals its angle of reflection. We need to go on to think about refraction to explore this idea further.

Refraction of ripples

Refraction occurs when the speed of light changes. We can see the same effect for ripples in a ripple tank (Figure 16.11b). The water in part of the tank is made shallower by immersing a glass plate in the water. Here the ripples move more slowly because they drag on the bottom of the tank. In the photograph, you can see that these ripples lag behind the faster-moving ripples in the deeper water. Also, their direction of travel has changed.

Figure 16.11b shows the same effect, but as a wave front diagram. On the left, the ripples are in deeper water and moving faster. They advance steadily forwards. On the right, the ripples are moving more slowly. The lower end of a ripple is the first part to enter the

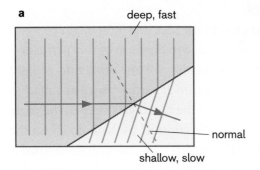

Figure 16.11 **a** This wave front diagram shows the pattern of waves when they slow down. The rays, drawn at right angles to the ripples, show that the refracted ray is closer to the normal. This is what happens when light slows down on entering glass. **b** This photo shows the same pattern. A submerged glass plate makes the water shallower on the right. In this region the ripples move more slowly so that they lag behind the ripples in the deeper water.

shallower water, so it has spent longer moving at a slow speed. Hence the right-hand end of each ripple lags further behind.

The rays marked on Figure 16.11b show the direction in which the ripples are moving. They are always at right-angles to the ripples. They emphasise how the ripples turn so their direction is closer to the normal as they slow down, just as we saw with the refraction of light (Figure 14.4 on page 213.)

You may have noticed that, at the beach, waves usually arrive roughly parallel to the beach. You may even have wondered why this is. Now you can explain it. If a wave approaches a beach at an angle, one end reaches the beach first. This end slows down because it is in shallow water. The other end of the wave carries on moving quickly, and gradually the whole wave changes direction as it reaches the beach. You can see this happening in the aerial photograph shown in Figure 16.12.

Figure 16.12 Waves out at sea may be in any direction. As they approach the shore, they tend to be turned so that they are parallel to the beach. This is a refraction effect. The waves travel more slowly in shallow water, so the end nearer the beach lags behind. The end further out to sea keeps moving fast, and so the whole wave swings round to be parallel to the shore.

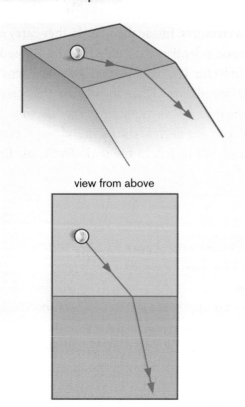

view from above

Figure 16.13 Newton's idea of refraction. The marble speeds up and changes direction as the slope of the board changes. The pattern is the same as we see when a ray of light is refracted. However, Newton was wrong: light bends towards the normal when it slows down, not when it speeds up.

Waves or particles? – again

Isaac Newton was never happy with the idea that light might be a type of wave. He believed that light travelled in the form of tiny particles or 'corpuscles'. He had his own explanation for the refraction of light, shown in Figure 16.13. He pictured a small particle (such as a marble) rolling down a sloping board. When the board gets steeper, the particles moves faster. It also changes direction. If we look down on this model from above, we see that the particle turns towards the normal as it speeds up. This is the opposite to what we observe for ripples; they bend towards the normal when they slow down.

Hence Newton's particle theory predicted that light speeds up when it enters glass. The competing wave theory predicted that light slows down when it enters glass. Unfortunately, at the time there was no way of measuring the speed of light in glass, so the question was unresolved. Today, we know that light travels more slowly in glass than in air, so Newton's idea was flawed. However, his influence was so strong that his corpuscle theory of light was favoured by physicists for a century or so after his death.

Refraction of sound

Sound waves can be refracted, just like ripples or light. Recall that refraction happens when the speed of waves changes. You may have noticed that, at night, you can often hear sounds over much greater distances than during the day. This can be explained by refraction of sound waves, as follows. At night, the ground cools off as heat radiates upwards. The air near the ground is cooler than air higher up, and sound travels more slowly in cold air than in warm air (because the air molecules are moving more slowly). Sound waves travelling upwards are refracted back towards the ground (Figure 16.14). This makes it possible to hear things at greater distances at night than during the day. During the day, temperatures are higher near the ground, so sound waves tend to refract away from the ground.

Figure 16.14 At night, sound waves are refracted towards the ground. They travel more quickly higher up where the air is warmer, and this causes them to change direction. In the daytime, the temperature difference is reversed because the ground absorbs sunlight and heats up the air. Sound waves are then refracted away from the ground.

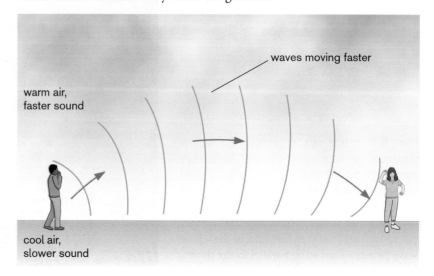

waves moving faster

warm air, faster sound

cool air, slower sound

Sperm whales are large sea creatures. Inside their heads, they carry a large block of a waxy substance. Scientists have only recently guessed what this strange organ might be for. It is believed that it acts as a 'lens' for sound. The whale emits sounds, which are focused by the waxy block into a beam. The whale uses this as a sonar device, directing it around its environment and listening for reflections. In this way it can avoid rocks and track down shoals of fish in the dark depths of the ocean, or at night.

? Questions

16.14 Draw a diagram to show what happens to plane waves when they strike a flat reflector placed at 45° to their direction of travel.

16.15 How can the speed of ripples in a ripple tank be changed?

16.16 Explain why the law of reflection does not help us to decide whether light travels as a wave or as particles.

16.17 Look at Figure 16.14. Draw a similar diagram to show how the refraction of sound waves makes it difficult to hear sounds from a distant source during the daytime.

16.4 Diffraction

We can see an interesting phenomenon when we look at how ripples behave when they go past the edge of a barrier, or through a gap in a barrier. Figure 16.15 shows what happens.

a Ripples passing the edge of a barrier curve 'round the corner', into the space behind the barrier.

b Ripples passing through a gap in a barrier spread out into the space beyond the barrier.

Figure 16.15 Ripples are diffracted: **a** as they pass the edge of a barrier; or **b** as they pass through a gap in a barrier. In both cases, they spread into the space behind the barrier.

These are examples of a phenomenon called **diffraction**. The effect is biggest when the gap is similar in size to the wavelength of the ripples – see Figure 16.16.

Diffraction is something that can be observed with waves, but we would not expect particles to behave in this way. A beam of particles would pass through a gap and continue in their original direction.

Hence diffraction is something we see with waves, not with particles. We can explain diffraction as follows: As the ripples arrive at the gap in the barrier, the water at the edge of the gap moves up and down. This sets off new *circular* ripples, which spread out behind the barrier. (You might notice diffraction of water waves in a harbour. The waves enter the harbour mouth and spread around corners, so that no part of the harbour is entirely undisturbed. Boats bob up and down on the diffracted waves.)

Now we can look for diffraction effects with sound and light, to help us to decide whether they travel as waves or as particles.

Diffraction of sound

Imagine that you come across a shoot-out in the street between two gangs of dastardly criminals. You hurry around the corner to evade the flying bullets. Even around the corner, you can hear their shouts and the occasional gunshot, but you know that you will not be hit. You can hear the sounds of fighting because sound diffracts around the corner; bullets are particles and do not diffract, so you should not be in danger. (Bad luck if one ricochets off another building and reaches you around the corner!)

So sound can diffract. We can calculate the wavelengths of the sounds we hear using the equation

$$v = f\lambda$$

as follows:

- Lowest audible frequency = 20 Hz
  speed of sound in air = 300 m/s

  wavelength $\lambda = \dfrac{v}{f} = \dfrac{300\,\text{m/s}}{20\,\text{Hz}} = 15\,\text{m}$

- Highest audible frequency = 20 kHz
  wavelength = 15 mm

So audible wavelengths range from 15 mm to 15 m. Such waves are readily diffracted around corners of buildings. They are also diffracted as they pass through doorways and open windows. We rely on the diffraction of sound every day to hear what is going on in the next room. This supports the idea that sound travels as a wave.

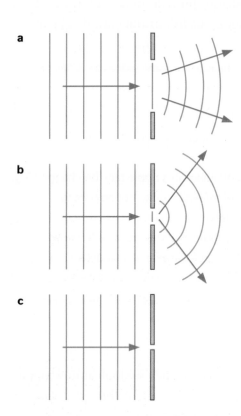

a

b

c

Figure 16.16 Diffraction is greatest when the width of the gap is similar to the wavelength of the waves being diffracted. When the gap is much smaller than the wavelength, the waves do not pass through at all.

Diffraction of light

When rays of light pass the edge of a solid object, we are used to seeing shadows. Shadows have sharp edges, and this might suggest that light is not diffracted. However, we are not looking in the right place to see the effects we want. The clue is in the connection between wavelength and the size of the gap that causes diffraction. As shown in Figure 16.16, the gap should be similar to the wavelength of light to have the maximum effect. Light has a very small wavelength – less than a thousandth of a millimetre – so we need to look for some very tiny gaps.

Figure 16.17 shows what happens when light from a laser is shone through a narrow slit between two straight-sided pieces of metal. When the light reaches a screen, it has spread out sideways to form a diffraction pattern. So light can be shown to diffract.

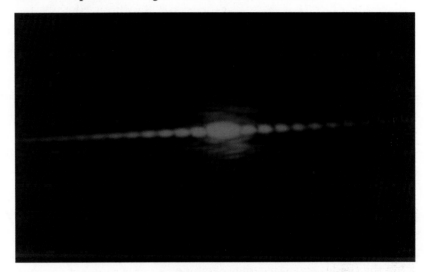

Figure 16.17 This diffraction pattern was produced by shining laser light through a narrow slit. The light spreads out beyond the slit, proving that light can be diffracted if the gap through which it passes is narrow enough.

You may have seen diffraction effects with light. For example, if you see a streetlight on a misty night, you may notice a glowing ring of light around it. This is light that has been diffracted by the tiny droplets of water that make up the mist. Think about how the light has reached your eyes: It has travelled outwards from the lamp, and has then been bent towards you by the mist, so that it doesn't appear to be coming directly from the light. (You may see a similar effect looking through a steamed-up car windscreen at the head-lamps of cars coming towards you.)

Now we know that light can be diffracted, like a wave. It is better not to say that 'light is a wave'; it is better to say that 'under certain circumstances, light behaves like a wave'. The reason for this is that, as Einstein showed 200 years after Newton, light sometimes behaves like particles. Light is strange stuff.

Radio waves (and any other type of electromagnetic wave) can be diffracted, too. There may be a hill between your radio or TV aerial and the transmitter, blocking your direct line of sight to the transmitter, but the radio waves diffract around the hill and you can still pick up a signal.

Interference of waves

What happens when two sets of waves meet? We saw that, when ripples are reflected, the two sets of ripples pass through each other. (This is what we see with light: one ray of light can cross the path of another and continue unaffected.) However, there is more to it than this.

In a ripple tank, we can produce two sets of circular ripples using a pair of dippers that vibrate up and down together (Figure 16.18). Where the ripples overlap, we see an interesting pattern. At some points the ripples combine to produce a bigger ripple; at others, they tend to cancel out. This is **interference**.

Each point in the ripple tank receives one set of ripples from one dipper, and another set from the other dipper. The result depends on whether the ripples are in step or not – see Figure 16.19.

a If the ripples are in step, they combine to give a bigger ripple with twice the amplitude; this is **constructive interference**.

b If the ripples are out of step, they cancel to give no ripple; this is **destructive interference**.

(At most points, the ripples are neither exactly in step nor exactly out of step, and they may not have exactly the same amplitude, so the outcome is somewhere in between the two extremes shown in the diagram.)

If two light waves arrive exactly in step, they will give constructive interference and we will see a brighter light. If they arrive exactly out of step, they will interfere destructively and we will see no light.

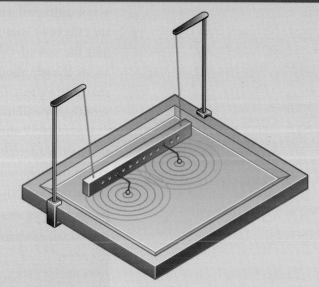

Figure 16.18 An interference pattern in a ripple tank. The two sets of circular ripples overlap. At some points, they combine to give a large variation. At others, they tend to cancel out.

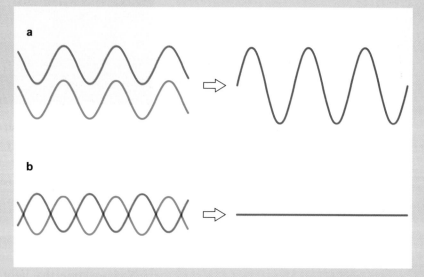

Figure 16.19 **a** Identical waves that are exactly in step show constructive interference. **b** If the waves are exactly out of step, they show destructive interference.

It is tricky to observe this, because of the short wavelength of light. However, the experiment was demonstrated in 1801 by Thomas Young, who passed light through two narrow slits and observed an interference pattern of light and dark areas on a screen beyond the slits. From his measurements he was able to calculate the wavelength of light.

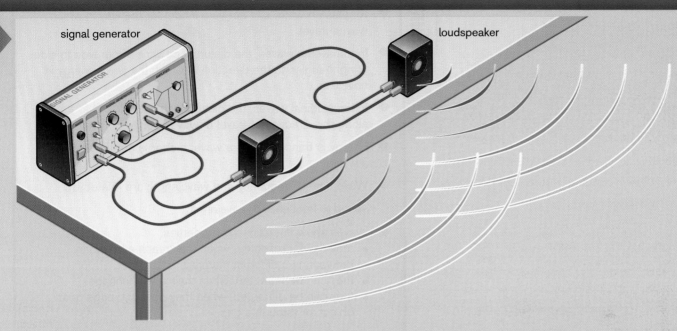

signal generator

loudspeaker

Figure 16.20 How to observe an interference pattern for sound. Moving around the room, you will find loud areas (constructive interference) and quiet areas (destructive interference). It helps if you put a finger in one ear so that you are only listening with one ear.

Similarly interference occurs with sound waves. You can observe this with two loudspeakers connected to the same signal generator, so that they produce identical sound waves (Figure 16.20). At some points in the room, you will hear a loud sound (constructive interference); at other points, you will observe silence (destructive interference). The waves set off in step with one another from the loudspeakers. However, they may have to travel different distances to reach your ear. We say that there is a **path difference** between them. If the two waves have travelled exactly the same distance to your ear, the path difference is zero and the waves interfere constructively to give a loud sound. If one wave has travelled exactly half a wavelength further than the other (i.e. the path difference is half a wavelength), they will interfere destructively to produce silence.

Questions

16.18 Diffraction may be observed when a wave passes through a gap. When else may it be observed?

16.19 What is observed when ripples pass through a gap in a barrier?

16.20 What can you say about the width of a gap if it is to produce the greatest diffraction effect?

16.21 Why is it difficult to observe diffraction effects with light?

16.22 Give an example of a situation where diffraction allows you to hear a sound.

Summary

◆ A wave is a regularly varying disturbance that travels from place to place.

◆ Ripples on water can act as a model for the way in which waves travel.

◆ In transverse waves, the disturbance varies from side to side, at right-angles to the direction in which the wave energy is travelling.

◆ In longitudinal waves, the disturbance is back and forth, along the direction of travel of wave energy.

◆ Energy is transferred by a wave; matter is not transferred by a wave.

◆ Wave speed, frequency and wavelength are related by:

speed = frequency × wavelength

◆ Waves show the following properties:
- they can be reflected, when they reach a boundary between two different materials;
- they can be refracted, when their speed changes;
- they can be diffracted, when they pass the edge of an object, or through a gap.

◈ *Waves can also show interference effects, when two similar waves meet.*

◆ Light shows all of these wave properties, which suggests that light travels as a wave.

Further questions

The numbering is continued from the in-chapter questions.

Chapter 12

12.21

Sounds are produced by vibrating objects.

a When a wind instrument such as a trumpet produces a sound, what is it that is made to vibrate by the player?

b When a stringed instrument such as a violin is played, what is it that is made to vibrate by the player?

c Explain how the sound from the instrument travels through the air to the listener's ears.

12.22

a In which material does a sound travel faster, a solid or a gas?

b Give one piece of evidence that shows that sound can travel through solid materials.

c Describe a method for measuring the speed of sound in air, in the laboratory. What measurements are made, and how is the speed of sound calculated from them?

12.23

The vibrations of a sound can be detected using a microphone and then displayed on an oscilloscope screen. The figure shows three such traces.

a Which trace shows the loudest sound? Explain your answer.

b Which trace shows the sound with the highest pitch? Explain your answer.

12.24

To measure the length of a long metal rod, engineers send a pulse of sound into one end of it. The sound travels to the other end and is reflected back. The engineers detect this echo, and determine the time taken for the sound to travel from one end of the rod to the other.

When making measurements on a steel rod of length 400 m, they find that the echo returns 0.16 s after the initial pulse. What is the speed of sound in steel?

12.25

Human beings can hear sounds over a wide range of frequencies.

a Give approximate values for the highest and lowest frequencies that a young person can hear.

b How does the upper limit of the audible range change as we get older?

c What name is given to sounds whose frequency is higher than the upper limit?

d Give one example of a way in which such inaudible sound is used.

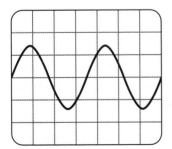 a

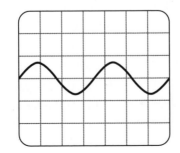 b

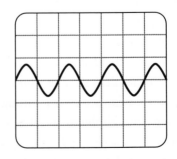 c

Figure Q12.23

Chapter 13

13.11

The speed of light in air is approximately 300 000 000 m/s, or 3×10^8 m/s.

a How long does it take for light to travel from the Sun to the Earth, a distance of 150 000 000 km?

b How far will light travel in the course of one year?

c What can you say about the speed of light in glass, compared to its speed in air?

13.12

The law of reflection says that: 'When a ray of light is reflected at a surface, the **angle of incidence** is equal to the **angle of reflection**.'

Draw a diagram to indicate how a ray of light is reflected by a flat mirror, and mark the two angles mentioned in the law.

13.13

A small lamp is placed at a distance of 4 cm from a plane mirror.

a Draw an accurate ray diagram to show where the image of the lamp in the mirror is formed.

b Explain how you have used the law of reflection in drawing your diagram.

c What does it mean to say that the image of the lamp is a *virtual* image?

Chapter 14

14.25

Windows usually have a flat sheet of glass, so that we can see clearly through them. Frosted glass has an irregular surface, so that we do not see a clear image through it.

a Draw a ray diagram to show how a ray of light passes through a parallel-sided glass block, if it hits the glass at 90° (i.e. perpendicular to the glass).

b Draw a ray diagram to show how a ray of light passes through a parallel-sided glass block, if it hits the glass at an angle other than 90° (i.e. obliquely to the glass).

c Explain why we can see clearly through a flat sheet of glass, even though light is refracted as it passes through.

d Explain how refraction prevents us from seeing clearly through frosted glass.

14.26

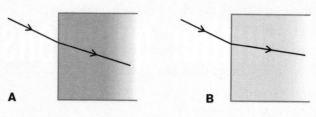

A **B**

Figure Q14.26

The figure shows what happens when a ray of light enters blocks of two different materials, A and B.

a In which material does the light travel more slowly, A or B? Explain how you can tell from the diagrams.

b Which material, A or B, has the greater refractive index?

14.27

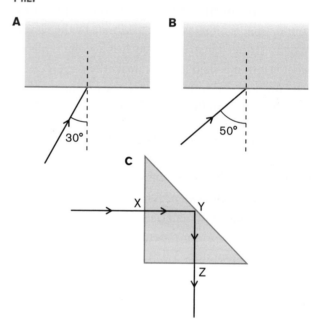

Figure Q14.28

The first two diagrams in the figure show two blocks of a material whose critical angle is 40°. In block A, the ray strikes the inner surface with an angle of incidence of 30°; in block B, the ray's angle of incidence is 50°.

a Copy and complete each diagram to show what happens when the ray strikes the surface.

b Use the diagrams to help you to explain what is meant by *total internal reflection*.

The third diagram in the figure shows how a right-angled prism can be used to reflect a ray of light through 90°.

c Explain why the ray in prism C is undeflected at points X and Z, but reflected at point Y.

d What advantage does this method of reflecting light have over the use of a plane mirror?

e Draw a diagram to show how a right-angled prism can be used to reflect a ray of light through 180°.

14.29

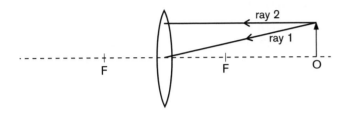

Figure Q14.29

The figure shows an incomplete ray diagram that represents the following situation: A converging lens has a focal length of 4 cm. Its focal points are marked F. An object O is placed at a distance of 10 cm from the lens. Ray 1 passes through the centre of the lens. Ray 2 is parallel to the axis of the lens.

a Copy and complete the ray diagram, to find the position of the image formed by the lens.

b Explain whether the diagram shows that the image is real or virtual.

c Explain whether the diagram shows that the image is magnified or diminished (smaller than the object).

d Explain whether the diagram shows that the image is upright or inverted.

14.30

When white light passes through a prism, it may be dispersed to form a spectrum.

a Draw a diagram to show how a ray of light may be dispersed by a prism.

b Which colour of the spectrum is refracted most by the prism?

c Why are some colours refracted more than others?

y

Chapter 15

15.21

Here is a list of eight forms of wave:

visible light   ultraviolet waves   microwaves   sound
X-rays   radio waves   gamma rays   infrared waves

a Which of the above is *not* a form of electromagnetic wave?

b Put the others in their correct order as they appear in the electromagnetic spectrum, starting with the form with the *shortest* wavelength.

c At what speed do electromagnetic waves travel through empty space?

15.22

Explain how electromagnetic radiation:

a can cause cancer;

b can be used to detect cancer;

c can be used to cure cancer.

In each case, state the type or types of electromagnetic radiation involved.

15.23

For each of the following forms of electromagnetic radiation, state one way in which it may be produced, and one way in which it may be detected:

a infrared radiation;

b X-rays;

c radio waves.

Chapter 16

16.23

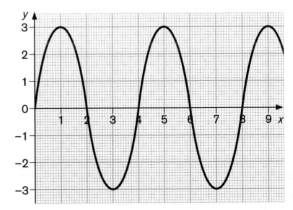

Figure Q16.23 The horizontal and vertical scales are in cm.

section c

Look at the wave shown in the figure.
a What is its wavelength?
b What is its amplitude?
c If this wave is moving at a speed of 10 cm/s, what is its frequency?
d On graph paper, sketch a wave having half this amplitude and twice this wavelength.

16.24

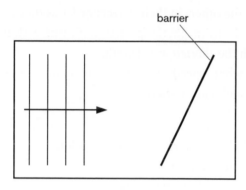

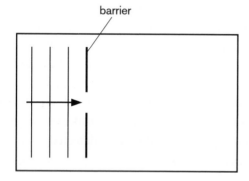

Figure Q16.24

Copy and complete the diagrams in the figure to show how the following effects appear in a ripple tank:
a plane waves are *reflected* by a straight barrier;
b plane waves are *diffracted* as they pass through a narrow gap.

16.25

When light passes from air into glass, do the following quantities increase, decrease, or stay the same?
a speed
b frequency
c wavelength

16.26

a Give an equation that relates the speed, frequency and wavelength of a wave.
b Light waves of frequency 6×10^{14} Hz have a wavelength of 3.75×10^{-7} m in water. What is their speed in water?

Static electricity

Topics in this chapter

◆ positive and negative electric charges

◆ attractive and repulsive forces between charges

◆ charging by induction

◆ charge and electrons

ⓔ *electrolysis*

◆ uses and hazards of static electricity

Benjamin Franklin was an American, born in Boston in 1706. He was a scientist, as well as many other things – politician, printer, economist, musician and publisher, among various other occupations. His most famous experiment (Figure 17.1), carried out in 1752, involved him in a most dangerous activity – flying a kite in a thunderstorm. He was investigating lightning as part of his studies of static electricity.

In the middle of the eighteenth century, static electricity was a subject of much popular interest – see Figure 17.2. Scientists gave demonstration lectures and sold equipment to members of the public

Figure 17.1 Benjamin Franklin, flying a kite in an attempt to capture a bolt of lightning. Franklin showed that lightning is similar to the sparks produced in experiments on static electricity. Shortly after, a Swedish scientist called Richtmann was killed when he tried to repeat Franklin's experiment. Richtmann's body was dissected to discover the effect of electricity on his organs.

Figure 17.2 Interest in static electricity made it something of a hobby for people in the eighteenth century. These Americans are rubbing rods to produce an electric charge. Reproduced by permission of the Library Company of Philadelphia.

so that they could try the experiments for themselves. Benjamin Franklin believed that lightning was simply a form of static electricity. He pointed out that a lightning flash was similar in shape and colour to the sparks that could be produced in the laboratory. They seemed to travel with similar speeds, and both were known to kill animals. He devised an experiment in which a man stood inside a tall 'sentry box' hut on top of a high tower. Using a long iron rod protruding from the top of the box, the man would draw sparks from storm clouds passing overhead.

In a further demonstration, Franklin attached a sharp-pointed metal wire to the top of a kite. He expected to draw down a spark from a lightning bolt. To avoid being electrocuted, he included a metal key at the bottom of the kite string, and attached a length of ribbon to the key. Holding the ribbon, he was relatively safe from electrocution (although other people were killed when they repeated his experiment). As a bolt of lightning struck the kite, Franklin saw the fibres of the kite string stand on end and a spark jumped from the key to the ground.

Franklin noticed that electrical sparks tend to jump from sharp points. He made use of this when he devised the lightning conductor. Today, most tall buildings have a sharp-pointed metal rod projecting from their roofs, with a continuous metal rod running down the outside of the building and into the ground. When lightning strikes, it is most likely to hit a lightning conductor and be safely channelled to the ground. Franklin's invention was enormously popular with insurance companies (who required the buildings they insured to install them), and the number of fires caused by lightning decreased dramatically.

Franklin had shown that lightning was a form of static electricity. He also showed that an electrically charged object could have either positive or negative charge. However, he had no way of knowing what causes lightning. Why does static electricity build up in storm clouds? This question took a long time to answer – it is very difficult to monitor what is going on inside a cloud.

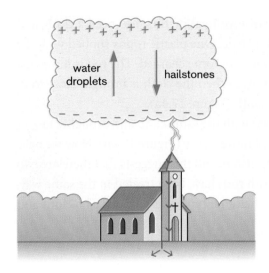

Figure 17.3 In a storm cloud, friction between water droplets and hailstones causes them to become electrically charged. The water droplets drift upwards, giving the top of the cloud a positive charge. Hailstones falling to the bottom of the cloud bring negative charge.

The answer seems to be that, for a cloud to become electrically charged, its temperature must be close to 0 °C, the freezing point of water. Inside the cloud, there is a mixture of water droplets and hailstones – see Figure 17.3. The droplets are carried upwards, perhaps by convection currents. The hailstones drift downwards. There is friction between them, and this leaves the water droplets with a positive charge and the hailstones with a negative charge. The top of the cloud thus becomes positively charged, and the bottom is negatively charged. When lightning strikes, negative charge from the bottom of the cloud leaps down through the air to the ground. Positive charge from the ground may also rush upwards to the cloud – a giant electric current is flowing through the air.

17.1 Charging and discharging

As well as lightning flashes, we experience static electricity in a number of ways in everyday life. You may have noticed tiny sparks when taking off clothes made of synthetic fibres. You may have felt a small shock when getting out of a car. Static electricity builds up on the car and then discharges through you when you touch the metal door. You have probably rubbed a balloon on your clothes and seen how it will stick to a wall or ceiling.

Before Benjamin Franklin and other scientists started carrying out their systematic experiments on static electricity, little was known about it. It had been known for centuries that amber, when rubbed, could attract small pieces of cloth or paper. Amber is a form of resin from trees which has become fossilised. It looks like clear, orange plastic. The Greek name for amber is *electron*, and this is where we get the name of the tiny charged particles that account for electricity.

Franklin and those who worked on the problem at the same time as him had no idea about electrons – these particles were not discovered until a hundred years later. However, that didn't stop them from developing a good understanding of static electricity. In the discussion that follows, we *will* talk about electrons. After all, they were discovered over a century ago, and they make it much easier to understand what is going on in all aspects of electricity.

Charging up

If you rub a plastic ruler with a cloth, both are likely to become electrically charged. You can tell that this is so by holding the ruler and then the cloth close to your hair – they attract the hair. (If your hair is not attracted, try some tiny scraps of paper instead.) You have observed that static electricity is generated by rubbing. You have also observed that a charged object may attract uncharged objects.

Now we have to think systematically about how to investigate this phenomenon. Firstly, how do two charged objects affect one another?

Figure 17.4 shows one way of investigating this. You need a cloth, and two rods made of the same plastic. One plastic rod is rubbed with the cloth so that both rod and cloth become charged. The rod is hung in a cradle so that it is free to move. When the cloth is brought close to it, the rod moves towards the cloth (Figure 17.4a).

If the second rod is rubbed with the same cloth and brought close to the first rod, the hanging rod moves away (Figure 17.4b). Now we have seen both attraction and repulsion, and this suggests that there are two types of static electricity. Both rods have been treated in the same way, so we expect them to have the same type of electricity. The cloth and the rods must have different types.

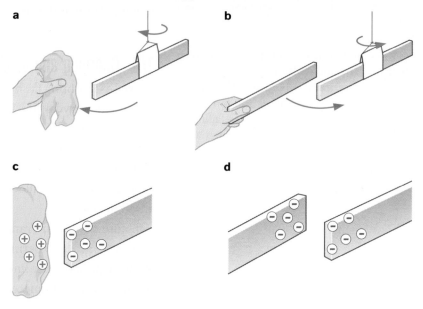

Figure 17.4 Two experiments to show the existence of two, opposite types of static electricity. **a** The charged rod and cloth attract one another. **b** The two charged rods repel one another. **c** The rod and the cloth have opposite electrical charges. **d** The two rods have electrical charges of the same sign.

The two types of static electricity are referred to as positive charge and negative charge. We can explain the experiments shown in Figures 17.4a and b by saying that the process of rubbing gives the rods one type of electric charge (say, negative), while the cloth is given the opposite type (positive). Figures 17.4c and d show details of the two experiments with the charges marked.

From these experiments, we can also say something about the forces that electrical charges exert on each other:

- like charges repel;
- unlike charges attract.

('Like charges' means both positive, or both negative. 'Unlike charges' means opposite charges – one positive and the other negative. People often remember this rule as 'opposites attract'.)

Friction and charging

It is the force of friction that causes charging. When a plastic rod is rubbed on a cloth, friction transfers tiny particles called **electrons** from one material to the other. If the rod is made of polythene, it is

Material	
Perspex (acrylic)	*most positive*
glass	
human hair	
nylon	
wool	
silk	
paper	
polyester	
polythene	
PVC	
Teflon	*most negative*

Table 17.1 A list of materials ranked according to how strongly they attract electrons when rubbed. This allows us to say that, for example, polythene will become negatively charged when rubbed with wool; the wool will become positively charged. (This list is rather like the electrochemical series, in which a substance higher up the series is more reactive than one lower down, and will replace it in a reaction.)

usually the case that electrons are rubbed off the cloth and onto the rod.

Electrons are a part of every atom. They are negatively charged, and they are found on the outside of the atom. Since they are relatively weakly held in the atom, they can be readily pulled away by the force of friction. An atom has no overall electric charge – we say that it is **neutral**. When an atom has lost an electron, it becomes a positively charged ion.

A polythene rod becomes negatively charged when it is rubbed with a silk cloth, so we can imagine electrons being rubbed from the cloth onto the rod – see Figure 17.5. It is difficult to explain why one material pulls electrons from another. The atoms that make up polythene must attract electrons more strongly than do the atoms of the silk cloth. Experiments have shown that materials can be ranked in order, according to how strongly they attract electrons when rubbed. The results are shown in Table 17.1. The table shows a competitive ranking: a material near the bottom of the table attracts electrons more strongly than a material higher up. For example, a nylon rod rubbed on silk will become positively charged, but if the same rod is rubbed on human hair, it will become negatively charged.

Notice that the materials listed in Table 17.1 are all insulators. It is possible to charge a good conductor such as a metal, but not by rubbing.

When Benjamin Franklin was studying static electricity 250 years ago, he imagined that both positive and negative charges could move around. Now we know that, when a material is charged by rubbing, it is the negatively charged electrons that are mobile.

The van de Graaff generator

Rubbing plastic rods on cloth is not a very satisfactory way to produce electric charge. A good way of producing a lot of charge is to use a van de Graaff generator (Figure 17.6). A motor or handle drives a belt, which carries electric charge up to the silver dome on the top of the

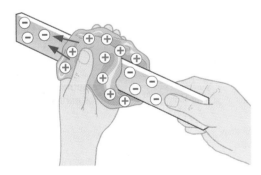

Figure 17.5 When a polythene rod is rubbed with a silk cloth, electrons are transferred from the silk to the polythene. The silk is left with a positive charge.

Figure 17.6 Generating large amounts of electric charge using a van de Graaff generator. The shiny dome shares its charge with the girl. Electrons spread out all over her hair, so that each strand repels every other strand. The fact that electric charges spread throughout the girl's body shows that humans are not perfect electrical insulators.

machine. The dome usually becomes negatively charged, with large numbers of extra electrons spread all over its surface. Any object touching the dome also becomes negatively charged. In the photo, the girl is touching the dome so that electrons flow into her. Each strand of her hair becomes negatively charged, so that they all repel one another.

Discharging static electricity

Static electricity tends to disappear. Positive and negative charges attract one another, and if possible they will move to neutralise one another. If you get an electric shock when you touch a car door, it is because an electric charge has built up on the car – because of friction between the car and the air. When your finger gets close to the metal car door, the charge leaps across the gap and you feel a shock. The car discharges through you and is no longer charged.

The Earth is like a giant 'sink' for electric charge. Negatively charged electrons will run into the Earth from a negatively charged object; and electrons will move from the Earth to neutralise a positively charged object (Figure 17.7). For this to happen, there must be a conducting path between the charged object and the Earth. We say that the object is 'connected to earth', or more simply that the object is 'earthed'. (Benjamin Franklin was providing a conducting path when he invented the lightning conductor.) Metals are good conductors, of course, but even wood can provide a path for electrons to flow into the ground. A wooden metre rule will conduct electrons away from a charged van de Graaff generator.

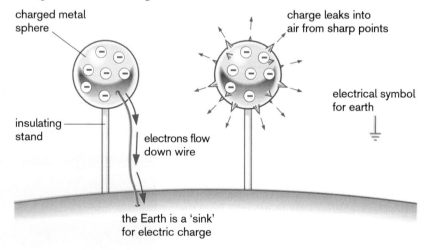

Figure 17.7 The Earth is neutral – it has a balance of positive and negative charges. When there is a conducting path between a charged object and the Earth, electrons will flow to discharge the object. Charge can also leak away into the air.

The air, too, can conduct away charge, particularly if it is damp. A tiny current flows from a charged object, particularly if there are sharp points on it. (The electric field is very strong around the tip of a sharp point; this ionises the air, and the charge leaks away.)

Occasionally, a spark will jump from a charged object as it discharges. You can see this with a van de Graaff generator. Charge up the dome, and bring a second, uncharged metal sphere close to it. A spark jumps between the two spheres as the dome discharges itself. Notice

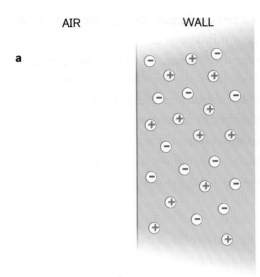

a

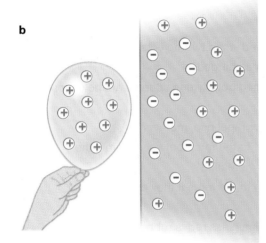

b

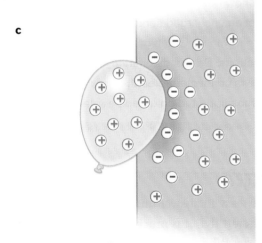

c

Figure 17.8 **a** The wall is neutral, because it has equal amounts of positive and negative charge. **b** The charged balloon attracts the negative charges in the wall, so that they move towards it. **c** The positive balloon and the negative surface of the wall stick together.

that this is an electrical spark; it is a current flowing through the air. The air is heated, and glows brightly for an instant. It is not the same as a chemical spark, the sort you see when a firework goes off, for example. In this kind of spark, a tiny piece of chemical is burning in the air. Electrical sparks can cause chemical sparks; for example, when a spark is used to ignite a gas cooker.

Why electrostatic experiments are tricky

Experiments with static electricity have a reputation for going wrong. There are several reasons why this can happen. The main one is that charged objects quickly lose their charge. Charge can leak away to the air, especially when the air is damp. To avoid this, it is best to work on a dry day when the humidity is low. Drying the surface of the object to be charged using a hairdryer also helps.

Also, if the charged object is not a perfect insulator, charge can conduct away from it. Charged objects need to be supported by materials that are good insulators – Perspex stands or nylon threads, for example. Wooden stands and cotton threads can conduct and charge will escape.

If you do a lot of experiments on electrically charged objects, you will begin to wish that you could get positively and negatively charged objects out of the cupboard, just as you can get ready-made magnets with north and south poles.

Charging by induction

A charged object can attract uncharged objects. For example, scatter some tiny pieces of paper on the bench. Rub a polythene rod on a woollen cloth. Both the charged rod and the charged cloth will attract the paper. This is the same effect as rubbing a balloon on your clothes and then sticking it to the wall. An uncharged object (the wall) is attracted by a charged object (the balloon). How does this happen?

Suppose the balloon has a positive charge. It must be attracted to a negative charge in the wall. The wall itself is neutral (uncharged), but its atoms are made up of positively and negatively charged particles – see Figure 17.8. When the balloon is brought close to the wall, the negative charges (electrons) in the wall move towards the balloon, because they are attracted by it. They may not move very far, but the effect is enough to give the surface of the wall a negative charge, which attracts the balloon.

We say that a negative charge has been **induced** on the wall; and this process is known as **charging by induction**. The same process occurs when the charged rod and charged cloth attract scraps of paper. The negative rod induces a positive charge on the surface of the paper, by repelling electrons away; the positive cloth attracts the electrons.

We can use charging by induction to charge a metal sphere, as shown in Figure 17.9. The sphere is charged by holding it *near* the

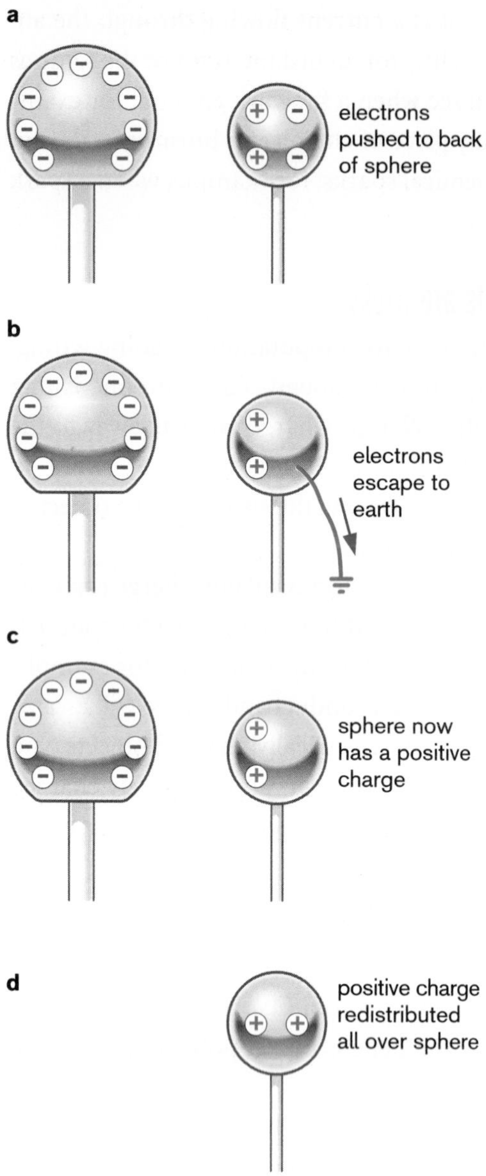

a

electrons
pushed to back
of sphere

b

electrons
escape to
earth

c

sphere now
has a positive
charge

d

positive charge
redistributed
all over sphere

Figure 17.9 The four steps in charging a metal sphere by induction. Note that the sphere and the charged van de Graaff dome never touch. The sphere gets a charge that is opposite in sign to that of the dome.

charged dome of a van de Graaff generator, though the two metal objects *do not touch*. Here is how it is done:

a The generator dome has a negative charge. When the metal sphere is placed near it, electrons in the sphere are repelled away. The front of the sphere (near the dome) has an induced positive charge.

b Now the sphere is touched, either by a hand or by a wire connected to earth. This allows electrons to escape from the sphere.

c The connection is removed. Now the sphere has a positive charge.

d Finally, the sphere is taken away from the dome. It has a uniformly distributed positive charge all over it.

Note that the connection to earth must be disconnected *before* the sphere is moved away from the dome; otherwise, the electrons would simply run back up to the sphere to neutralise its positive charge.

Questions

17.1 What force is involved when two objects are rubbed together and become charged?

17.2 Two positively charged polystyrene spheres are held close to one another.

    a Will they attract or repel one another?

    b What will happen to the force between them if the charge on one is increased?

    c What will happen to the force if they are held closer together?

17.3 Look at Table 17.1. If a glass rod is rubbed with a woollen cloth, will the rod become positively or negatively charged?

17.4 Draw a diagram to show how a negatively charged polythene rod can attract an uncharged scrap of paper.

17.5 The dome of a charged van de Graaff generator stores a large number of electrons. Draw a diagram to show what happens if the dome is connected to earth by a copper wire. Why is the dome supported on a Perspex stand?

17.2 What is electric charge?

In physics, we find it relatively easy to answer questions like 'What is a rainbow?' or 'How does an aircraft fly?' It is much harder to answer an apparently simple question like 'What is electric charge?' We have to answer it by saying how objects with electric charge behave. Objects with the same sign of charge repel one another; objects with opposite charge attract. This is not a very satisfying answer, because magnetic poles behave in the same way (north poles repel north poles and attract south poles). Because electric charge is a fundamental property of matter, we have to get a feel for it, rather than having a clear definition.

The electric force between two charged objects is one of the fundamental forces of Nature. (The force of gravity between two masses is another fundamental force.) The electric force holds together the particles that make up an atom; it holds atoms together to make molecules; and it holds molecules together to make solid objects. Without the electric force holding molecules together, we would fall through the floor. It is a very important force.

Charged particles

We have already seen that electrons are the charged particles that are transferred from one object to another when the objects are rubbed together. Electric charge is a property of the particles that make up atoms.

Charge is measured in **coulombs** (C), named after Charles de Coulomb, a French physicist who worked on static electricity at about the same time as Benjamin Franklin. He discovered that the force between two charged objects depends on how big their charges are and on how far apart they are, as we saw earlier.

An electron is a negatively charged particle. It is much smaller than an atom, and an outer electron is only weakly attached to the outside of the atom. It is held there by the attraction of the positively charged nucleus of the atom. The atomic nucleus is positively charged because it contains positively charged particles called protons.

An **electron** has a very tiny amount of negative electric charge:

$$\text{electron charge} = -0.000\,000\,000\,000\,000\,000\,16\,\text{C} = -1.6 \times 10^{-19}\,\text{C}$$

The electron charge is so small that it takes over six million million million electrons to make 1 C of charge.

A **proton** has exactly the same amount of charge as an electron, but positive:

$$\text{proton charge} = +0.000\,000\,000\,000\,000\,000\,16\,\text{C} = +1.6 \times 10^{-19}\,\text{C}$$

No-one knows why these values are *exactly* the same (or even if they *are* exactly the same), but it is fortunate that they are because it means that an atom that contains, say, six protons and six neutrons is electrically neutral. If all the objects around us were made of charged atoms, we would live in a shocking world!

Charge and voltage

When the metal dome of a van de Graaff generator is charged up, it has many millions of extra electrons, giving it a negative charge. The electrons all repel one another, so they are spread out all over the surface of the dome. The electrons want to escape from one another, and to get to earth (or to any positive charge). If the charged dome is left for a while, the charge will gradually leak away into the air.

Figure 17.10 The high voltage of the charged Van de Graaff dome makes a spark jump through the air. The electrons on the dome repel one another, and this is enough to make them leap the gap and discharge the dome.

The dome of the van de Graaff generator is charged up to a high voltage – hundreds of thousands of volts. Such a high voltage is enough to make a spark jump through a few centimetres of air. If you should get a spark from a van de Graaff, you would feel quite a jolt, as you would expect from such a high voltage (Figure 17.10). Of course, as the spark jumps, the dome loses its electric charge and so the spark is short-lived. The voltage that made the spark jump has disappeared.

Similarly high voltages can be developed when your clothes rub together. Synthetic fibres such as polyester and nylon are particularly good for this, as they tend to be good insulators, so that the charge cannot run away. If you pull off a sweater over your head so that it rubs on a shirt beneath, the two become charged up. High voltages develop. When the voltage at a point is high enough, a spark jumps to discharge the fabric. You can see that sparks literally do fly, especially if you undress in the dark.

This tells us something about what we mean by **voltage**. A negatively charged object (such as the dome of the van de Graaff generator) stores a lot of electrons. The electrons repel one another, so there is a strong force between them. If there is a conducting path for them to move along, the force will push them along it until the object is discharged. We can say that the electrons move because of the force pushing them; alternatively, we can say that there is a voltage that makes them move. The two explanations are equivalent.

There is much more about voltage and charge in Chapters 18 and 19.

Extension material

Electrolysis

So far, we have considered electrons as the charged particles that move when an object becomes charged, or when it discharges. Electrons are charged particles, and they are mobile. It is often the case that the movement of electrons can explain electrical phenomena. Metals contain many electrons, which are relatively free to move about. (If you have studied Chapter 10, you will recall that these free electrons also explain why metals are good conductors of heat.)

However, electrons are not the only charged particles that can move about, and this is particularly important in the case of electrolysis.

Electrolysis is the process of splitting up an ionic compound by passing an electric current through it.

Figure 17.11 shows what happens when an electric current is passed through molten sodium chloride. (The sodium chloride must be heated to melt it; no current will flow through solid sodium chloride.) The molten sodium chloride is not made up of neutral atoms. Rather, it is made up of charged sodium ions and chloride ions:

- Sodium ions (Na^+) are sodium atoms that have lost an electron.
- Chloride ions (Cl^-) are chlorine atoms that have gained an extra electron.

An **ion** is an atom (or a group of atoms) that has gained or lost one or more electrons.

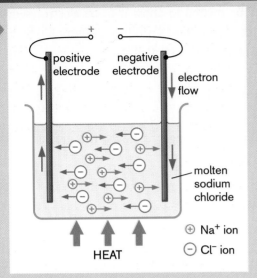

Figure 17.11 An electric current flowing through molten sodium chloride is carried by sodium ions and chloride ions.

A positive ion has lost one or more electrons; a negative ion has gained one or more electrons. From the symbol for the ion, you can tell how many electrons have been lost or gained; for example, a zinc ion Zn^{2+} has lost two electrons, and the sulphate ion SO_4^{2-} has gained two electrons. In solid sodium chloride, the sodium and chloride ions stick together because they have opposite charges. In liquid form, they are free to move around.

To electrolyse the sodium chloride, two **electrodes** are placed in it, connected to the positive and negative terminals of a battery or power supply. Now the ions begin to move. The positive ions are attracted to the negative electrode, and vice versa.

When a sodium ion arrives at the negative electrode, it gains an electron:

$$Na^+ + e^- \rightarrow Na$$

The ion has become a neutral atom of sodium. (Note that we write e^- to represent an electron and its negative charge.) For each sodium ion that reaches the electrode, an electron flows down from the battery.

At the positive electrode, each chloride ion loses an electron; they join together in pairs to make chlorine molecules:

$$2Cl^- - 2e^- \rightarrow Cl_2$$

The electrons given up by the ions flow along the wire to the battery.

There are two outcomes of this process:

- The compound sodium chloride is split into two separate, simpler substances, the elements sodium and chlorine.
- There is a flow of electrons around the circuit, from the negative terminal of the battery to the positive terminal.

Hence a current has flowed through the liquid, but it has been carried by moving ions, rather than by electrons.

Figure 17.12 The industrial electrolysis of aluminium oxide to produce aluminium. Aluminium sinks to the bottom of these large electrolysis cells. The electrodes are made of graphite (a form of carbon). The oxygen released by electrolysis reacts with the electrodes to form carbon dioxide gas, which escapes. The electrodes are rapidly used up and have to be replaced. Electricity is expensive, and this makes the price of aluminium higher than that of other common metals such as steel or lead.

The meaning of electrolysis

The word *electrolysis* means *splitting up by electricity*. It is a very important process. Figure 17.12 shows the industrial electrolysis of aluminium oxide to extract aluminium. Hundreds of amps of electric current pass through the molten aluminium oxide to release the metal from its compound. For each aluminium ion (Al^{3+}) that becomes an aluminium atom (Al), three electrons must be supplied by the negative electrode.

An ionic compound may be melted to allow it to be electrolysed; alternatively, it may be dissolved in water to produce a solution which will conduct electricity. The characteristics of electrolysis are:

- An electric current is passed through a liquid.
- A compound is broken down into simpler substances, often the elements from which the compound is made.
- The bigger the current, and the longer it flows, the greater the masses of the substances released.

? Questions

17.6 What charge does an electron have, positive or negative?

17.7 Would two electrons attract or repel one another?

17.8 Explain why an oxygen atom containing eight protons and eight electrons is electrically neutral.

17.9 Two identical metal spheres are placed close to one another. One is given a large negative charge. The two are then connected by a wire.

    a Use the idea of *electrical force* to explain what happens next.

    b Then use the idea of *voltage* to explain what happens.

17.3 The hazards and uses of static electricity

Hazards

Static electricity can be a problem – for example, it can make your hair stand on end if you brush it vigorously after washing it with too much conditioner. But it can be much more of a problem than this.

Disasters can happen when static electricity builds up as a result of friction. For example, when oil is pumped on-board a tanker, friction between the oil and the pipe can result in a build-up of charge – see Figure 17.13. A spark may jump between the negatively charged oil and the positively charged pipe. This spark may ignite the mixture of vapour and air in the hold of the tanker.

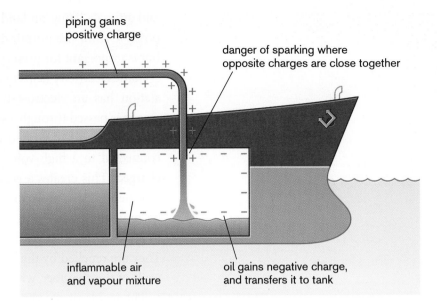

piping gains
positive charge

danger of sparking where
opposite charges are close together

inflammable air
and vapour mixture

oil gains negative charge,
and transfers it to tank

Figure 17.13 The hold of an oil tanker is likely to contain a dangerously inflammable mixture of oil vapour and air. Sparks must therefore be avoided. Problems arise when the oil flows through the pipe; friction gives rise to static electricity. The positive and negative charges must be given the chance to neutralise one another or a spark may result.

To avoid this, a good electrical connection must be made between the oil and all the metal parts of the tanker, including the pipes. A similar problem can arise when fuel is being pumped into an aircraft, or when the storage tanks at a petrol station are being refilled. The tanker supplying the fuel must be connected with a thick cable to the tank it is filling. Then any static charge that builds up as the fuel runs through the pipe will be discharged. Look out for the cable the next time you see a tanker refuelling a petrol station.

Similar problems can arise when dry powders flow along pipes. Friction produces static charges. Small amounts of powder in the air can be inflammable, and a spark can set off an explosion. This is a particular problem in the food industry – breakfast cereals and custard powder can both be ignited if care isn't taken to provide a method for electric charges to discharge themselves harmlessly.

Ink jet printer

The ink jet printer attached to many computers makes use of static electricity (Figure 17.14). The printer gun produces a jet of tiny droplets of ink. These have to be directed onto the paper to form the appropriate pattern of letters. To direct the beam across the paper, the droplets are electrically charged. Then they can be moved across the page by means of the pair of deflecting plates. Increasing the voltage of the supply pushes more positive charge onto the positive plate and the jet moves further across the page.

Electrostatic smoke precipitators

Power stations produce a great deal of smoke, which can pollute the environment for hundreds of kilometres around. The smoke consists of very fine particles, which may be carried high into the atmosphere, falling to ground a long way off. These particles cause damage to plants

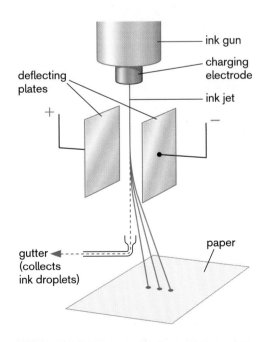

ink gun

charging
electrode

deflecting
plates

ink jet

gutter
(collects
ink droplets)

paper

Figure 17.14 An ink jet printer uses static electricity to move a jet of charged ink droplets across the page. This process can be extremely fast, printing a whole sheet of text in a few seconds.

and animals living on land and in water. Removing as much dust as possible from the output of power stations is an expensive business, but is important for preserving valuable ecosystems.

Static electricity helps to capture the smoke particles. When a power station has an electrostatic smoke precipitator (Figure 17.15), the smoke is passed through a special chamber before it goes up the chimney. The chamber is fitted with a series of metal wires. The wires are connected to a high-voltage supply, so that they become negatively charged. This creates a very strong electric field within the chamber. The neutral gas molecules in the air passing through the chamber become ionised as electrons are ripped from them. The electrons tend to stick to the dust particles, and these are then negatively charged. They are repelled by the negatively charged wires and attracted to the walls of the chamber, where they stick.

The inside of the chamber becomes caked with dust, and periodically large hammers strike its walls, causing the dust to fall to the bottom. Here it is collected up and removed for safe disposal. In this way, over 99% of the dust is removed from the exhaust gases coming from the power station's furnaces.

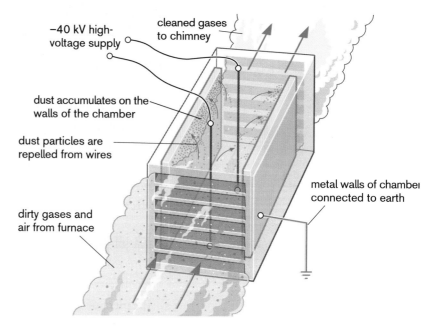

−40 kV high-voltage supply

cleaned gases to chimney

dust accumulates on the walls of the chamber

dust particles are repelled from wires

metal walls of chamber connected to earth

dirty gases and air from furnace

Figure 17.15 At a power station, an electrostatic precipitator removes dust from the exhaust gases produced by the furnace. Some homes, restaurants and other public buildings have air conditioning systems that are fitted with dust precipitators. These remove dust from the air entering the buildings, and this can be of great benefit to asthma sufferers.

Other uses of static electricity

Static electricity has many other uses, such as in photocopying, where the 'toner' (ink) is guided onto the paper using static electricity. In industry, paint is often sprayed electrostatically. This ensures that paint reaches all sides of an object such as part of a car body, and as little paint as possible is wasted.

Questions

17.10 Look at the diagram of the ink jet printer (Figure 17.16).

   a Are the ink droplets given a positive or negative charge?

   b Explain how you can tell.

17.11 **a** Explain how a danger of explosion may arise when flour passes down a pipe into a storage silo.

   b How can this danger be avoided?

17.12 Insect pests often hide on the underside of a plant's leaves. When farmers spray insecticide, it lands on the top surface of the leaf and the insects escape. How could static electricity be used to help overcome this problem? (Think about the example of paint spraying. Don't suggest giving the insects an electric shock!)

Summary

◆ When one object is rubbed against another, the force of friction may transfer electrons from one object to the other.

◆ Electrons have a negative charge, so the object that gains electrons becomes negatively charged; the object that loses electrons becomes positively charged.

◆ Charged objects exert forces on each other. Like charges repel; unlike charges attract.

◆ The greater the charges and the closer the objects are to each other, the greater the force between them.

◆ A charged object may attract an uncharged object. Electrons in the uncharged object move slightly, so that the object becomes charged by induction.

◆ Electric charge is measured in coulombs, C.

⊖ *In electrolysis, an electric current is passed through a liquid, which is split into simpler substances. The charged particles that move in the liquid are ions (atoms which are charged, because they have gained or lost electrons).*

◆ Static electricity can be hazardous, particularly because of the danger of sparks igniting explosive mixtures.

◆ Static electricity has many uses: for example, in printing, photocopying and paint spraying, and in electrostatic dust precipitation.

Electric circuits

Topics in this chapter

- the need for a complete circuit
- current, charge and electrons
- electrical resistance
- Ohm's law
- resistive components
- resistors in series and parallel
- *potential divider circuits*

No doubt, you have made electric circuits in the lab, and looked at some real-life circuits. The circuits that you have experimented with are **models** for the circuits that have real purposes in the world. They are models because they present a simplified view of how circuits work. Practical circuits are usually more complex, but it makes sense to start with simple circuits to build up a picture of how electric current flows.

The photographs in Figures 18.1 and 18.2 show two rather different types of electric circuit.

Figure 18.1 These cables carry large electric currents. Energy is being transferred from a power station to an industrial plant where it will be used to turn machinery, split chemicals and so on.

Figure 18.1 shows part of the electric circuit that carries energy from a large generating station to the industrial complex where the energy is used. Electric current is flowing through thick metal cables, held above the ground by tall pylons.

Figure 18.2 shows the electrical circuits inside a computer. There are several 'chips' (integrated circuits) in the computer. In these, electric current flows through silicon, a semiconducting material. (A semiconductor is not such a good conductor as a metal.) Engineers design chips to be as small as possible. This is because, although electric current flows quickly, it is not instantaneous, and so current takes less time to flow around a small component than a larger one.

Figure 18.2 The electric circuits of a computer are highly engineered. Each of the chips (the rectangular objects with many legs) contains many millions of electric circuits, which work to process information at high speed.

These two pictures illustrate the two general uses that we have for electric circuits:

● Electricity can be used to transport **energy** from place to place. A circuit contains devices for transforming energy. Think of a simple circuit like a torch. Energy is *transferred* electrically from the battery to the bulb, where it is *transformed* into light and heat.

● Electricity can be used to transport **information** from one place to another. Digital information comes into the computer, and its circuits then manipulate the information to produce pictures, sounds and new data. We even have electrical circuits in our bodies for handling information – our brain and nerves work electrically, and it is possible to trace the flow of electricity around our bodies.

In this chapter and the next, we will look at electric circuits in detail, and extend your understanding of the different components which are used in circuits to control the current that flows and the energy that is transferred.

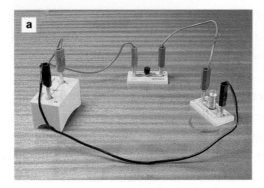

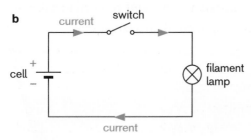

Figure 18.3 **a** A simple electrical circuit, set up in a laboratory using a circuit board. **b** The same circuit represented as a circuit diagram.

18.1 Current in electric circuits

If an electric current is to flow, two things are needed:
- a complete circuit for it to flow around, and
- something to push it around the circuit.

The 'push' might be provided by a battery or power supply. In most familiar circuits, metals such as copper or steel provide the circuit for the current to flow around. Figure18.3a shows how a simple circuit can be set up in the laboratory, using a circuit board. Once the switch is closed, there is a continuous metal path for the current to flow along. Current flows from the positive terminal of the battery (or cell); it flows through the switch and the filament lamp, back to the negative terminal of the battery.

Figure 18.3b shows the same circuit, represented by a circuit diagram. Each component has its own standard symbol. If you imagine the switch being pushed so that it closes, it is clear from the diagram that there is a continuous path for the current to flow around the circuit.

It is obvious how the switch in Figure 18.3a works: the button on the switch is pushed down until contact is made. Then the current can flow through it. Most switches work by bringing two pieces of metal into contact with one another, though you cannot usually see this happening. It is worth having a look inside some switches to see how they work.

Good conductors, bad conductors

Metals are good conductors of electric current because they contain **conduction electrons**. (These are the 'free electrons' already mentioned in Chapters 10 and 17.) The idea is that, in a bad conductor such as most plastics, *all* of the electrons in the material are tightly bound within the molecules, so that they cannot move. Metals are different. Whereas *most* of the electrons in a metal *are* tightly bound within their atoms, some are free to move about within the material – see Figure 18.4. A voltage, such as that provided by a battery or power supply, can start these conduction electrons moving in one direction

Figure 18.4 In a metal, some electrons are free to move about. These are known as conduction electrons; in copper, there is one conduction electron for each atom of the metal. The atoms, having lost an electron, become positively charged ions. A battery pushes the conduction electrons through the metal; the force is the attraction between unlike charges that was discussed in Chapter 17.

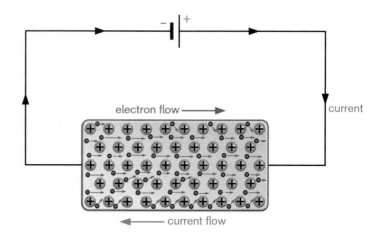

through the metal, and an electric current flows. Since electrons have a negative electric charge, they are attracted to the positive terminal of the battery.

In between good conductors (most metals) and good insulators (such as Perspex or polythene), there are many materials that do conduct electricity, but not very well. For example, liquids may conduct, but they are generally poor conductors. An electric current passing through a liquid is often carried by ions (charged atoms), and these do not move as freely as conduction electrons in metals. (The movement of ions through a liquid was discussed in Chapter 17, on page 273.)

People can conduct electricity – that's what happens when you get an electric shock. A current passes through your body and, if it is big enough, it makes your muscles contract violently. Your heart may stop and burns may also result. You can test your own conductivity in a safe way, using a multimeter. This passes a small current through any object connected between its terminals. Since it is battery-powered, you cannot give yourself a shock with it. Try holding a terminal in each hand. The meter will show the resistance of your body as the current flows up one arm, across your chest and down the other arm. Although dry skin is a good insulator, once the current is inside your body, it can flow relatively easily through the watery fluids inside your cells. Moisten your skin and repeat the experiment – your resistance will be much less. Now, touch a terminal to each of your ears to measure the resistance of your head. This will be very high, because the current cannot penetrate the bone of your skull. (This does not prove that there is a vacuum in there!)

Two pictures: current and electrons

The word *electricity* is a rather vague term. In everyday life, we might say things like:

'She got a shock when the mains electricity went through her.'

'This train runs on electricity.'

The first is really a statement about *electric current*. The second is a statement about *electrical energy*. We need to keep these ideas separate in our heads, and so it is best to avoid talking about electricity. When you read a statement such as 'People can conduct electricity', you should be able to translate this as 'People can conduct electric current'. Ideas about electrical energy are dealt with in detail in the next chapter. Here we will concentrate on the idea of electric current.

When we are trying to explain what happens in an electric circuit, we often talk about electric current. An electric current is a flow of electrical charge – the same charge that explains effects in static electricity (Chapter 17). An electric current may flow in a wire, or through a liquid, or as a spark through the air. We say:

Electric **current** is a flow of charge, from positive to negative.

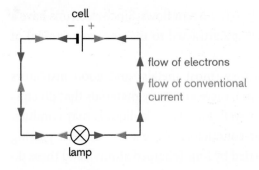

cell

flow of electrons

flow of conventional current

lamp

Figure 18.5 Two ways of picturing what happens in an electric circuit: conventional current flows from positive to negative; electrons flow from negative to positive.

Figure 18.5 shows the direction of flow of charge around a simple circuit. In the circuit symbol for a cell, the longer line represents the positive terminal. We picture positive charge flowing out of the positive terminal, around the circuit and back into the cell at the negative terminal.

Now, we know that in a metal it is negatively charged electrons that move. They leave the negative terminal of the cell, and flow around to the positive terminal, in the opposite direction to the current. Hence we have two different pictures of what is going on in a circuit:

- *Conventional current* We can think of conventional current, a flow of positive charge, moving from positive to negative. Conventional current is rather like a fluid moving through the wires, just like water moving through pipes. This picture doesn't tell us anything about what is going on inside the wires or components of a circuit. However, it is perfectly good for working out many things to do with a circuit – what the voltage will be across a particular component, for example, or how much electrical energy will be transferred to a particular resistor.

- *Electron flow* Alternatively, we can think of electron flow, a movement of conduction electrons, from negative to positive. As we will see shortly, this picture can allow us to think about what is going on inside the components of a circuit – why a resistor gets warm when a current flows through it, for example, or why a diode allows current to flow in one direction only. It is important to bear in mind that, as we discussed above, some materials conduct because they contain mobile ions rather than electrons.

The electron flow picture is a *microscopic model*, since it tells us what is going on at the level of very tiny particles (electrons and ions). The conventional current picture is a *macroscopic model* (a large-scale model).

The electrons in a circuit flow in the opposite direction to the electric current. It is a nuisance to have to remember this. It stems from the early days of experiments on static electricity. Benjamin Franklin realised that there were two types of electric charge, which he called 'positive' and 'negative'. He had to choose which type he would call positive, and his choice was to say that, when amber was rubbed with a silk cloth, the amber acquired a negative charge. Franklin was setting up a *convention*, which other scientists then followed; hence the term *conventional current*. Franklin had no way of knowing that electrons were being rubbed from the silk to the amber, but his choice meant that we now say that electrons have a negative charge. If Franklin had made the opposite choice, we would now say that conventional current and electrons both flow from positive to negative.

From time to time, people have tried to reverse Franklin's convention. This would mean re-labelling all batteries, power supplies, circuit diagrams and so on, so that both electrons and conventional current would flow in the same direction around a circuit. However, the idea has never caught on. The conventional current model works perfectly well, and it is not too difficult to picture electrons moving in the opposite direction to the current.

Measuring electric current

To measure electric current, we use an **ammeter**. There are two types, as shown in Figure 18.6:

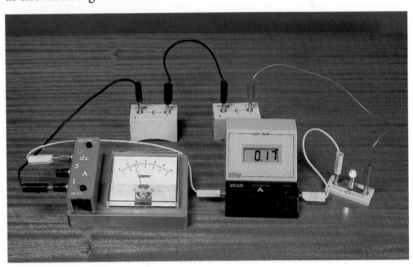

Figure 18.6 Ammeters measure electrical current, in amps (A). There are two types: analogue (on the left) and digital (on the right).

- An **analogue meter** has a needle that moves across a scale. With this type of meter, it is easy to see when the current flowing is increasing or decreasing. You have to make a judgement of the position of the needle against the scale.
- A **digital meter** gives a direct read-out in figures. There is no judgement involved in taking a reading. Data-loggers and personal computers use digital data.

An ammeter is always connected into a circuit *in series*; that is to say, the current flows in through one terminal (red, positive) and out through the other (black, negative). If the meter is connected the wrong way round, it will give negative readings. To add an ammeter to a circuit, the circuit must be broken – see Figure 18.7.

In a simple series circuit like the one shown in Figure 18.7, it does not matter where the ammeter is added, since the current is the same all the way round the circuit. We can understand this by thinking about the electrons that are flowing around the circuit. They leave the negative terminal of the cell; they are attracted to its positive terminal. To get there, there must be an uninterrupted circuit. They do not get used up as they pass through the lamp or other components in the circuit.

The reading on an ammeter is in amperes (A). The ampere (shortened to amp) is the SI unit of current. Smaller currents may be measured in milliamps or microamps:

$$1 \text{ milliamp} = 1 \text{ mA} = 0.001 \text{ A} = 10^{-3} \text{ A}$$
$$1 \text{ microamp} = 1 \text{ μA} = 0.000\,001 \text{ A} = 10^{-6} \text{ A}$$

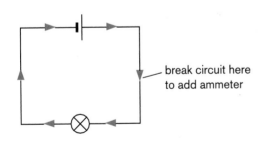

break circuit here to add ammeter

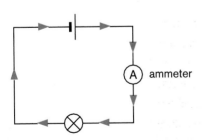

(A) ammeter

Figure 18.7 Adding an ammeter to a circuit; the ammeter is connected in series, so that the current can flow through it.

Current and charge

An ammeter measures the rate at which electric charge flows past a point in a circuit; in other words, the amount of charge that passes per second. We can write this relationship between current and charge as an equation, using the symbols shown in Table 18.1:

$$\text{current (A)} = \frac{\text{charge (C)}}{\text{time (s)}}$$

$$I = \frac{Q}{t}$$

So a current of 10 A passing a point means that 10 C of charge flows past that point every second.

You may find it easier to remember this relationship in the following form:

$$\text{charge (C)} = \text{current (A)} \times \text{time (s)}$$

$$Q = It$$

So if a current of 10 A flows around a circuit for 5 s, 50 C of charge flows past a point in the circuit.

Table 18.1 Symbols and units for some electrical quantities.

Quantity	Symbol for quantity	Unit	Symbol for unit
current	I	amps	A
charge	Q	coulombs	C
time	t	seconds	s

Worked example 1

A current of 150 mA flows around a circuit for 1 minute. How much electrical charge flows past a point in the circuit in this time?

● *Step 1* Write down what you know, and what you want to know, putting all quantities in the units shown in Table 18.1:

$I = 150\,\text{mA} = 0.15\,\text{A}$ (or $150 \times 10^{-3}\,\text{A}$)

$t = 1\,\text{minute} = 60\,\text{s}$

$Q = ?$

● *Step 2* Write down an appropriate form of the equation relating Q, I and t:

$Q = It$

Substitute values and calculate the answer:

$Q = 0.15\,\text{A} \times 60\,\text{s} = 12\,\text{C}$

So 12 coulombs of charge flow past a point in the circuit.

? Questions

18.1   **a** In which direction does conventional current flow around a circuit?

    b In which direction do electrons flow?

18.2   **a** What instrument is used to measure electric current?

    b How should it be connected in a circuit?

    c Draw its circuit symbol.

Questions continued

18.3 **a** What is the unit of electric current?

b What is the unit of electric charge?

18.4 Which of the following equations shows the correct relationship between electrical units?

1 A = 1 C/s,   1 C = 1 A/s

18.5 If 20 C of charge pass a point in a circuit in 1 s, what current is flowing?

18.6 A current of 4 A flows around a circuit for 10 s. How much charge flows past a point in the circuit in this time?

18.7 **a** How many milliamps are there in 1 amp?

b How many microamps are there in 1 amp?

18.2 Electrical resistance

If you use a short length of wire to connect the positive and negative terminals of a cell (a battery) together, you can do a lot of damage. The wire and the cell may both get hot, as a large current will flow through them. There is very little **electrical resistance** in the circuit, so the current is large. Power supplies are protected by trip switches, which cause them to cut out if too large a current flows.

The current flowing in a circuit can be controlled by adding components with electrical resistance to the circuit. The greater the resistance, the smaller the current that will flow. Figure 18.8 shows a circuit in which a cell pushes a current through a resistor. The cell provides the voltage needed to push the current through the resistor. Here 'voltage' is a rather loose term, and we should say that there is a **potential difference** across the resistor. Potential difference (or p.d. in short) is another term for voltage, and it indicates that there is a difference in electrical potential across the resistor. This difference is rather like the difference in height that makes a ball roll from a high place to a lower place.

We use the symbol V (in italics) to stand for p.d.; and its units are volts, V (not in italics). Take care not to confuse these two symbols! In Chapter 19, we will look in more detail at what we mean by potential difference. In the meantime, we will think of the p.d. across a component as the 'push' that is making current flow through the component.

In a circuit powered by a cell, how much current can flow through a resistor? This depends on the resistance of the resistor – the greater its resistance, the smaller the current that will flow through it. The resistance of a component is measured in ohms (Ω) and is defined by this equation:

$$\text{resistance } (\Omega) = \frac{\text{potential difference (V)}}{\text{current (A)}}$$

$$R = \frac{V}{I}$$

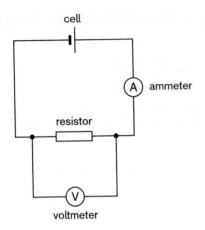

Figure 18.8 The cell provides the p.d. needed to push the current around the circuit. The amount of current depends on the p.d. and the resistance of the resistor. The ammeter measures the current flowing through the resistor. The voltmeter measures the p.d. across the resistor. This circuit can thus be used to find the resistance of the resistor.

There are three arrangements of this equation that you are likely to find useful:

$$R = \frac{V}{I} \qquad I = \frac{V}{R} \qquad V = IR$$

The circuit shown in Figure 18.8 illustrates how we can measure the resistance of a resistor (or any other component). We need to know the current flowing through the resistor, measured by the ammeter. We also need to know the p.d. across it, and this is measured by the **voltmeter** connected across it. A voltmeter is always connected *in parallel* with the relevant component, because it is measuring the potential difference *between the two ends* of the component.

Worked example 2 shows how to calculate the resistance of a resistor from these measurements of current and p.d.

Worked example 2

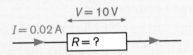

Figure 18.9 The quantities involved in worked example 2. Notice that we show the current as an arrow entering (or leaving) the resistor. The p.d. is shown by a double-headed arrow (or two separate arrows), to indicate that it is measured across the resistor. The resistance is simply shown as a label on or next to the resistor; it doesn't have a direction.

A resistor allows a current of 0.02 A to flow through it when there is a p.d. of 10.0 V between its ends. What is its resistance?

● *Step 1* Write down what you know, and what you want to know (you may prefer to write these quantities on a sketch of the situation – see Figure 18.9):

current $I = 0.02$ A

p.d. $V = 10.0$ V

resistance $R = ?$

● *Step 2* Write down the equation for R:

$$R = \frac{V}{I}$$

Substitute values and calculate the answer:

$$R = \frac{10.0\,\text{V}}{0.02\,\text{A}} = 500\,\Omega$$

So the resistance of the resistor is 500 Ω.

What is an ohm?

If we think about the equation

$$R = \frac{V}{I}$$

that defines what we mean by resistance, we can see that it takes a p.d. of 10 V to make a current of 1 A flow through a 10 Ω resistor; it takes

20 V to make 1 A flow through a 20 Ω resistor; and so on. Hence resistance (in Ω) tells us how many volts are needed to make 1 A flow through that resistance. To put it another way:

an ohm is a volt per amp	$1\,\Omega = 1\,V/A$

In the case of worked example 2, it would take 500 V to make 1 A flow through the 500 Ω resistor.

A note on language

It is helpful to use the correct terminology when talking, thinking or writing about electric circuits:

- *Charge* We can talk about the charge that flows *around* a circuit, or *through* a component.
- *Current* Similarly, we can talk about the current that flows *around* a circuit, or *through* a component. (Some people prefer to talk about the current *in* a circuit, because a current must be flowing or it isn't a current.)
- *Potential difference* We can talk about the p.d. or voltage *across* a component, or *between* two points in a circuit.

Remembering these ways of talking will remind you of how to connect meters correctly:

- *Ammeter* – connected in series with a component, so that the current can flow through it.
- *Voltmeter* – connected across (in parallel with) a component, to measure the p.d. across it.

The origins of resistance

An electric circuit is like an obstacle course. The current flows around because the cell provides it with energy. To travel all the way round the circuit, it must push its way through various components. The greater the resistance of the component, the harder it is for the current to get through, and so the smaller the current will be. If we think about the conduction electrons moving round the circuit, we can understand why some components have more resistance than others. We can also understand why components tend to get hot, especially when a large current flows through them.

Figure 18.10 shows how a piece of metal might look to an electron. The atoms of the metal are arranged in long, evenly spaced lines. (We say that the metal has a crystalline structure, or lattice.) Each atom is vibrating about a fixed position. At low temperatures, this vibration does not seriously impede the movement of the electrons. It is relatively easy for the electrons to whizz through the metal. However, if the metal is warm, its atoms are vibrating more vigorously. There is a greater danger that an electron will collide with a vibrating atom. Also, if there are impurities in the metal, these may have atoms of a different size. Again, electrons may collide with these. So the electrons go through the metal colliding with vibrating atoms and with impurity atoms. At each collision, they are deflected from their passage through the metal. They lose some of their energy to the atoms with which they collide, and in this way energy is transferred from the electrons to the atoms of the metal.

Figure 18.10 Electrons can move rapidly through a piece of metal. Their progress is impeded by any irregularity in the structure of the metal; for example, by vibrating atoms, or by impurity atoms of a different size. Electrons lose energy every time they collide with an atom.

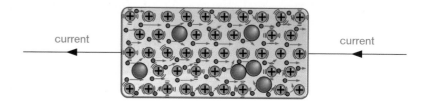

[There is an old-fashioned game called bagatelle, in which a marble is fired by a spring so that it runs up a sloping board. As it rolls back down the board, it speeds up. However, the board has various pins sticking out of it, and the marble keeps bouncing off the pins. At each bounce, it loses energy. The marble is like an electron in a metal, and the pins are like the atoms that impede its free movement through the metal. Bagatelle has been replaced by pinball machines.]

This model of resistance tells us two things:

● The hotter a metal is, the more its atoms vibrate. They will impede electrons more, and so the resistance of a metal must increase as it gets hotter.

● The more impure a metal is, the more likely it is that an electron will collide with an impurity atom. So pure metals have less resistance than impure ones.

Both of these ideas can be checked by measuring the resistances of different metals at different temperatures.

Measuring resistance

The circuit shown in Figure 18.8 on page 286 could be used to find the resistance of a resistor (which we call resistor P, for reasons that will soon become clear). However, this circuit would only provide a single value each for the p.d. V across resistor P and the current I through it. A better technique is shown in Figure 18.11. In place of the cell is a power supply, which can be adjusted to give several different values of p.d. across resistor P. For each value, the current through P is measured, and results like those shown in Table 18.2 are found.

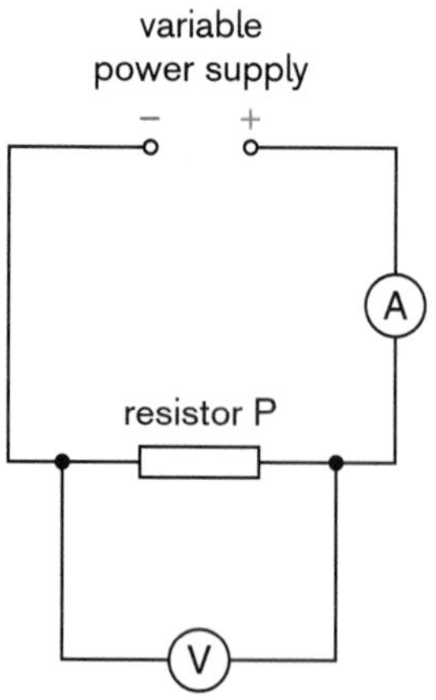

The last column in Table 18.2 shows calculated values for R. These could be averaged. A better approach is to use a graph, as shown in Figure 18.12. The axes of the graph are p.d. and current. It is clear that the points all fall close to a straight line.

A graphical method has the advantage that it is easier to spot results that do not fit the pattern. Also, the points on the graph are inevitably slightly scattered about a straight line, and a 'best fit' line can be drawn

Figure 18.11 A circuit for investigating the current–voltage characteristics of a resistor (which we call P). The power supply can be adjusted to give a range of values of p.d. (typically from 0 V to 12 V) across P. For each value of p.d., the current through resistor P is recorded.

Potential difference, V (V)	Current, I (A)	Resistance, R (Ω)
2.0	0.08	25.0
4.0	0.17	23.5
6.0	0.34	17.6
8.0	0.31	25.8
10.0	0.40	25.0
12.0	0.49	24.5

Table 18.2 Typical results for an experimental measurement of resistance. The values of resistance of resistor P are calculated using $R = V/I$.

Figure 18.12 A graph of current against p.d. for the data shown in Table 18.2. See worked example 3.

to smooth out this scatter. The gradient (slope) of the line can be used to find the value of the resistance of resistor P – see worked example 3.

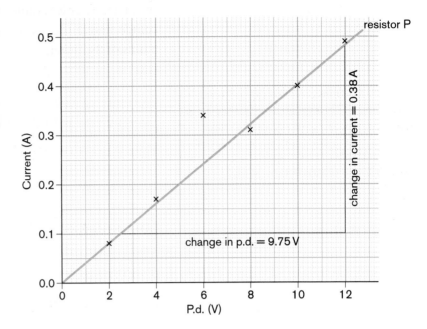

Worked example 3

Use a graphical method to find the resistance of the resistor P using the results shown in Table 18.2.

● *Step 1* Draw a graph to show the data. Plot p.d. *V* on the *x*-axis and current *I* on the *y*-axis.

The graph is shown in Figure 18.12.

● *Step 2* Draw a line of best fit through the points. (Identify any points that clearly do not lie on the line, and ignore them.) The line should pass close to the origin.

The line of best fit is shown in Figure 18.12. The point at 6.0 V has been ignored. (You might guess that the value of current has been incorrectly recorded. It should have been 0.24 A, but you can't assume this. You would need to repeat this measurement.)

● *Step 3* Draw a large triangle to find values for change in p.d. and change in current:

change in p.d. = 12.0 V – 2.5 V = 9.5 V
change in current = 0.48 A – 0.10 A = 0.38 A

● *Step 4* Calculate the resistance of resistor P from the equation:

$$\text{resistance } R = \frac{\text{change in p.d.}}{\text{change in current}}$$

(This is 1/gradient of the line.) Substitute values to get:

$$R = \frac{9.5 \text{ V}}{0.38 \text{A}} = 25 \, \Omega$$

So the resistance of resistor P is 25 Ω.

Ohm's law

A graph like that shown in Figure 18.12 is known as a current–voltage characteristic graph. It shows how the current through a component depends on the p.d. across it. For the resistor P whose *I–V* characteristic is as shown in Figure 18.12, the graph is a straight line passing through the origin, so we can say that the current that flows through the resistor increases in proportion to the p.d. across it.

Another way of summarising this graph is to say that the resistance of the resistor is constant, and does not depend on the p.d. across it. This relationship was first found by Georg Ohm, a German physicist working in 1827, and it is now known as **Ohm's law**:

> A component obeys Ohm's law if the current that flows through it is proportional to the potential difference across it.

Usually, for a component to obey Ohm's law, its temperature must remain constant. As we saw above, the resistance of a metal increases as its temperature increases.

More characteristic graphs

Figure 18.13a shows a smaller version of Figure 18.12, for resistor P. Now imagine reversing the contacts to resistor P in Figure 18.11. The p.d. across P would be reversed and the current would flow through P in the opposite direction. The current and p.d. now have negative values. This is shown by the curve in Figure 18.13b. We can combine Figures 18.13a and b on a single graph, and this is shown as the curve labelled 'resistor P' in Figure 18.13c. The curve is a straight line through the origin. This shows that the resistor has the same resistance in both directions. Figure 18.13c also shows typical results for another resistor, labelled 'resistor Q'. Again the curve is a straight line through

Figure 18.13 **a, b** A resistor has the same resistance in both directions. **c** Current–voltage characteristics for two resistors, P and Q. **d** Current–voltage characteristic for a filament lamp.

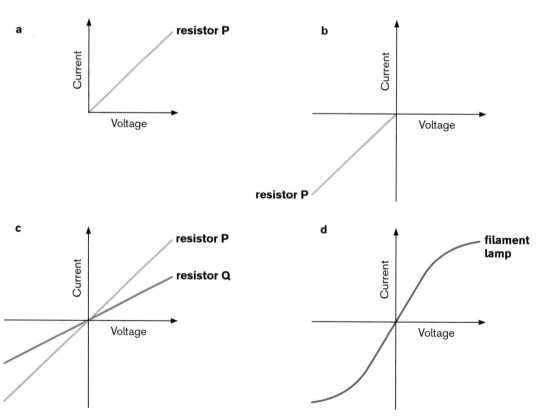

the origin. Resistor Q has a higher resistance than resistor P. You can tell this because, for any given p.d., resistor Q lets through less current.

Figure 18.13d shows the results for a filament lamp. The graph starts off from the origin as a roughly straight line, but it gradually curves over. The current passing through the filament causes it to get hot, and this increases its resistance. As a consequence, the current flowing through the filament does not increase as rapidly as it would do if its temperature remained constant.

Questions

18.8 **a** What do the letters p.d. stand for?
     b What meter is used to measure p.d.?
     c Draw the symbol for this meter.

18.9 What p.d. is needed to make a current of 1 A flow through a 20 Ω resistor?

18.10 What is the resistance of a resistor if a p.d. of 20 V across it causes a current of 2 A to flow through it?

18.11 **a** How does the resistance of a metal change if its temperature decreases?
     b How does the presence of impurities in a metal affect its resistance?

18.12 Look at the graph shown in Figure 18.13c. How can you tell from the graph that the two resistors obey Ohm's law?

18.13 Look at the graph shown in Figure 18.13d. How can you tell from the graph that the lamp's resistance increases as the p.d. across it increases?

18.3 Resistive components

Resistors (Figure 18.14) can be used to control the amount of current flowing around a circuit. They have two terminals, so that the current can flow in one end and out the other. They may be made from metal wire (usually an alloy – a mixture of two or more metals with a high resistance) or from carbon. Carbon (like the graphite 'lead' in a pencil) conducts electricity, but not as well as most metals. Hence high-resistance resistors tend to be made from graphite, particularly as it has a very high melting point.

A **variable resistor** can be used to alter the current flowing in a circuit. Figure 18.15a shows the inside of a variable resistor; notice that it has three terminals. As the control is turned, the contact slides over the resistive track. The current enters at one end and flows through the track until it reaches the contact, where it leaves the resistor. The amount of track through which it flows depends on the position of the contact. Variable resistors like this are often used for the volume

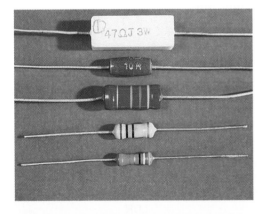

Figure 18.14 A selection of resistors. Some have colour-coded stripes to indicate their value; others use a number code.

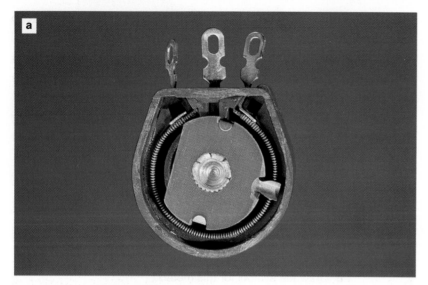

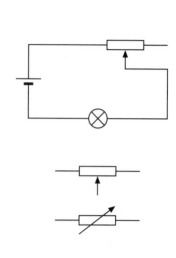

Figure 18.15 **a** A variable resistor: the resistance is provided by a 'track' of resistive wire or carbon. The resistance in the circuit depends on the position of the sliding contact. **b** The current flowing around this circuit depends on the position of the slider on the variable resistor. Imagine sliding the arrow to the right; the current has to flow through more resistance, and so the current will decrease. Also shown are two different circuit symbols for a variable resistor.

control of a radio or stereo system. (You may have come across a **rheostat**, which is a laboratory version of a variable resistor.)

Figure 18.15b shows two different circuit symbols for a variable resistor, together with an example of a circuit that makes use of one. Note that the upper symbol has three terminals (like the resistor itself), but only two are made use of in this circuit. All three terminals are used when a variable resistor is used in a potential divider circuit – see page 297.

Light-dependent resistors (LDR)

This is another type of 'variable resistor', but this time one whose resistance depends on the amount of light falling on it (Figure 18.16). In the dark, a light-dependent resistor (LDR) has a high resistance, often over 1 MΩ; shine light on it and its resistance decreases. In bright light, its resistance may fall to 400 Ω.

An LDR is made of a material that does not normally conduct well because its electrons are bound to their atoms. However, light can provide the energy needed for some electrons to break free. Now there are free conduction electrons, which can move through the resistor, and this means that a current can flow much more easily.

Figure 18.16 **a** A light-dependent resistor (LDR). The gold parts are the two terminals through which the current enters and leaves the resistor. In between is the resistive material. When light falls on it, electrons break free and can carry the current. **b** Two alternative circuit symbols for an LDR – the circle is optional. The arrows represent light shining on the LDR.

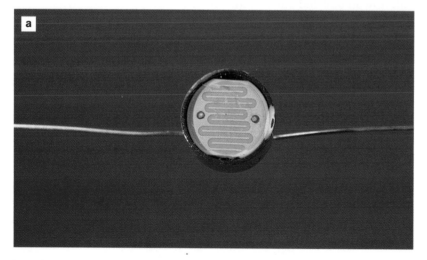

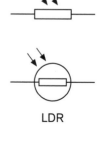

LDR

LDRs are used in circuits to detect the level of light, for example in security lights that switch on automatically at night. Some digital clocks have one fitted. When the room is brightly lit, the display is automatically brightened so that it can be seen against its bright surroundings. In a darkened room, the display need only be dim.

Thermistors

A thermistor (Figure 18.17) is another type of resistor whose resistance depends on its environment. In this case, its resistance depends on its temperature. The resistance changes by a large amount over a narrow range of temperatures.

For some thermistors, the resistance *decreases* as they are heated – perhaps from $2\,k\Omega$ at room temperature to $20\,\Omega$ at $100\,°C$. These thermistors are thus useful for temperature probes – see the discussion of thermometers on page 143.

For other thermistors, the resistance *increases* over a similar temperature range. These are included in circuits where you want to prevent overheating. If the current flowing is large, components may burn out. With a thermistor in the circuit, the resistance increases as the temperature rises and the high current is reduced.

Figure 18.17 **a** A thermistor. **b** The resistance of a thermistor depends on the temperature – in this case, its resistance drops a lot as the temperature increases by a small amount. The rise in temperature provides the energy needed for electrons to break free, and this makes it much easier for the current to flow. This type of thermistor is often used in electronic temperature sensors. **c** In the circuit symbol, the line through the resistor indicates that its resistance is not fixed but depends on an external factor (in this case, the temperature).

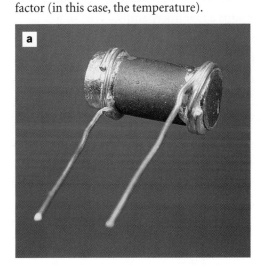

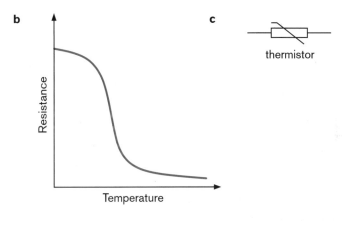

Diodes

A diode is a component that allows electric current to flow in one direction only. Its circuit symbol (Figure 18.18a) represents this by showing an arrow to indicate the direction in which current can flow; the bar shows that current is stopped if it tries to flow in the opposite direction. It can help to think of a diode as being a 'waterfall' in the circuit (Figure 18.18b). Charge can flow over the waterfall, but it cannot flow in the opposite direction, which would be up-hill.

Some diodes give out light when a current flows through them. These are light-emitting diodes (LEDs). We can extend our 'waterfall analogy' to deal with this. As the charge flows over the waterfall, some of the energy it loses is given out as light.

a

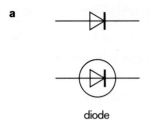

diode

b

charge can flow
this way ⟶

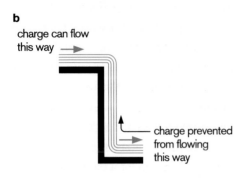

charge prevented
from flowing
this way

c

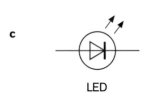

LED

Figure 18.18 **a** Two alternative circuit symbols for a diode – the circle is optional. Diodes allow current to flow in one direction only – in the direction of the arrow. **b** A diode is rather like a waterfall; charge can flow down-hill, but is prevented from flowing back up-hill. **c** The circuit symbol for a light-emitting diode (LED) – the arrows represent the light that is emitted when a current flows through the LED.

Figure 18.19 These modern LEDs have now been developed into full size traffic lights. They are much more robust than traditional light bulbs, and they use much less electrical energy, so they are cheaper to run.

Diodes are useful for converting alternating current (which varies back and forth) into direct current (which flows in one direction only). This is necessary, for example, in a radio that operates from the mains supply. Mains electricity is alternating current (a.c.) but the radio works using direct current (d.c.).

Light-emitting diodes are familiar in many pieces of electronic equipment. For example, they are used as the small indicator lights that show whether a stereo system is on. Recently, large LEDs have been developed which can be used in traffic lights (Figure 18.19). These use very little energy, so they are much cheaper to run than traditional lights; and they rarely fail, so that they do not need to be replaced frequently.

Figure 18.20 shows the current–voltage characteristic for a diode. When the p.d. across the diode is positive, a current flows. The bigger the p.d., the greater the current. However, note that the current doesn't increase in proportion to the p.d. You can tell this because the graph is not a straight line through the origin. Instead, it increases slowly at first and then curves upwards.

When the p.d. across the diode is negative, it is trying to push a current through the diode in the forbidden direction. In fact, a very small current does flow – perhaps a few microamps.

Because the *I–V* characteristic graph is not a straight line through the origin, we can say that the current flowing is not proportional to the p.d. In other words, the diode does not obey Ohm's law.

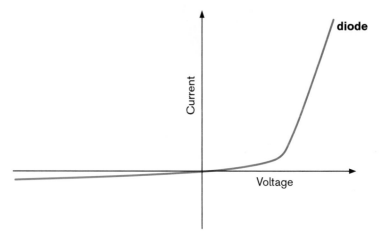

Figure 18.20 The current–voltage characteristic graph for a diode. A large current flows only when the p.d. across the diode is positive. For a negative p.d., a tiny current flows. The graph is curved, which tells us that the resistance of a diode does not obey Ohm's law.

? **Questions**

18.14 Draw the circuit symbols for: **a** resistor and **b** variable resistor.

18.15 **a** What does LDR stand for?

    b Draw its circuit symbol.

    c What happens to the resistance of an LDR when light is shone on it?

18.16 **a** Draw the circuit symbol for a thermistor.

    b Give one use for a thermistor.

    c Explain why a thermistor is suitable for this use.

18.17 **a** What does LED stand for?

    b Name one item in your home that uses an LED.

    c What is indicated when the LED lights up?

18.18 **a** Sketch the *I–V* characteristic graph for a diode.

    b How can you tell from the graph that the resistance of the diode does not obey Ohm's law?

18.4 Combinations of resistors

If you have two resistors, there are two ways in which they can be connected together in a circuit: **in series** or **in parallel**. This is illustrated for two 10 Ω resistors in Figure 18.21.

To recognise when two resistors are connected in series, trace the path of the current around the circuit. If it flows through one resistor and then through the other, they are connected in series. The resistors are connected end-to-end. For resistors in parallel, the current flows differently. It flows around the circuit until it reaches a point where the circuit divides (point X in Figure 18.21b). Then some of the current flows through one resistor, and some flows through the other. Then the two currents recombine at point Y and return to the cell. Resistors in parallel are connected side-by-side.

Resistors in series

Festive lights, such as those used on Christmas trees, are often wired together in series. This is because each bulb works on a small voltage; if a single bulb was connected to the mains supply, the p.d. across it would be too great. By connecting them in series, the mains voltage is shared out between them. The disadvantage of this is that, if one bulb fails (its filament breaks), they all go out because there is no longer a complete circuit for the current to flow around.

The same current flows in each resistor – remember, current can't be used up, because electrons can't disappear.

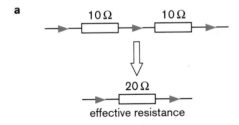

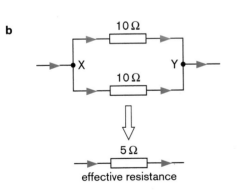

Figure 18.21 Two ways of connecting two resistors in a circuit: **a** in series and **b** in parallel.

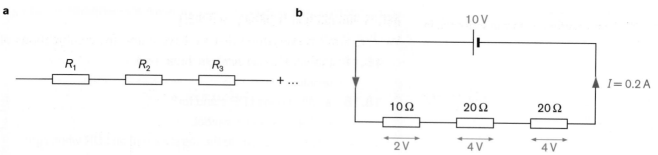

a

R_1 R_2 R_3

+ ...

b

10 V

$I = 0.2$ A

10 Ω   20 Ω   20 Ω

2 V   4 V   4 V

Figure 18.22 **a** Several resistors connected in series. **b** Values of current and p.d. in a series circuit. The p.d. of the supply is shared between the resistors.

There is a p.d. across each resistor. From the numerical example shown in Figure 18.22b, you can see that adding up the p.d.s across the separate resistors gives the p.d. of the power supply. In other words, the p.d. of the supply is shared between the resistors.

Resistors in parallel

The lights in a conventional house are connected in parallel with one another. The reason for this is that each one requires the full voltage of the mains supply to work properly. If they were connected in series, the p.d. would be shared between them and they would be dim. In parallel, each one can be provided with its own switch so that it can be operated separately. If one bulb fails, the others remain lit.

The effective resistance of several resistors connected in parallel (Figure 18.23a) is less than that of the individual resistors. This is because it is easier for the current to flow. Because the resistors are connected side-by-side, each feels the full voltage of the supply.

Current flows through each resistor. From the numerical example shown in Figure 18.23b, you can see that adding up the currents through the separate resistors gives the current flowing in to and out of the power supply. In other words, the current from the supply is shared between the resistors.

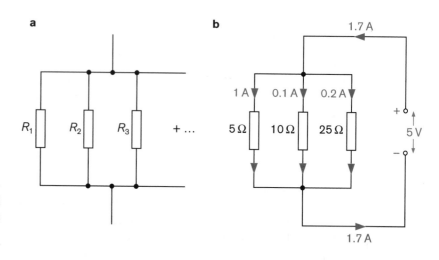

a

R_1 R_2 R_3 + ...

b

1.7 A

1 A   0.1 A   0.2 A

5 Ω   10 Ω   25 Ω

+

5 V

−

1.7 A

Figure 18.23 **a** Several resistors connected in parallel. **b** Values of current and p.d. in a parallel circuit. The current flowing from the supply is shared between the resistors.

Table 18.3 Summary for resistors in series and in parallel.

Series and parallel resistors: summary

We can sum up everything that we have found for combinations of resistors in a table. This is shown in Table 18.3.

	Resistors in series	Resistors in parallel
diagram	R_1 R_2 R_3 + ...	R_1 R_2 R_3 + ...
current	same through all resistors	shared between resistors
potential difference	shared between resistors	same across all resistors

Extension material

Potential divider circuits

Often, a power supply or a battery provides a fixed potential difference. To obtain a smaller p.d., or a variable p.d., this fixed p.d. must be split up using a circuit called a **potential divider**. Figure 18.24 shows the simplest form of potential divider.

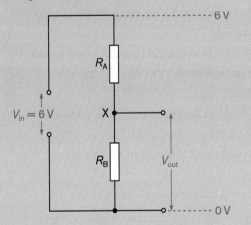

Figure 18.24 A simple potential divider circuit. The output voltage V_{out} is a fraction of the input voltage V_{in}. The input voltage is divided according to the relative values of the two resistors.

In the circuit shown, two resistors with resistances R_A and R_B are connected in series across the 6 V power supply. The p.d. across the pair is thus 6 V, and we call this the input voltage V_{in}. (It helps to think of the bottom line as representing 0 V and the top line as 6 V.) What is the p.d. at point X, between the two resistors?

The input voltage V_{in} is shared or divided by the two resistors; the bigger resistor gets the bigger share. Suppose $R_A = 10\,k\Omega$ and $R_B = 20\,k\Omega$. Since R_B is twice as big as R_A, its share of the p.d. is twice as great. Hence the p.d. across R_B is 4 V. So the output voltage V_{out} is 4 V.

We can write a formula for calculating V_{out}:

$$V_{out} = \frac{V_{in}\,R_B}{(R_A + R_B)}$$

A variable resistor can be connected in place of the two resistors; this makes use of the variable resistor's three terminals. The output voltage can then be varied from 0 up to V_{in}.

Using potential divider circuits

A potential divider circuit can be used as part of a light-sensing circuit. Figure 18.25 shows how. One of the resistors R_A is replaced by a light-dependent resistor. When light falls on the LDR, its resistance decreases. This means that its share of V_{in} decreases, so the p.d. across the fixed resistor R_B increases. Hence the output p.d. increases when the light

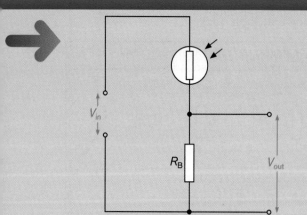

Figure 18.25 Using a potential divider circuit to produce a p.d. that changes when the light level changes. The resistance of the LDR depends on the intensity of the light, and so the output p.d. changes with the light level.

level increases, and this can then be used to trigger an electronic circuit, which responds in some way. If the circuit has detected a burglar's torch-light, it might sound an alarm. If it has detected the morning sun, it might switch off a street-light.

If the two resistors in this circuit are swapped over, the output p.d. will increase when the light level decreases. This could be used in a similar way to trigger an electronic circuit.

The circuit could also be adapted by using a variable resistor in place of the fixed one. Then the light level at which the electronic circuit is triggered could be set by adjusting the variable resistor.

For a circuit that detects changes in temperature, a thermistor could be used in place of the LDR. An increase in temperature would make the thermistor's resistance decrease, and V_{out} would increase.

? Questions

18.19 Use the idea of resistors in series to explain why a long wire has more resistance than a short wire (of the same thickness and material).

18.20 Use the idea of resistors in parallel to explain why a thick wire has less resistance than a thin wire (of the same length and material).

18.21 A $10\,\Omega$ resistor is connected in series with a $20\,\Omega$ resistor and a $15\,V$ power supply.

a What can you say about the current flowing around the circuit?

b Which resistor will have the larger share of the p.d. across it?

Summary

◆ Conventional current is a flow of positive charge from positive to negative. In metals, electrons flow from negative to positive.

◆ Current (in amps) is measured using an ammeter connected in series in a circuit. The potential difference (in volts, V) across a component is measured using a voltmeter, connected across the component.

◆ Charge, current and time are related by:
charge = current × time   or $Q = It$

◆ Resistance (in ohms, Ω) is defined by:
resistance $= \dfrac{\text{p.d.}}{\text{current}}$ or $R = \dfrac{V}{I}$

◆ A component obeys Ohm's law if the current that flows through it is proportional to the p.d. across it. Its current–voltage characteristic graph is a straight line passing through the origin.

◆ A light-dependent resistor has a resistance that decreases as the intensity of the light falling on it increases.

◆ A thermistor has a resistance that changes (increases or decreases) as its temperature increases.

◆ A diode allows current to flow through it in one direction only. It does not obey Ohm's law.

◆ Resistors in *series*: the same current flows through all resistors; the p.d. of the supply is shared between them; their effective resistance is the sum of their individual resistances:
$R = R_1 + R_2 + R_3 + \cdots$

◆ Resistors in *parallel*: they have the same p.d. across them; the current flowing is shared between them; their effective resistance is calculated from:
$\dfrac{1}{R} = \dfrac{1}{R_1} + \dfrac{1}{R_2} + \dfrac{1}{R_3} + \cdots$

⊖ *In a potential divider circuit, two resistors are connected in series across the input p.d., which is divided in proportion to their resistances. The output p.d. is given by:*
$V_{out} = \dfrac{V_{in}\, R_B}{(R_A + R_B)}$

⊖ *A potential divider circuit can include an LDR so that the output p.d. depends on the light level, or a thermistor so that the output p.d. depends on the temperature.*

Electricity and energy

Topics in this chapter

◆ energy transformations in electrical appliances

◆ the cost of using electrical power

◆ the meaning of voltage (p.d. and e.m.f.)

◆ calculating electrical power and energy transferred

◆ domestic electricity supplies

◆ electrical safety

In developed countries, most houses and other buildings are served by a mains electricity supply. Electricity travels round the building in wiring hidden in the walls or under the floor. We take it for granted that we can plug in an appliance – a heater, perhaps, or a computer – and it will work instantly. Mains electricity is a means of transferring energy to the appliances we use every day.

Mains electricity is usually supplied at a fairly high voltage – typically 230 V. This is dangerously high, because such a voltage can result in a fatal current passing through anyone who is unlucky enough to touch a live wire (Figure 19.1). Another potential hazard is fire. If the

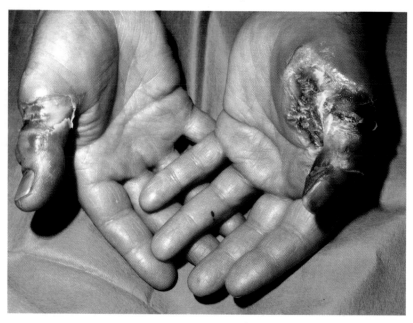

Figure 19.1 This man suffered a severe electric shock. A current passing through your body causes heating, which can lead to burns. The man survived, but months of medical treatment were needed to repair the damage done.

Figure 19.2 A fire broke out in this building after the owner tampered with the fuses at the point where the mains supply enters the building. An excessive current was able to flow, so that wiring overheated and the insulation caught fire.

wiring in a house is faulty, or if the householder has interfered with any of the safety features fitted, an electric current may flow where it is not intended. This can cause heating, leading to a fire (Figure 19.2).

The mains electricity supply is an excellent way of transferring energy to our homes, but it must be treated with care. This chapter looks at how we use energy supplied electrically, and how we can do so safely.

19.1 Using electrical appliances

We use electrical appliances for many different purposes. Often, we use them for heating – for example, electric heaters and ovens. Alternatively, we may use electricity to make something move, or to produce light or sound. Table 19.1 summarises some of these applications.

Table 19.1 Energy transformations in electrical appliances. The last column shows the energy transformation for which we use the appliance. However, most appliances transform some of the electrical energy supplied to other forms that we do not want. In other words, they are less than 100% efficient.

Function of appliances	Electrical appliances	Desired energy transformation
heating	heater radiator oven	electrical energy transformed to heat (thermal) energy
movement	motor fan food processor	electrical energy transformed to kinetic energy
lighting	filament lamp light-emitting diode television set computer monitor	electrical energy transformed to light energy
making sounds	loudspeaker	electrical energy transformed to sound energy
production of microwaves	microwave oven	electrical energy transformed to energy carried by electromagnetic waves

An electrical appliance is supplied with electrical energy, carried by an electric current. We say that electricity is a way of **transferring** energy from place to place. The appliance then **transforms** the electrical energy into another form of energy, such as heat energy or kinetic energy. The ideas of energy transfers and energy transformations were discussed in detail in Chapter 7.

If you have studied Chapter 7, you will recall that energy transformations are not always 100% efficient; that is, some of the energy may be transformed into a form we do not want. For example, we want a food processor to spin around and cut up pieces of food. Its motor makes it spin, so that it has kinetic energy, which we want. However, it also makes a lot of noise, and this is wasted energy. A lot of energy is also wasted as heat.

Electrical power

Most electrical appliances have a label that shows their power rating. An example is shown in Figure 19.3. Power ratings are indicated in watts (W) or kilowatts (kW). Typical values for some domestic appliances are shown in Table 19.2.

From Table 19.2, you can see that light bulbs come in several different power ratings. A 40 W bulb is much less bright than a 150 W bulb (although each runs from the same 230 V mains supply). In other words, it transforms energy at a slower rate. The power rating of an appliance shows the rate at which it transforms energy.

Power is the rate at which energy is transferred (from place to place) or transformed (from one form to another):

$$\text{power (W)} = \frac{\text{energy transferred (J)}}{\text{time (s)}}$$
$$P = \frac{E}{t}$$

If you have studied Chapter 8, you will recognise this definition of power. It applies to all energy transfers and transformations, not just electrical ones. Another way to write this is:

$$\text{energy transferred (J)} = \text{power (W)} \times \text{time (s)}$$
$$E = Pt$$

We use the symbol E to represent energy transferred. You may also come across W for energy transferred, as this is short for *work done*. But we will use E for energy, rather than W, as this can be confused with W for watts.

The equation for power also reminds us of the definition of the unit of power, the watt, W:

1 watt = 1 joule per second $1\text{ W} = 1\text{ J/s}$

Figure 19.3 This label is fixed to the back of a microwave oven. The power rating indicates the maximum power it draws from the mains supply when the oven is operating at full power.

Appliance	Power rating
washing machine	3 kW
electric heaters	1 kW, 2 kW, 3 kW
light bulbs	40 W, 60 W, 100 W, 150 W
television set	150 W
stereo system	100 W
refrigerator	100 W
portable radio	5 W
personal stereo	1 W
calculator	0.0004 W

Table 19.2 Typical power ratings for some domestic electrical appliances. Items that produce a lot of heat, such as heaters and washing machines, have a high power rating. Small electrical appliances that can run from batteries, such as personal stereos and calculators, have much lower power ratings. (These are only rough values; power ratings may vary quite a lot from one model to another.)

Figure 19.4 A domestic electricity meter. The read-out shows the number of kilowatt-hours (sometimes simply called 'units') of electricity that have been used. If you can see inside the meter, you may notice a metal disc spinning steadily round. This spins faster the more power you are using, and the figures on the read-out then change faster.

Paying for energy

The longer an appliance is used, the more energy it transforms and the more you will have to pay. An electricity meter is fitted near where the mains supply enters the house, and this records the total consumption (Figure 19.4). An electricity meter records consumption in units called kilowatt-hours (kWh). This is a unit of energy:

> energy transferred (kWh) = power (kW) × time (h)

The kilowatt-hour is not a standard SI unit. The reason for using the kilowatt-hour rather than the SI unit, the joule, is that the joule is a very small unit of energy; the kilowatt-hour is more practicable. Take care! It is a kilowatt-hour, not a kilowatt per hour. If you run a 2 kW heater for 3 hours, the energy transferred is 6 kWh. This should remind you that you multiply the kilowatts by the hours, rather than dividing:

> 1 kilowatt-hour is the energy transferred when an appliance transfers energy at the rate of 1 kW for 1 hour.

From the meter reading, the electricity supply company knows how many kilowatt-hours of electricity have been used. Given the price of an individual unit, they can then work out the total cost:

> cost = number of kilowatt-hours × price per kilowatt-hour

Worked example 1 shows how to make such calculations.

Worked example 1

A student uses two 150 W lamps for 6 hours. If the price per unit of electricity is 10 p (10 pence), what is the cost of this?

- *Step 1* Calculate the power being used, in kW:
  power = 2 × 150 W = 300 W = 0.3 kW
- *Step 2* Calculate the energy transferred, in kWh:
  energy transferred = power × time = 0.3 kW × 6 h = 1.8 kWh
- *Step 3* Calculate the cost:
  cost = number of kilowatt-hours × price per unit
  = 1.8 kWh × 10 p = 18 p

Note that you could combine steps 2 and 3 into a single calculation.

A note on language

We talk about 'using electricity' or 'consuming electrical power'. In a sense, an electrical appliance does 'use electrical energy', because it transforms it into other forms of energy. However, to be more technically correct when talking about electrical appliances, we should say:

'An electrical appliance transforms electrical energy into other forms of energy.'

'Power is the rate at which electrical energy is transformed.'

If you are not sure about how to describe energy transfers and transformations, look back to Chapter 7.

19.2 Voltage and energy

We use electric current to transfer energy from place to place. As we mentioned in Chapter 18, current is the flow of electric charge, brought about by the energy provided by a cell, battery or power supply connected into a circuit. How can we understand the transfer of energy by moving electric charges?

A cell is a device that transforms chemical energy into electrical energy. A battery is several cells connected together. You are unlikely to get a shock from a 1.5 V cell or from a 6 V battery. But you might be killed by the 230 V mains supply. This tells us something about the connection between voltage and energy. The higher the voltage, the greater the energy carried by the charges that move as a result of the voltage. The higher the voltage marked on a cell (Figure 19.5a), the greater the energy that is transferred to the charge by the cell.

If several cells are joined together to make a battery, the voltage they provide is the sum of their individual voltages (Figure 19.5b). Technically,

Figure 19.5 **a** Most cells and batteries are marked with the voltage they provide. **b** When cells are joined in series to make a battery, its voltage is the sum of the individual voltages.

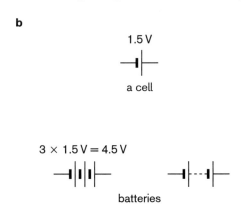

1.5 V

a cell

$3 \times 1.5\,V = 4.5\,V$

batteries

a battery is two or more cells connected in series (end-to-end). For the voltages to add up, the cells must all be connected the same way round.

Hence the voltage of a supply tells us about how much energy it transfers to charges flowing around the circuit. The greater the current flowing around the circuit, the faster that energy is transferred. Hence the rate at which energy is transferred in the circuit (the power P) depends on both the p.d. V of the supply and the current I that it pushes round the circuit. The following equation shows how to calculate the power:

$$\text{power (W)} = \text{p.d. (V)} \times \text{current (A)}$$
$$P = VI$$

You may prefer to remember this as an equation relating units:

$$\text{watts} = \text{volts} \times \text{amps}$$

There is an alternative way of writing the equation for power. From Chapter 18, page 286, the p.d. V across a resistor can be expressed by the equation $V = IR$. So we can eliminate V from the above equation $P = VI$ to get:

$$\text{power} = \text{current}^2 \times \text{resistance}$$
$$P = I^2R$$

Choose the most suitable form of the equation according to the information available to you – see worked examples 2 and 3.

Worked example 2

An electric fan runs from the 230 V mains. The current flowing through it is 0.4 A. At what rate is electrical energy transformed by the fan?

● *Step 1* Write down what you know and what you want to know:

$V = 230\,\text{V}$

$I = 0.4\,\text{A}$

$P = ?$

● *Step 2* Write down the equation for power that involves V and I:

$P = VI$

Substitute values and solve:

$P = 230\,\text{V} \times 0.4\,\text{A} = 92\,\text{W}$

So the fan's power is 92 W.

Worked example 3

A heating coil has a resistance of 200 Ω. At what rate will heat be produced in it when a current of 2.5 A flows through it?

● *Step 1* Write down what you know and what you want to know:

$R = 200\,\Omega$

$I = 2.5\,\text{A}$

$P = ?$

continued on next page

Worked example 3 continued

Step 2 Write down the equation for power that involves I and R:

$$P = I^2R$$

Substitute values and solve:

$$P = (2.5\,A)^2 \times 200\,\Omega = 1250\,W$$

So energy is transferred by the heater at a rate of 1250 W.

Calculating energy

Since, from earlier in this chapter, we have

$$\text{energy transferred} = \text{power} \times \text{time}$$
$$E = Pt$$

we can use the equation $P = VI$ to eliminate P from this to give a different equation for energy transferred E:

$$\text{energy transferred (J)} = \text{p.d. (V)} \times \text{current (A)} \times \text{time (s)}$$
$$E = VIt$$

The meaning of voltage

We should distinguish between two different types of voltage.

- A cell, battery or power supply provides a voltage which gives energy to charges to move them around a circuit. Energy is transferred *to the charges*, which then move around the circuit. This type of voltage is called an **e.m.f.** (short for electromotive force).

- In a circuit, there is a voltage across components such as resistors or lamps. Energy is transferred *from the charges* to the components as they pass through them. This type of voltage is called a **p.d.** (short for potential difference).

So the e.m.f. of a supply transfers energy to charges. As they pass through a p.d., they give up that energy. You can see both types of voltage in the circuit shown in Figure 19.6. In this circuit, the charges are given energy as they pass through the 3 V battery. They lose some of the energy as they pass through the first resistor, and the rest of the energy in the second resistor.

The e.m.f. of a supply tells us how much energy it transfers to each coulomb of charge passing through it. A 3 V battery gives 3 J of energy to each coulomb of charge. A 6 V battery gives 6 J to each coulomb, and so on. If 2 C pass through a 6 V battery, 12 J of energy are transferred. In other words:

$$\text{energy transferred (J)} = \text{p.d. (V)} \times \text{charge (C)}$$
$$E = VQ$$

Figure 19.6 Thinking about voltage and energy transfers around an electric circuit. Charges flow around the circuit; energy is transferred to them by the battery; they lose energy as they pass through the resistors.

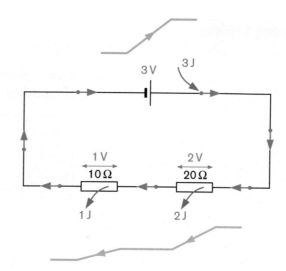

Another way to think of this is in terms of units:

1 volt = 1 joule per coulomb   1 V = 1 J/C

Now we can trace the path of one coulomb (1 C) of charge as it moves around the circuit shown in Figure 19.6. It gains 3 J of energy as it passes through the battery; it loses 2 J as it passes through the first resistor; it loses the last 1 J as it passes through the second resistor. This shows us why voltages must add up around a circuit. The voltage across the battery tells us about the energy gained by the charge; while the voltages across the resistors tell us about the same energy as it is transferred from the charges to the resistors.

The diagram shows another way of thinking about voltages. The battery pushes the charges up-hill; then they roll down-hill as they pass through the resistors. When you push something up-hill, you give it gravitational potential energy (GPE – see Chapter 8). When a battery pushes a charge 'up-hill', it gives it **electrical potential energy**. Now you may be able to see why we talk about 'potential differences' between points in an electric circuit. We can use the same idea to define what we mean by the e.m.f. of a cell or power supply:

The e.m.f. of a supply is the energy transferred by the supply in moving one coulomb of charge past a point in a circuit.

Worked example 4

An electric heater is connected to the 230 V mains supply. A current of 8 A flows through the heater. How much charge flows around the circuit each second? How much energy is transferred to the heater each second?

● *Step 1* Knowing the current $I = 8$ A, we can calculate the amount of charge Q flowing each second (using an equation from Chapter 18):

charge $Q = It = 8\,\text{A} \times 1\,\text{s} = 8\,\text{C}$

(8 A means 8 C per second.)

continued on next page

Worked example 4 continued

- *Step 2* Knowing the p.d. across the heater $V = 230\,V$, we can calculate the energy transferred:

  energy transferred = p.d. × charge

  $E = VQ = 230\,V \times 8\,C = 1840\,J$

  (230 V means 230 J transferred by each coulomb.)

  Hence 1840 J of energy are transferred to the heater each second. We could have arrived at the same result directly using $E = VIt$.

? **Questions**

19.6 What e.m.f. is provided by a battery of three 1.5 V cells connected in series?

19.7 Draw a diagram to show how four 1.5 V cells can be connected to give an e.m.f. of 3 V.

19.8 Write down an equation linking watts, volts and amps.

19.9 A 10 V power supply causes a 5 A current in a resistor. At what rate is energy transferred to the resistor?

19.10 Which of the following statements correctly defines a volt?

a volt is a joule per amp

a volt is a joule per coulomb

19.11 How much energy is transferred by a 12 V power supply to each coulomb of charge which it moves around a circuit?

19.3 Domestic electricity supply

The electricity supply to most homes is at a fairly high voltage, usually between 220 V and 250 V. Table 19.3 shows the supply voltages used in different parts of the world. You may notice that the supply voltage in North America and the Caribbean is only 110 V, half that of most other countries. Why is this?

A mains supply at 230 V is hazardous and must be handled with care. This section looks at some of the problems of using such a high voltage. A 110 V supply is less hazardous – you are much less likely to die if you get a shock from the live wire. However, to supply the same amount of electrical power at half the voltage, the current that flows must be twice as great. This follows from the equation for power, $P = VI$; if V is halved, I must be doubled to give the same value for P.

To carry a higher current, the wiring in a house must be thicker, and this is expensive. If thin wire is used, its resistance may be too great and it may overheat, leading to a fire.

Table 19.3 The mains electricity supply is different in different countries. The table shows the voltage used, as well as the frequency of the alternating supply.

Country or region	Domestic mains voltage (V)	Mains frequency (Hz)
European Union (including UK), Switzerland	230	50
India, China, Hong Kong	220	50
Singapore	220–240	50
South Africa	220–230	50
Australia	240–250	50
New Zealand	230	50
USA, most of Caribbean	110–120	60
Japan	100	50 or 60

Three wires and ring mains

The cables that pass around inside a house consist of three separate wires:

- The **live** wire – this is the wire that is at a high voltage, and in effect brings energy into the house.
- The **neutral** wire – this is connected to earth just outside the house, so that it is close to 0 V.
- The **earth** wire – this is a safety feature, which we will discuss shortly.

When we refer to 'the 230 V mains', we are talking about the p.d. between the live wire and the neutral wire. When you plug an appliance into a wall socket, you are connecting it between these two wires, so that current flows from the live wire, through the appliance, and out into the neutral wire.

Electricity enters a house near the fuse box and meter (Figure 19.7). From there, cables run around inside the house, connecting each socket to the supply. Usually, these cables are connected in a particular way,

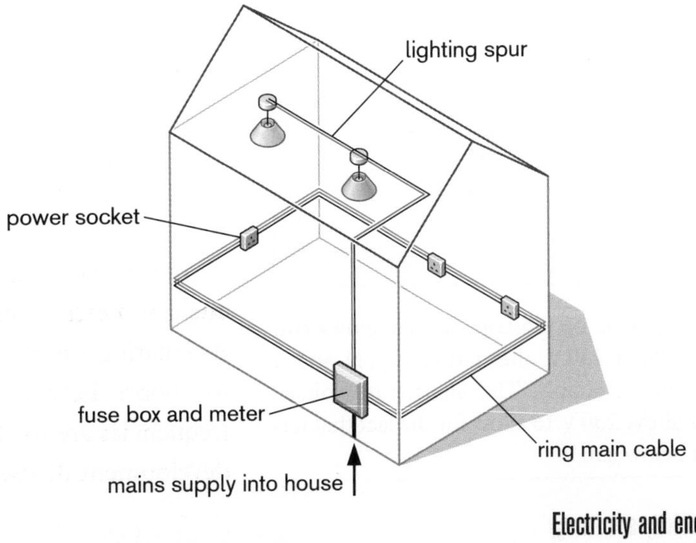

Figure 19.7 This drawing shows part of the electricity supply cabling in a house. The supply enters the house via the meter and fuse box. A ring main then runs around the ground floor. Each socket is connected to all three wires in the cable. Plugging in an appliance connects it to all three wires. Current flows to the appliance along the live wire, around both halves of the ring.

called a **ring main circuit**. The cable runs from the fuse box, around part of the house and back to the fuse box. Each of the three wires (live, neutral and earth) thus forms a loop, with several sockets around the loop. When an appliance is connected to a socket, current in the live wire can flow both ways around the loop to reach the appliance. This means that there are two routes for the current, so there is less resistance in the circuit. This allows the wires to be made thinner than if the cable was a single-ended 'spur' from the fuse box. Similarly, the current has two routes along which to flow back to the fuse box, along the neutral wire.

Lighting circuits may not be ring circuits. A cable leads out from the fuse box to supply several lights, but it does not make a complete loop. This is because lights do not require high currents. This means that the cable can be thinner, too.

Alternating current and direct current

In most countries today, the mains electricity supply provides alternating current (a.c.). This means that the current flows back and forth along the wires, rather than flowing steadily in one direction (direct current, d.c.). Batteries supply direct current. When public electricity supplies were first developed roughly a century ago, the choice of a.c. or d.c. was hotly debated. Thomas Edison, the American inventor, declared that alternating current would be far too dangerous and that its use should never be contemplated. How wrong he was!

The frequency of an alternating supply is usually 50 or 60 Hz; that is, the p.d. between the live and neutral wires varies from positive to negative and back again 50 or 60 times each second. If an alternating supply is connected to an oscilloscope, you can see how it varies. (A voltmeter cannot keep up with the rapid changes.) Figure 19.8 shows what we see on the oscilloscope screen for a 230 V, 50 Hz supply. The wavy line is the alternating voltage; the steady, horizontal line is a 230 V d.c. supply. Notice that the a.c. supply goes up much higher than 230 V at its peaks. This is because, to give an average of 230 V, the peaks must reach 325 V. So, if someone inadvertently touches the live wire of a 230 V supply, they will get a maximum shock of 325 V.

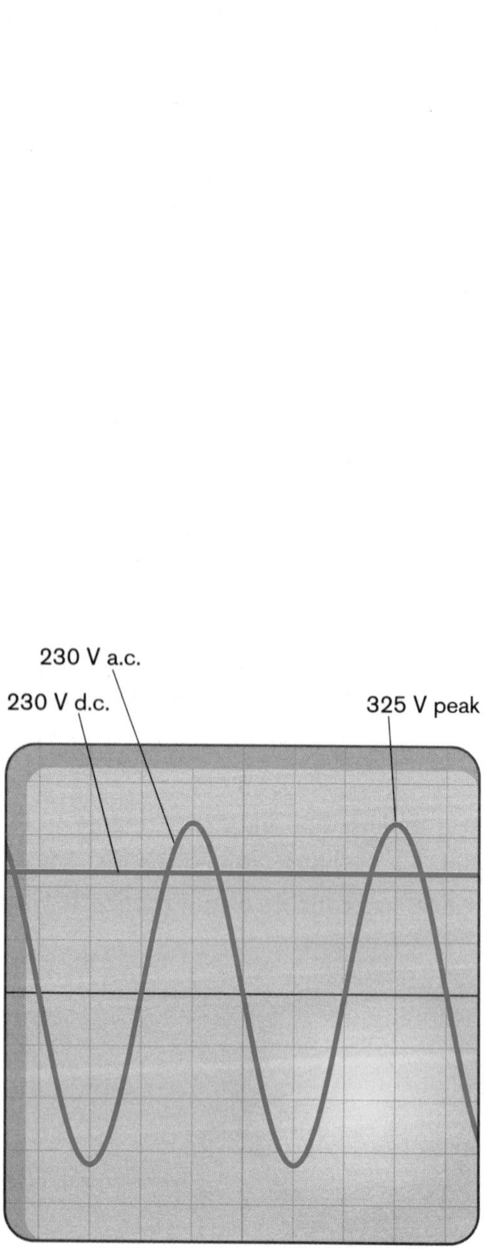

Alternating current is generally chosen for a variety of reasons:

- a.c. is easier to generate and to transmit from place to place;
- a.c. is good for electric motors, since they can be made to spin 50 or 60 times per second;
- a.c. can be readily converted (rectified) to d.c., whereas it is harder to convert d.c. to a.c;
- a.c. can easily have its voltage changed.

Alternating supplies are usually 50 or 60 Hz; there is nothing much to choose between these. It is a historical accident that different frequencies are used in different parts of the world, left over from the development of the systems in the early twentieth century. In Japan,

230 V a.c.

230 V d.c.

325 V peak

Figure 19.8 This oscilloscope screen shows two traces, for a 230 V alternating supply and a 230 V direct supply. The alternating voltage peaks above 230 V, to allow for the fact that it is often below 230 V.

both frequencies are used. A food processor may spin 20% faster if you move house from one area to another.

Cables and plugs

The cables that carry electric current around a house are carefully chosen. Figure 19.9 shows some examples. Each is labelled with the maximum current it is designed to carry. A 5 A cable is relatively thin; this might be used for a lighting circuit, since lights do not require much power, so the current flowing is relatively small. The wires in the 30 A cable are much thicker. This might be used for an electric cooker, which requires much bigger currents than a lighting circuit.

The wires in each cable are insulated from one another, and the whole cable has more protective insulation around the outside. If an excessive current flows in the wires, they will heat up and the insulation may melt. It may emit poisonous fumes or even catch fire. Thus it is vital to avoid using appliances that draw too much current from the supply. Fuses help to prevent this from happening – see next subsection. Just as different national electricity supply systems have their own choice of mains voltage and frequency, so they have their own design of plug and socket. Figure 19.10 shows a typical 13 A plug, as used in the United Kingdom. It has been designed to have a number of safety features:

- The pins are made of brass, a metal that is unlikely to corrode. Each pin has a shroud, so that you cannot touch the live metal when plugging in.
- The case is made of plastic, a good insulating material.
- The wires in the flex that leads to the appliance are colour-coded, so that it is less likely that they will be connected to the wrong pins.
- The wires are wrapped round the pins and screwed firmly into place.
- The flex is held by a cable grip, so that it is impossible to pull the wires from the pins.
- The earth pin is longer than the other pins so that this is the first to be connected and the last to be disconnected.
- An appropriate fuse is fitted, to protect the wiring from high currents. Today, manufacturers of electrical appliances generally fit plugs so that it is unnecessary for the user to do so.

Fuses

Fuses are included in circuits to stop excessive currents from flowing. If the current gets too high, cables can burn out and fires can start – see Figure 19.2. A fuse contains a thin section of wire, designed to melt and break if the current gets above a certain value – see Figure 19.11. Usually, fuses are contained in cartridges, which makes it easy to replace them; but some fuses use fuse wire, as shown in the photograph. The thicker the wire, the higher the current that is needed to

Figure 19.9 Cables of different thicknesses are chosen according to the maximum current they are likely to have flowing through them. Each cable has live, neutral and earth wires, which are colour-coded.

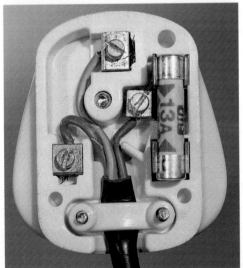
Figure 19.10 A 13 A plug from the UK. If you live in another country, compare the design of your plugs with this one.

Figure 19.11 Cartridge fuses and fuse wire. The thicker the wire, the higher the current that causes it to blow.

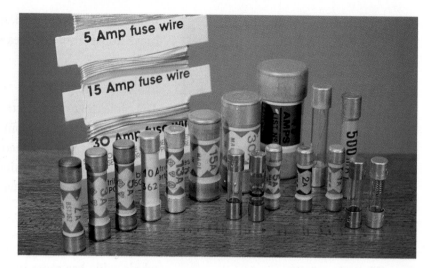

make it 'blow'. A fuse represents a weak link in the electricity supply chain. Replacing a fuse is preferable to having to rewire a whole house!

It is important to choose the correct value of fuse to protect an appliance. Its current rating should be just above the value of the current that flows when the appliance is operating normally. Worked example 5 shows how to do this.

Worked example 5

A 2 kW heater works on a 230 V mains supply. What current rating would a suitable fuse have? Choose from 3 A, 13 A and 30 A.

● *Step 1* Calculate the current that flows during normal operation. We use the equation $P = VI$, and need to rearrange it to give:

$$I = \frac{P}{V}$$

Substituting values gives:

$$I = \frac{2000\,\text{W}}{230\,\text{V}} = 8.7\,\text{A}$$

● *Step 2* Choose a fuse.

The 3 A fuse has too low a rating; it would blow when the heater was switched on. The 13 A fuse is the correct choice, since it has the lowest rating above the normal operating current.

Circuit breakers and earthing

There are two types of circuit breaker used in electrical safety – try not to confuse them. Both work using electromagnets, but we will not consider the detail of their construction here.

● *Trip switch* A trip switch can replace a fuse, and so protects the wiring and the appliance. When the current flowing through the trip exceeds a certain value, the switch 'trips', breaking the circuit. Some modern house wiring systems use trips instead of fuses in the fuse box. You have probably come across trips on laboratory power supplies. If too much current starts to flow, the supply itself might overheat and be damaged. The trip jumps out, and you may have to wait a short while before you can reset it.

● *Residual current device* A residual current device (RCD) protects the user rather than an appliance or cable. In normal circumstances, the currents flowing in the live and neutral wires are the same – see Figure 19.12. However, there may be a fault. Someone may have accidentally touched the live wire, perhaps by running over the flex of the lawnmower. Some current flows through the user, rather than along the neutral wire. Now more current flows in the live wire than the neutral, and the RCD detects this and switches off the supply. Houses often have RCDs fitted next to the fuse box. School laboratories usually have one too, to protect students and teachers.

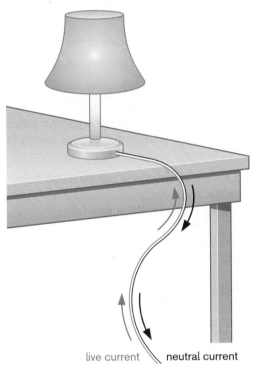

live current neutral current

DANGER: Never tamper with live electrical equipment.

current through child

Figure 19.12 In normal use, the current in the neutral wire is the same as that in the live wire. The small child has cut into the mains flex. A small current flows through the child, so that the live and neutral currents no longer balance. The RCD detects this and switches off the supply.

Many electrical appliances have an **earth connection**. This is particularly important for appliances with metal cases, including heaters and washing machines. The case is connected via a wire to the earth wiring in the plug, and from there to the earth outside the house. The idea is that, if a fault develops so that the metal case comes into contact with the live wire, the user will not get a shock. Instead, any dangerous current is conducted away to earth.

Appliances with plastic cases, including computers and hair dryers, are designed so that it is very difficult for the user to come into contact with the mains electricity inside. Such appliances are described as having **double insulation**, and they do not require an earth connection.

? **Questions**

19.12 Explain why it is more dangerous to touch the live wire of a mains supply, rather than the neutral wire.

?

Questions continued

19.13 What is the difference between alternating current and direct current?

19.14 In normal use, a current of 3.5 A flows through a hair dryer. Choose a suitable fuse from the following:

3 A, 5 A, 13 A, 30 A

19.15 Look at Figure 19.10. List the colours of the three wires in the flex connected to the plug.

19.16 **a** Why are fuses fitted in the fuse box of a domestic electricity supply?

b What device could be used in place of the fuses?

Summary

◆ Electricity is a convenient way to transfer energy from place to place. Electrical appliances transform electrical energy into other useful forms of energy.

◆ Energy transferred in various situations can be found from the following equations:
- energy transferred (J) = power (W) × time (s)

$$E = Pt$$

- energy transferred (kWh) = power (kW) × time (h)
- energy transferred (J) = p.d. (V) × current (A) × time (s)

$$E = VIt$$

- energy transferred (J) = p.d. (V) × charge (C)

$$E = VQ$$

◆ One kilowatt-hour (1 kWh) is the energy transferred when an appliance transfers energy at the rate of 1 kW for 1 hour.

◆ Paying for energy:
cost = number of kilowatt-hours × price per kilowatt-hour

◆ Power in an electrical circuit:
power (W) = p.d. (V) × current (A)

$$P = VI$$

◆ Equations relating units:
watts = volts × amps
1 volt = 1 joule per coulomb   1 V = 1 J/C

◆ A domestic electricity supply is alternating current (a.c.). The current flows back and forth in the wires.

◆ Fuses protect the mains wiring in a house. The current rating of the fuse should be just above the normal operating current.

Electromagnetic forces and electric motors

Topics in this chapter

◆ electromagnets and their magnetic fields

◆ uses of electromagnets

◆ d.c. electric motors

◆ magnetic force on a current-carrying conductor (the motor effect)

◆ Fleming's left-hand rule

ℯ *the force on a beam of charged particles*

◆ magnetic forces on a current-carrying coil

We make good use of electric motors in our everyday lives. They spin our CDs and computer disk drives. They turn our washing machines and food processors. They blow the hot air out of our hair dryers, and they cool us (and our computers) by turning fans.

There are many other electric motors at work, making our highly technological lives possible, but perhaps they are less evident to us. Here are some less obvious examples: An electric motor (the starter motor) is needed to get a petrol-driven car started (Figure 20.1). Electric motors turn the wheels of many trains, and the wheels of the electric cars that can help to reduce air pollution in cities (Figure 20.2). Giant electric motors operate the pumps that bring us fresh water, and other pumps that take away our sewage. Some of the electricity generated by a power station is needed by the power station itself, to power electric motors that pump cooling water through the condensers.

Figure 20.1 Most cars have an engine that is a type of internal combustion engine, fuelled by petrol. The engine will continue to operate once it has started turning. Today, cars have electric starter motors to give them their initial spin. In the early days of motoring, someone had to use a crank handle to start the motor. You may have seen this in old movies. An electric motor has the convenience that it will start to turn as soon as a current flows through it when you turn the ignition key.

Figure 20.2 This electric car is designed to be used in towns and cities. It has an electric motor to turn each wheel, as well as motors to operate the windscreen wipers and the door locks. Electric cars like this can help to reduce both noise and air pollution in city centres.

In this chapter, we will first look at electromagnets. We will then look at how electric motors are constructed, and consider two different ways of explaining how they work.

20.1 Electromagnets

Using magnetic materials is only one way of making a magnet. An alternative method is to use an electromagnet. A typical electromagnet is made from a coil of copper wire. When a current flows through the wire, there is a magnetic field around the coil (Figure 20.3). A coil like this is sometimes called a **solenoid**. Copper wire is often used, because of its low resistance, though other metals will do. The coil does not have to be made from a magnetic material. The point is that it is the electric current that produces the magnetic field.

From Figure 20.3, you can see that the magnetic field around a solenoid is similar to that around a bar magnet. One end of the coil is a north pole, the other is a south pole. Note that the field lines go all the way through the centre of the coil. If you were to place a tiny compass at a point in the field, it would align itself along the field line at that point. We use a convention that says that lines of force come out of north magnetic poles and go in to south poles. The field direction is the direction of the force on a north pole.

There are three ways to increase the strength of an electromagnet:
- Increase the *current* flowing through it – the greater the current, the greater the strength of the field.
- Increase the *number of turns* of wire on the coil – this doesn't mean making the coil longer, but packing more turns into the same space to concentrate the field.
- Add a soft iron *core*.

An iron core becomes strongly magnetised by the field, and this makes the whole magnetic field much stronger.

Electromagnets have the great advantage that they can be switched on and off. Simply switch off the current and the field around the coil disappears. This is made use of in a number of applications – for

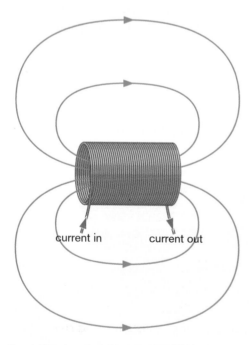

Figure 20.3 A solenoid. When a current flows through the wire, a magnetic field is produced. The field is similar in shape to that of a bar magnet.

current in   current out

Figure 20.4 Using an electromagnet in a scrap-yard. A steel object can be lifted and moved; then the current is switched off to release it.

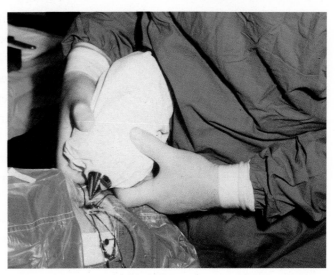

Figure 20.5 A surgeon can use an electromagnet to remove scraps of metal that have entered a patient's eye. The procedure must be carried out very gently, to avoid causing further damage to the eye. The surgeon can control the current flowing to the electromagnet to provide just the right force to remove the metal.

example, in the electromagnetic cranes that move large pieces of metal around in a scrap-yard (Figure 20.4). The current is switched on to energise the magnet and pick up a wrecked car. When it has been manoeuvred to the correct position, the current is switched off and the metal is released. Figure 20.5 shows a medical use for an electromagnet.

The field around a current

If you uncoil a solenoid, you will have a straight wire. With a current flowing through it, it will have a magnetic field around it as shown in Figure 20.6. The field lines are circles around the wire. The field is weaker than that of the solenoid, because winding the wire into a coil is a way of concentrating the field around the current.

The **corkscrew rule** (or pencil sharpener rule) tells you the direction of the field lines. Imagine screwing a corkscrew in the direction of the current; the direction you turn it in is the direction of the magnetic lines of force.

This arrangement is similar to that which originally revealed the connection between electricity and magnetism. Hans Christian Oersted was a Danish scientist, working in the early years of the nineteenth century. He noticed that both static electricity and magnetism showed similar patterns – attractive and repulsive forces, two types of charge or pole, a force that gets weaker at a distance, and so on. Most other scientists thought that this was just an interesting coincidence, but Oersted thought that there was more to it than this. He was sure that he could find a link between electricity and magnetism, and eventually he did so.

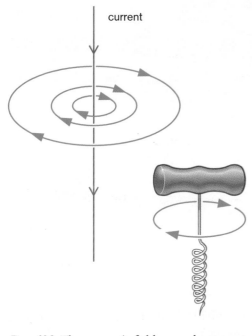

current

Figure 20.6 The magnetic field around a current in a straight wire. The field lines are circles around the wire. The further away from the wire, the weaker is the field.

It was early in 1820 that Oersted gave a public lecture on electricity. He described a report of a ship that had been struck by lightning. Its compass was affected, so that its north and south poles were reversed. He declared himself certain that electricity and magnetism were linked. Then a sudden thought struck him – there was an experiment he could try there and then to test his idea. On his demonstration bench, he had a wire and a compass (Figure 20.7). He placed the compass under the wire. When his assistant connected the wire to a large battery so that a current flowed through it, the compass needle moved. At the time, no-one was very impressed – not even Oersted himself. However, the more he thought about it, the more he realised that he had observed something of fundamental significance. The current in the wire was producing a magnetic effect that acted on the compass needle. By moving the compass around near the wire, he discovered that the magnetic effect showed a circular pattern around the current. The study of electromagnetism had begun.

Figure 20.7 During a public lecture, Oersted thought up an experiment that he hoped would show the link between electricity and magnetism. He tested his idea as soon as he had thought of it. Here, you can see Oersted and his assistant, who is holding two wires connected to a tall battery. The compass lies on the table. When a current flowed through the wire, the compass needle moved. It was responding to the magnetic field around the current.

Questions

20.1 Sketch a diagram of the magnetic field pattern of a solenoid. How would the pattern change if the current through the solenoid was reversed?

20.2 List three ways in which the magnetic field of a solenoid can be increased.

Questions continued

20.3 A current flows downwards in a wire that passes vertically through a table top. Will the magnetic field lines around it go clockwise or anticlockwise, when viewed from above the table?

20.4 Look at the magnetic field pattern shown in Figure 20.6. How can you tell from the pattern that the field gets weaker as you get further from the wire?

20.5 Describe how an electromagnet could be used to separate copper from iron in a scrap-yard.

20.2 Uses of electromagnets

A huge number of electromagnets are in use world-wide in many different situations. For example, each electric motor that is manufactured has at least one electromagnet. The applications that we shall consider in this book are the following:

● electric motors
● electric bells
● circuit breakers
● relays
● loudspeakers

However, because motors are considered in detail in Chapter 21, we will not look at them here. Instead, we will concentrate on the remaining four uses in our list above.

Electric bells

An electric door bell is a surprisingly clever device. It works using direct current from a battery, but it makes a hammer move repeatedly back and forth to strike the gong and produce the sound that tells us that someone is at the door. Figure 20.8 shows the construction of a

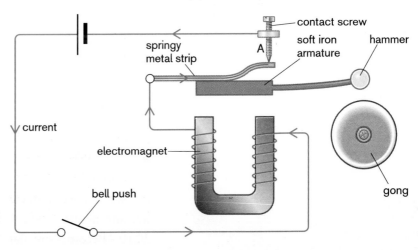

Figure 20.8 The construction of an electric bell. For as long as the bell push is depressed, the hammer springs back and forth, striking the gong. The contact screw at A can be adjusted to ensure that the circuit breaks each time the hammer is attracted by the electromagnet.

typical door bell. Notice that the hammer is attached to a springy metal strip, and is normally not in contact with the gong.

- When someone presses on the bell push, the circuit is completed. Current flows from the battery round through the electromagnet coil and the springy strip, and back to the battery via the contact point A.
- The coil is now magnetised and attracts the springy strip. Two things now happen: the hammer strikes the gong, and the circuit breaks at point A.
- The current stops, the coil is no longer magnetised, and the strip springs back to its original position.
- Now the circuit is complete again, and a current flows once more. The coil is magnetised and attracts the iron again, the hammer strikes the gong, and so on.
- This process repeats itself for as long as the bell push is depressed.

Circuit breakers

Two different devices known as 'circuit breakers' make use of electromagnets. The functions of these devices were discussed in Chapter 19 (pages 312–13).

An **electromagnetic trip switch** can be used in place of a fuse. It 'trips' (breaks the circuit) when the current flowing becomes too big and exceeds a certain limit. Figure 20.9 shows the construction of such a trip switch.

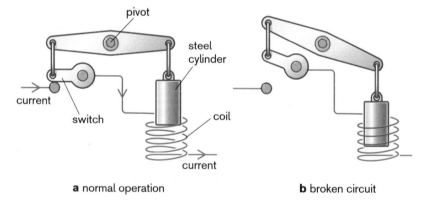

Figure 20.9 An electromagnetic trip switch. Like a fuse, this prevents an excessive current from flowing in a circuit. A trip switch cannot be relied on to prevent people from getting electric shocks.

a normal operation   **b** broken circuit

- The current in the circuit flows through the switch and the coil.
- When the current is small, the electromagnet is not strong enough to pull the steel cylinder down.
- When the current reaches the maximum value allowed for the circuit, the electromagnet pulls strongly enough to attract the steel cylinder downwards and open the switch.
- The trip switch is reset by pushing down on the lever arm to close the switch.

A **residual current device** (RCD) compares the currents flowing in the live and neutral wires. If they are unequal, the iron bar – see Figure 20.10 – becomes unbalanced and the circuit is broken.

Figure 20.10 The principle of an RCD. When the live and neutral currents are equal, the two coils pull equally on the iron bar. If the live current is greater than the neutral, the bar tips to the right, pulling the switch open. This can happen in one-hundredth of a second, saving the user from a potentially fatal shock.

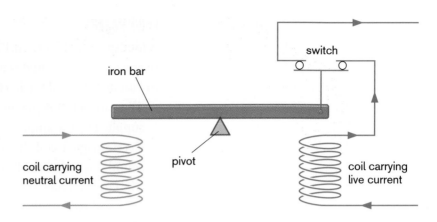

Relays

A relay is a switch operated by an electromagnet. Two types are shown in Figure 20.11, together with the circuit symbol.

The first **relay** (Figure 20.11a) is used to make a small current switch a larger current on and off. For example, when a driver turns the ignition key to start a car, a small current flows to a relay in the engine compartment. This closes a switch to complete the circuit which brings a high current to the starter motor from the battery.

- When switch A is closed, a small current flows around a circuit through the coil of the electromagnet.
- The electromagnet attracts the iron armature. As the armature tips, it pushes the two contacts at B together, completing the second circuit.

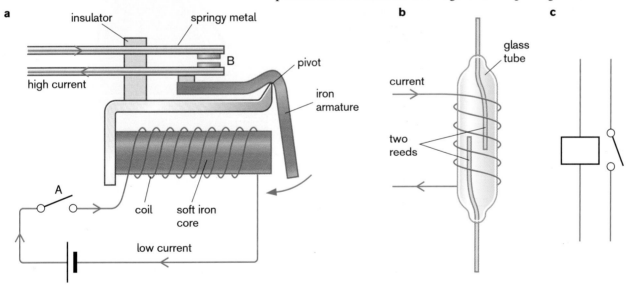

Figure 20.11 **a** A relay, capable of switching a circuit carrying hundreds of amps. **b** A reed relay can be switched on and off hundreds of times each second. **c** The circuit symbol for a relay; the rectangle represents the electromagnet coil.

The second type of relay, a **reed relay** (Figure 20.11b) is often used in electronic circuits because it can open and close many times a second. Inside the glass tube are two springy metal 'reeds', made of a magnetic material. Normally, they are separated by a small gap.

- When a current flows through the coil, the reeds become magnetised and attract one another.
- Now the circuit is complete and a current can flow through the switch.

Loudspeakers

A loudspeaker (Figure 20.12) has a permanent magnet and an electromagnet. To make sound waves in the air, the paper cone must be made to vibrate back and forth. Here is the principle of how this is done.

- The current flowing in the coil is an alternating current (a.c.) supplied by the amplifier. It flows back and forth in the wires of the electromagnet coil. Its oscillations are an electrical version of the sound waves that the listener wants to hear.
- The current flows one way around the coil, turning it into a magnet. One end is a north pole and the other is a south pole. When the current changes direction, the poles reverse.
- The permanent magnet has unchanging poles, north at one end and south at the other. When the current flows one way through the coil, it is attracted by the permanent magnet; when the current reverses, the coil is repelled.
- This means that the coil is pushed back and forth. It is attached to the paper cone, so the cone also moves back and forth.
- The cone pushes the air, sending oscillations to the listener's ears. These oscillations are sound waves.

Figure 20.12 How a loudspeaker is constructed. The electromagnet coil is attached to the cone, so that, as it is attracted and repelled by the permanent magnet, the cone pushes the air to make sound waves.

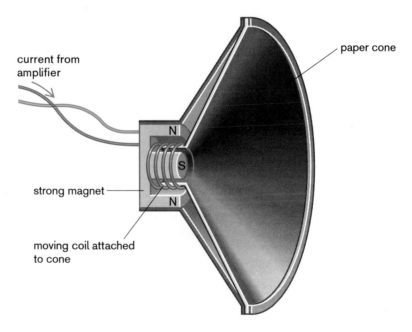

current from amplifier

paper cone

strong magnet

moving coil attached to cone

? Questions

20.6 Look at the diagram of the electric bell (Figure 20.8).
  a Why is the armature made of iron?
  b Why must *soft* iron be used?

20.7 Suppose that an RCD was wired up incorrectly, with the live and neutral currents passing through the wrong coils. Would it still function properly?

20.8 Look at the diagram of the relay (Figure 20.11a). Why is the coil fitted with a soft iron core?

20.9 A TV star switches on the Christmas lights in a shopping centre. She closes a switch, which operates a relay. The relay completes the circuit for the lights. Draw a circuit diagram for this, using the symbol shown in Figure 20.11c. (Remember that there will be two circuits, one to operate the electromagnet coil, the other to power the lights.)

20.10 The earphones used with a personal stereo are miniature loudspeakers. Explain why the permanent magnets in them should be made from a material that has a low density and is very strongly magnetic.

20.3 How electric motors are constructed

The idea of an electric motor is this: There is a magnetic field around an electric current. This magnetic field can be attracted or repelled by another magnetic field to produce movement. It isn't obvious how to do this so that continuous movement is produced. If you put two magnets together so that they repel, they move apart and stop. Electric motors are cleverly designed to produce movement that continues as long as the current flows.

You may have constructed a model electric motor like the one shown in Figure 20.13. This is designed to be easy to build and easy to understand. Its essential features are:

- a **coil of wire** – which acts as an electromagnet when a direct current flows through it;
- two **magnets** – to provide a steady magnetic field passing through the coil;
- a **split-ring commutator** and two **brushes** – through which current reaches the coil.

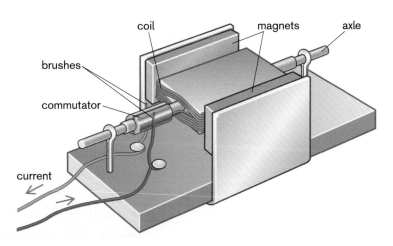

Figure 20.13 This model is used to show the principles of operation of an electric motor.

The split-ring commutator is in two sections, and each section is connected to one end of the coil. The whole commutator rotates with the coil. The brushes are springy wires that press against the two metal sections of the commutator.

Here is our first explanation of how an electric motor works. The important features of the motor are shown in Figure 20.14:

1 A current flows in through the right-hand brush, around the coil, and out through the other brush.

2 At the instant shown, its north pole is above the coil and its south pole is below the coil (see page 316). So, the electromagnet rotates as shown, to bring its north pole nearer to the south pole of the permanent magnet on the left.

3 This is where the commutator comes in. The coil is attracted round by the two permanent magnets. Its momentum carries it past the vertical position. Now, the brush connections to the two halves of the commutator are reversed. The current flows the opposite way around the coil.

4 We again have a magnetic north pole above the coil, so it turns another 180° anticlockwise.

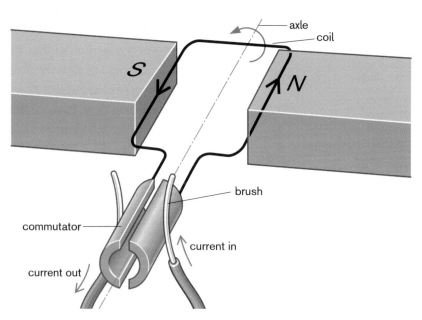

Figure 20.14 A spinning electric motor. The coil is an electromagnet, which is attracted round by the permanent magnets. Every half-turn, the commutator reverses the current flowing through the coil so that it keeps turning.

Without the commutator, the coil would simply turn until it was vertical. The commutator cleverly reverses the current through the coil every half-turn, so that the coil keeps on turning. If you have made a model like the one shown in Figure 20.13, you may have noticed electrical sparks flashing around the commutator. These happen as the contact between the brush and one commutator segment is broken, and as it makes contact with the other segment.

For a d.c. motor like this to be of any use, its axle must be connected to something that is to be turned – a wheel, a pulley or a pump, for example. This simple motor is not very powerful. The turning effect can be increased by supplying a bigger current, using stronger magnets, or increasing the area of the coil and the number of turns of wire.

Practical electric motors

The model electric motor is a good design if you want to understand how an electric motor works, but it doesn't function very well as a practical motor. There are several ways in which the design can be improved.

The rotating coil is known as the rotor. Many motors have three (or more) rotor coils, fixed at 60° (or smaller angles) to each other. Each in turn is attracted round by the permanent magnets, and this makes for a much smoother rotation. It is not necessary to rely on the coil's momentum to carry it past the vertical position, as there is always at least one coil that is being strongly attracted by the magnets. The commutator has six (or more) segments, two for each coil.

The permanent magnets may be replaced by electromagnets. Figure 20.15 shows an electric motor, partially dismantled to show the rotor coils that turn inside the fixed (stator) coils.

The motors we have been considering are d.c. motors (they work on direct current). Many motors run on alternating current, and they spin at the frequency of the supply (usually 50 or 60 Hz) or a multiple of this (e.g. 100 or 120 Hz).

Figure 20.15 This electric motor has been partly disassembled to show the rotor and stator. The stator coils provide the magnetic field that causes the rotor to spin when a current flows through it.

Questions

20.11 Give three everyday uses for electric motors. In each case, state whether the motor uses direct current or alternating current.

20.12 Look at the motor shown in Figure 20.14 and the explanation of how it works. Suppose that the two magnets were turned round so that there was a north magnetic pole on the left. Explain how the coil would move.

20.13 a In a d.c. motor, why must the current to the rotor coil be reversed twice during each rotation?

  b What device reverses the current?

20.14 List four ways in which the turning effect of a d.c. motor can be increased.

20.4 The motor effect

An electric motor has a coil with a current flowing around it (an electromagnet) in a magnetic field. It turns because the two magnetic fields interact with each other. However, it is not essential to have a coil to produce movement. The basic requirements are:

● a magnetic field;
● a current flowing *across* the magnetic field.

Figure 20.16 shows a way of demonstrating this in the laboratory. The copper rod is free to roll along the two steel support rods. The current from the power supply flows along one wire and support rod, through the copper rod, and out through the other support rod and wire. The two magnets provide a vertical magnetic field.

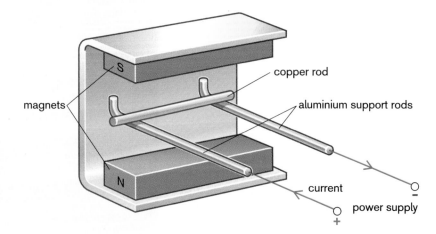

Figure 20.16 Demonstrating the motor effect. There is a magnetic field around the current in the copper rod. This interacts with the field of the magnets, and the result is a horizontal force on the rod. A copper rod is used because it is a non-magnetic material. (A steel rod would be attracted to the magnets.)

What happens when the current starts to flow? The copper rod rolls horizontally along the support rods. It is pushed by a horizontal force. The force comes about because the magnetic field around the current is repelled by the magnetic field of the permanent magnets. The force can be increased in two ways: by increasing the current, and by using magnets with a stronger magnetic field. This force, which is made use of in every electric motor, is known as the **motor effect**.

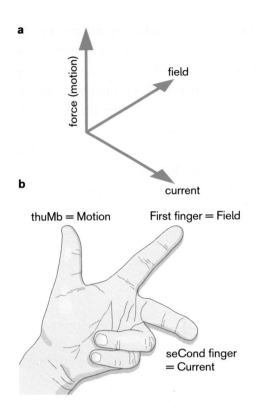

a

force (motion)

field

b

current

thuMb = Motion

First finger = Field

seCond finger = Current

Figure 20.17 **a** Force, field and current are at right-angles to each other. **b** Fleming's left-hand rule. Check that it correctly predicts the direction of the force on the current in Figure 20.16.

Fleming's left-hand rule

In Figure 20.16, there are three things with direction (three *vector* quantities – see chapter 1). These are:

- the magnetic field;
- the current;
- the force.

The magnetic field is vertical. The current and the force are horizontal, and at right angles to each other. Hence we have three things that are all mutually at right angles to each other (Figure 20.17a). To remember how they are arranged, physicists use Fleming's left-hand rule (Figure 20.17b). It is worth practising holding your thumb and first two fingers at right angles like this. Then learn what each finger represents, as shown in the diagram.

We use Fleming's left-hand rule to predict the direction of the force on a current-carrying conductor in a magnetic field. By keeping your thumb and fingers rigidly at right angles to each other, you can predict that:

- If the direction of the current is reversed, the force will also be reversed.
- If the direction of the magnetic field is reversed, the force will also be reversed.

(Don't try changing the direction of individual fingers. You have to twist your whole hand around at the wrist.)

From Fleming's left-hand rule, you can see why the current must flow *across* the magnetic field. If the current flowed along the field, you could not represent the field and current by two fingers at 90°. Figure 20.18 shows another way of thinking about the motor effect, in terms of the interacting magnetic fields. On one side of the conductor, the fields are in the same direction, so they add up. On the other side, they are opposed and cancel out. The strong field on one side pushes the conductor towards the weak field.

Michael Faraday, who made great strides in our understanding of electricity and magnetism, designed a slightly odd electric motor,

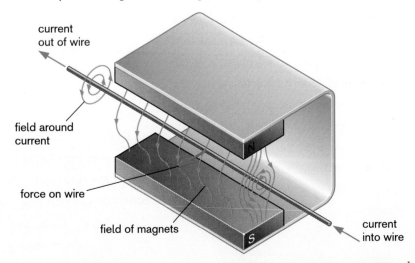

current out of wire

field around current

force on wire

field of magnets

current into wire

N

S

Figure 20.18 The motor effect, explained in terms of magnetic fields. The field around the current cancels out the field of the magnets on one side, and adds to it on the other side. The conductor is pushed towards the side where the field is weaker.

shown in Figure 20.19. A metal wire is suspended above a small magnet. A current flows from the battery, down through the wire and back to the battery through the mercury in the dish. The current is flowing across the magnetic field and this produces a horizontal force on the wire, causing it to rotate around the magnet. So, for the first time, movement had been produced from electricity.

[Faraday had solved the problem of getting the current into the moving conductor in two ways: using the hanging loop at the top, and the mercury at the bottom. An electric motor uses a commutator for the same purpose. There is more about Faraday's work on electromagnetism in Chapter 21.]

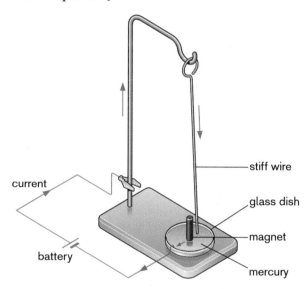

Figure 20.19 Faraday's model electric motor. The current flowing in the wire has a magnetic field around it. This interacts with the magnetic field of the magnet to produce a horizontal force on the wire, pushing it around in a circle. This was the world's first electric motor.

Extension material

The force on a beam of charged particles

In Chapter 18, we saw that a current is a flow of charged particles. Often, a current is a flow of electrons in a wire. However, a current could also take the form of ions moving in a liquid. In addition, it could be a beam of charged particles, like the beam of electrons in a television tube. Recall that, since electrons are negatively charged particles and current is the flow of positive charge, the current flows in the opposite direction to the movement of the electrons.

A beam of electrons can be deflected by the electric field between two charged plates. Now we can see that a magnetic field can also be used to deflect a beam of electrons. This can be demonstrated in the laboratory using a vacuum tube (Figure 20.20). Hence there is a force on any moving charge that crosses a magnetic field. In fact, when a current-carrying conductor is placed in a magnetic field, it is the electrons that feel the force; they then transmit it to the conductor. Looking back at Figure 20.16, you can imagine the electrons flowing in the copper rod and being pushed to the right as they cross the magnetic field.

A television tube usually has two sets of electromagnet coils mounted on it (Figure 20.21). The top-and-bottom pair produce a magnetic field that moves the electron beam from side to side; the left-and-right pair deflect the electron beam up and down. Fleming's left-hand rule should convince you that this is correct. Electromagnet coils are excellent for this job, because the current through them can be changed very rapidly. In this way, the electron beam can be scanned across the screen thousands of times each second to produce the images we see when watching a television programme.

Expensive experiments

Many physicists work on experiments to find out about the nature of the fundamental particles of which matter is made – for example, electrons and positrons (positively charged electrons), and the quarks of which protons and neutrons are made. They use particle accelerators to produce fast-moving beams of these particles, which then collide to produce sprays of energetic particles. Accelerators can be very large; the electron–positron collider at the European nuclear laboratory at CERN, Geneva, is 27 km in circumference. The magnetic force on moving charges plays two roles in this type of experiment:

- The beams of electrons and positrons travel through an evacuated tube. They are forced to travel around this curved tube by giant electromagnets (Figure 20.22a).

- The particle detectors that detect the tracks of particles produced in high-energy collisions use magnetic fields to determine their charges. In Figure 20.22b, you can see tracks spiralling in opposite directions. These are the tracks of oppositely charged particles. Detailed measurements can be made to determine the charge and mass of each particle. These experiments are very large and need teams of hundreds of physicists

Figure 20.20 An electron beam is travelling from left to right in this vacuum tube. The two electromagnet coils (front and back) produce a horizontal magnetic field. The electrons feel an upward force, and this causes the beam to curve. (Checking with Fleming's left-hand rule: current is right to left; magnetic field is towards the back; the force must be downwards on a positive charge. Electrons are negative so they are deflected upwards.)

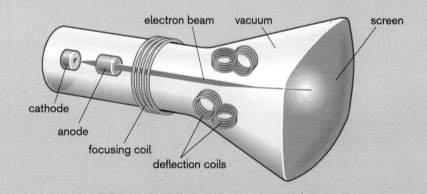

Figure 20.21 Electromagnet coils are mounted on the outside of a modern television tube, to deflect the electron beam across the screen. One pair of coils moves the beam horizontally, the other pair moves it vertically. As the beam moves across the screen, it builds up the picture. Usually, each picture is made up of 625 horizontal lines, and 50 or 60 are shown each second.

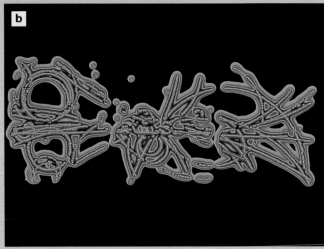

Figure 20.22 **a** Electromagnets provide the force needed to make beams of charged particles travel around a circular path in one of the accelerators at CERN. **b** The tracks of charged particles are curved when they enter a magnetic field. These tracks can be analysed to find out about the charges and masses of the particles. Then physicists can deduce the reactions that produced them.

and engineers to operate them. This makes them very expensive, but they have revealed much about the fundamental structure of matter. They are used to simulate conditions in the Universe shortly after the Big Bang when matter was highly compressed and very hot.

For every giant accelerator like this, there are hundreds of much smaller ones used for a great range of applications. Some are found in hospitals, where they provide energetic beams of electrons. The electrons crash into a metal target and produce high-energy X-rays, which can be used to destroy tumorous tissues in cancer patients.

Questions

20.15 For Fleming's left-hand rule, write down the three things that are at 90° to each other, and next to each one write down the finger (or thumb) that represents it.

20.16 List two ways to increase the force on a current-carrying conductor in a magnetic field.

20.17 What is the force on a current-carrying conductor that is *parallel to* a magnetic field?

20.18 Look at the picture of Faraday's electric motor (Figure 20.19). How would its motion change if the connections to the battery were reversed?

20.5 Electric motors revisited

Now that we have the idea that there is a force on a current crossing a magnetic field, we can think again about how electric motors work. (Previously, we said that the coil was an electromagnet attracted around by the permanent magnets. That was correct, but we can now picture the situation in a different way.)

Figure 20.23a shows a simple electric motor with its coil horizontal in a horizontal magnetic field. The coil is rectangular. What forces act on each of its four sides?

- *Side AB* The current flows from A to B, across the magnetic field. Fleming's left-hand rule shows that a force acts on it, vertically upwards.
- *Side CD* The current is flowing from C to D, in the opposite direction to AB, so the force on CD is downwards.
- *Sides BC and DA* The current here is parallel to the field. Since it does not cross the field, there is no force on these sides.

Figure 20.23b shows an end-on view of the coil. The two forces acting on it are shown; they cause the coil to turn anticlockwise. The two forces provide a turning effect (or **torque**), which causes the coil to turn. From Figure 20.23c, you can see that the forces will not turn the coil when it is vertical. This is where we have to rely on the coil's momentum to carry it further round.

Figure 20.23 **a** A simple electric motor; only the two longer sides experience a force, since their currents cut across the magnetic field. **b** The two forces provide the turning effect needed to make the coil rotate. **c** When the coil is in the vertical position, the forces have no turning effect.

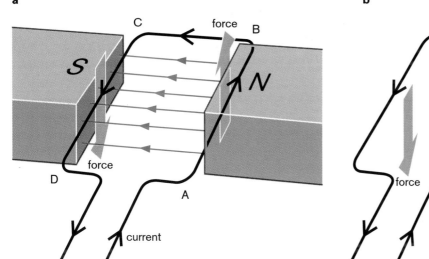

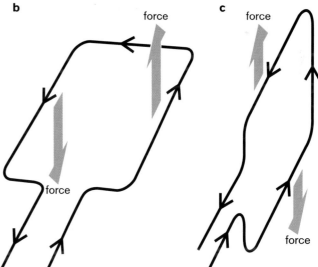

The diagrams show the coil as if it were a single turn of wire. In practice, the coil might have hundreds of turns of wire, resulting in forces hundreds of times as great. A coil with many turns causes the current to flow across the magnetic field many times, and each time it feels a force. A coil is simply a way of multiplying the effect that would be experienced using a single length of wire.

The torque of an electric motor can be increased in four ways.

- Increase the current.
- Use a stronger magnetic field.

- Use a bigger coil.
- Increase the number of turns on the coil.
- Use more than one coil, the coils being at an angle to one another.

Loudspeakers again

We can use the same approach to provide a second explanation of how a loudspeaker works. On page 322, we said that the coil carrying the alternating current was attracted and repelled by the permanent magnet. Now we can say that the current in the coil flows across the magnetic field. There is therefore a force at right angles to the coil, and this pushes the coil. As the current flows first one way then the other, the force pushes the coil alternately backwards and forwards.

? **Questions**

20.19 Explain why the forces shown in Figure 20.23c have no turning effect on the coil.

20.20 Use your understanding of the moment (turning effect) of a force to explain why increasing the current through the coil of an electric motor will increase the torque it provides.

20.21 What effect would using a coil of bigger area have on the moment of the forces? Draw a diagram like that shown in Figure 20.23b to support your answer.

20.22 How would the turning effect on a current-carrying coil be affected if stronger magnets were used?

Summary

- Electromagnets have the advantage over permanent magnets in that they can be switched on and off.

- Electromagnets have many uses, including electric motors, electric door bells, circuit breakers, relays and loudspeakers.

- An electric motor is a current-carrying coil in a magnetic field. In a d.c. motor, the commutator automatically reverses the current in the coil twice in each rotation, to ensure that the coil keeps spinning.

- A force is exerted on any current-carrying conductor that crosses a magnetic field.

- The relative directions of force, field and current are given by Fleming's left-hand rule.

- *A beam of charged particles can be thought of as a current, and will experience a force if it crosses a magnetic field. This is used to control the direction of beams of charged particles in television tubes, particle accelerators, etc.*

- The forces on opposite sides of a current-carrying coil in a magnetic field provide the torque that spins the motor.

- The torque can be increased by increasing the strength of the magnetic field, the area and number of turns of the coil, and the current.

Electromagnetic induction

Topics in this chapter

- ◆ generators and dynamos
- ◆ principles of electromagnetic induction
- ◆ power lines
- ◆ transformers
- ℯ *transformer calculations*

Houses, offices, factories, shops and schools – all must be supplied with electricity to maintain the lifestyle that we are used to if we live in a modern, developed country. Typically, we consume electrical energy at the average rate of about 1 kW (that is, about 1000 joules per second), although in the USA the average rate is more than twice this. This chapter is about how most of this electricity is generated and how it reaches us.

Fortunately, we usually don't have to think about the electricity we use. We plug in a computer or switch on a light and they work. Often, we have no idea where the electricity we use is generated or how it gets to us. You may have noticed some clues as you travel around. Figure 21.1 shows what to look out for.

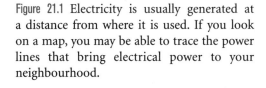

Figure 21.1 Electricity is usually generated at a distance from where it is used. If you look on a map, you may be able to trace the power lines that bring electrical power to your neighbourhood.

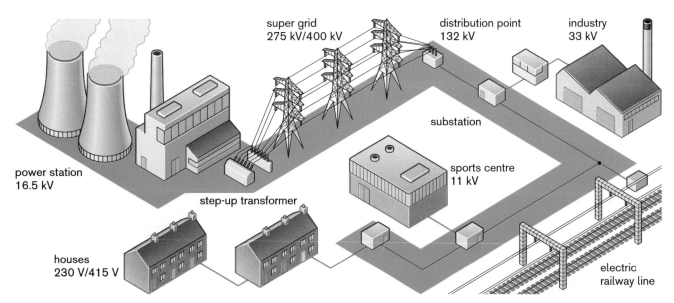

super grid
275 kV/400 kV

distribution point
132 kV

industry
33 kV

power station
16.5 kV

substation

sports centre
11 kV

step-up transformer

houses
230 V/415 V

electric
railway line

Power stations may be 100 km or more from the places where the electricity they generate is used. They are positioned close to a reliable source of fuel and where cooling water is readily available – on the banks of a river or lake, or near the sea. You may have noticed their cooling towers, which often have clouds of water vapour pouring out into the sky.

High-voltage electricity leaves the power station complex. Its voltage may be as much as one million volts. To avoid danger to people, it is usually carried in cables slung high above the ground between tall pylons. Lines of pylons stride across the countryside, heading for the urban and industrial areas that need the power.

When the power lines approach the area where the power is to be used, they enter a local distribution centre. Here the voltage is reduced to a less hazardous level, and the power is sent through more cables (overhead or underground) to local substations. Wherever you live, there is likely to be a substation in the neighbourhood. Its electrical equipment may be in a securely locked building, or it may be surrounded by fencing that carries notices warning of the hazard (Figure 21.2).

From the substation, electricity is distributed around the neighbouring houses. Larger buildings such as shopping malls, hospitals or sports centres may have their own substation. In some countries, the power is carried in cables buried underground. Other countries use tall 'poles' that hold the cables above the level of traffic in the street to distribute the power. Overhead power lines and cables can be an eyesore, but the cost of burying cables underground can be ten or a hundred times as great.

Figure 21.2 Look out for electricity substations in your neighbourhood. Here the voltage of the supply is reduced and power is distributed to all the nearby buildings. Warning signs indicate the extreme hazard of entering the substation. In this picture, you can see the transformers, which reduce the voltage to the local supply voltage, typically 230 V.

21.1 Generating electricity

A *motor* is a device for transforming electrical energy into mechanical (kinetic) energy. To generate electricity, we need a device that will do the opposite: it must transform mechanical energy into electrical energy. Fortunately, we can simply use an electric motor in reverse.

If you connect up an electric motor to a meter and spin its axle, the meter will show that you have generated a voltage (Figure 21.3). Inside

Figure 21.3 A motor can act as a generator. Spin the motor and the meter shows that an induced current flows around the circuit.

the motor, the coil is spinning around in the magnetic field provided by the permanent magnets. A current is *induced* to flow in the coil, and this is shown by the meter. The motor is acting as a **generator**.

There are many different designs of generator, just as there are many different designs of electric motor. Some generate direct current, others generate alternating current. Some use permanent magnets, while others use electromagnets.

The power station generators shown in Figure 21.4 generate alternating current at a voltage of about 25 kV. A **turbine** is made to spin by high-pressure steam from the boiler. The generator is on the same axle as the turbine, so it spins too. The generator spins around inside some fixed electromagnets, which provide a magnetic field. The coils inside the generator are therefore spinning in a magnetic field. A large current is then induced in these rotating coils, and this is the current that the power station supplies to consumers. A fraction of this current is used to supply the electromagnets of the generator itself.

Figure 21.4 The turbines and generators in the generating hall of a modern power station.

If you have a bicycle, then you may have a generator of a different design – a **dynamo** – for powering the lights. In a dynamo, the coil is fixed, while a permanent magnet spins around inside the coil (Figure 21.5). The magnet is on an axle that is made to turn by the knurled wheel that rubs on the cycle's tyre. Look at the coil of wire on the left. First the magnet's north pole moves past it, and the induced current flows in one direction. Then the south pole moves past, and the induced current flows the other way. In other words, an alternating current has been induced in the coil, and it is this current that makes the lamps light up.

Bicycle dynamos are designed like this because they have to be robust. A permanent magnet spinning around is more robust than a spinning coil, and there is no problem about making electrical connections to a spinning coil. Some wind generators use spinning permanent magnets to induce currents in fixed coils.

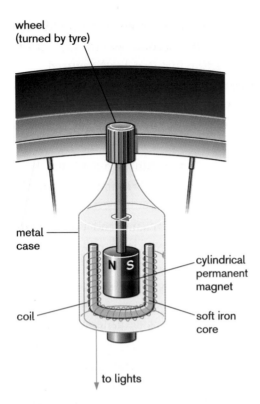

wheel
(turned by tyre)

metal
case

N S

cylindrical
permanent
magnet

coil

soft iron
core

to lights

Figure 21.5 A bicycle dynamo generates an alternating current that works the bicycle's lights.

All of these generators have three things in common:
- a magnetic field (provided by magnets or electromagnets);
- a coil of wire (fixed or moving);
- movement (the coil and magnetic field move *relative* to one another).

When the coil and the magnetic field move relative to each other, a current flows in the coil. This is known as an **induced current**. If the coil is part of a complete circuit, the current will flow all the way around. If the generator is not connected up to a circuit, there will be an **induced voltage** (or induced e.m.f.) across its ends, ready to make a current flow around a circuit.

> **Questions**
>
> **21.1** Draw a diagram to show the energy transformations in an electric motor and a generator. Remember that neither is 100% efficient.
>
> **21.2** If you hold a coil of wire next to a magnet, no current will flow. What else is needed to induce a current?
>
> **21.3** In this section, what alternative word is used to mean 'generator'?
>
> **21.4** How is the magnetic field provided in the generators found in large power stations?

21.2 The principles of electromagnetic induction

Electromagnetic induction is the process of generating electricity from motion. The science of electromagnetism was largely developed by Michael Faraday (Figure 21.6). He came up with the idea of the magnetic field to explain his observations, and drew field lines to represent it. As we saw earlier (page 328), he invented the first electric motor.

Figure 21.6 Michael Faraday delivering a Christmas lecture at the Royal Institution in London on 27 December 1855. He was a great populariser of science, and his lectures attracted many famous people. The artist, Alexander Blaikley, has included several members of the Royal Family in the audience, as well as famous scientists, including Charles Darwin, although it is unlikely that they were all present at this lecture. The Royal Institution Christmas Lectures started in 1826 and continue to this day. They are still presented in the same lecture theatre. Each year a different scientist presents illustrated talks and demonstrations on different subjects. You may have seen them on television, as they are broadcast around the world.

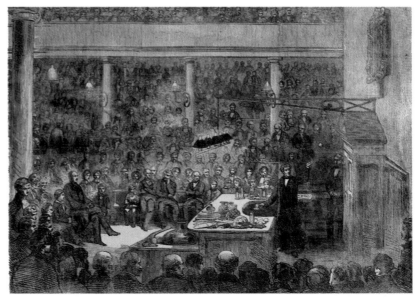

Then he extended his studies to show how the motor effect could work in reverse to generate electricity. In this section, we will look at the principles of electromagnetic induction that Faraday discovered.

As we have seen, a coil of wire and a magnet moving relative to each other are needed to generate electricity. In fact, a simple wire is enough, as shown in Figure 21.7a. The wire is connected to a sensitive meter to show when a current is flowing. Move one pole of the magnet downwards past the wire and a current flows. Move the magnet back upwards, and a current flows in the opposite direction. Alternatively, the magnet can be stationary and the wire can be moved up and down next to it. You can see similar effects using a magnet and a coil (Figure 21.7b). Pushing the magnet in and out of the coil induces a current that flows back and forth in the coil. Here are four further observations.

- Move the magnet or the wire more slowly and the induced current is smaller.
- With the magnet further from the wire or coil, the induced current is smaller (because the field is weaker).
- Reverse the magnet to use the opposite pole and the current flows in the opposite direction.
- Hold the magnet stationary next to the wire or coil, and no current flows. They must move relative to each other, or nothing will happen.

(This provides a good test of how steady your hand is. Hold a strong magnet next to a coil of wire. If your hand trembles, the meter will show that a current is flowing in the wire.)

Induction and lines of force

Figure 21.7 **a** Move a magnet up and down next to a stationary wire and an induced current will flow. **b** Similarly, moving a magnet in and out of a coil of wire induces a current. Michael Faraday first did experiments like this in 1831.

We can understand electromagnetic induction using Faraday's idea of lines of magnetic force. Picture the lines of force coming out of each pole of the magnets shown in Figure 21.7. As the magnet is moved, the lines of force are cut by the wire, and it is this cutting of lines of force

a

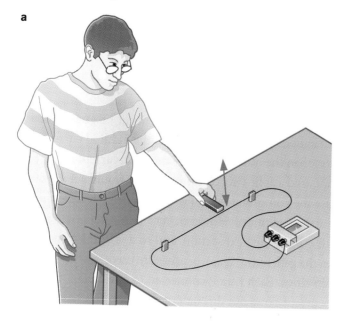

b

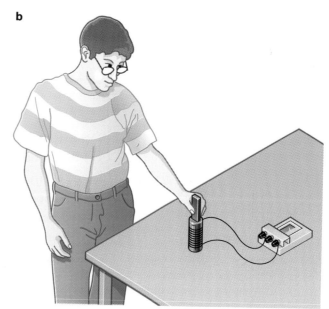

that induces the current. If the magnet is stationary, there is no cutting of lines of force, and so no current is induced. If the magnet is further from the wire, the lines of force are further apart and so fewer are cut, giving a smaller current. If the magnet is moved quickly, the lines are cut more quickly, and a bigger current flows.

As usual, a coil gives a bigger effect than a single wire. This is because each turn of wire cuts the magnetic field lines and each therefore contributes to the induced current.

An a.c. generator

Faraday's discovery of electromagnetic induction led to the development of the electricity supply industry. In particular, it allowed engineers to design generators that could supply electricity. At first, this was only done on a small scale, but gradually generators got bigger and bigger until, like the ones shown in Figure 21.4, they were capable of supplying the electricity demands of thousands of homes.

Figure 21.8 shows a simple a.c. generator. In principle, this is like a d.c. motor, working in reverse: the axle is made to turn so that the coil spins around in the magnetic field, and a current is induced. The other difference is in the way in which the coil is connected to the circuit beyond. A d.c. motor uses a split-ring commutator, whereas an a.c. generator uses slip rings.

Figure 21.8 A simple a.c. generator works like a motor in reverse. The slip rings and brushes are used to connect the alternating current to the external circuit. The small graph shows how the alternating current varies.

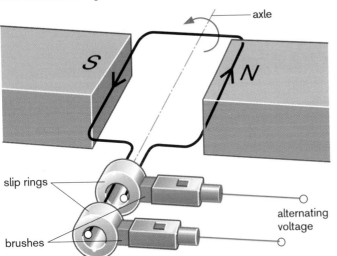

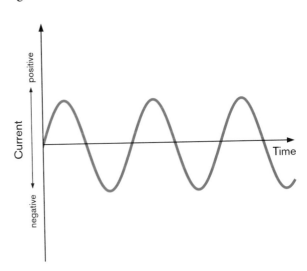

As the coil rotates, each side passes first the north magnetic pole and then the south magnetic pole. This means that the induced current flows first one way, and then the other. In other words, the current in the coil is alternating. If we used a split-ring commutator, we would get direct current out, because the commutator would automatically reverse the connection every half-revolution. However, a.c. has certain advantages, which we will discuss in the next section, and so it is useful to be able to extract a.c. from the generator. Again, brushes are used, but this time they press against **slip rings**. Each ring is connected to one end of the coil, so the alternating current flows out through the brushes.

There are four ways of increasing the voltage generated by an a.c. generator like this:

- Turn the coil more rapidly.
- Use a coil with more turns of wire.
- Use a bigger coil.
- Use stronger magnets.

Each of these has the effect of increasing the rate at which magnetic field lines are cut, and so the induced voltage is greater.

For the a.c. generator shown in Figure 21.8, each revolution of the coil generates one cycle of alternating current. Spin the coil 50 times each second and the a.c. generated has a frequency of 50 Hz. Practical generators often have three coils, set at angles of 60° to each other. Each has its own pair of slip rings and produces its own alternating current. The three currents are out of step with each other by one-third of a cycle. Practical generators generally use electromagnets instead of permanent magnets.

? Questions

21.5 The north pole of a magnet is moved towards a coil of wire, as shown in Figure 21.7b, so that an induced current flows. How would the current change if the magnet's south pole was used instead?

21.6 State two ways in which the current induced in the coil (Figure 21.7b) could be increased.

21.7 A magnet lies inside a coil of wire. Why does no induced current flow?

21.8 When you cycle faster, the bicycle's dynamo (Figure 21.5) spins faster. In what two ways will the induced alternating current supplied by the dynamo change?

21.9 List the features of a large a.c. generator from a power station (Figure 21.4) that make it capable of generating a higher voltage than the model a.c. generator shown in Figure 21.8.

21.3 Power lines and transformers

Electrical power is distributed around the country from power stations in a grid of high-voltage power lines. Figure 21.9 shows the national grid in the UK. From this map, you can see that there are loops which ensure that, when a local power station is switched off, electricity can still reach all of the consumers in the area. You can also see that the national grid in the UK is linked to the French grid by cables under the English Channel. France produces more electricity than it needs, and exports large quantities to neighbouring countries.

Figure 21.9 The UK national grid carries electrical power the length and breadth of the island. Power stations and power distribution lines are concentrated in the industrial urban areas. More than 22 000 pylons (towers) are needed to support the power lines.

Figure 21.10 Engineers sometimes have to work on power lines even when they are at high voltage. They can safely touch the cables so long as they are not in contact with the pylon or the ground, so that current cannot flow through them. For the same reason, it is safe for birds to sit on power lines.

The engineers in the photograph (Figure 21.10) are working on high-voltage power lines of an electricity grid. Sometimes it is necessary for them to work on the cables when they are at their high operating voltage, 275 kV or 400 kV. Currents of thousands of amps flow in the cables. This is hazardous, but, as long as they avoid becoming part of a circuit between the cable and the ground, they can avoid electrocution. In this section, we will look at why such high voltages are used, and how they are produced using transformers.

Why use high voltages?

The high voltages used to transmit electrical power around a country are dangerous. That is why the cables that carry the power are supported high above people, traffic and buildings on tall pylons (towers). Sometimes the cables are buried underground, but this is much more expensive, and the cables must be safely insulated. There is a good reason for using high voltages: it means that the current flowing in the cables is relatively low, and this wastes less energy. We can understand this as follows.

When a current flows in a wire or cable, some of the energy it is carrying is lost because of the cable's resistance – the cables get hot. A small current wastes less energy than a high current. To transmit a certain power, P, we can use a small current, I, if we transmit the power at high voltage, V. We can see this from the following numerical worked example.

Worked example 1

Suppose a power station generates 500 MW of power. What current will flow from the power station if it transmits this power at 50 kV? What current will flow if it transmits it at 1 MV?

Rearranging $P = IV$, we have the equation that we need to use:

$$I = \frac{P}{V}$$

Substituting values for the first case ($P = 500\,\text{MW} = 500 \times 10^6\,\text{W}$, $V = 50\,\text{kV} = 50 \times 10^3\,\text{V}$) gives the current as

$$I = \frac{500 \times 10^6\,\text{W}}{50 \times 10^3\,\text{V}} = 10\,000\,\text{A}$$

Now, consider the second case, when the power is transmitted at 1 MV ($10^6\,\text{V}$) – the operating voltage of some national grids. We now have that the current is given by

$$I = \frac{500 \times 10^6\,\text{W}}{10^6\,\text{V}} = 500\,\text{A}$$

Hence increasing the voltage by a factor of 20 reduces the current by the same factor of 20. This greatly reduces the power lost in the cables, and means that thinner cables can safely be used.

If we think of the current flowing in the cables as a flow of coulombs of charge, at high voltage we have fewer coulombs flowing but each coulomb carries more energy with it.

Transformers

Figure 21.11 **a** The structure of a transformer. This is a step-up transformer because there are more turns on the secondary coil than on the primary. If the connection to it were reversed it would be a step-up transformer. **b** The circuit symbol for a transformer shows two coils with the core between them.

Power stations typically generate electricity at 25 kV. This has to be converted to the grid voltage – say 250 kV – using transformers. For these voltages, we say that the voltage is stepped up by a factor of 10. Figure 21.11 shows the construction of a suitable transformer.

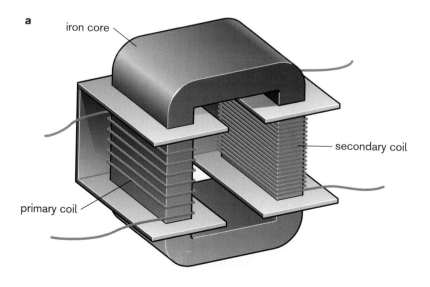

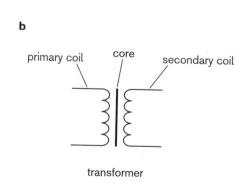

Every transformer has three parts:
- *Primary coil* – the incoming voltage V_p (voltage across primary coil) is connected across this coil.
- *Secondary coil* – this provides the voltage V_s (voltage across secondary coil) to the external circuit.
- *Iron core* – this links the two coils.

Notice that there is *no electrical connection* between the two coils, which are constructed using isolated wire. They are linked together by the iron core.

To step up the input voltage by a factor of 10, there must be 10 times as many turns on the secondary coil as on the primary. The **turns ratio** thus tells us the factor by which the voltage will be changed.

> A **step-up transformer** increases the voltage – there are more turns on the secondary than on the primary.
> A **step-down transformer** reduces the voltage – there are fewer turns on the secondary than on the primary.

(Note that, if the voltage is stepped up, the current must be stepped down, and vice versa.)

Hence we can write an equation, known as the **transformer equation**, relating the two voltages V_p and V_s to the numbers of turns on each coil, N_p and N_s:

$$\frac{\text{voltage across primary coil}}{\text{voltage across secondary coil}} = \frac{\text{number of turns on primary}}{\text{number of turns on secondary}}$$
$$\frac{V_p}{V_s} = \frac{N_p}{N_s}$$

How transformers work

Transformers only work with alternating current (a.c.). To understand why this is, we need to look at how a transformer works (Figure 21.12).
- The primary coil has alternating current flowing through it. It is thus an electromagnet, and produces an alternating magnetic field.
- The core transports this alternating field around to the secondary coil.
- Now the secondary coil is a conductor in a changing magnetic field. A current is induced in the coil. (This is another example of electromagnetic induction at work.)

If the secondary coil has only a few turns, the p.d. induced across it is small. If it has a lot of turns, the p.d. will be large. Hence to get a high voltage out, we need a secondary coil with a lot of turns compared to the primary.

If direct current is connected to a transformer, there is no output voltage. This is because the magnetic field produced by the primary coil is unchanging. With an *unchanging* field passing through the secondary coil, no voltage is induced in it.

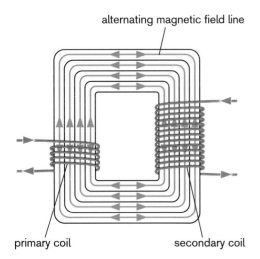

alternating magnetic field line

primary coil   secondary coil

Figure 21.12 The alternating current in the primary coil produces a varying magnetic field in the core. This induces a varying current in the secondary coil. The core of a transformer is often made in sheets (laminated); the magnetic field lines follow the sheets around from the primary coil to the secondary.

Notice from Figure 21.12 that the magnetic field links the primary and secondary coils. The energy being brought by the current in the primary coil is transferred to the secondary by the magnetic field. This means that the core must be very good at transferring magnetic energy. A soft magnetic material must be used – usually an alloy of iron with a small amount of silicon. Even in a well-designed transformer, some energy is lost because of the resistance of the wires, and because the core 'resists the flow' of the changing magnetic field.

Practical transformers

Figure 21.13 shows two very different transformers: the world's first transformer, made by Michael Faraday (Figure 21.13a), and a modern high-power transformer at a power station (Figure 21.13b). Transformers are found in many different situations.

- Transformers step up the voltage at a power station, and step it down again at the substations that supply local users.
- A portable radio may run off the mains, or from batteries. The mains voltage is reduced to a suitable low value by a built-in transformer.
- Mains adapters are often used with computer games and personal stereos. These are heavy because of the weight of the transformer core and coils that they contain.
- Theatre lighting may be dimmed and brightened using variable transformers.

Figure 21.13 Transformers old and new. **a** This transformer was made by Michael Faraday in 1831. The core is an iron ring. It is hard to see, but there are two separate coils of wire wrapped around the ring. **b** Transformers at a modern power station. The coils and core are entirely enclosed. A small fraction of the power passing through the transformer is wasted as heat. The tanks contain cooling fluid, which is pumped around to remove the heat.

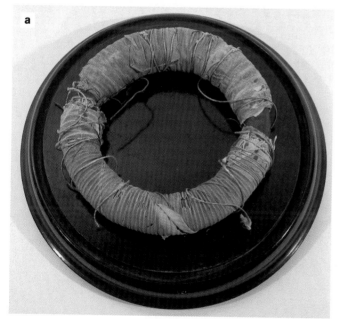

Extension material

Transformer calculations

We can use the transformer equation

$$\frac{V_p}{V_s} = \frac{N_p}{N_s}$$

to solve problems. Worked example 2 gives an example of the use of this equation.

If a transformer is 100% efficient, no power is lost in its coils or core. Then

> power into primary coil = power out of secondary coil

This is a reasonable approximation – well-designed transformers like the one shown in Figure 21.13b waste only about 0.1% of the power transferred through them. This allows us to write the **transformer power equation** relating the primary and secondary p.d.s to the currents I_p and I_s flowing in the primary and secondary coils, using $P = IV$:

> power into primary coil = power out of secondary coil
> $$I_p\, V_p = I_s\, V_s$$

Worked example 3 shows how to use this equation.

Worked example 2

A transformer is needed to step down the 230 V mains supply to 6 V. If the primary coil has 1000 turns, how many turns must the secondary have?

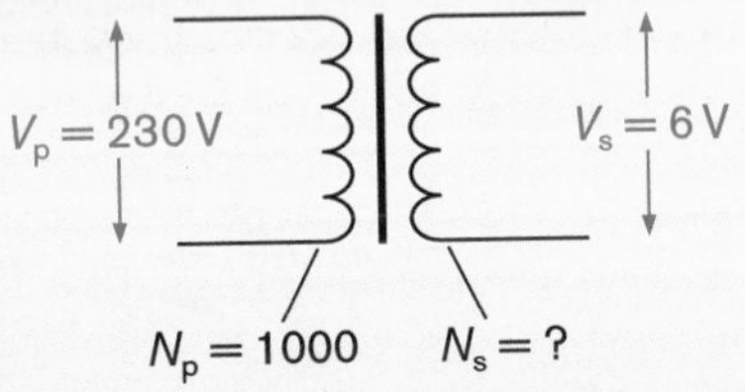

$V_p = 230\,V$ $V_s = 6\,V$

$N_p = 1000$ $N_s = ?$

Figure 21.14 For worked example 2.

● *Step 1* Draw a transformer symbol and mark on it the information from the question.

See Figure 21.14.

● *Step 2* Think about what a reasonable answer might be.

The voltage has to be reduced, so the number of turns on the secondary coil must be much less than 1000. Mental arithmetic shows that the voltage has to be reduced by a factor of about 40 (from 230 V to 6 V), so the number of turns must be reduced by the same factor. So number of turns on the primary will be about 1000/40 = 25. This is an *approximate* answer.

● *Step 3* Write down the transformer equation:

$$\frac{V_p}{V_s} = \frac{N_p}{N_s}$$

● *Step 4* Substitute values from the question:

$$\frac{230\,V}{6\,V} = \frac{1000}{N_s}$$

● *Step 5* Rearrange and solve for N_s:

$$N_s = \frac{1000 \times 6\,V}{230\,V} = 26.1 \text{ turns}$$

So the secondary coil must have 26 turns. This is in close agreement with our approximate answer in step 2.

Worked example 3

The primary coil of a transformer is connected to a 12 V alternating supply, and carries a current of 5 A. If the output voltage is 240 V, what current flows in the secondary circuit? Assume that the transformer is 100% efficient.

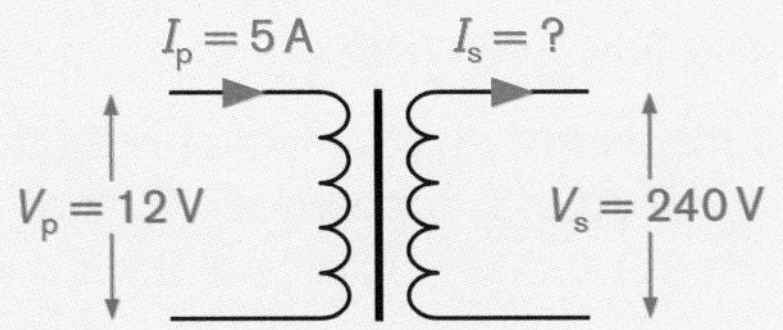

$I_p = 5\,A \qquad I_s = ?$

$V_p = 12\,V \qquad V_s = 240\,V$

Figure 21.15 For worked example 3.

● *Step 1* Draw a transformer symbol and mark on it the information from the question.

See Figure 21.15.

● *Step 2* Think about what a reasonable answer might be.

The voltage is being stepped up by a factor of 20 (from 12 V to 240 V). So the current will be stepped down by the same factor. You can probably see that the secondary current will be 1/20th of the primary current, or (5 A)/20 = $\frac{1}{4}$ A.

[This is the correct answer, but we will press on with the formal calculation.]

● *Step 3* Write down the transformer power equation:

$$I_p\, V_p = I_s\, V_s$$

● *Step 4* Substitute values from the question:

$$5\,A \times 12\,V = I_s \times 240\,V$$

● *Step 5* Rearrange and solve for I_s:

$$I_s = \frac{5\,A \times 12\,V}{240\,V} = 0.25\,A$$

Hence, as we found by mental arithmetic in step 2, the current supplied by the secondary coil is 0.25 A. So, in stepping up the voltage, the transformer has stepped down the current. If both had been stepped up, we would be getting something for nothing – impossible!

? Questions

21.10 Why is electrical power transmitted in the grid at high voltage?

21.11 What are the three essential parts of any transformer?

21.12 **a** What is the function of the core of a transformer?
b Why must it be made of a soft magnetic material?

21.13 Explain why a transformer will not work with direct current.

21.14 A portable radio has a built-in transformer so that it can work from the mains instead of batteries. Is this a step-up or step-down transformer?

Questions continued

21.15 A transformer has 200 turns on the primary coil and 5000 on the secondary. Is this a step-up or step-down transformer?

21.16 In a step-up transformer, is the current in the secondary coil greater than or less than the current in the primary coil?

Summary

♦ When a conductor is moved so that it cuts across a magnetic field, a p.d. is induced between its ends. If the conductor is part of a complete circuit, an induced current will flow. This is electromagnetic induction.

♦ To generate electricity, a magnet or electromagnet is rotated inside a coil of wire. An induced p.d. appears across the ends of the coil.

♦ Electrical power is transmitted at high voltages. This allows the current to be relatively low, so resistive losses of energy in the cables are low and thinner cables can be used.

♦ A transformer changes the voltage of an alternating supply.

♦ A transformer consists of primary and secondary coils, linked by an iron core. The changing magnetic field produced by the primary coil induces an alternating current in the secondary coil.

♦ A step-up transformer increases the voltage of the supply.

♦ The transformer equation relates the voltages and the numbers of turns:
$$\frac{V_p}{V_s} = \frac{N_p}{N_s}$$

⊕ *For a 100% efficient transformer (in which no power is wasted):*
power in = power out
$$I_p V_p = I_s V_s$$

Electronic control circuits

Topics in this chapter

◆ input–process–output systems

◆ AND, OR and NOT gates

◆ truth tables

◆ using a transistor as a buffer

ℯ *NAND and NOR gates*

◆ input devices

ℯ *capacitors in time delay circuits*

◆ output devices

ℯ *feedback and latches*

Today, much of the work of manufacturing things is done by robots. Fifty years ago, the same work was done by people. In a modern car factory (Figure 22.1), robotic machines position parts with great accuracy, weld them together, paint them, and so on. Computers control the robots, so that they select the correct parts and fix them in the right places. On the production lines, each car has to be built differently – they have different engine capacities, different fixtures and fittings, and are painted different colours. The computers make sure that each car comes off the line with all the right features.

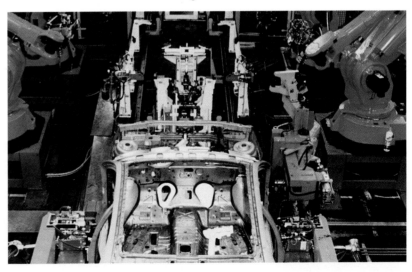

Figure 22.1 This car production line uses robots to perform many different operations. Robotic tools have built-in sensors that detect their positions. This information is used by a computer to control the tool.

The robots are fitted with sensors. These detect the position of its 'arms' and send the information back to the controlling computers. The computers can then send signals to the motors, which move the robot arms so that they can be correctly positioned for the required task.

All of this automated control is carried out by electronic circuits. When it is working well, it can produce goods of very high quality, relatively cheaply. Electronic systems have replaced many workers. If you are lucky enough to have a job, you will be able to enjoy the products of modern manufacturing industries.

Automatic control systems have arrived in many aspects of life. Farming and food growing are increasingly automated. The giant greenhouse shown in Figure 22.2 covers the area of several football pitches and is operated by one person. Sensors detect the levels of light, humidity, temperature and carbon dioxide. A computer uses this information to decide when to water the plants, open the windows, switch on the heating, or burn gas to produce more carbon dioxide. If anything goes wrong at night, it can even telephone the operator at home to give an alarm call!

Figure 22.2 At most times, only one person is needed to manage this giant glasshouse where tens of millions of lettuces are grown each year. Environmental sensors make measurements of temperature, humidity, etc., and this allows the watering and heating systems to be automatically operated. Only the lettuce picking requires much human labour.

In this chapter, we will look at some of the basic functions of electronic control systems, and some of the components used in them.

22.1 Electronic processors

In the glasshouse shown in Figure 22.2, the roof windows open automatically when the temperature rises. This requires a control system that will detect when the temperature reaches a certain level, and then switch on the motors that open the windows. We can picture this system as shown in Figure 22.3.

Figure 22.3 A block diagram for a simple control system. This system automatically opens the windows in the glasshouse when the temperature rises above a certain level.

temperature sensor	processor	motors
detects the temperature	decides whether the temperature is high enough to need the windows open	open the windows

In the past, someone might have looked at a thermometer and then turned the handles that open the windows. This person has now been replaced by the **processor**. A simple processor might be a single electronic component, but in the glasshouse a computer is used. A single computer can perform many operations like this each second; a person takes much longer.

Figure 22.4 shows a general block diagram that we can use to think about *any* control system. An **input device**, such as a temperature sensor, sends information to a processor, which then sends an appropriate signal to an **output device**, such as the motors that open the windows. The difference between electronic control systems and other control systems is that they work on electrical voltages. So we need to think about input sensors that produce voltages, and processors which can respond by supplying voltages to output devices.

Figure 22.4 A block diagram for a simple electronic control system. (In fact, this diagram could represent any control system, including mechanical ones, where the processor might be a person.)

input device	processor	output device

In earlier chapters, we have looked at devices whose electrical resistance changes with temperature (thermistors), light level (LDRs) and so on. These can form the basis of electronic sensors. We have also looked at some possible output devices that produce motion (motors), light (lamps, LEDs), etc. In this section, we will look at some electronic components that can work as processors. They have to receive a voltage from an input device, and provide a voltage to operate an output device.

Logic gates

A logic gate is a device that receives one or more electrical input signals, and produces an output signal that depends on those input signals. These signals are voltages.

- A high voltage is referred to as ON and is represented by the symbol 1.
- A low voltage is referred to as OFF and is represented by the symbol 0.

It is easiest to understand this by looking at three specific examples: the AND, OR and NOT gates, whose standard circuit symbols are shown in Figure 22.5. Each symbol has inputs on the left and a single output on the right.

a An AND gate functions like this: its output is ON if *both* input 1 **and** input 2 are ON.

Figure 22.5 The standard circuit symbols for three logic gates: **a** AND gate; **b** OR gate; and **c** NOT gate. (The symbol for an AND gate looks rather like the letter D in AND.)

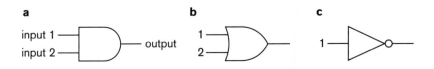

a AND gate

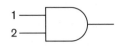

input 1	input 2	output
0	0	0
1	0	0
0	1	0
1	1	1

b OR gate

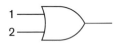

input 1	input 2	output
0	0	0
1	0	1
0	1	1
1	1	1

c NOT gate

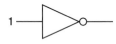

input	output
0	1
1	0

Figure 22.6 Truth tables for three logic gates: **a** AND gate; **b** OR gate; and **c** NOT gate. In a truth table, 0 stands for OFF or a low voltage; 1 stands for ON or a high voltage.

b An OR gate functions like this: its output is ON if one input is ON **or** if both inputs are ON.

c A NOT gate functions like this: its output is ON if its input is **not** ON.

Let's look at a concrete example. An OR gate might be useful in a domestic heating system. There might be temperature sensors in two rooms. If a room was cold, the sensor in that room would send an ON signal to the OR gate. If either room was cold, the output of the gate would be ON, and this would switch on the central heating.

The way in which these three gates operates is clear from their names. Another way to remember how they operate is by learning their **truth tables**, shown in Figure 22.6. In a truth table, we use 0 to stand for OFF and 1 to stand for ON.

A truth table shows all the possible combinations of inputs, and the output that results from each combination. A NOT gate has only one input, which can be ON or OFF, so this is the simplest table. AND and OR gates have two inputs. There are four possible combinations of inputs, and there is a corresponding output for each. For example, you can see from the last line in the truth table for the AND gate that two input 1's give an output 1; for all other combinations of inputs the output is 0. You should check that you understand how these truth tables represent the same information as in the sentences above that describe these gates.

Combining logic gates

Computer chips (microprocessors) are made up of many millions of logic gates. They combine together to produce outputs that depend on many different inputs. We will restrict ourselves to some simple examples involving just a few gates, to illustrate the principles involved.

Figure 22.7a shows an AND gate with a NOT gate connected to its output. We can work out the truth table for this combination by realising that the *output* of the AND gate is the *input* of the NOT gate; when the AND gate output is 1, the NOT gate turns this into a 0.

Figure 22.7b shows the same gates but differently connected, together with the resulting truth table.

a AND NOT

input 1	input 2	output
0	0	1
1	0	1
0	1	1
1	1	0

b NOT AND

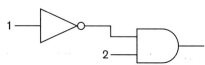

input 1	input 2	output
0	0	0
1	0	0
0	1	1
1	1	0

Figure 22.7 Two ways of combining a NOT gate and an AND gate, together with the resulting truth tables.

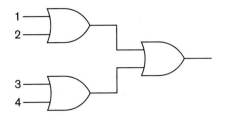

Figure 22.8 Three OR gates connected together. The combination has four inputs, so there are 16 different possible combinations of input signals. If one or more inputs is ON, the output is ON.

Figure 22.8 shows a combination of three OR gates. This might function like this: A building has smoke detectors in four different places. Their outputs are connected via this combination of gates to a single alarm siren. If any detector gives an ON signal, the siren will be switched ON. This saves the expense of a separate siren for each detector.

Transistors

A logic gate can provide an output *voltage* that acts as a signal to control an output device (such as a relay switch or a lamp). However, it cannot provide enough *current* to operate these devices. To overcome this problem, a **transistor** is often connected to the output of the gate, and this draws the necessary current from the power supply.

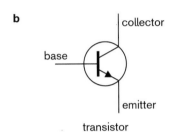

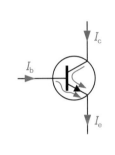

Figure 22.9 **a** Some transistors. **b** The circuit symbol for a transistor. **c** With no current flowing into the base, no current can flow down through the transistor. When a small current flows into the base, a large current flows into the collector, through the transistor and out through the emitter. (The arrow shows the direction of current flow; the emitter emits electrons in the opposite direction to the flow of conventional current, and the collector collects them.)

A transistor is an electronic component with three terminals or connections. Figure 22.9 shows some examples, together with the circuit symbol. The three terminals are called the collector, base and emitter. In the circuits we are interested in, a transistor acts as a device for controlling the flow of current. It works like this:

The transistor is connected so that there is a p.d. of 6 V between the collector (c) and the emitter (e). A current wants to flow downwards from the collector to the emitter; the arrow indicates the direction of current flow. However, the transistor has a very high resistance, so no current flows. If a small current flows into the base (b), this greatly reduces the transistor's resistance, and a large current flows downwards from the collector to the emitter. Hence a small base current I_b permits a large current I_c to flow into the collector. The two currents join together and flow out through the emitter:

base current + collector current = emitter current
$$I_b + I_c = I_e$$

Hence a small current (I_b) controls a large current (I_c).

Now we will look at an example of a circuit that includes a transistor so that sufficient current can flow to operate a buzzer (Figure 22.10). This circuit sounds an alarm when either of two sensors gets hot – it could be part of a fire alarm system. The sensors are omitted from the diagram, to make its operation simpler to understand.

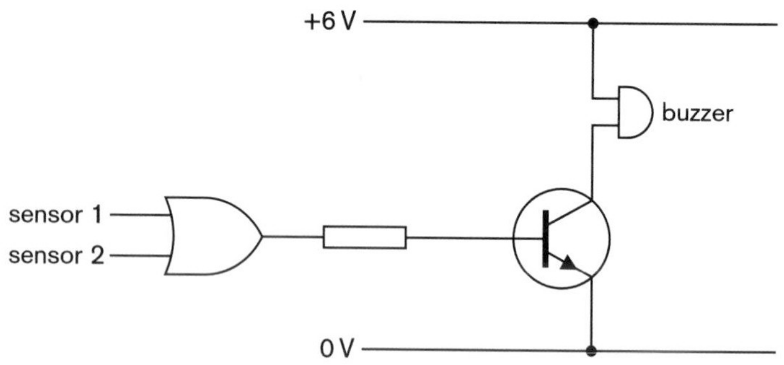

Figure 22.10 A control circuit in which a transistor is switched on by a current supplied by an OR gate. The base current controls whether or not a large current flows through the buzzer. For clarity, the input devices (two temperature sensors) are not shown.

- If either sensor supplies an ON signal to the OR gate, the gate's output is ON.
- This high voltage makes a small current flow into the base of the transistor. (The resistor is there to make sure the current doesn't get too big.)
- This allows a large current to flow down through the transistor. It also flows through the buzzer, which buzzes.

(If neither of the OR gate's inputs is ON, its output is OFF. No current flows to the base, so no current flows through the transistor or the buzzer.)

A transistor used like this is sometimes described as a 'buffer' between the output of the logic gate and the output device.

Extension material

Two more logic gates

Figure 22.11 shows the symbols for two more logic gates; like the AND and OR gate, each has two inputs. Their truth tables are also shown. From the truth tables, you should see that these gates can be described as follows:

a A NAND gate functions like this: its output is OFF if *both* input 1 **and** input 2 are ON.

Figure 22.11 Symbols for **a** NAND and **b** NOR gates, together with their truth tables. The little circle on each symbol is like the circle on the NOT gate symbol (Figure 22.5).

a NAND gate

input 1	input 2	output
0	0	1
1	0	1
0	1	1
1	1	0

b NOR gate

input 1	input 2	output
0	0	1
1	0	0
0	1	0
1	1	0

b A NOR gate functions like this: its output is ON if *neither* input 1 **nor** input 2 is ON.

You could construct a NAND gate by connecting a NOT gate to the output of an AND gate (compare Figures 22.11a and 23.7a); similarly, OR + NOT = NOR.

? Questions

22.1 The output of a NOT gate is connected to the input of another NOT gate.

    a Draw up a truth table for this arrangement.

    b Write a sentence to describe its effect.

22.2 Look at the combination of gates shown in Figure 22.7b, together with its truth table.

    a Draw the same combination of gates, but with the NOT gate connected to the other input of the AND gate.

    b Work out the corresponding truth table.

22.3 **a** Using the correct symbols, show the following: two AND gates with their outputs connected to the inputs of a third AND gate.

    b When will the output of this third gate be ON?

    c Suggest a use for this combination of gates.

22.4 Draw the circuit symbol for a transistor, and label each of the three terminals with its correct name.

22.5 Why is a transistor needed in the circuit shown in Figure 22.10?

22.6 **a** Draw a similar circuit to that shown in Figure 22.10 but in which the transistor turns on an LED when the two inputs are both ON.

    b Suggest a use for such a circuit.

22.2 Input devices

Transducers

Figure 22.12 shows a security light. It comes on at night if it detects anything moving in the vicinity. To do this, it incorporates two sensors: at the bottom is a movement detector, and in the top is a light detector. Sensors like this are also known as transducers.

> A **transducer** is any device that produces a voltage in response to some change in the environment.

Figure 22.12 A security light with two built-in sensors. You can see the movement sensor at the bottom, and there is a light sensor in the top.

Similarly, an output device can be a transducer. A buzzer changes an electrical signal into a sound signal.

The security light comes on if *both* the movement sensor *and* the light sensor tell it to. An AND gate is part of the circuit, to combine the two inputs. The lamp comes on if the AND gate output is ON.

In Chapter 18, we saw some devices that are suitable as input sensors:
- thermistors, whose resistance decreases (usually) over a narrow range of temperatures;
- light-dependent resistors (LDRs), whose resistance decreases when light shines on them;
- variable resistors, whose resistance depends on the position of the control knob or slider.

To this list we can add:
- microphones, which produce a voltage output in response to a sound;
- moisture detectors, whose resistance decreases when they get damp;
- a variety of switches, which respond to pressure, tilting or magnetic fields.

Using a potential divider

In Chapter 18, we also saw how to connect two resistors together to make a potential divider. Such a circuit is often used with one of the above devices to make a sensor that can supply the necessary voltage to a logic gate. Figure 22.13 shows an example of how this can be done using a resistor and a thermistor.

Figure 22.13 Using a thermistor in a potential divider circuit to act as a temperature sensor. This might be used, for example, to switch off a computer if it is in danger of overheating.

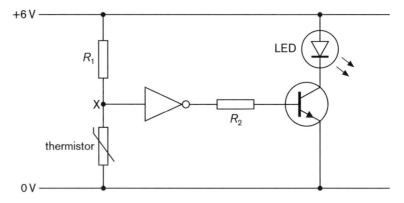

We will see how this circuit could be used to provide a warning light when an electrical appliance overheats. When the thermistor is cold, its resistance is high (much higher than R_1). It therefore has a large share of the supply voltage across it, so the voltage at point X is high. The input to the NOT gate is therefore ON, so its output is OFF. No current flows to the base of the transistor, so it too is OFF. The LED is unlit.

When the thermistor becomes hot, its resistance drops (it becomes much less than R_1). The p.d. across it therefore decreases, and the voltage at X becomes low. The input to the NOT gate is now OFF, so its output is ON. This high voltage causes a current in the resistor R_2 into the base of the transistor, permitting a large current to flow down through the transistor. This current passes through the LED, and it lights up.

Note the reason for using a NOT gate here: As the thermistor warms up, its resistance decreases gradually. The voltage at X therefore decreases slowly. Without the NOT gate, this would produce a gradually increasing current in the transistor, and the LED would light up dimly at first, gradually getting brighter. With the NOT gate present, the LED lights up suddenly at a critical temperature. Replacing the resistor R_1 with a variable resistor would allow the user to set the temperature at which the LED lit up.

Extension material

Using a capacitor

A **capacitor** is a component that can be used in an electric circuit to store charge. We will look at how a capacitor can be charged and discharged (Figure 22.14). Then we will see how a capacitor can be used to provide a time delay in a circuit.

a A capacitor can be thought of as a tiny rechargeable battery in a circuit. If it is connected to a cell (Figure 22.14a), it becomes charged up to the voltage of the cell. A current flows through the resistor R_C and delivers charge to the capacitor C. The bigger the resistor R_C, the smaller the current, and the longer it takes to charge up the capacitor.

b Now, if the capacitor is disconnected from the cell (Figure 22.14b), it retains its stored charge. (It also stores energy, because the cell does work in pushing the charge into the capacitor.)

c If the charged capacitor C is now connected across another resistor R_D, it discharges (Figure 22.14c). The bigger the resistor R_D, the longer it takes to discharge.

Figure 22.15 A time delay circuit. Close the switch to discharge the capacitor and the LED goes off. Open the switch and, after a time delay, the LED lights up again.

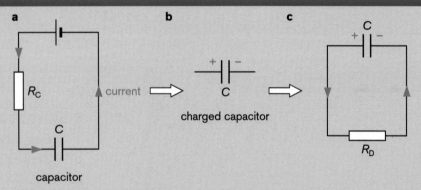

Figure 22.14 a Using a cell to charge a capacitor C through a resistor R_C. **b** The charged capacitor. **c** Discharging the capacitor C through another resistor R_D.

Creating a time delay

Now that we have looked at the basics of how a capacitor can be charged and discharged, we can see how it can work in a circuit that switches a light on after a certain time delay. Figure 22.15 shows the circuit, which is the same as the one shown in Figure 22.13 but with a capacitor C and a resistor R forming a potential divider. There is an additional switch, connected across C.

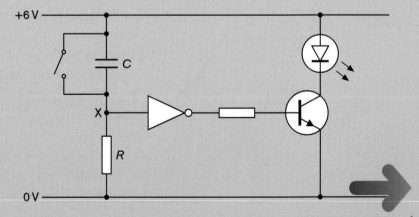

At first, C is uncharged. The p.d. across it is 0 V, so the p.d. across R is 6 V. The p.d. at X is therefore 6 V, and the output of the NOT gate is OFF. The LED is not lit.

Then, a current flows in the potential divider circuit, charging up the capacitor. The p.d. across C increases, so the p.d. across R decreases. (Together, these p.d.s add up to 6 V.) The voltage at X thus gradually decreases. Eventually, this means that the input to the NOT gate goes low (OFF) and its output becomes ON. The LED lights up.

Now we can see the purpose of the switch. Close the switch and the capacitor discharges. The p.d. at X becomes 6 V and the LED is not lit. Open the switch and the capacitor starts to charge up. After a short while, the LED lights up. We have made a time delay circuit. The LED lights up a certain time after the switch is opened. We can alter this time by using different values of R. A high-value resistor allows only a small charging current to flow, and so it takes longer for C to charge up enough for the LED to light up.

> **Questions**
>
> **22.7**   **a**   Which of the following can be used as input devices in electronic control circuits?
>   **b**   What does each respond to?
>   LED,   LDR,   thermistor,   microphone,   buzzer
>
> **22.8**   How could the circuit shown in Figure 22.13 be altered so that the LED goes *off* when the temperature rises to a certain level?
>
> **22.9**   Draw a circuit similar to the one in Figure 22.13 to show how an LED could be made to come on when an LDR detects a fall in light level.
>
> **22.10**   If the resistor R_1 in Figure 22.13 was replaced with one of lower resistance, how would the temperature at which the LED lights up be altered?

22.3   Output devices

We have looked at electronic circuits that make LEDs light up or buzzers sound. There are many different output devices that can be operated by an electronic circuit:

● LEDs and filament lamps;
● buzzers, bells and loudspeakers;
● heaters;
● motors;
● electromagnets and relays.

The processing part of a circuit (usually involving logic gates or transistors) provides a voltage signal to operate these devices.

Unfortunately, the current that it can supply is usually limited, so powerful devices like motors and heaters cannot be operated directly. This is where a relay (see Chapter 20) can prove very useful. Figure 22.16 shows a circuit where a relay is used to switch on a circuit that includes a heater.

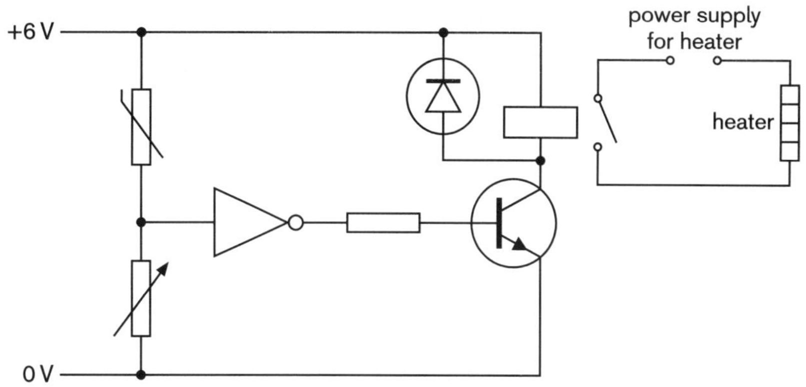

Figure 22.16 This circuit switches on a heater when the temperature falls. Because the heater requires a large current, it is connected in a separate circuit with its own power supply. This circuit is switched on by the relay, which is operated by the electronic circuit.

Note how we can divide the circuit into separate input–processing–output sections, as in Figure 22.4. When the temperature drops, the transistor is switched on (in the same way as we saw in the earlier circuits, Figures 22.13 and 22.15). A current flows through the relay coil, which becomes magnetised. It attracts the switch in the heater circuit, switching on the heater. When the temperature rises again, the relay switches off and the heater circuit is broken.

You will notice in this circuit that a diode is connected across the relay coil. Normally, no current flows through it. However, when the relay coil is switched off, there is a sudden short burst of current, and this escapes (or 'shorts') through the diode. Otherwise it would damage the transistor. This is known as **diode protection**, and is a standard part of any electronic circuit that includes a relay.

Extension material

Feedback in control systems

If your body gets hot, you start to sweat; and that cools you down. If you get cold, you shiver; and that warms up your muscles. These are two aspects of the way in which your body controls its temperature. (They are part of the general process of homeostasis, the way in which organisms maintain themselves in a constant condition.) Your body is using **feedback** to keep its temperature stable. Figure 22.17 shows the principles of feedback.

Nerves in your skin detect its temperature. This information is fed back to the systems that control your metabolism and speed them up if you are too cold, or slow them down if you are too hot. From the diagram, you can see why this is termed 'feedback': the system operates from left to right, but the nerves send a signal from the output back to affect the input. In this case, we have negative feedback, so-called because a decreasing temperature is made to increase, and an increasing temperature is made to decrease.

Electronic systems often use feedback. Many houses use negative feedback to control their heating system – see Figure 22.18. The

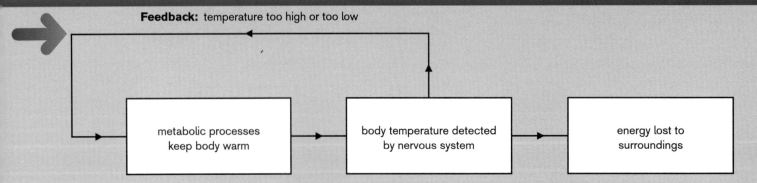

Feedback: temperature too high or too low

Figure 22.17 Feedback in the body's temperature control system. This is an example of negative feedback. If the body temperature goes down, the body reacts to bring it back up. If it goes up, the body reacts to bring it down.

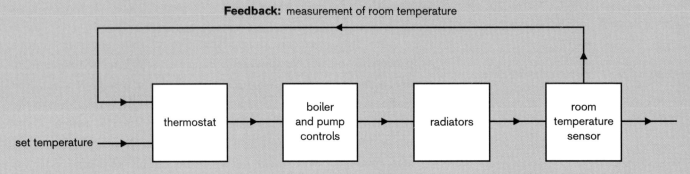

Feedback: measurement of room temperature

Figure 22.18 Feedback in a heating system.

thermostat has a dial to set the desired temperature. The boiler supplies hot water to radiators, which warm the air. If the thermostat detects that the temperature is above the set temperature, it switches off the boiler. If the temperature drops, it switches the boiler back on. The feedback loop carries information about the system output (the temperature of the room) back to the input (the thermostat).

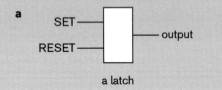

a

a latch

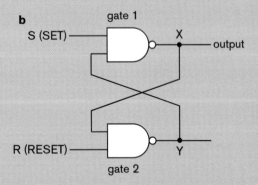

b

gate 1

gate 2

Figure 22.19 **a** A latch switches ON when the SET input becomes ON. It remains ON until the RESET input becomes ON. **b** A latch can be constructed using two NAND gates, with the output of each fed back to the input of the other. This combination of gates is sometimes known as a bistable, because it has two stable states.

Latching

The security lamp shown in Figure 22.12 switches on after dark when it detects someone moving nearby. If the person stops moving, we want the lamp to stay on. To do this, we use an electronic processor called a **latch**. Figure 22.19a shows how this is represented. It has two inputs, labelled SET and RESET.

- When SET becomes ON, the output switches ON.
- Now, even if SET becomes OFF, the output remains ON. It is said to be latched.
- To return the output to OFF, the RESET must become ON.

You can see how this would be useful in a burglar alarm. If a burglar is detected, the latch switches on and sounds the alarm. It doesn't stop sounding until the latch is reset. The same sort of system can be used in many other situations – for example, if the electricity supply to a domestic freezer fails, its contents warm up and a warning light comes on. When power is restored, the freezer cools down again, but the owner still needs to know that the frozen food may have thawed out. A latch keeps the warning light on.

Figure 22.19b shows how a latch can be constructed from two NAND gates. The output of one NAND gate acts as one of the inputs to the other NAND gate – this is feedback at work. (The output of a NAND gate is ON unless both inputs are ON.)

- When S is ON, one of the inputs to gate 1 is ON, and so point X is ON.
- This provides an ON input to gate 2, so its output (point Y) is ON.
- This feeds back to the other input of gate 1, so gate 1 remains ON, even if R goes OFF. The output is latched ON.
- To reset the latch: When R is switched ON, both inputs to gate 2 are ON so its output Y goes OFF.
- Now both inputs to gate 1 are OFF, and its output switches. The latch has been reset.

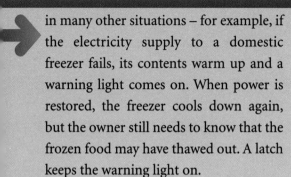

?

Questions

22.11 Name three output devices that produce sound.

22.12 Look at the circuit shown in Figure 22.16. How can the temperature at which the heater switches on be altered?

22.13 Draw a circuit diagram to show how the circuit of Figure 22.16 can be modified for use in a greenhouse. It has to operate a motor that will open the windows when the temperature rises above a certain level.

Summary

- Electronic control systems can be broken down into input, process and output blocks.

- Processing is often carried out by logic gates. The operation of each type of gate is represented by a truth table.

- A transistor may be used as an electronic switch, controlled by logic gates. The transistor allows sufficient current to flow to operate some low-power output devices.

- Input devices such as LDRs and thermistors are often used in potential divider circuits to provide a voltage to a processor. They are transducers – they produce an electrical signal related to some property of the environment.

- *Capacitors store charge (and energy) in electrical circuits. They can be incorporated in electronic systems to provide time delays.*

- Output devices are transducers. They take an electrical signal and produce an output signal of another form (e.g. sound, light).

- *Feedback is used in electronic control systems to produce a stable output. A latch is an example of an electronic device with built-in feedback.*

Further questions

The numbering is continued from the in-chapter questions.

Chapter 17

17.13

When a Perspex rod is rubbed on a woollen cloth, the rod acquires a negative electric charge.

a What type of electric charge does the cloth acquire?

b What can you say about the amounts of charge on the two charged items?

c What force gives rise to the charge on the rod and the cloth?

d Explain how the movement of electrons accounts for the two items becoming charged.

e If you had two Perspex rods charged up in this way, how could you show that they both have electric charges of the same sign?

17.14

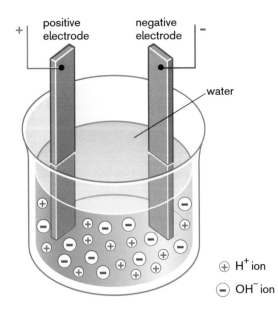

Figure Q17.14

The figure shows how an electric current can be made to flow through water. To make the water conduct better, a small amount of acid is added to it; this increases the number of ions in the water. Hydrogen gas is released at one electrode, and oxygen gas at the other.

a Explain what is meant by an ion.

b The water contains hydrogen ions (H^+) and hydroxyl ions (OH^-). In which direction will each of these ions move in the arrangement shown in the diagram?

c Initially, a current of 0.1 A flows for 5 minutes, and hydrogen gas is collected. State two ways in which the amount of hydrogen gas collected could be increased.

d The process illustrated here is an example of electrolysis. What is meant by the term *electrolysis*?

17.15

a The build-up of positive and negative static electric charges can lead to problems, particularly when sparks result. Give an example of a situation where such a hazard may arise. Explain how the hazard can be avoided.

b The picture on a television screen is produced by a moving beam of electrons. The screen often acquires a negative electric charge, which then attracts particles of dust from the air. Explain how the charged screen can attract uncharged dust particles.

c Static electricity has many uses. In a television tube, the direction of the beam of moving electrons may be controlled using charged plates, as shown in the figure. If the electron beam in the diagram is to be deflected upwards, which of the two plates (upper or lower) must be given a positive charge?

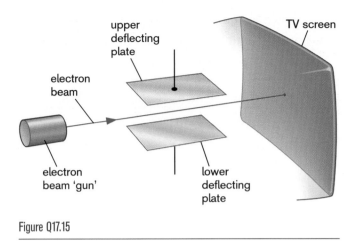

Figure Q17.15

c Explain whether the wire's resistance appears to obey Ohm's law. What other measurements would you need to help you be more certain of your answer?

p.d. across wire (V)	Current through wire (A)
2.1	0.15
4.3	0.32
5.9	0.46
8.0	0.61
10.1	0.73
12.0	0.92

Chapter 18

18.22

A 5 V power supply is connected to two 20 Ω resistors, which are joined together in series.

a Draw a circuit diagram to represent this. Add an arrow to indicate the direction of conventional current flow in the circuit.

b Explain the difference between *conventional current* and *electron flow* in a circuit like this.

c What is the effective resistance of the two resistors?

d Calculate the current that flows from the power supply.

e What is the p.d. across each resistor?

18.23

To determine the resistance R of a resistor, an ammeter and a voltmeter can be used.

a Draw a circuit diagram to show how you would use these instruments, together with a variable power supply, to determine R.

b What quantity does each of these meters measure?

c If the voltmeter gave a reading of 6.5 V and the ammeter gave a reading of 1.25 A, what would be the value of R?

18.24

The current through a metal wire is measured for various values of the p.d. across the wire. The table shows the results obtained.

a Use the results shown in the table to plot a current–voltage graph for the wire.

b From the graph, deduce a value for the wire's resistance.

18.25

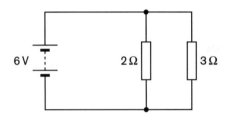

Figure Q18.25

The figure shows an electric circuit in which current flows from a 6 V battery through two resistors.

a Are the resistors connected in series with each other, or in parallel?

b For each resistor, state the p.d. across it.

c The current flowing from the battery is shared between the resistors. Which resistor will have a bigger share of the current?

d Calculate the effective resistance of the two resistors, and the current that flows from the battery.

18.26

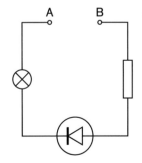

Figure Q18.26

The figure shows a circuit that includes a diode.

a Copy the diagram and add the label 'diode' in the right place.

b Between points A and B, add the symbol for a cell. The cell must be connected in such a way that a current flows through the resistor.

c Add a labelled arrow to show the direction in which electrons move through the resistor when the current flows.

d A diode is a non-ohmic conductor (its resistance does not obey Ohm's law). Sketch a current–voltage characteristic graph for a diode, and explain how this shows that a diode is non-ohmic.

Chapter 19

19.17

Electrical appliances are used to transform electrical energy into other, more useful, forms of energy.

a Into what useful form of energy does a filament lamp transform electrical energy?

b Into what other, less useful, form is electrical energy transformed by the lamp?

c A lamp is labelled '12 V, 36 W'. This indicates that it should be used with a 12 V supply. What other information does the label provide?

d How much electrical energy does the lamp transform in 1 minute?

e The lamp is connected to a 12 V supply. Use the relationship $P = VI$ to calculate the current that flows through it.

f Which of the following fuses would be appropriate to use to protect the lamp?

3 A, 5 A, 13 A

Explain your choice.

19.18

An electric heater is rated at 2 kW. It is switched on for 4 hours.

a How many kilowatt-hours of energy does it transfer to the room in this time?

b If one kilowatt-hour costs 8 pence, how much does it cost to use the heater for 4 hours?

c A student reads her electricity meter each Monday morning for three consecutive Mondays. Her readings are shown in the table. From the readings, calculate the average number of kilowatt-hours of electricity she uses each day during this time.

Date	Meter reading
Monday March 1st	40271
Monday March 8th	40332
Monday March 15th	40411

19.19

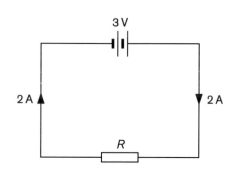

Figure Q19.19

The figure shows a circuit in which a 3 V battery causes a current of 2 A to flow.

a How much charge flows past a point in the circuit each second?

b How much energy does the battery transfer to each coulomb of charge that flows around the circuit?

c How much energy does the current transfer to the resistor each second?

19.20

An electric cooker has an oven and four hotplates. When all are fully switched on, its power rating is 6.0 kW. The cooker runs from a 250 V mains supply.

a Calculate the maximum current that flows through the cooker.

b Explain whether the oven and the hotplates should be connected in series or in parallel with one another. Draw a circuit diagram to support your answer

c Electric cookers are usually connected to a special socket, which is individually wired, using thick cables, to the fuse box. Explain why this is so.

d What is the function of the fuses in the fuse box ('consumer unit') of a domestic electricity supply?

Chapter 20

20.23

An electromagnet is a coil of wire through which a current can be passed.

a State three ways in which the strength of the electromagnet can be increased.

b An electromagnet can be switched on and off. Suggest one situation where this would be an advantage over the constant field of a permanent magnet.

20.24

The figure shows the construction of an electric bell. Put the following sentences in the correct order to explain how the bell operates.

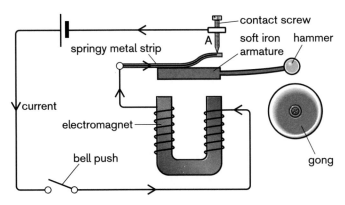

Figure Q20.19

- A current flows through the electromagnet.
- At the same time, the circuit is broken at point A.
- Someone presses the bell push.
- The circuit is completed again at A.
- The electromagnet attracts the iron armature.
- The hammer strikes the gong.
- The springy metal pulls the hammer back.

20.25

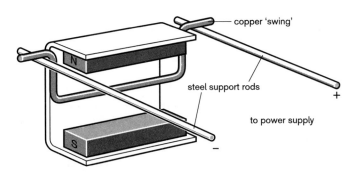

Figure Q20.25

The motor effect is sometimes demonstrated using the apparatus shown in the figure. A current flows through a wire 'swing'. The swing hangs in a magnetic field. When the current is switched on, the swing is pushed out of the field.

a In which direction is the magnetic field between the two magnets?

b In which direction will the swing be pushed?

c What will happen if the connections to the power supply are reversed?

20.26

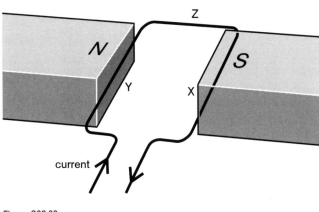

Figure Q20.26

The figure shows a simplified diagram of a d.c. electric motor. The loop of wire is horizontal in a horizontal magnetic field.

a What does the term 'd.c.' indicate?

b In which direction is the force on side X of the wire loop?

c In which direction is the force on side Y of the wire loop?

d Explain how these forces cause the loop to rotate.

e What can you say about the force on side Z?

20.27

a What desired energy transformation takes place in an electric motor?

b What undesired energy transformation also takes place in an electric motor?

c A d.c. electric motor is essentially a current-carrying coil in a magnetic field. State four ways in which the torque provided by a d.c. motor can be increased.

Chapter 21

21.17

A student holds a bent piece of wire in a horizontal magnetic field, as shown in the figure. She moves the wire downwards through the field, and then upwards.

a Explain why a p.d. is induced between the ends of the wire.

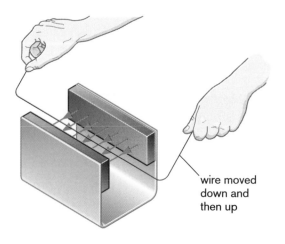

wire moved down and then up

Figure Q21.17

b How will the p.d. differ between moving the wire downwards and moving it upwards.

c Suggest how she could move the wire to induce a bigger p.d.

d She now moves the wire horizontally from side to side in the magnetic field. Will a p.d. be induced? Give a reason to support your answer.

21.18

In a simple d.c. generator, a coil rotates in the magnetic field provided by permanent magnets.

a Suggest two ways in which the coil could be altered to induce a bigger p.d.

b Suggest two other ways in which the p.d. could be increased.

c The current flows into and out of a d.c. generator via brushes pressing on a split-ring commutator. What replaces the commutator in an a.c. generator?

d Describe the essential difference between alternating current and direct current. Include a diagram to support your answer.

21.19

Electrical power is often transmitted over long distances in high-voltage power lines (cables). Transformers are used to increase the voltage provided by the power station, and to reduce the voltage for the final user.

a Explain why, if the same power were transmitted at a lower voltage, the cables would have to be thicker.

b A transformer has 10 turns of wire on its primary coil, and 200 turns on its secondary coil. If the p.d. across the primary coil is 3 V a.c., what will be the p.d. across the secondary? Assume that there are no power losses in the transformer.

c How could the same transformer be used as a step-down transformer?

Chapter 22

22.14

Logic gates are often used in electronic control circuits. The operation of a logic gate can be represented by a truth table.

a What logic gate is represented by the truth table shown in the first diagram? Write a sentence to describe its operation.

0 = OFF

1 = ON

input 1	input 2	output
0	0	0
1	0	0
0	1	0
1	1	1

Figure Q22.14a

b The output of a gate called an 'exclusive OR' gate is ON if just one of its two inputs is ON; otherwise it is OFF. Draw a truth table to represent this.

c What will be the output of the combination of gates shown in the second diagram if both inputs are ON?

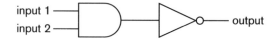

Figure Q22.14c

22.15

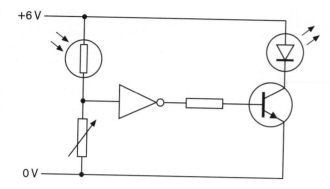

Figure Q22.15

The figure shows an electronic control circuit.

a Name the two components that form the potential divider.

b What type of logic gate is being used here?

c Copy the circuit symbol for the transistor and label the three terminals with their appropriate names.

d Why is it necessary to include a transistor in this circuit?

e What is the function of this circuit?

f It is desired to alter the circuit so that it controls a mains-powered lamp rather than an LED. A relay must be incorporated as part of the circuit. Draw a complete circuit diagram to show how the control circuit must be modified to achieve this.

Atoms, nuclei and electrons

Topics in this chapter

◆ the size of atoms

◆ evidence for the existence of electrons

◆ cathode rays

◆ models of the atom

◆ Rutherford's alpha scattering experiment

◆ protons, neutrons and electrons

◆ electrons and quarks as fundamental particles

◆ elements and isotopes

You probably have the idea in your head that 'all matter is made of atoms' – and that is more or less true. Most of the matter around you – buildings, the air, your body, this book – is made of tiny atoms, far too small to be seen individually. You have probably also seen an image of an atom like the one shown on the coin in Figure 23.1. This is a Greek 10-drachma coin, and on the other side it shows Democritus, the Greek philosopher who is usually credited with first suggesting the idea that matter was made of tiny, indivisible particles called 'atoms'.

If you look at the image of the atom, you will see that it shows a tiny nucleus at the centre, with three electrons travelling around it along circular paths. (The paths are shown as ellipses because of the perspective view.) This image of an atom is like a tiny solar system, and it is not how Democritus would have pictured an atom. He believed that atoms were the smallest building blocks of matter, so they could not be divided into anything smaller; the word 'a-tom' means 'not-divisible'.

Figure 23.1 One side of this Greek 10-drachma coin shows Democritus, a philosopher who lived almost 2500 years ago. According to his atomic theory, matter is made up of vast numbers of tiny particles, which come together in different combinations to make the things we see around us. The reverse side of the coin shows a modern image of a single atom. Democritus would not have imagined that an atom could be subdivided into a nucleus and electrons.

The mini-solar-system picture of the atom was developed in the early years of the twentieth century, and it is still quite a useful model. Today, most scientists would picture an atom rather differently. This chapter looks at some of what we know about atoms, and how the scientific picture of atoms has been changed in the centuries since Democritus.

23.1 The size of atoms

At one time, physics textbooks would say that atoms are very tiny, too tiny to be seen. Certainly, a single atom is too small to be seen using a conventional light (optical) microscope. But technology has made great advances, and now there is more than one kind of microscope that can be used to show individual atoms. Figure 23.2 shows a photograph made using a scanning tunnelling microscope. The picture shows carbon atoms on the surface of a piece of graphite (the material from which pencil leads are made). You can see that the atoms are arranged in a regular hexagonal pattern. Each individual atom is about 0.000 000 000 16 m across. A scanning tunnelling microscope can achieve a magnification of about 10 000 000 000. A good light microscope can only magnify by about 1000 times.

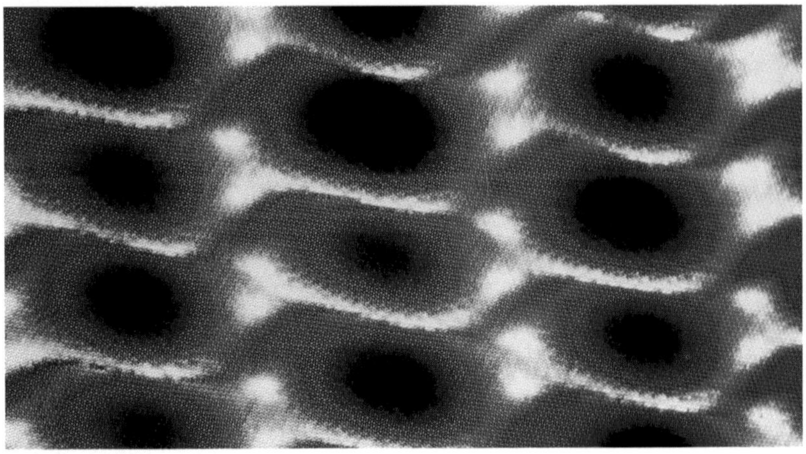

Figure 23.2 Carbon atoms seen using a scanning tunnelling microscope. This microscope uses a fine probe to track across the sample, just above the surface. A small electric current flows between the probe and the sample – the closer the sample, the bigger the current. A computer monitors the current and produces a picture of the surface. The atoms have been 'coloured in' by the computer. The microscope only 'sees' in black and white, because you need to use visible light to see the colours of things.

Knowing the diameter of a single carbon atom, you can work out how many fit into one metre. Picture a long line of carbon atoms, lying side by side, and stretching 1 m. You can calculate how many there are by calculating how many times the diameter fits into 1 m:

diameter of one atom = 0.000 000 000 16 m = 1.6×10^{-10} m

number of atoms per metre = $\dfrac{1\,\text{m}}{1.6 \times 10^{-10}\,\text{m}}$ = 6 000 000 000

So 6 000 000 000 (6×10^9) atoms fit into 1 m.

Atoms come in different sizes, though the diameter of the biggest is only about six times as great as the diameter of the smallest. Table 23.1 shows some approximate values. (The values can only be approximate because they depend on the method used to measure them.)

Atom	Diameter (m)
hydrogen	0.8×10^{-10}
carbon	1.6×10^{-10}
copper	2.3×10^{-10}
sodium	3.8×10^{-10}
potassium	4.7×10^{-10}

Table 23.1 Diameters of some atoms.

? **Questions**

23.1 If 6 000 000 000 carbon atoms fit into 1 m, how many fit into 1 mm?

23.2 For each of the atoms in Table 23.1 on page 367, calculate how many would fit side by side into 1 m.

23.2 Electrons

Atoms are tiny, and it wasn't until 1980 that the first photograph showing individual atoms (like the photo in Figure 23.2) was obtained. For several decades before this, most scientists had had no doubt that atoms existed – ideas about atoms helped to explain many phenomena, including much of chemistry. So we don't insist on having photographic proof to know that something exists.

Electrons are much tinier than atoms – their mass is about one two-thousandth of the mass of the lightest atom. We don't know how big an electron is – indeed, they may have no size at all, which is very hard to imagine. Nor do we have any pictures of individual electrons. But scientists have been sure of their existence ever since their discovery by the British physicist J. J. Thomson in 1897 – see Figure 23.3. His work is an interesting example of how a particle can be discovered without actually being seen, and this throws some light on the work of today's scientists, who use giant accelerators in an attempt to discover other fundamental particles.

Figure 23.3 Joseph John (J. J.) Thomson, discoverer of the electron. Here he is demonstrating the evacuated glass tube that he used in his investigations of cathode rays. His work was only possible because of the invention of the vacuum pump, which removed almost all of the air from inside the tube.

In the 1890s, scientists were investigating how an electric current flows through a gas. A glass tube was fitted with two electrodes, the cathode (negative) and the anode (positive). When the electrodes were connected to a power supply, the gas in the tube glowed. Coloured rays appeared to be streaming out from the cathode, and it was these 'cathode rays' that J. J. Thomson set about studying.

Thomson's evacuated tube is shown in Figure 23.4. At the right is the heated cathode. When there was a sufficiently high voltage between the two electrodes, he knew that cathode rays would be emitted by the cathode and travel towards the anode. A clever part of the design is the hole in the anode through which the rays passed; this was how Thomson knew that the rays were coming from the cathode rather than the anode. The rays travelled across the space beyond the anode and struck the fluorescent screen at the end of the tube. The screen glowed, showing where it was hit by the rays.

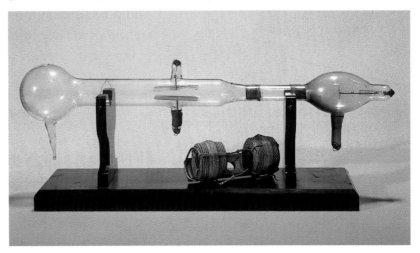

Figure 23.4 J. J. Thomson's tube for deflecting cathode rays. The beam of cathode rays (electrons) passed through a hole in the anode, so that Thomson could experiment with them in the space beyond. The rays were invisible in the tube, but their presence was detected when they made the fluorescent screen glow.

Thomson called his tube a 'deflection tube', because two metal plates beyond the anode could be used to deflect the cathode rays. With the top plate connected to a positive voltage, the rays were deflected upwards. With the top plate negative, they were deflected downwards. Thomson found that he could deflect the rays using a magnetic field, too. What was he to make of these results?

- The rays came from the cathode, which is negative; they were attracted by a positively charged plate and repelled by a negatively charged plate. He deduced that the rays carried negative charge.
- The rays travelled in a straight line through the tube; they weren't pulled down by gravity. They must have been moving very fast.
- Thomson's calculations showed that the rays were moving slower than the speed of light. They were probably streams of tiny particles, rather than a form of radiation. (We now think that charge cannot exist alone without mass.)
- The rays were easily deflected by electric and magnetic fields. They must be very light. In fact, Thomson showed that their mass was less than one thousandth of the mass of a hydrogen atom.
- When the rays were deflected, they did not split up or broaden out into a wider beam. This showed that they were made up of many identical particles all travelling at the same speed.

This was quite a lot to deduce from one experiment! For the first time, a particle lighter than an atom had been identified – the electron. Thomson had solved the mystery of the 'cathode rays'.

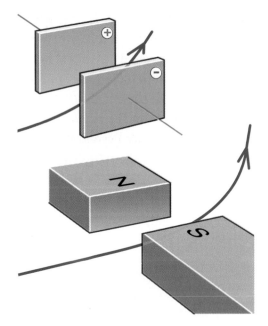

Figure 23.5 **a** A beam of electrons is deflected as it passes between two charged plates. Electrons are negatively charged, so the beam is attracted towards the positive plate and repelled by the negative one. **b** An electron beam is also deflected by a magnetic field. The left-hand rule shows the direction in which it is deflected.

Figure 23.6 A television tube: the electron gun produces a beam of electrons, which is then controlled by magnetic fields. Compare the design of this tube with the deflection tube (Figure 23.4), which J. J. Thomson used to investigate cathode rays. A TV tube is still sometimes referred to as a 'cathode ray tube'.

Electron beams

A beam of electrons can be deflected by electric and magnetic fields. In Thomson's experiment, he used the two metal plates to deflect the beam using an electric field. As shown in Figure 23.5a, the beam is attracted towards a positively charged plate and repelled by a negatively charged one. This is simply an example of static electricity at work (see Chapter 17). Electrons have negative charge and are attracted by an opposite, positive charge.

Figure 23.5b shows an electron beam being deflected by a magnetic field. A beam of electrons is, in effect, an electric current. The electrons are shown moving from left to right; because a current is a flow of positive charge, we say that a current is flowing from right to left. An electric current is pushed by a magnetic field; this is the motor effect (see Chapter 20). We can use the left-hand rule to check the direction in which the current is pushed – in this case, upwards.

TV tubes and particle accelerators

J. J. Thomson's deflection tube was important because it led to the discovery of the electron. But it had another great importance. It led to the invention of many other devices that made use of beams of electrons travelling through a vacuum. One example is the television tube (Figure 23.6), used in TV sets and computer monitors. We shall now look at how a 'black-and-white' television tube works.

At the back on the right is the electron gun. The cathode is connected to a negative voltage. It is made of a metal in which the electrons are only weakly bound. When it is heated, these electrons gain energy and can escape from the cathode. (This process is called **thermionic emission**.) When you switch on a TV set, you usually have to wait a few seconds for the cathode to heat up (unless you have left it on standby). The electrons are accelerated by the attractive force of the anode, so that they go faster and faster as they approach it. Then they pass through the hole in the anode and travel at a steady speed in the space beyond. Because electrons are charged particles, they constitute an electric current. Their charge is negative, so the conventional current is in the opposite direction to the movement of the electrons.

To make a picture on the screen, the beam must scan across it in a regular pattern. This is usually done using magnetic fields provided by the electromagnetic coils attached to the outside of the tube. One pair of coils moves the beam from side to side; the other pair moves it up and down, so that it can be directed to any point on the screen. To make bright and dark areas of the picture, the intensity of the beam is increased and decreased.

The main problem with a television tube like this is its size. It is usually 20 or 30 cm from the back, where the electron gun is, to the screen at the front, so television sets and computer monitors are rather bulky. Flat-screen televisions have a different way of producing pictures using a liquid-crystal display, like the displays used in lap-top computers. These are more portable, but they are generally not very bright and you need to sit directly in front to see a clear picture.

A television tube is a common example of a particle accelerator. Today, the biggest particle accelerators are used by physicists investigating the fundamental particles of Nature and the forces that hold them together. These accelerators may be several kilometres in length and cost billions of euros. Many more accelerators are used for more routine purposes: in medicine, where they produce radiation for diagnosing and treating illnesses; and in industry, where the radiation they produce is used to investigate the structures of materials.

Cathode ray oscilloscope

A cathode ray oscilloscope has a vacuum tube similar to a television tube, but the electron beam is deflected by electric fields rather than magnetic fields. You have probably seen varying voltages displayed on an oscilloscope screen, for example to show the wave-like behaviour of sound. The oscilloscope looks complicated, with many controls, but its principle is simple: An electron beam produces a dot on the screen; the dot is moved steadily across the screen by one voltage, while another voltage moves it up and down.

Figure 23.7 shows the construction of an oscilloscope. An electron gun produces a focused beam of electrons, just as in a television tube. The beam is deflected when it passes between two pairs of metal plates. The beam is moved up and down by the Y plates, and from side to side by the X plates.

- To move the beam steadily across the screen, an increasing voltage is applied to the X plates. This is negative at first, but becomes positive.
- The varying voltage is applied to the Y plates. A positive voltage attracts the beam upwards, so that the spot moves up the screen; a negative voltage moves the spot downwards.

Fig 23.7 The construction of a cathode ray oscilloscope. An electron beam is produced by an electron gun; the beam is deflected by the positive and negative charges on the X and Y plates.

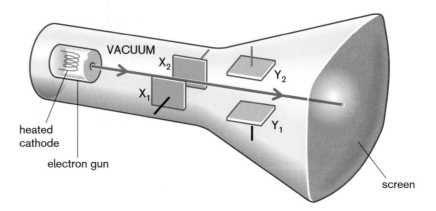

You can think of an oscilloscope as a kind of voltmeter; the spot on the screen is deflected more by bigger voltages. It can show a voltage that is rapidly varying; a meter with a needle and scale would not be able to move quickly enough.

> ### Questions
>
> **23.3** **a** Of what particles are cathode rays made?
> **b** Why are they called *cathode* rays?
>
> **23.4** What is meant by thermionic emission?
>
> **23.5** How did J. J. Thomson know that the particles he had observed were all of the same mass and moving at the same speed?
>
> **23.6** An electron beam moves from the cathode to the anode in a television tube. In which direction does the conventional current flow?
>
> **23.7** Why do electrons accelerate as they move from the cathode towards the anode in a vacuum tube?
>
> **23.8** Look at the diagram of the cathode ray oscilloscope (Figure 23.7).
> **a** If plates X_1 and Y_1 have a negative charge, and plates X_2 and Y_2 have a positive charge, in which direction will the electron beam be deflected?
> **b** If the spot appears at the centre of the bottom of the screen, what can you say about the charges on the plates?

23.3 Inside atoms

J. J. Thomson realised that electrons were much smaller than atoms, at least one thousand times lighter than a hydrogen atom. (Now we can be more accurate and say that the mass of an electron is about 1/1836 of that of a hydrogen atom.) He guessed, correctly, that electrons were part of atoms. He even suggested that atoms were made up entirely of

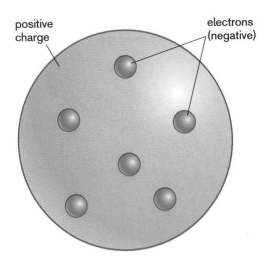

Figure 23.8 The plum pudding model of an atom. Electrons form the plums stuck in a positively charged, spherical pudding.

electrons, spinning in such a way that they stuck together. This was not a very successful model.

Other scientists argued that, since electrons have negative charge, there must be other particles in an atom with an equal amount of positive charge, so that an atom has no overall charge – it is neutral. Since electrons have very little mass, the positive charge must also account for most of the mass of the atom. Figure 23.8 shows a model that illustrates this. The atom is formed from a sphere of positively charged matter with tiny, negatively charged electrons embedded in it. This is the famous 'plum pudding model', where the electrons are the plums in the positively charged pudding. You can see that this is a different model from the 'solar system' model we described earlier (Figure 23.1).

So why do we no longer think that atoms are like plum puddings? The answer comes from some work done by the New Zealander Ernest Rutherford and his colleagues, about ten years after Thomson's discovery of the electron.

Radioactivity had been discovered at about the same time as the electron. Rutherford understood that the radiation coming from radioactive substances – alpha, beta and gamma radiation – was a result of changes happening in individual atoms. Tiny particles or rays were being spat out from inside atoms, and he thought that he could use this radiation to investigate other atoms. (You will find more about radioactivity and the different types of radiation in Chapter 24.) Rutherford decided to use alpha radiation to probe the atoms in a sample of gold.

Alpha radiation consists of tiny, fast-moving positively charged particles. Rutherford's colleagues Geiger and Marsden set up an experiment (Figure 23.9) in which alpha radiation was directed at a thin gold foil. They expected the alpha particles to be deflected as they passed through the foil, because their paths would be affected by the positive and negative charges of the atoms. (You might be surprised to think of anything passing though something as solid as gold. Rutherford pictured the alpha particles as tiny bullets, fired through a wall of plum puddings.)

Everyone was surprised by the results of this experiment. Geiger and Marsden found that most of the alpha particles passed straight through the gold foil, scarcely deflected; however, a very few bounced back towards the source of the radiation. It was as if there was something very hard in the gold foil – like a ball-bearing buried inside the plum pudding. What was going on?

Rutherford realised that the answer was to do with static electricity. Alpha particles are charged. If they are repelled back from the gold foil, it must be by another 'like' charge. If only a few were repelled, it was because the charge of the gold atoms was concentrated in a tiny space within each atom. Most alpha particles passed straight through because they never went near this concentration of charge – see Figure

Figure 23.9 The experiment to show alpha particle scattering by a gold foil, also known as Rutherford scattering. Alpha particles from the source on the left strike the gold foil. Most pass straight through but a few – about one in 8000 – are scattered back towards the source.

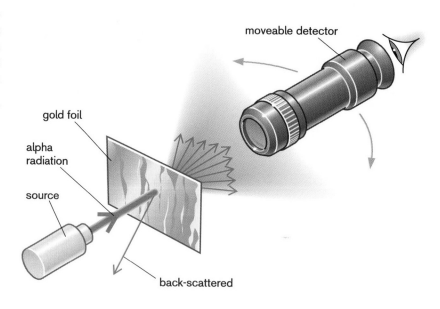

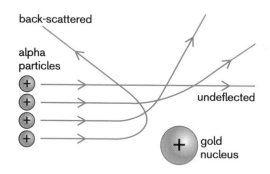

Figure 23.10 Most alpha particles pass straight through the gold foil, because they do not pass close to the atomic nucleus. Only those which score a 'direct hit' are reflected straight back.

23.10. This speck of concentrated charge, at the heart of every atom, is what we now call the atom's **nucleus**.

In later years, Rutherford often spoke of the surprising results of the alpha scattering experiment. He said:

'It was quite the most incredible event that ever happened to me in my life. It was as if you fired a fifteen-inch artillery shell at a piece of tissue paper and it came back and hit you.'

A sense of scale

Rutherford was able to analyse the results from Geiger and Marsden's experiment to work out just how big the nucleus of a gold atom was. An atom is small – about 10^{-10} m across – but its nucleus is very much smaller – about 10^{-15} m in diameter. Around the nucleus travel the electrons. They are even tinier than the nucleus; and the rest of the atom is simply empty space.

It is hard to imagine these relative sizes. Try picturing a glass marble about 1 cm in diameter, placed at the centre of the Millennium Dome, in London, to represent the nucleus of an atom. Then the electrons are like tiny grains of dust, orbiting the nucleus at different distances, right out to the edge of the Dome.

It's even harder to imagine, when you stub your toe on a rock, that the atoms of the rock (and your toe) are almost entirely empty space!

A successful model

Rutherford's picture of the atom rapidly gained acceptance among scientists. It gave a clear explanation of the alpha scattering experiment, and further tests with other metals confirmed Rutherford's ideas.

Thomson had the idea that the atom was made of many electrons spinning in such a way that they stuck together. This was a rather unclear model, and it was swept away by Rutherford's simpler picture.

Rutherford's model also allowed scientists to think about other questions. Chemists wanted to know how atoms bonded together. Physicists wanted to understand why some atoms are unstable and emit radiation. These were all questions to which we now have good answers, and Rutherford's discovery of the atomic nucleus did a lot to help answer them.

Today, practising scientists have rather different ideas about atoms. They want to calculate many different quantities, and so models of the atom are much more mathematical. Quantum theory, developed not long after Rutherford's work, made the atom seem like a much fuzzier thing, not a collection of little spheres orbiting around each other. However, the important thing about a model is that it should help us to understand things better, and help us to make new predictions, and Rutherford's model of the nuclear atom has certainly done that.

? Questions

23.9 Explain why, in Geiger and Marsden's experiment, some alpha particles were 'back–scattered' when they came near the nucleus of a gold atom.

23.10 Explain why only a very few alpha particles were back–scattered.

23.11 In the plum pudding model of the atom: **a** what are the plums; and **b** what is the pudding?

23.12 In the 'solar system' model of the atom, what force holds the electrons in their orbits around the nucleus?

23.4 Protons, neutrons and electrons

Ernest Rutherford's discovery of the atomic nucleus gave rise to the 'solar system' model of the atom, described earlier. In this model, the negatively charged electrons orbit a positively charged nucleus. The electrons are attracted to the nucleus (because of its opposite charge), but their speed prevents them from falling into it.

Nowadays we know that the nucleus is made up of two types of particle, protons and neutrons. The protons carry the positive charge of the nucleus, while the neutrons are neutral. Otherwise, these two particles have similar masses, and they account for most of the mass of the atom (because electrons are so light). Together, protons and neutrons are known as **nucleons**.

Table 23.2 summarises this information about the masses and charges of these three sub-atomic particles.

Protons and neutrons are very different from electrons.

- The electron is a **fundamental particle**; most physicists believe that it cannot be sub-divided into smaller particles.
- Protons and neutrons are each made of three fundamental particles, called **quarks**.

Particle accelerators have been used to probe protons and neutrons, and the results show that they do indeed have some structure inside them, but so far no-one has been able to identify an individual , isolated quark. It seems that they always go around in twos and threes, bound together to form more massive particles.

Particle	Position	Charge (C)	Relative charge	Mass (kg)	Relative mass
proton	in nucleus	$+1.6 \times 10^{-19}$	$+1$	1.67×10^{-27}	1
neutron	in nucleus	0	0	1.67×10^{-27}	1
electron	orbiting nucleus	-1.6×10^{-19}	-1	9.11×10^{-31}	1/1836 (approx 0)

Table 23.2 Charges and masses of the three sub–atomic particles. The columns headed 'Relative charge' and 'Relative mass' give the charge and mass of each particle compared to that of a proton. It is much easier to remember these values, rather than the values in coulombs (C) and kilograms (kg).

Atoms and elements

Once the particles that make up atoms were identified, it was much easier to understand the Periodic Table of the elements (Figure 23.11). This shows the elements in order, starting with the lightest (hydrogen, then helium) and working up to the heaviest. In fact, it is not the *masses* of the atoms that determine the order in which they appear, but the *number of protons* in each atom. Every atom of hydrogen has one proton in its nucleus, so hydrogen is element number 1. Every helium atom has two protons, so helium is element number 2, and so on.

Each element has its own symbol, such as H for hydrogen. Sometimes an atom is represented by this symbol, with two numbers alongside:

$$^4_2\text{He}$$

This represents an atom of helium. The numbers tell us that there are two protons in the nucleus of the atom, and a total of four nucleons. (From this, it is simple to work out that there must be two neutrons in the nucleus.)

In general, we can represent the nucleus of an atom of element E like this:

$$^A_Z\text{E}$$

Z is the **proton number** – the number of protons in the nucleus, also known as the atomic number.

A is the **nucleon number** – the number of nucleons (protons and neutrons) in the nucleus, also known as the mass number.

H₁																	He₂

H 1																	He 2
Li 3	Be 4											B 5	C 6	N 7	O 8	F 9	Ne 10
Na 11	Mg 12											Al 13	Si 14	P 15	S 16	Cl 17	Ar 18
K 19	Ca 20	Sc 21	Ti 22	V 23	Cr 24	Mn 25	Fe 26	Co 27	Ni 28	Cu 29	Zn 30	Ga 31	Ge 32	As 33	Se 34	Br 35	Kr 36
Rb 37	Sr 38	Y 39	Zr 40	Nb 41	Mo 42	Tc 43	Ru 44	Rh 45	Pd 46	Ag 47	Cd 48	In 49	Sn 50	Sb 51	Te 52	I 53	Xe 54
Cs 55	Ba 56	La to Lu 72	Hf 72	Ta 73	W 74	Re 75	Os 76	Ir 77	Pt 78	Au 79	Hg 80	Tl 81	Pb 82	Bi 83	Po 84	At 85	Rn 86
Fr 87	Ra 88	Ac to Lr															

La 57	Ce 58	Pr 59	Nd 60	Pm 61	Sm 62	Eu 63	Gd 64	Tb 65	Dy 66	Ho 67	Er 68	Tm 69	Yb 70	Lu 71
Ac 89	Th 90	Pa 91	U 92	Np 93	Pu 94	Am 95	Cm 96	Bk 97	Cf 98	Es 99	Fm 100	Md 101	No 102	Lr 103

Figure 23.11 The Periodic Table of the elements is a way of organising what we know about the different elements, based on their atomic structures. They are arranged in order according to their atomic number (the number of protons in the nucleus of an atom of the element).

A neutral atom of element E will also have Z electrons orbiting the nucleus. From Z and A you can work out a third number:

N is the **neutron number** – the number of neutrons in the nucleus.

So we have

proton number + neutron number = nucleon number
$$Z + N = A$$

Elements and isotopes

It is the proton number Z that tells us to which element an atom belongs. For example, a small atom with just two protons in its nucleus ($Z = 2$) is a helium atom; a much bigger atom with 92 protons in its nucleus is a uranium atom, because uranium is element 92.

The atoms of all elements exist in more than one form. For example, Table 23.3 shows three types of hydrogen atom. Each has just one proton in its nucleus, but they have different numbers of neutrons (zero, one and two). They are described as different **isotopes** of hydrogen.

Isotopes of an element have the same number of protons but different numbers of neutrons in their nuclei.

Figure 23.11 shows atoms of two isotopes of helium, $^4_2$He (the commonest isotope), and $^3_2$He (a lighter and much rarer isotope).

Table 23.3 Three isotopes of hydrogen, and two isotopes of uranium.

Symbol for isotope	Proton number, Z	Neutron number, N	Nucleon number, A
$^{1}_{1}\text{H}$	1	0	1
$^{2}_{1}\text{H}$	1	1	2
$^{3}_{1}\text{H}$	1	2	3
$^{235}_{92}\text{U}$	92	143	235
$^{238}_{92}\text{U}$	92	146	238

Figure 23.12 These drawings represent two isotopes of helium. Each has two protons in the nucleus and two electrons orbiting it, but the lighter isotope $^{3}_{2}\text{He}$ has only one neutron.

Figure 23.13 **a** An atom represented as a miniature solar system. Electrons with more energy orbit the nucleus at a greater distance. **b** An atom shown with its electrons smeared out into 'orbitals', rather than orbits. Chemists find this a useful way of working out how atoms combine to form molecules. **c** Two hydrogen atoms, bonded together to form a hydrogen molecule. The electron of one atom is represented by a dot, and that of the other by a cross. Of course, the two electrons are identical, but showing them differently helps to show what is going on when the atoms join together.

Picturing atoms

We started this chapter with a discussion of the existence of atoms. Today we know for sure that atoms exist, and we know a lot about the sub-atomic particles of which they are made. But we can't really say that we know 'what atoms look like'. We may think of protons, neutrons and electrons as tiny, hard spheres, like the ones shown in Figure 23.12. But we don't think that they really look like that – and they certainly aren't red, black, blue, orange, green or any other colour!

We have many different ways of picturing atoms, and none of them is 'correct'. Three different pictures are shown in Figure 23.13. Each has its merits and shows some aspects of what an atom is like. However, atoms are part of a world that we can only explore indirectly, probing it with radiation (as Rutherford did), and we shouldn't expect this world to be just a miniature version of the everyday, large–scale world that we inhabit.

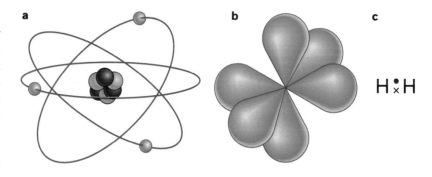

? Questions

23.13 **a** Which particles make up the nucleus of an atom?

b Which particles orbit around the nucleus?

23.14 An atom of a particular isotope of oxygen is written $^{17}_{8}O$.

a What is its nucleon number?

b What are its proton number and neutron number?

23.15 An atom of a particular isotope of lead (symbol Pb) contains 82 protons and 128 neutrons. Write down the symbol for this atom.

23.16 How many protons, neutrons and electrons are there in a neutral atom of silver, $^{107}_{47}Ag$?

23.17 **a** What is the same for the atoms of two different isotopes of an element?

b What is different for them?

23.18 How many times greater is the mass of a proton than the mass of an electron?

Summary

♦ The diameter of an atom is of the order of 10^{-10} m.

♦ 'Cathode rays' are beams of electrons. Electrostatic attraction drags them away from a heated cathode. The electrons are produced by thermionic emission.

♦ Electrons are negatively charged with a mass much smaller than that of an atom.

♦ The direction of an electron beam can be changed using magnetic or electric fields.

♦ In Rutherford's alpha particle scattering experiment, fast-moving alpha particles were deflected as they passed through a gold foil. Some were back-scattered, which showed that the mass and charge of the atom was concentrated in a tiny space at the centre of the atom.

♦ Negatively charged electrons orbit the positively charged nucleus, held in their orbits by the electrostatic attraction between them.

♦ Atoms of isotopes of an element have the same number of protons in their nuclei, but different numbers of neutrons.

♦ Nucleons are made of quarks; electrons and quarks are thought to be fundamental (indivisible) particles.

♦ The nucleus of an atom of element E can be represented as $^{A}_{Z}E$, where Z is the proton number and A is the nucleon number.

Radioactivity

Topics in this chapter

◆ background and artificial radiation

◆ detecting radiation

◆ the nature of alpha, beta and gamma radiation

◆ ionisation

◆ using radioactive substances

◆ radioactive decay and half-life

ℯ nuclear equations to represent decay

ℯ patterns of stability and instability in the N–Z plot

Radioactivity is a serious topic. You can tell that because people make lots of jokes about it.

'If you go on a school visit to a nuclear power station, you will come back with two heads.'

'If you have radiation treatment in hospital, you will glow in the dark.'

As with many jokes, there is a small element of truth here, and a great deal of fear of the unknown.

When radioactivity was first discovered, people became very excited by it. Some doctors claimed that it had great health-promoting effects. They sold radioactive water, and added radioactive substances to chocolate, bread and toothpaste (Figure 24.1). There were radioactive cures for baldness, and contraceptive cream containing radium. This attitude still lingers on today, with some alpine spas offering residents the chance to breathe radioactive air in old mine tunnels!

Figure 24.1 In the 1930s, you could buy bulbs of radioactive radon gas to dissolve in your drinking water. An American called Ethan Byers drank a bottle a day for five years – he died of cancer of the jaw.

Figure 24.2 An atomic bomb being tested. Only two atomic bombs have been used in warfare, but many others have been tested. Such tests have released large quantities of radioactive materials into the environment. Their main impact has been on the power struggles between different countries and blocs around the world.

Our use of radioactive substances, particularly by the most technologically advanced countries, has had some very damaging effects that stick in people's imaginations. The dropping of atomic bombs on the Japanese cities of Hiroshima and Nagasaki at the end of the Second World War is one example (Figure 24.2). The positive side of our use of radioactive materials has been less obvious, but today millions of people who would once have died of cancer are now alive thanks to scanning (Figure 24.3) and radiation therapy.

Radioactive materials produce radiation. We have eyes to see light, and we can detect infrared radiation with our skin, but we have no organ for detecting the radiation from radioactive materials which is all around us. We make little use of radioactive materials in our everyday lives, so they remain unfamiliar to us. We learn about them from a teacher who handles radioactive samples with great care. It is not surprising that we are cautious, if not downright scared, when the topic of radioactivity is raised.

In this chapter, we will look at radioactive substances and the radiation they produce, and discuss how they can be used safely.

24.1 Radioactivity all around

We need to distinguish between two things: **radioactive substances**, and the **radiation** that they give out. Many naturally occurring substances are radioactive; usually these are not very concentrated, so that they don't cause a problem. There are two ways in which radioactive substances can cause us problems.

- If a radioactive substance gets inside us, its radiation can harm us – we have been **contaminated**.
- If the radiation they produce hits our bodies, we say that we have received a dose of radiation – we have been **irradiated**.

In fact, we are exposed to low levels of radiation all the time; this is known as **background radiation**. In addition, we may be exposed to radiation from artificial sources, such as the radiation we receive if we have a medical X-ray.

Figure 24.4 shows the different sources that contribute to the average dose of radiation received by people in the United Kingdom. It is divided into natural background radiation (about 87%) and radiation from artificial sources (about 13%). We will look at these different sources in turn.

Sources of background radiation

- Air is radioactive. It contains a radioactive gas called radon, which seeps up to the Earth's surface from radioactive rocks underground. Because we breathe in air all the time, we are exposed to radiation from this substance. This contributes about half of our annual exposure. (This varies widely from one part of the country to

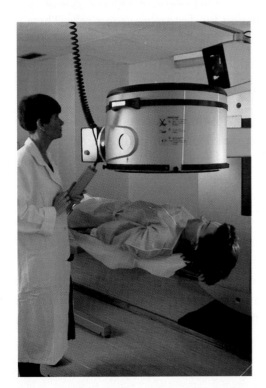

Figure 24.3 The positive side of radioactivity. Here, a patient is being prepared for a scan to check for cancer.

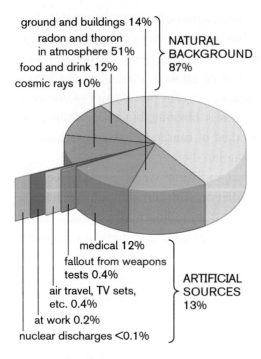

ground and buildings 14%
radon and thoron
in atmosphere 51%
food and drink 12%
cosmic rays 10%

NATURAL
BACKGROUND
87%

medical 12%
fallout from weapons
tests 0.4%
air travel, TV sets,
etc. 0.4%
at work 0.2%
nuclear discharges <0.1%

ARTIFICIAL
SOURCES
13%

Figure 24.4 This chart shows the different sources of radiation and how they contribute to the average dose of radiation received each year by someone living in the United Kingdom. The main division is between natural background radiation and radiation from artificial sources.

another, depending on how much uranium there is in the underlying rocks.)

- The ground contains radioactive substances; we use materials from the ground to build our houses, so we are exposed to radiation from these.
- Our food and drink are also slightly radioactive. Living things grow by taking in materials from the air and the ground, so they are bound to be radioactive. Inside our bodies, our food then exposes us to radiation.
- Radiation reaches us from space in the form of cosmic rays. Some of this radiation comes from the Sun, some from further out in space. Most cosmic rays are stopped by the Earth's atmosphere; if you live up a mountain, you will be exposed to more radiation from this source.
- If you fly in an aircraft, you are high in the atmosphere. You are exposed to more cosmic rays. This is not a serious problem for the occasional flier, but airline crews have to keep a check on their exposure.

Because natural background radiation is around us all the time, we have to take account of it in experiments. It may be necessary to measure the background level and subtract it from experimental measurements.

Sources of artificial radiation

- Most radiation from artificial sources comes from medical sources. This includes the use of X-rays and gamma rays for seeing inside the body, and the use of radiation for destroying cancer cells. There is always a danger that exposure to such radiation may trigger cancer. Medical physicists are always working to reduce the levels of radiation used in medical procedures. Overall, many more lives are saved than lost through this beneficial use of radiation.
- Today, most nuclear weapons testing is done underground. But in the past, bombs were detonated on land or in the air, and this contributed much more to the radiation dose received by people around the world.
- Many people, such as medical radiographers and staff in a nuclear power station, work with radiation. Overall, this does not add much to the national average dose, but for individuals it can increase their dose by up to 10%.
- Finally, small amounts of radioactive substances escape from the nuclear industry, which processes uranium for use as fuel in nuclear power stations, and handles the highly radioactive spent fuel after it has been used.

Detecting radiation

Radioactivity was discovered by a French physicist, Henri Becquerel, in 1896. He had been investigating some phosphorescent rocks – rocks that glow for a while after they have been left under a bright light. His

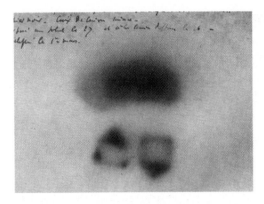

Figure 24.5 One of Henri Becquerel's first photographic records of the radiation produced by uranium. The two black blobs are the outlines of two crystals containing uranium. To show that the radiation would pass through metal, he placed a copper cross between one of the crystals and the photographic film. You can see the 'shadow' of the cross on the photograph. The writing is Becquerel's: the last line says 'développé le 1er mars' – developed on the first of March (1896).

Figure 24.6 Using a Geiger counter to monitor radiation levels close to a nuclear power station. Regular checks are made on samples of air, soil and water for 20 km around.

method was to leave a rock on his window sill in the light. Then he put it in a dark drawer on a piece of photographic film to record the light it gave out. He suspected that rocks containing uranium might be good for this, but he discovered something even more dramatic: the photographic film was blackened even when the rock had not been exposed to light. He realised that some kind of invisible radiation was coming from the uranium. What was more, the longer he left it, the darker the photographic film became. Uranium gives out radiation all the time, without any obvious supply of energy.

Becquerel had discovered a way of revealing the presence of invisible radiation, using photographic film. This method is still used today. One of his first photographs of radiation is shown in Figure 24.5.

It takes a while to expose and develop a photographic film. For a quicker measurement of radiation, we can use a Geiger counter (Figure 24.6). The detector is a Geiger–Muller tube, which is held close to a suspected source of radiation. The radiation enters the tube, which produces an electrical pulse every time it detects any radiation. The electronic counter adds up these pulses; it can give a click or beep for each pulse. In the photograph, a Geiger counter is being used to check that radiation levels close to a nuclear power station are safe.

Radiation dose units

Radiation doses are measured in units called sieverts (Sv). The average annual dose in the UK is about 0.002 Sv, or 2000 microsieverts (μSv). Hence the pie chart shown in Figure 24.4 represents 2000 μSv. This measurement takes into account the total amount of radiation to which the person is exposed and how seriously it affects the different organs of the body.

Any exposure to radiation can be harmful. An annual exposure of 2000 μSv is not thought to be very damaging. It is estimated that, each year in the UK, a few thousand deaths may be the result of radiation exposure. This should be compared with roughly 40 000 deaths each year caused by smoking-related diseases.

? Questions

24.1 What is the biggest contributor to background radiation?

24.2 Why are people who live high above sea-level likely to be exposed to higher levels of background radiation?

24.3 What fraction of our annual average dose of radiation is from artificial sources?

24.4 List three sources of exposure to artificial radiation.

24.5 Name two methods of detecting radiation from radioactive materials.

24.2 The microscopic picture

To understand the nature of radioactivity, we need to picture what is going on at a microscopic level, on the level of atoms and nuclei. The two questions we need to answer are: 'Why are some atoms radioactive and while others are not?' and 'What is the nature of the radiation they produce?'

Radiation is emitted by the nucleus of some atoms. We say that the nucleus is unstable; it emits radiation to become more stable. Fortunately, most of the atoms around us have stable nuclei. The unstable nuclei emit radiation in an attempt to become more stable. When the Earth formed, about 4500 million years ago, there were many more radioactive atoms around. However, as those millions of years have passed, most have decayed to become stable. In the distant past, the level of background radiation was much higher than it is today.

Any element comes in several forms or isotopes (see page 377). Some may be stable, others are unstable. For example, carbon has two stable isotopes ($^{12}_{6}C$ and $^{13}_{6}C$), but $^{14}_{6}C$ is an unstable isotope. Unstable (radioactive) isotopes are known as **radioisotopes**.

Three types of radiation

There are three types of radiation emitted by radioactive substances (Table 24.1). These are named after the first three letters of the Greek alphabet, alpha (α), beta (β) and gamma (γ). Alpha and beta are particles; gamma is a form of electromagnetic radiation (see Chapter 15).

Name	Symbol	Made of	Mass	Charge	Speed (m/s)
alpha	α or $^{4}_{2}He$	two protons + two neutrons	approx. (mass of proton) $\times$ 4	+2	$\sim 3 \times 10^{7}$
beta	β or $^{0}_{-1}e$	an electron	approx. (mass of proton)/1840	−1	$\sim 2.9 \times 10^{8}$
gamma	γ	photon of electromagnetic radiation	0	0	3×10^{8}

Table 24.1 Three types of radiation produced by naturally occurring radioactive substances. To these we should add neutrons and positively charged beta radiation, produced by some artificial radioactive substances.

- An **alpha particle** is made up of two protons and two neutrons. (This is the same as the nucleus of a helium atom, $^{4}_{2}He$.) Because it contains protons, it is positively charged.
- A **beta particle** is an electron. It is not one of the electrons that orbit the nucleus – it comes from inside the nucleus. It is negatively charged, and its mass is much less than that of an alpha particle.
- A **gamma ray** is a form of electromagnetic radiation. We can think of it as a wave with a very short wavelength (similar to an X-ray, but even more energetic). Alternatively, we can picture it as a 'photon', a particle of electromagnetic energy.

An atom of a radioactive substance emits either an alpha particle or a beta particle; in addition, it may emit some energy in the form of a gamma ray. The gamma ray is usually emitted at the same time as the

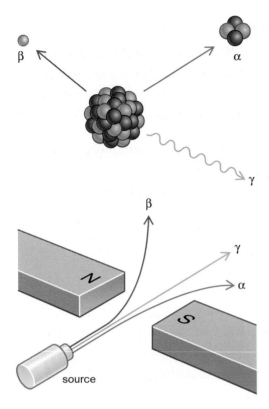

Figure 24.7 **a** Radiation comes from the nucleus of a radioactive atom. **b** Alpha and beta particles are charged, so they constitute an electric current. Because of their opposite signs, the forces on them in a magnetic field are in opposite directions. Gamma rays are undeflected.

Figure 24.8 The penetrating power of radiation is greatest for gamma radiation and least for alpha radiation. This is related to their ability to ionise the materials through which they are passing – gamma is the least ionising.

alpha or beta particle, but it may be emitted some time later. Because they have opposite charges, alpha and beta particles are deflected in opposite directions when they pass through a magnetic field (Figure 24.7). Gamma rays are undeflected. This is how the three types of radiation were first distinguished.

Alpha particles have a much greater mass than beta particles, so they travel more slowly. Gamma rays travel at the speed of light.

Energy released

Radioactive substances release energy when they decay. Before they decay, this energy is stored in the nucleus of the atom. When it is released, it is in two forms:

- An alpha or beta particle is fast-moving. The nucleus that has emitted it recoils (Newton's third law of motion). Both have **kinetic energy**.
- A gamma ray transfers energy as **electromagnetic radiation**.

Penetrating power

When physicists were trying to understand the nature of radioactivity, they noticed that radiation can pass through solid materials. (In Figure 24.5, we saw how Becquerel showed that some of the radiation from uranium could pass through copper.) Different types of radiation can penetrate different thicknesses of materials.

- Alpha particles are the most easily absorbed. They can travel about 5 cm in air before they are absorbed; they are absorbed by a thin sheet of paper.
- Beta particles can travel fairly easily through air or paper, but are absorbed by a few millimetres of aluminium.
- Gamma radiation is the most penetrating. It takes several centimetres of a dense metal like lead, or several metres of concrete, to absorb most of it.

These ideas are represented in Figure 24.8.

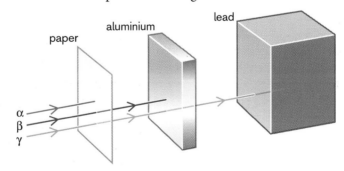

A radiation film badge

People who work with radiation have to monitor the amount of radiation to which they are exposed (their radiation dose). Two types of detector are shown in Figures 24.9a and b – a solid state detector, which is plugged into a machine to give a read-out, and a film badge dosimeter. Figure 24.9c shows the construction of a film badge. The radiation is detected by a piece of photographic film inside the badge. The badge's cover has various 'windows', holes filled with different materials. The section of film behind the open window detects all of the radiation that enters through the window. (This is the only window that allows alpha radiation to reach the film.) The other windows allow through radiation of different energies; only the most energetic radiation can penetrate the lead window. In this way, when the film is developed, it is possible to say whether someone had a high or low dose of radiation, and how much of it was alpha, beta and gamma rays of different energies.

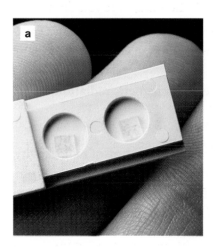
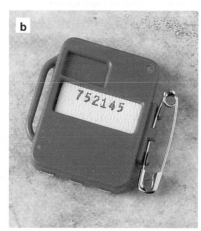
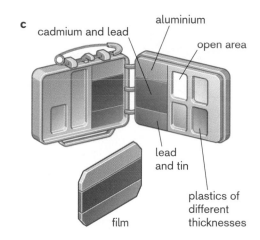

Figure 24.9 **a,b** Two types of personal radiation dosimeter, a solid state detector and a film badge. **c** The windows of the film badge allow different energy ranges to penetrate to the film. Once the film is developed, a technician can work out how much radiation of each type the wearer has been exposed to.

Ionisation

Picture an alpha particle passing through air. As it collides with a molecule of the air, it may knock an electron from it, so that the air molecule becomes charged. We say that the air molecule has become **ionised**. The alpha particle loses a little of its energy; it must ionise thousands of molecules before it loses all of its energy and comes to a halt.

A beta particle can similarly ionise air molecules. However, it is less ionising for two reasons: its charge is less than that of an alpha particle, and it is moving faster so that it is more likely to whizz straight past an air molecule without interacting with it. This is why beta radiation can travel further through air without being absorbed.

Gamma radiation is uncharged and it moves fastest of all, so it is the least readily absorbed. Lead is a good absorber because it is dense (its atoms are packed closely together), and its nuclei are relatively large so they present an easy target for the gamma rays.

Because the radiation from radioactive substances causes ionisation of the materials which absorb it, it is often known as **ionising radiation**. You should be able to see the pattern linking ionising power and absorption:

● Alpha radiation is the most strongly ionising, so it is the most easily absorbed and the least penetrating.

● Gamma radiation is the least strongly ionising, so it is the least easily absorbed and the most penetrating.

X-rays also cause ionisation in the materials they pass through, and so they are also classed as ionising radiation. X-rays are very similar to gamma rays; they usually have less energy (longer wavelength), and they are produced by X-ray machines, by stars, etc., rather than by radioactive substances.

When something has been exposed to radiation, we say that it has been **irradiated**. Although it absorbs the radiation, it does not itself become radioactive. Things only become radioactive if they absorb a radioactive substance. So you do not become radioactive if you absorb cosmic rays (which you do all the time), but you do become radioactive if you consume a radioactive substance – coffee, for example, contains measurable amounts of radioactive potassium.

Ionising radiation and cells

There are three ways in which radiation can damage living cells.

● An intense dose of radiation causes a lot of ionisation in a cell; this can kill the cell. This is what happens when someone suffers radiation burns. The cells affected simply die, as if they had been burned. If the sufferer is lucky and receives suitable treatment, the tissue may regrow.

● If the DNA in the cell nucleus is damaged, the mechanisms that control the cell may break down. The cell may divide uncontrollably, and a tumour forms. This is how radiation can cause cancer.

● If the affected cell is a gamete (a sperm or egg cell), the damaged DNA of its genes may be passed on to future generations. This is how radiation can produce genetic mutations. Occasionally a mutation can be beneficial to the offspring, but more usually it is harmful. A fertilised egg cell may not develop at all, or the baby may have some form of genetic disorder.

We are least likely to be harmed by alpha radiation coming from a source outside our bodies. This is because the radiation is entirely absorbed by the layer of dead skin cells on the outside of our bodies (and by our clothes). However, if an alpha source gets inside us, it can be very damaging, because its radiation is highly ionising. That is why radon and thoron gases are so dangerous; we breathe them into our lungs where they irradiate us from the inside. The result can be lung cancer.

Figure 24.10 shows a storage box used for keeping radioactive sources in a school laboratory. Each source is kept in its own lead-lined compartment, and the whole box should be stored in a metal cabinet with a hazard warning sign.

Today, we know more about radiation and the safe handling of radioactive materials than ever before. Knowing how to reduce the hazards of radiation means that we can learn to live safely with it. In the next section, we will see how radiation can be used for many worthwhile purposes.

Figure 24.10 A storage box for laboratory radioactive sources, and the metal cupboard in which it is stored when not in use.

? **Questions**

24.6 Name four types of ionising radiation.

24.7 **a** Which radiation from a radioactive substance is positively charged?

b Which is negatively charged?

24.8 What type of sub-atomic particle is a beta particle?

24.9 Which type of radiation is a form of electromagnetic radiation?

24.10 **a** Which travels fastest, alpha, beta or gamma radiation?

b Which travels most slowly?

24.11 Why are gamma rays undeflected in a magnetic field?

24.12 **a** Which type of radiation from a radioactive source is the most highly ionising?

b What does this tell you about how easily it is absorbed?

24.3 Using radioactive substances

We will look at the uses of radioactive substances under three main headings, namely uses related to:

- their different penetrating powers,
- the damage their radiation causes to living cells,
- the fact that we can detect tiny quantities of radioactive substances.

Uses related to penetrating power

Smoke detectors

These are often found in domestic kitchens, and in public buildings such as offices and hotels. If you open a smoke detector to replace the battery, you may see a yellow and black radiation hazard warning sign (Figure 24.11). The radioactive material used is americium-241, a source of alpha radiation. Here is how it works.

- Radiation from the source falls on a detector. Since alpha radiation is charged, a small current flows in the detector. The output from the processing circuit is OFF, so the alarm is silent.
- When smoke enters the gap between the source and the detector, it absorbs the radiation. Now no current flows in the detector and the processing circuit switches ON, sounding the alarm.

In this application, a source of alpha radiation is chosen because alpha radiation is easily absorbed.

Thickness measurements

In industry, beta radiation is often used in the measurement of thickness. Manufacturers of paper need to be sure that their product is of a uniform

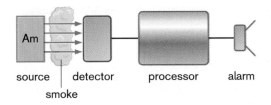

Figure 24.11 The photograph shows a smoke detector; the source of radiation is a small amount of americium-241. The block diagram shows the circuit, which sounds the alarm when smoke absorbs the alpha radiation. Americium is an interesting element. It is not found in Nature, but must be made in nuclear reactors. It is element 94 in the Periodic Table, and is described as a transuranic (beyond uranium).

thickness. To do this, beta radiation is directed through the paper as it comes off the production line. A detector measures the amount of radiation getting through. If the paper is too thick, the radiation level will be low, and an automatic control system adjusts the thickness. The same technique is used in the manufacture of plastic sheeting.

Beta radiation is used in this application because alpha radiation would be entirely absorbed by the paper or plastic; gamma radiation would hardly be affected, because it is the most penetrating.

Medical diagnosis

The diagnosis of some diseases may be carried out using a source of gamma radiation. The patient is injected with a radioactive chemical that targets the problem area (it may accumulate in bone, for example). Then a camera detects the radiation coming from the chemical and gives an image of the tissue under investigation.

Fault detection

Faults in manufactured goods are sometimes detected using gamma rays. Figure 24.12 shows an example, where engineers are looking for any faults in some pipework. The radioactive source is strapped to the outside of the pipe, and a photographic film is placed on the inside. When the film is developed, it looks like an X-ray picture, and shows any faults in the welding.

Figure 24.12 Checking for faults in a metal pipe. The gamma source is stored in the box, but is pushed through the long tube to reach the pipe. The engineers are checking that no radiation is escaping from the storage box.

Uses related to cell damage

Radiation therapy

The patient shown earlier in Figure 24.3 is receiving radiation treatment as part of a cure for cancer. A source of gamma rays (or X-rays) is directed at the tumour that is to be destroyed. The source moves around the patient, always aiming at the tumour. In this way, other tissues receive only a small dose of radiation. Radiation therapy is often combined with chemotherapy, using chemical drugs to target and kill the cancerous cells.

Food irradiation

This is a way of preserving food. Food often decays because of the action of microbes; these can be killed using intense gamma rays. Because these organisms are single-celled, any cell damage kills the entire organism. Different countries permit different foods to be irradiated. The sterile food that results has been used on space missions (where long life is important) and for some hospital patients whose resistance to infection by microbes may be low.

Sterilisation

Sterilisation of medical products works in the same way as in food irradiation. Syringes, scalpels and other instruments are sealed in plastic bags and then exposed to gamma radiation. Any microbes present are killed so that, when the packaging is opened, the item can be guaranteed to be sterile. The same technique is used to sterilise sanitary towels and tampons.

Uses related to detectability

Radioactive tracing

Every time you hear a Geiger counter click, it has detected the radioactive decay of a single atom. This means that we can use radiation to detect tiny quantities of substances, far smaller than can be detected by chemical means. Such techniques are often known as radioactive tracing.

For example, engineers may want to trace underground water flows. They may be constructing a new waste dump, and they need to be sure that poisonous water from the dump will not flow into the local water supply. Under high pressure, they inject water containing a radioactive chemical into a hole in the ground. Then they monitor how it moves through underground cracks using gamma detectors at ground level (Figure 24.13).

Biochemical monitoring

Biochemists use radioactively labelled chemicals to monitor chemical reactions. The chemicals bond to particular parts of the molecules of interest, so that they can be tracked throughout a complicated

Figure 24.13 Detecting the movement of underground water. Engineers need to know how water will move underground. This can affect the stability of buildings on the site. Water containing a source of gamma radiation is pumped underground, and its passage through cracks is monitored at ground level.

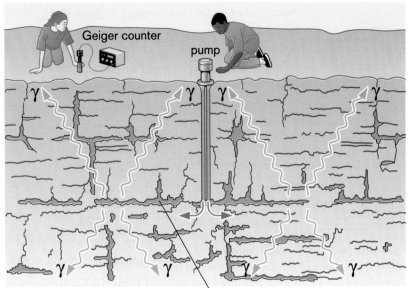

Figure 24.14 A DNA (genetic) fingerprint appears as a series of bands. Each band comes from a fragment of DNA labelled with a radioactive chemical. They show up on a photographic film.

sequence of reactions. The same technique is used to show up the pattern of a genetic fingerprint (Figure 24.14).

> **Questions**
>
> **24.13** Why would beta radiation not be suitable for use in a smoke detector?
>
> **24.14** Why must gamma radiation be used for inspecting a welded pipe?
>
> **24.15** When medical equipment is to be sterilised, it is first sealed in a plastic wrapper. Why does this not absorb the radiation used?
>
> **24.16** Why must the engineers shown in Figure 24.13 use a source of gamma radiation?

24.4 Radioactive decay

Henri Becquerel discovered the radioactivity of uranium. What surprised him was that uranium appears to be able to emit radiation endlessly, without ever running out of energy. This would go against the principle of conservation of energy. What he did not realise was that the uranium he used was undergoing very gradual decay. The problem was that uranium decays very slowly so that, even if Becquerel had carried on with his experiments for a thousand years, he would not have noticed any decrease in the activity of his samples. In fact, the uranium he was working with had been decaying gradually ever since the Earth formed, over 4500 million years ago.

Different radioactive substances decay at different rates, some much faster than others. However, they all decay with the same pattern, as

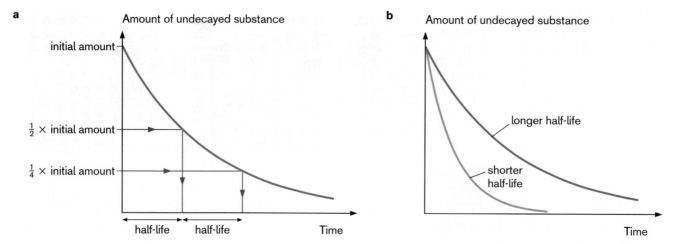

a

Amount of undecayed substance

initial amount

$\frac{1}{2} \times$ initial amount

$\frac{1}{4} \times$ initial amount

half-life   half-life   Time

b

Amount of undecayed substance

longer half-life

shorter half-life

Time

Figure 24.15 **a** A decay graph for a radioactive substance. A curve of this shape is known as an exponential decay graph. **b** A steep graph shows that a substance has a short half-life.

shown in Figure 24.15. The graph shows that the amount of a radioactive substance decreases rapidly at first, and then more and more slowly. In fact, because the graph tails off more and more slowly, we cannot say when the last atoms will decay.

Because we cannot say when the substance will have entirely decayed, we have to think of another way of describing the rate of decay. As shown on the graph, we identify the half-life of the substance:

> The **half-life** of a radioactive substance is the average time taken for half of the atoms in a sample to decay.

Uranium decays slowly because it has a very long half-life. The radioactive samples used in schools usually have half-lives of a few years, so that they have to be replaced once in a while. Some radioactive substances have half-lives that are less than a microsecond. No sooner are they formed than they decay into something else.

Explaining half-life

After one half-life, half of the atoms in a radioactive sample have decayed. However, this does not mean that, after two half-lives, all of the atoms will have decayed. From the graph of Figure 24.15, you can see that one quarter will still remain. Why is this?

Figure 24.16 shows one way of thinking about what is going on. We picture a sample of 100 undecayed atoms of a radioactive substance. They decay randomly; each one has a fifty-fifty chance of decaying in the course of one half-life.

- After one half-life, a random selection of 50 atoms has decayed.
- During the next half-life, a random selection of the remaining 50 atoms decays, leaving 25 undecayed at the end of two half-lives.
- During the third half-life, half of the remaining atoms decay, leaving 12 or 13 undecayed (of course, you can't have half an atom).

So the number of undecayed atoms goes $100 - 50 - 25 - 12 - \ldots$ and so on. It is because radioactive atoms decay in a random fashion that we get this pattern of decay. Notice that, just because one atom has not

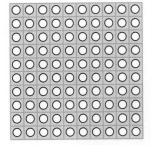 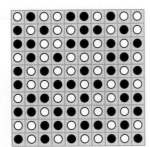 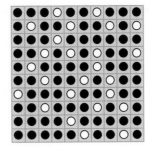 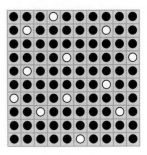

Figure 24.16 The pattern of radioactive decay comes about because the decay of individual atoms is random. Half decay during each half-life, but we have no way of predicting which individual atoms decay.

decayed in the first half-life does not mean that it is more likely to decay in the next half-life. It has no way of remembering its past.

Usually, we cannot measure the numbers of atoms in a sample. Instead, we measure the **count rate** using a Geiger counter or some other detector. We might also determine the activity of a sample:

> The **activity** of a sample is the number of atoms that decay each second, and is measured in becquerels (Bq).

An activity of one becquerel (1 Bq) is one decay per second. The count rate and activity both decrease following the same pattern as the number of undecayed atoms.

We will look further at what some of these things mean by considering a simple numerical worked example.

Worked example 1

A sample of a radioactive element X has an activity of 240 Bq. If the half-life of element X is 3 years, what will its activity be after 12 years?

● *Step 1* Calculate the number of half-lives in 12 years:

$$\frac{12 \text{ years}}{3 \text{ years}} = 4 \text{ half-lives}$$

Hence we want to know the activity of the sample after 4 half-lives.

● *Step 2* Calculate the activity after 1, 2, 3 and 4 half-lives (divide by 2 each time):

initial activity	= 240 Bq
activity after 1 half-life	= 120 Bq
activity after 2 half-lives	= 60 Bq
activity after 3 half-lives	= 30 Bq
activity after 4 half-lives	= 15 Bq

So the activity of the sample has fallen to 15 Bq after 12 years. [Another way to do this is as follows: 12 years is 4 half-lives, so we need to divide the initial activity by 2^4, which is 16, giving (240 Bq)/16 = 15 Bq.]

Measuring a half-life

Figure 24.17 shows how the half-life of a particular substance, protactinium-234, is measured in the laboratory. After the bottle has been shaken, the upper layer of liquid contains protactinium, which emits beta radiation as it decays. Because its half-life is 70 s, the count rate decreases quickly. The number of counts in successive intervals of 10 s is recorded, and a graph is plotted. Then the half-life can be deduced from the decay graph as shown in Figure 24.18.

Radioactivity | 393

Figure 24.17 The practical arrangement for measuring the half-life of the radioactive decay of protactinium-234.

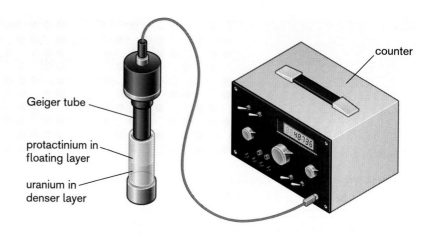

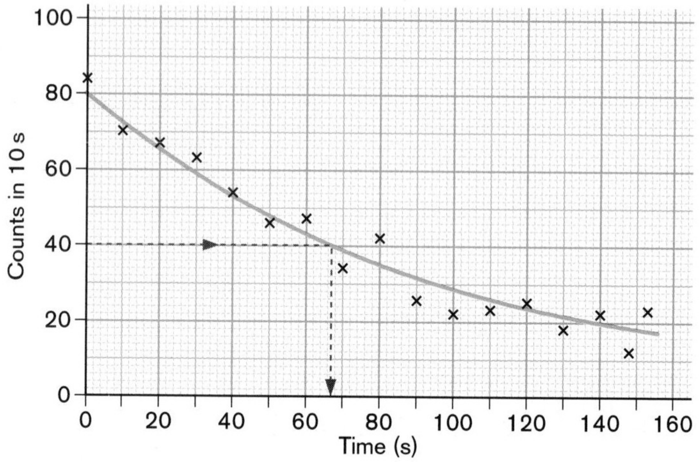

Geiger tube

protactinium in floating layer

uranium in denser layer

counter

Figure 24.18 The count rate for protactinium-234 decreases rapidly. The points show some experimental scatter, so a smooth curve is drawn. From this, the half-life can be deduced. This particular experiment gives the value as 67 s.

Half-life and dating

Because radioactive substances decay at a rate we can determine, we can use them to discover how old objects and materials are. The best-known example of this is **radiocarbon dating**.

All living things contain carbon. Plants get this from atmospheric carbon dioxide, which they use in photosynthesis. Animals get it from the plants they eat to build their bodies. Most carbon is carbon-12 ($^{12}_{6}C$), which is not radioactive. A tiny fraction is radioactive carbon-14 ($^{14}_{6}C$), with a half-life of 5370 years. (It emits beta radiation.)

The idea of radiocarbon dating is this: When a living organism dies, the carbon-14 in its body decays. As time passes, the amount remaining decreases. If we can measure the amount remaining, we can work out when the organism was alive. There are two ways to measure the amount of carbon-14 present in an object:

- by measuring the activity of the sample using a detector such as a Geiger counter;
- by counting the number of carbon-14 atoms using a mass spectrometer.

The Turin Shroud (Figure 24.19) was famously dated in 1988 using a mass spectrometer. (This is a large machine that uses magnetic fields to

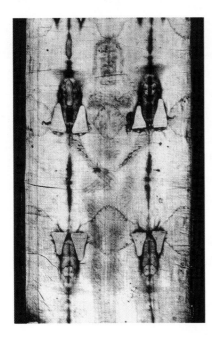

Figure 24.19 The Turin Shroud was dated by radiocarbon dating. It was found to date from the fourteenth century, which matched the dates of the earliest historical records of its existence.

separate atoms according to their mass and charge.) The Shroud was dated to 1325 ± 33 AD, showing that it did not date from Biblical times.

Problems can arise with radiocarbon dating. It may be that the amount of carbon-14 present in the atmosphere was different in the past. Certainly, nuclear weapons testing added extra carbon-14 to the atmosphere during the 1950s and 1960s. This means that living objects that died then have an excess of carbon-14, making them appear younger than they really are.

Geologists use a radioactive dating technique to find the age of some rocks. Many rocks contain a radioactive isotope, potassium-40 ($^{40}_{19}K$), which decays by beta emission to a stable isotope of argon ($^{40}_{18}Ar$). Argon is a gas, and it is trapped in the rock as the potassium decays. Here is how the dating system works:

- The rocks of interest form from molten material (e.g. in a volcano). There is no argon in the molten rock because it can bubble out.
- After the rock solidifies, the amount of trapped argon gradually increases as the potassium decays.
- Geologists take a sample and measure the relative amounts of argon and potassium. The greater the proportion of argon, the older the rock must be.

Extension material

Nuclear decay equations

When an atom of a radioactive substance decays, it becomes an atom of another element. This is because, in alpha and beta decay, the number of protons in the nucleus changes. We can represent any radioactive decay by an equation using the notation explained in Chapter 23 (page 376).

- Here is an example of an equation for **alpha decay**:
$$^{241}_{94}Am \rightarrow \, ^{237}_{92}U + \, ^{4}_{2}He + energy$$
This represents the decay of americium-241, the isotope used in smoke detectors. It emits an alpha particle (represented as a helium nucleus) and becomes an isotope of uranium. Notice that the numbers in this equation must balance, because we cannot lose mass or charge:

nucleon numbers: $241 \rightarrow 237 + 4$

proton numbers: $94 \rightarrow 92 + 2$

- Here is an example for **beta decay**:
$$^{14}_{6}C \rightarrow \, ^{14}_{7}N + \, ^{0}_{-1}e + energy$$
This is the decay that is used in radiocarbon dating. A carbon-14 nucleus decays to become a nitrogen-14 nucleus. (The beta particle, an electron, is represented by $^{0}_{-1}e$.) If we could see inside the nucleus, we would see that a single neutron has decayed to become a proton:
$$^{1}_{0}n \rightarrow \, ^{1}_{1}p + \, ^{0}_{-1}e$$
For each of these two beta decay equations, you should be able to see that the nucleon numbers and proton numbers are balanced. We say that, in radioactive decay, nucleon number and proton number are **conserved**.

Nuclear stability

Why are some nuclei stable while others are unstable? If you think about an atomic nucleus (Figure 24.20), you might expect it to blow

Figure 24.20 An atomic nucleus is made up of protons and neutrons. The protons are positively charged, so they tend to repel one another. In a stable nucleus, the neutrons dilute this effect so that the nuclear strong force is enough to balance the repulsion between the protons.

apart because all of its protons repel one another (because their positive charges repel). In fact, this repulsion is balanced by another force, the **nuclear strong force**, which holds the nucleus together against the repulsion of like charges. The strong force is one of the fundamental forces of Nature, and it acts between all nucleons (protons and neutrons) regardless of their charge.

In a stable nucleus, the strong force and the electrostatic force balance each other. We can think of the neutrons as keeping the protons apart, so that the electrostatic force is diluted. In an unstable (radioactive) nucleus, the forces are unbalanced. The nucleus decays in an attempt to become more stable.

- A nucleus with too few neutrons (too many protons) must lose some positive charge. An alpha particle is emitted.
- A nucleus with too many neutrons (too few protons) must increase its positive charge. A beta particle is emitted (a neutron becomes a proton).

Stable and unstable isotopes

The atoms of an element come in several forms – its isotopes. All of the isotopes of a particular element have the same number of protons, Z, but they differ in their number of neutrons, N. Some isotopes are stable, while others undergo radioactive decay. What pattern can we find in those which are stable and those which decay?

Figure 24.21 is a graph which can help you answer this question. Each dot represents a stable isotope. From the axes of the graph, you can read off the values of proton number Z and neutron number N. The dots form the **line of stability**. This line starts off as a roughly straight line through the origin, but soon curves upwards. Here is the patttern it reveals for stable isotopes:

- For the lightest elements, Z and N are roughly equal. Stable nuclei such as $^{4}_{2}$He, $^{12}_{6}$C and $^{40}_{20}$Ca have equal numbers of protons and neutrons.
- For the heavier elements, N is greater than Z. There are more neutrons than protons in stable nuclei such as $^{138}_{56}$Ba and $^{200}_{80}$Hg. They are needed to dilute the repulsion between the protons.
- No isotopes beyond $Z = 93$ are stable.

The graph of Figure 24.21 also shows how unstable isotopes decay.

More isotopes beyond the lines of stability (i.e. those with proton number greater than 83) decay by emitting an alpha particle .

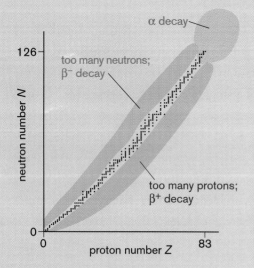

Figure 24.21 This graph is known as an 'N–Z plot'. It shows values of proton number and neutron number for all the known stable isotopes. The heavier isotopes have more neutrons than protons.

An isotope which lies above the line of stability has too many neutrons. It decays by emitting a beta particle (an electron). A neutron has become a proton and an electron. This is known as beta-minus (β^-) decay because the particle emitted has a negative charge:

neutron → proton + electron $n \rightarrow p + \beta^-$ (β^- decay)

There is another possibility: an unstable isotope lies below the line of stability. These isotopes have too many protons. They can reduce this by emitting a *positively*-charged electron, a particle known as a **positron**. A positron is identical to an electron, except that its charge is positive. This is known as beta-plus (β^+) decay; a proton is decaying to become a neutron and a positron:

proton → neutron + positron $p \rightarrow n + \beta^+$ (β^+ decay)

Figure 24.22 shows what is going on inside protons and neutrons when they decay. There is a change in the **quarks**, the fundamental particles of which the nucleons are made.

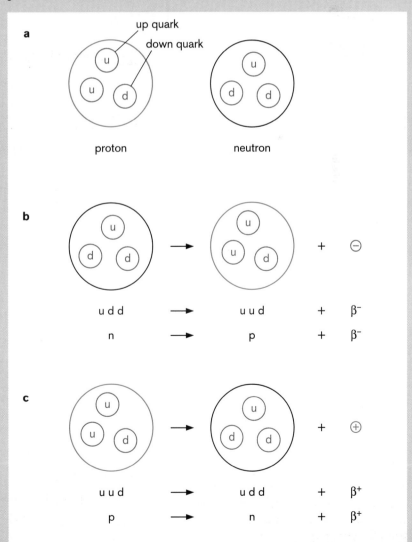

Figure 24.22 The underlying processes of beta decay. **a** A proton is made up of two up quarks and a down quark; a neutron is two downs and an up. **b** In β^- decay, a down quark in a neutron becomes an up quark, and an electron is emitted. **c** In β^+ decay, an up quark in a proton becomes a down quark, and a positron is emitted.

?

Questions

24.17 What is the SI unit of activity of a radioactive element?

24.18 What word is missing from this definition of half-life? 'The half-life of a radioactive substance is the time taken for half of the atoms in a sample to decay.'

24.19 A sample of a radioactive substance contains 200 undecayed atoms. How many will remain undecayed after 3 half-lives?

24.20 The half-life of radioisotope X is 10 days. A sample gives an initial count rate of 440 counts per second. What will be the count rate after 30 days?

24.21 Radioisotope Y has a half-life of 2000 years. How long will it take the activity of a sample of Y to decrease to one-eighth of its initial value?

Summary

- We are constantly exposed to background radiation from a variety of sources. We are also exposed to radiation from artificial sources.

- Radiation can be detected using photographic film, Geiger counters and other detectors.

- Naturally occurring radioactive substances produce alpha (α) and beta (β) particles, and gamma (γ) rays (a form of electromagnetic radiation).

- The radiation from radioactive substances causes ionisation in the materials through which they pass, and so they are known as ionising radiations.

- Radioactive substances have many uses. Suitable substances are selected according to the penetrating power of their radiation, the effect of their radiation on cells, their detectability (as tracers) and their half-life.

- The half-life of a radioactive substance is the average time taken for half of the atoms in a sample to decay.

- The activity of a sample of a radioactive substance is the number of atoms that decay per second, measured in becquerels (1 Bq = one decay per second).

- *The radioactive decay of a radioisotope may be represented by a balanced equation. In radioactive decay, nucleon number and proton number are conserved.*

- *A plot of neutron number N against proton number Z can be used to show the pattern of stability and instability among nuclei of different compositions.*

Nuclear fission

Topics in this chapter

◆ nuclear fission

◆ chain reactions

ℯ *how nuclear power stations work*

The nuclear power industry has had a troubled history. Nuclear power stations produce electricity that is the same as the electricity from any other power station. However, rather than burning a fuel such as coal or gas, a nuclear power station uses a completely different mechanism: nuclear fission, the splitting of uranium atoms. In its early days, half a century ago, nuclear power was seen as a cheap, clean and safe way of providing electricity on a large scale. Today, a significant proportion of the world's energy resources come from nuclear power – roughly 20% of the UK's electricity, more than 75% of France's (Figure 25.1).

The first countries to develop nuclear power were those which had developed nuclear weapons during the Second World War – the USA,

Figure 25.1 Most of France's electricity is produced in nuclear power stations like this one at Penly, near Dieppe. The sea provides the necessary cooling water. France's reserves of fossil fuels are more limited than those of other European countries, but they do have uranium mines, so they have embraced nuclear technology with more enthusiasm.

the UK and the Soviet Union (now Russia, Ukraine, etc.). Some people opposed this development because early reactors were often designed to produce plutonium for use in nuclear weapons, as well as electricity. There is still concern that, when nuclear power technology is sold to other countries, they are being given the means to produce nuclear weapons.

Any method of generating electricity is bound to damage the environment. Burning fossil fuels produces carbon dioxide and contributes to the greenhouse effect. A dam for a hydroelectric scheme can flood useful farmland and displace local people. Nuclear power stations produce radioactive waste. This is the major environmental concern in relation to nuclear power. How should the waste be handled? Should it be dumped underground, or stored above ground where its condition can be monitored to ensure that it stays safe for decades into the future?

Cost is another concern with nuclear power. All power stations are expensive to build, and the operator gets no return on investment until electricity is generated. This may be as long as ten years from the start of planning and construction. Dealing with the radioactive waste produced is expensive. Finally, at the end of its life, a nuclear power station must be dismantled and made safe (Figure 25.2). The site must be looked after for up to a hundred years. All this adds to the cost, so that the original idea of electricity 'so cheap that it would not be worth the expense of metering' proved an over-optimistic dream.

In some ways, the nuclear industry has had a raw deal. It is very easy to spot any leaks, because (as we saw in Chapter 24), even very tiny amounts of radioactive substances can be detected with a Geiger counter; that is what makes such substances useful as tracers. At the same time, we have become very conscious of the environmental impact of all of our industrial activities. If, one hundred years ago, we had been aware of the damage that was being done to the atmosphere and to water supplies by the large-scale burning of fossil fuels, we might have developed cleaner coal-fired power stations.

The nuclear industry has inevitably led to deaths. The Chernobyl disaster (Figure 25.3) may eventually result in hundreds of deaths, and other leaks and accidents add to the death toll. Even so, the numbers affected are small compared to the numbers who have died or suffered long-term health problems in coal-mining or in extracting oil and gas from hostile environments around the world.

At the same time, we should be conscious of the benefits that have come from the nuclear industry. The radioisotopes that are used in medicine (for detecting and treating diseases) are all made in nuclear reactors, as are the radioisotopes used in the other industrial applications discussed in Chapter 24.

In this chapter, we will look at the physics of nuclear fission, the process by which energy is extracted from uranium. We will also take a

Figure 25.2 Berkeley, in the west of England, was one of the UK's first nuclear power stations. At the end of its working life, much of it was dismantled. Here you can see the large rusty-red boilers being laid down on the ground. Eventually levels of radioactivity will be low enough for the whole site to be grassed over.

Figure 25.3 In 1986, the power station at Chernobyl, in the Ukraine, exploded after the operating engineers ignored instructions in the safety manual and the nuclear chain reaction went out of control. Large amounts of radioactive material were spread over a wide area. The cloud of radioactive gas and dust that resulted was detected as it travelled right round the world.

glance at nuclear fusion, another nuclear process, which releases energy in the Sun and which may, one day, be a useful source of energy here on Earth.

25.1 Nuclear fission

In Chapter 24, we saw why radioactive decay occurs: an unstable nucleus becomes more stable by emitting a small particle (alpha or beta), and usually some electromagnetic radiation (a gamma ray).

In **nuclear fission**, a large nucleus splits in two to form two smaller nuclei – in the process, some neutrons are also released.

(The word *fission* means 'splitting'. Think of a fissure, which is a large crack in a rock.)

There are two ways in which fission can occur. Sometimes a large unstable nucleus will split spontaneously; this is *spontaneous fission*. In the other kind of fission, a neutron collides with a large nucleus, making it even more unstable and causing it to split; this is *neutron-induced fission*. We will concentrate on this second mechanism, because it is the one that is used in nuclear power stations and in nuclear bombs.

Figure 25.4 shows a uranium nucleus undergoing fission. A neutron hits the uranium nucleus and is absorbed. The nucleus is now very unstable and starts to deform. Soon, it splits completely in two, to form two 'daughter' nuclei of about the same size. At the same time, two or three neutrons are released.

Releasing energy

This process releases energy that was previously stored in the uranium nucleus. This energy takes the following forms.

- The daughter nuclei move apart; they have kinetic energy.

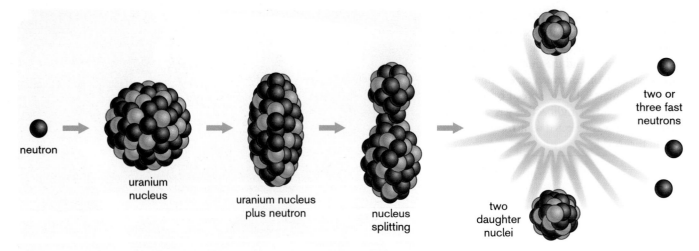

neutron

uranium
nucleus

uranium nucleus
plus neutron

nucleus
splitting

two
daughter
nuclei

two or
three fast
neutrons

Figure 25.4 A uranium nucleus undergoing neutron-induced fission. In the process, a lot of energy is released. Two daughter nuclei of about the same size are formed, and two or three neutrons are released. These neutrons may go on to cause more uranium nuclei to split.

- The neutrons also fly off at high speed; they too have kinetic energy.
- Gamma rays are released; this is energy in the form of photons of electromagnetic radiation.

(Sometimes, people talk about 'nuclear energy'. We might use this name for the potential energy stored by the uranium nucleus. This energy is converted to the kinetic energy of the particles, and the energy of the gamma radiation.)

When a single uranium nucleus splits like this, the energy released is about 10^{-11} J. This is a tiny amount, but it is much more than the energy released in a chemical reaction. For example, when two hydrogen atoms and an oxygen atom bond together to form a molecule of water, the energy released is less than one-millionth of that released by the fission of a uranium nucleus. Hence, we can think of uranium as a highly concentrated store of energy, roughly one million times as concentrated as an equal mass of coal and oxygen. That is what attracted physicists to the idea of using uranium as a fuel for electricity generation.

Chain reaction

Fission releases neutrons, which fly off at high speed – perhaps 10^7 m/s. Each of these neutrons may collide with another uranium nucleus and cause it to split. The result can be a **chain reaction** – see Figure 25.5.

- In a nuclear power station, the chain reaction is kept under control. The reactor is designed so that just one of the neutrons goes on to cause another nucleus to split. The other neutrons escape from the uranium and are absorbed by control rods or by the surrounding concrete.
- In a nuclear bomb, the idea is to get as many uranium nuclei as possible to undergo fission in a very short time. From the first fission, perhaps two neutrons go on to cause uranium nuclei to split, releasing four neutrons that cause fission, then eight, then 16, and so

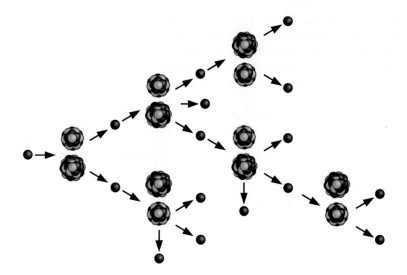

Figure 25.5 A nuclear chain reaction. It does not really happen in straight lines like this. The neutrons released fly off in all directions, and they may travel some distance through the uranium before they strike another nucleus and cause it to split.

on. The nuclear reaction escalates out of control and vast amounts of energy are released in a fraction of a second.

The reactor in a nuclear power station is designed so that the conditions needed for a bomb cannot happen. The biggest danger is that the reaction may go so fast that the uranium overheats. It may melt, and the reactor may burst into flames.

Radioactive products

A uranium nucleus splits to produce two daughter nuclei. These are (obviously) no longer uranium nuclei, but the nuclei of atoms of different elements such as krypton, rubidium, caesium and barium. These daughter nuclei are almost always unstable; that is, they are radioisotopes that undergo radioactive decay. Here is an equation that shows one way in which a uranium nucleus may split:

$$^{235}_{92}U \ + \ ^{1}_{0}n \ \rightarrow \ ^{141}_{56}Ba \ + \ ^{92}_{36}Kr \ + \ 3^{1}_{0}n \ + \ energy$$

parent + 1 neutron → 2 daughter + 3 neutrons + energy
nucleus   nuclei

Here, the daughter nuclei are isotopes of barium and krypton, and both are radioactive.

This is the big problem with using uranium as a fuel; it doesn't result in ash (as when coal is burned). Instead, radioactive waste is produced and has to be dealt with. Some of the radioisotopes are highly radioactive, but that can be a good thing. After a few years, their activity will have decreased to a safe level. Others are less radioactive, and this means that they must be stored safely for a long time, perhaps centuries, until they are safe to release to the environment. Figure 25.6 shows how the activity of nuclear waste decreases over the years.

It is difficult to decide the best way to deal with these dangerous materials. Is it best to concentrate them so that only a small volume of highly dangerous material must be stored, or is it best to keep them in a more dilute form?

Figure 25.6 Nuclear waste is a mixture of radioactive substances, some with short half-lives, others with long half-lives. Its activity decreases rapidly at first, but the longer-lived isotopes may be active for thousands of years.

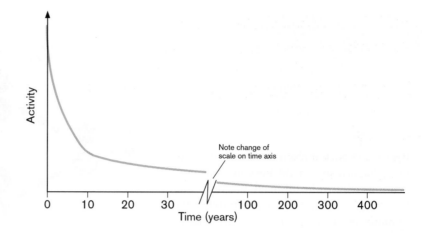

A second problem is that the chain reaction in uranium usually comes to a halt long before all of the uranium nuclei have been split. This is because it has become too dilute. There are no longer enough uranium nuclei present to ensure that at least one neutron from each fission event goes on to cause another fission. The spent fuel must be processed to re-concentrate the uranium and to remove the hazardous daughter products. Such reprocessing requires great technical skill to avoid releasing hazardous materials to the environment. Because there are only a handful of reprocessing plants in the world (Figure 25.7), spent fuel must be transported over large distances, and this is another cause for concern. An accident might result in the release of radioactive material; a terrorist attack might put bomb-making material in the hands of dangerous groups.

A note on language

We often talk about uranium as the 'fuel' for a nuclear power station. Sometimes, we even talk about uranium 'burning' in a reactor; of course, it isn't really burning. Uranium isn't a fuel in the same sense that coal, oil and gas are fuels; it doesn't combine with oxygen to release energy.

Radioactive waste may also be described as 'hot', which means that it is highly radioactive. Its temperature may be high at first, because energy is released rapidly as it first decays. Later it cools down, but it may still be described as 'hot'.

This is rather picturesque language, which tends to highlight the similarities between the processes of extracting energy stored in fossil fuels and in uranium. It is important not to forget that fundamentally different chemical and physical processes are at work here.

Figure 25.7 This nuclear reprocessing plant at Cap de la Hague in northern France receives shipments of spent uranium fuel from many countries. It separates out the radioactive daughter products and re-concentrates the uranium for re-use in power stations.

Extension material

Inside a nuclear power station

The electricity generated by a nuclear power station is exactly the same as the electricity from any other power station. Figure 25.8 compares a nuclear station with a coal-fired power station. The principal difference is at the left-hand side.

- In a nuclear reactor, heat is generated by the fission of uranium. This energy is transferred by a **coolant** (such as carbon dioxide gas) to a boiler, which generates steam.

- In a coal-fired station, burning coal produces heat, which heats the water in the boiler to make steam.

In both cases, steam from the boiler is used to turn turbines, which turn generators.

Inside a nuclear reactor

There are several different designs of nuclear reactor in use around the world. Figure 25.9 shows a 'Magnox' reactor, a type that has been in use in the United Kingdom and elsewhere for 40 years. Some features to notice are the following.

- The fuel is in the form of rods. Inside each **fuel rod**, the fuel is in the form of pellets. A spent rod can be removed and replaced while the reactor is running.

- Between the fuel rods are blocks of graphite (carbon), which form the **moderator**. Without the moderator, the neutrons would tend to fly straight out of the reactor. The neutrons are slowed down as they pass through the graphite, making them more likely to interact with uranium nuclei.

- Also passing through the graphite are **control rods**. These are made of a material (boron) that is good at absorbing neutrons. They can be lowered into the reactor to slow down or stop the reaction; they can be removed to speed it up. They are designed to drop in automatically if the reactor overheats.

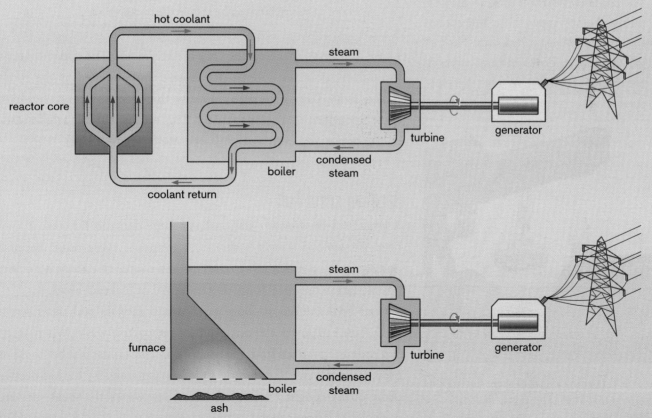

Figure 25.8 These block diagrams show the similarities between nuclear and coal-fired power stations. The main difference is in the way heat is produced and transferred to the boiler.

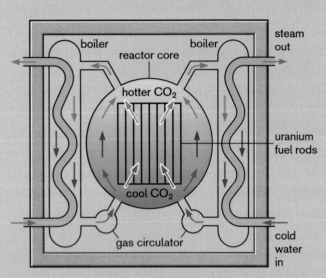

Figure 25.9 The core of a Magnox-type reactor. The chain reaction occurs in the uranium fuel; its heat is carried away by the coolant.

- The **coolant** is carbon dioxide gas. It is pumped along pipes in the hot core of the reactor, where it heats up. The hot gas then passes down through pipes in the boiler, resulting in high-pressure steam.

Figure 25.11 Loading a flask of spent nuclear fuel onto a transporter. The metal flask must be strong enough to withstand any impacts *en route* to the reprocessing plant.

Figure 25.10 These engineers are working on top of the core (marked **A**) of a nuclear reactor in a power station. To replace individual fuel rods, a machine lifts one of the blocks in the floor, pulls up the spent rod and replaces it with a fresh one. The machine can be seen in the background.

These four parts make up the core of the reactor. The coolant passes through pipes in the core so that it isn't contaminated by the core's radioactivity. The core is surrounded by thick layers of concrete which absorb neutrons that escape from it. This means that it is safe to work on top of the core even when it is operating (Figure 25.10).

Handling spent fuel

A large coal-fired power station has a large demand for coal. It may need a *train*load – over a thousand tonnes – every hour. Because nuclear fuel is a much more concentrated source of energy, a nuclear power station may need only one *truck*load of fuel each week.

Coal-fired stations produce ash, carbon dioxide and other waste gases. Nuclear power stations produce radioactive waste. When spent fuel rods are removed from the reactor core, they must first be stored in deep tanks of water. This removes the heat generated by the radioactive decay of the daughter products. After a few weeks, the spent rods are packed into a strong metal container (Figure 25.11) and transported to a reprocessing plant.

Questions

25.1 What is the meaning of the word 'fission'?

25.2 What particle can induce the fission of a uranium nucleus?

25.3 Look at Figure 25.4. How can you tell that the daughter nuclei are not uranium nuclei but the nuclei of other elements?

25.4 Look at the equation for the fission of a uranium nucleus on page 403. Show that this is a balanced equation by checking that both proton number and nucleon number are conserved (i.e. that the total number of protons on the left equals the total number of protons on the right, and so on).

25.5 What is the difference between a controlled chain reaction (as in a nuclear reactor) and an uncontrolled chain reaction (as in a nuclear bomb)?

25.6 Why must spent nuclear fuel be handled with extreme care?

Summary

◆ Fission is the splitting of heavy nuclei to form two lighter daughter nuclei of about the same size. In the process, neutrons are released.

◆ Energy is also released in fission, in the form of the kinetic energy of the particles produced, plus gamma rays.

◆ A heavy nucleus may be induced to undergo fission when it captures a neutron. This allows a chain reaction to be established.

◆ The daughter products of nuclear fission are highly radioactive.

◈ *In a nuclear power station, the energy released by the fission of uranium or plutonium is carried away by a coolant; it is used to heat water in a boiler.*

◈ *The radioactive daughter products of nuclear fission contaminate the nuclear fuel. Short-lived isotopes decay quickly but make the waste hot. Long-lived isotopes require the waste to be stored for a long time.*

Further questions

The numbering is continued from the in-chapter questions.

Chapter 23

23.19

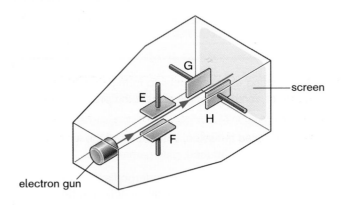

Figure Q23.19

The diagram shows a simple cathode ray tube. A beam of particles, emitted by the cathode, strikes the centre of the screen.

a What are the particles emitted by the cathode?

b Explain why the cathode must be heated.

c Describe how the speed of the particles changes as they travel from the cathode to the screen.

d What is the principal energy change that occurs when the beam strikes the screen?

e Which of the four deflecting plates (E, F, G or H) should be connected to a positive voltage if the spot on the screen is to be moved upwards?

f Describe what you would expect to see on the screen if the two deflecting plates G and H were connected to an alternating voltage supply.

23.20

Ernest Rutherford devised an experiment in which alpha particles were directed at a thin gold foil. The results of this experiment showed that every atom has a nucleus, and the 'plum pudding' model of the atom had to be discarded.

a Consider these three particles: alpha particle, gold nucleus, electron.

   i What type of charge (positive or negative) does each have?

   ii List the three particles in order, from smallest to largest.

b Describe the 'plum pudding' model of the atom.

c Draw a diagram to show how an alpha particle could be scattered backwards by a gold atom, towards the source from which it came.

d Explain why most alpha particles passed straight through the gold foil.

23.21

Diamond is a form of carbon. It is made up (almost entirely) of carbon-12 atoms. The symbol for the nucleus of a carbon-12 atom is $^{12}_{6}C$.

a i How many protons are there in a carbon-12 atom?

   ii How many neutrons?

b How many electrons are there in a neutral carbon-12 atom?

Using the following data, it is possible to estimate the size of a carbon atom:

   density of diamond = $3500 \, kg/m^3$

   12 g of carbon-12 contains 6.0×10^{23} atoms

c Calculate the volume of 12 g of diamond.

d Calculate the volume occupied by each atom of carbon in diamond.

As shown in the diagram, we can picture each atom occupying a tiny cube of side length d, equal to the diameter of the atom, so that the volume occupied by the atom $V = d^3$.

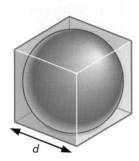

Figure Q23.21

e Use your answer to part **d** to estimate the diameter d of a carbon atom. Explain why your answer is only an estimate. Would you expect the true value of d to be greater than, or less than, your estimate?

Chapter 24

24.22

Alpha, beta and gamma radiations are three types of radiation produced by radioactive substances.

a Copy and complete the table to show the nature of these radiations.

Radiation	Symbol	Type of particle or electromagnetic radiation	Mass	Charge
alpha				
beta				
gamma				

b A school has two radioactive sources for use in physics experiments. One is a source of alpha radiation, the other of beta radiation. They have lost their labels, and the teacher wants to check which is which. Use your knowledge of the different penetrating powers of these radiations to suggest how this might be done.

24.23

Alpha, beta and gamma radiations are produced by radioactive substances. They are sometimes described as *ionising radiations.*

a Explain what is meant by the term *ionisation.*

b Name another type of ionising radiation.

c Ionising radiation can damage living cells. Describe three possible consequences of this.

24.24

The radiation produced by radioactive substances has many uses.

a Describe a use of gamma radiation that makes use of its ability to damage living tissues.

b Describe a use of beta radiation that makes use of the fact that it is absorbed by a few millimetres of solid matter.

24.25

In an experiment to determine the half-life of a radioisotope, the graph shown was obtained.

a From the graph, what was the background count rate?

b What was the initial count rate from the sample (i.e. disregarding the background count rate)?

c From the graph, deduce the half-life of the radioisotope. Draw a sketch graph to illustrate your method.

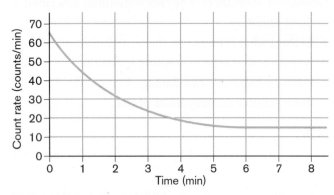

Figure Q24.25

Chapter 25

25.7

In nuclear fission, a massive nucleus (such as uranium or plutonium) splits. Two daughter nuclei are produced, and energy is released.

a What other particles are produced?

b In what two forms is the energy that is released?

c Explain how a chain reaction can be established in a mass of uranium.

d The daughter nuclei produced in fission are usually unstable. What important consequence does this have for the nuclear power industry?

The active Earth

Topics in this chapter

◆ structure of the Earth

◆ seismic waves

◆ plate tectonics

Figure 26.1 Alfred Wegener (1880–1930) was a German meteorologist (he studied the weather). He was the first scientist to produce a reasoned theory of continental drift. Amongst his evidence was the discovery of tropical ferns among fossils on the Arctic island of Spitzbergen. Either the climate had once been very warm close to the North Pole, or the land itself had once been closer to the equator.

Alfred Wegener (Figure 26.1) was a good scientist but an unfortunate man. He was interested in the idea of continental drift. This is the idea that the continents were once joined together – a very old idea, which came about when the first maps of the world were drawn. It seemed obvious that the shapes of Africa and South America fitted together, and many people suggested that these two continents had drifted apart. Perhaps all of the continents had once been a single landmass that had gradually broken up, with individual continents moving slowly across the surface of the Earth.

Wegener published his book *Our Wandering Continents* in 1915. He didn't simply base his theory on the jigsaw puzzle pattern of the continents. He brought much more evidence to bear on the idea. These are some of the things he noticed.

● The sequence of rock types along the west coast of Africa matched the rock types along the east coast of South America.

● Fossils of a small sea-living reptile called *Mesosaurus* were found in rocks of the same age on both sides of the Atlantic Ocean.

● Similar collections of plant species were also found fossilised on both sides of the Atlantic.

This convinced Wegener that these two continents had once been joined. He went further than this: he produced evidence that all the continents had once been joined in a single landmass, which he called *Pangaea* (meaning 'all the Earth') – see Figure 26.2.

Finally, perhaps Wegener's most astonishing idea came from the discovery that many rocks in Africa showed signs of having been weathered by the action of ice. He suggested not only that the continents moved across the surface of the Earth, but also that they might have moved from the poles to the tropics. Today's Antarctica was once a tropical island; Africa was once beneath the ice of the South Pole.

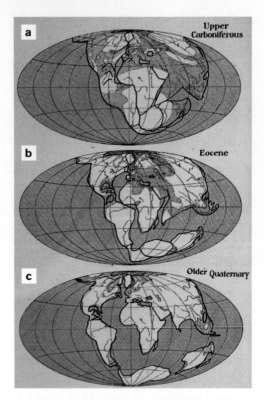

Figure 26.2 **a** Alfred Wegener's map of Pangaea, the single landmass formed when all of today's continents were joined together about 220 million years ago. **b,c** Pangaea starts to break up and drift apart, and our modern continents begin to form.

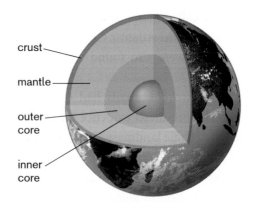

Figure 26.3 The internal structure of the Earth. The densest materials are at the centre; the least dense rocks form the crust. The highest temperatures are also at the centre.

All this was too much for many scientists. There were two problems:

1 They could not see any direct evidence of the continents moving. If they truly were still on the move, they could only be moving very slowly. The Earth was thought to be a few tens of millions of years old, and this didn't seem to allow time for these great movements.

2 It was difficult to imagine a mechanism that would provide the huge forces needed to move such giant masses.

Although Wegener had many supporters, and he had drawn on a great many sources of evidence, his ideas were broadly rejected by the scientific establishment. Physicists in particular, led by Lord Kelvin, discounted the theory. They regarded his observations of similar patterns of rocks and fossils on distant continents as simply an interesting coincidence. Wegener was right and the physicists were wrong, but the influence of Wegener's opponents was so great that it was fifty years before his ideas were seen to be justified. The unfortunate Wegener did not live to see his theory triumph.

Later in this chapter we will see how the theory of plate tectonics came about, and how it justified Wegener's ideas. Before that, we will look at what we know about the structure of the Earth.

26.1 Inside the Earth

We live on the surface of a spherical Earth. In fact, the Earth is not perfectly spherical; it is slightly soft and, as it spins, it widens slightly around the equator. Its equatorial radius is about 20 km greater than its polar radius. Inside the Earth, geologists have identified three distinct layers (Figure 26.3):

● *Crust* or *lithosphere* This is the Earth's hard outer shell. The oldest rocks (up to 3.8 billion years) are found in the continental crust, beneath the continental landmasses. This part of the crust is up to 70 km thick. The oceanic crust, beneath the oceans, is younger (up to 200 million years) and thinner (6–11 km).

● *Mantle* This is about 3000 km thick and accounts for 80% of the Earth's volume. The mantle rocks are denser than those of the crust, which is why the crust floats on the mantle. They are also hotter, so that they are partially molten.

● *Core* This has a radius of about 3500 km. The core is a sphere of iron and nickel, two dense metallic elements. The outer core is hot enough to be molten. The inner core is even hotter – up to 6000 °C, a similar temperature to the surface of the Sun. However, here the pressure is so great that the metal remains solid.

Looking inside

Geologists know most about the rocks of the crust. Some can be seen on the surface of the Earth. Others have been examined by mining or drilling to see what lies below the surface. The deepest boreholes go no deeper than about 15 km (although that is a great achievement), so how do we know what lies below the crust?

Evidence comes from earthquakes. An earthquake is a violent rearrangement of rocks in the crust or upper mantle. Shock waves called **seismic waves** spread out from the centre or focus of an earthquake, and these can tell us about the nature of the material through which they are moving. Earthquake recording laboratories are stationed all around the globe, and these use **seismographs** to pick up details of the tremors produced by an earthquake, which may be on the other side of the Earth. Figure 26.4 shows an example of the trace produced by a seismograph during a major earthquake.

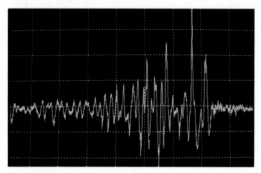

Figure 26.4 The screen display of a seismograph at the University of Tokyo, Japan. The trace shows the tremors detected during the Kobe earthquake of 16 January 1996, which measured 7.1 on the Richter scale. The vertical divisions represent time intervals of 5 seconds.

When an earthquake occurs, it is recorded by most seismographs. The further they are from the focus, the longer it takes the seismic waves to arrive. Geologists can then deduce how long the waves have been travelling. They can also work out something about the materials through which the waves have been moving.

Two types of seismic waves can be identified: **primary** or **P waves**, and **secondary** or **S waves**. P waves travel faster than S waves, so they arrive first at a detector – hence the words 'primary' and 'secondary'. The differences between these are summarised in Table 26.1. Figure 26.5 shows representations of both types. P waves are longitudinal – a sequence of compressions and rarefactions, similar to sound waves. S waves are transverse, and do not pass through liquids. A consequence of this is that S waves cannot pass through the core, since the outer core is liquid.

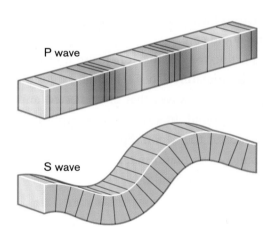

Figure 26.5 The nature of P and S seismic waves. P waves are longitudinal, whereas S waves are transverse.

Refracted waves

As P and S waves travel outwards from the focus of an earthquake, their directions change. This is because they are *refracted* by the material through which they are moving. Figure 26.6 shows typical paths of such waves. You will notice that the biggest changes of direction occur when P waves enter or leave the core. This is because their speed

Table 26.1 The properties of P and S seismic waves.

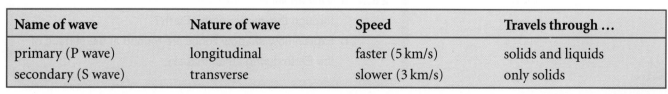

Name of wave	Nature of wave	Speed	Travels through ...
primary (P wave)	longitudinal	faster (5 km/s)	solids and liquids
secondary (S wave)	transverse	slower (3 km/s)	only solids

changes dramatically here. The waves also curve slightly within the mantle and core, because the material does not have a uniform density, so the waves gradually change speed. The S waves travel only within the mantle; they are absorbed by the liquid core.

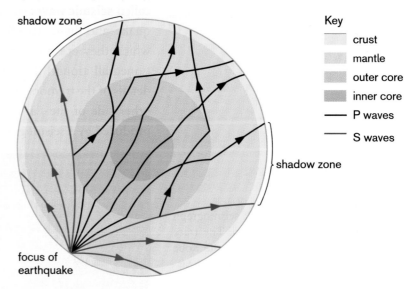

Figure 26.6 Geologists have learnt about the interior of the Earth by studying the movement of seismic waves (P and S waves) through it. The waves are refracted as their speed changes. Refraction by the core results in shadow zones, where no waves arrive at the surface.

From Figure 26.6, you can see that there are regions of the Earth's surface where no waves arrive. These are known as **shadow zones**. These result from the fact that P waves are refracted away by the core, while S waves are absorbed. This is the most striking evidence we have for the existence of the Earth's liquid core.

When geologists are prospecting for oil, they often use a seismic technique, like an earthquake in miniature. They set off an explosion on the Earth's surface and detect the waves that are reflected and refracted by layers of rock underground. In a similar way, explosions have been set off on the surface of the Moon. Spaceprobes on the surface have detected the seismic waves that result, and these data are used to find out about the interior of the Moon.

Questions

26.1 Which layer within the Earth is: **a** liquid; **b** partially molten; **c** made of iron and nickel; and **d** also known as the lithosphere?

26.2 There are two types of seismic wave: P waves and S waves. Which of these: **a** travels fastest through the Earth; **b** is a transverse wave; and **c** can travel through the Earth's core?

26.3 **a** Why do seismic waves change direction as they pass through the interior of the Earth?

b Explain how shadow zones are formed at the surface of the Earth during an earthquake.

26.2 Plate tectonics

An understanding of the structure of the Earth was essential to the development of the theory of **plate tectonics**, the theory that followed on from Alfred Wegener's theory of continental drift, which we considered at the start of this chapter. The rocks of the crust are solid, but they float on the more liquid material of the mantle. It is movement of the rocky material on the mantle that gives rise to continental drift.

The crust of the Earth is divided into many plates, nine large ones and a dozen or so smaller ones (Figure 26.7). Each continent sits on a large plate, and other large plates make up the ocean floor. It is the gradual movement of these plates that accounts for continental drift.

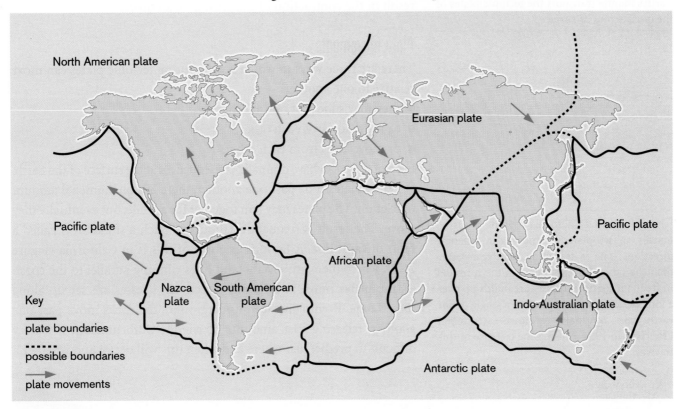

Figure 26.7 The tectonic plates that make up the surface of the Earth. As the plates move, they carry the continents with them.

How can we explain the movement of such giant objects as tectonic plates? Remember that the Earth's crust is less dense than the mantle, so that it floats on it. The mantle is hot and partially liquid. The mantle is also hotter than the crust. Great convection currents flow in the mantle, bringing up hotter material from deep inside the Earth – see Figure 26.8. The moving material of the mantle carries the crustal plates across the Earth's surface, like passengers on a giant conveyor belt. The rate of movement is generally slow – only a few centimetres each year – which means that it is difficult to make direct measurements.

These convection currents in the mantle transfer heat energy from deep inside the Earth to its surface. The inside of the Earth is hot for two reasons.

1 The Earth formed from a mass of hot gas and dust, which still retains some of its heat.

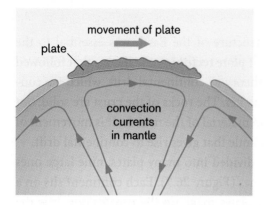

Figure 26.8 Convection currents within the Earth's mantle transport the tectonic plates of the crust across its surface.

2 The rocks of the Earth contain radioactive elements such as uranium and radium. These are gradually decaying (and have been since the Earth formed). Radioactive decay releases energy (see Chapter 24), and this is the origin of most of the heat inside the Earth.

When Wegener's theory of continental drift was being debated, early in the twentieth century, no-one had any idea of the vast amounts of energy that are being released by radioactive materials inside the Earth. This was why so many noted scientists rejected his theory. They preferred an older theory: that the Earth had gradually cooled and solidified, and that its surface features were formed as it cooled. The wrinkles of mountain ranges and the dips of oceans were simply the result of the contraction of the crust as it solidified.

Plate movements

There are three ways in which neighbouring tectonic plates can move relative to one another:

- they may slide past one another;
- or move towards each other;
- or move away from each other.

Each of these can have dramatic consequences at the surface of the Earth.

When plates slide past one another, there is a phenomenal amount of friction. The plates may jam together for a while, but eventually they move. The result is frequent earthquakes. Such a situation is called a **fault** or **fault line**. A famous example of this is in California (Figure 26.9), where there are several fault lines running parallel to the coast. As the plates move in different directions, stresses are set up along these faults. Eventually, deep underground, the rocks move past one another, releasing vast amounts of energy. Unfortunately, it is very difficult to predict just where and when this will occur, and whether a

Figure 26.9 Coastal California is prone to earthquakes. **a** Two plates are moving in different directions; one is travelling 5 cm/year faster than the other. Friction between them results in frequent tremors. If pressure builds up over a long period, the result may be a single major earthquake. **b** A major earthquake struck San Francisco in 1994, causing the collapse of this freeway.

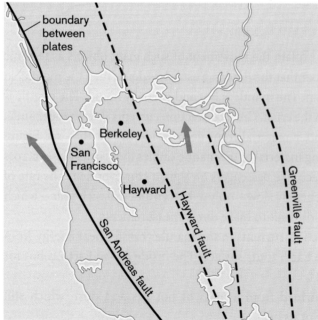

single large earthquake will be the result, or many minor tremors. This means that earthquake prediction is a very difficult business.

Two tectonic plates are colliding with one another on the western coast of South America. The Nazca plate is an oceanic plate, thinner and denser than the South American plate. As they collide, the oceanic plate is pushed downwards (or subducted) beneath the continental plate (Figure 26.10), forming a **subduction zone**. The continental plate is compressed so that it wrinkles up, forming a **mountain range** – the Andes in this case. As the oceanic plate dives down into the Earth's hot interior, it melts and becomes part of the mantle. Some of the molten material pushes upwards through the solid continental plate and emerges at the Earth's surface in the form of a volcano. The Andes range contains several active volcanoes, such as Cotopaxi in Ecuador.

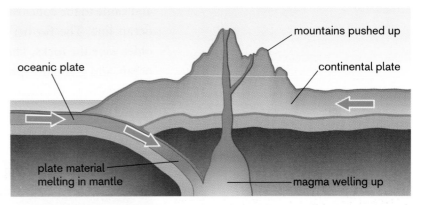

Figure 26.10 In a subduction zone, an oceanic plate is pushed down beneath a continental plate. The continental plate crinkles up to form a mountain range. The material that dips down into the Earth becomes partially molten; some of it pushes back up to the surface and emerges as a volcano. The high temperatures generated result in the conversion of sedimentary rocks into metamorphic rocks.

Finally, two tectonic plates may pull apart from one another. As they move in opposite directions, the resulting fracture in the Earth's surface fills up with magma, molten rock pushing up from the mantle below. This forms new oceanic crust (Figure 26.11) – a **mid-oceanic ridge** forms. This is what is happening in the mid-Atlantic, for example. This situation is associated with hot vents or 'smokers' (see

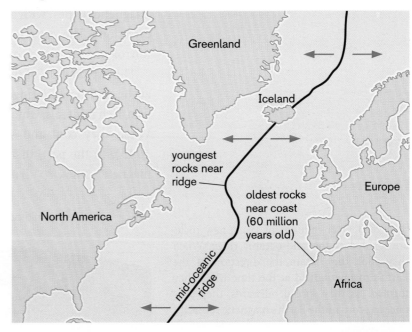

Figure 26.11 In the mid-Atlantic, two oceanic plates are moving apart in opposite directions. New oceanic crust is formed from material welling up from the hot mantle below.

Figure 6.1 on page 84), where boiling, sulphurous water is bubbling up from deep under the ocean bed.

Evidence for plate movements

It is possible to guess the positions of tectonic plate boundaries by mapping where earthquakes and volcanoes occur. Mountain ranges such as the Alps and Himalayas mark where plates are colliding. However, the most convincing evidence for the movement of plates comes from measurements of the ocean floor.

In the late 1960s, geologists collected rock samples from the bed of the Atlantic Ocean. They were looking for possible oil and gas fields beneath the sea. What they discovered was surprising: they found the age of the rocks using radioactive dating methods (see Chapter 24), and came to the conclusion that the youngest rocks lay along the mid-ocean line. The further they moved away from the mid-ocean, the older were the rocks. This suggested that the sea-floor formed at mid-ocean, and gradually spread outwards (Figure 26.12).

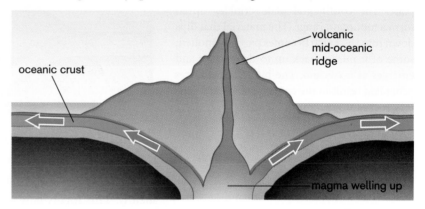

Figure 26.12 An oceanic ridge lies along the middle of the Atlantic Ocean. The youngest rocks lie close to the ridge; the oldest rocks, about 60 million years old, lie furthest from the ridge.

Previously, scientists measuring the magnetism of ocean-bed rocks had found another interesting pattern. The rocks carry a pattern of 'magnetic stripes', with alternate bands of rock magnetised in opposite directions. The patterns on opposite sides of the mid-ocean line are mirror images of each other.

The explanation of this is as follows. As molten rock wells upwards at the mid-oceanic ridge, it gradually cools and solidifies. It contains iron-rich minerals, which are magnetised by the Earth's magnetic field. When they cool and solidify, they retain this magnetism (Figure 26.13). In the past, there have been periodic reversals of the Earth's magnetic poles, so that the direction of the Earth's magnetic field

Figure 26.13 Over millions of years, new rocks are formed at the mid-oceanic ridge. When they cool, they retain the direction of the Earth's magnetic field at the time when they formed. As they spread outwards, they produce a record of the Earth's magnetic reversals.

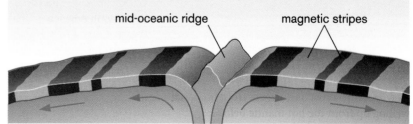

reverses every few million years. Hence the rocks showed a record of these reversals. Knowing the ages of the rocks, it was possible to work out just when these reversals had occurred.

These two patterns (magnetic stripes and age of rocks) confirmed the idea that the ocean floor is gradually spreading out from the mid-ocean line, as two oceanic plates move apart from one another. This is the strongest evidence we have for the theory of plate tectonics.

Questions

26.4 Why is it difficult to make accurate predictions of the timing and magnitude of earthquakes?

26.5 Japan is an island group formed by the relative movement of two tectonic plates. Use Figure 26.7 to help you identify these plates.
  a How are they moving relative to one another?
  b Explain how this accounts for the presence of active volcanoes in Japan.

26.6 Look at the map of the Earth's tectonic plates (Figure 26.7).
  a Which plates are moving to give rise to the mid-Atlantic oceanic ridge?
  b Explain why you would expect the movement of the Nazca and Pacific plates to give rise to a mid-oceanic ridge.

Summary

- The Earth consists of a core, mantle and crust. The hottest, densest material is at the centre.

- Seismic waves travel out from an earthquake. Observations of primary (P) and secondary (S) waves have allowed geologists to deduce the interior structure of the Earth.

- The Earth's crust is divided into tectonic plates. These are moved by giant convection currents flowing in the mantle.

- The relative motion of plates results in earthquakes, volcanoes, the formation of mountain ranges and the spreading of the sea-floor.

- Evidence for the movement of tectonic plates comes from patterns in the ages of rocks from the sea-floor, and in their magnetism.

Around the Earth

Topics in this chapter

- ◆ gravity
- ◆ orbiting under gravity
- ◆ *weightlessness*
- ◆ satellites

To see the Earth from space must be a marvellous thing. The first astronauts, who went into space in the early 1960s, were in orbits less than 200 km above the Earth's surface. This meant that they could only see a part of the Earth. However, when astronauts reached the Moon, they could look back and see the whole of the Earth, a light blue ball in the darkness of space, flecked with white clouds, and with the brown and green shapes of the continental landmasses (Figure 27.1).

To see the Earth like this, you need to board a spacecraft, which will lift you upwards, pushing against the pull of the Earth's gravity. It takes a lot of energy to do this. Today, we are familiar with the sight of giant rockets launching the latest satellites into orbit. The fuel they burn provides the energy needed to lift the spacecraft (and the rocket itself) up through the Earth's gravitational field. We are familiar, too, with the

Figure 27.1 The Earth rising behind the Moon. Although such images are familiar today, they had a dramatic impact on people's view of the Earth when they were first published. This picture was taken from Apollo 11 by NASA astronauts who visited the Moon in 1969.

Figure 27.2 Bangladesh, viewed from a satellite in space. This low-lying country stands on the delta of the Ganges and Brahmaputra rivers. It is threatened by rising sea-levels, a consequence of global warming. Satellite observation can help to monitor the development of this problem.

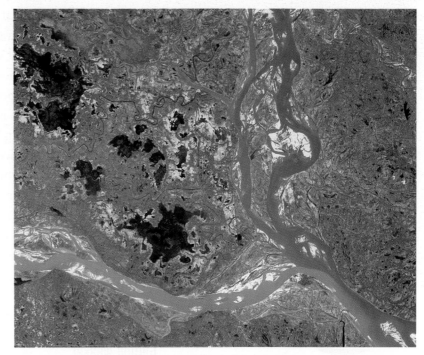

images sent back from orbiting satellites (Figure 27.2). These are shown every day in weather forecasts, but they have many other uses, such as in prospecting for minerals, observing the growth of crops, and spying on a potential enemy's military operations.

Would space be a desirable holiday destination? In the 1990s, the first tickets were sold to would-be space holidaymakers. For tens of thousands of pounds, they were promised a trip in a shuttle and a stay in a space hotel in low-Earth orbit. Although the first flight was fully booked, the tickets showed no departure date.

27.1 Gravity

The Earth's gravity pulls us down. If we jump upwards, we return to the ground because of gravity. The force that ensures we do not disappear into space is our weight, the name we give to the force of gravity that acts on us (see Chapter 2).

The Earth's gravity pulls on everything in its vicinity. It pulls on people, other animals, plants, soil and rocks, birds as they fly and satellites as they orbit. It pulls on the atmosphere, ensuring that it does not escape. It even pulls on the Moon, keeping it in orbit around the Earth.

In fact, as we shall see in Chapter 28, without gravity the Earth would never have formed.

Explaining gravity

How can we understand gravity? Gravity is one of the fundamental forces of Nature that underlie all of the forces we experience in everyday life. The Earth exerts a gravitational pull on us because it has mass. In fact, the Earth has a very large mass (about 6×10^{24} kg), and it is only

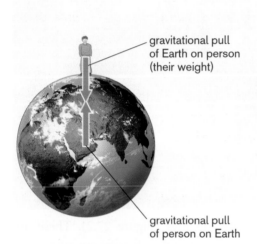

Figure 27.3 The Earth's gravitational pull on a person is their weight. It is caused by the Earth's mass, acting at the Earth's centre pulling on the person's mass. Equally, the person exerts a gravitational pull on the Earth. We show each of these forces by an arrow at the centre of gravity of the object on which it is acting. Newton's third law tells us that the two forces must be equal and opposite; they are an example of action and reaction.

Figure 27.4 The Earth exerts a gravitational pull on other objects. This is represented by its gravitational field, shown by radiating lines of force to the Earth's centre. The field gets weaker the further you are from the Earth's surface.

because its mass is so great that we notice its effects. The Moon's mass is much smaller and its gravity is therefore weaker. If astronauts visited a small asteroid, they would find that its gravity was very weak indeed, so that it would not hold them in place.

The Earth's gravity depends on its mass. It attracts any other object that has mass – gravity is the force of attraction between masses. People also have mass, but because our masses are so small, we do not attract things with a noticeable force. In fact, we do attract the Earth with a force equal to our weight – see Figure 27.3. The Earth pulls us down with a force *mg*, and we pull back on the Earth with an equal force. These two forces must be equal and opposite; this is a consequence of Newton's third law of motion (see page 58). The Earth's pull on us has a large effect, because we are small. Our pull on the Earth has very little effect, because the Earth is so large. If your weight is 500 N, your pull on the Earth is 500 N, and you can imagine that this will have only a minuscule effect on an object of mass 6×10^{24} kg.

Getting weaker

As a space rocket lifts off, it starts its climb upwards, away from the Earth. It is moving upwards through the Earth's gravitational field. We imagine this as the region around the Earth in which its gravity acts. We can represent it as shown in Figure 27.4, by lines of force, rather like the lines of force of a magnetic field. The arrows show the direction in which the Earth's gravity pulls. This diagram shows us two things about the Earth's gravitational field:

1 As the rocket gets higher, the pull of the Earth's gravity gets weaker. This is shown by the lines of force becoming further apart the further you are from the Earth. In fact, if the rocket doubles its distance (measured from the centre of the Earth), the pull of gravity decreases to a quarter of its previous value.

2 The lines of force extend outwards for ever. This tells us that the Earth's gravity extends far out into space – in fact, the Earth exerts a gravitational pull on every other object in the Universe. Of course, for most objects this pull is very tiny indeed. However, the Sun's pull on the Earth must be significant, even though the Sun is 150 million kilometres away; otherwise we would not continue in our orbit around the Sun.

Some wrong explanations

It was Isaac Newton who first came up with a modern explanation of gravity. He realised that the Earth's gravity could do two things:

● it could pull an apple downwards as it fell from a tree, and
● it could keep the Moon in its orbit around the Earth.

He realised that it was the *masses* of the Earth, the apple and the Moon that caused these forces – not their colour, or their chemical composition, or their magnetism or electric charge.

Although we have known that mass causes gravity for three centuries, people still have other strange explanations. It is worth asking people for their ideas. You may get explanations like this:

'Gravity is caused by the Earth spinning; if it stopped, we would all fall off.'
Wrong! The same people often think that, if the Earth started spinning faster and faster, we would all fly off into space, which is true.

'Gravity is caused by the Earth's magnetism.'
Wrong! Gravity and magnetism are two, unrelated, fundamental forces of Nature.

'Gravity is caused by the Earth's atmosphere.'
Wrong again! Perhaps people think this because they are remembering that the Moon's gravity is weak, and there is no atmosphere on the Moon. They have got cause and effect the wrong way round: the weak gravity means that there is no atmosphere.

Gravity acts between every pair of objects in the Universe that have mass. Your mass pulls on the most distant star, but your effect is tiny. The planets pull on you, but their effects are tiny, too. That is one of the reasons why physicists find it hard to accept the claims of astrologers that we are influenced by the positions of the stars and planets.

Questions

27.1 What name is given to the force exerted by the Earth's gravity on an object?

27.2 Table 27.1 shows the masses of three astronauts, and their distances from the centre of the Earth.

   a Which astronaut will feel the strongest gravitational pull?

   b Which will feel the weakest?

Astronaut	Mass (kg)	Distance from centre of Earth (km)
A	80	7000
B	60	8000
C	80	8000

Table 27.1 Information for question 27.2.

27.3 Here are two statements comparing the Moon and the Earth.

   (i) The mass of the Earth is 80 times the mass of the Moon.

   (ii) The radius of the Earth is four times the radius of the Moon.

   a Explain why statement (i) suggests that an astronaut standing on the Moon's surface will weigh less than back home on the Earth's surface.

   b Explain why statement (ii) suggests that the astronaut will not weigh 80 times more on the Earth than on the Moon.

27.2 Into orbit

The Moon is the Earth's natural satellite. It orbits the Earth at an average distance of 380 000 km, and takes about four weeks to do so. Isaac Newton used a 'thought experiment' to explain how gravity could hold an object in orbit around the Earth (Figure 27.5). Picture a very high mountain on the Earth. At the top of the mountain stands a large cannon. The cannon can fire a shell horizontally. When a shell is fired, its path depends on its initial speed. The diagram shows four typical tracks.

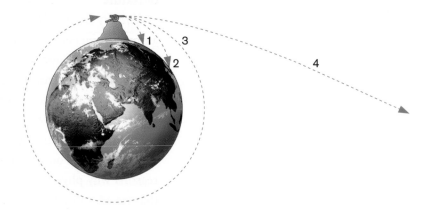

Figure 27.5 Newton's thought experiment. He wanted to explain how gravity could hold an object in a circular orbit around the Earth. An object moving too slowly will fall to the ground; an object moving too fast will fly off into space.

1 This shell is the slowest. It follows a curved path down to the ground.
2 Shell 2 is faster than shell 1, so that it travels farther before it reaches the ground. Notice that, because of the curvature of the Earth, it travels a greater distance than if the Earth had been flat.
3 This shell is faster still. In fact, it is fired at just the right speed so that its curved path follows the curve of the Earth. Gravity is constantly pulling it towards the centre of the Earth, but, at the same time, the surface of the Earth is curving away below it. As a consequence, it continues along a circular path around the Earth – it is in orbit.
4 Shell 4 is the fastest. Gravity pulls on it so that its path is slightly curved. However, because it is travelling so fast, gravity is not strong enough to prevent it from flying off into space.

If you could do this experiment in practice, you would find that a shell with an initial speed of 8 km/s would stay in a circular orbit, just above the Earth's surface. This is the speed of spacecraft that travel a few hundred kilometres above the Earth.

Force, mass and acceleration

Many spacecraft orbit the Earth along circular paths. Gravity keeps them in their orbits – in fact, gravity is the only force acting on them (Figure 27.6). The diagram shows that, as a spacecraft travels around the Earth:

● its weight (the pull of gravity) is always directed towards the centre of the Earth;
● its velocity is always at right angles to its weight.

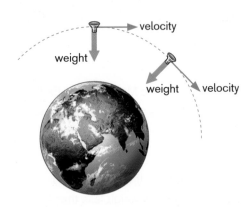

Figure 27.6 The only force acting on a spacecraft in a circular orbit around the Earth is its weight – the pull of the Earth's gravity on it. Its velocity is always at 90° to this force.

Gravity makes the spacecraft accelerate towards the centre of the Earth. This means that its *velocity* is changing. However, its *speed* is not changing. You should recall the difference between speed and velocity (see Chapter 1): speed is a scalar, whereas velocity is a vector. Although the spacecraft is travelling at a constant speed, its direction is changing. Change in direction means change in velocity, i.e. acceleration.

When a spacecraft orbits the Earth, it does not need to keep its rocket motors working. Why does it need no source of energy?

- The spacecraft is travelling at steady speed, so its kinetic energy is not changing.
- It is travelling at a constant height above the Earth, so its gravitational potential energy is not changing.

Hence, in a circular orbit at constant speed, a spacecraft's energy does not change, and so no source of energy is required. Another way to think of this is as follows. Gravity is pulling the spacecraft towards the Earth. However, it does not get any closer to the Earth. This means that the force of gravity does no work on the spacecraft, so the energy of the spacecraft does not change. (Recall from Chapter 8 that: work done by a force = force × distance moved *in the direction of the force*; the spacecraft is moving at right angles to the force.)

Notice that, since there is only one force acting on the spacecraft, it is not in equilibrium. If the forces on it were balanced, it would travel in a straight line.

Higher still

Some satellites are in orbit far out from the Earth – for example, the communications satellites used for satellite television transmission. Here, the Earth's gravitational field is weak and so they do not need to travel so quickly to avoid being pulled down to the Earth's surface. The greater the distance from the centre of the Earth, the slower the orbiting satellite must travel.

A consequence of this is that, the greater the radius of a satellite's orbit, the longer it takes to orbit the Earth. An extreme example is the Moon. It is about 400 000 km from the Earth. At this distance, it need only move at 1 km/s to stay in orbit. This is why it takes four weeks to complete one orbit.

The Earth is not the only object with satellites. The Solar System is a collection of planets orbiting the Sun under the influence of its gravity. The most distant planets (Uranus, Neptune and Pluto) travel most slowly and take the longest time to complete one orbit. The Solar System itself orbits the centre of gravity of our Galaxy, the Milky Way.

We now know of more planets outside the Solar System than in it. Astronomers looking at a nearby star may notice a tell-tale wobble in its motion. This is caused by a massive planet in orbit around it. It is more correct to say that the star and the planet are in orbit around their mutual centre of gravity (Figure 27.7). The star, which has the

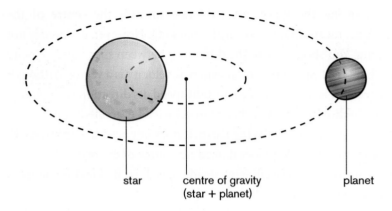

star   centre of gravity   planet
        (star + planet)

Figure 27.7 How to detect an invisible planet around a star. The star and the massive planet orbit around the centre of gravity of the combination. To an observing astronomer on Earth, the star appears to be moving first forwards and then backwards. Although the planet itself cannot be seen, it is possible to deduce its presence from the wobble of the star.

greater mass, orbits closest to the centre of gravity; the planet, being less massive, orbits further out. When astronomers see evidence of a star moving back and forth like this, they know that they have evidence for a large planet in orbit around it.

Extension material

Figure 27.8 Fun and games in a spacecraft. This astronaut is experiencing weightlessness. In practice, this state can be a problem. Eating, drinking and going to the toilet are difficult, and having no sense of which direction is down can lead to sickness. Modern spacecraft are designed so that the occupants all sit and work the same way up, so as not to confuse the brain.

Weightlessness

If you see film or video of astronauts floating around inside their spacecraft (Figure 27.8), apparently weightless, it can look like fun. This freedom to move about, unhindered by gravity, is something many of us would like to experience. However, in practice, astronauts find it rather difficult to cope with weightlessness. The sight of one of their colleagues coming towards them upside down or, worse still, on their side, can lead to feelings of nausea. An attack of sickness in a spacecraft is no laughing matter!

Humans like to know which direction is 'down'. We have organs, the semicircular canals in our ears, which sense gravity and allow us to divide the world into up and down. Problems arise when what we see conflicts with what we sense. An upside-down person looks wrong, and we imagine that we are the wrong way up. This mental confusion is what leads to sickness.

What is going on when astronauts experience weightlessness? Some people imagine that they are so far above the Earth that they are beyond its gravitational pull, but this is not so. Typical orbits for manned spacecraft are less than 1000 km above the Earth's surface, and here its gravity is only 25% less than we experience at ground level. So the astronauts still have weight, even if it is a bit less than on Earth. Indeed, if the spacecraft did not experience the Earth's pull, it would not orbit at all – it would disappear off into space.

In fact, when you experience weightlessness, you are constantly accelerating towards the Earth. Your weight makes you accelerate, and this keeps you on your curved path around the Earth. An astronaut, and the spacecraft in which he or

she is travelling, are both accelerating downwards under the pull of gravity. Because they both have the same acceleration, they fall at the same rate and the astronaut never reaches the floor of the spacecraft.

You could experience the same thing here on Earth. Imagine being inside a lift (an elevator). The cable that supports it snaps, and it accelerates downwards. You also fall under the pull of gravity. Take your feet off the floor of the lift, and you will hover in mid-air until the nasty moment when the lift reaches the bottom of the shaft. For a few seconds, you will have been 'weightless'.

Being weightless while in orbit is thus the same as being in free fall: you are moving freely under the pull of gravity; the only force acting on you is your weight.

Questions

27.4 A satellite orbits the Earth at a constant speed and at a constant height above the Earth's surface.
  a Explain why a force is needed to keep it in its orbit.
  b What is this force?
  c Explain whether the satellite is in equilibrium.
  d Which of the following remain constant as the satellite orbits:
      its velocity   its acceleration   its kinetic energy.
27.5 Venus orbits the Sun. Its orbit is closer to the Sun than the Earth's orbit.
  a Which travels at a greater speed around the Sun, Venus or the Earth?
  b Which takes longer to orbit the Sun?
27.6 The Moon follows a roughly circular path around the Earth. Explain how its path would change if:
  a the Moon's speed suddenly halved;
  b its speed suddenly doubled.

27.3 Spacecraft at work

Spacecraft have many different uses, and they have made a big difference to our everyday lives. (The word 'satellite' is often used instead of 'spacecraft'. Strictly speaking, a satellite is in orbit around a larger object; some spacecraft are not satellites.) Here are some uses of spacecraft.

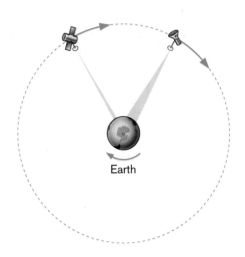

Figure 27.9 Geosynchronous satellites are used for satellite TV transmissions. They travel once around the Earth in 24 hours, remaining above the same point on the equator.

Communications satellites

Hundreds of communications satellites are in orbit above the equator. These are used for beaming television broadcasts down to Earth; individual consumers fit a dish receiver to the wall or roof of their home to collect the electromagnetic waves transmitted by the satellite.

Such satellites are described as geostationary or geosynchronous. This means that they orbit the Earth once each day. As they orbit, the Earth turns below them, so that they stay above the same point on the Earth's surface all the time (Figure 27.9). The receiving dish does not have to alter its position to track the satellite. Geostationary orbits are a long way off in space; their radius is about six times the radius of the Earth.

Only a limited number of geostationary satellites (about 400) can be put in place. This is because, if two were close together, a dish receiver would collect signals from both, and the signals would interfere with each other.

Other satellites, used by mobile phone networks, are in low orbit over the equator, typically 200 km up. Signals are sent up from a ground station and back down to receivers. These satellites move rapidly across the sky, so they must be tracked by turning the transmitting and receiving dishes to follow them. They suffer from friction with the atmosphere, even though it is thin at this height. This slows them down, so they tend to drift downwards. Rockets push them back to their desired orbit, but when their fuel supply runs out, they slowly fall towards Earth, eventually burning up.

Polar-orbiting satellites

As well as satellites whose orbits are over the equator, there are satellites that orbit the Earth from pole to pole (Figure 27.10). It takes such a satellite about 90 minutes to complete one orbit of the Earth if it is just a few hundred kilometres above the surface. As the Earth turns beneath it, it can scan the Earth's surface. In the course of a day, it can send back images of a large part of the Earth. Such monitoring satellites have many uses:

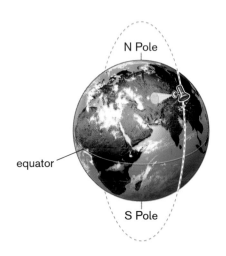

Figure 27.10 A polar-orbiting satellite travels around the Earth in an orbit that takes it directly over the North and South Poles. On each orbit, it can monitor a strip of the Earth's surface.

- taking weather measurements – cloud cover, pressure, wind speed and direction, temperature, etc., for use by meteorologists;
- observing environmental features of the Earth – such as crops and other vegetation, rock formations for mineral prospecting, and changes in sea-levels;
- making astronomical observations (Figure 27.11) – ground-based telescopes produce poor images because the atmosphere absorbs or distorts much of the radiation;
- for military purposes – including spying and possibly carrying weapons.

At night, you may be able to see a polar-orbiting satellite. They look like a bright star, moving steadily across the sky, heading north or

Figure 27.11 The Hubble Space Telescope has produced many images to excite astronomers. Because it is positioned above the Earth's atmosphere, it has a much clearer view of space. The stars it sees do not 'twinkle', since their light has not been distorted by irregularities in the atmosphere.

south, taking perhaps 20 minutes to cross your field of view. Some newspapers publish details of when you may see a satellite such as the International Space Station.

The Global Positioning Satellite (GPS) system uses a network of satellites orbiting the Earth. Each satellite transmits radio signals, which can be detected on Earth. At any one time, four or five satellites are above the horizon for an observer on Earth. Someone who requires an accurate measurement of their own position uses a receiver that picks up the signals from these satellites. A tiny computer measures the time it has taken each signal to reach the receiver, and works out the distance of each satellite. From this, it can calculate the receiver's position on the Earth to within a fraction of a metre. GPS receivers have proved a great benefit to people who enjoy sailing and wilderness walking.

? Questions

27.7 Every geostationary satellite orbits the Earth once every 24 hours. The radius of its orbit is 42 300 km.

   a Calculate the speed of a geostationary satellite.

   b Is a geostationary satellite in equilibrium? Explain your answer.

   c Explain why a geostationary satellite remains above the same point on the Earth's surface as it orbits.

27.8 What benefits can come from having an astronomical telescope on board a spacecraft orbiting the Earth?

Summary

◆ Gravity is an attractive force that acts between any two objects that have mass. The greater their masses, the stronger the force.

◆ The Earth's gravity decreases the further you are above the Earth's surface.

◆ An object that orbits another object under its influence is not in equilibrium. The force of gravity causes it to accelerate, holding it in its orbit.

◆ The farther an orbiting object is from the Earth, the slower it must move to remain in orbit, and the longer it takes to complete each orbit.

◈ *Orbiting objects are in free fall. They appear weightless, although they are still acted on by the force of gravity.*

◆ Satellites have many uses, including communications, Earth-observation, astronomy and military applications.

The Solar System

Topics in this chapter

◆ rotation of the Earth

◆ the Moon and the Sun

◆ the nine planets

◆ orbits of planets and comets

℮ the search for life elsewhere

Roughly four-and-a-half billion years ago, a giant, swirling cloud of dust and gas condensed to form the Solar System, where we live today. Gravity was the force that led to this condensation. Each particle in the cloud attracted every other particle, and they gradually came together. At the centre of the cloud, a mass of hydrogen gas collected. It got hotter and hotter, glowing more and more brightly – the Sun had formed. Further out, dust and ice particles stuck together to form the planets (Figure 28.1).

Figure 28.1 The Solar System is thought to have formed from a swirling cloud of dust and gas. The Sun and the planets formed at the same time. In this impression, the new Sun is beginning to glow, while the surrounding cloud of dust and ice is condensing to form the planets. The force of gravity pulls all this material together.

When the Solar System formed, the Universe was already about ten billion years old. Many stars had already formed, lived and died. Some of the material from these dead stars was incorporated into the new Solar System.

Why did the Sun become hot? The hydrogen particles of which it is made were attracted together by gravity, because of their mass. As they fell towards the centre of the cloud, they speeded up. Colliding with one another, they shared out their kinetic energy. So gravitational potential energy was transformed to kinetic energy. A gas of fast-moving particles (with a lot of KE) is very hot. So, as the gas condensed, it became hotter. Eventually, when the temperature reached several million degrees, the process of nuclear fusion started up. This released more energy, and the Sun still shines today thanks to nuclear fusion.

When astronomers look out into space with their most high-powered telescopes, they can see new solar systems forming. Figure 28.2 shows a new star surrounded by a disc of dust in which planets are forming.

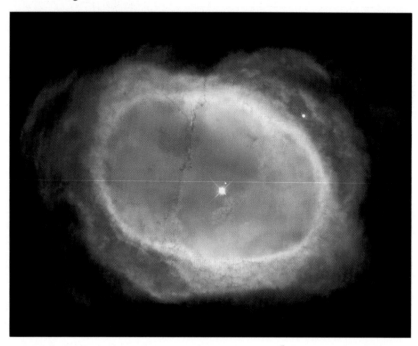

Figure 28.2 New 'solar systems' are thought to be forming all the time, as new stars are formed in distant parts of our Galaxy. This image was made by the Hubble Space Telescope, and shows a cloud of dust around a new star. The dust will gradually condense under the pull of its own gravity to form planets. The clouds are disc-shaped, so that the planets will all move around the star in a flat plane, just like our own Solar System.

In this chapter we will look at the planets of the Solar System, what they are made of and how they move. We will end by looking at the possibility that life may exist on other planets, and how we might be able to detect signs of life in other planetary systems far off in space.

28.1 The moving Earth

The rotation of the Earth

Today, most people accept that the Earth is a rotating sphere, and that it orbits around the Sun. This picture took a long time to become the conventional view – it is easier to believe that the Earth is at the centre of things, with the Sun moving around the Earth. Figure 28.3 shows a fifteenth-century view of the Universe, with the Earth at the centre and the Sun (shown as a star) in an orbit around the Earth.

The Earth travels around the Sun in an orbit that is almost a perfect circle – see Figure 28.4. (In fact, the orbit is very slightly distorted from circular; it is an ellipse.) It takes one year to travel around this orbit. Of course, there are no signposts in space to tell us when we have returned to our starting point, so it is difficult to measure the length of a year.

Figure 28.3 A drawing from the fifteenth century, representing the Solar System. The Earth is at the centre, with the Moon in the nearest orbit to it. Then come Mercury, Venus and the Sun (shown as a star). Beyond are three more planets: Mars, Jupiter and Saturn, followed by the sphere of fixed stars. Although the relative positions of the Earth and Sun are incorrect, this diagram shows the other planets in the correct order.

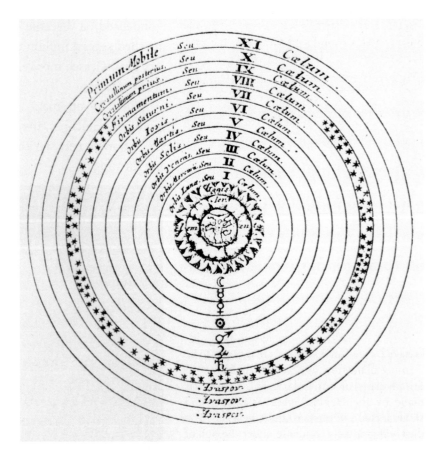

You could count the days from the shortest winter day to the shortest day a year later. Alternatively, you could notice where the Sun rises above the horizon on a particular day, then count the days until it rises again at the same point. You would find that the length of a year is roughly 365 days. In fact, a very accurate value is 365 days, 5 hours, 48 minutes and 45.96768 seconds! Simple techniques could never hope to achieve such precision.

As well as moving around the Sun, the Earth also rotates about an axis that passes through the North and South Poles. This, of course, is why we experience night and day. The Sun appears to move across the sky from east to west; in fact, the Earth is rotating from west to east.

Although we think of the Earth turning once each day, this is not strictly correct. After 24 hours, the Sun returns to the same point in the sky; however, the Earth has turned through slightly more than one complete revolution in this time. Figure 28.4 shows why.

In position 1, the Sun is directly overhead as seen from point X on the Earth. In position 2, the Earth has turned through 360°. However, the Earth has moved a short distance along its orbit, and X is no longer pointing straight at the Sun. The Earth must turn a little more until X is pointing directly at the Sun and the Sun is overhead again. It takes 23 hours 56 minutes to travel from position 1 to position 2, and an extra 4 minutes to turn so that X is facing the Sun again. That makes 24 hours in total, and the Earth has rotated through a little more than 360°.

Figure 28.4 The Earth in its orbit around the Sun. The Earth completes one orbit in a year. The movement of the Earth from one day to the next (indicated by positions 1 and 2) has been exaggerated.

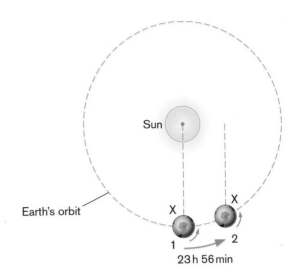

Questions

28.1 What mathematical name is given to the shape of the Earth's (not quite circular) orbit around the Sun?

28.2 The Earth spins once on its axis every 23 hours 56 minutes. A day lasts 24 hours. If the Earth rotated around its axis at the same rate but in the opposite direction, how long would a day be? (Looking at Figure 29.4 may help you to answer this.)

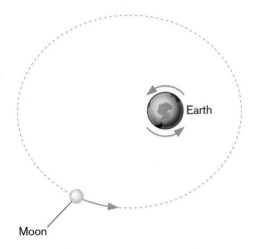

Figure 28.5 The Moon's orbit around the Earth is slightly elliptical (although the effect is exaggerated in this picture). This means that at certain times it is closer to the Earth than at others. Hence its apparent size in the sky changes slightly, although this is not noticeable to the naked eye.

28.2 Moon and Sun

The Sun travels across the sky during the day, a result of the Earth's rotation. The Moon also crosses the sky, following a similar path to the Sun. This motion is also caused by the rotation of the Earth. However, there is a difference: the Moon's position in the sky changes slightly more slowly than the Sun's. This is because the Moon is slowly orbiting around the Earth, from west to east – see Figure 28.5. The Moon's orbit is slightly elliptical, so that it is closer to us at some times than at others. It takes about one month to make one complete orbit.

There is also another difference between the Moon and the Sun. The Sun is the source of its own light; we see the Moon because it reflects sunlight to us.

The origin of the Moon is uncertain. There are several theories, each with its own supporters:

● The Moon may have formed as a separate, small planet. Later, it was attracted out of its orbit by the gravitational pull of the Earth.

● The Moon and the Earth may both have formed at the same time, close to one another, along with the rest of the Solar System. They have continued to travel together ever since.

- The Earth may have initially spun much faster than today. The Moon may have arisen from matter thrown off by the rapidly spinning Earth.
- The Earth may have been subjected to a violent impact from another large object – a small planet or a large comet or asteroid. Material from the damaged Earth collected together to form the Moon.

This last theory has the widest support among astronomers. However, more samples will need to be collected to allow geologists to compare rocks from Earth and Moon, to see which theory is best supported by the evidence.

Questions

28.3 Which is a source of its own light, the Sun or the Moon?

28.4 Explain why the Sun and the Moon have the same apparent size when viewed from Earth, despite the fact that the Sun is many times bigger than the Moon.

28.5 Some people say:

'The Sun is in the sky during the day, the Moon is in the sky during the night.'

What is incorrect about this statement?

28.3 The nine planets

The planets and their orbits

Five planets (Mercury, Venus, Mars, Jupiter and Saturn) appear in the night sky. To the naked eye, they look like stars. They move steadily across the sky, just like the stars, as the Earth turns on its axis. However, if you watch them night after night, you will notice that their positions change gradually relative to the stars (Figure 28.6). The planets are different from the stars because they appear to 'wander' about the sky. In fact, the word 'planet' comes from the Greek word *planetes* meaning 'wanderer'.

[This 'wandering' is why astrologers say things like: 'Jane was born when Mars was in Leo.' This means that, on the day when Jane was born, the planet Mars appeared against the background of the stars that make up the constellation Leo. Later, as the position of Mars changes, it would appear in a different constellation.]

Ancient peoples had a clear view of the night sky, unpolluted by the lights of cities and motorways. To them, the different behaviour of the planets was easy to spot, and they attributed all sorts of significance to these heavenly bodies. Today, spacecraft have visited most of the planets, so we have a very different view of them.

Figure 28.6 This map shows part of the night sky, with the position of Mars as seen over the course of a year. Several dates of measurement are marked. Mars appears to move slowly against the background of fixed stars.

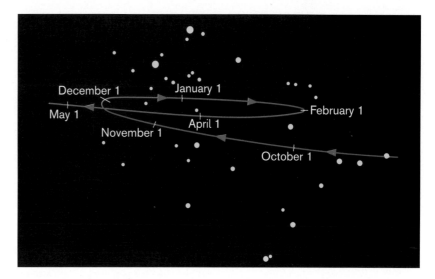

Table 28.1 Data relating to the orbits of the nine planets.

Planet	Time for one orbit, T (Earth years)	Average radius of orbit, d (10^6 km)
Mercury	0.24	58
Venus	0.62	108
Earth	1.00	150
Mars	1.88	228
Jupiter	11.86	778
Saturn	29.46	1427
Uranus	84.01	2870
Neptune	164.79	4497
Pluto	247.70	5902

As you might expect, there *is* a pattern in the 'wandering' of the planets. We can only explain it satisfactorily by assuming that the Earth and the other planets are orbiting around the Sun. Like the Earth, the other planets travel around the Sun in slightly elliptical orbits. These orbits are at different distances from the Sun, and the planets move through space at different speeds, taking different times to complete their orbits. Table 28.1 shows data for the period T (time for one orbit around the Sun) and distance d from the Sun for the nine planets, listed in order outwards from the Sun.

Now we are in a position to see why Mars appears to move, relative to the background of the fixed stars (Figure 28.7).

● Imagine being on the Earth in position 1, looking out towards Mars. You would see Mars against a background of a particular constellation, Aries say.

● A month later, the Earth has moved one-twelfth of the way around its orbit to position 2. Mars has moved about one-twentieth of the way around its orbit. Now when you look from Earth to Mars, you would see Mars against a background of a different constellation, perhaps Taurus.

Figure 28.7 When we observe the planets, we are looking at moving objects from our position on another moving object, the Earth. As we move from position 1 to position 2, we see Mars against a different background of stars.

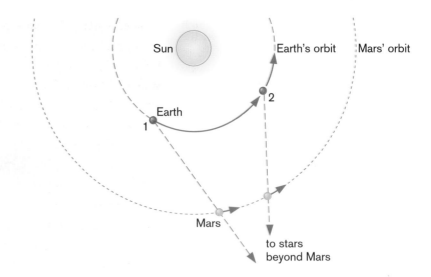

Discovering planets

Only six planets (including the Earth!) are visible to the naked eye. The other three (Uranus, Neptune and Pluto) were only discovered once telescopes had been invented.

Uranus was discovered in 1781 by an amateur astronomer, William Herschel (who also discovered infrared radiation). He was mapping stars in a particular region of the sky, and noticed a greenish object whose position appeared to change from one night to the next. He deduced that it was a planet, whose distance from the Sun was twice as far as Saturn's.

Careful measurements of the motion of Uranus showed that at times it appeared to speed up; at other times it slowed down. It seemed that another, undiscovered, planet was affecting its motion. Figure 28.8 shows how one planet can affect the motion of another.

Recall that, the further a planet is from the Sun, the slower it moves and the longer it takes for a complete orbit. Uranus orbits more quickly than Neptune, rather like two runners on a circular track; as Uranus catches up on Neptune, it is pulled forwards by Neptune's gravity. This makes it speed up (and slows Neptune down). Once Uranus has passed Neptune on the inside, it is pulled back by Neptune's gravity, so that it slows down to its original speed. This accounts for Uranus' changing speed as it travels around its orbit.

Mathematicians were able to calculate the position of Neptune, and astronomers turned their telescopes in that direction – and there it was, exactly as predicted. This discovery, in 1846, was a triumph for Newton's theories of motion and gravitation.

Figure 28.8 Planets orbiting the Sun can affect each other by their gravitational pull. As the inner planet (Uranus) catches up on the outer one (Neptune), it is pulled forward so that it speeds up. Once it has passed Neptune, the gravitational pull on it slows it down again. Neptune is affected in the opposite way: it first decelerates, then it accelerates.

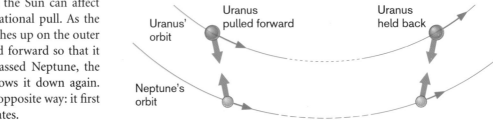

Later, when even more precise data were available, further calculations predicted the existence of a ninth planet. Pluto was discovered in 1930. This is probably the last planet to be discovered in the Solar System although, from time to time, suggestions are made that a tenth planet, 'Planet X', may exist. Whether or not further planets are discovered in the Solar System, many more remain to be found in orbit around other stars (see Chapter 27, page 425–6).

The asteroids lie in a belt between Mars and Jupiter. They are lumps of rock, all orbiting the Sun in parallel orbits. It is thought that they may represent a planet that never formed. Each time Jupiter's orbit brought it near to this material, its gravitational pull disrupted it so that it never had a chance to coalesce and become a single planet. Every now and then, asteroids collide with one another. This knocks them out of their orbits, and some fragments may reach the Earth. This is one source of 'shooting stars', seen as bright streaks across the night sky as they burn up in the atmosphere.

Types of planet

We can divide the planets into two types: rocky, and gas giants.

- The four planets closest to the Sun (Mercury, Venus, Earth and Mars) are relatively small and rocky. Each has a core, mantle and crust, like the Earth (see Chapter 26), surrounded by a relatively thin atmosphere.
- The next four planets (Jupiter, Saturn, Uranus and Neptune) are much larger. They each have a rocky core, but the bulk of their volume is made up of frozen gases – hydrogen, methane, ammonia, etc.
- Pluto is a small lump of rock and ice, in the coldest reaches of the Solar System.

The Sun is the source of heat and light for the Solar System. The further a planet is from the Sun, the smaller the amount of energy it receives from the Sun. Figure 28.9 shows how the temperature decreases with distance from the Sun. This graph can help us to understand why the inner planets are rocky, while the outer ones are gassy.

The inner planets are in the warmer part of the Solar System. In this region, gases such as hydrogen and carbon dioxide do not freeze. Thus, when these planets formed, only materials such as iron and silicon with high melting points joined together.

It is much colder where the outer planets formed. Here, substances that we think of as gases became solid and formed the bulk of these giant planets.

Surface gravity

Gravity is the most important force in the story of the Solar System. Gravity caused a cloud of dust and gas to condense and form the Sun and planets. Each planet came together because of the gravitational

Figure 28.9 The further you are from the Sun, the colder it is. Beyond the orbit of Mars, the temperature is low enough for gases such as hydrogen and carbon dioxide to condense.

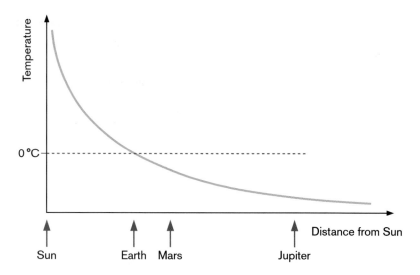

pull of all of its particles on each other. The planets remain in their orbits because of the pull of the Sun's gravity.

Here, on the surface of the Earth, we experience the pull of its gravity. It pulls with a force of about 9.8 N on each kilogram of our mass, so we say that the strength of the Earth's surface gravity is 9.8 N/kg. The Moon's mass is smaller, so that its surface gravity is less, about 1.6 N/kg.

Table 28.2 shows the surface gravity of each planet, together with some other related factors. The surface gravity g of a planet depends on two things:

- its *mass* – the greater the mass, the greater the value of g;
- its *radius* – the greater the radius, the smaller the value of g (because, on the surface, you are further from the centre of gravity).

Looking at Table 28.2 we can see that Venus and Earth have very similar sizes, but the mass of Venus is about 20% less than that of the Earth. Its surface gravity is therefore less than Earth's.

Table 28.2 Some important quantities for objects in the Solar System. From this information, you can understand how surface gravity is related to the mass and radius of a planet.

It is interesting to compare Saturn with the Earth. Its mass is about 100 times Earth's, but its radius is about 10 times Earth's. The result is that its value of g is very similar to Earth's. (Saturn's density is the low-

Object	Radius (km)	Mass (10^{23} kg)	Density (kg/m^3)	Surface gravity (N/kg)
Sun	700 000	20 000 000	1 400	270
Moon	1 740	0.7	3 340	1.6
Mercury	2 400	3.3	5 430	3.8
Venus	6 000	49	5 250	8.8
Earth	6 400	60	5 520	9.8
Mars	3 400	6.4	4 000	3.8
Jupiter	71 000	19 000	1 330	24.9
Saturn	58 000	5 700	690	9.1
Uranus	25 000	870	1 290	7.7
Neptune	24 000	1 000	1 640	11.0
Pluto	1 100	5	2 000	0.4

est of all the planets. It is less than $1000\,kg/m^3$ so, if you had a large enough tank of water, you could float Saturn in it.)

Jupiter's surface gravity is almost three times Earth's. If you travelled by spacecraft to land on Jupiter, you would find it extremely difficult to escape from its pull. Most fuels would not be able to supply enough energy to lift you free of its gravity.

The orbits of comets

Several comets are likely to be detected each year, but only occasionally can they be seen without a telescope. A comet is a dramatic object in the sky (Figure 28.10); it moves across the background of the fixed stars, at a rate much greater than that of a planet. For a long time, it was believed that they were visitors from outside the Solar System, and that they foretold significant events. (Indeed, it seems likely that the Star of Bethlehem was a comet that was visible from the Middle East in 5 BC.)

Now we know that comets are objects from the outer edges of the Solar System. They are lumps of rock and ice that follow highly elliptical orbits around the Sun. The fact that their orbits are much more elliptical than those of the planets means that they behave in a different way to planets. A planet travels at more-or-less steady speed around its orbit. Figure 28.11 shows how a comet's speed varies as it travels around the Sun.

- As the comet 'falls' towards the Sun, it speeds up. It is losing GPE and gaining KE.
- As it moves away from the Sun, it is slowed down by the Sun's gravity, and so it moves more and more slowly.

A comet moves most slowly when it is furthest from the Sun. This means that it creeps along in the furthest depths of the Solar System, perhaps for hundreds of years, before it plunges back in towards the Sun.

Figure 28.10 A comet develops its tail as it approaches the Sun. The comet warms up, and frozen material starts to evaporate from it. Electrically charged particles streaming outwards from the Sun push the tail so that it always points away from the Sun; this also causes the tail to glow.

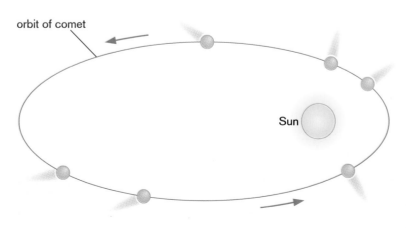

Figure 28.11 A comet travels along an elliptical path around the Sun. It speeds up as it plunges in towards the Sun, then slows down again as it goes back out into the depths of the Solar System.

Extension material

Searching for life

Scientists (and others) have endlessly debated whether life might exist on other planets, or elsewhere in space. Mars is a similar planet to Earth, and seemed a likely place for other creatures to live. At the end of the nineteenth century, a wealthy American called Percival Lowell built a private observatory in order to study Mars at a time when its orbit brought it close to Earth. There had been earlier suggestions that the surface of Mars was covered with channels caused by the flow of water. When Lowell looked through his new telescope, he was convinced that he could see a network of artificial canals. Figure 28.12 shows one of his drawings. He believed that there must be intelligent beings on Mars, and that they had developed a system of irrigation canals to water the surface of the dry planet.

Today, spacecraft have orbited Mars and landed on its surface. There is no evidence of water there, though there may have been in the distant past. Percival Lowell's pictures indicate the low power of his telescope's lenses and the high power of his imagination.

What should we look for if we hope to detect life elsewhere in space? This depends on whether we are looking for life in general (which might mean relatively simple organisms, such as bacteria), or intelligent life. The Search for Extra-Terrestrial Intelligence project, known as SETI, has been going on for several decades, but without any positive results.

Signs of intelligence

The Earth is constantly sending radiation out into space. All of our many broadcasting stations produce signals (radio waves), which spread out from a transmitter, and much ends up in space, travelling outwards at the speed of light. It is just possible that we might pick up similar signals coming to us from intelligent beings on another planet.

It is more likely that such beings might deliberately transmit signals that could be picked up by us (or creatures elsewhere) and would convince us of their intelligence. The SETI project has been using radio telescopes since the 1960s to look for such signals, but as yet they have found nothing.

Signs of life

It seems more likely that we might find evidence of less intelligent life by one of two other means:

We might obtain material from elsewhere in the Solar System. For example, spacecraft might visit other planets or their moons and use robots to collect material. This might be examined on-site, or brought back to Earth for laboratory investigation. We could look for evidence

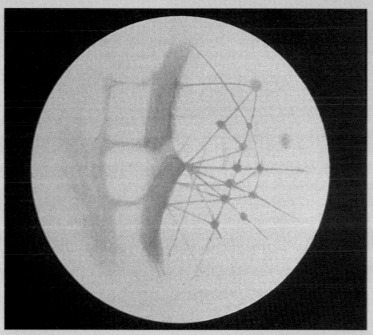

Figure 28.12 A drawing of the surface of Mars, made by Percival Lowell in 1894/95. He believed that he could see a network of irrigation canals, evidence of the presence of intelligent beings. It is thought that many of the parallel lines that he could see were a result of slight defects in the lenses of his telescope.

of fossil organisms in rocks. Alternatively, we might hope to find creatures such as bacteria actually living on these planets or moons. A few lumps of rock that originally came from Mars have been found on Earth; they were knocked from Mars by the impact of a comet that collided with the planet. In 1996, a group of scientists caused a stir by claiming that they had found evidence of fossilised bacteria in one of these rocks (Figure 28.13), but this was disputed by other scientists.

Another possibility is to examine the atmospheres of other planets or moons. Our atmosphere contains a large proportion of oxygen (20%). This is because of the presence of green plants, which produce oxygen as a by-product of photosynthesis. Signs of oxygen in a planet's atmosphere would then be a good indication of the presence of life. It is not essential to visit a planet to know about its atmosphere. Instead, its composition can be deduced by looking at the spectrum of light coming from it.

Jupiter and Saturn are gas giants, and so are unlikely to harbour life. However, they have several rocky moons, which are similar in size to the Earth, and might be sensible places to look for signs of life.

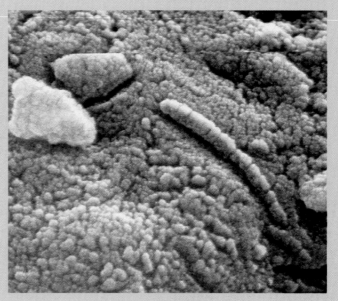

Figure 28.13 This piece of rock, found on the Earth, came originally from Mars. In 1996 it was suggested that the thread-like markings (right) are the fossils of micro-organisms, evidence that life had once existed on Mars, although only a minority of scientists accepted this at the time.

? **Questions**

28.6 **a** What is meant by the surface gravity g of a planet?

b Which two factors determine g?

28.7 Look at the data in Table 28.2.

a Work out the values of mass/radius^2 for each planet.

b Plot a graph to show how surface gravity g of a planet depends on mass/radius^2.

c Describe any pattern you see in the graph.

28.8 The planets nearest the Sun are described as 'rocky', whereas the further planets are 'gas giants'.

a Explain what is meant by these terms.

b Why are gas giant planets only found at great distances from the Sun?

28.9 **a** At what point in a comet's orbit is it moving fastest?

b Describe how the kinetic energy and gravitational potential energy of a comet change as it travels around its orbit.

Summary

◆ The Solar System is believed to have formed from a swirling cloud of dust and gas. Gravitational attraction between particles in the cloud caused the Sun and planets to form.

◆ Night and day occur because of the rotation of the Earth about its axis.

◆ The planets orbit the Sun in orbits that are slightly elliptical (like squashed circles). Comets have orbits that are much more elliptical.

◆ The planets nearest the Sun are small and rocky; the further planets are cold, gas giants.

◆ The surface gravity of a planet depends on its mass and radius.

◉ *Scientists looking for life elsewhere in space look for micro-organisms or their fossils; alternatively they may look for evidence of life in the composition of a planet's atmosphere.*

◉ *Intelligent life might be sending signals to us, to indicate its existence.*

The Universe

Topics in this chapter

- stars, galaxies and the Universe
- light-years
- fusion and the elements
- life cycle of stars
- evidence for an expanding Universe
- the Big Bang

The Universe contains everything we can see – planets, stars, distant galaxies (Figure 29.1). It contains much that we cannot see – dark clouds of dust and gas with many galaxies hidden from view behind them. We think of the Universe as containing everything that we *could* know about; the word 'universe' means that it contains everything.

Now some physicists have suggested that our Universe may be just one of many universes. Where are the others? To answer this, we need to think a little about black holes.

When some very massive stars come to the ends of their lives, they collapse inwards. Their own gravity pulls them inwards until they are very, very dense. In fact, the density of matter at the centre of such a

Figure 29.1 Our idea of the Universe has changed radically over the years. It is less than two centuries since astronomers agreed that there were galaxies beyond our own Galaxy, the Milky Way. Now powerful telescopes have shown that there are billions of other galaxies, spread throughout the vastness of space. This photograph, made by David Malin of the Anglo-Australian Observatory, shows a spiral galaxy similar to the Milky Way. If this were our Galaxy, the Sun would be on the edge of one of the spiral arms, about two-thirds of the way out from the centre.

black hole is thought to be infinite. Matter anywhere near a black hole is sucked in, disappearing down a giant 'plug-hole' in space.

Some physicists have come up with the idea that, when a black hole forms, a new baby universe appears from within it. This new universe is not inside our Universe; it is elsewhere, with its own three dimensions of space. The new universe expands outwards from a point, just as it appears that our Universe is expanding from a Big Bang that occurred billions of years ago.

We cannot hope to look into a black hole and see a baby universe. The gravitational pull of a black hole is so great that light cannot escape from it; that is why it is black. However, this does not mean that the 'many-universe theory' cannot be tested. The theory tries to explain many of the interesting features of our own Universe: why it has existed for so long; why there appear to be many black holes; how it started, and how it will eventually end. If a successful theory answers such questions and also predicts the existence of baby universes, then it may turn out that our Universe is just one of many that exist.

29.1 Stars and galaxies

The Sun is a star. It is just one of many billions that make up our Galaxy, the Milky Way. If you live somewhere where the night sky is free of light pollution (or if you holiday in such a place), you will have seen the bright band of stars in the Milky Way crossing the sky. Although the Milky Way is a spiral galaxy like the one shown in Figure 29.1, we do not see it as a spiral. We are looking at it edge-on; we see a bright band of stars across the sky because we are looking inwards, towards its centre. Figure 29.2 shows an image of the Milky Way, made by combining many separate photographs of different regions of the Galaxy.

If you know where to look, you can see one or two more galaxies with the naked eye. A galaxy is a cluster of many billions of stars – there

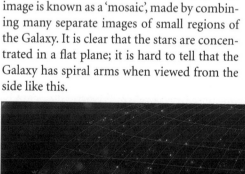

Figure 29.2 The Milky Way, our Galaxy. This image is known as a 'mosaic', made by combining many separate images of small regions of the Galaxy. It is clear that the stars are concentrated in a flat plane; it is hard to tell that the Galaxy has spiral arms when viewed from the side like this.

are perhaps one hundred billion stars in the Milky Way. The Milky Way occupies only a tiny fraction of the Universe, and beyond the Milky Way lie many billions of galaxies. If there are 10^{11} galaxies in the Universe, and each contains 10^{11} stars, that makes a total of 10^{22} stars:

10 000 000 000 000 000 000 000 stars in the Universe

A galaxy is held together by the gravitational attraction that each star has for the others. In a similar way, we now know that galaxies, too, tend to cluster together. The force of gravity extends throughout the Universe, and is the force that explains the formation of planets, stars, galaxies and clusters of galaxies.

The scale of things

It is difficult to determine how far away the Sun is. It is much harder still to measure the distance to the stars. Looking at the night sky, you might imagine them all to be equally distant. In fact, the nearest star (other than the Sun) is 250 000 times as far away as the Sun; the most distant stars that we can see in the Milky Way are a thousand times farther away than this.

We could give all of these distances in metres or kilometres. However, for such large distances, it is easier to think in terms of a much bigger unit of length, the light-year (ly):

One **light-year** (1 ly) is the distance travelled by light in one year.

Notice that the light-year is a unit of *distance*, even though it may sound like a unit of time. Since light travels at 3×10^8 m/s and there are roughly 3×10^7 s in one year, it follows that:

$1\,\text{ly} \sim 10^{16}\,\text{m} = 10\,000\,000\,000\,000\,000\,\text{m}$

Table 29.1 shows the distances from Earth to some significant astronomical objects, measured in light-years. (The distance to the Sun is given as 500 light-seconds (ls); this means that light takes 500 s to reach us from the Sun. Its distance is a small fraction of a light-year.)

When we see a distant star, say one that is 1000 ly away, its light has taken 1000 years to reach us. This means that we are seeing it as it was 1000 years ago. We see the Sun as it was 500 s (about 8 minutes) ago.

Table 29.1 Some astronomical distances, given in light-seconds (ls) and light-years (ly). One light-second (1 ls) is the distance travelled by light in a second, about 3×10^8 m.

Object	Distance from Earth
Sun	500 ls
edge of Solar System	25 000 ls
next nearest star	4.2 ly
far edge of Milky Way	100 000 ly
next nearest galaxy	170 000 ly
most distant observed stars	10 000 000 000 ly

Looking out into space is like looking back in time. Since the most distant stars we can see are about 10 billion light-years away, this suggests that the Universe itself may be about 10 billion light-years across. We might also guess that it is about 10 billion years old, and this agrees with other methods for determining the age of the Universe.

The Universe contains a lot of empty space. There may be many stars in a galaxy, and many galaxies in the Universe, but there is also a lot of empty space in between. This is another consequence of gravity. The stars attract one another to form a galaxy, and galaxies attract one another to form clusters. This leaves a lot of empty space in between.

?

Questions

29.1 **a** What name is given to our Galaxy?

b What shape does it have?

c Explain why it is difficult for an observer on the Earth to tell that it has this shape.

29.2 Barnard's Star is at a distance of 5.9 ly from the Earth. How long does it take light to travel from Barnard's Star to an observer on the Earth?

29.3 Jupiter is at a distance of 780 000 000 km from the Sun. The speed of light in empty space is 3×10^8 s.

a How long does it take light to travel from the Sun to Jupiter?

b How far is Jupiter from the Sun, in light-seconds?

29.2 The life of a star

Stars (including the Sun) produce light by the process of nuclear fusion. In fusion, the nuclei of light elements join together to form the nuclei of heavier elements. For example, four hydrogen nuclei may fuse to form a helium nucleus. In the process, energy is released, and this is the source of the star's radiation. For fusion to occur, very high temperatures are needed. The temperature inside a star reaches millions of degrees, so fusion is possible.

During the twentieth century, scientists unravelled the story of how stars form, how nuclear fusion starts, and how they eventually die. In this section, we will look at that story.

How stars form

We have already discussed the importance of gravity in astronomy. A star forms when a cloud of dust and gas pulls itself together by its own gravitational attraction. Each particle is attracted by each of the others, so that each feels itself pulled towards the centre of gravity of the mass. As the cloud collapses inwards, it gets hotter and hotter. Gravitational potential energy is being transformed to kinetic energy (see page 430). The material at the centre of the cloud becomes a star; and planets may form around it. Figure 28.2 (on page 431) shows what are thought to be new stars forming, surrounded by a disc of material that will become planets. Figure 29.3 shows a region of our own Galaxy where new stars are forming in a region of space that is rich with gas and dust.

Figure 29.3 New stars are seen here in the Eagle Nebula, forming from clouds of dust and gas.

The temperature in the central core of a star is millions of degrees. The particles of which it is made are rushing around very energetically. They press outwards, preventing the star from collapsing any further under its own gravity – see Figure 29.4. Thus the outward force provided by the pressure of the moving particles balances the inward force of gravity. The two forces are in equilibrium.

Inside the star, where it is hottest, fusion is going on at a steady rate. Energy is being released, and eventually this energy escapes from the surface of the star. A star can remain like this for billions of years. The Sun has been glowing for over four-and-a-half billion years, and is probably only half-way through its life.

How stars die

Telescopes allow us to see millions of stars. By looking at the differences between them, we can work out how stars form, live and die. Most of the stars that we see are in the steady, equilibrium state, producing energy at a constant rate. Some are at the end of their lives. How they die depends on their masses – see Figure 29.5.

The Sun is a fairly typical, middle-aged star. In a few billion years, it will start to run out of fuel and the nuclear fusion process will come to an end. As this happens, the Sun will blow up to form an enormous **red giant** star, engulfing the nearest planets, including the Earth. The cool outer layers will then blow off into space. The inner material will collapse inwards (due to gravity), and form a small **white dwarf** star (see Figure 29.6). Eventually this will simply fade away.

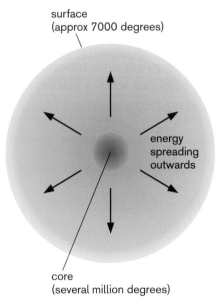

surface
(approx 7000 degrees)

energy
spreading
outwards

core
(several million degrees)

Figure 29.4 Inside a star. The surface temperature of a star is a few thousand degrees. Inside, in its dense core, it is much hotter. This is where the process of nuclear fusion is going on, releasing energy. The inward force of gravity, tending to make the star collapse inwards, is balanced by the outward pressure of the moving particles.

Figure 29.5 The way in which a star dies depends on its mass. It may end up as a white dwarf, a neutron star or a black hole.

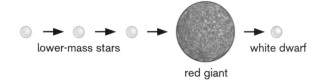

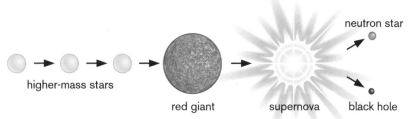

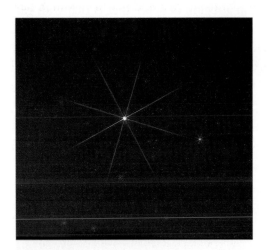

Figure 29.6 The Dog Star (Sirius) is one of our nearest neighbours in the Solar System. It has a companion, a white dwarf star known as the Pup, which is the remains of a star that was once similar to Sirius. A white dwarf star is no bigger than a large planet.

If a star is more massive than the Sun, it dies in a more spectacular way. It forms a red giant with a heavy core, which collapses more and more. In a sudden searing flash, it bursts apart in a gigantic explosion. This is a **supernova**. Each year, astronomers detect a few of these catastrophic events out there in the Universe.

The remnant of a supernova may be either a **neutron star**, which is a planet-sized object made mostly of neutrons, or, if the star was supermassive, a **black hole**. A black hole consists of matter that has collapsed inwards under its own gravity. Its density is so great and its gravitational pull is so strong that nothing can escape from it, not even light. You might think that a black hole would be very difficult to see, and you would be right. One way in which their presence *can* be detected is by the X-rays that are produced when a black hole rips material from a nearby star – see Figure 29.7.

Figure 29.7 A black hole is rather like a plug-hole in space. Any object that comes near to it is likely to be sucked in. Here, material is being dragged from a nearby star. As it accelerates into the black hole, it loses energy in the form of X-rays. Detecting X-rays coming from the site of a supernova hints at the existence of a black hole where a star used to be.

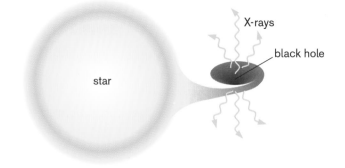

Recycling stardust

In the process of nuclear fusion, a star produces new elements. A star like the Sun turns hydrogen into helium, carbon, oxygen and so on. These are the lightest elements, at the start of the Periodic Table. However, bigger stars produce heavier elements.

As a massive star reaches the end of its life, its core contracts and gets hotter and hotter. These are the conditions needed to fuse carbon nuclei together to form elements such as silicon and iron. When it explodes as a supernova, the temperature is high enough to form the heaviest elements, including uranium. These substances are then blasted out into space to join the clouds of dust and gas from which new stars are formed.

The Solar System contains some of the heaviest elements. There is uranium in the Earth's rocks, and the Earth's core is mostly iron and nickel. These elements could not have been created in the Sun. This suggests that the Solar System must have formed from 'stardust', material that was blown out into space in the course of a supernova explosion. Your body contains iron, carbon, oxygen, potassium, sodium and so on – these elements were created by fusion in a long-dead star.

Questions

29.4 When a star dies, it may become a white dwarf, a neutron star or a black hole. What factor determines which of these it becomes?

29.5 a What process is going on inside a star to release energy?

b Why does a star not collapse completely under its own gravitational pull?

29.3 The life of the Universe

In the course of four centuries, physicists and astronomers have made great changes in how we view our place in the Universe. The fifteenth-century chart of the Solar System shown in Figure 28.3 (page 432) places the Earth at the centre, with the Sun and planets orbiting the Earth, and a ring of stars beyond the outermost planet. At the time, many people believed that Jerusalem was the very hub of the Universe, and that the Universe did not extend much beyond the orbit of Saturn.

Since then, observational astronomy has taken off and we have a very different view of things. We live on a small planet circling an average star, towards the edge of a spiral galaxy. Our star is just one of billions of stars in the Galaxy, which is just one of many billions of galaxies. Our importance at the centre of things seems to have evaporated. Many scientists argue that there must be many more planets like the Earth, and some must have intelligent life on them. (Many other scientists disagree with this – it's a hot debate.)

Today, astronomers believe that the most distant stars in the Universe are 10–15 billion light-years distant, and that the Universe itself is 10–15 billion years old. What evidence do they have to support this idea?

Figure 29.8 Two American astronomers. **a** Henrietta Leavitt found a method of measuring the distance to other galaxies. **b** Edwin Hubble discovered that distant galaxies are moving away from us. The Hubble Space Telescope is named after him.

The expanding Universe

The Universe is expanding. This discovery was made in the 1930s, and was based on the work of two American astronomers (Figure 29.8).

● Henrietta Leavitt made detailed observations of variable stars. These are stars whose brightness varies from day to day, in a regular way. By finding a pattern that related a star's brightness and the rate at which it varied, she was able to work out how far a variable star was from the Earth. This meant that astronomers could work out how far away other galaxies were.

● Edwin Hubble looked at the light from stars in other galaxies. He noticed that the light from distant stars was redder than that from nearby stars. He realised that this 'red-shift', or change in frequency, occurred because the stars were speeding away from us.

The **red-shift** that Hubble noticed is related to the Doppler effect. You may have noticed that, when an emergency vehicle approaches you and then goes past, the note of its siren drops – this is the **Doppler effect**. In a similar way, the light waves coming from a distant star are stretched out as the star moves away from us (Figure 29.9). Their wavelength is longer, so they are closer to the red end of the spectrum.

Figure 29.9 Light waves reach us from a distant star. If the star is moving away from us, the waves are stretched out and the light looks redder.

What Hubble discovered was that almost all galaxies appear to be moving away from us; their light is red-shifted. What is more, the further away the galaxy, the faster it is moving.

Imagine such a Universe. It is full of galaxies, all rushing outwards, away from each other. Now imagine how this Universe must have been in the past. Run the movie backwards in your mind: all of the galaxies rush back together, so that they meet at a single point. That point in space and time was the start of the Universe.

The Big Bang

Most physicists and astronomers now accept this picture of the start of the Universe. It began with a gigantic explosion. All of the matter and energy that is now in the Universe exploded out of a single point – this was the Big Bang. In the first seconds of the life of the Universe, it was incredibly dense and incredibly hot. In the billions of years that have followed, it has expanded and cooled. Stars and galaxies have formed, planets have appeared, with life on at least one of them.

From initial temperatures of billions of degrees, space has cooled as it has expanded. The energy of the Big Bang is spread thinly throughout space, so that the average temperature is only about 3 K (three degrees above absolute zero). Physicists have detected this background radiation, known as the **microwave background** because it consists of low-energy microwaves. This is one of the main pieces of evidence that the Universe really did come into existence as a result of a Big Bang.

How will it all end? No-one is sure about this. Figure 29.10 shows two possibilities.

- *Low-mass Universe* As the Universe expands, it gradually slows down. The gravitational attraction of the galaxies for each other causes them to decelerate. This may not be enough to stop them from moving apart for ever.
- *High-mass Universe* However, if there is enough matter in the Universe, the galaxies may eventually slow down, go into reverse and head back towards one another. The Universe will end in a Big Crunch.

None of us will live to see this happen. However, the work of the next generation of physicists will almost certainly allow us to know what is the likely fate of the Universe.

Figure 29.10 The fate of the Universe depends on the amount of mass it contains. If there is sufficient, its expansion may stop and it will contract to a Big Crunch. If there is less mass, it will continue to expand for ever.

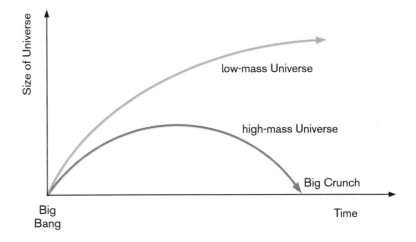

? Questions

29.6 Most galaxies are moving away from us, but a few nearby galaxies are moving towards us; their light is shifted towards the blue end of the spectrum. Draw a diagram like Figure 29.9 to show why the wavelength of light from an approaching star is blue-shifted.

29.7 Imagine that Edwin Hubble had discovered that the light from distant galaxies was not red-shifted, but that it was the same as light from stars in our own Galaxy.
  a What would this tell you about the Universe?
  b Why would this make it difficult to determine the age of the Universe?

Summary

◆ Our star, the Sun, is just one star in our Galaxy, the Milky Way. Their are billions of stars in a galaxy, and billions of galaxies in the Universe.

◆ Astronomical distances are often measured in light-years. One light-year is the distance travelled by light in one year.

◆ A star forms from a cloud of dust and gas, contracting under its own gravitational pull.

◆ Nuclear fusion is the energy source of a star. Light elements are fused together to form heavier ones.

◆ The fate of a star depends on its mass. It may end up as a white dwarf, a neutron star or a black hole.

◆ The Universe is thought to have come into existence as the result of a huge explosion, the Big Bang.

◆ Since then, the Universe has been expanding. The galaxies are moving rapidly apart. The evidence for this comes from the fact that their light shows a red-shift.

Further questions

The numbering is continued from the in-chapter questions.

Chapter 26

26.7

During an earthquake, P and S waves travel outwards from the centre or focus of the tremor.

a Which of these waves could be described as a sequence of compressions and rarefactions? Is this a transverse or longitudinal wave?

b Describe how the other type of seismic wave travels through the Earth.

c Which of these waves travels fastest?

d Give another example of a transverse wave.

e Give another example of a longitudinal wave.

26.8

The inner structure of the Earth is revealed by seismic waves. It consists of the core, mantle and crust. Compare these three regions in terms of:

a volume;

b density;

c temperature.

26.9

The Atlantic Ocean is gradually widening, as a result of the movement of tectonic plates (see Figure 27.11 on page 417). Use the following information to estimate the rate at which it is widening.

The newest rocks are in the mid-Atlantic.
The oldest rocks, approximately 60 million years old, are found at either side of the Atlantic Ocean.
The Atlantic Ocean is approximately 5000 km wide.

Chapter 27

27.9

A satellite orbits the Earth at a height of 2000 km above the Earth's surface. Its orbital speed is 6.9 km/s. [The radius of the Earth is 6400 km]

a Calculate the distance travelled by the satellite in one complete orbit.

b Calculate the time it takes the satellite to complete one orbit.

c Calculate the number of times the satellite orbits the Earth in one day.

d Suggest some uses for such a satellite.

27.10

A satellite is held in its circular orbit around the Earth by the Earth's gravitational pull on it.

a How does the size of this force compare with the gravitational pull of the satellite on the Earth?

b Draw a diagram to show the directions of these two forces.

c On your diagram, indicate the orbit of the satellite. Show how the satellite would move if the Earth's gravitational pull should suddenly stop acting on it.

Chapter 28

You will need to use the data for the nine planets given in Table 28.1 (page 435) to answer questions 28.10 to 28.12.

28.10

Look at the data in Table 28.1.

a Does T increase or decrease as d increases?

b In the early seventeenth century, Johannes Kepler looked at data similar to these and deduced that T^2 is proportional to d^3. Using a spreadsheet (or otherwise), check this relationship, and say whether it is true or false.

c Draw a graph of T^2 against d^3.

28.11

a Use the data in Table 28.1 to calculate the speed at which each planet orbits the Sun.

b What pattern can you find in these data?

28.12

Most of the asteroids lie in the asteroid belt, between Mars and Jupiter. Ceres is the largest asteroid; it orbits the Sun once every 4.61 years. Use the data in Table 28.1 to help you to estimate its average distance from the Sun.

28.13

Astronomers can examine the light coming from the atmosphere of a distant planet and deduce its composition. This could help in the search for life beyond the Earth. Which of the following gases might indicate the presence of life on another planet?

   hydrogen,   oxygen,   water vapour,
   carbon dioxide,   nitrogen

Chapter 29

29.8

How do the following support the theory that the Universe began with a Big Bang?

a The light from distant galaxies shows a red-shift.

b Space is filled with low-energy microwave radiation with a temperature of about 3 K.

29.9

a Explain what is meant by a light-year.

b Why is this a useful unit in astronomy?

29.10

A cloud of dust and gas in space condenses to form a star.

a What force causes it to contract?

b What energy transformation is happening as the star becomes hotter and starts to glow?

c What process results in the production of energy during the main lifespan of a star?

Index

absolute zero, 144–5, 157, 171
absorption of sound, 187
acceleration, 12–15, 28–31
acceleration, measurement 14–15, 40–1
acceleration, units 13–14
accelerators, 368, 371, 376
acid rain, 95
action and reaction, 58
activity, 393
air resistance, 38–9, 104
alpha (α) particle, 384–5
alpha (α) radiation, 373
alternating current, 310–11
ammeter, 283, 287
ampere (amp, A), 283
amplitude, 191, 243–4
analogue meter, 283
AND gate, 349–50
angle of incidence, 205, 212, 215–16
angle of reflection, 205
angle of refraction, 212
Aristotle, 119
astrologers, 423, 434
astronauts, 35–6
atom, models of, 136
atomic bombs, 381
atoms, size of, 367
attractive forces (between particles), 133–4
audiogram, 192
average speed, 2, 7

baby universes, 444
background radiation, 381–2
balanced forces, 31–2
barrels of oil, 92
base, 351
battery, 304
becquerel (Bq), 393
Becquerel, Edmond, 228–9
Becquerel, Henri, 382–3, 385, 391
beta (β) particle, 384–5
beta (β) radiation, 373
Big Bang, 450–1
Big Crunch, 451
binoculars, 216–17
biochemical monitoring, 390
biomass fuels (biofuels), 86
black holes, 443–4, 448
boiling point, 129
bonds (between particles), 133–4
Boyle's law, 167–9, 171, 172. 173
Boyle, Robert, 167
braking distance, 22–4
brushes, 323–5

cable TV, 217
cables, electrical, 311
calories (kcal), 91
cameras, 221–2
cancer, 229, 239, 382, 387
capacitor, 355–6
cataracts in eye, 235
cathode ray oscilloscope, 371
cathode rays, 368
cavity walls, 159–60
cell, 304
cell damage, 390
Celsius scale, 142–3, 144–5
Celsius, Anders, 142
centre of mass, 68–70
centripetal force, 46–7
CERN, 330
chain reaction, 402–3
changes of state, 128–31
characteristic graphs, current-voltage, 289–91
charge, electrical, 266, 270–2, 287
charged particle beams, 328–30
charging by induction, 269
charging, static electricity, 265–8
Charles' law, 170–2, 173
Charles, Jacques, 170
chemical energy, 99
Chernobyl, 40–1
circuit breakers, 312–13, 320–1
circular motion, 46–7, 123
circular orbits, 424–6
cleaning with ultrasound, 198
coal, 87–8
collector, 351
collisions, 50–5
colour, 224–5
combustion, 87
comets, 439, 441
communications satellites, 428
commutator, 338
commutator, split ring, 323–5
compressions, 194, 245–6
computers, 279, 347–8
Concorde, 56
condensing, 129
conduction (of heat), 148–51
conduction electrons, 150–1, 280–1
conservation of energy, 107
constellations, 434
constructive interference, 256–7
contact force, 42, 67, 123
continental drift, 411–12, 415–16
control rods, 405

convection, 152–4
convection current, 95, 152–4
conventional current, 282–3
converging lenses, 219–23
coolant, 405–6
cooling curve, 128–9
core of Earth, 412–4
core, iron, 316–17
corkscrew rule, 317
cosmic rays, 382, 387
coulomb (C), 271
Coulomb, Charles de, 271
count rate, 393
critical angle, 216
crumple zone, 59, 77
crust, 412
CT scanning, 238
current and electrons, 281–3
current, electric, 279, 287
current, measurement, 283

data-logger, 128
daughter nuclei, 402–3
deceleration, 17
Democritus, 366
density, 72–3, 154, 165
destructive interference, 256–7
detergent additives, 234
diffraction, 253–5
diffraction of light, 255
diffraction of sound, 254
diffusion, 133
digital meter, 283
diode, 293–4
diode protection, 357
direct current, 310–11
discharging, static electricity, 268–9
dispersion, 225
displacement, 7
distance travelled, 2, 8, 18–20
distance-time graphs, 357–71
diverging lenses, 219–20
DNA fingerprint, 391
Doppler effect, 2, 450
double insulation, 313
drag, 36–9
dynamo, 335–6

Earth, 434–9
Earth connection, 313
earth wire, 309–10
Earth's magnetic field, reversal, 418–19
Earth, gravity of, 41–2, 46
earthing, electrical, 312–13

earthquakes, 413–14, 416
echo-sounding, 197, 200
echoes, 186
Edison, Thomas, 310
efficiency, 108–9
Einstein, Albert, 202
elastic deformation, 74–6
elastic energy, 99–100
elastic limit, 76–7
electric bells, 319–20
electric circuits, 278–99
electric motors, 315–16,
electric motors, construction, 323–5
electric motors, explanation, 331–2
electric motors,practical, 325
electrical appliances, 301–2
electrical energy, 100
electrical potential energy, 307
electrical power, 125, 302
electrical resistance, 285–91
electricity and energy, 300–14
electricity generation, 334–6
electricity meter, 303, 309–10
electricity supply, domestic, 308–13
electrolysis, 272–4
electromagnetic forces, 315–32
electromagnetic induction, 333–46
electromagnetic induction, principles of, 336–8
electromagnetic radiation, 100, 155
electromagnetic spectrum, 227–40
electromagnetic waves, 230–1, 243
electromagnets, 316–8
electromagnets, uses of, 319–22
electromotive force (e.m.f.), 306–7
electron beams, 328–30, 370–2
electron gun, 370
electronic sounds, 192–3
electrons, 150–1, 265, 271, 287–8, 368–72, 375–6
electrons and current, 281–3
elements, 377–8
emitter, 351
endoscopes, 217–18
energy consumption, 86
energy efficiency, 108–9
energy resources, 86, 90
energy transfers, 98–110
energy transformations, 98–110
energy, definition, 90, 96
energy, electricity and, 279
environmental damage, 96
equations of motion, 20–2
equilibrium, 64, 67
evaporation, 129, 30
explosions, 50–5
extension, 75–6
extrapolation (of graph), 171
eyes, 221–2

Fahrenheit scale, 142
Fahrenheit, Daniel, 142
Faraday, Michael, 327, 336, 343
fault detection, 389
fault lines, 416
feedback, 357–9
film badge, 385–6
first law of reflection, 205

fixed points (of temperature scale), 142
Fleming's left-hand rule, 327–9
flex, electrical, 311
flight, 58–9
fluorescence, 234
fluorescent lights, 233–4
focal length, 219–20
focal point, 219
focus, 219
food irradiation, 390
foods, 91–2
force and acceleration, 27–31
force, electrical, 266
forced convection, 153
forces and momentum, 56–9
forms of energy, 98–103
fossil fuels, 86–96, 400
Franklin, Benjamin, 263–4, 267, 271, 282
free electrons, 150–1, 280
freezing point, 129
frequency, 190–2, 195, 230–1, 244–5, 247–9
friction, 31–2, 36–9, 104
friction, and static electricity, 266–7
friction, measurement, 37–8
fuel rods, 405
fuels, 90
fundamental particles, 368, 376
fuse box, 309–10
fuses, 311–2

galaxies, 443, 444–6
Galileo Galilei, 33–4, 42–4, 118–20, 142, 218
gamma (γ) radiation, 373, 384–5
gamma (γ) rays, 100, 238–40
gas laws, 164–77
gas syringe, 167
gases, 73, 87–8, 132
gases, properties of, 164–6
Geiger counter, 383, 390
Geiger, Hans, 373–4
Geiger-Muller tube, 383
generator, van de Graaff, 267–70, 271–2
generators, 335–6
generators, a.c., 338–9
genetic fingerprint, 391
geothermal energy, 95
Global Positioning Satellite (GPS) system, 429
global warming, 95–6
GPS (Global Positioning Satellite) system, 429
gravitational field (of Earth), 420
gravitational potential energy (GPE), 99, 117–18, 430–1, 446–7
gravitational potential energy (GPE), calculation, 113–15
gravity, 39–46, 421–7, 430–1
gravity, explanations of, 421–3
gravity, origin of, 41–2
greenhouse effect, 95–6, 400

half-life, 392–3
half-life, measurement of, 393–5
heat energy, 100
heat flow, 151
heat sink, 158

helicopters, 61
Herschel, William, 228, 436
hertz (Hz), 190
Highway Code, 22–4
home insulation, 159–60
Hooke's law, 75–6
Hooke, Robert, 75
Hubble, Edwin, 450
hydro-electricity, 89
hydrocarbons, 87
hydrogen, 92

ideal gas law, 176
ideal gases, 175–6
incident ray, 205, 212
inelastic behaviour, 77
information, electricity and, 279
infrared energy, 100
infrared radiation, 155–7, 228–9, 231, 232–3
infrared radiation, hazards of, 233
infrared radiation, uses of, 233
infrasound, 192, 197–8
inner core, 412–14
input devices, 349, 353–4
instantaneous speed, 7
insulation (thermal), 158–60
intelligent life, 440–1
interference, 256–7
internal energy, 100, 138–40, 141
International System of units, 3
internet, 217
interrupt card, 6, 15, 30
ionisation, 386–7
ionising radiation, 386–7
ions, 281, 272–4
iron core, 342
isotopes, 377–8

joule (J), 122, 303
Jupiter, 434–5, 437–9

Kelvin scale, 144–5, 157
Kelvin, Lord (William Thomson), 144, 412
kilojoule (kJ), 91
kilowatt (kW), 125
kilowatt-hour (kWh), 92, 303
kinetic energy (KE), 99, 117–18, 385, 430–1, 447
kinetic energy (KE), calculation of, 115–17
kinetic model of matter, 127–45, 169

laser, 200–2
latching, 358–9
laws of reflection, 215
laws of reflection of light, 205–6
LDR (light-dependent resistor), 292–3, 354
Leavitt, Henrietta, 450
LED (light-emitting diode), 294, 356
lenses, 218–23
levity, 43
life, 440–1
lift, 47, 59
light, 100, 200–9
light energy, 100
light, as particles, 250, 252
light, as waves, 250, 252

light-dependent resistor (LDR), 292–3
light-emitting diode (LED), 294, 356
light-gates, 6–7, 15, 30
light-year (ly), 445
lightning, 264–5
lightning conductor, 264
line of stability, 396–7
linear air track, 30–31
linearity (of scale), 143
lines of magnetic force, 337
liquid-crystal display, 371
liquids, 73, 132
lithosphere, 412
live wire, 309–10
load, 75–6
logic gates, 349–53
longitudinal waves, 245–6
loudness, 191
loudspeakers, 322, 332
Lowell, Percival, 440

magnifying glass, 223
mains electricity, 300–1
mantle, 412
Mars, 434–5, 437–9, 441
Marsden, 373–4
mass, 28–30, 165
mass spectrometer, 394
Maxwell, James Clerk, 230–1
medical diagnosis, 389
medical imaging, 238
megajoule (MJ), 91
megawatt (MW), 125
melting point, 129
Mercury, 434–5, 437–9
metals, 150–1, 279, 287–8
microamp (μA), 283
microphone, 188, 189, 354
microprocessors, 350
microscope, light, 367
microscope, scanning tunnelling, 367
microsievert (μSv), 383
microwave background radiation, 451
microwave heating, 237
microwave ovens, 237
microwaves, 100, 235–7
mid-oceanic ridge, 417
Milky Way, 425, 443, 444–5
milliamp (mA), 283
mixture, 130
mobile phones, 237
models (in physics), 136, 242, 249, 278, 367
moderator, 405
moisture detector, 354
moment of a force, 64–7
momentum, 51–62, 116
monochromatic light, 225
Moon, 46, 433–4
Moon, gravity, 41
Moon, origin of, 433–4
motion in a circle, 46–7
motion sensor, 357–74
motor effect, 326–8
multiflash photograph, 4–5, 43–4
musical instruments, 184–5

NAND gate, 352–3

natural frequency, 195–6
negative charge, 266
negative feedback, 357
Neptune, 436, 437–9
neutral wire, 309–10
neutron number, 377
neutron star, 448
neutron-induced fission, 401
neutrons, 375–8
newton (N), 26–9
Newton's first law of motion, 34
Newton's second law of motion, 35–6
Newton's third law of motion, 58–9, 385, 422
Newton, Isaac, 29, 34, 42–44, 57, 96, 122, 225–7, 252, 422
non-metals, 150
non-renewable energy resources, 93–6
NOR gate, 352–3
normal, 205, 212
NOT gate, 349–50
nuclear bomb, 403
nuclear decay equations, 395
nuclear energy, 99, 402
nuclear fission, 399–407
nuclear fuels, 88–9, 382
nuclear fusion, 448–9
nuclear power, 399–401
nuclear power stations, 402–3
nuclear stability, 395–7
nuclear strong force, 396
nuclear weapons, 382, 399–400
nucleon number, 376–7
nucleons, 375–6

Oersted, Hans Christian, 317–18
ohm (Ω), 285–7
Ohm's law, 289–91
Ohm, Georg, 290
oil, 87–8
optical fibres, 217
OR gate, 349–51
orbiting under gravity, 424–6
oscilloscope, 189–91, 194, 310, 371
outer core, 412–14
output devices, 349, 356–7
ozone layer, 229

P waves, 413–14
paint-spraying, electrostatic, 276
Pangaea, 411
parachuting, 45–6
particle model of matter, 127–45
pascal (Pa), 169
path difference, 257
penetrating power, 385–6, 388–9
percussion instruments, 185
period, 190, 244–5
Periodic Table, 376–7
periscopes, 216
photocopying, 276
photon, 384
photosynthesis, 86–7
photovoltaic cell, 94, 106
pitch, 191, 195
pivot, 64–9
plane mirror, 206
Planet X, 437

planets (and see individual planets), 425–6, 431, 434–9
plasma, 135
plastic deformation, 74–7
plate tectonics, 415–19
plugs, electrical, 311
plum pudding model, 373
Pluto, 436–9
plutonium, 85–6, 88, 400
positive charge, 266
positron, 397
potential difference (p.d.), 285, 287, 306–7
potential divider, 297–8, 354–5
potential energy, 102–3
power, 124–5
power equation, transformers, 344
power lines, 334, 339–41
power stations, 334
pre-natal scanning, 198–9
pressure, 165
pressure law, 173–5
pressure, units, 169
primary (P) waves, 413–14
primary coil, 342
principle of conservation of energy, 105
principle of conservation on momentum, 52–5, 57
printer, ink jet, 275
processors, electronic, 348–9
proton number, 376–7
protons, 271, 375–8

quality control with ultrasound, 197–8
quarks, 376, 397

radar speed gun, 2
radiation (heat transfer), 154–60
radiation therapy, 390
radio, 236
radio telescopes, 236
radio waves, 100, 235–7
radioactive dating, 418
radioactive decay, 391–7
radioactive materials, 85, 88, 381
radioactive sources, 387
radioactive substances, uses of, 388–91
radioactive tracing, 390
radioactivity, 380–98
radiocarbon dating, 394
radiographers, 382
radioisotopes, 384
radon, 381–2
rainbow, 225, 2277
range (of thermometer), 143
range of hearing, 192
rarefactions, 194, 245–6
ray box, 201, 212, 215
ray diagrams, 206–8, 220–1, 223
RCD (residual current device), 313
reactor, nuclear, 405–6
real image, 206, 219–20
red giant, 447–8
red-shift, 450
reed relay, 321
reflected ray, 205
reflection of light, 205–8
reflection of sound, 187
reflection of waves, 249–51

refracted ray, 212, 215
refraction of light, 210–26
refraction of light, definition of, 213
refraction of light, explanation of, 213–14
refraction of sound, 252–3
refraction of waves, 249–53, 413–14
refractive index, 204, 214
relays, 321, 356, 357
renewable energy resources, 93–6
reprocessing of nuclear fuel, 404
residual current device (RCD), 313, 320–1
resistance, measurement of, 288–9
resistance, origins of, 287
resistors, 291
resistors, in parallel, 295–7
resistors, in series, 295–7
resistors, combinations of, 295–7
resonance, 195–6
respiration, 91
resultant force, 32
rheostat, 292
ring mains, 309–10
ripple tank, 242–3, 245–6
ripples, refraction of, 250–1
robots, 347–8
rockets, 60, 101, 422
roller-coaster ride, 6, 14, 117
Romer, Ole, 203
rotation of Earth, 431–3
Rutherford, Ernest, 373–5, 378

S waves, 413–14
Sankey diagrams, 104–
satellites, 427–9
satellites, communication using, 236–7
satellites, polar-orbiting, 428–9
Saturn, 434–5, 437–9, 449
scalar quantities, 8, 425
second law of reflection, 206
secondary (S) waves, 413–14
secondary coil, 342
security checking, 238–9
security marking, 234
seismograph, 413
semiconductors, 279
sensitivity (of thermometer), 143
sensors, 348
shadow zones, 414
SI system, 52
SI units, 3, 29, 52, 72, 122, 169, 283, 303
sievert (Sv), 383
signal generator, 190
slide projector, 221–2
slip rings, 338
smoke detectors, 388
smoke precipitator, electrostatic, 275–6
smokers, 417–18
solar cell, 94
solar panel, 94
Solar System, 425, 430–442, 449
solenoid, 316–7
solids, 73–7, 132
solution, 130
sound, 183–99
sound energy, 100
sound waves, 194–5, 243
Space Shuttle, 26
spacecraft (see also satellites), 85, 420–1,
427–9
specific heat capacity, 160–2
specific heat capacity of water, 162
spectrum, 224–5, 227
speed, 2–12
speed of light, 202–4
speed of sound, 185–8
speed of sound, measurement of, 188
speed, measurement of, 3–11
speed of waves, 247–9
speed-time graphs, 16
spontaneous fission, 401
springs, 75–6
stability, 68
stardust, 448–9
stars, 443, 444–9
stars, death of, 447–9
stars, formation of, 446–7
stars, life of, 446–9
states of matter, 128–31, 135
static electricity, 263–77
static electricity, hazards of, 274–5
static electricity, uses of, 275–6
sterilisation, 239–40, 390
stopping distance, 22–4
strain energy, 99–100
stringed instruments, 184
sub-atomic particles, 55
subduction zone, 417
sublimation, 129
substation, electricity, 334
sulphur dioxide (SO2), 95
Sun, 229, 433–4
Sun, gravity of, 46
supernova, 448, 449
surface gravity, 437–9
switches, 354
synthesiser, 192–3
Système Internationale, 3

tectonic plates, 415–19
telecommunications, 217
telescope, 210–11
television, 236
television tube, 370–1
temperature, 140–2, 165
temperature difference, 149
temperature scales, 142–3
terminal velocity, 45–6
thermal energy flow, 151
thermal energy transfers, 147–63
thermal equilibrium, 141
thermistor, 143, 293
thermocouple, 143
thermometers, 140–4
thickness measurements, 388–9
thinking distance, 22–4
Thomson, J.J., 368–70, 372
thrust, 59
ticker tape, 5, 15
ticker-timer, 5, 15
tidal power, 89
tides, 89
time delay, electronic, 355–6
time of flight (of sound), 188
timer, electronic, 40
top speed (see also terminal velocity),
38–9
torque, 331–2
total internal reflection, 215–18, 224, 225
total internal reflection, uses of, 216–18
transducers, 353–5
transformers, 341–5
transformers, calculations involving,
344–5
transformers, operation of, 342–3
transformers, power equation of, 344
transistors, 351–2, 357
transverse waves, 245–6
trip switch, 312, 320
truth tables, 350, 352
Turin shroud, 394–5
turning effect of a force, 64, 331–2

ultrasound, 11, 192, 197–9
ultraviolet radiation, 100, 228–9, 231,
233–5
ultraviolet radiation, hazards of, 234
ultraviolet radiation, uses of, 233–4
unbalanced forces, 31–2
Universe, 430–1, 443–52
Universe, age of, 446
Universe, life of, 449–51
upthrust, 42
uranium, 88
uranium burning, 404
Uranus, 436, 437–9

van de Graaff generator, 267–70, 271–2
van Leeuwenhoek, Anton, 219
variable resistors, 291–2, 354
vector quantities, 7, 32, 54, 425
velocity, 7
velocity of sound, 187–8
velocity-time graphs, 16–20
Venus, 434–5, 437–9
vibrations, 185, 195–6
video camera, 355–53
virtual image, 206, 220
volt (V), 285
voltage, 272, 280
voltage and energy, 304–8
voltage, meaning of, 306–7
voltmeter, 286, 287, 372
volume, 165

waste energy, 106
water power, 89
watt (W), 125, 302
wave model of light, 230–1
wavefronts, 249–51
wavelength, 230–1, 243–4, 247–9
waves, 241–58
waves, and energy, 246
waves, description of, 242–6
Wegener, Alfred, 411–12, 415–16
weight, 41–2
weightlessness, 426-7
white dwarf, 447–8
William Thomson, 144
wind energy, 95
wind instruments, 184–5
work done, calculating, 121–4
work, doing, 107, 120–4

X-rays, 199, 238–40, 384, 387, 448